CIVIL RIGHTS UNIONISM

CIVIL RIGHTS UNIONISM

Tobacco Workers and the
Struggle for Democracy in the
Mid-Twentieth-Century South

ROBERT RODGERS KORSTAD

The
University
of North
Carolina
Press

Chapel Hill
and London

This book was published with the assistance of the
William Rand Kenan Jr. Fund of the University of
North Carolina Press.

Designed by April Leidig-Higgins
Set in Minion by Copperline Book Services, Inc.

The paper in this book meets the guidelines for
permanence and durability of the Committee on
Production Guidelines for Book Longevity of the
Council on Library Resources.

Library of Congress Cataloging-in-Publication Data
Korstad, Robert Rodgers.
Civil rights unionism: tobacco workers and the
struggle for democracy in the mid-twentieth-century
South / by Robert Rodgers Korstad.
p. cm.   Includes bibliographical references and index.
ISBN 0-8078-2781-9 (cloth: alk. paper)
ISBN 0-8078-5454-9 (pbk.: alk. paper)
1. Tobacco workers—Labor unions—Southern
States—history—20th century.   2. Civil rights
movements—Southern States—History—20th
century.   3. Food, Tobacco, Agricultural, and Allied
Workers Union of America—History—20th
century.   I. Title.
HD6515.T6 K67 2003
331.88'17973'0975667—dc21   2002152319

cloth   07 06 05 04 03   5 4 3 2 1
paper   07 06 05   5 4 3 2

For Frances and Karl
and for Jacquelyn

CONTENTS

ILLUSTRATIONS AND MAPS

Illustrations

Maps

ABBREVIATIONS

AFL   American Federation of Labor

CIO   Congress of Industrial Organizations

CIO-PAC   Congress of Industrial Organizations–Political Action Committee

CPA   Communist Political Association

CRP   Community Relations Project

DPOWA   Distributive, Processing, and Office Workers of America

FBI   Federal Bureau of Investigation

FDR   Franklin Delano Roosevelt

FEPC   Fair Employment Practices Committee

FLSA   Fair Labor Standards Act

FTA   Food, Tobacco, Agricultural, and Allied Workers of America

HUAC   House Committee on Un-American Activities

NAACP   National Association for the Advancement of Colored People

NIRA   National Industrial Recovery Act

NLRB   National Labor Relations Board

NRA   National Recovery Administration

NTWU   National Textile Workers Union

NWLB   National War Labor Board

PAC   Political Action Committee

SCHW   Southern Conference for Human Welfare

SNYC   Southern Negro Youth Congress

STFU   Southern Tenant Farmers Union

TUUL   Trade Union Unity League

TWIU   Tobacco Workers International Union

TWOC   Tobacco Workers Organizing Committee

UCAPAWA   United Cannery, Agricultural, Packing, and Allied Workers of America

UTSE   United Transport Service Employees

WPA   Works Progress Administration

YMCA   Young Men's Christian Association

YWCA   Young Women's Christian Association

CIVIL RIGHTS UNIONISM

INTRODUCTION

Civil Rights Unionism tells the story of a working-class-led, union-based civil rights movement that tried to change the arc of American history in the years surrounding World War II. Its protagonists consist of roughly 10,000 tobacco manufacturing workers, mostly African Americans but including several hundred whites, who through Local 22 of the Food, Tobacco, Agricultural, and Allied Workers–Congress of Industrial Organizations (FTA-CIO) initiated and sustained a broad-based challenge to economic exploitation, political disfranchisement, and racial discrimination in Winston-Salem, North Carolina, throughout the decade of the 1940s. Arrayed against them were the managers of the R. J. Reynolds Tobacco Company and an industrial oligarchy that wielded enormous power in the city, the region, and the nation. This social drama mobilized a supporting cast that was national and even international in scope: it included officers and staff from FTA; a group of mostly white workers who opposed unionization; sectors of the black middle class; officials from various branches of the federal government; and Communist Party activists, many of whom were native North Carolinians. Political, labor, civil rights, and religious leaders from across the political spectrum made cameo appearances. Among them were Henry Wallace, Mary McLeod Bethune, Philip Murray, Richard Nixon, Paul Robeson, Norman Vincent Peale, Lucy Randolph Mason, and Woody Guthrie, all of whom were critical players in the larger struggle of which Local 22 was a part. At its heart, however, this was a local movement mounted by local people with leaders whose names, until now, have been largely lost to history: Robert

Black, Viola Brown, Willie Grier, Etta Hobson, Velma Hopkins, Ruby Jones, Robert Lathan, Clark Sheppard, Theodosia Simpson, Moranda Smith, and others.[1]

One of the South's first truly modern businesses, the R. J. Reynolds Tobacco Company revolutionized the tobacco industry in the years after World War I, when its Camel cigarette campaign made smoking a wildly popular American pastime. Through brand-name advertising, integrated manufacturing and distribution systems, and the cultivation of global markets, Reynolds helped to generate a landscape of modernity, even as it based its profits on the super-exploitation of black labor and concentrated its operations in a tightly controlled southern town. By 1940 the company operated the largest tobacco manufacturing facility in the world, and its approximately 12,000 employees (plus the several thousand seasonal workers in the city's independent leaf houses) represented one of the largest concentrations of industrial workers in the region. Two-thirds of the workers were African American, and over one-half of them were women.[2]

FTA drew on the solidarities created by this dense concentration of African American workers. It also built on a long process of social learning that began with the mass migration of rural southerners to the city in the early 1920s. Taking advantage of the window of opportunity that opened during World War II, the union won collective bargaining rights at Reynolds and three smaller independent leaf houses in 1943. Men and women who had been disfranchised and discounted as backward, uneducated tobacco "mules" found themselves negotiating head to head with the state's most powerful men as they hammered out contracts that brought major improvements in wages, benefits, and working conditions. Equally important, they replaced an arbitrary, personalistic, and often abusive system of labor-management relations—which harked back to the nineteenth century and stood in sharp contrast to the company's modern, sophisticated public face—with one based on a workplace bill of rights and implemented by militant shop floor stewards. Women such as Moranda Smith, a sharecropper's daughter who became the first black woman to serve on the executive board of an international union, took the lead in this process of movement and institution building, and their actions proved especially subversive of existing social relations.[3]

Local 22 rekindled the political activism among African Americans that had been smoldering since the turn-of-the-century white supremacy campaign. From the outset, the union blurred the boundaries between home and work, sacred and secular, play and politics, consumption and production. In a society in which the exploitation of black laborers went hand in hand with their exclusion from politics and most social services, black unionists could hardly avoid linking workplace issues to community concerns. Local 22's brand of race-inflected "civic unionism" thus expressed the experience and perspective of its African American workers, who combined class consciousness with race solidarity and looked to cross-class institutions such as the black church as a key base of support, as well as the outlook of progressive-minded unionists generally, who saw trade unions not just as a means of advancing the interests of their members but as the generative force in a larger struggle for economic democracy.[4]

Women's leadership forwarded this dual emphasis as well. Winston-Salem was not only a city of blue-collar workers, it was a city of *women* workers. Men led the World War I–era exodus to the North, but women fled to southern cities in numbers that equaled or exceeded those of men. At a time when the vast majority of urban black women workers in this country had no choice but to labor in white homes, more than half of Winston-Salem's gainfully employed women found work in the tobacco factories. Working women did double duty as workers and household managers, and their complex consciousness as proletarians, consumers, women, and African Americans helped to reinforce the connections between the community and the shop floor.[5]

Local 22 registered thousands of black voters, revitalized the local chapter of the National Association for the Advancement of Colored People (NAACP), and spearheaded the election of a black minister to the Winston-Salem Board of Aldermen, the first African American to defeat a white opponent in the South since the turn of the century. During the CIO's postwar southern organizing drive, dubbed "Operation Dixie," Local 22 carried the union message to the poorest, most repressive area of the state, stimulating the organization of an additional 10,000 workers in the leaf houses of eastern North Carolina. Activists also demanded a greater voice for citizens in the day-to-day operations of city government and the enactment of civil rights legislation. Their consumerist, social welfare agenda included calls for low-income housing, price controls, unemployment compensation, and equalization of educational opportunities. In 1948 FTA and Local 22 threw their energies into the Progressive Party and the presidential campaign of Henry Wallace, a last-ditch attempt to extend the social democratic impulses of the New Deal into the postwar world.

These actions placed Winston-Salem unionists on the front lines of efforts to advance the boundaries of democratic culture in the workplace, in civil society, and in personal relationships. Local 22 was the prize local in what was arguably the most diverse left-led union in the country. If FTA could, in one unionist's words, "bring that big giant," R. J. Reynolds, "down to earth," there was hope for a new kind of labor movement, one built around women, blacks, Hispanics, and other vulnerable workers and committed to civil rights and a broad social welfare agenda.[6]

By the 1940s, moreover, the South had emerged as the critical battleground in the efforts of liberals and leftists to maintain the momentum of the New Deal. The region was home to the country's largest bloc of unorganized workers, and the long-term success of the CIO depended on its ability to bring southern workers into the house of labor. Likewise, two out of three African Americans lived below the Mason-Dixon line, and the vast majority of these were working class. To succeed, the emerging struggle for civil rights had to mobilize the millions of black workers who labored in the region's factories, farms, households, mines, and lumber camps. To survive and expand, New Dealers had to break the stranglehold of conservative southern Democrats, who owed their seniority and thus their domination of congressional committees to the South's constricted electorate and one-party rule.[7]

Local 22 thus stood at the nexus of at least half a dozen interrelated democratic projects that emerged in the United States in the 1930s and 1940s. First and foremost, its members were in the vanguard of efforts to transform midcentury race relations. World War II was a major watershed in the development of the modern civil rights movement. The number of black voters doubled in the North between 1940 and 1948, and in the eleven states of the former Confederacy black registration more than quadrupled. Likewise, membership in the NAACP soared. The half-million black workers who joined unions affiliated with the CIO put themselves in the front ranks of this movement, as civil rights advocates increasingly looked to mass unionization as the best hope for overcoming the tangle of oppressions that excluded blacks from full participation in American life. The wartime rhetoric of democracy, the imprimatur of the federal government, and the booming economy generated a rights consciousness that gave working-class black militancy a moral justification similar to that evoked by Afro-Christianity a generation later. In the automobile factories of Detroit, the cotton presses of Memphis, the steel mills of Pittsburgh and Birmingham, the stockyards of Chicago and Louisville, the shipyards of Baltimore and Oakland, and the tobacco factories of Richmond, Charleston, and Winston-Salem, the mobilization of black workers made civil rights an issue that could not be ignored by union officers, white executives, or government officials.[8]

Civil rights unionism, in turn, represented the finest flowering of the industrial union project initiated in the 1930s by the CIO, which sought to extend trade unionism beyond the skilled trades and bring industrial democracy to the mass-production industries.[9] It was also central to what may be called the "Southern Front," a loose coalition of labor unionists, civil rights activists, and southern New Dealers that saw a strong labor movement and the reenfranchisement of the southern poor as the keys to reforming the South and a reformed South as central to the survival and expansion of the New Deal.[10] The linkage between race and class that animated this phase of the black freedom struggle also drew black activists into the Communist orbit. The Communist Party, in turn, helped to tie the movement to liberation struggles around the world.[11] Local 22 drew strategically on ideas and resources from all of these streams. At the same time, events in Winston-Salem shaped the trajectories of these larger movements, and all are illuminated by a fine-grained study at the local level.

The key events in this history of working-class insurgency took place between 1942 and 1950, and their telling forms the heart of this book. But the institutions and processes that influenced that mobilization have a much longer history. Structured as a narrative of a local workers' movement, *Civil Rights Unionism* moves back and forth between the action on the ground and the larger forces at play. It begins by cutting directly to the 1943 strike that sparked the formation of Local 22. It then moves back in time to examine the late-nineteenth-century coup d'état in which North Carolina industrialists and planters snatched power from a coalition of workers, African Americans, Populist farmers, and Republicans. These Bourbon Democrats, so called by their Populist opponents because of their elitist base and goals, established a system of racial capitalism that they called "white supremacy," a term that helped to obscure the class presumptions of their undemocratic project. Racial subordination lay at the heart of white supremacy, but it encompassed class and gender inequalities as well. In fact, it was the interpenetration of gender, race, and class hierarchies that was the defining feature of this social formation.[12]

More than four decades elapsed between the turn-of-the-century "reactionary revolution" and the rise of the workers' movement in Winston-Salem. The consolidation of racial capitalism created a separate low-wage labor market in the South that depended on the exploitation of black labor, served as a magnet for runaway northern industries, undercut the labor movement, and pulled national wage standards down. This economic structure so circumscribed consumer buying power that by 1938 President Franklin D. Roosevelt declared the South "the Nation's No. 1 economic problem." The region's political system also underwrote the power of conservative Democrats who allied with Republicans in Congress to block or dilute social welfare measures and progressive labor laws. Racial capitalism thus became at the same time the context, the subject, and the object of Winston-Salem workers' democratic endeavors.[13]

The roots of Local 22's struggle lie deep in the past in another way as well. Lawrence Goodwyn has warned historians not to truncate their search for the origins of social movements, reminding us that a long process of social learning and movement building precedes what seem to be spontaneous uprisings.[14] The involvement of working men and women in the rich associational life of Winston-Salem's black community gave them self-confidence and organizational and leadership skills. In the 1920s and 1930s, a cohort of aspiring workers, confined by discrimination and economic structures to the tobacco plants, used the local efforts of the American Federation of Labor's Tobacco Workers International Union, the Communist Party, and the FTA to transform themselves into the organic intellectuals, astute leaders, and institution builders of the 1940s. Accordingly, this study looks carefully at the quarter century preceding the explosion of the workers' movement, first outlining the spatial and material processes of urbanization and proletarianization, then tracing the social learning that took place during earlier efforts at unionization and political participation, and finally documenting the building of Local 22 and its ultimate defeat in the midst of the postwar red scare.

At times I doubted that I could capture the movement in full bloom, much less find its deeper roots. Most local union documents ended up in trash barrels, and a flood destroyed FTA records. Company lawyers, bent on concealing evidence that could be used against them in antitobacco lawsuits, refused to give me access to their archives. For twenty years, Reynolds officials even held up the publication of a laudatory history of the company by the historian Nannie Mae Tilley. The repression surrounding Local 22's defeat muzzled former union members, and black and white citizens alike tried to forget the intense discrimination that prevailed in the years before the advent of the union.[15]

In part because of the city's tight control by corporate interests, Winston-Salem experienced neither the full brunt of the civil rights movement of the 1950s and 1960s nor the magnifying glass of civil rights historiography. Accordingly, much of the experience of the city's black community still remained, as C. Vann Woodward has put it, "in the twilight zone between living memory and written history." In order to overcome those silences, probe the dynamics of life under Jim Crow, and trace the legacy of the "great fear," I looked to the only first-person sources available to me: more than one hundred oral history interviews, most of which I conducted myself. I also drew on newspaper accounts, Federal Bureau of Investigation (FBI) records, government documents, and the like, reading those contemporary sources against retrospective interviews with an eye to the competing narratives they contain as well as to what they can tell us about the texture of everyday life and the substance of workers' politics and practices.[16]

For help in making sense of the rise and fall of Local 22, I turned to the interdisciplinary scholarship on social movements. The framework provided by historians, sociologists, and political scientists helped me to isolate the multiple and contingent factors that gave rise to this effort, account for continuity and change, and place the movement's evolution in both a local and a global context. I looked especially at what social movement theorists call "the structure of political opportunities," the circumstances that made the political system receptive to change. In this case the special circumstances included the New Deal, the rise of the CIO, the coalescence of the Southern Front, and the patriotic rhetoric and economic boom of World War II. Understanding this "macro level," however, solves only part of the riddle; equally important is unraveling the complex motives that lead individuals to participate in social movements, the subjective meanings those movements acquire, and the sources of hope and political courage that enable people to risk so much for a cause. I remain all too aware of what I cannot know, of how much mystery remains.[17]

Although the main concern of this study is to trace a social movement from the ground up, I also emphasize the national dynamics that made this mobilization possible. Ruby Jones, one of Local 22's more outspoken rank-and-file leaders, remembered that it was "like being reconstructed when the union came." Her reference to that earlier effort to build a democratic, interracial political order from the ashes of slavery affirmed the crucial link between the initiative of African Americans and the intercession of the federal government. Just as freedmen and women had sought the support of white allies in their fight for political rights and a share of the region's economic resources after emancipation, so too did black workers in Winston-Salem enlist the aid of the federal government, the trade union movement, and radical activists in their effort to remake the political, economic, and social landscape of Winston-Salem.

Historians have seen two of these allies—the federal government and the Communist Party—as especially problematic. By and large, previous scholars have underscored the potentially enervating effects of labor's reliance on the system of legalistic, top-down state regulation that began with the Wagner Act and peaked with the establishment of the National War Labor Board. This critique, however, applies mainly to the North and to white male workers. For the South, and especially for black southern workers, the federally imposed system of what came to be known as "industrial jurisprudence" was quite simply indispensable, and the actions of pro-labor federal agencies did in fact constitute a second "reconstruction." Disadvantaged by their class, race, and sex, black women especially benefited from the dynamic relation among the union, the state, and the public, which shaped labor law, forwarded democratic participation, and offered protection from retaliation and sexual exploitation.[18]

No one who writes about the Communist movement in the United States can escape the ideological charge that history continues to carry. An older historiography, which reflected the preoccupations of the Cold War, stressed the Party's ties to the Comintern and the Soviet Union and dismissed its connections to indigenous American radicalism. That approach reasserted itself with new vigor after the collapse of the Soviet Union in the 1980s. Other scholars have emphasized the flexibility and creativity of the Party at the grassroots level and its responsiveness to local conditions and leaders, while also criticizing the Party's attachment to the USSR and its dogmatism. In the case of Winston-Salem, I see the Communist Party as a controversial but important ally, whose impact on the course of local events was eclipsed by forces ranging from indigenous black activism to technological innovation and anti-Communist hysteria. Although I pay attention to the Party's ideas and actions, my chief emphasis is on the larger Popular Front, especially its distinctive southern wing, which *did* shape the movement in Winston-Salem profoundly. The Popular Front, in the sense in which I use the term, was not a short-lived product of Party policy, but a broad-based coalition of laborites, independent radicals, progressive New Dealers, and Party activists, with interracial, left-led CIO unions at its core.[19]

Marshaling its enormous economic power and drawing on the larger corporate backlash in which it participated, Reynolds responded to Local 22's challenge to its community and workplace control with a strategy that included both the carrot of welfare capitalism and the stick of race- and red-baiting and automation. Soon after the war, the company began a mechanization campaign that eliminated several predominantly black departments. When contract negotiations began in 1947, Reynolds forced a strike. In a pattern replicated throughout industrial America in those years, Communist influence in the union became the key issue around which management and its allies mounted their attack. The *Winston-Salem Journal* charged that the Communist Party, which had recruited several dozen members among the union's local leaders, had "captured Local 22, the Reynolds union of the C.I.O. tobacco workers—lock, stock, and barrel."[20] Although the company and the union finally reached a settlement on June 7, 1947, it proved to be the last collective bargaining agreement signed by the Reynolds Tobacco Company. Three years later, after a controversial National Labor Relations Board ruling that effectively disfranchised black seasonal workers and allowed lower-level white supervisors to vote in a recertification election, Local 22 lost the right to represent Reynolds workers.

This study ends with an examination of the causes of Local 22's demise, stressing what I call the metamorphosis of white supremacy: the decision by white elites to relax some of the harsher features of Jim Crow while maintaining a system of race, class, and gender subordination. Reynolds was in the forefront of a coordinated campaign by the nation's leading industrialists to contain and, where possible, dismantle the union-based working-class movement that had dramatically altered the distribution of power since the 1930s. Yet even Reynolds found it necessary to modify some of its policies in response to workers' demands.

Civil Rights Unionism places the Reynolds campaign in the context of this national corporate counteroffensive. In doing so, it embraces the arguments of recent historians who have questioned the depth of the postwar "settlement" between capital and labor, in which major corporations tied higher wages and benefits to productivity gains. Reynolds, like many other key corporations, never accepted the notion that collective bargaining could serve as a useful prop to oligopolistic pricing. Rather, it routinized paternalism by updating welfare capitalism and bided its time until the Cold War created a climate in which it could join with other businesses to check labor's growth.[21]

In much the same way, Winston-Salem power brokers ameliorated some aspects of racial discrimination while keeping the larger system of racial capitalism in place. Local officials reluctantly extended voting rights, built low-income housing, and formed biracial committees on community relations. They brought in selected members of the black middle class to sit on governmental boards and on the board of the local black college. They increased spending on social services and philanthropy to the black community. This metamorphosis widened class divisions in the black community and undercut civil rights unionism, but it also created cracks in the edifice of segregation that revealed the irrationality of the whole structure. These cracks, in turn, became the "free spaces" in which the civil rights movement of the 1950s and 1960s would grow.[22]

In the end, however, the breakup of the workers' movement in Winston-Salem and in the United States required an extraordinary feat of political repression. It was the post–World War II red scare that finally silenced dissident voices and contained political debate. Although the anti-Communist crusade singled out individuals and organizations, the real targets were the broad social movements begun in the 1930s. Anti-Communism not only damaged the left-led unions and civil rights groups, it also constrained the labor movement and civil rights activism more generally. CIO president Philip Murray and NAACP head Walter White, strong anti-

Communists themselves, were just as much "victims" of the red scare as FTA president Donald Henderson or Paul Robeson, the leading symbol of the culture of the Popular Front, although they certainly did not pay as high a personal price. More generally, the postwar repression scotched any prospect for what Henry Wallace called the "Century of the Common Man," the internationalist, social democratic alternative to what *Time*'s Henry Luce dubbed the "American Century."[23]

The Cold War isolated the workers' movement from its most important allies. As in the first reconstruction, once the political tides shifted with the end of World War II, the Republican capture of Congress, and the advent of the Cold War, the federal government moved quickly from ally to adversary. I therefore raise critical questions about the national government's participation in local and regional systems of subordination while also stressing the importance of the moments when federal officials act against local elites. I emphasize the dialectical relations between citizens' movements, which give legislation its political force, and state action, which can legitimate and undergird social movements or tip the scales toward capital and against labor.[24]

Congressional action, or inaction, undermined the thrust of the workers' movement in other ways as well. Congress's failure to create universalistic social welfare programs—national health insurance, full employment, unemployment compensation, and social security—helped to fracture working-class unity. Large CIO unions had little choice but to pursue benefits such as health insurance and pensions within collective bargaining agreements, creating an "uneven pattern of social provision" in which organized workers, who were mostly white and male, enjoyed protections denied to blacks, women, and nonunion white workers. Those who were left out, in turn, could not look to unionized workers for strong allies in their drive for more generous social spending.[25]

By the time Local 22 faced its final NLRB election in 1950, Reynolds had eliminated enough black jobs and hired enough new white workers to achieve a fifty-fifty racial split in the workforce. Until then, Local 22 had based its success on its ability to gain the allegiance of practically the entire black workforce along with the active participation of several hundred whites and the votes of some other white employees who never officially joined the union. Still, neither local black leaders nor FTA officials ever gave up on recruiting white workers. They believed that in the long run only an interracial labor movement could achieve their broader goals. They also believed that despite the overdetermined blend of company pressure, racialist ideology, fear, fragmentation, and social ostracism that kept whites from joining a left-wing, black-led union, sensitive, dedicated organizers would eventually be able to tap a reservoir of underlying grievances against the company and support for the union's goals.

Taking this optimism seriously, I attend to the common interests that made interracial unionism thinkable; to the events, such as the Great Depression and the immense popularity of the New Deal, that enabled some white workers to put their class interests ahead of their tenuous racial advantages; and to the remarkable steadfastness of the union's small core group of white supporters, who acted bravely and against type. I also underscore the division of labor and social life enforced by four decades of official segregation, the continued deployment of sexualized racism, and the new uses of anti-Communism, as well as the many other barriers that kept black and white workers apart.[26]

In all this, I draw on the rich scholarship on the wages of whiteness, especially on works that emphasize the fact that white workers' racism was never static and instinctual and that their consciousness shifted "back and forth along the axes of race, class, and gender" in tandem with changes in the cultural and political terrain. White workers' racial identities and attitudes, however, are not the focus of this book, in part because I do not see them as a primary cause of the movement's defeat. In a predominately black industry, the particular strategies of Reynolds, the national postwar corporate counteroffensive, the broader structures of racial capitalism, and the political repression associated with the Cold War were more important. Moreover, a focus on the well-known and relatively easily understood racism of white workers would decenter the black workers who are the main protagonists of this book. It would also shift attention away from the role of "great corporations in constructing and maintaining racism" and thus replicate a long tradition of blaming poor whites for the worst aspects of southern history and letting the discursively and economically powerful off the hook.[27]

The collapse of civil rights unionism cast a long shadow over the second half of the twentieth century. The disintegration of the movements of the Popular Front era ensured that when the civil rights struggle of the 1960s emerged it would have a different social character and a different political agenda, which in the end proved inadequate to the immense social problems that lay before it. Like the workers' movement of the 1940s, the protests of the 1960s mobilized an African American community that was overwhelmingly working class. The key institutions of the new movement, however, were not the trade unions but the black church and independent protest organizations. As Martin Luther King Jr. and others well knew, winning the vote and ending discrimination in public accommodations and education could not overturn the forces that impoverished African Americans. After 1965 such activists sought to raise issues of economic equality and working-class empowerment to the moral high ground occupied by the assault on disfranchisement and segregation. Yet they found themselves hamstrung by the institutional and cultural rifts between the civil rights and labor movements and by the divisions between the haves and have-nots within the working class. Most important, perhaps, they could not build on the alternative social vision of the 1940s, for that vision had been largely lost to memory, destroyed by the political repression of the McCarthy era.[28]

There were other repercussions as well, for the South, for labor, for the women's movement, and for American political culture. The South has prospered in ways that the activists of the 1940s could never have imagined or foreseen, but it still suffers from its historical reluctance to invest in health, education, and other dimensions of "human capital." Just as leftists feared, conservative southern congressmen did help to push through an edifice of labor law that hampers the labor movement to this day. The South, along with reservoirs of even cheaper labor abroad, continues to lure runaway shops, ensuring that capital will retain the advantage of infinite mobility over labor. The CIO's embrace of Cold War ideology, its thralldom to the Democratic Party, and its attempt to forge a postwar "settlement" with leading corporations ended the industrial union project of the 1930s. The purge of the left-led unions deprived that movement of organizers oriented toward the heterogeneous workforce that would emerge after World War II. McCarthyism cut the women's liberation movement off from one strand of its history, the multiethnic-left feminism represented by the women of Local 22, leaving the movement vulnerable to the charge of being racially exclusive and middle class. The list could go on. All the ills that beset America cannot be chalked up to the outcome of the struggles of the 1940s. But that outcome does stand as a watershed. And the United States *is* distinguished by the lowest rates of unionization and the most miserly social provisions in the industrialized world.[29]

None of this could have been predicted. Nothing was inevitable. To the workers who rose in the wee hours of the morning to make their way toward the R. J. Reynolds Building, June 17, 1943, was simply another day of toil. Yet ahead of them lay seven years of high-stakes conflict. Some would suffer for their participation in the events that were about to unfold. For others, those years would be the glory of a lifetime. Few in the town could escape the drama altogether. And few who were drawn into it, or tried to write about it, would emerge unchanged.

CHAPTER ONE

Those Who Were Not Afraid

At dawn on June 17, 1943, the haze that has developed during the cool early morning hours slowly begins to burn away. Seen from atop the R. J. Reynolds Building, far above the trees and church steeples, the city of Winston-Salem, North Carolina, slowly comes alive. The heat wave of the past two weeks continues. The ever-present smell of tobacco fills the air, a sickly-sweet odor that ties all the city's inhabitants to the giant company.

In the valley known as Monkey Bottom on the east side of town, men and women emerge from dilapidated shotgun houses and slowly begin their ascent by foot up Third, Fourth, and Fifth Streets to the R. J. Reynolds Tobacco Company, the largest tobacco manufacturing complex in the world. Farther to the east, the buses of the black-owned Safe Bus Company make their rounds. At each stop Reynolds employees climb aboard, joined by hundreds of household workers headed for the white homes of Winston-Salem. From the north and south of town come white Reynolds employees, some on foot, some in cars, and some riding Duke Power buses. More white workers stream in from the foothills of the Blue Ridge Mountains to the west, in cars with four and five passengers. Many of these daily migrants from Forsyth, Stokes, Wilkes, and Yadkin Counties have been up since daybreak, tending to the livestock on their farms or putting in an hour on their own tobacco crop before leaving for work.[1]

It is Thursday, and the increased workload in place since early May is taking its toll. Black and white workers move slowly into separate lines as they file through the factory gates for the 7:30 A.M. starting time. They barely notice the "White only" and "Colored" markers at each of the seventy-two entrances, even as they obey and absorb these vivid reminders of the segregated world they all inhabit.[2]

Other Reynolds employees are readying themselves for the day ahead as well. On his 120-acre farm in western Winston-Salem, John Clarke Whitaker, vice president of the company, glances at the headlines in the *Winston-Salem Journal*: the Allies had attacked Italy, and Churchill was planning his Balkan drive. The war was going well, but it was causing problems for tobacco manufacturers. The demand for cigarettes far exceeded all possible production; the military alone bought 20 percent of the company's product. Yet the company found new machinery almost impossible to obtain. The labor shortage in the Carolina Piedmont also threatened the green leaf tobacco season that began in August. Reynolds needed 1,500 seasonal workers, and many who traditionally filled these positions had joined the armed forces or secured war-industry jobs.[3]

The son of a local tobacco manufacturer, John Whitaker had begun working for Reynolds in 1913 after graduating from the University of North Carolina, and he prided himself on having operated Reynolds's first cigarette-making machine. He joined the navy during World War I and then returned to Winston-Salem to head the company's new employment office. He became vice president in charge of manufacturing in 1937 and fifteen years later would become chairman of the company. Whitaker knew the ins and outs of the Reynolds Tobacco Company firsthand. He was worried about the labor shortages and aware that his employees were being pushed to work harder than ever before.[4]

Theodosia Gaither Simpson was one those overworked employees. A slender young African American woman, Simpson was fated to be John Whitaker's antagonist. The two rivals, each with deep roots in North Carolina, shared a strong sense of family and a bedrock faith in education. Theodosia Simpson's maternal grandfather moved from nearby Mocksville to teach school in Forsyth County. The rest of the family found work in town at Reynolds. Theodosia seemed destined to follow in the footsteps of her grandfather, but in 1936 the Depression forced her to drop out of Winston-Salem Teachers College after one year and go to work in the tobacco stemmeries to help support her family. Like Whitaker, Simpson knew all about tobacco production, indeed, more than she cared to know. This morning she caught the bus at the corner near her apartment on North Cherry Street, where she and her husband, Buck Simpson, lived, and headed reluctantly for her job on the fifth floor in the stemmery of Plant Number 65.[5]

African American women, ranging in age from late teens to sixties, performed

Theodosia Gaither Simpson
(*UCAPAWA News*)

almost all the stemming in the Reynolds plants. They removed the hard center core from the tobacco leaf, a key step in the process that transformed the aged tobacco leaves into cigarettes, smoking tobacco, and chewing tobacco. Until the mid-1930s, hand stemming predominated; by 1943 most stemmers worked on a machine that cut the leaf away from the stem.

Three women worked at each of the fifth floor's sixty-six stemming machines. Black men from the nearby casing room brought the tobacco to the machines in large boxes. One woman removed a "hand" of tobacco from the box, untied it, and passed it on to a coworker who spread the leaves out on top of the machine. A third woman fed the tobacco onto a moving chain that carried it between two circular knives that cut out the stem. Each job required dexterity and intense concentration. The room was hot, the work numbingly repetitive, and the dust from the leaf covered everyone from head to foot by the end of the day. The tobacco moved con-

John Clarke Whitaker
(Forsyth County Public
Library Photograph
Collection)

tinuously, with the speed of the work in the stemmery geared to the needs of the manufacturing division it supplied. But the manufacturing division also depended on the product from the stemmery, a fact that made the women stemmers a linchpin in the entire production process.[6]

By 1943, workers at Reynolds had gained a modicum of protection under the 1938 Fair Labor Standards Act, which mandated a forty-hour week and a minimum wage of forty cents per hour plus time-and-a-half for overtime. The work was regular, but the $16 to $20 a week that most women took home still amounted to only half the annual income the federal government calculated as a "minimum subsistence of living" in cities like Winston-Salem. Few stemmers made more than ten cents above minimum wage, even those who had worked at Reynolds for many years. The company manipulated small wage differentials to create divisions among the workers and encourage dependence on the foreman's goodwill.[7]

Reynolds had responded to the soaring wartime demand for cigarettes by speeding up production and then, in early May, by jacking up quotas throughout the factory. The foremen and subforemen who walked the lines of machines hour after hour, checking the work and disciplining the women, saw nothing out of the ordinary. But beneath the surface lay a hidden reality of unrest and self-organization that had begun in 1942 when a small but dedicated group of rank-and-file workers and organizers from the United Cannery, Agricultural, Packing, and Affiliated Workers of America–Congress of Industrial Organizations (UCAPAWA-CIO) formed the Tobacco Workers Organizing Committee (TWOC) and slowly began to sign up members.[8]

"We was catching so much hell in Reynolds that we had to do something," said Geneva McClendon, a close friend of Theodosia Simpson and one of the small group of union supporters in Plant Number 65 in 1943. "In the first place they gave you a great big workload, more than you could do," McClendon continued. "Instead of cutting down on the boxes of work, if the foreman discovered a box not tightly packed, he would roll it back to the casing room to be repacked. If you'd tell them they put too much work on you, they'd fire you. And then they stood over you and cussed you out about doing it: 'If you can't get this work out, get your clothes and get out.' . . . Everybody would almost cry every day the way they would work you and talk to you. Working conditions was so bad you needed God and a union." Finally, McClendon remembered, "it got so we wasn't going to take it any more; we had had it."[9]

Sit-down

The confrontation erupted on the hot, muggy morning of June 17. Theodosia Simpson remembered exactly how it began. "The lady who worked on the machine next to me, she was a widow with five kids, and she was sick that day. Oh, you could get sick up there in a minute, the way you had to work. She couldn't keep up with her work." Other workers would often pick up the slack when one of their number fell behind, but "she didn't have too good a relationship with the other two people on the machine, so they weren't helping her. The foreman came up and told her that if she didn't catch up, 'there was the door that the carpenter left.' She started crying because she had these children to rear and nobody working but her. And that sort of got next to me. I called a couple of people I thought I could trust 'down house,' down to the lavatory. I said, 'When we come in here tomorrow, let's not work until we get some understanding on how these people are going to be treated.'" The line foreman, Will, found out about the women's plans, apparently from someone in Simpson's group. Recalled Geneva McClendon, "He came around telling everybody, 'We hear there's going to be a work stoppage. You better not do that. You'll lose your job.' And that frightened a few people. So at lunchtime we got together, and decided instead of doing it tomorrow morning, let's do it after lunch."[10]

The conspirators told Leon Edwards and the other men who worked in the adjoining casing room about the planned strike. "They said, 'We want you all to stick with us,'" Edwards remembered. When the women filed back in after their lunch break, Edwards saw that they really meant business. The company "had a little whistle they'd blow [when it was time to start work] and when that whistle went 'whwhwh,' them women about-faced just the same as if they were in the army. Everyone turned their back to the machine. You [never saw] anybody turn so quick."[11]

"The foreman looked at us as if we were crazy," McClendon remembered. "He pulled the whistle again and nobody moved. He asked what was wrong. Several of us told him that we weren't going to work until our working conditions were improved, our workload cut to where we could get our work out, and we wanted our wages equalized. The foreman said he couldn't do nothing and if we didn't want to work to get out. We told him we wanted to work but not under those conditions and if he couldn't do nothing we would like to talk to the person that did have the authority to remedy the situation."[12]

At that moment, the conflict took a dramatic turn. James McCardell, a thirty-eight-year-old "draft boy" who had worked for fifteen years putting boxes of tobacco on the women's machines, stepped forward to make it clear to the foreman that the men from the casing room were going to back the stemmers' refusal to work. "If these women'll stand up for their rights, I'm with them," he proclaimed. No sooner had the words left McCardell's mouth than he crashed to the floor. The few machines that were still running stopped as everyone rushed to see what was wrong. "Some fellows grabbed him and carried him to the nurse," Simpson recalled. "One came back and said, 'He's already dead.' He had been sick that whole week, going back and forth to the nurse. Instead of staying home, he would come to work and feel bad. He would go to the nurse, but she said he wasn't sick and sent him back to the floor to work." Doctors later determined that McCardell had died of a cerebral hemorrhage.[13]

Whether or not the heightened emotion of the moment caused McCardell's death, his collapse was like a match in a tinderbox. Suddenly, everyone was yelling. Milling around the head foreman, Samuel Strader, the stemmers shouted that neglect and overwork had killed McCardell and the company was to blame. Management had thoroughly schooled Strader in how to handle the complaints of individual employees. But the official "Memorandum on Grievances" ill prepared the foreman for a simultaneous work stoppage by 200 women. He had been cautioned "that the farther away a problem or dispute gets from the place it started, the larger it grows, and the more importance it assumes. The foreman must learn from his experience how to prevent disputes, and if not successful, to settle them before they go up the management ladder." It was clear from the outset that this case could not be contained, and Strader immediately telephoned the executive offices to ask for help.[14]

Meanwhile, word of the strike and McCardell's death swept quickly through the factory. The stemmed tobacco that normally fell to the searching tables on the fourth floor was not moving. "Why?" the women below asked. Elevator operators passed the word: "They're sitting down." Within minutes, the 198 women on the fourth floor and the 25 on the third floor were standing idly by their machines. Soon company officials ordered all the doors locked so that no one could enter or leave the building.[15]

As the women waited, union members circulated quietly on their respective floors. "'Sit right there, don't move,'" they told their coworkers. "'Just stay there until time to go home. If you've got to go to the bathroom, go to the bathroom, come right back on your job.' You wasn't running around all over the place," Edwards remembered. "Right there where you worked is right there where you'd be."[16]

Stories of hurt and hardship, many of which had been told before, traveled from group to group as the workers sat at their machines talking among themselves. What were they going to ask for? Surely an end to the increased workload. They all needed more money. What about enlarging the dressing rooms? They didn't see why people should have to work when they were sick. Respect. They would demand that the foremen treat them with respect.[17]

It did not take the company officials long to get to Number 65; the main office was only two blocks away. Within minutes, the strikers looked up to see B. C. Johnson, superintendent of the stemmeries, Edgar Bumgardner, head of the employment office, and John C. Whitaker, vice president in charge of manufacturing, walking through the door. Bumgardner asked the women what was wrong. "We told him that we were tired of the workload," McClendon remembered, "tired of the bosses standing over us with a whip in his hand. We wanted better working conditions, and we wanted more money. We wanted equal pay for equal work." Then Johnson introduced Whitaker, who climbed up on one of the machines to address the workers. This was the first time that most of them had ever laid eyes on the Reynolds vice president, though some had been with the company as long as he had.[18]

John Whitaker personified the official style of Reynolds management. His calm but forceful manner combined the charm of the Old South with the practicality of the New. He did not operate like the foremen who worked for him. He did not threaten the men and women in Number 65; there were no raised voices, no curses as he tried to persuade them to return to work. He had the power to hire and fire, reward and discipline everyone in the factories, even the foremen. But he presented himself as a reasonable man who, because of his experience and position in the company, could be trusted to act in the best interest of the workers. As the creator of the employment office, Whitaker had formulated the rules by which foremen were supposed to live, although few abided by them. "Foremen should quietly, and certainly with no show of antagonism, discuss any grievance," he had written. They should "discuss the matter from every possible angle, being careful to bring out the employee's point of view" and "make it easy for the employee to back down if wrong."[19]

With these guidelines in mind, John Whitaker spoke to the workers around him.

Let me first remind you of the very important responsibility we all have to maintain production during this very crucial period of the war. Neither you nor I want to have our boys overseas think badly of our effort here in Winston-Salem. I know you have some grievances, and I want you to tell me about them so that the company can study them and make some changes where they are necessary. I want you to remember, however, that this is a very large company, and many different people make different demands on our time and resources. Your demands are part of that, but so are the workers over in Number 12, or the stockholders who furnish us with the capital to operate.[20]

Theodosia Simpson described what followed. "One girl who was supposed to be a little off, she tugged at his tie a couple of times. We had to get her back. Everybody started mumbling and finally a few talked out loud."

"We can't work this hard."

"I don't make enough money to give my family a decent meal."

"We're tired of those foremen treating us like dirt."[21]

Finally Whitaker reclaimed the floor. He promised that the company would take note of all the complaints, investigate them, and make changes where needed. He reminded the workers that the company was operating under wartime wage controls. Even if it wanted to raise wages, it could not do so without the federal government's permission.[22]

Whitaker had responded coolly to the unprecedented experience of being jostled and interrupted by a roomful of women workers. But he was unnerved by what happened next, for instead of being silenced by his expertise, Simpson took up the debate. "I guess he thought we were going to be afraid of him," said Simpson. "Well, at this point it didn't matter to me. I was twenty-three years old. I had a husband who was working, and I had no children. I figured I was going to get along."

"Mr. Whitaker, according to the Little Steel formula you can give us a wage increase."

"Who told you about the Little Steel formula?"

"Whether you know it or not, I can read and I can think. It's been in all the newspapers."

"I don't know anything about the Little Steel formula, but I'll have the company attorneys look into it."

"Well, you start talking to them about that wage increase."[23]

Simpson went on the describe the foreman's abuse of the widow and the death of James McCardell. Other women joined in. The complaints multiplied, and the details became more precise. The interchange was remarkable. Never before had these women, en masse, spoken so honestly and fearlessly to the chief representative of a company that wielded tremendous control over all their lives. Equally important, they challenged management's monopoly on expert knowledge, one of the prerogatives of power, and aligned themselves with the federal government, whose ability to intervene in labor-management disputes was at an all-time high.[24]

Finally, Whitaker told the workers to select a committee to meet with him the following morning. In so doing, he surrendered a crucial weapon in management's arsenal: its ability to divide and isolate individual workers. Asking the women in Number 65 to form a committee to discuss their grievances, moreover, legitimated both their complaints and the process of collective action. And it violated one of the cardinal rules of management: instead of responding to their complaints on the spot, Whitaker gave the dispute time to spread. As he himself had predicted, the farther the conflict moved from its place of origin, the larger it grew.[25]

As soon as Whitaker left the room, the men who moved the tobacco and cleaned the floors, along with the women stemmers, selected a committee with Simpson as its spokesperson. Simpson had been a stalwart among the small group of rank-and-file workers in the TWOC and had initiated the sit-down that morning. Most of the other committee members knew about the union, but being on the committee at this point was mostly "a matter of who was willing to do it," as Theodosia Simpson remembered. Geneva McClendon was both knowledgeable and willing. "Every worker should be in a union," she believed. "In the union you take the whip out of the boss's hand. I knew about unions from reading newspapers and the pamphlets. I read about the benefits the union had gotten. I figured the CIO was a good union."[26]

News of the afternoon's events passed quickly to workers in other buildings as the truck drivers made their rounds. When the workers finally left Number 65, night shift workers in Number 12, where the stemmed tobacco from the building was made into cigarettes, met them at the gates. Soon women from the stemmeries in Numbers 8 and 256, led by TWOC member Velma Hopkins, hurried down Chestnut Street to see what was going on.

Simpson and McClendon, meanwhile, went straight to the union office to talk with UCAPAWA organizers William DeBerry and Frank Hargrove. The women described the events of the afternoon. They told of the selection of the committee and the meeting scheduled for the following morning and asked for suggestions about what to do next.

DeBerry and Hargrove were excited. Months of meetings, discussions, and training had paid off. The union had neither planned nor foreseen the protest in Number 65, but solid preparation had carried the sit-down in its direction. TWOC members had been in the forefront of the action, and they were among the most articulate workers and quick-witted leaders. Their tactical maneuvering and articulation of workers' grievances had transformed the protest into a sit-down strike.

Still, the UCAPAWA organizers found themselves in a quandary. The union supported the "no strike pledge" taken by the CIO for the duration of the war. It was important, therefore, to try to arrange a settlement so that production of tobacco, which was considered a vital war commodity, could be resumed. At the same time, the sit-down presented a great opportunity to bring more people into the union. The situation had to be handled carefully. "Hargrove didn't want the company to get the idea that the union was keeping the workers out," said Simpson. "He wanted to keep it as much a workers' thing as a union thing at that particular time." The organizers' official position was that UCAPAWA was not involved, that the work stoppages were a "spontaneous act on the employees' part without discussion with the union," and that the workers should return to their jobs, but not "under previously existing working conditions," which they described as "unbearable."[27]

The TWOC decided to arrange a meeting that evening at the Union Mission Holy Church, pastored by the Reverend Frank O'Neal, a Reynolds worker. "A big good-looking guy," O'Neal reportedly made more money than any other black worker at Reynolds. He was a roller in the plug department at Number 8, known for his speed and dexterity. He had not been an active participant in the organizing drive, but his church had served as an occasional meeting place during the previous year.[28]

The meeting that evening proved larger than anyone expected. Over fifty people came, most from Number 65 but some from other stemmeries as well. Simpson took the floor, explaining in detail what had happened that afternoon. She told of the workers' promise to return to work in exchange for a meeting with Reynolds officials. The union organizers assured the workers "that the company was not going to fire them, a bunch of people." Simpson remembered DeBerry and Hargrove stressing the power of collective action. "If you'd go to them one at a time you might get fired, but if you stick together, they're not going to fire you."[29]

All spring the papers had been filled with stories about strikes and walkouts by miners, rubber workers, and auto workers, many of which had resulted in higher wages and better working conditions. As women from the other stemmeries listened to Simpson and the UCAPAWA organizers, they thought about those victories and the conditions in their own departments. First Lola Love spoke up, then Janie Wilson, then Velma Hopkins and others. Things were just as bad where they worked.

"The speed-up in May, that was the last straw for me."

"People are tired of these conditions."

"It's now or never."

"Why not sit down too?"

The women had examples of courage, and they were determined to follow them. "The main thing," said Simpson, "was to get someone who wasn't afraid to say something to that company."[30]

Meanwhile, in the black neighborhoods around the Reynolds plants, women gathered on street corners and front porches. The porch was their traditional meeting place, especially in the summer when the tin-roofed houses remained stifling until well past midnight. Sitting outside, they could see the bright lights in the Reynolds office building and hear the noise of the night shift, reminding them of the long, hot, dusty day they had spent in the factory. That night the groups outside seemed larger than usual, the mood more electric. Everyone talked of one thing— what had happened in Number 65. Few knew all the details, but they knew that people in the TWOC were involved. They heard that Theodosia Simpson had talked back to John Whitaker and he had not fired her. Should they follow her example? Could they organize similar protests in their own departments?[31]

As the meeting at the church broke up, stemmery workers hurried back through the streets to urge their neighbors to expand the sit-down. Relying on a network of family and friends, they passed the word that on Friday morning people should report to the factory but refuse to work until the company agreed to respond to their grievances. Each department with a predominantly black workforce had one or two TWOC members who could be relied on to offer leadership and explain the tactic to the other workers. A number of people who had shown interest but until then had not come forward could be counted on as well. The organizational base was in place, but no one could predict the reaction of the hundreds of workers in the stemmeries.

Friday, June 18, began much like the day before. To be sure, a front-page story in the morning newspaper hinted that something might be astir. "The Simpson woman," as the *Journal* called her, said that workers had staged a sit-down in Number 65 and were meeting with Reynolds management that morning to demand "equalization of wages among the several types of laborers at the stemming machines on the fifth floor; a reduction of an additional work load . . . placed on the stemming workers recently; and general improvement of working conditions." But as company officials prepared to meet with the committee in Number 65, they had no way of sensing the rebellious current that had gathered force in the black community the night before.[32]

When the women approached the largest stemmeries of Reynolds—Number 60 and Number 60 Extension—it became obvious that something had changed. Instead of entering one by one, they stopped. They whispered among themselves, passing the word. Then they made their way to the dressing rooms, changed clothes, and streamed out onto the plant floor. Sixteen hundred women took up their positions. The whistle blew, but all but a few stood stiffly still. Quickly the few machines that had started screeched to a halt. An eerie silence fell. When the superintendent came out, a TWOC spokeswoman stepped forward to say that the company's problems were not limited to Number 65. Workers in Number 60 also had grievances; they too wanted a face-to-face meeting with the executives over in the Reynolds Building. And they demanded that the company allow Robert "Chick" Black to help them present their demands.[33]

Black worked in the experimental division of Number 64, a "secret operation" in which stems from the tobacco leaf were cut into fine pieces for use in cigarettes and smoking tobacco—in contradiction to Reynolds's claim that it used 100 percent leaf tobacco. The company would not allow union organizers in the plants, and the night before Black's wife, Minnie, who worked in Number 60, had raised the possibility of her husband representing the women in her department. Despite their obvious assertiveness and organizational abilities, in this case the women fell back on the tradition of looking to male leadership. "I think they called on Brother Black because they knew he was honest and he was a good talker," one worker remembered. "He had nerve," another observed, "and he could talk and explain things to you."[34]

Shortly after the sit-down started, John Whitaker and Ed Bumgardner went into Number 64 to see Black. Determined not to listen to the complaints until the women went back to work and confident of his ability to command Black's help, Whitaker defined the situation this way: "Robert," he said, "we've got a problem over there in Numbers 60 and 60 Extension. We've got 1,500 or 1,600 of your

Robert "Chick" Black
(Courtesy of Donald Black)

women who are sitting down at their machines refusing to go to work. They want you to come over there and ask them to go back to work." Once again, Reynolds managers found themselves confronting not just resistance, but an explicit, head-to-head challenge to their command. "Now Mr. Whitaker," Black replied, "you want me to go over there and speak for the company. I'm not going to do that. I've got a wife working over there. Just to let you know how I feel about it, we're going to close down this plant. I think it's wrong for me working in Number 64, with my wife over in Number 60 trying to better her condition with all those other people. I'm going to send word up and down this five-floor factory and in thirty minutes we'll have everyone of these machines at a standstill." To show that he meant business, Black then walked over to Maso Fields and asked him to tell the men to cut off the machines. "He just held his hand up and all four machines went down," Black remembered, and "in less than twenty minutes there wasn't a machine running in that whole building."[35]

Robert Black's threat to close the plant had not been an idle boast. His participation in the TWOC and his interventions on behalf of his fellow workers had prepared him, like Theodosia Simpson, to assume leadership. "I had been begging people to go to the foreman and demand more money," he explained. "They would quiet me by slipping me a three and four cent raise. I would show my envelope to the other guys and say, 'Man, why don't you get that man to give you more money?' Therefore they felt that I was trying to help them get better pay. They had confidence in me. I was confident that if I went back there and asked them to close it down, they would do it. We just had that kind of relationship."[36]

Sizing up the situation, Whitaker responded with his usual blend of reasonableness and determination. The foreman called Black back into the office. Whitaker was still there, only now he had Black's employment record. "You have years of exemplary service, with only three days' absence in all that time," Whitaker said. "You are one of the highest paid colored workers in all the company. You should be proud of that record and you should do everything you can to help the company continue its production. We've got a war going on. You don't want those soldiers overseas to find out that you people are refusing to produce cigarettes for them."[37]

Whitaker, however, had more than Black's record and the war effort on his mind. The work on Black's floor consisted of cutting up tobacco stems after they had been processed with conditioners and simmered under pressure in large, tightly packed bins. If the stems sat too long, they could burst into flames. "Robert," Whitaker said, "you know that tobacco can't sit in those bins over the weekend. The whole factory will burn down. I want to appeal to you to process the tobacco that's in the bins. We'll give the men an extra hour's pay, and then you all can go home." Black agreed to this arrangement but in exchange asked for a pass to go to the union office and then to go speak with the women in Numbers 60 and 60 Extension.[38]

The foreman wrote the pass. Black returned to the floor and asked the men to process the remaining product. They were confused by his request. "Why should we work, when everybody else has quit?" one man demanded. "Now, I'm not on the company's side," Black told them. "But why let this whole department burn up when we expect to come back to work, under better conditions." The men finally agreed, though one man said, "I'm going to stay and work the day, because I need the money." The other workers would have none of that. "You're going to work until that damn tobacco's run out," they told him, "and when that tobacco's run out, you, and us and everybody else is going." Not every group of employees proved as cooperative as those in Number 64. According to foreman R. F. Hamrick, workers in Number 97 Casing and Cutting refused to finish processing the tobacco. Hamrick had to enlist white workers and supervisory personnel to work all weekend to clean out the bins.[39]

As events unfolded elsewhere, employees from Number 65 gathered outside the factory. The committee chosen in the wake of the sit-down had prepared a list of grievances and was ready to meet with Whitaker. Simpson recounted the previous evening's meeting at the Union Mission Church and reminded everyone that they were to report to their jobs while the committee talked with management. Soon, the workers made their way up the stairs to their respective floors.

The committee waited by the foreman's office, but Whitaker never came. The work stoppages in other departments required his immediate attention. Ed Bumgardner, personnel director, and B. C. Johnson, stemming superintendent, finally showed up. They hastily promised to reduce the workload and to consider wage increases, but they were less concerned with a few hundred workers in Number 65 than with the thousands of idle hands throughout the factory. After Bumgardner and Johnson left, the women in Number 65 saw no reason to go back to work. "Instead of working, people would just cut off the machine and go down the line and talk with someone on another machine," Simpson recalled. "A lot of people got joy from not working. [The foreman] was afraid to say too much, so they just did as they pleased that Friday."[40]

By early afternoon, thousands of black workers were on the streets around the factories. Numbers 60, 60 Extension, and 64 were closed. Number 65 was idle. TWOC members made the rounds, exhorting their fellow workers to follow the lead of the women in the stemmeries. "Chick and all the rest of them came over [to my plant]," remembered Willie Grier, "and said, 'Come on out, come on out. We're on strike.'" Soon, departments in Numbers 8, 256, and 97 joined the sit-down. "The thing that really hurt Reynolds," Robert Black observed, "was these workers, none of them went home. They were just out in the streets. Out on the company's premises. That was really embarrassing for the company. Everybody knew."[41]

An air of joy and excitement, relief and expectation surrounded the day's events. On the streets, boasts of what was going to happen to "old man so-and-so" mingled with propositions for later meetings. Like a fire alarm that unexpectedly disturbs the day's routine, the protest uprooted workers from their jobs in the factories and mixed them up on the streets below. For Theodosia Simpson, it didn't matter what motivated workers' actions; what was important was that "it got them out."[42]

As the workers left the factories and came out into the fresh air, they found TWOC members at the gates with union cards. Hundreds signed up that afternoon. Initiation fees filled the pockets and aprons of the union members. Impromptu speeches solidified support for the union. "If you want to pin a contract on the company," Black told a group of women at Number 60, "stay together. I can't promise you anything, but if you stick together and don't let the company intimidate you, we'll build a union in Reynolds."[43]

That evening, TWOC leaders left the union office and made their way to a meeting at the home of Boyd Byrd. There were thousands of people "all out in the streets, all back out in the yard, everywhere." The momentum of the expanding protest had brought along many of the timid souls who had remained on the sidelines up to now. What had started out as a sit-down in Number 65 quickly captured the imagination of the larger black community, and hundreds of people who did not work at Reynolds joined the crowds and lent their support. The police promptly arrived on the scene, but their usual high-handedness gave way to cooperation in the face of such a large crowd. They told people not to block the streets and suggested that the meeting move to the Woodland Avenue School, a few blocks away. They agreed to see that someone turned on the lights at the school grounds.[44]

Slowly the workers made their way up the street. Trailing behind, seeing all the people, TWOC officials tried to prepare themselves for what had become a volatile mass meeting. The situation seemed critical, and only a few of the local people had union experience on which to draw. "We didn't know whether the company would hire thugs to start something," Simpson recalled. "That was a fear of the union people. Our people being hot under the collar and a little bit angry, the company could very easily have sent people in there and started a mass riot. If we had had any sort of disturbance, everything would have gone downhill."[45]

Simpson's fears were not unfounded. Racial tensions had reached a boiling point all across the United States that June. The "Zoot suit" riots in Los Angeles sparked a series of bloody conflagrations that engulfed San Diego, Philadelphia, and Chicago. That very weekend, blacks and whites in Detroit confronted each other in one of the worst race riots in the nation's history. Thirty-four people died, nine whites and twenty-five blacks, the majority of whom were killed by police. It was not unthinkable that something similar could happen in Winston-Salem. Across the South, police and local militia had been used throughout the 1930s and 1940s to disrupt organizing drives and break strikes. Black activists, including UCAPAWA organizers, had repeatedly faced the fists, sticks, and guns of official and unofficial enforcers of the status quo. An atmosphere of defiance surrounded the gathering crowd. "The people, after they realized Reynolds could be conquered, all the years of sweat, the blood and the cursing just came out," Black observed.[46]

As it happened, the protest remained remarkably peaceful. No white thugs or policemen intruded. No hotheaded workers tried to channel the group's anger in a violent direction. Someone produced an old megaphone and brought a car around to serve as a platform for the speakers. The Reverend Frank O'Neal climbed up to give the invocation, and then Simpson led the group in singing what would become a union favorite, the spiritual "Do Lord, Remember Me." Simpson described what had happened in Number 65 on Thursday. "I told them they had nothing to be afraid of. Because we had stood together, the company couldn't do anything to us. I told them if they stood together, they could make the company listen to them." Black followed with a salute to the workers' determination to fight the "giant company." Frank Hargrove spoke of UCAPAWA's policy of industrial unionism and nondiscrimination and of the great gains made by the CIO. He said that the company had agreed to meet with a committee the next morning in an effort to resolve the issues before work started on Monday.[47]

As these leaders addressed the assembly, other TWOC members circulated through the crowd, signing up new members and collecting initiation fees. "During the meeting people would come up and submit their names and the names of other people in their department that hadn't joined the strike. 'We want to be part of it too. We want to be representatives.'" By the end of the evening, the group had elected a committee to meet with company officials on Saturday morning.[48]

The gathering on the school grounds that Friday night solidified the workers' movement. Its very size indicated the depth of the union's support and reinforced its members determination. The cooperative attitude of the police showed that there would be no overt retaliation—at least not yet—by Reynolds or the city fathers. The peaceful nature of the protest reassured the larger black community and gained the TWOC and the strikers an added measure of legitimacy and respect.

Marching, Marching

On Saturday morning, mourners gathered at the Second Institutional Baptist Church for the funeral of James McCardell. His death in Number 65 on Thursday had hastened the initial sit-down, yet the conflict unfolding in downtown Winston-Salem had already overshadowed the fate of one man. As soon as the services ended, the negotiating committee left for the Reynolds Building to present the workers' grievances. At 3:00 P.M. Whitaker issued a statement formally promising to examine the grievances and to explore the possibility of seeking permission for wage increases from the War Labor Board.[49]

The TWOC and the workers' committee studied the company's proposal. Although it did recognize that problems existed, the proposal offered nothing but vague assurances. The TWOC feared that the company would fire all the leaders as soon as production resumed, something Reynolds had done repeatedly in past organizing drives and a possibility that all the rank-and-filers understood. "The only way we knew we could beat Reynolds," Robert Black observed, "was to keep those people out of those plants. The trick was once they got them back in there to running those machines, the first person that stepped out, he or she would get fired.

And that would intimidate and throw fear into the others." Accordingly, the TWOC demanded that Whitaker sign a written statement promising not to discriminate against strikers. Union leaders also decided to call a mass meeting for Sunday afternoon, at which time they would discuss the company's proposal and ask the workers to continue the strike. The rank-and-file's response would determine what happened next.[50]

Sunday morning in any southern town revolved around the church, and that June 20 was no exception. Gathering in churchyards before Sunday school, striking Reynolds workers and their families talked about the walkout. TWOC leaders—all active church members—made their way through the various congregations, urging everyone to come to the meeting that afternoon.[51] The evening before, they had made a point of talking to virtually every minister in the black community. Reynolds workers and their families accounted for a large portion of most congregations. Many of the ministers, particularly those with small churches, even worked in the factories. Some had allowed the TWOC to hold union meetings in their churches and had openly supported the union. The ministers' understanding and support was vital to the workers' efforts. Willie Grier, a member at Mt. Zion Baptist Church, talked to his pastor, the Reverend Kelley Goodwin; Theodosia Simpson consulted her minister, the Reverend Jerry Drayton at New Bethel Baptist.[52]

Geneva McClendon and Velma Hopkins belonged to Shiloh Baptist Church, pastored by the Reverend R. M. Pitts. They had gone to him on Saturday to ask for his assistance. "At the time," McClendon remembered, "Shiloh Baptist had about 500 members, and at least 400 of them worked for Reynolds. A lot of us were in the union." An imposing, eloquent man, loved and respected by his congregation and the black community, Pitts was a forthright opponent of racial discrimination, and he had quickly taken a stand in favor of the union. "He was the first minister to support it," McClendon recalled. "In fact, he was the most outspoken minister. That Sunday he told us to stick together and all those that weren't in the union to join it." "He preached organization and the people respected him," Robert Black remembered. "He was trying to get the black maids, domestic workers, to build an organization to force the people that they were working for under slave conditions to recognize their ability and to make stronger efforts to see that they earned a living wage and were treated like decent people."[53]

Barred for the most part from participation in the city's political life, African Americans used their churches as a base for social, educational, and community involvement, and church activities provided a training ground for the men and women who would become union leaders. The church also served as a channel of communication in the black community and on this Sunday offered the means by

Reverend R. M. Pitts, pastor
of Shiloh Baptist Church
(*The Expected*, Virginia
Baptist State Convention)

which the union could contact workers, discuss the issues in small groups, and respond to questions and concerns. To be sure, church leaders commonly viewed
unions with suspicion, on the grounds that they discriminated against blacks or
upset the balance of race relations. Some, as Robert Black put it, "were more concerned about keeping their church and the collection plate going." Those concerns
had not disappeared overnight, and the leaders of some black churches refused to
support the TWOC efforts. In all but a few services, however, ministers at least mentioned the strike. Citing a long history of poor working conditions and low pay,
they joined Pitts in urging their members to join the union.[54]

After church, everyone went home for dinner and then gathered on the Woodland Avenue School grounds. It was a "nice, sunshiny" afternoon, and the brick
school building wedged in the corner at Eleventh Street and Cleveland Avenue provided a natural gathering place for the 9,000 to 10,000 people who attended the
TWOC meeting. "People were out in the streets, on sidewalks, in parked cars, standing on the top of their cars. People were in trees. They were everywhere; everywhere they could find a spot."[55]

A few hundred white workers joined the gathering, some as curious spectators,
others as union supporters. Just the day before, white TWOC members led by Clark

"Slim" Sheppard, a machine operator in the Number 12 cigarette-making department, made known their support for the black workers' protest and requested a meeting with Reynolds officials to discuss their own grievances. The white workers' involvement, limited as it was, strengthened the TWOC's claim to leadership of an interracial class-based movement.[56]

Organizers erected a small platform and set up a loudspeaker system. At 3:00 P.M. Pitts opened the meeting with an invocation. He blessed the spirit of the workers and the courage of their leaders. As the people echoed his final "Amen," the fervor of the crowd began to build. Once again, Theodosia Simpson told the story of the sit-down in Number 65. Shouts of "Amen" and "Tell it, sister" interrupted her time and again. "The lesson," she concluded, "was that you have to stick together and stand up to the company." Conrad Espe, UCAPAWA international vice president, brought greetings from the international union, from President Donald Henderson, and from the CIO. He promised full support for the workers in Winston-Salem. William DeBerry, the most respected of the organizers, continued the thanks offered by the UCAPAWA staff. He had worked closely with the workers' committee, met with church groups, passed out leaflets at the factory gates, and gone door to door in the black community. This day he spoke of his experiences as an organizer among sharecroppers in the South, telling about how he had been shot and had had to hide in the bushes to escape arrest. "The dramatics of that experience really hit home with the workers," Theodosia Simpson recalled. "We felt those guys can really take it. We had a lot of respect for DeBerry."[57]

The last to speak was Robert Black. As he climbed up on the platform, someone passed the word that Whitaker had been spotted on the front porch of a nearby house. "To begin I gave [Whitaker] a big greeting from the platform and asked him to come over and hear what we had to say." Black's reputation as a talker was on the line as he addressed the huge crowd. "It gave me a chance to pour out all the bitterness against the company. All I had to do was open my mouth and the words just rolled out." Although he had never aspired to the ministry, the sit-down seemed to have transformed Black into a charismatic, prophetic preacher.[58]

Black provided details of the Saturday meeting between the workers' committee and management. He read Whitaker's statement, pointing out the lack of any binding agreement that would protect the workers when they returned to work. He suggested that the workers reject the company proposal and continue the strike. "After we shut that company down," Black reflected, "we realized all the years that we had took cursings and abuses and slave driving off of that company, and we saw, just by sticking together, how we could manhandle that big giant."[59] As he finished speaking, Black called for a vote on the company's proposal. Workers defiantly registered their stand: no agreement, no work. "Well, since we have voted not to go back to work," Black responded, "we won't have to call Mr. Whitaker. We can tell him now." With that, another "No!" echoed from the crowd.[60]

The night shift at Reynolds that June included only the departments that manufactured cigarettes and smoking tobacco. But the sit-downs in the stemmeries on Friday had halted the flow of tobacco for fabrication, so the workers on the Sunday night shift had nothing to do. The black workers who were in town that evening saw a concrete illustration of their power: they had shut down the plants.[61]

The real test, however, came on Monday morning. The *Journal* forecast another hot summer day. The view from the top floor of the Reynolds Building suggested nothing different from a thousand previous Mondays: workers, black and white, "loaded the streets." But down on those streets, a new spirit reigned. Black workers walked in groups, not alone. They looked straight ahead, not down. They reinforced their pledge to one another to remain on strike. The men and women who made their way up Third, Fourth, and Fifth Streets were not the same people they had been the week before.

"The company had the plant gates open, but we instructed the workers to follow their leaders," Black recalled. "If the company had not signed an agreement, they were not to go inside. They came with their aprons, their overalls, and their lunches. The streets were full of people. The foremen said, 'Y'all come on in.' But the people said, 'No, sir.' We went around to the gates and told them an agreement had not been signed, not to go to work. The people went on back home."[62]

The 7:30 whistle blew as usual, but no one was there to turn on the machines. Production in the giant factories of the R. J. Reynolds Tobacco Company had ground to a halt. More than 10,000 workers (56 percent of whom were women and approximately 60 percent of whom were African American) stayed off their jobs. For the first time in the company's history, a critical mass of workers had exercised the power of refusing to work as a means of improving the conditions of their labor. The TWOC had been successful; unity had been maintained. "We had Reynolds by his tail," Black remarked, "and he wasn't going anywhere unless he settled with us."[63]

Nonstriking whites, who numbered a little over 3,000, reported to the plant but left when the company told them there was nothing for them to do. Some black workers reported seeing young, rural white men entering the factories and finding themselves assigned to jobs ordinarily filled by blacks. One such position was in the priming bins, where workers packed tobacco with their feet. The bins were miserably hot and the work was physically demanding. The rumor spread that the white men had been unable to do it and had been sent home.[64]

The rebellion was infectious: by Monday, Winston-Salem was in the midst of a general strike as hundreds of workers from other companies joined the thousands on strike at Reynolds. At Brown & Williamson Tobacco Company, approximately 600 members of the Tobacco Workers International Union—American Federation of Labor (TWIU-AFL) continued a wildcat strike that had begun the previous Friday. Although the TWIU segregated blacks and whites in separate locals, in this case the locals made common cause, demanding higher wages and better working conditions for all. Workers at the Mengel Company, a supplier of wooden products for the tobacco industry, struck Monday morning to protest a delay in a settlement by the National War Labor Board. Black workers at Hanes Knitting Company and maids at the Robert E. Lee Hotel staged work stoppages as well.[65]

R. W. Goodrick from the U.S. Conciliation Service had arrived in Winston-Salem on Sunday night at the request of UCAPAWA officials. On Monday he contacted Conrad Espe at the TWOC office, who told him that the Reynolds workers would be willing to return to work if management entered into a discussion of grievances with the workers' committee. Goodrick conveyed the demand to Whitaker, who agreed to meet with the workers. Members of the committee also asked Goodrick to obtain written and binding assurances from the company that no disciplinary action would be taken against workers and that negotiations would take place on company time. In exchange for these assurances, they would ask everyone to go back to work. Goodrick promised to secure such a written agreement from Whitaker by that evening.[66]

At 6:00 P.M. the TWOC held another mass meeting at the Woodland Avenue School. Black reported that the company had agreed to recognize the committee but that Whitaker had not yet signed the agreement. The strikers agreed to return to work upon receipt of a signed statement but not before. The negotiating committee members then adjourned to the TWOC office to wait for Whitaker's statement so that they could begin spreading the word to go back to work. Hours passed, but nothing came from the Reynolds Building.

UCAPAWA officials, anxious to get workers back on the job because of the union's no-strike pledge, felt that the company's willingness to meet with workers was adequate assurance that they would not begin firing union activists. But Black and the other workers had long memories. They had not forgotten 1928, when the company fired more than 2,000 union-minded workers, black and white. They were well aware of the dozens of workers since then who had been let go as soon as a foreman found out they were attending union meetings. "We need that stipulation," Black told UCAPAWA officials, "in case they ever try to intimidate, and they will." The company might not single out and fire leaders like Black, but it would

Workers massed outside factory doors during a 1948 protest (Ed. T. Simons, Winston-Salem, N.C., for United Tobacco Workers Local 22. Courtesy of the Reference Center for Marxist Studies, New York; Mark Rosenzweig, Archivist.)

quietly pick off rank and filers. "Once the workers realized that the company could still do that and get by with it, it would scare their britches off."[67]

By Monday evening idle tobacco workers crowded the downtown streets. Robert Black remembered the angry mood. "They had allowed that company to ride roughshod over them all those years, with their heads bowed. When they realized they could stop that big giant, they got bitter." To lessen the potential for violence among angry workers, the union asked City Hall to close all the beer gardens and wine rooms in town. Ignoring the union's initiative, the *Journal* claimed that police authorities had halted the sale of beer and wine. The newspaper also reported ominously that "the State Guard held an unofficial mobilization."[68]

Under the circumstances, Whitaker apparently decided to stall; he did not sign the statement Monday evening, nor did he call the workers' committee back for another meeting. Nevertheless, at 11:30 P.M., Commissioner Goodrick, assuming that Whitaker had complied with his request, issued a statement urging all workers to return to work. The TWOC did not find out about Goodrick's statement until the next morning. Black remembered: "Somebody went on the radio to tell the workers that the company had met with the employees' committee, that they signed a document that bound the workers, and that Robert C. Black and John C. Whitaker had signed the document." It was a prescription for mass confusion. There was no telling what the next morning would bring.[69]

"That Tuesday morning people were marching, marching," Black recalled. "The streets were just full of people. One of the workers came to my house. We had a meeting and I hadn't gotten to bed 'till 4:00. He said the people were going in the factories. A neighbor of mine had a Ford with a rumble seat. So I got in the back of the car and we went around to the plants where we had designated leaders. We asked them to keep the people outdoors. The workers went back to the factory expecting that the thing had been signed. So I told them, 'The Reynolds Tobacco Company has pulled a sneak.'"[70]

Black's efforts paid off: the workers stayed out on the streets. Once more the machines remained silent in the cavernous plants. The events of Tuesday morning testified to the workers' discipline and solidarity and to their trust in such rank-and-file leaders.

Later that morning, Reynolds officials called the workers' committee and Commissioner Goodrick back to the Reynolds Building. Black asked Whitaker whether he was going to sign the document. "The lawyers tell me it's not binding," replied Whitaker. "We want something to protect those workers," said Black. "We're going to have a written statement with your signature on it. I'll take the responsibility with the elected workers' committee of guaranteeing you that once we get this thing behind us, more than 95 percent of our members will be in the plants ready to work. But not until."[71]

Commissioner Goodrick advised the managers to sign the agreement. Finally, Whitaker agreed. In turn, Black promised to go on the radio and talk to the newspapers to let people know the agreement had been signed. The *Winston-Salem Sentinel* carried his statement in its late edition. The TWOC held a mass meeting that night at the Woodland Avenue School, and the workers voted unanimously to return to their jobs. "Folks said they wasn't ready to go back to work. It was June. It was hot. They wanted to stay out a month. But they went back. The company said they had the lowest absentee record of any day when we went back."[72]

Anatomy of a Sit-down Strike

The momentum behind the sit-down and the eventual walkout had been gathering for some time. But social movements rarely evolve in a predictable manner. Indeed, most embryonic campaigns fail to leave any imprint on the historical record. Why, on those steamy summer days in June 1943, did the walls of repression and fear, accommodation and fatalism come tumbling down?[73]

Given the volatility of the situation at Reynolds and the emergence of rank-and-file leaders within the TWOC, skirmishes between workers and supervisors might have broken out in a number of places. Robert Black, Eddie Gallimore, and Velma Hopkins were all capable of leading revolts in their departments. As it happened, it was the reaction of Theodosia Simpson and her confederates to the tears of a hard-pressed woman and the death of an ailing man that led to the sit-down in Number 65 and sparked the subsequent protest in Number 60 and Number 60 Extension. The chain of events continued with the walkout of almost the entire black workforce, the expansion of union membership from hundreds to thousands, and the selection of a committee to meet with management.

No one explanation will suffice. The TWOC had not planned to bring production to a halt in order to enlist thousands of new members, as management believed. But neither was this a purely "spontaneous act on the part of the employees," as union organizer Frank Hargrove claimed. A series of contingent events and preexisting conditions conspired to produce a walkout of historic proportions.[74]

Changes in labor law, the policies of the New Deal, the intense demand for labor, and the patriotic egalitarianism of the war all provided a context that was favorable to organization. Just as important, workers in the TWOC had spent two years preparing themselves and their fellow workers to act. This favorable context and deliberate self-organization helped to undermine one of the major barriers to collective action: the fear that kept workers in line. Acting in unison and with backing from a national union and federal mediators, they could dare to take actions that might cost them their jobs—jobs that, for all of their shortcomings, were the lifelines of the black working class. Workers in other departments could see that the people in Number 65 had not been fired when they sat down that Thursday. The breakdown of structures of authority, like the rise of social movements, follows no set course or immutable laws. But one thing is predictable: cracks in the edifice help create the conditions for future deterioration. And sometimes that deterioration, however long in coming, appears to happen virtually overnight.[75]

The particular confluence of race, class, and gender inequalities in the stemmeries provided a critical impetus for the workers' actions. In Number 65, for instance, gender-specific grievances and gender-defined responses were at the heart of the situation. The decision by the older woman's coworkers not to help her keep up with her work—a decision influenced by the company's effective use of wage differentials and favoritism—warns against the assumption that a preexisting solidarity explains collective action. Nevertheless, the woman's tears evoked a reaction from Simpson and her friends that was strongly influenced by their common experiences and socialization as women. Who among them had not responded—or wanted to respond—in a similar way to the abuse of a foreman, father, or husband, or to the stress of too much work and too few rewards?[76] The women in Number 65 could also comprehend the seriousness of the woman's plight: she was a black woman raising children on her own, with the family dependent on her wages for support. If others in Number 65 were not in the same situation, they had friends and relatives who were. The white foreman's abusive treatment had both a gender- and race-specific meaning as well as a history that helped solidify the reaction of the other women workers. To be sure, foremen often treated white women and black men disrespectfully as well, but there were virtually no constraints when it came to black women. "The woman was a little more oppressed," Theodosia Simpson, observed. "They had to put up with the men patting on them and talking all kinds of talk to them. They were anxious to get out from under it."[77]

The racial stratification of the workplace also helped to mobilize the protest. All the authority figures in the factory—the superintendents, the foremen, the nurses—were white. There were no black supervisors, even at the lowest levels, to discipline workers and defuse black resentment toward white managers. Even slave owners understood the value of such intermediaries. This raw display of the prerogatives of white men differentiated black and white workers. True, white workers were subject to supervision that could be as harsh and demanding as that faced by blacks. But that discipline was always mediated by whiteness, and sometimes by social and family connections.[78]

Finally, class divisions were critical. They directed workers' anger at the policies and personnel of the Reynolds Tobacco Company, not just at the larger structures of racial subordination. Class inequalities also provided the basis for the union's demands: more money, less work, better treatment.

Within this context, a series of events propelled the workers toward action. First, there was a change in routine that not only set people on edge but also drew their attention to other problems, such as harsh treatment by the foremen and wage inequalities. The catalyst in this case was the speed-up in the stemmeries, but a wage cut, layoff, or other event could have played the same role. Second, there were two triggering incidents—the threatened firing of the woman and the death of

McCardell—that helped focus and magnify those resentments. Here, too, other events, such as the firing of a union leader or a serious accident, might have had the same result. Third, the workers had leaders who could initiate, direct, and maintain the protest. Simpson started the action rolling, acting not as an isolated individual, but as a representative of the group.

Simpson's relationship with her family, her husband's support, her friendship with Geneva McClendon, her participation in her church, her relations with the other workers in Number 65, and her membership in the TWOC all enabled her to speak as her fellow workers would have spoken, had they had her special abilities. When she acted, they followed because they trusted her and shared her outrage. In the process, they overcame their isolation and sensed the strength they possessed when they stood together. The silence of the machines represented this fusion. No one individual, no matter how heroic, could stop the whir of production in the plant, but hundreds of workers, acting collectively, could do so. Once that had happened, and the foreman had to call the Reynolds Building for help, the conflict progressed to a new level.

After Number 65 had taken action, the rank-and-file TWOC leaders provided critical direction to the mounting protest. They helped explain the circumstances to their fellow workers. "If it had not been for the steps that the [TWOC] took during the course [of organizing]," Robert Black said, "we would have had nothing there to have looked to at the time of this tragedy. But you see, our people were so spread out into so many plants that it was a perfect setting for us. [On Tuesday morning,] when I went to 65, Theodosia Simpson closed down 65. I would go to 256; Velma Hopkins closed down 256. Ninety-seven, Bro Malone closed down. Vander Rogers closed down Number 12. The Rev. Frank O'Neal closed down Number 8. That gave us such an advantage."[79]

Finally, TWOC leaders had a strategy for immediate action and a direction for further mobilization. Simpson did not try to mobilize the women in Number 65 by asking them to go on strike or join the union. She simply suggested, "Let's not work until we get some understanding of how these people are going to be treated." These were not great expectations and might reasonably be attained. In fact, the workers in Number 65 accomplished their initial goal: work *did* come to a halt, and the men from the Reynolds Building *did* agree to discuss the women's grievances. The same was true for the larger protest. Workers asked that management meet with a committee and sign a statement guaranteeing that workers would not be fired, a demand that could be, and was, quickly met.[80]

Under other conditions such immediate responses on the part of the company might have stopped the protest in its tracks. Instead, over the next few days hundreds of workers who had had nothing to do with the TWOC's eighteen-month campaign joined the union. Why, suddenly, would so many workers do what only a day before they might have been afraid to do?

First, while the workers' committee was negotiating with the company, the TWOC deftly seized the moment to transform the mounting protest into a recruiting drive. TWOC members, with their hands full of authorization cards, hit the streets on the afternoon of the walkout, signing up recruits and collecting initiation dues. The TWOC's actions, moreover, were backed by the resources of UCAPAWA. The union had an organizational structure, human and financial assets, and national and local leaders who were well trained and ready to carry out their responsibilities. Those leaders could muster support from outside Winston-Salem, certainly from the CIO unions and often from the federal government itself.

And finally, workers themselves endowed the union with a larger meaning that transcended any concerns they might have had about its appropriateness as an organizational vehicle for their protests. It became the secular expression of their resistance to racial injustice and a manifestation of their determination to change the structures of power in which they were ensnared. By the time the workers' committee met with management on Saturday morning, a protest movement had been born in the form of a union.

On Thursday morning, June 17, no one could have predicted what occurred over the next six days, but by Wednesday, June 23, there seemed to be no way to stop what had been put in motion. The willingness of thousands of black workers to walk off their jobs at some risk to themselves and their families represented a rare and remarkable moment in southern history. The walkout, the rapid membership drive, and the mass meetings gave them reason for hope. Out of such hope, Local 22 would be born.

CHAPTER TWO

Industrial and Political Revolutions

Although union officials described the sit-down in Number 65 as "spontaneous" and company officials attributed it to "outside agitators," the roots of the conflict that engulfed Winston-Salem in June of 1943 lay deep in the history of the town and the region. The pivotal moment in that history was a late-nineteenth-century coup d'état carried out by a planter-industrialist coalition in which Reynolds Tobacco Company played a critical role. The outcome of this turn-of-the-century struggle defined the social formation known as white supremacy, which rested on class and gender hierarchies as well as racial subordination. It was this larger system, not just the inequities in the workplace, that Winston-Salem tobacco unionists fought to transform in the 1940s.

The Rise of R. J. Reynolds Tobacco Company

The Civil War devastated the Piedmont South, but within adversity there was opportunity. Some saw the future in cotton textiles; others seized on tobacco as the vehicle for their own and the region's recovery. In Salem, where Moravians seeking religious freedom and economic self-sufficiency had settled during the eighteenth century, and in Winston, created nearby in 1849 as the county seat for Forsyth County, the two industries grew up side by side. By the time Winston and

Salem joined in 1913, however, it was tobacco that had put the "Twin City" on the map.[1]

Moravian leaders created Salem as the town center for a religious community of small farmers and artisans. By the antebellum period, Salem had emerged as the hub of a vigorous economy based on farming, small-scale craft production, and merchandising. But beginning in 1836, cotton textiles and other types of manufacturing gained ascendancy, and the subsistence farmers and small craftsmen producing for a regional market soon diminished in importance. Although Salem retained the pious posture of its congregational beginnings, by the end of the nineteenth century industry and commerce also shaped the ethos of the community.[2]

By contrast, the quest for power and profit suffused Winston from its very beginning. The antebellum tobacco industry had centered in Virginia, where slaves on tobacco plantations shaped the leaf into products for local consumption. North Carolina farmers too had long produced tobacco for chewing and smoking, peddling it in the backcountry as a sideline. The explosive growth of the industry in the 1870s depended on Bright leaf tobacco, a thin, mild-tasting leaf that flourished in the silty soils of the northern Piedmont along the Virginia border and was processed by flue-curing rather than by Virginia's open-fire method. The Union and Confederate soldiers who passed through the area took a taste for the mild leaf home with them, and demand for North Carolina Bright tobacco after the war encouraged more and more farmers in the ten counties that came to be known as the "Bright Belt" to risk their labor and capital on tobacco cultivation.[3]

Winston entrepreneurs quickly grasped the possibilities for turning an indigenous agricultural product into a major business. Not only were raw materials readily available, but Bright leaf tobacco presented an unparalleled marketing opportunity. In most industries, southern manufacturers had to compete against established businesses in the Northeast and Midwest, the nation's most dynamic industrial regions. Tobacco met no such competition. Tobacco, moreover, was a consumer product readily differentiated by taste and the use of brand names; it was also addictive, providing entrepreneurs with an ideal opportunity to *create* desire and thus assure themselves of a market. In addition, tobacco had two important advantages over textiles, the South's leading industry, both of which were critical in a region strapped for capital and dependent on distribution networks based in the North. First, start-up costs were low because, while textile manufacturing was already highly mechanized, tobacco products were still largely made by hand. Second, unlike cotton mill owners, who continued to depend on northern commission agents to market their products, tobacco manufacturers quickly learned to peddle their own wares. Taken together, low demands for capital, a protected regional market, control over distribution, and an understanding of the money to be made through brand-name recognition, creative packaging, and consumer loyalty prepared tobacco entrepreneurs to create modern enterprises and then "take on the world."[4]

Among the young men who responded to tobacco's lure was Richard Joshua (R. J.) Reynolds. His father was a successful farmer, merchant, and tobacco manufacturer in Patrick County, Virginia, who owned nearly one hundred slaves. Too young to fight in the Civil War, R. J. spent two years at Emory and Henry College before he returned home to learn the tobacco manufacturing trade. Traveling the back roads of the Appalachians peddling his father's tobacco taught him the tricks of merchandising. In 1875 he headed south to Winston, drawn by the success of local businessmen in lobbying for an extension of the North Carolina Railroad from Greensboro through Winston and Salem and on to the Virginia line and by the town's location "in the center of the belt in which the finest tobacco in the world is grown." Like the Carrs and Dukes of Durham, who became his chief rivals, R. J. put his faith in advertising, strove to dominate a regional market, and began invading the Midwest and Northeast as well. Within ten years, R. J. Reynolds Tobacco Company had catapulted to the top of the plug and twist chewing tobacco industry.[5]

By 1890 Winston's population had reached 8,000, half of whom labored in the twenty-two tobacco plants that dotted the town. Other businesses grew directly from tobacco: wagon makers supplied vehicles for factories and farms; numerous mercantile stores, taverns, and hotels served the workers and entrepreneurs who flocked to town; and Wachovia Bank and Trust filled its vaults with tobacco deposits and stocks. In Salem two established mills and the new Artista mill provided employment for several hundred, mostly white workers.[6]

Textiles and tobacco adopted strikingly divergent labor recruitment strategies. Following a pattern established in the antebellum period, textile manufacturers hired white workers, especially widows and single women fleeing the ravaged countryside, to tend their looms and spinning machines. They relegated black men to menial positions such as sweeping floors and unloading and unpacking cotton bales and employed almost no black women. They also built mill villages, provided housing, and kept an intrusive eye on workers' lives. The tobacco industry, by contrast, relied heavily on African American workers. Donning a few of the trappings of paternalism, R. J. sometimes paid transportation costs to Winston, tried to recruit whole families, hired the relatives of current workers, and made a point of roaming through the factories and knowing his workers by name. By and large, African American tobacco workers neither benefited from the subsidized housing in the mill villages nor suffered from the surveillance and isolation that mill hands endured.[7]

The dominance of tobacco guaranteed that Winston would have a large black population, and in 1880 a full 47 percent of the town's residents were African American. The black population, however, waxed and waned with the seasons, for tobacco work, based as it was on an agricultural crop, was a highly seasonal endeavor. Blacks labored in the factories in the spring and summer and then returned to the countryside. Gradually, however, more and more people stayed on in Winston, started new families, and began to find other local jobs during the off season.[8]

As was the case with white mill hands, most black tobacco workers were young and single, and a large proportion of them were women. The two groups were similar in other ways as well. Both textile and tobacco workers labored in difficult and dirty conditions for eleven or twelve hours a day. Both earned rock-bottom wages: an average of sixty-nine cents a day for men and fifty-five cents for women in the county's textile mills, as compared to $1 for men and sixty-four cents for women in tobacco. Yet these two industries provided virtually the only road out of rural poverty as well as a critical means by which struggling farm families acquired the margin of income that allowed them to cling to the land.[9]

While a new class made up of successful manufacturers and merchants prospered and increasingly directed the destiny of the towns, craftsmen, who had dominated the antebellum economy, watched their independence steadily slip away. The coming of the railroad and the intrusion of mass-produced goods from the North, together with indigenous industrialization, created an environment in which fewer and fewer young men could look forward to becoming master craftsmen. The lucky and ambitious might aspire to positions as foremen, clerks, or small proprietors. Others found themselves scrambling for jobs as day laborers or as operatives in the towns' new textile and tobacco plants.[10]

Reynolds's success in dominating the plug chewing tobacco industry made the company a prime target for the monopolistic ambitions of James B. ("Buck") Duke in the 1890s. A long-time rival, Duke had made his fortune in nearby Durham, but he quickly moved his American Tobacco Company to New York. There he developed the financial contacts that enabled him to create a virtual monopoly modeled on John D. Rockefeller's Standard Oil Company. The Trust, as Duke's company was called, was among the nation's first modern businesses, and it quickly gained control of the country's fledgling cigarette market and then of the northern chewing tobacco business.[11]

Initially, R. J. Reynolds managed to hold out against Duke. But in 1899, his need for access to northern capital and the very real possibility that the Trust might run him out of business forced him to capitulate. R. J. Reynolds Tobacco Company re-organized as a New Jersey corporation, and American Tobacco acquired a two-thirds stake in the new company. Duke and other American officials joined the board of directors, and much of the profit migrated to New York. Reynolds To-bacco Company kept its corporate identity, however. R. J. remained as president with his office in Winston, and local executives continued to manage the company.[12]

R. J. hated what he regarded as Yankee control. He particularly despised his quar-terly trips to the North to report to what he called the "New York crowd." But he also thrived by deploying the Trust's financial clout and powers of intimidation. His job was to consolidate ownership of the plug chewing tobacco industry in the South, and Reynolds Tobacco Company was soon gobbling up firms in Virginia and North Carolina. In 1900 the company acquired its three major competitors in Winston, and within a few years it controlled 90 percent of the industry.[13]

R. J. also came up with the idea for a nationally distributed pipe tobacco. He named the secret mixture Prince Albert, after the coat worn by the popular Prince of Wales, who had become the English monarch Edward VII, and retained a major New York advertising firm, N. W. Ayer & Sons, to market it throughout the coun-try. Founded in 1869, Ayer & Sons played a central role in formulating the tasks of the modern advertising agency: to help corporations identify their products with progress and to rid advertising of its association with peddlers and other marginal operators who depended on face-to-face communication in local markets—men like R. J. himself in his younger days. With Ayer's advertising, northern capital, and an effective national sales force, Reynolds increased its annual production of Prince Albert from 250,000 pounds in 1907 to more than 14 million by 1911.[14]

When Theodore Roosevelt's "trustbusters" prevailed and the U.S. Supreme Court dissolved the American Tobacco Company Trust in 1911, Reynolds emerged as the smallest of the "big four" independent companies: American, Liggett & Myers, P. Lorillard, and Reynolds. R. J., however, was determined to "give Buck Duke hell" for earlier humiliations. A few days after the company regained its inde-pendence, a new electrical billboard lit up the Manhattan skyline. It featured a giant likeness of King Edward VII in his Prince Albert jacket, with the brand's slo-gan "The Nation's Joy Smoke" followed by a pointed statement of personal, re-gional, and company pride: "R. J. Reynolds Tobacco Company, Winston-Salem, N.C."[15]

In 1913 R. J. took a step that ushered in a new era in the industry. Although Reynolds Tobacco Company retained most of its chewing tobacco brands after the dissolution of the Trust, it received none of the increasingly lucrative cigarette mar-ket. R. J. moved to remedy that situation by introducing a new, lighter brand of cigarettes made from a blend of Turkish and domestic tobaccos, giving it a name that evoked not the small tobacco farmers of the Piedmont but the more exotic climes from which Reynolds imported the tobacco that he mixed with North Carolina Bright leaf and Kentucky burley to give Camels their distinctive taste.[16]

In the late nineteenth century, when numerous brands competed in local and regional markets, entrepreneurs sold tobacco plugs under names like Johnny Reb, Rebel Girl, Confederate, and Blood Hounds. Reynolds's $1.5 million Camels campaign, on the other hand, shied away from regional references. Camel ads neither acknowledged black consumers nor featured the pickaninnies, mammies, and other black stereotypes that filled advertising copy at the time. Instead they pictured wealthy white men and women in drawing rooms, marbled hallways, and fancy cars, on the assumption that the masses would emulate the tastes of the upper classes. At the same time, a pack of Camels sold for a dime, a nickel less than other brands. Marketed as a means of "magical regeneration through purchase," a modern, democratic, "product for the masses," and a "boon for the breathless age," Camels promised quick relief for the rushed urban dweller. Unlike cigars and pipes, which took time to smoke, cigarettes were "short, snappy, easily attempted, easily completed or just as easily discarded before completion." They were, as a *New York Times* editorial put it, the ultimate symbol of leisure in a hectic "machine age in which the ultimate cogs and wheels and levers are human nerves."[17]

Reynolds's profits continued to skyrocket during the 1920s as cigarettes became the emblem of the Jazz Age. The opulent climax of that decade was the opening of the twenty-two-story Reynolds Building in 1929, the tallest structure in North Carolina at the time. The company asked New York architects Shreve and Lamb (who later used the Winston-Salem design as a model for the Empire State Building) to design a headquarters that was striking, but not flashy. Marble from Missouri, France, Belgium, and Vermont lined the lobby, corridors, and restrooms. Gold leaf covered the lobby ceiling.[18]

The Reynolds Building rose skyward out of the factory district, dominating the visual landscape of Winston-Salem much as the company dominated the economic environment. It would not have been far-fetched to construe the twenty-two-story edifice as an elaborate guard tower from which company executives could keep watch over their subordinates at home, work, or play. From the observation tower on the building's east side, the naked eye could easily monitor the comings and goings of most of the city's black inhabitants. But while the nineteenth-floor executive offices did, in fact, become the command center for local power brokers, the implements of control were more subtle and far-reaching.[19]

Reynolds's one hundred acres of production facilities spread out in a crescent to the north, south, and east of the headquarters building, creating one of the most densely packed manufacturing districts in the country. That concentration made economic sense since large production units were critical for realizing economies of scale. But the company's decision to centralize its production facilities was not driven by rational economic choice alone. In fact, dispersion would have offered some advantages, such as lower real estate costs and the flexibility to seek out ever cheaper labor. Many national corporations had begun moving plants to suburban locations after the turn of the twentieth century as a way of avoiding the labor unrest they associated with urban life. Even Reynolds would flirt with decentralization during labor troubles at the end of World War I, but after a few years the company closed its small plants in New Jersey, Virginia, and Kentucky and consolidated all its operations in Winston-Salem.[20]

Reynolds's strong identification with the city prevailed. To R. J., his factory buildings were not simply spaces for production, they were the personification of his success. The town was not just a place to do business, it was the embodiment of the company's wealth and power. Winston-Salem, North Carolina, *was* R. J. Reynolds Tobacco Company and vice versa, an equation that was nicely illustrated by the proximity of the company's offices and factories to the city and county governmental buildings. By the 1920s, the company paid a fourth of the city's property taxes and contributed $1 of every $2.50 in state corporate income taxes. Commentators regularly described Winston-Salem as a "company town" or "extended mill village," and by all reports, the men who paid the piper called the tune.[21]

Reynolds's blend of national market dominance, modern advertising techniques, and a localistic corporate identity had far-reaching consequences. On the one hand, such concentration made tobacco manufacturers in general more vulnerable to unionization than the textile industry, where companies could transfer production from one locale to another and unions had to organize countless small businesses in order to affect the industry as a whole. On the other hand, Reynolds's particularly close identification with Winston-Salem gave it enormous economic and political leverage, and its corporate culture, which combined a self-image of paternalism with a drive system of managing black labor, made it more resistant to unions than the other major tobacco companies. In the long run, the tobacco giant forwarded regional economic development by creating worldwide markets for North Carolina products and drawing immense amounts of capital into the state. Yet tobacco's dominance also constricted development in Winston-Salem and other communities, short-circuiting the emergence of a strong local economy based on small, diverse, indigenous enterprises.[22]

Looking back, a local lawyer observed: "Once there were a hundred and forty in-

Aerial view of the factory district, Winston-Salem, ca. 1950 (Winston-Salem City Council Planning Department)

dependent tobacco factories in Winston-Salem. But the [Reynolds] trust turned the town from a thriving little city of small shops and moderate incomes into a city with one company so great, so rich, so powerful that the city itself became relatively insignificant. The little tobacco men disappeared and the big tobacco men took their places. The balance and interplay of interest and personalities also disappeared. No interest could conceivably have importance beside the overwhelming factory."[23]

Moreover, Reynolds's connection of its thoroughly modern business techniques with highly exploitative labor policies contributed little to the development of human capital. Unlike the textile industry, in which cutthroat competition among small companies kept profit margins low, tobacco became a virtually depression-proof oligopoly. Yet Reynolds did not follow the route of paying high wages in order to boost economic development and consumer demand. By taking advantage of the seemingly bottomless reservoir of poor, unskilled labor in the countryside, pursuing a low-wage strategy that discriminated against black workers, and using its lock on power to help perpetuate the underdevelopment of the workforce in the region, Reynolds Tobacco Company enriched itself and Winston-Salem's local elite while perpetuating the racial and class subordination that made the South the nation's poorest and least democratic region.[24]

"Prejudice and Passion"

The industrial and commercial transformations that underlay Reynolds's economic success went hand in hand with a reactionary political revolution that disfranchised the South's African Americans and poor whites. Post–Civil War politics was a hotly contested terrain, and by the late nineteenth century, North Carolina had developed the South's most democratic—and thus most volatile—political system. The struggle for power in Winston-Salem was representative of the political battles that took place in urban areas across the South.

Forsyth County citizens had overwhelmingly opposed secession in 1861, and during Reconstruction local Unionists joined freed blacks in the Republican Party, forging a biracial coalition that exercised substantial power until the end of the century. Although denied formal access to the vote, black women participated alongside men in the party's mass meetings and in myriad ways asserted their right to a voice in the public sphere. Winston's local newspaper, the *Union Republican*, articulated the city's Republican citizens' support for civil rights for freedmen and women as well as increased government spending for education and social services. For a time, the Republicans were quite successful: they controlled access to elected office until the late 1870s, when conservative Democrats, dominated by tobacco manufacturers, emerged as the most powerful political force in the area.[25]

Merchants, bankers, manufacturers, and large farmers from eastern North Carolina dominated the Democratic Party's leadership, and they opposed local self-government, state restrictions on private enterprise, government intervention in labor-management relations, and increased taxes for schools and public works. The Knights of Labor and the Farmers' Alliance gave voice to the grievances of shopkeepers, mechanics, workers, and farmers who saw their status and livelihood declining with the rise of industry and commercial agriculture. In 1886 and 1887, workers in Winston and Salem organized three Knights of Labor assemblies, one for black tobacco workers, one for white textile workers, and a mixed-trades assembly for whites. The local assemblies supported labor tickets in a series of municipal elections, with some limited success, and black Knights used the organization to further the social and educational interests of their own community. In the Knights of Labor hall in predominately black East Winston, weekly discussions focused on how to improve the political and economic status of artisans whose livelihoods were being undermined by the encroaching market economy as well as on plans for raising money for the black school. In 1889 the hall served as headquarters for a "general strike" by tobacco rollers protesting wage cuts.[26]

The Democratic-controlled state legislature responded to this interracial working-class political mobilization by passing a more restrictive election law in 1889. Winston was divided into three multimember wards, which local Democrats gerrymandered so that two of them were controlled by the largely white population in the northern and western part of town, which represented only one-third of the citizenry. Blacks, most of whom were registered Republicans, found themselves confined to a single ward in what would eventually become all-black East Winston. Although blatantly undemocratic, the Third Ward's demographics offered blacks the possibility for representation at City Hall. In 1890 they ran an independent Colored Men's Ticket. The Democrats nominated R. J. Reynolds, perhaps thinking he could command his employees' support. But the vote went against him, and black Republicans won the ward's three seats. Such assertions of black electoral power convinced the Democrats that confining the black vote was not enough, and they began searching for ways to eliminate it. In 1892 they challenged black registrants and intimidated those who tried to vote. Despite the harassment, three Republicans—two black and one white—won election in the Third Ward in 1892 and 1894.[27]

Increasing dissatisfaction with the political and economic policies of the Democratic Party, along with a series of failed crops and the first tremors of the economic crisis of 1893, spurred the growth of the Farmers' Alliance in North Carolina and throughout the South. In 1892 Alliance advocates formed the People's (Populist) Party to challenge Democratic rule locally and nationally. In the 1894 state elections, Populists joined Republicans to support a Fusion ticket. To the astonishment of North Carolina's ruling elite, this coalition swept into control of both houses of the General Assembly.[28]

Fusionists immediately enacted a program of unprecedented reforms, including lower interest rates on bank loans, increased expenditures for public education, higher taxes on corporations and railroads, and more generous appropriations for charitable and correctional institutions. To expand political participation among illiterate citizens, they required party symbols to be printed on all ballots. And they reversed the state's autocratic control of municipal politics. In Winston this reform meant an increase in the number of wards (from three to five) and aldermen (from nine to fifteen), a more equitable distribution of black voters among the wards, the popular election of the mayor and other local officials, and fairer registration and voting procedures. Although the dispersion of black voters lessened their chance to elect black candidates, it gave them unprecedented influence in the Republican Party and in city politics at large.[29]

Voters rushed to the polls in the 1896 state and national elections, creating the largest voter turnout in post-Reconstruction North Carolina. As a result of Fusionist electoral reforms, an astounding 85 percent of eligible North Carolina black voters cast their ballots, giving Republicans the margin of victory in a close gubernatorial contest. The significance was clear: if small farmers, shopkeepers, workers, and African Americans voted together, they could control politics in North Carolina. Thanks to a doubling of black voter registration, Republicans in Winston won the mayoral and nine aldermanic races. Then, with black voters holding a large majority in Winston, two black tobacco workers won election to the Board of Aldermen in 1898.[30]

Labeling Fusionist government "Negro rule," Democrats whipped up fears that the new regime was bent on turning social hierarchies upside down. In 1898 two white women bicyclists encountered a crowd of black women leaving work at one of Winston's tobacco factories. A black worker blocked the path of one of the white bicyclists, who had to dismount and walk around her. The *Winston Free Press* claimed that the other black women, whom it called "impudent wenches," "laughed loudly and clapped their hands at making her dismount." The paper commented that "such exasperating occurrences would not have happened but for the fact that the negro party is in power in North Carolina." Whatever the truth of the story, the reaction of the white press indicated just how threatened whites felt by the growing assertiveness of black men and women, whether in business, education, and politics or in daily life. "The condition is becoming unbearable," the editor of the *Free Press* continued. "We have proper regard for good negroes who know and keep their places, but for mean, impudent, and unruly negroes we have the utmost contempt. The rule of the fusionists has served to develop in the bad negroes all their mean traits."[31]

That place, according to the disfranchisement and segregation statutes that were proliferating in the Deep South, was away from the ballot box, in the rear of the streetcar, in the balcony of the theater, outside the ice cream parlor, at the back door of the house, in the kitchens and laundry rooms of white homes, and in the fields of cotton plantations. At first, black North Carolinians hoped that their state might resist these draconian measures. But white Democrats kept up a drumbeat of threats that created a thickening atmosphere of foreboding. "It is rapidly approaching the point where the patience of all true white men will be exhausted," the *Free Press* warned. "Such men will take the law in their own hands and by organized force make the negroes behave themselves."[32]

A cabal made up of some of the state's most prominent citizens decided to do just that in the 1898 elections. Led by future U.S. senator Furnifold Simmons and with strong support from tobacco and textile barons and the legal community, the Democrats began with an all-out campaign to win back control of the General Assembly. Their strategy was threefold. First, they threatened blacks who refused to abandon electoral politics with violence or economic sanctions. Second, they unleashed the Negrophobe extremists whom previous Democratic administrations, with an eye on federal Republican intervention, had kept under wraps. And finally, they appealed to white Fusionists who had deserted the Democratic Party to return to the "white man's party," their true political home.[33]

A few days before voters went to the polls, the *Winston Journal* published a letter that forcefully articulated the Democrats' assumptions about the right of the wealthy to rule and the proper place of blacks in the New South social order. Written by a "Democrat" and addressed "To the Colored People," the letter reminded black voters of their obligation to "white Democrats in whose factories you work, for whom you drive, who visit your barber shops, and give you all other kinds of employment." These were the people, the writer stressed, who paid the bulk of the taxes in Winston and Forsyth County, taxes that funded black schools and other social services. Loyalty and deference, the writer implied, were the price of that modicum of social support. But instead of allying themselves with their "superiors," blacks had joined forces with those who were out to destroy the very foundations of elite power. "Our people have become TIRED of your INGRATITUDE and will RESENT it. On the day of the election, we will keep a list of those who HELP US and those who vote against us and after the election we will REWARD those who aid us and TURN AWAY from those who TRY TO INJURE US."[34]

The same edition of the *Journal* made clear that this appeal to African Americans to support the interests of their patrons and employers did not imply a place for black voters in Democratic Party politics. The local Democratic Club, the *Journal* reported, had changed its name to the "Winston-Salem White Man's Club" and opened its doors to all men "who believe in white supremacy and good government in North Carolina" and "who love their race." The 600-plus charter members included the city's "very best and most influential businessmen." It went without saying that the "best men" were white.[35]

To win at the polls, however, Democrats had to have the votes not just of the best men but of the disaffected white farmers, workers, and shopkeepers who had supported Fusion in 1894 and 1896. They used a variety of tactics to win that support and, where that proved impossible, to keep poor whites from the polls. State Democratic Party chairman Furnifold Simmons orchestrated the campaign for white hearts and minds, railroad lawyer and future governor Charles B. Aycock supplied the oratory, and Raleigh *News and Observer* publisher Josephus Daniels penned the news stories and editorials that fanned the flames of racial distrust. This rhetorical blitz included appeals to white chauvinism, exposés on the corruption of black officeholders, and reports of black impertinence like those on the streets of Winston-Salem. Those insolent black women had been bad enough, but white Democrats claimed to see lurking behind them an even more sinister threat: black men, who, having secured the ballot, now desired that other prerogative of white manhood, access to white women. Creating a black-on-white rape scare, Democrats accused Fusionists of sacrificing their own women by allying themselves with black men.[36]

Republicans and Populists did their best to stem the tide. They charged that Democrats were appealing to "prejudice and passion" because they could not win a free and fair election. Republicans predicted that Democrats were plotting not only to disfranchise black voters, but also to exclude whites with whom they disagreed. If the Democrats won, charged one Republican leader, they would "rob our citizens of their right of franchise, and rivet on us the chains of lasting and hopeless slavery."[37]

In the end, prejudice and passion, along with intimidation and outright violence, prevailed, and Democrats narrowly, but with great fanfare, took control of both houses of the General Assembly. The *Union Republican* charged that in Winston "there were crowds of men who gathered around the polls in each ward and openly and boldly drove a large per cent of the colored Republican voters and a good many white voters away from the polls." White men left the Populist Party in droves, and Republicans, still hoping to challenge Democratic power, increasingly marginalized and excluded black voters.[38]

Democrats usually cast this struggle in stark images of black and white, yet what they feared most was an interracial coalition. In a moment of candor, the *Charlotte Daily Observer* characterized the Democratic campaign as "the struggle of the white people of North Carolina to rid themselves of the danger of the rule of Negroes and the lower classes of whites." Sure enough, just as Republicans had predicted, once in power the Democrats immediately set to work to disfranchise the black and poor white voters who were the backbone of the Republican and Populist Parties. Their main weapon was an amendment to the state constitution that required voters to pay a poll tax and pass a literacy test. To ensure its passage, Democratic legislators rewrote the Fusionist election laws to make registration and voting more difficult. When Populists charged that the amendment would disfranchise whites as well as blacks, Democrats added a "grandfather clause." It exempted from the literacy test until 1908 all men whose ancestors had been eligible to vote in 1867. A greatly diminished electorate ratified the amendment in 1900 and elected white supremacist governor Charles B. Aycock. The challenge to planter/industrial rule had been turned back.[39]

In addition to restricting the vote in state elections, the 1898 General Assembly severely limited democracy at the local level. Under the new election laws, Winston citizens lost the right to elect the mayor, the Board of Aldermen reverted to its pre-1895 form of three wards and nine aldermen, and registration restrictions disfranchised most black voters. In the 1900 municipal elections, even before the passage of the disfranchisement amendment, only Democrats ran for office and only 580 of over 2,500 potential voters cast ballots. Democratic registrars simply refused to register black voters. The *Union Republican* predicted that "of fully 1000 negroes who list and pay [poll] taxes in Winston only 147 will be allowed to vote."[40]

Blacks in Winston refused to surrender the franchise quietly. In 1902 twenty-four men filed charges against two Democratic registrars, claiming that they had been deprived of their constitutional rights. Typical was William H. Mebane, who was born in slavery in Rockingham County and had moved to Winston in 1878. Despite the fact that Mebane had been a property owner, taxpayer, and voter for twenty-two years, the registrar told him that someone from his home county would have to vouch for his identity. The Republican district attorney indicted the registrars, but a Democratic judge dismissed the case before it went to trial. By the end of the year, the *Union Republican* counted only fifty-seven black registrants in the city, of whom less than half voted.[41]

The Political Economy of White Supremacy

Through fraud, intimidation, and violence, North Carolina's emerging business and professional class, in coalition with large landowners, had instituted a new political and social order. The Winston-Salem White Men's Club and its counterparts across the state celebrated their "Glorious Victory" against the "negroizing of North Carolina." Having disfranchised blacks and many poor whites and regained control of the political machinery of state and local government, Democrats spent the next decade hammering out the public policies that secured their "reactionary revolution." These policies, many of which remained in place until the 1960s, made clear that while racial rhetoric had dominated the electoral battle, white supremacy was a political project that not only cloaked elite control of wealth but mandated class and gender hierarchies as well.[42]

A belief in the natural superiority of prosperous white men, or the "propertied

interest," fueled the Democrats' reaction to democratic insurgency. This belief remained a cornerstone of their vision of the new society. True, they had been forced
by the rebelliousness of their white social inferiors to hide those assumptions behind the veil of race. They had deployed the rhetoric of Herrenvolk democracy in
an effort to persuade whites of all classes to see themselves as members of the ruling race, but the winners' actions betrayed their true intent. They meant to be the
rulers of the ruling race and the sovereigns of the social order.[43]

Black subordination within a biracial society headed the Democrats' agenda and
functioned as the linchpin of the new order. The breakdown of personalized relations of authority and the need to contain the aspirations of laborers in an urban-
izing, industrializing region seemed to mandate new forms of social control. In the
anonymity of the city, masterless men and women moved about all too freely. The
Winston Free Press, for example, knew the names of both of the white women bicyclists, but not of the black women tobacco workers who confronted them: they
were simply "impudent wenches." Only by separating the races could whites protect themselves against the assertiveness of blacks in public places and black men's
supposed rapacious desire for white women, not to mention the threat of conta-
gious disease, which, as the germ theory gained credence in the late nineteenth century, became increasingly associated with blacks. Racist ideologues, moreover,
branded black men as emotional, irrational, and dependent—the very antithesis
of the ideal male citizen—and blamed their lack of restraint on the supposed im-
morality of black women. Turn-of-the-century science gave the idea of inherent
racial differences the stamp of objective truth, and even reform-minded white
southerners came to see segregation as a modern, progressive way to maintain
order in a biracial society.[44]

This system of racial segregation went by the name of Jim Crow, a reference to
early-nineteenth-century minstrelsy that came to connote black subordination.
But the spatial separation of blacks from whites was only part of the larger pattern
of inequality, discrimination, and unfreedom. Nor did this system rest on racist
ideas alone. Segregation developed from the very strategy that white supremacists
had used to regain control of the state. Having asserted, and worked hard to make
themselves believe, that race, not class, was the fundamental division in society and
that all blacks were inferior to all whites, white supremacists implemented policies
to instantiate this imagined racial hierarchy—to make it seem natural, inevitable,
and real.

The myriad segregation statutes and customary practices that developed during
the early twentieth century went a long way toward accomplishing this goal. Jim
Crow laws, mostly local ordinances mandating separate railway cars, schools, water

fountains, prisons, waiting rooms, and burial grounds, served as intraracial levelers, affirming the superiority of all whites and lumping blacks together regardless of social or economic status, thereby obfuscating class differences. The ubiquitous "Whites only" and "Colored" signs, often hung without legal mandate, aggressively drew the color line. The indicators of class privilege appeared everywhere as well, barring entrance to country clubs, large estates, executive offices, and private railway cars, but those markers were mostly assumed, not proclaimed.[45]

Jim Crow wore the badge of statutory authority, but over time it was increasingly enforced by customs that mandated second-class citizenship for blacks, many of which had been invented in the wake of the white supremacy campaign. Fear also enforced deference. Anyone who had not experienced white violence had heard stories of the harsh authority exercised over blacks by the police, courts, private individuals, and vigilante groups. Stateways and folkways, backed by violence, conspired so perfectly that by midcentury many southerners, both black and white, saw segregation and discrimination not as tactics but as timeless expressions of the natural order of things.[46]

Although Jim Crow seemed mainly intended to prescribe the proper place and behaviors of blacks, it defined the place of whites as well. Whites were not free to associate with whomever they pleased, whenever they pleased, and however they pleased. Such strictures were particularly effective as a means of maintaining (or instituting) divisions between and among poor and middling blacks and whites. By prescribing where members of each race could live, work, and socialize, Jim Crow effectively bifurcated the institutions—churches, lodges, sporting teams, musical groups, labor unions—that might have served as sites of interracial cooperation and resistance to elite rule. In the end, it erected "a nearly insurmountable wall between the blacks and poor whites who had risen to challenge Democratic power."[47]

That wall effectively blocked black political participation, but it did not literally separate blacks from whites. Rather, it prescribed a subordinate place—somewhat separate, and decidedly unequal—for blacks within a racialized social order. Racist zealots might have wished to ship blacks back to Africa, and blacks might have hoped to create their own businesses or tend their own patches of land far off the main road, but African American labor was as crucial to the development of the New South as it had been to the Old. It was inevitable, then, that blacks and whites would encounter each other on the farm, in the factory, in white homes, and on the streets and sidewalks of small towns and cities. And in all these places Jim Crow intervened to enforce caste hierarchies and police the behavior of whites as well as blacks.[48]

Yet the question remains, Why, in this bustling age of commerce and industry, where the free flow of capital and labor were the marketplace's sine qua non, would planters and industrialists demand so many restrictions on personal freedom? The answer lies in white supremacy's dual function as a means of political subordination and a method of labor control and allocation. For these New South elites, the accumulation of wealth went hand in hand with political usurpation and racial subordination, and they required any number of coercive labor policies to ensure the profitability of their farms, factories, and financial institutions. In the transition to a fully developed industrial capitalist economy, remnants of old labor relations contributed to the fashioning of new ones.[49]

What might be called racial capitalism structured labor relations in the South's growing industrial sector through a mixture of laissez-faire and social control. The most telling feature of southern industry was the near exclusion of blacks from skilled and semiskilled positions. Textiles, where whites claimed the machine-tending jobs, offered the most extreme case. But even in steel, tobacco, and other industries where blacks worked in large numbers, segregated job hierarchies forced blacks to the lowest positions. In contrast to public accommodations, however, elites made few attempts to write job segregation into law. Manufacturers always wanted the flexibility to replace, or threaten to replace, whites with blacks, and vice versa, if workers tried to organize.[50]

Textile mill owners were key supporters of the Democratic Party in North Carolina, and their attitudes and policies toward their workers manifested white supremacy's deep-seated class assumptions most starkly. Being white got you a job in the mill but few other spoils of the new order. Low wages guaranteed that it took a houseful of workers to make ends meet. Children could perform many jobs, and mill owners adamantly opposed child labor laws. As with blacks, economics combined with social stigmas to segregate most millhands in villages built and controlled by manufacturers. Unions were simply beyond the pale.

Authority over state and local taxes mattered as much to southern manufacturers as labor control. Fusionist policies had addressed the need for social accumulation—the creation of schools, hospitals, and regulatory agencies—through higher taxation. And for a few short years under Fusion, North Carolina spent more on social welfare programs than any other southern state. But Democrats quickly reversed the tax codes and corporate regulatory measures put in place by Republican and Populist reformers. Having regained direction of the machinery of state, Winston industrialists and their allies across North Carolina built their fortunes unhampered by regulation, high taxation, or working-class organization.

The stabilization of politics had been a central goal of the white supremacist takeover of state and local government. Having disfranchised opponents through literacy tests, poll taxes, and registration laws and eliminated the chance of a biracial challenge, white supremacists aimed to structure an orderly process within a one-party state through the Democratic primary. Under this system, the party chose its nominees for the general election in a primary restricted to Democrats, with all the candidates pledging to support the winner of the primary in the general election. All personal and political conflict (which was plentiful) took place within the party, and it became almost impossible for candidates from other parties to gain office. The white primary worked effectively to prevent Democratic factions from turning to blacks or Republicans for support. Moreover, the South's restricted electorate and its one-party system allowed southern Democrats to return to their seats in Congress year after year and thus to dominate key committees and exercise inordinate national power.[51]

Firmly allied in their commitment to industrial capitalism, the one-party state, and African American subordination, North Carolina Democrats did spar over a number of critical social policy issues during the first decade of their rule. All agreed on the goal of ending the distributive social welfare policies of the Fusionist governments, but there was less consensus on what policies should take their place. Dubbed the Progressive Era, the decades after the turn of the twentieth century witnessed the rise of reformers who advocated state intervention, while planters and industrialists continued to fight public spending on health, education, and welfare, insisting that employer beneficence and local philanthropy or outright neglect were appropriate responses to the plight of the poor.

Despite the best efforts of reformers, limited state outlays marginally improved poor whites' capacities as workers and consumers and maintained their perception of advantage over blacks but did virtually nothing to level the economic playing field or create opportunities for upward mobility. Well into the twentieth century, white industrial workers, particularly in textiles, had to rely on the paternalism of employers even for the rudiments of education. Blacks received even less attention. The underdevelopment of human capital among both African Americans and poor whites was a defining feature of racial capitalism.[52]

Discrimination against African Americans, moreover, pulled all workers' wages down. It thus served as the linchpin in what became in effect a separate southern political economy. A captive labor force of low-wage laborers—both black and white—helped to enrich the few but ensured that the South would remain the nation's poorest, most underdeveloped region.

The imposition of racial capitalism rested on the federal government's abandonment of its obligation to protect the former slaves' rights, the co-optation of poor whites, and the coercive power of the state. The staying power of the social order, however, ultimately depended on the degree to which white elites could normalize the class/race/gender hierarchies they had built. The more natural the dictates of white supremacy appeared, the greater the stability and longevity of the system.[53]

Racism, however, was not instinctive, and normalization remained a difficult task. It relied on the stringent enforcement of the law, the coercive power of state institutions, and control of key economic resources, such as jobs and credit. But it also depended on the power of invented tradition. The late nineteenth century had been marked by great flux and experimentation; a new etiquette of white supremacy had to be learned as well as enforced. The more often a white woman received a deferential gesture from a black man, the more normal deference became. Each time the mayor came from a particular neighborhood and church, the more it seemed that that had always been and would always be the case. Each year that a sharecropper, white or black, ended in debt, the more it seemed that unfreedom was a fixed way of life. Each morning on which a black tobacco worker entered a factory through the "Colored" door, the more segregation came to seem timeless and inevitable.

A pernicious process of indoctrination reinforced, indeed created, "tradition." The young were its chief objects, since white supremacy, in all its manifestations and for all of its participants, had to be learned. Racially segregated and class stratified schools taught lessons in hierarchy by their very existence. But such lessons were not left to chance. Hand-me-down books, where they existed at all, reminded blacks of their second-class citizenship. School terms built around the needs of the planting and harvesting seasons stressed the limited purposes of education for rural black and white children alike. Resource-rich urban schools located in the heart of white, middle-class residential districts perpetuated class privileges. School holidays for Confederate Memorial Day tied the present to the past.[54]

Still, lessons learned in school might not last a lifetime, and personal experience might not be enough to enforce oppressive social roles. Indoctrination must extend to every nook and cranny of life. North Carolina native Thomas Dixon's novels *The Leopard's Spots: A Romance of the White Man's Burden, 1865–1900* and *The Clansman: An Historical Romance of the Ku Klux Klan* confirmed the conservative view of the Civil War and Reconstruction. Movies such as *Birth of a Nation*, which was based on *The Clansman*, and later *Gone with the Wind*, the film version of Margaret Mitchell's 1936 novel, carried these interpretations to an even wider audience. History textbooks written by apologists for white supremacists were little more than rationalizations for the system itself. Newspapers focused on the sensationalized aspects of black life and seldom printed a story, good or bad, about white workers.[55]

But no matter how powerful the means of persuasion, white supremacy was not normal, was not embedded in the unchanging folkways of the South, was not the only possible way in which social life could be ordered. Despite the best efforts of their betters, the everyday actions of subordinate groups, black and white, could work to undermine the system. Any act that required Jim Crow to be explicitly enforced called its normalcy into question. Any suggestion that this was a construct imposed on subordinate groups without their consent revealed its artificial character. The black domestic worker who quit her job when cursed by the lady of the house, the brilliant black student who went north and earned a degree at an Ivy League college, the black and white neighbors whose children ate lunch at each others' houses all through the summer, the gadfly politician who railed against the arrogance of local elites—all of these made hegemony hard work. To the extent that white workers believed in the inherent inferiority of blacks, they accommodated themselves to a key premise of white supremacy. But when they refused to believe in their own inferiority in relation to the better classes, then they too challenged the hierarchical assumptions of white supremacy.

Such individual actions, moreover, fed larger forces that threatened white supremacy's mechanisms of control. The massing together of blacks in towns like Winston-Salem created solidarities and capacities for collective action that would have been impossible in the countryside. The autonomous institutions of black life—the church, the lodge, fraternities and sororities—constructed a base from which to attack Jim Crow. The textile mill villages, despite their intent, nurtured a tight-knit working-class community that defended millhands from the condescension of the middle class and sometimes supported labor protest, even as they undercut the possibilities for interracial solidarity. It would be half a century after disfranchisement before Winston-Salem would elect its next black alderman. In the meantime, workers and managers, blacks and whites struggled daily over the strange fruit of the late-nineteenth-century white supremacy campaigns.

CHAPTER THREE

Winston-Salem, North Carolina

Country Small Town Grown Big Town Rich—and Poor

The meteoric rise of Reynolds Tobacco Company to leadership in the tobacco industry transformed Winston-Salem from a county-seat town of shops and modest incomes into North Carolina's largest city and the largest producer of tobacco products in the world. Reynolds's profits also underwrote the rise of a tightly knit group of merchants, manufacturers, and financiers who sat atop the city's social pyramid and controlled its political and economic life. Equipped with all the tools of wealth and power, this oligarchy attempted to sculpt the physical and social landscape in its own interests, which it equated with the good of the whole.[1]

The black workers who streamed into Winston-Salem from the farms and small towns of central and eastern North Carolina and upcountry South Carolina put their stamp on the city as well. Excluded from employment in most southern industries and pushed to the bottom of the agricultural ladder, they jumped at the chance to work in the city's tobacco warehouses and leaf houses and, especially, in the manufacturing plants of the R. J. Reynolds Company. The strictures of Jim Crow combined with class demarcations to confine these new migrants to the neighborhoods north and east of the factories. There, in concert and conflict with the black middle class, they built a densely populated and tightly interwoven world, a world of suffering and poverty, to be sure, but also one that nurtured resistance and cultural innovation.

Map 1. Points of interest, Winston-Salem, North Carolina, ca. 1945

R. J. Reynolds Buildings

1 Main Building
2 Number 4 Plant
3 Number 12 Plant
4 Number 38 Plant
5 Number 60 Plant
6 Number 60 Extensions
7 Number 64 Plant
8 Number 65 Plant
9 Number 97 Plant
10 Number 256 Plant

Union Halls

11 Local 22 headquarters
12 AFL offices

Other Tobacco Companies and Businesses

13 Brown & Williamson
14 Export Leaf
15 Winston Leaf
16 Piedmont Leaf
17 Imperial Leaf
18 P. H. Hanes Knitting Company

African American Churches

19 First Baptist Church
20 First Institutional Baptist Church
21 Holy Trinity Baptist Church
22 Mt. Zion Baptist Church
23 Shiloh Baptist Church
24 Union Mission Holy Church
25 Golar Memorial AME Zion Church
26 St. Paul AME Church

African American Businesses

27 Camel City Laundry
28 Howard Robinson Funeral Home
29 Winston Mutual Life Insurance
30 Safe Bus Company
31 Bruce Building

African American Schools and Business Associations

32 Atkins High School
33 Fourteenth Street School
34 Woodland Avenue School
35 Winston-Salem State Teachers College
36 Phillis Wheatley Home
37 Pythian Hall
38 YMCA
39 YWCA

African American Theaters, Parks, and Libraries

40 Lincoln Theatre
41 Lafayette Theatre
42 George Moses Horton Branch,
   Winston-Salem Public Library
43 Fourteenth Street Park

Government Buildings

44 City Hall
45 County Courthouse

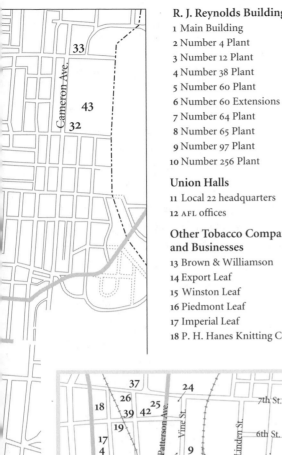

"The Solidarity of the Solidly Fixed"

Winston-Salem was a company town, but it was not literally a one-company town. There had been cotton mills from the beginning, and Reynolds's buy-out of the tobacco interests of the brothers Pleasant Henderson Hanes and John Wesley Hanes freed capital and entrepreneurial imagination for the development of hosiery and knitting factories, a relatively new and increasingly lucrative branch of the textile industry. As with Reynolds Tobacco, the Haneses' enterprises took off during World War I, fueled by the army's demand for men's underwear. Undercut by the South's cheap labor, northern factories closed their doors or migrated southward; by the Depression decade North Carolina dominated the hosiery industry, and Winston-Salem became the largest manufacturer of knit underwear in the world. The interests of Wachovia Bank and Trust Company, founded in 1879 by James A. Gray and others, were inextricably intertwined with those of the tobacco company as well; two of James A. Gray's sons, Bowman and James Jr., became chairmen of Reynolds Tobacco after the death of R. J. Reynolds. That relationship helped Wachovia to become one of the largest banks in the Southeast. Chatham Manufacturing Company, a maker of wool and cotton blankets in Elkin, North Carolina, moved its headquarters to Winston early in the century, completing the small circle of large enterprises. Furniture plants and other businesses added to the economic mix.[2]

Three families were at the top of Winston-Salem's social hierarchy: the Reynoldses, the Haneses, and the Grays. Jonathan Daniels, the liberal son of the white supremacist publisher Josephus Daniels and editor of the Raleigh *News and Observer*, dubbed them and their allies the "air-*stock*-racy" and described their cohesiveness as the "solidarity of the solidly fixed." "They were the city's patriarchs," the son of a lesser Reynolds executive told Daniels, "autocratic and unapologetic about it, and few aspects of Winston business or social and cultural life escaped their indelicate mastery." "Winston-Salem is not the village of a company, but in it is a company of people . . . who know what they have and what they want," Daniels concluded. "No stock ownership, no interlocking directorates (though there are some) are necessary to bind them together. They do not have to plot around a table; they can wave at a dance or exchange a mutual conviction on the steps of a church or over a glass. They do not have to conspire, they are already agreed. Not many people have to be cajoled into guarding a gold mine."[3]

The men who ran Winston-Salem also helped to run the state. Writing in 1949, the political scientist V. O. Key observed: "An aggressive aristocracy of manufacturing and banking, centered around Greensboro, Winston-Salem, Charlotte, and

Durham, has had a tremendous stake in state policy and has not been remiss in protecting and advancing what it visualizes as its interests. Consequently a sympathetic respect for the problems of corporate capital and of large employers permeates the state's politics and government. For half a century an economic oligarchy has held sway."[4]

While the top corporate officials did not normally run for public office, a Reynolds, Hanes, or Gray might occasionally occupy a key position when he thought the city, county, or state needed decisive leadership. James G. Hanes, son of the founder and long-time president of Hanes Hosiery, had a special penchant for politics. He served two terms as mayor before taking over as chairman of the board of county commissioners in Forsyth County in 1925, a post he held for twenty-two years. Known for his political and economic ruthlessness, Hanes ran both his business and the county with an iron hand. His brother, Robert M. Hanes, president of Wachovia Bank and Trust, served two terms in the North Carolina House of Representatives and one term in the Senate, where he led the fight for a state sales tax. James A. Gray Jr., vice president of Wachovia and then chairman of Reynolds, served as a state senator and as chairman of the Senate finance committee. R. J. Reynolds's son, R. J. ("Dick") Reynolds Jr., briefly occupied the mayor's seat. Gordon Gray, Bowman Gray's son and, beginning in the late 1930s, publisher of the *Winston-Salem Journal*, spent three terms in the North Carolina Senate and helped to author the state's right-to-work law; he went on to become secretary of the army in the Truman administration. Thurmond Chatham Jr. represented North Carolina's Fifth Congressional District beginning in 1949. Generally, younger company officials, relatives, or business partners took care of electoral politics. Combining political participation with informal power, "the major businessmen and industrialists of Winston-Salem had virtually complete control."[5]

The ruling families, which had thrown their weight behind the Democratic restoration in the late 1890s, maintained close ties to Furnifold Simmons, the Democratic Party boss who parlayed his success as the architect of North Carolina's white supremacy campaign into a seat in the U.S. Senate from 1900 to 1930. Winston-Salem's influence in the state capital increased even more with the election of O. Max Gardner as governor in 1928 and the establishment of the "Shelby Dynasty." Gardner, a college classmate of Robert Hanes, had purchased 1,000 shares of Reynolds stock with the help of James Gray, and he continued to rely on the two men for political and financial advice. When Gardner opened a law firm in Washington in 1933, Reynolds Tobacco Company became a client. S. Clay Williams, chairman of the board at Reynolds from 1935 to 1949, did a stint in Washington as head of the

National Industrial Recovery Board during the New Deal, and Franklin Roosevelt tapped Dick Reynolds to serve as treasurer of the Democratic National Committee in the early 1940s.[6]

These men exhibited their status through what one historian described as the "esthetics of plenty," and the estates and homes they created rivaled those of America's wealthiest families. Initially, the town's bankers and manufacturers built Victorian mansions along Fifth Street just blocks west of the factory district. The advent first of streetcars and then of automobiles, along with the enormous wealth generated by the success of Camels, made it possible for them to abandon the industrial environment that produced that wealth. Fleeing to the secluded enclaves of Country Club Estates and Buena Vista, they reconfigured Winston-Salem from a compact walking city into one marked by yawning economic and social divisions, insinuating white supremacy's rage for order into the layout of the city as well as the warp and woof of everyday social relations.[7]

R. J. Reynolds set the tone in 1917, when he and his wife, Katharine Smith Reynolds, built Reynolda House on 1,667 acres three miles west of the city. According to one observer, the sixty-room "bungalow," school, greenhouse, post office, and other buildings had "the appearance of a self-sustaining feudal manor with a staff of more than one hundred persons." One of R. J.'s younger brothers, Will Reynolds, and his wife, Kate, purchased a 1,117-acre Yadkin River estate that, in later years, the family transformed into sprawling Tanglewood Park. Other wealthy families followed suit. James G. Hanes constructed a stone replica of a sixteenth-century English manor house, and he also owned a 6,000-acre farm and hunting preserve in south Georgia named Senah Plantation. John C. Whitaker lived on a 120-acre farm not far from Reynolda. In the mid-1920s, the Chathams, Grays, Haneses, and Reynoldses spearheaded the development of a summer community in nearby Roaring Gap. There on the eastern edge of the Blue Ridge, dozens of "cottages" nestled on the hillside beneath the Graystone Inn. Positioned so they could keep close watch on Winston-Salem, the families spent their summers there with their servants in tow.[8]

"The air-stock-rats," observed Jonathan Daniels, "move in well-dressed packs to parties. They have a good time together." The Twin-City Club, the oldest male social club in town, dated back to the early 1880s. In 1910 many of the club's members founded Forsyth Country Club and built a golf course on the outskirts of town. In 1939 R. J.'s daughter Mary and her husband, Charles Babcock, who had bought Reynolda, gave a portion of the land for the new Old Town Country Club, which quickly became the city's most exclusive.[9]

Most of the daughters of the leading families finished at Salem College, were presented at the various debutante balls, and, in many cases, married local business and professional men. The sons usually prepared at Woodberry Forest School in Virginia. Beginning shortly before the turn of the century, virtually all matriculated at the University of North Carolina at Chapel Hill, including Bowman Gray Sr. and Jr., John Whitaker, James Hanes, Robert Hanes, and James Gray. Their names are prominent on the campus today, adorning campus buildings, endowed professorships, and athletic facilities. Gordon Gray was the academic star of the group. After prepping at Woodberry Forest, he entered the University of North Carolina in 1926, where he was first in his class, president of Phi Beta Kappa, and a member of the most prestigious fraternity and secret societies; he then went on to law school at Yale. Ties to Chapel Hill did not end with graduation: both Robert Hanes and James Gray served many years on the university's board of trustees, and Gordon Gray did a turn as president of the consolidated university system from 1950 to 1955. Even as the university, led by the crusading liberal Frank Porter Graham, gained a reputation as the South's chief fountain of intellectual dissent, Winston-Salem's millionaires, along with other members of the state's industrial elite, continued to steer its affairs.[10]

Ranking just below the millionaires in the Winston-Salem social hierarchy were their junior partners: smaller manufacturers, large retailers, managers, doctors, lawyers, and other professionals. Below these junior partners stood a middling group of townspeople and skilled workers, who tended to view Reynolds's largess with a "mixture of gratitude and misgiving." From their ranks came dissenters who would speak out more and more often as the Depression challenged complacency and threw conventional wisdom into doubt. The general secretary of the Young Women's Christian Association (YWCA) in the late 1930s articulated this latent unease. "Winston-Salem is just like a big mill village and controlled like such a village by the city fathers, who really say they have the welfare of the city at heart," she observed. "They are not *actively* in politics, but they dictate who serves the city in political capacities. However, they're *actively* on our large volunteer boards like Associated Charities, Council of School Agencies, and Juvenile Delinquency. And, they work hard on these boards. They *know* crime areas, bad housing areas, etc. And, due to their knowledge, they're competent to perform valuable services—such as donating hospitals, parks, schools. But, they feel it is up to them to recognize and serve the need. I do not call this democracy."[11]

The city fathers did indeed sit on the volunteer boards, but it was their wives who gave the oligarchy its reputation for combining "the Salem conscience" and "the Winston purse." R. J.'s widow, Katharine Smith Reynolds, in particular, symbolized the roles carved out by middle- and upper-class white women as they used their position as guardian of the home as a springboard into public life. A member of North Carolina's first generation of college women, Katharine Reynolds had attended the state Normal School, where a roommate described her as having "an active social conscience and a penchant for service." As a young bride, she turned Reynolda, her Forsyth County estate, into a model farm for demonstrating the benefits of diversified agriculture to farmers and nutritious food preparation to farmers' wives. She persuaded her husband to open the Reynolds Inn, a boardinghouse for the young white women who poured into town to run the cigarette-making machines during World War I, and she sat on the founding board of the YWCA, which provided dormitories, a lunchroom, and a gymnasium for white working women and offered courses to help industrial workers make the leap to clerical and sales positions. Over the years, she and her sister-in-law, Kate Bitting Reynolds, also donated land for a new public high school for white children, built a community auditorium, helped to start the city's first modern hospitals for whites and blacks, and created a trust to provide health care for the poor of the state. Given the stinginess of state allocations in this period, women's philanthropies and voluntary efforts were central to the improvements in public welfare that did occur. At the same time, these top-down activities, which were mostly for whites only, helped to institutionalize a system of what might be termed corporate maternalism, in which services to blacks and most poor whites depended on self-help, charity, or a penurious relief system rather than becoming an entitlement of citizenship or an employment contract.[12]

The Making of a Black Urban Working-Class World

Neither the Reynolds boardinghouse nor the YWCA nor the other services provided by Winston-Salem's government agencies and voluntary associations eased the transition of Robert Black's family from the farm to the factory. The Blacks were among the 1.5 million African Americans who left the rural South in the period from 1900 to 1920. More than half of these migrants settled in southern cities, and in North and South Carolina and Virginia many headed for tobacco manufacturing towns. Once there, they had to rely on their own labor, pool resources, and look to their own herculean voluntary efforts to survive the rigors of factory work and urban life.[13]

Born in 1905, Black spent his earliest years in Cabarrus County, outside of Concord, North Carolina, where his family farmed on shares. The third of six children, he began helping in the cotton field and vegetable garden before he was old enough for school. "Life in the country was a little hard," Black remembered, "because we toiled in the fields from morning until late in the afternoon. And then when we were able to catch up with our farm work, my daddy would hire us out to work in other people's fields. My dad had three of us old enough to work in the fields, and my mother worked in the fields, but we never seemed to get any farther ahead."[14]

The multiple hardships of sharecropping—poor soil, bad weather, dishonest landlords, the boll weevil, the crop lien—sent many southern farmers, black and white, searching for opportunities in the mines, mills, and factories of the North and South. But a father's infidelities provided the immediate stimulus for the Black family's move from farm to factory. "My mother was the type of a woman that wanted a loving home," Black remembered. "She wanted children, but she didn't feel that she should have to share her husband with a lot of other women that lived in the neighborhood. My dad pulled a few acts that really was unbecoming to a father. My mother was with child, the baby boy, and was expecting almost anytime. It was in the wintertime. My dad went to town during this time, and he stayed for about three days. It was snowing. We had a cow that was coming with calf at about the same time that my mother was expecting this last child. And the only thing that she had there in the house was one of her brother-in-laws, and he could cook a little and help there with the children, but he couldn't attend to that cow. The cow had the calf and the calf died, which meant the calf couldn't nurse the cow, and the cow's bag filled with milk, and it killed the cow. This baby brother of mine was born while my daddy was gone, and somehow or another, with the help of this uncle, my mother managed to survive. And I guess, when she put all those things together, she realized that each year there was an additional member to the family, that she just decided to make a change."[15]

Robert's mother, Eliza, moved first to Elizabeth, New Jersey, where two of her sisters lived. Then, after a failed attempt to reconcile with her husband, she decided to try her luck at Reynolds Tobacco Company, where jobs were opening up. Robert, his older brother and sister, and the three younger children moved with their mother to Winston-Salem on April 14, 1913. They found a three-room shotgun house in the neighborhood called Monkey Bottom, and Eliza Black started work the next day stemming tobacco leaves by hand at Reynolds. Robert was seven, Janie nine, and Ben ten.[16]

Robert and Janie were too small to hold jobs of their own, but they could help their mother. "My mother said we were going to get some schooling," Janie remembered, "so we went to work about six o'clock in the morning and we got to work until about a quarter of eight. We'd knock a little dust off us and go to school smelling like that strong tobacco. Many of the children worked there so nobody paid it any attention. We'd get off school and get to make a couple of hours. We got to make mother a little check that way." Robert remembered the long hours of labor in the same matter-of-fact way: "My mother was doing piece work—and we would work in that department and do all we could, as far as stemming the tobacco, and then we would leave that with her. Later in the day as they weighted her out, she would get paid. That was one way that we had of helping to earn our livelihood."[17]

Not long afterward, Janie got her own job. "You had to be able to earn so much a day to hold a stemmery bench," Robert said. "My sister had a bench and I would sit on the floor underneath that bench and they would hand me tobacco and I would stem that to supplement her." Years later Janie proudly remembered their exact wages. "He and I together would make my mother $2.50 a week. My oldest brother might make $1.50 or $1.75. My mother was a right good stemmer and she would make $4.50 and sometimes maybe $5.00 a week." Soon Robert too "got an hour job in Reynolds" doing stemming piece work.[18]

The tide of migration that brought the Blacks to Winston-Salem transformed the city, shaping its culture and character every bit as much as the industrial aristocracy did. Between 1890 and 1940, Winston-Salem's population increased from 13,650 to 78,815; 45 percent of its residents were African Americans, and almost 65 percent of those blacks who were employed held manufacturing jobs. By 1940 no other city in the state had a larger number of African American citizens; no major city in the country had a higher ratio of blacks to whites, and in no city in the South did a larger proportion of blacks hold manufacturing jobs.[19]

An extraordinary number of black migrants made their way to Winston-Salem specifically to work for R. J. Reynolds. In 1930, for instance, fully half of all of the city's gainfully employed black citizens worked for the company at some time during the year. Those who could not get jobs at the Reynolds plants looked to the dozens of tobacco warehouses and leaf houses that dotted the cityscape. Work there was seasonal and paid less than jobs at Reynolds, but when combined with domestic and casual labor, these jobs provided a livelihood for thousands of men and women.[20]

A significant number of the black workers who migrated to Winston-Salem were women. They came in response to pushes and pulls, active desire and demographics, individual choice and family decisions. Planters refused to rent land to women, and the sexual division of agricultural labor created many more jobs for men than for women. Cities, on the other hand, had a voracious need for domestic labor, and tobacco towns like Winston-Salem offered factory work to women and men alike. Families were more likely to encourage an unfettered man to try his luck in the North than to send a daughter to a strange and distant city. They also expected women to serve as "kinkeepers," taking responsibility for maintaining close ties with relatives rooted in the countryside and providing the ballast that kept transient families together. For all these reasons, female-headed households and families with many daughters were the first to abandon the countryside. The proportion of men in rural areas steadily increased throughout the interwar period, and women outnumbered men in every southern city.[21]

Once settled in Winston-Salem, most African American women had no choice but to do "public work." This was especially true for the many single, divorced, or widowed women in the city: a survey of tobacco workers in 1935 revealed that almost 60 percent of the women were on their own. Black men's low wages, moreover, meant that a larger proportion of black married women sought wage work as well. In 1940 more than 60 percent of black women over fourteen years of age were in the labor force, and they made up almost half of the city's black wage earners. Although the proportion of black women in domestic service decreased steadily, until World War II the vast majority of black urban women throughout the country continued to labor as laundresses or household workers in white homes, occupations that were shunned by trade unions and excluded even from the regulations that offered meager protections to industrial workers. In Winston-Salem, by contrast, more than half of black women wage earners held jobs in industry. Another 40 percent were service workers, but because women often worked in the tobacco plants only during the "green season," the ten to twelve weeks during the late summer when the leaf was being prepared for processing, many combined factory work with paid household labor, making the proportion of women with experience in industry even higher than the census figures would indicate.[22]

Black migrants to Winston-Salem shared not only a common work experience but the bonds that grew from the city's distinctive pattern of residential segregation. As newcomers arrived, they found their lives shaped by the nexus between race, space, and proletarianization. In Deep South cities, where most blacks worked as household workers or day laborers, an earlier pattern in which blacks lived in "pocket neighborhoods" near their employers left its mark on urban landscapes. Even in Winston-Salem, a pocket neighborhood called Silver Hill grew up near "Millionaire's Row" on Stratford Road when the city's wealthier citizens moved to the outskirts of town. But Reynolds's domination of Winston-Salem's economy combined with the formal and informal practices of Jim Crow to create a densely populated black working-class community known as East Winston, which spread slowly northward and eastward from the Reynolds factories in the heart of town. In most

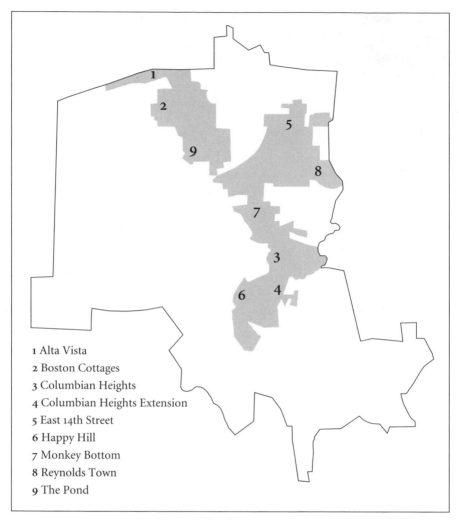

1 Alta Vista
2 Boston Cottages
3 Columbian Heights
4 Columbian Heights Extension
5 East 14th Street
6 Happy Hill
7 Monkey Bottom
8 Reynolds Town
9 The Pond

Map 2. African American neighborhoods in Winston-Salem, 1940. The shaded areas indicate city blocks where the census listed the population as more than two-thirds "nonwhite." The great majority of these blocks were "nonwhite only." (*Sources*: Opperman, *Winston-Salem's African-American Neighborhoods*; U.S. Department of Commerce, Bureau of the Census, *Sixteenth Census of the United States, 1940: Housing.*)

New South cities, by contrast, blacks lived in one to three large clusters, with smaller clusters scattered throughout older areas.[23]

White migrants streamed into Winston-Salem as well, intensifying competition for housing and jobs. As the city became more and more divided along lines of both race and class, whites gathered into distinctly working-class neighborhoods and labored in white-coded jobs. The 1,000-plus men, women, and children who worked at the spinning plant built by Hanes Knitting Company in 1910 lived in Hanes, an unincorporated, company-owned village just outside the city limits on the west side of town. Stigmatized as "lintheads," they attended their own schools and churches, were unable to participate in city elections, and had relatively little to do with the life of the town. Yet even as they confronted daily tokens of their lowly position in the social order, they were reminded that African Americans were more lowly yet. The company maintained housing for nine black families along a street behind the plant known as "colored row." A few blacks managed to get a toe-hold in the mill. Baxter Holman, for one, made the best of limited opportunities. "I started off working with a woman scrubbing in the mill, scrubbing floors and different things," he remembered. "I was pretty swift, so the yard foreman wanted me out there unloading cotton. I stayed on the yard for ten years and finally a job of running a machine came open in the opening room. After a number of years I got a chance to move up to the picker room." Most, however, never got past jobs as janitors, boiler stokers, openers, and yardmen, while their wives labored as do-mestics, mostly in the homes of managers but also for mill workers who, despite their subsistence wages, could still pay the pittance a black domestic worker could command.[24]

The Hanes knitting and finishing mills stood near the center of town, and jobs in those mills were eagerly sought after. The machinery was less dangerous than that in the textile mills, where workers could expect to be mangled by the machines almost as a matter of course; the air was not filled with cotton dust; there were more opportunities for skilled work, at least for men; and workers did not live on the mill hill, under the constant surveillance of a boss. Moreover, a skilled male worker, usually a machine fixer, could purchase a circular knitting machine, which was small and relatively portable and inexpensive, and set himself up as an inde-pendent entrepreneur in a garage or outbuilding, producing goods at night or off his shift, often with the help of his wife, to be sold to the large firms at low prices. This "shadow industry" offered opportunities for individual enterprise, while also relegating women to "homework," which could be isolating and exploitative.[25]

White tobacco workers were scattered throughout the city, with the largest con-centration in the working-class neighborhoods to the south of town, and many drove to work from rural communities to the north and west. Indeed, unlike their black counterparts, white workers often kept one foot in the factory and one foot on the farm. They were more likely to have come to Winston-Salem directly from the farm than from another urban area, and they maintained strong ties to the countryside even when they made the move to town.[26]

By contrast, poor blacks who could secure factory jobs made a permanent commitment to the city and to industrial labor early on, often moving first to small towns, then to larger cities like Winston-Salem, and sometimes on to the urban North. That difference in orientation would have a profound impact on the prospects for trade unionism: it engaged blacks in urban networks that were conducive to movement building, while isolating whites from one another as well as from blacks, and it ensured that, given the right conditions, black tobacco workers would be more likely than whites to cast their lots with a union, a quintessentially urban, industrial institution.[27]

As both the black and the white working-class populations mushroomed in the city, housing became a flash point of interracial tension. As the number of African American tobacco workers grew, the twin scourges of poverty and discrimination thrust them into the "bottoms" to the north and east of the tobacco plants. These low-lying areas along streams were prone to flooding, lacked sewage lines, paved roads, and street lights, and bred armies of rats, snakes, and mosquitoes. Monkey Bottom, the neighborhood where Robert Black grew up, was a fetid swamp within sight of the factories. When Theodosia Simpson married in 1942, she moved with her husband, Buck, to an apartment in an area known as the Pond. It got its name shortly after the turn of the twentieth century when the city reservoir collapsed its banks and flooded the streets. Within the Pond were neighborhoods with names like Spook Ranch, Peppercorn, Smokey Hollow, and the Shoe. Further north lay Boston Cottages, an area of shanties built by white developers in the late nineteenth century with lower-income black renters in mind.[28]

As the black factory workforce gradually pushed from the edge of the factory district into the neighborhoods that came to be known as East Winston, white real estate agents took advantage of blacks' desperate need for shelter and whites' racial fears by threatening white homeowners with deteriorating property values once blacks moved in, buying their houses cheaply, and selling them to other whites as rental property or to African Americans who could scrape together enough money for homes. In response to these block-busting techniques, residents pressured the Board of Aldermen to enact the city's first residential segregation ordinance. Passed on July 1, 1912, this law made it illegal for anyone—black or white—to occupy a house on any block in which the majority of the residents belonged to a different race.[29]

A black homeowner named William Darnell challenged the ordinance, taking his case to the state Supreme Court with the help of one of Winston's leading white attorneys. On April 8, 1914, Darnell won the case, scoring a victory for Winston-Salem blacks and helping to invalidate similar laws in other North Carolina cities. But in Winston-Salem, as in other southern towns, housing segregation resulted as much from economic pressures and informal discrimination as from Jim Crow laws: black workers simply could not afford to live in any but the most run-down neighborhoods, and as they filtered into those areas, whites rapidly moved out.[30]

Under these conditions, East Winston became a contested terrain. By 1939 Cameron Park, a predominately white neighborhood created by R. J. Reynolds, had become a mostly black neighborhood called Reynoldstown, and black residences formed a horseshoe around the remaining white areas of East Winston. As the economy picked up with the coming of World War II, the need for housing increased and racial tensions mounted. In the spring of 1941, an African American named Jasper Carpenter purchased a home in the white neighborhood near City Hospital. That night a group of whites stoned the house and drove him and his family away. But the die had been cast, and in 1942 whites began a mass exodus from the area; within twelve months East Winston was almost entirely black.[31]

Yet even as spatial segregation intensified, the two races continued to live "separate lives together," parallel and relational, each conditioned, however unequally or differently, by the other. Black neighborhoods abutted those occupied by poor whites, and the edges of working-class districts became interracial contact zones where neighborly relations as well as competition and violence flourished. Geneva McClendon remembered her white neighbors. "When we lived up on Eighth and Highland, a white family lived next door. We never thought nothing of it. We played together. They'd run in and out of our house; we'd run through their house. And we had a good time. There wasn't no fights, no nothing. I'm sure they was poor. Any neighborhood I lived in, you were poor. [Poor whites] lived on Highland from Eighth Street all the way down to First Street. And blacks lived right behind them, or in front of them. And it was never no problem."[32]

Theodosia Simpson had similar memories of her childhood on the edge of town. "In the section where I was born and reared [in Forsyth County], the blacks lived out on the highways, and on the back streets were the whites. But we were all neighbors. We played with the white kids. If somebody died in one of the other families we all went to the rescue. If the Gatewood kids were at our house at lunch time, my mama fed us all. If we were at Mrs. Gatewood's, she fed us all. This fellow John Farley, he was a little older than I was, but both of us liked to read, and we exchanged books. We had to pass a couple of white schools to get to the one we attended. And we went to different churches, although the whites came to our church when they got ready and there was a little small white church below us and we'd go there if we wanted to. I didn't really pay any attention to a difference."[33]

When Simpson and her rural neighbors ventured into town, however, they found themselves negotiating the intricate etiquette of urban segregation. "I went to work in Reynolds in 1937," Simpson remembered. "I was on the bus. There was a long seat at the back and then these two short seats. I sat on one of the short seats and this white woman got on and the seat beside me was vacant and she wouldn't sit down. This fellow John Farley cursed them [the whites on the bus] out. He cursed them all the way from City Hall to Lexington Road. Farley told them, 'These people come to your house and take care of your children and cook for you.'"[34]

Unlike McClendon and Simpson, Robert Black remembered relations with white children as "nothing but fighting and kicking. We had our neighborhood gangs. And if we were going to the baseball field or anything like that, somewhere along the line we had to pass through a white community. And if they knew we were coming, they would have their rocks piled up. And it was not that that was my way of life, but it was the system. I didn't want to fight nobody and things like that. But you had to fight to survive. That was just how it was. And if a bunch of black kids was to come into the community and say there's a bunch of white kids got a bunch of black kids pinned down up there in their neighborhood, and they're having a pretty hard time, well, I would go running. I didn't have hatred for whites, but I understood the separation of the two races. I didn't agree with it, but it was just a part of the system."

"There was nothing that I would have loved any better," Black lamented, "than to have played with the whites and mingled in their homes and they in mine, for what it was worth, but we just didn't live like that. But as I grew up, I lost all my prejudice. I began to understand that the whites being segregated, blacks being segregated, didn't make our lives any better. But now how many others could you convince of that? And you had to fight if you survived."[35]

Relationships between new migrants to the city and the "better class" of blacks were fraught with complications in very different ways. In Winston-Salem as in other southern towns, African Americans recognized significant distinctions among themselves, however hard white supremacists might try to lump them together as members of an inferior caste. The pre–World War I black elite, whom W. E. B. Du Bois called the "talented tenth," was composed of the sons and daughters of free blacks, the mulatto children of high-status white men, and those who through education, industriousness, or patronage had risen from more humble roots. United around values of morality, self-discipline, and social decorum, they sought respect from the white community and influence in their own, and they aspired to a position in southern society on the basis of their achievements, not the color of their skin. They had faith that once they had demonstrated their ability to function as respectable, hard-working citizens, whites would grant them full citizenship rights, and even the imposition of Jim Crow had not entirely crushed that hope.[36]

Simon Green Atkins was the unquestioned leader of black Winston-Salem's "better class." Born a slave in 1863, Atkins was a penniless country boy when he encountered a young schoolteacher, Anna Julia Haywood (later Cooper), the black feminist writer. Inspired by her, he became an educator especially dedicated to training women for teaching careers. Atkins arrived in Winston in the early 1890s to serve as principal of the Depot Elementary School, the city's first public school for black children, and he founded Slater Industrial Academy in 1892. Atkins lived through the horrors of the white supremacy campaigns, and he was devoted to making Winston-Salem a place in which African Americans could find a "permanent home and in which they could dwell in peace and safety and prosperity." Students built Slater Academy's first permanent building with their own hands, and when the school began issuing teaching certificates in 1905, the men and women who acquired them did yeoman service in black schools across the state and the region. It took twenty more years of struggle before Atkins, his faculty, and the black community managed to persuade the North Carolina General Assembly to transform the academy into Winston-Salem Teachers College. The struggle itself made the school a monument to black achievement and a symbol of hope for the future.[37]

Given the poverty of the black community, however, Atkins's success depended not only on such efforts, but also on access to the most powerful white men in the city. Enormous wealth, together with the conviction that disfranchisement and segregation had settled the "race problem" once and for all, gave Winston-Salem's power brokers a palpable aura of security. They could afford to cultivate what they regarded as "exceptional" African Americans to help manage race relations and to give themselves a point of entry into an increasingly distant and self-contained black community. Indeed, men like R. J. Reynolds exercised their power in part through noblesse oblige. They saw helping trusted black leaders to uplift the poor as a means of upgrading a workforce made up of undisciplined and unruly country folk as well as of influencing affairs in black precincts from which they were far removed.[38]

In 1891 Simon Atkins appeared before the Winston Board of Trade to seek help both in starting the teachers' college and in developing comfortable houses for black professionals and skilled craftsmen nearby. In response, a consortium of white men formed to assemble the land that became Columbian Heights, a suburb for black professionals. Once established, the college served as the chief point of contact between the white oligarchy and the black elite. Reynolds executives served on the board of trustees (no blacks were appointed until the late 1940s), and their wives attended events at the school. When Booker T. Washington paid a visit to the college (then still Slater Institute) in 1910, he was introduced by the mayor and entertained with the assistance of "silver and linen and two servants" sent by Katharine Smith Reynolds, one of the "richest white ladies in town."[39]

Atkins claimed to have had the honor of meeting R. J. Reynolds frequently and knowing him well. When speaking to white audiences, at least, he had nothing but praise for Reynolds and his ilk. They were, he said, committed to "promoting good race relations," one and all, and the fruits of that commitment (and of his own persistent diplomacy) could be seen in the "excellent homes" acquired by the black middle class, the black businesses that dotted the town, and, most of all, the educational attainments of the students at his school. Black progress, Atkins believed, depended on a trade-off that some might see as a Faustian bargain but that to men and women of his generation represented the only strategy that had a prayer of success. Atkins called that bargain the "Columbian Heights Method." It consisted of an acceptance of "voluntary segregation" in return for an "educational square deal" and "fair treatment by our city and justice in the courts." Atkins was no fool, and he was well aware both that segregation was anything but voluntary and that whites were far from having lived up to their part of the deal. For him, however, accentuating the positive was a necessary political tool.[40]

Speaking before the city's white ministerial association in 1929, Atkins addressed a development that threatened to upset the race's slow upward march: the surge of black rural folk into the city. When he arrived in Winston-Salem in 1890, Atkins explained, the black community was made up of native North Carolinians along with a few Virginians, all of whom were "eager to use every opportunity for improvement and progress." Now, however, the black population had exploded, undermining such unity of purpose. Moreover, these newcomers were drawn from a far-flung "submerged element." More interested in the wages to be earned in the factories and in the pleasures of the city than in the uplift efforts of the middle class, they multiplied the black community's "social, educational and religious problems."[41]

Denied the right to elect their own representatives during the Jim Crow interregnum, African Americans had little choice but to look to men such as Simon Atkins to manage their relationships with whites and to extract services from the state. To be sure, leaders did emerge in the black community without the imprimatur of whites. Workers might defer in community matters to the opinion of a successful businessperson, an effective minister, a well-regarded teacher, or the president of a local lodge. But whatever their origins, insofar as they acted as go-betweens for the black community, such spokespersons functioned, in Glenda Gilmore's apt metaphor, as "double agents," walking "a tightrope that required them to be forever careful, tense, and calculating." At the heart of their dilemma was the necessity of leaning on the weakest of reeds: the trust and generosity of whites. That dependency, as well as their own middle-class values, inevitably affected their stance toward the black migrants who, if only by their sheer numbers, increasingly set the tone of the city's black world.[42]

This change in the city's black population widened the gulf between the masses and the established black "better class" and created new tensions within the African American community. But it also underwrote economic and cultural expansion and the growth of a larger and more diverse middle class. By the beginning of World War II, Winston-Salem's black citizens fell into three main groups: a tiny elite made up of a small number of administrators, businessmen, and professionals, many of whom were associated with Winston-Salem Teachers College; a middle class of black teachers, clerical workers, and small business owners; and a large majority of industrial and household workers. In contrast to the white community, where class status was closely pegged to occupation and income, African Americans' class identities were derived as much from education and respectability as from occupation. Class lines were thus more permeable, and the markers of class more evanescent and variable. Some ministers, for instance, served relatively prosperous congregations; others headed storefront churches in poor neighborhoods. The latter often labored full-time in the tobacco factories alongside their working-class parishioners. Teachers, an increasing majority of whom were women, determinedly presented an aura of respectability, but they earned little more than tobacco workers, might supplement their salaries with seasonal industrial or household work, and often lived in modest working-class neighborhoods. Charged with the education of all the community's children, they pivoted between their cross-class responsibilities and their professional identities.[43]

Black-owned enterprises blended acquisitiveness with community-mindedness and a commitment to self-help. Small business owners sometimes extended credit to their customers and sometimes gouged them. Under political pressure, they vacillated between solidarity with their working-class neighbors and the acquisitive individualism they shared with their white counterparts. But these institutions were indispensable. They provided a measure of autonomy and security for the owners as well as for the black community. They also served as community centers, places where people could gather to gossip, socialize, and share the information on which movement building depended.[44]

A thriving black business district sprang up along Patterson Avenue, which ran north from the Reynolds plants to Liberty Street, the dividing line between East Winston and the white neighborhoods to the west. The ground floor of the Goler Building housed a barber shop, doctors' office, and café. Next door were lawyers' offices and a print shop. The city directory reported over 200 black-owned businesses in 1938, the large majority of which were barbershops (43), beauty parlors (35), grocery stores (57), cafés (52), and beer parlors (8). Most of these concerns remained one- or two-person operations. Their lack of capital, competition from whites (who wanted blacks' dollars however much they embraced Jim Crow), and the poverty of their customers contributed to high rates of failure, and small proprietors, like ministers, sometimes held factory jobs as well.[45]

Among the most successful of these black-owned enterprises was the Safe Bus Company, which, as the city grew, became the chief means by which blacks made their way back and forth from their homes to the plants and to the Duke Power buses that took them to white suburban homes. The streetcars that enabled whites to leave the city in the late nineteenth century did not extend to the black neighborhoods, and neither did the pavement that covered streets downtown and in the suburbs after the introduction of automobiles in the years before World War I. Horse-drawn carriages provided transportation in the black community, and later small buses, called jitneys, picked up passengers. The jitney trade flourished, despite the nearly impassable condition of the roads in wet weather, and in 1926 a group of drivers formed a bus company to provide more extensive and regular service to blacks. Within a decade Safe Bus boasted that it was the largest black-owned transportation company in the world.[46]

Subsistence-level wages in both manufacturing and domestic service, along with the marginal profitability of most businesses, severely limited wealth accumulation in the African American community. As a result, Winston-Salem had few black financial institutions. Mutual aid societies pooled the resources of members for help in times of trouble. In the early twentieth century, enterprising entrepreneurs began taking over this function and folding it into profit-making insurance companies. The unrivaled leader in this area was Durham's North Carolina Mutual Life Insurance Company, but Winston developed a moderately successful firm of its own. The Winston Industrial Association opened in 1906 to provide accident and sickness policies; a decade later it changed its name to the Winston Mutual Life Insurance Company and offered life insurance policies as well.[47]

Housing, as well as education and income, helped differentiate African Americans in Winston-Salem. Like their white counterparts, the "better living blacks" carved out their own distinctive communities, rushing to the suburbs early in the century, although without benefit of streetcars. They congregated first across the railroad tracks from East Winston, in Columbian Heights, the planned neighborhood near the college. Another middle-class neighborhood sprang up along East Fourteenth Street, where the families of men such as the bishop of the AME Zion Church, the principal of the Depot School, and the founders of the Safe Bus Company and Winston-Salem Mutual Life Insurance Company enjoyed comfortable, high-ceilinged homes and tree-shaded yards. A suburb called Alta Vista opened in 1929, claiming to be the only "restricted" black neighborhood in the South.[48]

The vast majority of African Americans could afford only the most wretched of rental housing. White real estate firms and developers built most of the units in black working-class districts and then sold them to white investors. Also, as Robert Black put it, "some of the better-living blacks started buying dilapidated houses and putting new boards and a slosh of paint on them and renting them to the blacks because there was a big profit." Rent collectors, whether white or black, were known for their ruthlessness. Theodosia Simpson recalled that "T. E. Johnson and the Newton brothers were the worst; they were real prejudiced. They actually didn't own the houses, they were just rental agents. Most of the houses were owned by absentee landlords, all of them white. Those apartments where we lived were owned by people who lived in Florida. You miss one week's rent, they'd have the sheriff setting your stuff outdoors." Robert Black concurred. "There wasn't no explaining to do. 'Have you got my money?' 'No.' You just as well go putting your things together 'cause when he went back to town the sheriff would be out there."[49]

Families, often including three generations, squeezed into tiny apartments and "4 ½s," a local variation of the shotgun house. Crowding was especially intense during World War I, when the demand for labor outstripped the housing supply. Reynolds took to paying recent migrants to go back home and recruit additional workers. "They would put them in boxcars like cattle," Robert Black remembered, "and bring them to Winston." These newcomers often doubled up in the homes of family and friends until they could find a place to stay. Black knew of situations where families had to "put a spread on the eating table and two or three people would get up on that table and sleep."[50]

Geneva McClendon lived at the corner of Eighth Street and Highland Avenue. To her the neighborhood was "a lot of different shacks, not houses. We didn't have lights, let alone indoor plumbing. You used lamps at night. We had windows, but we didn't have window panes in them." Robert Black described conditions in Monkey Bottom when he was growing up: "There were areas in there that had community water facilities, toilet and water. We had one set of toilets for six or seven houses. You had one faucet. Those people used newspapers back then, they wasn't able to buy toilet paper, they'd clog those things up and the filth would just run all

Housing in poor black neighborhood near Monkey Bottom, at rear of East Second Street, 1950 (Forsyth County Public Library Photograph Collection)

over the lawns. Your children would go out and play and the flies would eat out of it and come in and get on your plate. Didn't have no screen doors and all that kind of stuff. Very few of them had over three rooms. There was a front room and a middle room for a bedroom and a kitchen. Most people had to use what you would call a living room for a bedroom because there were too many in the family."[51]

"There wasn't a house in the neighborhood where I lived that didn't have a rat path," Black continued. "You'd block them out at one place with a piece of tin or something and the next thing you'd know you'd be lying·in bed at night and hear them running all through your house. You couldn't keep them out. In the cold wintertime you could sit in the house and look through the floor. You wasn't able to buy linoleum and things to shut out the cold. Half of the time you'd have to move the beds around when it was raining to keep it from raining on your bed, setting up tin tubs and all that kind of stuff. You wouldn't believe it, living in a country like America, that people would have to live under those conditions."[52]

Black middle-class leaders might prefer to distance themselves from the newcomers in their midst, but they could not separate their destiny from that of the race. The South's progressive reformers intensified their efforts in the 1920s and, despite the miserly contributions from the state, managed to bring about a significant expansion of social services and of the infrastructure necessary for urban growth. In Winston-Salem, however, instead of raising property taxes, which remained among the lowest in the state, the city fathers floated bonds to upgrade the city's facilities, and they spent a disproportionate share of these revenues on buildings and services for whites. In response, blacks redoubled both their voluntary activities and their demands for a fair share of state-funded services.[53]

These efforts focused initially on education. In 1910 Winston had only one public school for black children, the Depot School. Whites had three graded schools and a separate high school. During the next decade Winston-Salem built three more black schools: Trade Street, Oak Street, and Woodland Avenue (which became the scene of many mass meetings by unionized workers in the 1940s). Around the same time, the city also established a black high school at Columbian Heights. Its replacement, the Winston-Salem Negro High School (later renamed for Simon Atkins), opened in 1931 with support from the Rosenwald Fund and city bonds. With its modern classrooms, science labs, and workshops, Atkins High School represented a major advancement for African American students, who began to graduate from high school in higher numbers.[54]

Even with these hard-won improvements, educational opportunities available to blacks paled by every measure in comparison to those provided for whites, from student-teacher ratio to teachers' salaries and the value of buildings and equipment. Such comparative disadvantages stemmed in part from the advances of the white school system during the 1920s. At the start of the twentieth century, the city's entire public school system was abysmal. A thorough evaluation by a University of North Carolina researcher recommended major changes, and in the aftermath of World War I, city government and local philanthropists funneled millions of dollars into new buildings, higher salaries, and additional teachers. Within a few decades the white system was among the best in the state and region. The jewel in the crown was the R. J. Reynolds High School, built in the western part of town on land donated by R. J.'s widow, Katharine. For generations, the sons and daughters of the city's middle class received a private school education there free of charge. The city also built two more modest high schools for working-class whites, Hanes in the northern part of the city and Gray in the southern section. In 1929 roughly 9,000 white and 6,000 black children were enrolled in the public schools. There was one teacher for every 28 white students, but only one for every 37 blacks; there were 268 acres of school playgrounds for whites and 42 for blacks.[55]

Class was a great equalizer, however, as the disadvantages of poor children of both races were compounded by family economies that depended on child labor. Robert Black described his own predicament: "In our family, we three older children went into the factory because there was need for our little bit of income. This cut out our chances for education. Now my younger brothers and sister were able to go until they finished high school. College was almost out then, because people just didn't have enough money for college. A few was able to get a high school education and that was about it. And that held true among the working whites, too. It's hard to believe that person to person, you would find almost as many white children that had limited education. They weren't altogether exploited. They lived in better houses, and they had paved streets, most of them. But now there were some that were still victimized as badly as the Negro was."[56]

Poverty, squalid housing, and dangerous working conditions took a terrible toll on the bodies as well as the minds of the city's black workers. Not surprisingly, people who could not keep enough nutritious food on their tables and who lived in houses without screens and in neighborhoods without adequate water and sewer facilities died from treatable communicable diseases and suffered from high rates of maternal and infant mortality and low life expectancies. In fact, blacks in the city were worse off than those in the countryside, despite higher incomes and better access to medical care. Poor whites labored under similar disadvantages, but blacks had the added burden of racist doctors and nurses, hospitals that denied them care, and a shortage of black health care professionals.[57]

In the 1920s a black voluntary movement, together with a statewide public health offensive, made significant headway. By the early 1940s, Winston-Salem had three black public health nurses, more than any other North Carolina city except Charlotte and Greensboro, each of which had six. By World War II, blacks made up half the clients of the state's public health clinics, at a time when African Americans comprised approximately one-quarter of the population, and attendance at maternal and infant clinics was virtually all black.[58]

The struggle for hospital care was even more protracted. The Reynolds family played a key role, in part because in the industrialists' calculus proper treatment for illness would cut down on absenteeism among tobacco workers. R. J. and Katharine Reynolds had worked with Simon Atkins to establish Slater Hospital on the grounds of the Slater Industrial and Normal School. The hospital functioned from around 1902 until 1912, but it withered away because neither the city nor local industrialists were willing to cover its operating expenses. The merged towns of Winston and Salem constructed a new City Hospital in 1913 and in 1922 added a wing to accommodate black patients.

An openly racist administrator, Dr. J. B. Whittington, denied hospital privileges to African American physicians. After years of trying to persuade city officials to change this policy, the black Twin City Medical Society petitioned the mayor and Board of Aldermen to construct a separate hospital. A substantial gift from Will Reynolds led to the opening in 1938 of the Kate Bitting Reynolds Memorial Hospital, named in honor of his wife. The 198-bed facility and the accompanying nursing school dramatically increased blacks' access to health care and provided opportunities for black health care professionals. Still, it took another eight years before clamor from the African American community forced Whittington to turn over administrative responsibilities to blacks. Once the "Katie B." opened, moreover, City Memorial stopped admitting blacks entirely, making health care even more segregated than it had been before.[59]

There was one public service that did penetrate African American communities, albeit often in a threatening guise. In Winston-Salem, as in most southern towns, the police force was entirely white—and for the most part poorly educated, poorly trained, and poorly paid. The city did not hire a black officer until 1949, although the department retained a black detective beginning in the 1920s. Robert Black felt that the only requirement of a police job was to be a "Negro hater." "We had people on the force who couldn't read and write. As long as you were white, they'd give you a gun and a pair of handcuffs." "Policemen were pretty rough on the blacks," Theodosia Simpson remembered. "They circled the community pretty regularly on Friday, Saturday, and Sunday nights. They had their regular schedules. In areas where there were beer gardens and pool rooms you'd see them more often because you had more people congregated. You couldn't say, what am I being arrested for; if so, you were beaten a lot of times."[60]

Blacks were much more likely than whites to end up in prison and on death row. In 1942, when African Americans made up less than a third of the state's population, they comprised half of its prisoners. Out of 308 individuals executed between 1910 and 1943, 243 were black. Predominantly black road gangs built and repaired the highways in North Carolina, which called itself the "good roads state," and in 1942 a traveler could see more blacks working on the road gangs in Forsyth than in any other county in the state.[61]

In Winston-Salem, as in virtually all black communities, the church became the primary institutional expression of African American life. Combining African spirituality with Christian teaching, slaves before the Civil War developed forms of ecstatic expression that articulated their experiences and aspirations. After emancipation, freedmen and women formed their own churches, chose their own ministers, and developed their own denominational structures. From the outset, there were conflicts between the exuberant religious styles of the freedmen and the restraint of the black New Englanders who came South to civilize what they saw as a backward rural folk. Over time those tensions shaped southern religious life, as urban Baptists and Methodists began to frown on such Africanist practices as dancing and call-and-response singing and adopted European styles of singing from hymnals (which only the literate could do) and "rendering one self quiet in the house of the Lord." Black ministers accommodated white pressures in other ways as well, and increasingly the mainline black denominations came under fire for losing touch with the essence of black rural traditions and depoliticizing the church. Afro-Christianity, however, proved endlessly protean and inventive. The limits of freedom—segregation, white supremacy, and economic exploitation—ensured that it never lost its prophetic edge, and, beginning in the late nineteenth century, new Holiness-Pentecostal denominations sprang up to serve the urban poor.[62]

Moravians established the first of the city's African American churches when they created a separate congregation for slaves and free blacks in Salem in 1822. Independent black churches begin to appear by the 1880s. Among the earliest were the Tabernacle AME Zion Church, St. James AME Church, and the First Baptist Church, which attracted many of the black community's professional and business leaders. Tiny storefront churches proliferated after 1910, and during the Depression decade the number of Sanctified churches in Winston-Salem rose from seven to twenty-five, only six fewer than the Baptists, the black community's largest denomination, could claim.[63]

Of necessity, black churches became social service providers for the community. Sunday worship was punctuated by special collections for sick and needy parishioners. The church often provided classes in reading and writing and in some cases hosted public school classes as well. Women performed the lion's share of this church work in the mainstream as well as the Holiness churches, in part because they were the designated caregivers in their families and, by extension, their communities, and in part because among black parishioners in North Carolina they outnumbered men by two to one. In most denominations, women formed powerful, autonomous departments and fought to secure the right to ordination. Even when they were banned from preaching, they served as teachers, missionaries, and musical directors. In some of the Sanctified churches women gained full ordination, pastored their own churches, and created and headed their own separate denominations. White church women fought similar battles and created similar organizations, but, all in all, the black church offered women a greater variety of leadership opportunities. As a result, many black union activists had years of organizational experience.[64]

In Winston-Salem, moreover, black churches offered a space in which class differences narrowed and working-class sensibilities often prevailed. To be sure, men usually monopolized the pulpit, and middle-class delegates predominated in state and national church assemblies. But at the local level, a tobacco or domestic worker might occupy a respected position as a deaconess, Sunday school teacher or choir leader, and a preacher who moonlighted as a tobacco worker, working side-by-side with his parishioners, would be unlikely to set himself apart. Velma Hopkins, to take just one example, labored in the Reynolds plants all week, but in the evenings and on weekends, she orchestrated singing contests and helped organize Woman's Day at Shiloh Baptist Church.[65]

Under such circumstances, church was far from being just a Sunday morning affair: prayer services, committee meetings, and Bible study brought people to the church all through the week. In the larger, more financially secure churches, the minister and a secretary might look after day-to-day activities, but the congregants themselves provided much of the oversight and the support to keep the church running. Indeed, the church served as the locus of political life in the black community. "Excluded from the mainstream electoral process, black people voted and chose their leaders in their churches, selecting pastors, bishops, trustees, deacons and deaconesses, the presidents of the convention, women's auxiliaries, and the like," two church scholars observed. "This surrogate politics carried on in the Black Church became an intensive training ground of political experience with all of the triumphs and disappointments of which the political process is capable."[66]

African Americans created a rich associational life outside of the church as well, and many people belonged to multiple organizations. Greek-letter fraternities and sororities allowed the black middle class to distinguish itself from the masses; photographs of their dances, debutante balls, and scholarship drives filled the "Negro News" page of the Sunday *Journal and Sentinel*. The fraternal orders and secret societies that became popular in urban areas in the twentieth century were more likely to cut across class lines. Like the churches, clubs and lodges served as outlets for social and political aspirations and provided new migrants with a sense of participation and belonging.[67]

Black clubwomen and churchwomen focused especially on protecting young women from city dangers. Because the boardinghouse built by Reynolds was for whites only, black women formed the Phillis Wheatley Home and then a branch of the YWCA to provide housing for young black women who had migrated to Winston-Salem to work. Such efforts could reinforce the very stereotypes they were meant to counter, particularly the assumption that black women, especially poor women from the countryside, were inherently promiscuous, a belief that sparked "moral panics" among black elites as migrants crowded into both southern and northern cities and that most whites took as axiomatic. But these programs also made the point that black women deserved the same treatment as whites. Increasingly, the younger generation of YWCA leaders, especially those employed by its industrial department, did not defend black womanhood by making distinctions between themselves and the masses. Instead, they fought to position black migrants as *women workers* and as potential *leaders*, and to transform the race problem into an industrial problem, that is, a problem of gaining equal access for black women to business and industrial employment. The black woman, the industrial department leaders suggested, must "so entrench herself in the stronghold of trade and industry that the color of her skin can never again act successfully as a barrier to the realization of her highest ambitions."[68]

Such uplift enterprises were welcomed by aspiring members of the respectable working class. But front porches, movies, beer parlors, poolrooms, and juke joints offered black workers their most compelling sites of urban pleasure. As a child, Sidney Royal made sure that he saw two movies every Saturday. Before she married, Theodosia Simpson and her friends from work attended the movies three times a week, mostly to watch the westerns and serials that were popular with young people. By 1940 Winston-Salem had six movie houses. Two white theaters admitted blacks, but they had to enter through a separate entrance and sit in a balcony called the "buzzard's roost." There were two black-owned theaters and two that admitted only whites. One of those was the Winston. "We used to have a joke about the Winston Theater," Geneva McClendon remembered. "You can go to the Winston Theater if you know what side to sit on. The outside."[69]

The "race cinema" of the 1920s allowed black audiences to enjoy productions by black writers and producers, and in black theaters during the era of silent film, the sounds of ragtime and the blues accompanied the visual images flashing across the screen. These opportunities declined with the advent of the "talkies," as movies reduced blacks to images of nostalgia or buffoonery or erased them completely from view. But during World War II, as workers such as McClendon and Simpson began to demand all the rights of American citizenship, they could glimpse whole-souled black characters in mainstream Hollywood films for the first time. Physically separated though they were, black and white southerners alike found themselves watching movies that featured black heroes, condemned racism, and anticipated a "nation of nations" to which all races and ethnic groups contributed.[70]

Young people in the 1930s flocked to the juke joints and house parties that came alive in the late evening. Club 709, one of Winston-Salem's more popular nightspots, offered "food, refreshments, entertainment, and rendezvous." The jukebox provided the dance music on most nights, but local and traveling bands also performed. In winter and spring, social organizations rented a tobacco warehouse and sponsored dances with nationally known musicians such as Duke Ellington, Count Basie, and Cab Calloway. On occasion, both blacks and whites would attend, with a rope down the middle of the dance floor to keep the groups separated. The dance pavilion at Robinhood Park became a favorite gathering spot for young people after its opening in 1937.[71]

Black blues and gospel singers rooted in the tobacco towns of Virginia and the Carolinas and influenced by black labor activism created an explicitly political musical sound. The songster Josh White, the guitarist Walter Brown "Brownie" McGhee, and the blind blues harmonica player Sonny Terry were among the most talented and well known of these blues men. The Golden Gate Jubilee Quartet, which broadcast its music from a station in Columbia, South Carolina, influenced gospel singers throughout the urban corridor from the Carolinas to Virginia and New York. In 1938 Brownie McGhee toured Richmond, Durham, and Winston-Salem with James E. Jackson Jr., a founder of the left-wing Southern Negro Youth Congress (SNYC) and Communist Party member, playing for the operatives as they left the factories. McGhee's future partner, Sonny Terry, made his living playing for Durham tobacco workers. Josh White, one of the most successful artists on the "race" records of the 1930s, recorded songs like "No Segregation in Heaven," "Bad Housing Blues," and "Jim Crow Train" during the Great Depression.[72]

Music, like religion, flowed across class lines. Choral groups especially attracted African Americans from all walks of life. Indeed, no musical form more vividly illustrated the overlap between work and community and the degree to which the culture of tobacco work infused the life of the town. From antebellum times onward, blacks sang in the factories, and many choral groups grew from musical relationships formed at work. Often identified with a particular institution (the drivers and mechanics of the Safe Bus Company, for instance, formed a Choral Club in 1938), these singers competed against one another, staged benefits for community projects, traveled widely, and launched individuals on musical careers. Moreover, in the 1930s, when radio became the chief source of news and entertainment for millions of Americans, black choral groups appeared regularly on WSJS, the city's major radio station, offering compelling glimpses of black culture that countered the updated minstrelsy of *Amos 'n' Andy*, the most popular broadcast on the air.[73]

Only sports rivaled religion and music as a means of communal and individual expression. Baseball, a favorite pastime in the rural South, especially captured the imagination of young boys. Robert Black dreamed of being a professional player, but when he was growing up the major leagues were all white, and none supported minor-league teams for black players. Thousands of black children watched their talents go to waste in the small-town ballparks of the South. "I was devoted to base-

The Smith Choral Club (*UCAPAWA News*)

ball," Black recalled. "I started playing in the streets like most kids did; we didn't have playgrounds. I ended up playing professional baseball. We built a couple of ball teams in Winston-Salem. We played in Southside Park where the whites played. We would travel on the weekends. We would draw large crowds. I was like Satchel Paige and a lot of the others; we just never got a chance to play in major leagues." The sport was an important source of identity and pride for the city's young men. "I played outfield," Black continued. "Not patting myself on the back, but I was considered a pretty good outfielder. Pretty good guy at the plate and I could run pretty well. That's where I got the name 'Chick.' When I started chasing the ball, the fans would yell, 'Get that ball, chicken.'"[74]

Such glories added up to a vibrant social world. Within little more than a generation after disfranchisement, African Americans in Winston-Salem had built an intricate urban community that offered more than a refuge from a threatening white world: it also provided innumerable avenues for developing organizational and leadership skills. This was true for tobacco workers as well as teachers, women as well as men. Indeed, the lack of social services, the disfranchisement of men, and the centrality of the church combined to convince black women across the class spectrum that they had a special leadership role to play.

Black women's extraordinarily high rate of participation in industry had a host of implications as well. Few among the poor could choose not to enter the work-force, and domestic service constituted their main alternative. In Winston-Salem, as elsewhere in the South, domestic workers had already won a measure of inde-pendence by opening their own laundries and insisting on living "out" rather than in their employers' homes. They also found myriad ways to resist exploitation and find meaning in their work. Still, they often labored in isolation, seven days a week, from dawn to dusk, at their employers' beck and call. By contrast, the tobacco plants offered sociability, solidarity, and personal autonomy as well as higher wages. At the same time, because tobacco workers often spent part of the year working in white homes and were, in any case, only marginally more prosperous than domes-tic workers, there were no hard and fast lines between the two groups. Tobacco ac-tivists could look to their nonfactory working-class neighbors for support. More-over, factory workers who also performed domestic labor in the homes of whites, including the homes of Reynolds's managers and white-collar workers, had a keen understanding of the ruling class. Less compromised than middle-class go-be-tweens in labor disputes, they could also serve as intelligence gatherers and medi-ators, in effect as "double agents," working behind enemy lines.[75]

Whether they served as church leaders, as household heads, as individual wage earners, or as household workers, women were well positioned to shape the work-ers' movement of the 1940s in their own image. Mobilizing their complex identi-ties—as workers, mothers, consumers, and kin- and community-keepers—they helped dissolve the dichotomies that divided home from work, the secular from the sacred, play from politics. In the process, they gave the union its distinctive breadth and community orientation.

These gender and class dynamics blended with the rigid customs of racial segre-gation to create a strong sense of group identity. Middle-class status might provide a buffer against the worst assaults, but in the end it was no shield against Jim Crow. "If they had to go to the hospital," Theodosia Simpson recalled, "they had to go to the same little hospital that we went to. If they went to the Carolina Theater, they had to sit in the balcony just like we did." Distinctions based on class, family, occu-pation, skin color, and neighborhood would have important repercussions for union-building efforts. But because its black population was overwhelmingly work-ing class and everyone from preachers to shopkeepers to undertakers depended on a working-class clientele, Winston-Salem's African American community was ex-traordinarily cohesive, arguably more so than in any other industrial city in the United States.[76]

"All of my life wasn't bad," Robert Black said of his youth in Monkey Bottom. "I didn't starve when I was growing up. My mother did a good job of keeping the family together. We were part of the community. We attended the churches. We fought a little and played a little, just like normal kids would do. All of my life wasn't bitter. I did miss the presence of my daddy. But even though my mother and he weren't living together, if he felt that anything was needed he would come with the money. He didn't have a fortune, but he worked hard. He would order a big load of wood and come down to the house to find out if there was enough money for food. I still respected him as my father. It was hard for we six kids to understand why the two of them weren't together. You didn't see families breaking up then as you do now. But my mother was respected. She attended church. She didn't have too much time to participate in social affairs, but she was respected in the neighborhood and we children were respected. People would come to her for advice because she was an intelligent woman. She had a good education. We became a part of the neighborhood."[77]

White supremacy and Jim Crow constrained blacks' aspirations and accomplishments, and the stark realities of everyday life, the deprivations, and the soul-killing insults could not be missed. But behind the veil, African Americans forged a basis for resistance around solid, working-class-inflected institutions, rich cultural traditions, relative gender parity, and a history of self-help.

CHAPTER FOUR

R. J. Reynolds Tobacco Company

A Moneymaking Place

The ascent of the Reynolds Tobacco Company to the top echelons of corporate America required a complex operation attuned to the vicissitudes of the weather, as well as the whims of consumers, and capable of coordinating thousands of people, millions of dollars, tons of tobacco, hundreds of machines, and scores of advertising and distribution networks. By all accounts, Reynolds executives carried out their duties with remarkable success, at times using their political and economic muscle to rein in independent-minded farmers and when necessary colluding with other manufacturers to set prices. But profitability depended above all on the steady production of Camel cigarettes, Prince Albert smoking tobacco, and numerous brands of plug, and here Reynolds relied on the men, women, and children who made the products that made the profits for the company and its stockholders. Ownership of capital gave Reynolds's directors the upper hand in organizing the regimens of factory life, but workers had their own needs and interests, which they asserted in ways big and small.[1]

The Division of Labor

The process by which aged tobacco leaves were cleaned, conditioned, cut, and then made into cigarettes and smoking and chewing tobacco mixed manual techniques and mechanical processes. The highly automated, assembly-line technology of the manufacturing departments set the pace for the entire factory, but into the 1940s many tasks continued to be done by hand. It took thousands of men and women to satisfy the voracious appetites of the making machines and hundreds more to package and ship tobacco products to consumers. As a result, the hiring, deployment, and disciplining of labor became a chief preoccupation of Reynolds's owners and managers and a central means by which they made R. J. Reynolds a "money-making place."[2]

Their principal tool for allocating—and ultimately controlling—workers within the factory was the racial and gender division of labor, which both structured and reflected social relations in the larger society. As the sociologist Ruth Milkman has observed, the formative period is critical in establishing a long-term pattern of industrial segregation, because "once established, [it] quickly gains all the weight of tradition and becomes extraordinarily inflexible." In the case of tobacco, there were two defining moments. The first lay in the antebellum past when African Americans, free and slave, provided most of the labor in the factories. Here gender was the primary criterion for job typing, since virtually all workers were black. Women dominated the sorting, picking, and stemming of tobacco leaves while men moved raw materials, applied conditioners, and made plugs and twists of chewing tobacco. In general, men performed the jobs that required more physical strength, but they could be expected to do women's jobs when necessary. Before the Civil War, whites showed little inclination to compete with black labor, and manufacturers had little incentive for recruiting them. Even after the war, when blacks found themselves driven out of many of their former occupations, neither white workers nor employers questioned blacks' right to or suitability for existing jobs in tobacco.[3]

The second moment came with the introduction of new products, new technologies, and new positions in the 1870s, when large numbers of whites entered the tobacco factories for the first time. The perfection of granulating and packing machines for the production of smoking tobacco provided the initial impetus for change. White men and boys took up the new jobs and quickly became the mainstays of this growing branch of the industry. More important, whites got in on the ground floor in cigarette manufacturing. When cigarettes first gained popularity, southern manufacturers began hiring young white women to roll them by hand. White women were also the first to tend the high-speed, Bonsack cigarette-making machines that transformed the industry in the 1880s. As more white males left failing farms, they too found positions tending and fixing machines in the cigarette divisions. Although tobacco never carried textile's symbolic freight, both tobacco and textile manufacturers promoted factory work as a chance for poor white farmers to reap the benefits of New South economic development. Such appeals lured rural people to the city, while signaling to whites and blacks alike that the wages of industrialization would be distributed according to race and gender.[4]

The ruling conventions of late Victorian thought buttressed the bargain that reserved machine-tending for whites and consigned blacks primarily to manual labor. To white southerners who were launching a homegrown industrial revolution, machines symbolized both progress and the superiority of Western civilization. These products of Anglo-Saxon ingenuity served as the nineteenth century's chief symbol and mechanism of power, and they went hand in hand with presumptions regarding the hierarchy of labor: at the top stood occupations that required intelligence, dexterity, and mastery; at the bottom were jobs associated with physical exertion. Blacks got the lowly jobs because they were at the bottom of the social hierarchy, and, according to this circular reasoning, they were at the bottom of the hierarchy because they lacked the capacity for skilled labor. Such beliefs fit nicely with evolutionary thinking, which posited a continuum of human evolution from savagery to civilization, with the darker races at the bottom and "Nordic" whites at the top.[5]

The two-tiered process of machine and hand labor meshed with phobias about sexuality and gender as well. It served as a convenient means of ensuring that black men would not mingle with white women. "Negroes must not be over whites," one observer concluded, "and Negroes and whites must not work together without some visible division of labor." By confining black women to hard, dirty, largely unmechanized jobs, this division of labor reflected and reinforced their association— as blacks and as women—with soil and excrement, with licentiousness and bodily functions, with the materiality and removal of dirt. From slavery onward, black women had been exempt from the protections that surrounded respectable white women; they had tilled the soil, cleaned the houses, nursed the babies. The black woman, indeed, had been the "mule of the world." Even as factory owners ceased consciously to justify their practices in such terms, these assumptions and associations lived on in the culture of the tobacco industry, embedded in the practices of factory life.[6]

Following the introduction of Camels in 1913, Reynolds divided its production activities into two separate divisions: leaf preparation, often called prefabrication, and manufacturing, which included the smoking, chewing, and cigarette departments. The majority of black workers labored in the prefabrication division, where they occupied virtually all of the jobs in the stemmeries. Women fed tobacco through reordering machines, stemmed it, and removed foreign materials by hand. Men moved the tobacco from place to place, although at times they too stemmed it. Beginning in the mid-1930s, Reynolds introduced more machines into the stemmeries in response both to federal minimum wage laws, which raised the pay of hand stemmers, and to the increased militancy of women workers. Even then, black women were confined to the prefabrication department, where much of the picking and sorting continued to be done by hand, and most jobs remained sex-typed; men might do women's jobs, but women rarely took the place of men. In 1943, of the approximately 3,500 people at work in the cavernous rooms of Numbers 60 and 60 Extension or in one of the smaller departments such as Number 65, 80 percent were women.[7]

The manufacturing division, by contrast, employed nearly equal numbers of blacks and whites. Whites dominated positions in the cigarette departments as well as in the skilled crafts, and by the beginning of World War II, they made up slightly more than one-third of the overall workforce at Reynolds. White men monopolized the most desirable jobs as mechanics and craftsmen (carpenters, plumbers, millwrights, painters, steam fitters, and electricians), both because management preferred to hire them and because those positions required training from which blacks had been increasingly excluded. Cigarette-making machine operators and packing machine operators comprised the largest category of white male workers. White women inspected the output of making and packing machines and, in smaller numbers, operated machines or did clerical work in the factory. Black men clustered in the casing and drying and the casing and cutting departments, where flavorings—honey, rum, chocolate, vanilla, and various secret ingredients—were applied to the leaf. Both black men and women could be found in large numbers in the chewing tobacco departments.[8]

These divisions of labor prevailed until the late 1950s. They were not written in stone, however, and could be modified if production requirements or labor market conditions required. While Reynolds generally observed the etiquette of racial segregation, it made sure that workers understood that such policies were the company's prerogative, not the workers' right. In extraordinary circumstances—during the Christmas rush when the company needed maximum production or during hard times when whites were desperate for jobs—racial divisions (but not gender divisions) evaporated, and whites and blacks temporarily worked side by side. More often, Reynolds tinkered with this racialized division of labor by requiring blacks and whites to perform the same jobs on different floors or different shifts. The company occasionally operated a stemming department staffed by whites, and at various times the leaf houses used whites on one shift and blacks on another. Beginning in the early 1920s, Reynolds maintained one cigarette-making department using black workers. Apparently no other major cigarette manufacturer employed blacks in such a capacity, and Reynolds promoted this novel arrangement for public relations purposes. Middle-class blacks on factory tours were shown this department as evidence of the company's efforts to improve opportunities for black workers; black visitors, the company assumed, should not be allowed to watch whites at work.[9]

Neither the company nor the workers seem to have made much of these crossings of the color line, but one white worker who spoke to the sociologist Charles S. Johnson in 1935 understood the implications of such transgressions. "'The poor whites and niggers is worked together up at no. —,'" he explained. "'They is using the poor whites to whip the nigger and the nigger to whip the poor whites. If the poor whites sort of get out of line, they fire them and put niggers in their jobs and they do the niggers the same way.'"[10]

There in a nutshell was the underlying purpose of the division of labor in tobacco and, indeed, the central mechanism of white supremacy. Democrats had used the same divide and conquer approach to regain political power at the end of the nineteenth century, and it served as an effective labor management strategy well into the twentieth. A racially divided workforce gave manufacturers tremendous leverage in their dealings with workers of both races. Noting the absence of a union at Reynolds, a writer for *Fortune* observed in 1938 "that the workers are divided half white and half black, and this in the South weakens, where it does not forestall, every attempt to organize." There was nothing uniquely southern about this strategy; throughout industrial America management exacerbated or created racial, ethnic, and gender divisions as a means of weakening workers' power. But in the South, the institutionalization of segregation solidified this fragmentation.[11]

The division of labor in the factories, in turn, helped to normalize the racial hierarchy that existed outside the workplace. If a black man fell behind while feeding tobacco to a cigarette-making machine, he could expect to hear a few choice words from the white operator even though the operator lacked any supervisory authority. One worker trenchantly observed: "The whites does the bossing, the Negro does the work." Cultural conceptions of blacks as the "low other" also squared with their roles in the factory. "The [workers] would dip snuff and chew tobacco and all," Blanche Fishel remembered. "They had these old big metal cuspidors. These colored men would come around and take them things up every day. Then they had colored people who sweep the floors and things like that. We had dressing rooms to put our things, and then we had nice restrooms. We had a maid that kept them clean." Although not directly subordinate to white workers, blacks cleaned up after them, thus deepening whites' image of blacks as fit only for servitude. Such a division of labor contributed to whites' elevated sense of their own status and prerogatives and to their image of blacks as categorically different and inferior, while at the same time undergirding manufacturers' power. By creating separate environments and experiences for workers based on gender, race, and skills, it also short-circuited class-based solidarities.[12]

Yet, for all of its effectiveness, the system of racial privilege was inherently unstable, both in the factories and in the larger society. For one thing, racial discrimination and segregation did not prevent the development of *intra*racial class consciousness. In fact, by minimizing differences based on age, marital status, church affiliation, education, neighborhood, or birthplace, divisions based on race and sex could become points of solidarity and mobilization. On the other hand, when the company tinkered with the division of labor in order to assert its own power and play off one group against the other, it as much as admitted the interchangeability of blacks and whites and highlighted their common concerns. If Reynolds cared no more for racial solidarity than to "whip the poor whites" as well as the "niggers," why should poor whites side with the company against blacks? Those rare occasions when blacks and whites worked together offered a glimpse of an interracial solidarity that potentially could emerge. A black woman who worked in an integrated picking room at Reynolds remembered that they all "got along fine." Observing the capacity of common experiences to dissolve difference, she said, "All seem like one color." Indeed, covered in dust and sweat, the many skin pigments probably did blend into one color: dirt made everyone "black."[13]

Early Organizing Campaigns and the Rise of Welfare Capitalism

Reynolds faced the first serious opposition to its labor policies during World War I. Across the South, labor shortages stimulated union organizing campaigns. In order to recruit and retain workers, Reynolds raised wages, initiated attendance and performance bonuses, and offered subsidized housing. As soon as the war ended, however, the company curtailed these benefits. In response, Reynolds workers appealed for help to the Tobacco Workers International Union. Founded in 1895, the TWIU, an American Federation of Labor affiliate, usually limited itself to the promotion of the union label, offering manufacturers who agreed to abide by certain wage rates and work rules and to require their employees to belong to the union a small stamp of approval to be affixed to tobacco packages. The union label, in turn, was supposed to make these products more attractive to labor-supporting American consumers; cooperating firms also benefited from the TWIU's practice of eschewing strikes and promoting steady, skilled workmanship.[14]

Around the turn of the century, the TWIU made significant inroads into the country's smaller, independent tobacco manufacturers, including Winston's P. H. Hanes Company, which saw the union label as a way to fight James B. Duke's American Tobacco Company Trust. By 1900, ninety of these independents were affixing the label to their products. But the TWIU could never penetrate the Trust. The dissolution of the Trust in 1911 seemed to offer hope to the struggling union, but it took the domestic disruptions caused by World War I to force American, Liggett & Myers, P. Lorillard, and Reynolds to the bargaining table.[15]

Responding to appeals from Reynolds workers, Anthony McAndrews, the president of the TWIU, and James Brown, a black organizer from Richmond, Virginia, arrived in Winston-Salem in the spring of 1919, in the midst of a nationwide strike wave that constituted an "unprecedented revolt of the rank and file." The men's success in signing up members landed them in jail. A state official, undoubtedly acting at the behest of Reynolds, charged them with selling insurance—the union's sick and death benefits—without a license. The incident exemplified the collusion between business and government that helped to stymie labor organization in Winston-Salem and in North Carolina as a whole during the interwar years, although in this case the state eventually dropped the charges.[16]

By early summer the TWIU had enough members to charter two locals at Reynolds, one for whites and one for blacks. Segregated locals were common practice, and while the TWIU could not have tackled the South's Jim Crow system single-handedly, it could have treated its black locals with respect. Instead, national union leaders exhibited deep-seated prejudices of their own, manifested especially in their refusal to grant black locals the same control over finances and bargaining enjoyed by their white counterparts. Nevertheless, black workers enthusiastically supported the union drive.[17]

In Winston-Salem, as elsewhere, some members of the black business community were more skeptical. Echoing Booker T. Washington's accommodationist philosophy, they viewed union organizers as a threat to the edifice of racial peace, white patronage, and economic autonomy on which their prosperity and the race's progress depended. After all, the exclusionary and discriminatory practices of white unionists, who saw blacks mainly as potential strike-breakers and as cheap competitors who brought all wages down, had driven blacks from many crafts, particularly the building trades, and denied them access to newly created occupations.

Manufacturers who had jobs to give and less incentive to discriminate seemed to be the real friends of black working people. In a letter to the *Journal*, bank president J. H. Hill assailed the TWIU as "the most detrimental organization that ever came to our city. . . . There is no need for any poor laboring class of people to try to make demands on any rich corporations. We are dependent upon these corporations for employment." Without mentioning race as an issue, he implored "my people" not to be tempted by "strangers" from labor unions. Hill was not alone in his condemnation; several black merchants also spoke against the union.[18]

Black Reynolds workers were well aware of the disadvantages of affiliation with a Jim Crow union. They knew that to wrest concessions from powerful white employers they needed not only a biracial union but also broad black support, support that would always be hard won, contingent, and dependent on the political terrain. In this instance, as in later years, their choice of allies and strategies was dictated by the interweaving of their class needs with their racial and gender identities. Foreshadowing the consumerist tactics that would characterize Winston-Salem tobacco unionism in the years to come, they initiated informal boycotts of stores that refused to support the TWIU and threatened to withdraw their money from Hill's bank, using their power as customers to bring their black critics into line. The TWIU's newspaper, the *Tobacco Worker*, reported that "places where the members used to deal for household articles and barber shops who joined in the opposition to the union are now being passed up. The members' dimes and quarters and dollars are being spent in places where a friendly word for the union was given."[19]

Reynolds responded to the push for unionization by hurriedly introducing an industrial democracy scheme. The program, modeled on those being implemented by the War Labor Board and many of the nation's leading manufacturers, called for the creation of a factory council that functioned in effect as a company union, "initiated, nursed, protected and financed by the employers." Composed of supervisors selected by management and workers' representatives elected by their peers, 60 percent of whom would be black and 40 percent white, the council would serve as a vehicle through which workers could suggest efficiency measures and be rewarded through a profit-sharing plan. Confident of the support of black leaders who were dependent on the company's largess, Reynolds officials contacted Simon Atkins, urging him to convince the Negro Ministerial Association that the plan was in the best interests of the race. Black workers, however, did not look to the middle class for their cues. Asked to vote on the scheme, they rejected it with "hoots and jeers," according to future personnel director Edgar Bumgardner.[20]

Faced with a defiant workforce and hoping to avoid the fierce battles raging across industrial America, Reynolds reluctantly signed a contract with the TWIU. The company increased wages by 20 percent, reduced the workweek to forty-eight hours, and promised not to discriminate against union members. The TWIU signed similar agreements with Brown & Williamson, Bailey Brothers, and Taylor Brothers. By October 1919, the *Tobacco Worker* boldly dubbed Winston-Salem "A Union Town."[21]

The claim was premature. The postwar years were marked both by depression, which made labor more plentiful and workers less militant, and by political reaction. Across the country, antilabor violence, race riots, and a red scare sparked by the 1917 Russian Revolution decimated labor and radical movements. Emboldened by that repressive atmosphere, Reynolds began harassing unionists, forcing a rapid decline in membership. TWIU officials charged that the company's managers "ridiculed the union. They employed new workers who they would not let become members of the union, and created dissension, by pointing out to the union members that employees who did not belong to the union were getting as much as they were and not paying dues." When the TWIU's contract expired in 1921 and the union made no attempt to renegotiate, rumors spread that the company had bought off a local union official by giving him a farm in Forsyth County—a suspicion that reflected the rural orientation of many white tobacco workers as well as the ineptness of the union. Within a few months, Reynolds dismissed 1,500 workers (over 14 percent of the workforce), reduced wages by 20 percent, and established a fifty-five-hour workweek in the cigarette division. The company eventually rehired almost half of those it had laid off, but according to TWIU officials, these workers found their wages drastically reduced, and many union activists were never brought back. By 1923 there were no functioning TWIU locals left in Winston-Salem.[22]

Again Reynolds softened the fist of retaliation with the glove of paternalism, a pattern that would characterize its labor-management relations for years to come. Like other large corporations, the company instituted a program of welfare capitalism designed to strengthen workers' loyalty to and dependence on the company and to polish its public image. At the same time, it sought to moderate the arbitrary power of foremen, a perennial source of workers' discontent.[23]

The locus for these new policies was the Employment Office, created by John Whitaker in 1919, a year after the death of R. J. Reynolds. Whitaker's vision mixed older paternalistic impulses with the latest thinking of industrial relations experts. His father had owned a small chewing tobacco company until shortly before his death in 1912, and Whitaker had undoubtedly observed the informal, face-to-face interactions that characterized such operations. R. J. had brought him into the company as a young man, and as he rose through the ranks, he sought to emulate the founder's personalistic style. According to a long-time colleague, when Whitaker became superintendent of Reynolds's manufacturing division, "everybody in the factory considered Mr. Whitaker his friend. The workers carried problems to him for his aid and counsel. He visited the sick and attended funerals." In his new role, Whitaker aimed to routinize paternalism, temper the foremen's power, and instill an identification with the company in both workers and supervisors. "Management," commented company historian Nannie Mae Tilley, "was endeavoring to enter the twentieth century," carrying with it the penumbra of the past.[24]

Until the consolidation movement spurred by the American Tobacco Company Trust, R. J. Reynolds had wandered the factory floor himself, greeting workers by name and inquiring after their families. He exercised firm control over the workforce, motivating workers with a combination of "harsh discipline" and "inspiration" and regularly intervening in conflicts between workers and foremen. As in most early factories, however, foremen could hire, fire, and punish as they saw fit. As the company grew too large for R. J.'s personal oversight, the foremen began to operate like subcontractors with near dictatorial control. The favoritism that resulted could lead workers to feel a stronger allegiance to a particular foreman than to the company and to follow him as he moved to different departments or different companies. It could also be a source of resentment and volatility on the factory floor.[25]

Whitaker's new employment office took over responsibility for the selection and placement of workers within the factory and for enforcing state and federal laws regulating the employment of women and children. R. J. had been a staunch opponent of child labor legislation, but the passage of a tough federal law in 1919, a year after his death, convinced the company that it would have to begin screening job applicants or face heavy fines, for foremen could not be trusted to keep out underage workers. The removal of key personnel decisions to the executive offices also allowed the company to weed out what Whitaker called "misfits" and "undesirables," who might be fired by a foreman but then move undetected from plant to plant.[26]

The most ambitious, and ultimately least successful, of the office's initiatives was the effort to establish a companywide procedure for processing workers' suggestions and complaints. Having been rebuffed by unionists in 1919, Whitaker instituted a modified Factory Council made up entirely of management personnel. Writing about the goals of the council, Whitaker lamented the loss of personal relationships that accompanied corporate growth. "The question with which the student of industrial problems is now confronted," he wrote, "is how to re-establish this personal relation and co-operation. The answer . . . is through the establishment and operation of a proper means of close and easy communication between employer and employee."[27]

Whitaker's ideas met stiff resistance from many foremen and corporate officers, and the Factory Council was short-lived. The Employment Office took over a few key personnel functions, and Whitaker continued to lecture supervisors about the need to study human nature and lead by example. The employment of underage workers diminished, although children continued to lie about their age, and through the 1940s rumor had it that Reynolds resorted to hiring them during labor short-ages or union trouble. But foremen still ruled the factory floor, retaining the power to fire if not to hire. Company historian Nannie May Tilley observed that it took more than twenty years "for the [employment] department to gain the trust and support of foremen and top management."[28]

The company's corporate welfare programs proved more enduring. In its early years, Reynolds provided few benefits to its factory workers. But the agitations of the World War I era caused the company to rethink its policies. To its credit, and largely through the foresight of John Whitaker, Reynolds became one of the first of the major southern manufacturers to offer limited provisions for health care, housing, retirement, and vacations to its employees. These benefits improved the quality of workers' lives inside and outside the factory in small ways. But even a cursory examination of the timing and terms of such benefits shows that the company used these policies primarily to stabilize employment and limit dissatisfaction rather than to increase actual returns to workers for their labor. And, as with everything else in the factory, benefits followed race and gender lines: they helped whites more than blacks, men more than women, and skilled more than unskilled workers.[29]

By World War II, Reynolds had developed a management strategy similar in some ways to that adopted by other sophisticated non-union companies, which routinized paternalism and used welfare programs and personnel departments to secure workers' loyalty. But unlike its peers, Reynolds failed to check its foremen's shop-floor power. That strategy reflected the company's dual identity as both a modern, oligopolistic corporation unalterably opposed to collective bargaining and a southern manufacturer operating in a closed labor market and relying on the exploitation of a largely black labor force. Such practices also paralleled Reynolds's two-tiered, race-coded system of machine and hand labor: the personnel department was most effective in handling skilled and white-collar workers, while foremen continued to exercise a form of personal power over blacks and, to a lesser degree, white women that reflected social relations in the society at large. Unable to secure either the protection of a union or access to a career job ladder, such workers remained vulnerable to a level of coercion reminiscent of the early days of the industrial revolution.

Reynolds's welfare programs sought to secure workers' loyalty and stave off unionization by filling some of the gaps in the South's inadequate safety net. But as with public services, those programs discriminated against blacks and women, couching differential treatment in the language of skill, seniority, labor force commitment, and so on. After relegating black women to seasonal jobs, for instance, the company then excluded them from benefits on the grounds that they were a fly-by-night "floating population." Corporate welfare thus replicated the division of labor and the dual wage structure that gave white men advantages while depressing the living standards of the working class as a whole. If worker loyalty was the goal, moreover, the high turnover rates during the 1910s and 1920s suggest that Reynolds's welfare programs did not penetrate very deeply. Still, those programs made a difference: they ameliorated suffering; they gave workers the margin of security that might embolden them to risk their jobs in an organizing campaign; and they gave them a sense of entitlement, a taste of a world in which social welfare provisions might eliminate the threats that made working-class life so perilous and necessitated lives lived so close to the bone.

Race, Gender, and Authority

For thirty years, between the introduction of Camels and the sit-down in Number 65, thousands of workers made their way in and out of the factory's "White" and "Colored" entrances. Without access to company personnel records, it is impossible to know precisely who these men and women were, where they came from, where they lived, how old they were, whether they were married, single, or divorced, how long they worked for the company, or how much they earned. Census data yield some information, as do documents submitted by Reynolds to the federal government. Oral histories also provide important clues. But Reynolds's refusal to open its records to scholars makes a precise demographic profile impossible.

A survey of tobacco workers conducted by the sociologist Charles S. Johnson for the National Recovery Administration offers our best snapshot of the tobacco workforce in the city. In 1934 Johnson interviewed 373 workers in Winston-Salem. Forty-two percent were male, 58 percent female; 35 percent were white, and 65 percent black. A majority of those interviewed undoubtedly worked at Reynolds, and these percentages roughly reflected the demographics at the company during the interwar years.[30]

The birthplaces of Johnson's respondents attest to the massive migration that propelled the tobacco industry's growth. Less than 20 percent listed Winston-Salem as their birthplace. The large majority of whites were born in other parts of North Carolina, mostly in rural areas; counties north and west of Forsyth supplied most of these newcomers. Black migrants were evenly divided between North Carolina and other states, with South Carolina as the leading source of non-natives. Unlike whites, roughly half of blacks claimed an urban birthplace, evidence of the degree to which black workers were more rooted in town and factory life than were whites.[31]

Theodosia Simpson's intervention on behalf of the older woman in Number 65 testifies to the diversity of ages within the stemmeries. There was virtually no mobility out of those departments, and since few other jobs paid black women as much as factory work, workers tended to start at an early age and work for many years. The company's oldest and youngest employees often worked side by side. The average age for black women in Johnson's survey was thirty-four, and there were almost as many over forty-five as there were under twenty-five. Because there were fewer entry-level jobs in the departments where black men predominated, their average age was a bit higher. Johnson found that the average age of white men was comparable to that of black men and women, but that white women were about five years younger. They tended to have shorter stays in the factory, since, unlike black women, they left the labor force when they married and began having children.[32]

As one might expect, factory hands had little formal education. Johnson found that black men and women averaged just 5.5 years of schooling, while white males averaged 6.1 and white females 7.5 years. Such numbers meant that a significant number of white and black tobacco workers were illiterate. Those averages increased by the 1940s, as improvements in black education coupled with high black and white unemployment during the Depression kept children in school for longer periods of time. Moreover, as Theodosia Simpson and Wardell Boulware's experiences confirm, even a high school diploma did not guarantee blacks a job outside of the factory, and college-educated men and women were scattered throughout the workplace.[33]

More male than female tobacco workers married. Seventy-six percent of white men and 62 percent of black men were married at the time of the survey, while only 41 percent of both black and white women were. This disparity was due in part to the fact that there were more women than men over the age of twenty-one in the city's population, which meant that there were hundreds of women—particularly black women—who held jobs and lived on their own or with relatives. Of Johnson's informants, almost 30 percent of the white women and 20 percent of black women were single; the rest were separated, divorced, or widowed. Although black married women were more likely than their white counterparts to work outside the home, many such women found part-time jobs as domestics or did seasonal work in the tobacco factories rather than becoming full-time tobacco workers.[34]

The presence in the factories of the sons of Reynolds managers and white-collar employees complicated the identities of white workers. A stint on the factory floor was imperative for just about anyone who aspired to a supervisory or management position—even John Whitaker started out as a cigarette machine-tender —and many such young men began working during their summer breaks. A worker interviewed by the WPA felt that this practice enhanced the status of white operatives, at least of the men. "You know, it's a funny thing, but practically all the fellows in Reynolds are respected in high society all over town. I reckon it's because a lot of the boys come from families who are 'higher ups' in the company, and according to most people here in Winston, a fellow who works in the tobacco factory is as good as any white-collar man, and some of us makes better wages. Seems like it's kind of different with the girls. The 'higher ups' will let their boys go into the factory, but not their daughters. So I guess a girl who goes into the plant is just a 'factory girl.'" The sons of the "higher ups," of course, were preparing for management careers, occupations that were closed to their daughters.[35]

White male tobacco workers did occupy a position atop the ranks of blue-collar workers in Winston-Salem, but their status had less to do with the opinions of the higher ups than with wages, working conditions, and job security. White men enjoyed many more employment opportunities than their black or female counterparts. Few jobs in Winston-Salem provided higher wages, steadier income, or better working conditions than a skilled job in the tobacco industry. These benefits translated into markers of respectability: the ability of wives to leave the workforce, the opportunity to own a home, and the chance to acquire cars and other consumer goods.

Not only were the jobs held by blacks less secure and less lucrative, they also required considerable physical exertion—bending, pushing, lifting, walking, standing —all day long, day after day, year after year. Lifting heavy hogsheads, carrying boxes of tobacco, and stemming tobacco leaves exhausted even the younger workers. Where machines performed some of the production tasks, feeding or tending them demanded repetitive movements and constant attention. "At night we would come home and with the hustle and bustle of the day we would shake at night from being overworked," Willie Grier remembered. "Conditions was terrible," exclaimed

Ruby Jones. "Things was so bad, when you weren't in that plant, you relived them in the bed. You'd go through that motion at night."[36]

The foul and unhealthy environment of the departments where blacks worked exacerbated the physical demands of their jobs. In the prefabrication departments, the high humidity levels required to keep the tobacco from drying out and becoming brittle, combined with the heat from the machinery and various conditioning processes, made many rooms oppressive, even in winter. Before the introduction of air conditioning after World War II, the summers were almost unbearable. The women wore scarves around their necks and the men always had a handkerchief handy, but both were quickly saturated with perspiration. "It would be so hot in there sometimes," recalled Viola Brown. "Maybe they would let you raise the windows, then if they took a notion they say, 'Don't raise those windows, you're drying out the tobacco,' and me in there with perspiration rolling from head to foot. In the latter years, they would put some kind of little old fans up on the posts and maybe you would get a little breeze every now and then."[37]

Dust particles hung in the humid air, settling on workers' clothes and penetrating their bodies with every breath they took. "When you started to work you'd be just as nice and clean and in a half hour you could write your name on yourself," Viola Brown remembered. To keep the dust out of their hair, most of the women wore bandanas. A badge of slavery days, the wet and dirty headpieces reminded workers that they were only one step away from the cotton fields. "Most of the people walked home," Brown recalled. "They were ashamed to get on the bus."[38]

The casing and drying departments in the cigarette division, staffed mostly by black men, were among the worst places to work. After they applied conditioners, men forked the tobacco off the floor into the priming bins, where it had to sit for a few days to dry. To achieve the maximum effect from the conditioners, they had to pack the tobacco tightly. In the days before compression machines, the men used their feet, stomping down layers of tobacco until the room was filled almost to the ceiling. Lonnie Nesmith described the experience: "It was so hot, sometimes you couldn't catch your breath. When I'd come down from there and walk to the restroom, you could trail me from the water coming out of my shoes." A floor man with a mop often followed the men to the restroom so others wouldn't slip on the perspiration. "The only thing I would work in was my pants and shoes," Nesmith continued, "no socks, underwear or shirt. There wasn't a need to put them on, they were going to get wet anyway. I had to lay down many a night after I come out of that place. All that stuff was in my nostrils, and I was so sick I'd just gag. I couldn't even take a drink of water."[39]

In addition to the tired muscles and layers of sweat and dust workers carried home each day, conditions in the industry also gave rise to long-term health problems. "I can't hear good today on account of the noise in Reynolds," remembered one worker. "When I'd hit the street, it would be a roaring in my ear."[40]

Tuberculosis, in particular, was a scourge of the tobacco factories; in the 1940s, blacks in North Carolina succumbed to this silent killer at four times the rate of whites. An infectious bacterial disease that is primarily transmitted from person to person by coughing or spitting, tuberculosis spread readily in the hot, humid, and stale air of the prefabrication departments. The concomitants of poverty—poor nutrition, inadequate housing, and unsanitary living conditions—contributed to the prevalence of the disease. Dying by degrees, workers sometimes saw tobacco dust itself as the cause of their illness (it did abet a variety of other respiratory illnesses), and they resorted to remedies that made matters worse. One stemmer told Charles Johnson that many people died "with T.B. from sniffing that old tobacco dust in they nose all the time." "I dip snuff to keep from catching the T.B.'s," explained another worker. "You see we can spit all the time if we want to. So I keep snuff in my mouth all the time so I can spit all that old dust out of my mouth. Lots of people go out of here with T.B.'s."[41]

Many women stemmers believed that they required hysterectomies and suffered from miscarriages and other medical problems because of the physical exertion and the constant vibration of metal machinery. They experienced the stemming machines that came into use in the 1930s as a visceral threat. One stemmer wrote, "When you is working on the belt you have to press your stomach right up against the board all the time, that's why so many women have to be cut open all the time." Ruby Jones concurred: "There's a lot of women who had operations; who could never have children because of those steel things." Another woman declared, "I felt that all that standing while I stemmed tobacco was the reason I lost my two children."[42]

No aspect of the work was more galling than the tyrannical supervision in the prefabrication departments. Freedmen and women had successfully resisted planters' efforts to reintroduce work gangs after the Civil War, and black workers saw the regimentation of the labor process under the firm control of the foreman as a throwback to slavery days. They experienced the highly personalistic rule of the foreman as an assault on their manhood and womanhood as well as on their human dignity.

It went without saying that positions of authority belonged exclusively to white men. When asked if the company had ever hired blacks as foremen, personnel director Ed Bumgardner emphatically answered, "Never!" Odell Clayton remembered that blacks did everything in the factories but "boss." They could have said the same about women. Such practices prevailed throughout the industrial South, although it was possible to find an occasional white woman supervisor in the textile plants and black men supervising other black workers in the mines and sawmills.[43]

Despite the company's efforts to consolidate personnel decisions, the foreman remained the key figure in the workplace hierarchy at Reynolds, as in most of industrial America. "The superintendent would have charge of the whole plant," Robert Black remembered, "but each department would have a head foreman and straw foremen [also called line foremen or subforemen]. Now this foreman's job was to keep his crew under control and some of them were no better than prison guards. Back then the only requirement to get a job as a foreman was to be tough." Ruby Jones said her foreman had a simple motto: "We got three damn gets: Get in here, get to work, or get the hell out." Workers interviewed by Charles Johnson in the 1930s made particular mention of the "rigorous and abusive discipline" at Reynolds. There were some foremen who managed with a lighter hand, but workers' testimony indicates that most foremen, particularly those who supervised black women, exercised a harsh authority.[44]

Most complaints came from the prefabrication departments. Intrusive, personalized discipline was typical in the labor-intensive production processes where blacks were concentrated, in contrast to the cigarette departments where white workers were disciplined by the speed of the machines as much as by their foremen. Supervisors rarely used physical abuse to drive workers to maximum production, but they could raise a threatening voice at any time. If a worker did not respond by picking up her pace, she might be shown the door—or, as the saying went, "the hole the carpenter left." One worker told Charles Johnson: "That boss man makes them women cry; sometimes he cusses them out like a dog. I can't do a thing but grit my teeth. I wouldn't let my wife work there for I would kill him. When the nurse is around he is just as nice and wouldn't say a word out of the way to nobody, but as soon as she leaves he starts out again. They call Number 60 Reynolds's Hell Hole."[45]

"Oh, it was rough," recalled Geneva McClendon, "it was rough! . . . We'd get some foremen in there that I bet couldn't even read and write good. And the way they'd talk to you. In fact, I had a foreman tell me once if I couldn't keep up with my work to go on and play with my damn baby. I think at the time my baby was about, oh, maybe a year old. Boy, that burned me up, but you couldn't say nothing. If you'd talk back to them they'd fire you."[46]

The foremen "were real prejudiced," Theodosia Simpson remembered. "One girl who worked on the line was real beautiful and she was always smiling and laughing and talking with them. She got by pretty easy. But if you didn't have much to say to them or if you tried to be halfway intelligent, they didn't like it. A lot of times I didn't get to read the newspaper in the morning, and I'd bring it to read at lunchtime. They'd say, 'Whacha doin' with that newspaper, you came here to work.'"[47]

"My wife wasn't feeling good one day," a worker confided to Charles Johnson, "and she went to the door to get some air. The foreman, he saw her and cussed and say, 'Get out the do' nigger; what you standing in that do' for.' I come near quitting that day. My wife, it affected her so she was sick for a week." Evelyn Hairston experienced an equally crushing reminder of her second-class citizenship. Hairston took the Duke Power bus to work. "Come a thunderstorm up in the summertime and Mr. Lackey, my supervisor, and I got off on 5th Street and went in the door on the white side and he made me go back out there in all that rain and come in that black door around there. I couldn't hardly forgive him for that. I wasn't going to hurt nothing, but they were just going to make you a slave. That's all it was. You couldn't go in that door." Ruby Jones concluded: "You were just Jim Crowed all around. . . . The foremen didn't respect you unless you done their dirty work [spied on other workers] or went with them."[48]

Going with the foreman, of course, meant succumbing to his sexual advances, and the sexual exploitation of black women troubled men as well as women. Robert Black described the demeaning atmosphere of intimidation and favoritism that prevailed: "If there was a good-looking woman, even the black women, in that plant, and even if her husband worked in that same department, and that foreman wanted to pat on her or wanted to play with her or take her out to the office, [he would]. Those foremen would take one of these good-looking Negro women out to his desk and maybe hold her there for an hour, and all of these hundreds of people just looking. At the end of the day when you went to weigh your product, after he weighed most of the other people's product, these women that he had been toying with would come up one by one. He would reach over on the pile that had already been weighed and throw fifteen or twenty pounds onto their product. That was his way of compensating them. And better not nobody say anything about it. I've seen them just walk up and pat women on their fannies and they'd better not say anything. If her husband was working right next to her, that husband better not say anything." As Black made clear, the foreman's roving hands were an assertion of white men's dominion over black men as well as black women. Race thus fused with sexuality and gender to condition both men's and women's experiences.[49]

Under such circumstances, women's quest for privacy was also a quest for workers' rights. Women's restrooms in particular became sites of heated, symbolic conflict, as workers sought a place to attend to bodily needs and to enjoy a moment of respite from the foreman's gaze. For the company, every minute in the restroom represented lost production, whether the worker was on hourly or piece rates. "When you'd go to the rest room, you was timed," Ruby Jones remembered. "And if you didn't come out at that time, you went to the desk." Many foremen would "come in the dressing room, in the toilet where the women were . . . [and] say, 'You've been in here long enough. If you ain't done, you won't get done.' Now that's no respect."[50]

Although foremen targeted white women for sexual favors as well, they would not have dared to do so with such flagrancy, with the women's husbands helplessly looking on, nor would they have violated white women's privacy by entering dressing rooms and opening toilet stalls. Foremen were generally unaware of or unsympathetic toward the particular needs that pregnancy or menstruation could create for women, black or white. But they did display a modicum of restraint in dealing with women of their own race. Their refusal to extend common courtesies to black women carried unmistakable meanings. As Ruby Jones put it, the foremen "didn't regard you as much as an animal."[51]

Race and gender influenced how the foremen disciplined white women workers as well. While there was a certain respect for white women because of their race, the foremen also considered them subordinates who should submit to male authority. White women complained to Charles Johnson about the "rigid discipline" and the fact that the company paid men more than women for doing the same jobs. Sexual harassment seems to have been fairly widespread. Although there was less of the overt groping that went on in the stemmeries in other departments, sexual dynamics in the factory could easily lead to hard-to-refuse requests for dates after work or progress to demands for sexual favors as the price for keeping one's job.[52]

Supervision was different, though not necessarily better, for black men. They were spared the indignity of sexual harassment, but their gender did not protect them from harsh discipline. Willie Grier recalled, "We had a foreman, he was a rascal, his name was Newton. He came around bossing the line and said to me one day, 'If you don't get that tobacco out of that box by the time I get back, you get your clothes and your hat and get out of here.' We had to work like dogs to get that tobacco out." Robert Black concurred: "If you went to the bathroom, say, more than once or maybe twice on the morning shift before lunchtime, he would probably check with you and want to know what's wrong. He'd tell you, 'Okay, you've done been down to that place there enough times now. I want to see you go over there and get some work done.' That would let you know that if you went back in there again, he was going to see you and there was going to be a long hereafter."[53]

The harsh authority exercised by white foremen over black workers pervaded the factory like the sickening, sweet smell of the tobacco leaf. But it was never clear to workers whether these practices expressed company policy or simply the prejudices of their supervisors. "When I went into the company," Lonnie Nesmith observed, "it was rough. I don't know whether the people over there in the big office knowed what was going on. Some people said they didn't know, and some people said they knowed and didn't care. But I do know that the people didn't get no action, more or less. Many people got fired and never got back, just because Mr. So-and-So said, and that was it. Was this the policy of top management?" One of Charles Johnson's respondents concurred: "When the big folks come 'round them foremen quit cussin' and bawling' you out. They get so nice and considerate when they come round. But soon as they is gone, they starts cussing and pushin' you around again."[54]

The paper trail makes clear that John Whitaker and other top managers knew about the behavior of the foremen, even if they did not approve of it. From 1919 on, they issued memoranda advising supervisors to use modern personnel methods for motivating employees; if management had not perceived the problems in employee morale, there would have been little need for such admonishments. And company officials, not supervisory personnel, set the production quotas that each department had to meet. The company kept meticulous production records, and managers and supervisors drove their workers in part because they were themselves under intense pressure to meet their quotas while keeping costs low.

Black workers consistently evoked images of slavery in their descriptions of the workplace. Janie Black described the stemmeries as a "slave place." "You couldn't be a foreman in Reynolds if you was sympathetic to human beings," her brother Robert recalled. "You had to be a slave driver, get the full, maximum amount of work out of each employee, sick or well, day after day." A worker interviewed by Charles Johnson remembered his days in the factory before World War I. "When we worked for R. J. Reynolds, I was in bondage. You had to work like a slave over there." After being laid off, he got a job at Brown & Williamson, a smaller and, by many accounts, less hard-driving tobacco company. "There was freedom over there," he recalled. "There was nobody to watch you and you could go out to get water or to the toilet without somebody bawling you out and naggin at you all the time."[55]

The division of labor and the presumptions of white supremacy protected whites from the harder, dirtier work assigned to blacks. But whites, too, complained bitterly about working conditions and arbitrary supervision. The intricate making and packing machinery guaranteed that the cigarette departments would be cleaner than the stemmeries, but the heat, humidity, noise, and odor made conditions in those departments similar to those in other parts of the factory. "I reckon I was pretty glad to get a chance to go into the cigarette department," one worker told interviewers in the 1930s. "In the first place wages are higher, and it's a lot cleaner. The only objection is the noise, and you soon get used to that, too. The cigarette and packing machines run pretty smooth, but they still make more noise than two skeletons truckin' on a tin roof." "Oh, it was awful hot in the summer time, until they put in some kind of an air conditioning," Blanche Fishel recalled. "[But] it never was satisfactory. It blowed too much air at one place and not enough at another."[56]

Smell marked tobacco workers almost as clearly as lint identified cotton mill hands. Even white workers in the cigarette departments carried the factory home with them every day. Fishel did not pay much attention to the odor at work: "We was in it, you know, so much. But my clothes smelt like tobacco when I'd go home. I had two closets. I dared not put any of my clothes in the closet with my good clothes that I dressed to go out. I had them separate. You couldn't hardly wash that odor out of them. And of course, like a coat, you know, you wore in the winter time, or like sweaters and things like that. Now, I'd keep me a sweater. I'd fold it and put it up in my drawer where I kept my pocketbook, and I kept me a sweater over there all the time. And I didn't carry it home. Because things like that pick that odor up."[57]

Job assignments, wages, benefits, and working conditions almost always favored white workers over black. But in no arena did the company's policies advantage whites more than in promotion to the ranks of skilled workers and supervisors. Men garnered most of these advancements, but in the cigarette departments women could win prized positions as chief inspectors and record keepers. James McKensie's career reflects the opportunity structure available to ambitious white men, who were able to ascend the management ladder even without formal education. Born in nearby Germantown of lower-middle-class parents, McKensie moved to Winston-Salem in 1930 hoping to get a job at Reynolds. Although he had family in the plant, it took him five years to secure a position. Finally, in August 1935, he received a call from the employment office and went to work hanging tobacco in Number 1 Leaf House. Working alongside some recent college graduates preparing for management careers, McKensie realized that he would have to "prove himself, to do more than [he] was asked to do" in order to advance in the company. After six months he moved to the smoking tobacco division sacking tobacco. "I worked there for a year and a half," he remembered, "until an opening came up in the Turkish Department. All this time I was keeping in touch with personnel, [telling them,] 'I don't want to do this the rest of my life, and if something better comes up, give me an opportunity.'" He worked as a weigh master in Turkish tobacco and in 1940 was promoted to supervisor. "Several years later I was made a department supervisor and when the factory manager retired I was elevated to factory manager. That's the way Reynolds would do back at that time; within the department they would elevate people."[58]

Robert Black had all the skills and ambition he needed to work his way up the supervisory ladder as well, all, that is, except the right color of skin. A machine operator in Number 64, he remembered the many times he was passed over: "When they got ready to promote a foreman, I and Benny Blackshear and one or two other people knew more about that operation than any of the whites, even the foreman that was over me. When they got ready to add on another foreman they wouldn't come to me and say, 'Robert, we need a top supervisor in here or an assistant supervisor. We know you know this business and so the company has asked that you fill that position.' No, they bring a little young white guy in there and bring him over to me. 'Robert, this is John Smith and he's going to be working in here for a little while and we'd like for you to teach him the ropes.' And they'd bring him over there and I'd teach him all the ins and outs of the operation of that department. Six or eight weeks later, he's got on a collar and tie and they bring him back to me. 'Robert, this is Mr. So-and-So and from this day on he will be the assistant supervisor.' That was the policy of the company from way back."[59]

Resistance

Within these constrained surroundings, Reynolds workers found quotidian ways to resist the pressures of factory production and the petty tyrannies of the foremen and to pursue their desire for meaning and dignity. They waged this contest over simple, yet fundamental matters: how hard they would have to work, how much they would be paid for their efforts, whether they would be treated with a modicum of respect.

Chronic absenteeism and quitting expressed discontent as clearly as any manifesto. Workers often stayed home, returned to the countryside, or spent a day resting when they had something more pressing to do or had earned enough money to meet their weekly or monthly expenses. Blue Monday was a favorite holiday. Some workers stayed out to recover from weekend parties; others extended a trip back to the home place for an extra day. A bad day fishing beat even a good day at work. A child's illness might keep a mother at home. Excuses ranged from the truth to the truly inventive; funerals of distant relatives were a favorite. Quitting was a more serious expression of discontent, and every year hundreds of workers voted with their feet. Yearly turnover rates of 100 percent were common until the mid-1920s and only dropped significantly with the onset of the Depression.[60]

Once on the job, workers had little control over the number of hours they worked, but their desires, as well as the machine's speed and the foreman's scrutiny, determined the intensity of labor. Management wanted maximum effort from start to finish; workers needed time to rest and relieve the monotony of the job. Cooperative arrangements helped people reduce the work load when they were sick or tired or just unable to keep up. When one woman on a machine was ill, the others might take up the slack. If women on a stemming machine were falling behind, the man who supplied the tobacco might bring them loosely packed baskets. "Some of them women would be out there working and they would be wet from their collar on down," Leon Edwards remembered. "They had so many punches they had to get [for each box]. If they didn't get those punches, the little foreman he would get down on them. And sometimes they would get behind, then we could try to lighten up on the boxes. If the boss man wasn't watching too much then we could try to lighten up on the boxes."[61]

In these and other ways, workers extended an ethic of mutuality, forged in poverty, into the workplace and sabotaged management attempts to speed up production by encouraging them to compete against one another. Robert Black remembered one such instance. "They'd start pushing on us to turn out more tobacco. The foreman would come out and check my cards and if I was two or three hundred pounds ahead of those old machines he would say, 'Robert, you're having a good day. Go ahead, we want to have a test on these new machines against the old ones.'" Black knew the foreman would use his output to set higher production quotas for the whole department, so he had to think defensively. "These machines were more delicate, and all I had to do was feed them a little faster and overload it and the belts would break. When it split you had to run the tobacco in reverse to get it out, clean the whole machine out and then the mechanics would have to come and take all the broken links out of the belt. The machine would be down for two or three hours and I would end up running less tobacco than the old machines. We had to use all kind of techniques to protect ourselves and the other workers."[62]

Management had the upper hand when it was time to allocate the rewards of workers' labor, and as a result, black workers in the interwar years labored for near-subsistence wages. But at that level every penny counted, and workers and supervisors fought constantly over how much would appear in each week's pay envelope.

Hourly workers had two ways to increase their pay: they could work more hours or they could convince the foreman to give them a raise. The wages of piece-rate workers, on the other hand, could vary considerably from week to week. Any number of variables might determine their output: how fast they worked, the demand for their product, and/or the supply and quality of the materials they were working on.

A common complaint among hand stemmers centered on the company's refusal to let workers check the scales or question the foreman's judgment when he weighed their stems. It was bad enough that they were paid so little; it was infuriating to be cheated even out of that. At one point the company changed its policy and began weighing the leaves instead of the stems. This gave workers a chance to devise a new tactic for beating the system. Willie Grier described how it worked. "They took the tobacco that comes off the stems and put that on scales to be weighed. I can tell you something that not only I did, but a lot of other people did in order to make a living. Go and get a wet rag and wipe it on your head so everything was wet and you could pack it down. They were cheating us. We only had one way to make another penny." Unfortunately for the workers, the policy was short-lived. "They went back to the stems and they didn't weigh much."[63]

Tobacco products were portable consumer goods, and workers were sorely tempted to take them home for personal use or resale. "People would steal cigarettes and chewing tobacco," Robert Black remembered. "They would go by a bin of defective products with a lunch bucket and just load it up. This was done at quitting time. You had to do it and be on your way out. But when you got caught, there was no question that you were going to jail, because you were stealing from Mr. Reynolds." The more entrepreneurial workers, Black recalled, might "carry a paper bag full of chewing tobacco to the farmers market and trade it for a ham or vegetables. The stealing was done mostly among the husbands and fathers, because there was the greatest pressure for survival. I know of many people who followed this stealing thing over a period of years who were able to buy a little house and maybe help his family to live a little better. Once he got started doing it he couldn't afford to quit, because he had his deals adjusted to a point where he wouldn't have been able to pay his debts." The company was well aware of the practice, Blanche Fishel remembered, and kept an eye on suspected pilferers. "The ones that they knew took them out, they watched them, and if they caught them, they'd fire them."[64]

Coping with the power and prerogatives of individual foremen required patience and ingenuity, and both black men and women drew on a wide range of gender-based strategies. The more daring responded to the foreman's verbal aggression by giving as good as they got, which could cost them their jobs, earn them reputations as troublemakers, or gain them a bit of grudging respect. Some simply turned the other cheek, kept up with their work, and waited patiently for the shift to end. Others relied on the power of prayer. "People get mad and want to curse," Louise Smith explained, "[but] you can't fight your battle like that. Let God touch their hearts. He said, 'Be still and know that I am God.' So you have to fight your battle quietly. If you see somebody disturbed, you can pray to God to bless and change their mind and give them more love." More than one woman reported that she "played the fool"; the foreman thought she was crazy and unpredictable and left her alone. A union official remembered another tactic: "In one of the leaf houses the foreman had a bad heart condition and one of the women there knew about it. She would provoke him into a situation where he might be in danger of getting a heart attack. She used that as a weapon against him."[65]

Some individuals responded to the conditions of the factory in ways other workers might have considered less than exemplary. Young women, black and white, were known to trade on their attractiveness to get time away from their work, higher wages, or a better job. A small number of men and women workers participated in an intricate system of industrial espionage (as "picks," "pets," and spies), tattling on their fellow workers in an effort to curry favor with the boss. Workers received small favors in exchange for serving as the supervisor's eyes and ears, including more money or a lighter job; a supervisor might demand information as a payback for obligations incurred when a family member got a job or a worker had a run-in with the police.

Stereotyped by whites as lazy and untrustworthy, some black men performed their assigned role, while others asserted their manliness by working hard and providing for their families. There were psychic wages to be gained from prideful boasts of strength that turned white scorn for manual labor upside down. "Yes, they [whites] work alongside us," one man told Charles Johnson, "but they do the light work and we do the heavy work. They couldn't do the kind of work that we do. We go carrying around iron racks weighting from 90 pounds up. That would kill the whites. They tell me that the white man does the work in St. Louis where they work all whites, but these kind of whites couldn't stand this work, no sir!"[66]

Talking back to a foreman might earn a truce, but it was more likely to lead to dismissal. Physically striking a foreman was a sure route to jail. The penalties for physical retaliation were not as severe for white men, however. One worker recounted hitting the foreman in the department where his girlfriend worked after her boss called him a liar. "I lost my job all right," he said, "but it was worth it. I wasn't aiming for my girl to think that I was afraid of any foreman, job or no job."[67]

No aspect of black workers' behavior more powerfully expressed their solidarity and dignity than the group singing that suffused the labor-intensive departments. The mingling of song and work had a long tradition in the fields, forests, and factories of the South, both during and after slavery. Africans brought as slaves to the New World carried with them an understanding of the functions of song that differed radically from that of Anglo-European tradition. To them song could not be abstracted from life, and work songs served not only as vehicles for controlling the tempo and intensity of labor, but as a means of relating history, placating the deities, and voicing social critique.[68]

In the early plug chewing tobacco plants, distinctive songs accompanied each step in the production process. The stemmers, working at their own pace, sang rhythmically light melodies. Regularly paced cadences accompanied the molding of leaves into plugs, and slow chants paced the prizers who turned the massive presses that mashed the plugs into wood molds. All were rendered in a call-and-response pattern in which a single voice cried out a line and the group responded with a phrase or action. As tobacco manufacturing became increasingly mechanized the roar of machines silenced the voices of the workers, but in the hand stemmeries the tradition persisted virtually unchanged well into the twentieth century.[69]

At Reynolds, piece-rate workers in the stemming room used singing to set a steady pace, ensuring that they made their quotas or a few cents more each day. White visitors to the factories liked to think that the soulful sounds were evidence of the happiness and contentment of black workers. But the spirituals and gospel tunes, sometimes with words added to make them relevant to the work at hand, carried more complicated messages—about the pain of hard labor, the cruelty of bosses, and the longing for a better world. Most of all, perhaps, singing was a balm for the spirit. Velma Hopkins, who also organized singing groups at Shiloh Baptist Church, put it this way: "It made you forget how hard you were being worked and the treatment you were going through. Singing is something that is good for the soul, and we used to do lots of it. We had to."[70]

At Reynolds, singing could be a contested matter. One worker remembered that "up at Number 43, they didn't want you to talk but you could sing." Another commented that "you couldn't sing anything like the blues, you had to sing Christian songs." Some younger workers might have preferred to adapt the hot jazz music they heard in the juke joints on Saturday night to the religious songs they sang in church on Sunday; others loved the ragtime-influenced Piedmont blues or the fusion of blues and gospel represented by "race" record songsters. Still others were devoutly religious and considered the blues the devil's music. "A lot of older ladies up there were Christians and they would sing and get happy and have to be carried off the floor."[71]

There was something defiant about the singing. The hymns that rang out on the factory floor were a powerful assertion of the vitality of black culture and a reminder of the shared religious beliefs of black and white southerners. By singing, blacks claimed for themselves a space owned and defined by others. "I've had the foreman to ask me in 256—they didn't want us to talk. But we'd go to singing and he'd say, 'Velma, how can you sing? They're working the hell out of you.' And I said, 'I'm singing the hell out of you.'"[72]

CHAPTER FIVE

Social Learning

Visitors to Winston-Salem in the interwar years described it as a complacent town. Outsiders attributed this seeming quiescence to a combination of the iron-fisted control exercised by local authorities, the fierce antiunionism of tobacco and textile companies, and the divisions between black and white workers. But the absence of dramatic conflict did not mean that everyone accepted the industrialists' monopoly on power and privilege. There were apostates among both races, and simmering discontent, especially in the African American community, had fed post–World War I attempts at unionization. The Depression and New Deal changes in labor law, combined with the infrapolitics of the workplace and community, stimulated a new wave of organizational attempts and a cumulative process of social learning. Out of that dynamic came many of the leaders who would take the CIO to victory in the 1940s.

Southern Labor Stirs

The American labor movement found itself "becalmed and beleaguered" during the 1920s. By the end of the post–World War I economic downturn, union membership had shrunk by a third; the deportations and government repression that accompanied the red scare had blotted out radical activists and unions, and AFL leaders had decided to make peace with employers rather than risk further losses.

Antiunion campaigns, corporate welfare schemes, and bureaucratized management practices solidified employers' power in the workplace. Southern workers, adrift in a labor market swelling from the collapse of cotton farming brought on by the spread of the boll weevil, saw their income decline as their workload increased.[1]

Cautious at best, the TWIU reacted to these circumstances by becoming even more tepid. E. Lewis Evans, who had been secretary-treasurer of the union since its founding and president since 1925, remained firmly in control. Evans believed in the power of the union label and in his own right to rule. During his almost dictatorial reign the union held no conventions, and the TWIU constitution made it almost impossible for locals to call strikes. Workers across the country stayed away in droves.[2]

At the end of the decade, however, southern labor unexpectedly and dramatically stirred. Encouraged by a flush labor market, textile owners tightened the screws on workers, and white millhands from Tennessee through the Carolinas walked out in record numbers. The most dramatic conflict occurred in Gastonia, North Carolina, but there were dozens of rebellions across the Piedmont. The strike wave of 1929 was followed in 1934 by a general textile strike in which tens of thousands of southern workers walked off their jobs. Democratic officeholders used the power of the state to suppress both uprisings, but in doing so, they threw into question the precarious bargain between elites and the white workers who were thought to be dependable junior partners of the ruling race.

Technological rationalization spread through the tobacco industry as well, and in 1927 Reynolds imposed wage cuts, a speed-up, and a stretch-out in its manufacturing plants. In response, the TWIU sent in an organizer to tap discontent among black employees, while a local leader of the 1919 unionization drive built a volunteer organizing committee among whites. Apparently hundreds of black and white workers joined forces, creating consternation among Reynolds officials. When workers returned from the Christmas holidays, the company fired several hundred suspected union members and sympathizers. "We intend to break up that union," a foreman reportedly told one of those who lost his job. Robert Black, although not involved, remembered how easily that was accomplished. "The company planted stooges in the union meetings. And they would take the name and department you worked in, and you would be fired."[3]

The TWIU put the fired workers on its payroll, paying them each $5 a week plus a twenty-five-cent commission for every new member they signed up. Union officials claimed these worker-organizers brought in up to 7,000 of the 12,000 workers at the Reynolds plant. Despite such support, the union's repeated attempts to gain recognition and negotiate a contract went nowhere. In the climate of the late

1920s, Reynolds officials saw no reason to compromise. Instead, they continued to lay off union members. On one day in 1928, Reynolds reportedly discharged 1,700 employees. "If they thought you belonged to the union," remembered one worker, "then you were gone." Workers complained of wholesale evictions: landlords, they said, were pressured by the company to put unemployed workers out on the street when they fell behind on their rent.[4]

Unable to counter Reynolds's power within the factory, the TWIU mounted a national consumer boycott of Camels and Prince Albert smoking tobacco. Vivid descriptions of the effects of low wages and dreadful working conditions appeared in union newspapers, leaflets, and press releases. Union president E. Lewis Evans charged that Reynolds was "among the most autocratic corporations in existence." Using a metaphor that implicitly positioned tobacco workers as white working men and contrasted the freedom that was their birthright with the bondage of blacks, he told a national audience that Winston-Salem workers were "just as much slaves today as were the black slaves before the Civil War."[5]

The TWIU's final gambit consisted of a warning to Reynolds that the union represented the lesser of two evils. The real threat, according to Evans, came from the "Russian Communists." "You in your busy days perhaps do not get time to note their movements," he warned a Reynolds official. "It is their delight to step into a chaotic situation and make it worse." Foreshadowing the tactics that the AFL would employ with a vengeance in the 1940s, Evans went on to claim that Communists had opened an office in Winston-Salem and were distributing literature among the factory employees. He suggested that Reynolds and the TWIU put aside their past differences so that they could fight this "common enemy." The ploy fell on deaf ears. Moreover, Reynolds suffered no appreciable decline in its sales from the boycott and continued to stand firm in its refusal to negotiate with the union. Even as the company maintained a hard line with the union, it quietly improved its retirement and insurance plans, offering workers a minimum of security but making no concessions that compromised its unilateral power.[6]

The TWIU president's charges about the Communist presence in Winston-Salem contained a grain of truth. Sometime in late 1929, southern Party activists arrived in Winston-Salem as part of a regionwide organizing campaign. The Communist Party of the United States had formed in 1919 in the wake of the Bolshevik victory in Russia and the creation of the Soviet Union. Made up largely of immigrant workers, the Party's membership fluctuated wildly during its first decade, never exceeding more than a few thousand. Initially the Party hoped to create its own independent unions, but the red scare, coupled with the postwar economic recession, forced a change in tactics. Party members began to join the AFL, hoping to build a radical rank-and-file opposition within the established unions. That strategy ended in 1928 when the Communist International (Comintern), which coordinated the activities of parties outside of the USSR, determined that a "third period" (characterized first by economic crisis and then by revolutionary upheaval) had begun. To prepare workers for the coming battle, the Party decided to end its policy of cooperating with the AFL and instead to establish separate labor organizations under the umbrella of the Trade Union Unity League (TUUL). These dual unions concentrated on the most oppressed and least organized workers: those in textiles, tobacco, mining, and agriculture, many of whom were found south of the Mason-Dixon line.[7]

At the same time, the Comintern reformulated its position on the "Negro question." Prior to 1928, the Communists had maintained that the special problems of African Americans should be addressed by interracial, class-conscious organizations. Working-class blacks, however, increasingly channeled their discontent into nationalist groups such as Marcus Garvey's United Negro Improvement Association, which fostered feelings of solidarity between Africans and peoples of African descent and saw blacks in America not as a downtrodden national minority but as a global majority. Drawing on the earlier middle-class Pan African Congress movement, which placed American race relations in an international perspective, Garvey brought anticolonialism to a mass audience. The cross-fertilization between Communism and Pan Africanism after the Russian Revolution transformed both projects, confronting the left with the distinctive history of black laborers scattered around the globe and giving Pan Africanism a more universalistic and radical cast. Communist leaders, both black and white, began pressuring rank-and-file members to be more sensitive to the needs of blacks and aware of their own racism, while Soviet theorists considered the role of colonized peoples in the world revolution. By the late 1920s, Communist policy defined African Americans as an "oppressed nation" within the United States that had a right to "self-determination," including the creation of a separate republic in the southern black belt, that area of the South dominated by cotton growing and populated largely by African Americans. This vision, far-fetched as it was, had the effect of endowing the black struggle with dignity and importance and, in the process, of making the South a critical new site of Communist activity. Among southern Party activists, a deep and ongoing commitment to interracialism, integration, and black civil rights coexisted with an internationalist perspective that linked the fate of blacks at home with the exploitation of colonial peoples abroad.[8]

The Communist Party made its first significant appearance in the South during the strike wave of the late twenties. In 1929 the Party's National Textile Workers

Union (NTWU) helped to lead a prolonged walkout at the Loray Mill in Gastonia, North Carolina. The conflict attracted worldwide attention, particularly after the killings of the police chief and Ella May Wiggins, the union's balladeer. It also provoked the wrath of the local mill owners, who accused the organizers of fostering "race mixing" (notwithstanding the fact that the vast majority of millhands were white) and called in the National Guard to smash the strike. The Gastonia conflict invigorated the small Communist movement in North Carolina and the South. Soon organizers for the Trade Union Unity League had penetrated the region's mines, mills, and cotton fields. For a time, it looked as if the Party might offer industrial workers a real alternative to the conservative, craft-oriented AFL.[9]

From Winston-Salem, Robert Black followed the events in Gastonia. He was working at Brown & Williamson at the time, so he had not been involved in the abortive TWIU organizing campaign at Reynolds. He was, nevertheless, keenly interested in trade unionism. "I was encouraged by the struggle of the workers in Gastonia, North Carolina through the late '20s," Black recalled. "It was brutal, but it was educational. It caused me to realize that if you're ever going to beat the system, you've got to organize. You can't fight it alone. They'll either destroy you, or they'll form some other way of so browbeating and intimidating you that you will eventually give up the fight. But if you make up your mind to improve your condition, regardless as to the power and the support of the companies that you are fighting against, you can win if you properly organize and go out in the community. I knew what I had read in the press was not the real story of the struggle that was waged in Gastonia, where they brought in company stooges with guns, bombs, and beat up and intimidated and jailed most of the militant workers. Even though they weren't able to complete their union organization, they told a story to the working class. Once you attempt to improve your standards of living and working conditions, you must go through this period. The people in the Gastonia situation were workers just like us. And the companies had no right to go in with paid goons and beat up and destroy those peoples' opportunity of building an organization to defend their rights."[10]

The NTWU and the TUUL made racial equality and interracial cooperation cornerstones of their campaigns, even in the largely white textile industry, and they aggressively recruited African Americans into their organizations. The large concentration of black and white industrial workers in Winston-Salem made the city a natural target for Communist attention. Sometime in late 1929 or early 1930, representatives of the NTWU and TUUL, a number of whom had just emerged from the Gastonia strike, came to Winston-Salem to organize among workers at Hanes

Hosiery and Reynolds Tobacco. Going door to door in the mill villages and the black community, distributing leaflets at the factory gates during shift changes, and holding interracial meetings to protest the lynching of an elderly black woman in a nearby rural community, they drew the attention of the police, who raided the NTWU office and arrested one of the organizers, the former Loray Mill worker Dewey Martin, for writing a bad check. A local TWIU official reported that the judge who convicted him "stopped court for twenty minutes" to tell the "poor white and colored folks . . . that Martin and his kind were lower than dogs." In 1930 the Winston-Salem Board of Aldermen also passed an ordinance prohibiting the distribution of leaflets around the factories. Undeterred, another TUUL organizer, William G. Binkley, ran for Congress on the Communist Party ticket. Far from being the "outside agitators" that Communists were purported to be, both Martin and Binkley were native sons. Binkley had grown up in a log cabin on a farm in nearby Walnut Cove, gone to the University of North Carolina, and practiced law in Forsyth County. He would surface again in the Winston-Salem labor movement in the 1940s as an organizer for the fur and leather workers union and the husband of FTA Local 22's educational director.[11]

In the midst of this organizing drive, the Depression hit the country with full force, throwing millions of people out of work and undermining prospects for unionization. While the Republican president Herbert Hoover counseled patience and balanced budgets, the Communist Party created unemployed councils. Unemployment, leftists maintained, was not an aberration but an inevitable result of the booms and busts of a capitalist economy. Unemployed councils, which pressured local government agencies to provide direct relief to people who were out of work, functioned as loose coalitions of unemployed workers and political activists aimed at moderating capitalism's worst features and maintaining unity between those members of the working class who had jobs and those who did not. Although Party members played a key role in these organizations, membership was open to everyone.[12]

When Party activists launched an interracial unemployed council in Winston-Salem, Robert Black's mother, Eliza, was quick to join. "During the Hoover Depression," he remembered, "four or five people came to Winston-Salem and got a few blacks and whites together to form this unemployment league. They would go down to city hall or to the county commissioners and put pressure on them to appeal for government help. My mother," Black continued, "along with a few others were able to get some food and clothes, a ton of coal or a load of wood every now and then, and sometimes six or eight dollars to help pay the rent. Now it was nothing but just the roughest food, pinto beans and fatback meat, but it was something to keep you from starving."[13]

The council boasted modest success in convincing social service agencies to provide relief to black workers and in spreading its political message to the city's poorest residents. As part of a regionwide day of protest on March 6, 1930, a reported 1,500 to 2,000 people marched on City Hall. Local authorities broke up the demonstration and launched a campaign of red-baiting and intimidation. "The people who was running the county and city government," according to Black, "began to have these people picked up off the street—they were going from one house to another—and accused them of being Communists, just because they were trying to show people that their government was supposed to support them and clothe their nakedness." Like African Americans in Richmond, Charlotte, Birmingham, and other southern cities, where the unemployed movement enjoyed some success, Robert Black paid little attention to anti-Communist attacks. Whether or not they were initiated by "reds," the councils seemed to stand alone in their effort to help poor blacks in Winston-Salem.[14]

The Communist Party's Depression-era activities attracted a small but committed cohort of workers, black and white. Winston-Salem had a small functioning Party organization until the mid-1930s. These efforts helped to bring race issues to the nation's attention and to awaken a new generation of young, middle-class reformers to the region's ills. Southern writers associated with the Party, such as Grace Lumpkin, Myra Page, and Fielding Burke, contributed to a new genre of proletarian literature on the plight of the South's poor. In the early 1930s, the pilgrimage of young idealists to the South acquired the aura of daring and romance that would later send their counterparts to fight in the Spanish Civil War.[15]

Nothing did more to position the Party as a champion of blacks than its spirited defense of the Scottsboro Boys. In 1931 nine young black men were accused of raping two white women on a train outside Scottsboro, Alabama. In less than three weeks, eight of the defendants were found guilty and sentenced to death. With the support of the young men's parents, the International Labor Defense, a Party-influenced organization set up to provide legal support for American radicals, wrested the case from the NAACP and began a legal and political campaign to overturn the verdict. After two retrials, the International Labor Defense, in cooperation with other civil rights groups, arranged a plea bargain that saved the men's lives but sent most of them to prison. The national and international publicity generated by the case spurred efforts to reform the South's judicial system and enhanced the Communist movement's credibility in parts of the black community.[16]

New Deal Reforms

By the summer of 1932, the country had skidded to the bottom of the Depression. A quarter of the workforce was unemployed, breadlines extended for blocks in major cities, and bank closings had destroyed the savings of much of the middle class. Amid such calamities, Franklin Delano Roosevelt's presidential campaign promise of a "new deal" offered a ray of hope. The South responded enthusiastically to his candidacy, and southern working-class voters were among his strongest supporters. Sweeping to victory, FDR turned his attention first to the crises in banking and agriculture. When the New Dealers eventually addressed the problems besetting industry, the centerpiece of their effort was the National Industrial Recovery Act (NIRA), which aimed to promote recovery by setting "codes of fair competition." To employers, the NIRA's chief appeal lay in its relaxation of antitrust rules, which allowed competing firms to cooperate to control overproduction and the downward spiral of prices. Although Roosevelt still clung to the idea of industry self-regulation, the act represented the federal government's first peacetime attempt to regulate the hours and wages of adult workers, and it contained the seeds of a program of federal economic planning. Moreover, almost as an afterthought, Congress added Section 7(a) giving workers the right "to organize and bargain collectively through representatives of their own choosing."[17]

In the code-drafting process, each industry submitted a plan to National Recovery Administration (NRA) officials, who consulted with labor representatives and then held public hearings. Unorganized workers, who had the most to gain from higher labor standards, had virtually no voice in this process. Traveling through the South as the code hearings began, Lucy Randolph Mason, a Virginian who had just taken over as director of the National Consumers' League, became increasingly alarmed both by this lack of representation and by industry attempts to prescribe longer hours and lower wages for unskilled workers on the grounds that many of those workers were black. Writing to Department of Labor head Frances Perkins, Mason explained that without trade union protection, tobacco workers in Winston-Salem did not "feel safe in openly making demands." She urged Perkins to investigate the industry and planned to participate in the hearings herself.[18] She also issued a broadside refuting the arguments for racial discrimination point by point, coming down especially hard on the contention that equal wages would disturb "sociological conditions" in the South by enraging white workers and drawing blacks out of agriculture. Mason argued that discrimination poisoned race relations by perpetuating whites' fears of competition from low-paid black workers; she maintained that the large pool of cheap black labor in the countryside pulled all workers' wages down, decreasing spending power and contributing to the Depression. In the end, however, manufacturers succeeded in dominating the boards charged with enforcing the code provisions, and even without explicit provisions for racial discrimination, regional wage differentials—which often functioned mainly to camouflage lower wages for blacks—allowed southern manufacturers to maintain their grip on a separate market of low-cost labor.[19]

Unlike the highly competitive textile industry, which had pushed for the NRA, tobacco was already dominated by large firms that used advertising dollars and brand loyalty rather than low prices to compete for market shares. Stalling as long as they could, the tobacco companies refused to open hearings until the summer of 1934 and failed to get FDR's signature on a code of fair competition until a few months before the Supreme Court declared the NIRA unconstitutional on May 27, 1935. In the interim, however, Reynolds and the rest of the industry agreed to operate under the president's Reemployment Agreement, a baseline for NIRA standards. They also engaged in what workers called "code chiseling"—an evocative term for the many ways in which industries short-circuited the new wage and hour provisions.[20]

In 1933 Reynolds raised wages by 17 percent, the first wage increase it had instituted since the expiration of its post–World War I contract with the TWIU in 1921. It also limited hours to forty per week. The hour provisions had little effect since few people at Reynolds were working full-time. Workers welcomed the wage increase but found that they had no recourse when Reynolds moved to undermine their gains. Forced to raise wages in the hand stemmeries, the company installed stemming machines and transferred the faster hand stemmers to the machines. It also set quotas that workers had to meet in order to earn the minimum wage and laid off those who failed to make the quota. A stemmer summed up the net effect of these moves. "Sure, they have increased the wages of some of the stemmers; those that was making about $5.00 a week can now make about $9.00, but they done put the fastest stemmers on the machines and let the slower stemmers stem by hand. They sure are some smart people running this here Reynolds Tobacco Company."[21]

Another stemmer had an even more critical assessment of the NIRA. "They say they are working by the Code and they used to have a big eagle over there [an emblem signifying the company's compliance with the code] but he ain't never fly no more money to me. . . . I guess the eagle just give all the money to the white folks and none to the niggers, if they all like me. I ain't got none. This little ain't enough, but ain't no use talking, them white folks ain't caring nothing." Another Reynolds worker suggested that rather than give workers Blue Eagles to stick on their windows, "they better had been giving us some we could eat instead."[22]

Although the NIRA did discriminate against African Americans by establishing lower wages in all the job categories in which they predominated, the "white folks" who benefited were primarily the employers. Two hundred and fifty white Reynolds workers sent a letter to the NRA in the fall of 1933 complaining about the impact of the code. The petition suggested an alternative method for cutting unemployment while at the same time maintaining wages. "We do not know just how you feel about it but it looks to us that the real thing that should be done is to cut the speed of the machinery just half to what it is at present. . . . We are doing two times as much work for less pay than we were five years ago. So instead of cutting hours, why not cut the speed of the machinery down just half to what it is today and every one in the U.S. will be put back to work." Concerned that their letter might be dismissed as the work of radical agitators, the workers assured the NRA and the president of their loyalty. "You may think that we are Communists trying to stir up something but we are everyone of us born here in North Carolina and Virginia and we voted for beloved Franklin D. Roosevelt and believed in him and his policy."[23]

Despite its shortcomings and its brief lifespan, the NRA constituted an opening salvo in the assault on the dual wage structure that made discrimination against black workers the linchpin in the South's separate economy. It raised wages for common laborers and narrowed the gap between the South and the North. It encouraged public participation in government decision making, both by staging public hearings and by inspiring workers to engage in a vast letter-writing campaign. More generally, it raised workers expectations and signaled to them that the federal government could and would intervene on their behalf.[24]

Section 7(a), in particular, had a galvanizing effect. Encouraged by what appeared to be a guarantee of their right to organize, TWIU officials returned to Winston-Salem in 1933. They began recruiting Reynolds workers but scored their main victory by signing a national union label agreement with Brown & Williamson, a small British-owned producer of "economy brands," which hoped that the agreement would help it compete for consumers against the big four. Brown & Williamson signed a contract that called for a closed shop and a dues checkoff (which meant that workers had to join the union as a condition of employment and that the company would automatically deduct dues from their paychecks). To workers' dismay, the TWIU agreed to wages that were lower than those at Reynolds. When Charles S. Johnson conducted his study of tobacco workers in 1934, he interviewed numerous employees at Reynolds and Brown & Williamson about working conditions, the NIRA, and unions. At Brown & Williamson, the complaint of a black male stemmer was representative: "I say the company gets more out of the union than we does. The union can't do nothin' the company doesn't want it to do. . . . This is a company union. That's all it is." Just as it had in earlier years, the TWIU established segregated locals and denied black workers any control over their own affairs. Theodosia Simpson's mother told her about contract ratification meetings in which the white union leaders simply announced the terms of the contract to black workers without ever asking about their grievances and concerns. Members of the black local were known to advise their friends and neighbors who worked at Reynolds not to have anything to do with the TWIU.[25]

When the Supreme Court declared the NIRA unconstitutional in May 1935, the small beachhead established by the TWIU seemed unlikely to survive. But within a few weeks, Congress passed the National Labor Relations Act (known as the Wagner Act). Whereas Section 7(a) had lacked any real mechanism for enforcement, the Wagner Act put teeth in labor's right to organize independent unions and bargain collectively with employers. Among other things, it prohibited employers from supporting company unions, arbitrarily firing union activists, or employing industrial spies; established majority rule as a fundamental principle of representation; and created the National Labor Relations Board as a quasi-independent federal agency to oversee the administration of federal labor policy. Under the law, workers seeking representation could petition the board, which would determine the appropriate bargaining unit and then conduct an election.[26]

An Important Training Ground

The Wagner Act invigorated the whole labor movement, and even the TWIU benefited from tobacco workers' hunger for organization. Within a few years the union had negotiated contracts with Reynolds's major competitors. In Durham, North Carolina's other major tobacco manufacturing center, the TWIU achieved a permanent place in the city's factories. By the mid-1930s, white workers at Liggett & Myers and American Tobacco had negotiated contracts with their respective companies. Skilled black male workers at Liggett & Myers followed suit a few years later. Segregated locals at American's Reidsville plant also negotiated contracts in the mid-1930s.[27]

The TWIU's unprecedented success in convincing employers to sign union contracts was due less to its renewed vigor than to a new development on the labor scene: the emergence of the Congress of Industrial Organizations (CIO) in December 1935. Tobacco manufacturers, it seems, settled with the TWIU to avoid a confrontation with the more aggressive federation of industrial unions. The CIO began as a dissident committee of AFL unions headed by United Mine Workers president

John L. Lewis. Angered by the AFL's craft snobbery and its unwillingness to capital-
ize on the growing militancy of American workers, Lewis and his supporters bolted
from the group and vowed to organize workers in the mass production industries
without regard to craft, race, or nationality. In 1936 the industrial unions scored
stunning victories across the country and energized the southern labor movement.
With a strong foothold in the mining districts of the upper South, the CIO launched
an organizing drive in the Birmingham, Alabama, coalfields and formed a Textile
Workers Organizing Committee to take on the powerful and violently antiunion
textile industry. Rumors that the CIO was also contemplating a major organizing
drive among tobacco workers were enough to frighten some employers into settling with the tamer TWIU.[28]

The TWIU's success at Brown & Williamson and its growing membership in
Durham and Reidsville renewed the union's desire to organize Reynolds, and it returned to Winston-Salem in 1937. Once again, union organizers targeted white
workers in the cigarette factories, admitting blacks almost as an afterthought. This
continuing failure to mount a campaign focused on black workers—who, after all,
made up a large majority of Reynolds's employees—stemmed from a combination
of racial stereotyping and misunderstanding of black workers' potential. On the
one hand, TWIU leaders believed that blacks were too frightened and unreliable to
make good unionists: "The fear complex had been embedded into their souls," observed TWIU president Evans. "There are too many S. Carolina NIGS there to offer
any stable opportunity," explained another official, voicing the widely held belief—
among many blacks as well as whites—that migrants from South Carolina, unlike
earlier arrivals from North Carolina and Virginia, were country rubes. On the
other hand, the TWIU took black workers for granted. "Weaver and I have been
working together on the white workers mostly but have been putting in some time
with the Smoaks," a white organizer reported. "We feel that the Smoaks will almost
come in at our calling when we have something of a definite nature with the
whites." President Evans even demurred when a group of black citizens, responding to the new possibilities for interracial organizing opened by the CIO a few years
later, asked for the services of a black staffer to help organize Reynolds workers.
"We have tried that stunt at other times, with a total failure as a result," he wrote.
"The preachers and Doctors go into these movements with an eye to either acquir-
ing members in their parishes or medical clientele. And you know that the civic organizations have no love for the UNIONS."[29]

It was true that a climate of fear reigned in the Reynolds plants. Charles Johnson
summed up the situation this way: "So far as the organized labor movement in the
R. J. Reynolds Company plants was concerned, the impression seems to have been

one of utter futility. Workers who were earning just enough money to keep themselves above the starvation level in a place where there was practically no alternative work were careful not to jeopardize their jobs. This prevailing fear was everywhere in evidence. The subject of unions was taboo. The Reynolds Company had the labor situation 'well under control.'" As one worker explained, "They got so bad about those who joined the union that they would fire anybody for saying the word. Why one man got fired for talking about Western Union time. He said 'I got Western Union time.' They heard 'I got' and 'Union,' and just threw him out—put him out without telling him why." A group of women workers had a "pool association" that met regularly at the Negro Branch of the YWCA. One Sunday in March 1935, they invited Louis Austin, the crusading editor of Durham's black newspaper, the *Carolina Times*, to speak on how to "organize and raise wages and standard of living." When the city fathers learned of the meeting, the chairman of the Community Chest threatened to withhold funds from the YWCA and other agencies, and the meeting was canceled. Reynolds's imperviousness to unionization became as much an emblem of its corporate culture as the Camel on its cigarette pack.[30]

Resentment of the company's attempts to control workers on the job and in the community, however, was just as pervasive as fear. The TWIU's position, moreover, overlooked an important new development: the impact of the Depression and the rise of the interracial CIO on younger members of the black middle class, whose devotion to uplift and opposition to trade unionism was giving way to an embrace of unionization as a means of community advancement. That critical change of heart was manifested in the black citizens' call for a black TWIU organizer and in the economic militancy of Louis Austin and the black press. At the same time, the union did nothing to educate white workers about the need to build interracial alliances if they wanted to organize an industry in which a majority of workers were black.[31]

In 1938 union organizers finally began to make headway in the Reynolds plants. The catalyst was the company's response to the passage that year of the Fair Labor Standards Act (FLSA), the culmination of four decades of effort, dating back to the Progressive Era, to regulate wages and hours and prevent the most egregious abuses of labor. Conservative southern congressmen had led the resistance to the act, backed by the National Association of Manufacturers, which opposed all intervention in the "private" relationship between employers and workers. Southern lawmakers saw the FLSA, with justification, as an attack on the political economy of the South, which depended on a captive labor force of low-wage workers, and they fought bitterly, first to torpedo the bill altogether, then to keep labor standards as low as possible, and finally to maintain what they saw as the South's major "natural" advantage, its pool of cheap labor, by mandating regional wage differentials. Arrayed against them were northern textile manufacturers who were losing out to southern competitors, northern unionists whose strongholds were threatened by the migration of industry to the South, and an increasingly vocal and effective coalition of southern liberals and leftists who responded to the Depression by formulating a radical analysis of the region's ills. That analysis centered on the need for federal intervention and unionization to reform the South, both for the welfare of the region's people and to prevent its separate economy from depressing labor standards and impeding unionization everywhere. The FLSA's labor-liberal proponents prevailed, but only after lowering its standards, limiting its coverage, and barely staving off regional wage differentials. In the aftermath of that partial victory, moreover, they found themselves facing ongoing and intensifying efforts by conservatives to gut both the FLSA and the Wagner Act, the high points of early New Deal labor policy.[32]

The new law established a national minimum wage of forty cents an hour and a maximum workweek of forty hours for adult workers whose occupations were judged to be in the flow of interstate commerce. It exempted agricultural and domestic workers, who comprised the vast majority of the South's black labor force, as well as other categories of workers. But it struck at the heart of low-wage industries, the leading edge of the South's economy. In industries that employed large numbers of black workers, the FLSA extended a degree of federal protection to African American laborers they had never experienced before.[33]

Reynolds responded to the new law, as it had to the NRA, with further efficiency measures, including layoffs and increased workloads, and in the process spurred another burst of union activity. Workers claimed that while Reynolds paid skilled workers wages approximating those in union plants, employees rarely worked a full forty-hour week, and they were required to tend two machines rather than the one that union workers tended. Capitalizing on the unrest, the TWIU chartered Local 217, which, in a departure from the union's usual practice, included both blacks and whites. Reynolds retaliated with transfers, layoffs, preferential wage raises, and outright dismissals, in defiance of the Wagner Act's guarantees. Charles Johnson described the company's tactics: "It is the present policy of the company, according to many workers interviewed, not to fire workers out-right who are suspected of union affiliation, but to 'ease them out of their jobs' by systematic pressure of one sort or another. A case was cited where a worker was given tasks impossible to execute and continually reprimanded for failure on his job until, finally, grounds enough were manufactured to warrant his release on [the] basis of supposed inefficiency." The company used this strategy to drive out Local 217 president Ruel White, who got his walking papers in February 1940 after nine years of service as a machine operator. The NLRB later reinstated White, finding that he had been unfairly discharged for union activities. This was perhaps the first time a governmental agency had intervened in labor management relations at Reynolds.[34]

Despite such ongoing harassment, the union persisted. In January 1941 the TWIU asked Reynolds to recognize Local 217 as the bargaining agent for production and maintenance workers in the company's three cigarette plants. This unit included white making and packing machine operators as well as black workers. Citing provisions of the Wagner Act, the company said it would not bargain until the NLRB had certified the union. The TWIU then petitioned the NLRB for an election.

Faced with the possibility that the local might have majority support among black and white workers in the manufacturing division, Reynolds implemented a brilliant strategy for undermining this emerging interracial coalition and derailing the organizing effort. First, the company announced small wage increases. Then lower-level supervisors, along with a hastily formed "no union" movement, began covertly threatening union members. A local unionist described the situation to the national office: "Our efforts have been met with subtle opposition from the Supervisors, Foremen, Floorladies, and other groups of company dominated Employees. Floorladies are all handpicked for the purpose of talking to the employees about [the] union. . . . Foremen give floor ladies authority to roam all over the department, they in turn use this as a contact to speak to all the workers. . . . We have in this plant a horrible example of silent persecution, the workers are afraid to move in the direction of organization, afraid of the wrath that would be meted out to them by the loss of their livelihood."[35]

Apparently many of the supervisors' conversations with white workers focused on the interracial makeup of the bargaining unit and the membership of the local. Union opponents emphasized the prospect of black men associating with white women and rising to positions in which they would supervise white women's work. The TWIU, whose commitment to interracial organizing was shallow at best, responded by restricting Local 217's membership to white workers and chartering Local 224 for black workers. Although the prejudices of local white unionists may have played a part in this decision, it is more likely that it was a top-down effort to defuse antiunion propaganda. Many Local 217 officers, in fact, later joined the interracial CIO.[36]

When the NLRB opened hearings to determine an appropriate bargaining unit, Local 217 narrowed its definition of "production and maintenance" to "those engaged in the actual manufacture and packing of cigarettes." This excluded workers in the tobacco processing departments, 90 percent of whom were black. But even the new unit contained black workers in Plant Number 97, where Reynolds had for years maintained an all-black cigarette department. Responding to the company's race-baiting campaign by trying to define a racially exclusive bargaining unit, the TWIU found itself confronting company officials who now argued that there was no craft or community of interest specific to the designated workers. Reynolds thus worked both sides of the fence. In the factory, company officials pursued a whispering campaign that played on white workers' fears of allying themselves with blacks, while in NLRB hearings they took the TWIU's original position that all production and maintenance workers in the cigarette division, black and white, should be included in the same bargaining unit. The NLRB agreed with the company and dismissed the TWIU's petition for an election on the grounds that the unit was totally artificial. The union, derailed by the twists and turns of company strategy and its own racial bigotry, lost its chance to organize the tobacco industry's leading firm.[37]

For more than two decades, the TWIU had maintained a presence in Winston-Salem in an attempt to scale the walls of the "Ford of the South," the last of the large tobacco companies to be unionized. With the exception of a brief period during World War I, Reynolds had repelled every challenge. The TWIU's failure stemmed in part from the company's tenacious resistance. This locally owned and managed tobacco giant, which concentrated all its production facilities in a single, tightly controlled town, was a more determined opponent than American, Liggett & Myers, or Philip Morris, which all had a weaker ideological stake in remaining union free, more diffuse management, and decentralized production structures. But the TWIU's refusal to make black workers central to its campaign also played directly into the company's hands. The attitudes and policies of the AFL perhaps appealed to some whites but certainly alienated blacks, even though many put aside their objections and joined union organizing efforts. CIO organizers later found that to make headway, they had to confront the legacy of the TWIU's mistakes. "A lot of them remembered the old AFL trying to organize," Theodosia Simpson recalled. "A lot of them remembered the AFL down at Brown & Williamson, where they had segregated locals, and they didn't want to belong to anything like that."[38]

Despite these limitations and failures, the TWIU campaigns of the interwar years served as a valuable learning experience for Winston-Salem's working classes. Four major organizing drives had involved thousands of workers. R. J. Reynolds continued to tell itself that its employees were as satisfied as the consumers of its products, but the number of signed AFL membership cards belied these claims. A strong current of prounion sentiment persisted among Winston-Salem's workers, waiting to be tapped for future efforts.

Each organizing campaign also forced the company to expose the hand of power. The massive layoffs of the 1920s and the selective firings of later years may have contributed to a "fear complex" among workers, but they left a residue of anger as well as resignation. The paternalistic gestures of company officials carried limited weight with men and women whose family members and friends had lost their jobs and sometimes their homes for exercising their right to join a union.

The AFL unionization drives of the late thirties, moreover, proved to be an important training ground for future CIO leaders. Among the white officers of TWIU Local 217, Clark Sheppard, Henry Cofer, and John Henry Minor would become stalwarts in FTA's Local 22. Black officers and members of Local 224 included many future leaders of the CIO drive, among them Robert Black, Eddie Gallimore, and Lola Love. AFL efforts taught this cadre of men and women a number of valuable lessons. First, they learned which organizing tactics would doom them to failure. Attacking Reynolds without majority support was foolhardy, and dividing workers along skill, race, and gender lines only played into the hands of the company. Second, they learned which strategies might bring them success. They needed broad-based support, not only among men and women, blacks and whites, but in the larger community as well. They would also have to counter the company's shifting tactics, which had included race-baiting, sexual innuendo, trumped up no-union movements, intimidation by supervisors, and the recruitment of stool pigeons. Finally, they would need national allies. Although the NLRB ruling had gone against the AFL, the agency's very presence was an indication of the critical role the federal government was beginning to play in labor-management relations.

Political Openings

Labor unionists were not the only ones to rebel against what Winston-Salem's gadfly weekly *Thursday* characterized as industrialists' "unwarranted aggrandizement of money power." Conservative Democrats had dominated the state's political life since the turn of the century. Now, for the first time in decades, they confronted threats to their power: the Depression and the New Deal had encouraged workers to organize unions, farmers to clamor for looser credit and higher prices, and political reformers to call for regulation of corporations, expansion of the welfare state, and an enlarged federal presence in state and local affairs.[39]

As political leaders grappled with how to respond to these pressures and possibilities, fissures opened within the North Carolina Democratic Party. An emerging liberal wing hoped to use the New Deal to redistribute political and economic power within the state. It fought for higher taxes on corporations and the wealthy and federal aid for the poor and jobless. The ruling conservatives, who had overthrown the Fusionists at the turn of the century in order to pursue a development strategy based on cheap labor, low taxes, and limited social spending, now marshaled states' rights and laissez-faire arguments to oppose any programs that might temper the power or limit the profits of industrialists and planters. Although they accepted the help of New Deal relief agencies, they resisted genuine social reform, supported a balanced budget, and pushed a regressive sales tax through the state legislature. They also did their best to hijack New Deal reforms. Emblematic of that tactic was the appointment of former Winston-Salem mayor George Coan as head of the state's Works Progress Administration (WPA). Coan, a former Reynolds employee, had the strong support of business leaders in Winston-Salem and across the state, and he used the WPA in large part to dispense patronage for the North Carolina congressional delegation.[40]

The ideological split among southern Democrats widened during the presidential campaign of 1936. Throughout the country, the CIO, working through the Labor Non-Partisan League, organized get-out-the-vote campaigns among black and white workers. The Roosevelt administration continued to cultivate the support of southern Democrats, who acted as a brake on New Deal social policies, and FDR remained cautious on racial issues, but he did open federal jobs to blacks and bring black leaders into advisory roles, most notably Mary McLeod Bethune, one of the foremost members of a southern network of black women educators and club leaders. He also became increasingly equalitarian in symbolic ways, and he wooed the black vote energetically. Urged on by the NAACP and the CIO, black citizens throughout the South abandoned the Republican Party of their ancestors and stepped up their attempts to register and vote. Northern black voters helped provide FDR with a resounding victory.[41]

In the 1936 North Carolina gubernatorial primary, Democratic Party regulars supported either Clyde Hoey, a conservative lawyer from Shelby, a private prosecutor in the trial of the Gastonia strikers, and the brother-in-law of former governor O. Max Gardner (a close ally of Winston-Salem's leading industrialists), or the even more conservative lieutenant governor, Alexander Graham. The liberal candidate, Ralph McDonald, was a Forsyth County state legislator and former Salem College professor. A native of Illinois who had come south to earn a Ph.D. at Duke University, McDonald had emerged from political obscurity as the leader of the anti–sales tax forces in the 1934 General Assembly. His alternatives to the regressive sales tax included taxes on corporations, stock dividends, and personal incomes of over $1,000. McDonald won the support of *Winston-Salem Journal* publisher Owen Moon, also a Yankee transplant, and the enmity of local bankers and manufacturers. Although McDonald lost to Hoey in a runoff, he did carry Forsyth County, and his endorsement by the *Journal* so enraged local power brokers that they determined to take over the newspaper. A syndicate of Winston-Salem's ruling families pressured Moon into selling out and installed Gordon Gray, son of former Reynolds president Bowman Gray, as publisher.[42]

The loss of the *Journal* illustrated the weakness of the Democratic reformers, who were hamstrung by the disfranchisement of the black and white poor, which fatally narrowed their electoral base. For the moment, conservatives maintained control of the machinery of state. But the divisions within the Democratic Party did not heal and would widen over the following decades.

Taking advantage of that split, African Americans intensified their efforts to gain access to the ballot. North Carolina had repealed the poll tax in 1920, thus eliminating one of the most effective tools for restricting both white and black voter participation, and by the 1930s it had ceased formally to exclude blacks from the Democratic primary. Yet formidable barriers remained. The rule that voters had to be able to read and interpret the Constitution, which registrars manipulated in order to refuse most black requests; the long memory of the white supremacy campaigns; the coding of governmental processes as white—these and other forms of institutionalized racism continued to keep black voters away from the polls.[43]

In Raleigh, blacks organized a Negro Voters' League in 1931; by 1935 the *News and Observer* estimated that the capital city had over 2,000 black registered voters. In Durham, a League of Independent Voters appeared in 1931, and a few years later blacks organized the Committee on Negro Affairs, which retains its influence to this day. By 1936 leaders in both cities spearheaded the creation of the North Carolina Committee on Negro Affairs. More than 40,000 of the state's African Americans had registered as Democrats by the late 1930s.[44]

Blacks in Winston-Salem joined this slow move into the political arena. Taking advantage of the opening brought about by the enfranchisement of women in 1920, an estimated 326 black men and women had managed to register by the end of the decade. Throughout the 1930s African Americans continued to present themselves to the registrars and suffer the insult of being turned down. The capriciousness of the process often hurt as much as the actual denial. Jack Atkins, for instance, had been refused the right to register despite his position as a professor and son of Simon Atkins, the founder of Winston-Salem Teachers College, and his strong connections to people in the Reynolds Building. For the workers dependent on white employers, the bar remained even higher. "I worked in Reynolds," Robert Black recalled, "and if I wanted to register to vote, I would have to get the OK from my foreman before the registrar would even give me a chance to register."[45]

George Stoney, a white Winston-Salem native and recent graduate of the University of North Carolina, and Wilhelmina Jackson, an African American student at Howard University, visited Winston-Salem in 1939 and 1940 as field researchers for a study of race relations launched by Gunnar Myrdal for the Carnegie Corporation. Although Stoney and Jackson acknowledged the tight control of industrialists over local affairs, they also saw signs of black political ferment. In one instance these efforts smacked of political manipulation by white officials, but in others they signaled the emergence of a concerted drive by newly arrived black ministers to develop an independent black politics.[46]

In the 1939 mayoral election, the Republican Party fielded a candidate for the first time in twenty years, posing a real threat to a Democratic banker, James Fain, who was the choice of local industrialists. Odell Sapp campaigned against what he called "the machine," a none-too-veiled reference to the city's industrialists, and received his strongest support from white working-class precincts. A local black physician, Dr. W. H. Bruce, working with Bill Pfohl of the city's Democratic Executive Committee, took charge of delivering the black vote for the Democrats. Bruce, apparently with the support of white leaders, even ran for a seat on the Board of Aldermen in the Democratic primary in order to stimulate black registration, becoming the first African American to run for office in Winston-Salem in almost forty years. If Bruce was expecting white support in exchange for delivering black votes, he was sorely disappointed. The *Union Republican* reported that "his white cronies went back on him and he failed to land." In the general election, however, the black vote proved decisive in pushing the Democratic candidate to victory. A year later, Stoney noted, Pfohl, now secretary of the Democratic Committee, "was active in getting Negroes to register, and to register Democratic. . . . He has since formed an organization of Negro voters. Among its members are the leading Negro business and professional men."[47]

Although a far cry from full participation, the solicitation of black voters and the candidacy of Dr. Bruce, who ran and lost again in 1941, opened possibilities for new political activity by African Americans that young ministers were quick to exploit. The most outspoken was the Reverend J. S. Blaine, the recently arrived pastor of the Hanes Institutional CME Church. Blaine formed a Colored Improvement League in 1938 to "organize the Negroes in the interest of their economic and political freedom." Combining self-help with political protest, the league sought to mobilize consumers to support black businesses as well as to expand participation by blacks in local political affairs. As president of the league, Blaine criticized black as well as white leaders, including Bruce, for neglecting the needs of the black masses. "[Blaine] is very outspoken," Wilhelmina Jackson reported, "and, so, town gossip has it, has been told to go easy."[48]

The Reverend Thomas Kilgore also brought energy and imagination to local politics. A South Carolina native and graduate of Morehouse College, Kilgore assumed the pastorate of Friendship Baptist Church in December 1938 and quickly added to the membership and the treasury. Within a few years, he and his wife began organizing citizenship training classes in the church. "We got all the materials about what you had to do to vote," he remembered. "We had role playing. Someone would serve as one of those hard-nosed registrars who didn't fear calling you a 'nigger' or anything else. We'd [teach] them how not to loose their cool."

"Time came for a registration period for new voters," Kilgore continued. "I took five of these people who were the best trained and went to the polls. I had already registered. I had no trouble. They gave them the test, and they did pretty well, but the registrar failed everyone." Disappointed, the church members returned home. But Kilgore stayed to watch as other people came to register. "'Everybody who comes in here, you're going to give that test,'" he told the registrar. "'If anyone does more poorly than my group and you pass them, I'm going to have you put in jail.'" The registrar thought Kilgore "was crazy," but he asked later registrants, all of whom were white, to read and write sections of the state constitution. Most passed without a problem, but under Kilgore's watchful eye, the registrar turned down three or four white people who could not read. The next Saturday he took a larger group, and this time the registrar accepted every one of them, although "he didn't like it," Kilgore recalled. "That was sort of a break[through] in Winston-Salem."[49]

Blaine's and Kilgore's efforts set in motion a flurry of political activity in black Winston-Salem. The Winston-Salem Negro Chartered Democratic Club formed in May 1940 as part of a statewide group that had branches in all the major cities. The Young Negro Democratic Club of Forsyth County also surfaced that year, with the aim of stimulating black political participation. According to Wilhelmina Jackson, a by-invitation-only "Committee of 100 hoped to set up a central Negro leader democratically elected who can go down town and, having the force of a thousand or more votes behind him, actually goad officials into action on the Negro question." Known as "bronze mayors," such leaders were chosen in mock elections in a number of southern cities as symbols of blacks' disaffection and their determination to be represented by their own political leaders.[50]

In addition to these political initiatives, blacks challenged their exclusion from juries in Forsyth County courts. In 1940 the lawyer for a black defendant raised objections to the seating of a jury that contained no African Americans. Although the trial went forward, within a few weeks an elderly black man became what the independent weekly *Thursday* described as "the first negro to serve on a Forsyth superior court petit jury since—longer than most folks can remember." Court officials denied that there had been discrimination against blacks, saying that their names had always been in the jury box, but when drawn they had been "hard to reach, or could not be found."[51]

By the late 1930s a passion for change had taken root in Winston-Salem and in other black and working-class communities. The TWIU organizing drives, the advent of the CIO, the Communist Party's militant egalitarianism, the mobilization of the unemployed, the leftward drift of the New Deal, the candidacy of Dr. Bruce— none of these transformed class or race relations, but taken together they created an atmosphere of hope; they bred the self-confidence it takes to overcome fear and resignation. The dramatic, headline-grabbing revolts of white textile workers, first in 1929 and then in the 1934 general strike, also suggested the possibility of sea changes to come. It was by no means clear that poor whites would remain loyal to the regime hammered into place after the late-nineteenth-century white supremacy campaigns. For white and black workers alike, the bargain of paternalism crumbled under the pressures of economic collapse.

Within the biracial tobacco industry, workers continued to join separate locals, but they did so on the basis of shared experiences and grievances, and they took critical lessons from both their defeats and their moments of success. For African American workers, there was no question that economic and political citizenship had to go hand in hand. Most also understood that they could not go it alone. They needed allies in Congress and the White House; they needed the support of at least some sectors of the black middle class; and they needed the cooperation of white workers whose class interests outweighed their racial conditioning. These were the seeds of civil rights unionism, and they would bear fruit in the years ahead.

CHAPTER SIX

Talking Union

On December 7, 1941, the Japanese bombed Pearl Harbor, plunging the United States into war. At first, the defense build-up that lifted hundreds of thousands of unemployed whites out of the Depression seemed destined to bypass African Americans. Even the armed forces, which attracted blacks in unprecedented numbers, placed them in Jim Crow units and relegated them to jobs primarily as laborers and servants. Despite the biracial goals of the more progressive CIO unions, moreover, African American workers experienced nothing like the broad mobilization of white working-class ethnic groups that was so important to the Roosevelt coalition. Immediately the black press, the NAACP, and other black groups united around a "Double V" campaign—for victory over racism at home as well as fascism abroad.

A. Philip Randolph, the socialist founder of the Brotherhood of Sleeping Car Porters—AFL and former chairman of the National Negro Congress, took the lead in that effort. Responding to the discrimination against black soldiers and the feeble inclusion of blacks in the defense effort, Randolph announced plans to pressure the federal government to integrate the armed forces and provide jobs for black workers by threatening to march on Washington with thousands of protesters. Although hesitant at first, President Roosevelt and his advisors could not afford a war at home and acceded to some of Randolph's demands. Executive Order 8802, the "first presidential order on civil rights since Reconstruction," outlawed discrimination in defense industries and created a Fair Employment Practices Committee (FEPC).[1]

In the wake of that success, black workers and voters began mobilizing on a scale undreamed of since the 1890s. "We are living in the midst of perhaps the greatest revolution within human experience," wrote South Carolina political organizer Oscelo McKaine. "Nothing, no nation, will be as it was before when the peace comes. . . . There is no such thing as the status quo."[2]

Shortly before Pearl Harbor, the United Cannery, Agricultural, Packing, and Allied Workers of America arrived in Winston-Salem, bringing with it the CIO's militant new approach to unionization and political mobilization. In response, Reynolds workers embarked on a process of movement building that was shaped both by the social learning of the 1920s and 1930s and by rapidly unfolding developments in the South, in the nation, and around the globe. The Depression had shifted the whole force field of American politics to the left, giving birth to a broad, eclectic "Popular Front" with the CIO at its center. Independent radicals and New Dealers had struggled to wrest control of the southern Democratic Party away from the architects of white supremacy, loosen the influence of conservative congressmen on the Roosevelt administration, and forward the social democratic impulses of the New Deal. When the United States entered the war, that tug-of-war intensified, opening an unprecedented window of opportunity for African American workers. As the war economy heated up, the demand for labor skyrocketed, and the rhetoric of democracy in a war against fascism gave the "race question" a resonance it had never had before. These conditions, in combination with wartime protections for workers' rights in the name of national defense, helped to create a context in which Reynolds workers could take on the tobacco giant and hope to win.

The CIO and the Southern Front

UCAPAWA had emerged from the revolt in the AFL that launched the CIO. At its head stood an intense and energetic organizer named Donald Henderson. As a young economics instructor at Columbia University and a member of the Communist Party, Henderson had served as the unofficial advisor to a left-wing student movement that mushroomed in response to the Depression and the rise of fascism in Europe. Although upstaged by the protests of labor and the unemployed, student demonstrations during the Great Depression mobilized hundreds of thousands of students annually and had a profound impact on the nation's colleges. One student recalled that Henderson was among the "major faculty personalities of the era, and the bull sessions we had with [him] off the campus . . . had probably greater impact than anything said in the classroom." The instructor's activities did not go unnoticed, and in early 1933 he became one of a number of conspicuous radicals who lost their jobs because of their political convictions. Despite student protests, Henderson left academia. Joining the labor movement, he dedicated himself to organizing the country's agricultural workers.[3]

Henderson initially worked in southern New Jersey with the Cannery and Agricultural Industrial Union, which was affiliated with the Trade Union Unity League, the Communist Party's counter to the AFL. When the Party abandoned its strategy of dual unions in 1935, Henderson became president of the National Committee for Unity of Agricultural and Rural Workers, a loose coalition of small locals that were affiliated with the AFL. Unable to get the AFL to charter an international union of agricultural workers and increasingly drawn to the CIO's industrial union structure, Henderson and representatives from locals throughout the country met in Denver in July 1937 to form UCAPAWA, which promptly received a charter from the CIO.[4]

From the beginning, UCAPAWA represented a veritable rainbow of American workers. Mexican sugar beet workers from the Rocky Mountains, black sharecroppers from Arkansas and Missouri, cannery and farm workers from New Jersey, laborers from the Florida citrus groves, and Filipino, Chinese, and Japanese cannery workers in Washington were only a few of the dozens of occupations and nationalities involved. Henderson remembered organizing campaigns in which "we had to get out a leaflet in eight different languages." In addition to the challenges involved in molding this multicultural constituency into a forceful international union, UCAPAWA faced an almost insurmountable organizing task. Agricultural labor was notoriously difficult to organize: workers were migratory because of the seasonal nature of the industry; the relatively unskilled nature of the work created an oversupply of labor; most agricultural laborers came from minority groups that lacked social or political clout; and, because labor represented a high percentage of the cost of production, employers fought hard to keep unions out. Yet despite these difficulties, UCAPAWA enjoyed some early success, thanks in part to active organizing by established locals and the financial support of the CIO. By 1937 Henderson could report a membership of over 120,000 workers in more than 300 locals.[5]

Like a number of CIO presidents, Henderson relied heavily on the skill and commitment of activists affiliated with the Communist movement. Many of UCAPAWA's officers and organizers in the early days shared Henderson's political sympathies. Some had become unionists as a result of their politics; others had been drawn to

Donald Henderson
(*UCAPAWA News*)

Communism as a result of their organizing experiences. They saw little difference between being good trade unionists and loyal Party members. Other UCAPAWA leaders, while not Party members, saw themselves as participants in a radical cultural and political project in which the Party played an important, but not necessarily a defining, role.[6]

The Party and the CIO each had compelling reasons for making this alliance work. The new union movement desperately needed experienced organizers who could mobilize workers in the nation's most notoriously antiunion industries. None were more seasoned and dedicated than activists from the left wing of the labor, student, civil rights, and unemployed movements. At the same time, the Party needed a way to reach the American proletariat on which it pinned its hopes for revolutionary change.

Communists had put aside the sectarianism that had spurred dual unions in order to strengthen both the New Deal and the fight against fascism. Under this new "United Front" policy, the Trade Union Unity League dissolved and labor radicals turned to organizing within the AFL and CIO unions. Although always a small percentage of union members, Communists eventually attained highly influential positions in a number of CIO unions, including large organizations such as the United Electrical Workers and smaller ones such as UCAPAWA and the Mine, Mill, and Smelter Workers, both of which organized biracial locals in the South. From the outset there were tensions between these left-led unions and the CIO's more conservative affiliates, but through the mid-1940s a federation that one historian has called a "fragile juggernaut" remained united around common goals, foremost among which were a commitment to "organizing the unorganized" and support for the left wing of the New Deal.[7]

The young organizers recruited by the CIO and the Party in the 1930s differed from the first generation of Communist activists, most of whom were immigrants who looked to Europe for their ideological cues. Many of the new generation of activists came from middle- and upper-middle-class families, had attended college, and had been leaders in the student movement. They had been radicalized by the threat of fascism and the inequalities and injustices laid bare by the Depression. Others came from working-class backgrounds and had learned their lessons in the college of hard knocks. Many of these young men and women saw themselves as indigenous American radicals as well as members of an international movement.[8]

One of these idealistic recruits, Ed McCrea, became one of UCAPAWA's most successful leaders and an important actor in Winston-Salem. After a childhood spent in New York and Maryland, McCrea attended St. John's College and New York University. "When I got active in the Marxist movement," he remembered, "there were mostly young people like myself, who after the Depression, welcomed the chance to participate in the organization of the unions and became leaders in the left-wing unions. They went out in the coal fields, the mill towns, and met with people in the woods, built the unions. They were a part of the people. They didn't go in well dressed, in white shirts and ties and stuff. They were clean, decent looking, but it wasn't a business with them. All the people I knew before the war were that way, in the left wing. We built a lot of unions, too, with people who later became right-wing. But at the time it didn't make any difference really what wing you were from."[9]

That unity was sorely tested in 1939 when Stalin attempted to prevent Hitler from attacking the Soviet Union by entering into a nonaggression treaty with the Third Reich. In response the Communist Party abruptly abandoned its united front against fascism and urged nonparticipation in a war between European powers. Although it returned to its earlier strategy after the United States entered the war and Germany invaded the Soviet Union, the Party had alienated many of its former allies. As knowledge of Stalin's domestic terrorism spread, moreover, Communists found themselves under fire for defending a country ruled by a dictator comparable to Hitler.

For many on the left, however, the Popular Front had less to do with these twists and turns in the Party line than with a sea change in American political culture. They saw the Popular Front as a broad-based movement, even a "structure of feeling," with which reformers of a wide variety of political persuasions could identify. As such, it did not begin or end with decisions in New York or Moscow. Rather, it was paced by the rise of the CIO, marked by the emergence of working-class themes and sensibilities in American culture, and dedicated to realizing the broader, social democratic possibilities of the New Deal. Members of this progressive coalition might differ furiously on a range of issues, but they were linked by a commitment to industrial unionism, antiracism, the defense of civil liberties, and the international fight against fascism and preoccupied with a search for new forms through which to communicate their aesthetic and political vision.[10]

Three developments marked the emergence of the "Southern Front," or southern wing, of this larger Popular Front movement: the growing militancy of southern workers, the NAACP's decision in the mid-1930s to expand its base in the South and to put the situation of southern blacks at the core of its agenda, and the 1938 founding of the Southern Conference for Human Welfare (SCHW), a diverse group of New Deal officials, journalists, intellectuals, trade unionists, and civil rights advocates. SCHW's participants drew on the insights of the new regionalists, who argued against divisive sectionalism and for economic planning; on the economic theories associated with John Maynard Keynes, who maintained that recovery depended on regulating business in order to control production and raise mass purchasing power; and on American and European social democratic thought, which sought to promote an evolution toward socialism by extending the principles of democracy into economic life. Civil rights advocates, who drove home the links between racial oppression, economic exploitation, and regional underdevelopment, played an increasingly influential role in the organization.[11]

The Southern Front's chief concern was the welfare of the region. Those who identified themselves with this project believed that only a thoroughgoing redistribution of wealth and political power, both within the South and between the South and the North, could end the region's poverty, which stemmed from its own skewed political economy as well as from its role as a producer of raw materials for the industrial North. But they also saw that solving the "southern problem" was the key to national progress. The South's constricted electorate underwrote the power of conservative Democrats in Congress, whose seniority enabled them to dominate key congressional committees. Southern congressmen, in turn, allied with Republicans to block or dilute social welfare measures and progressive labor laws. This conservative alliance helped to perpetuate the South's separate low-wage labor market, which served as a magnet for runaway industries, undercut the labor movement, and pulled national wage standards down. To loosen its grip and crack the South's separate labor market, southern progressives sought to expand the electorate and use the political space opened up by the New Deal and the CIO to build a biracial movement on behalf of economic and political democracy. For more than a decade, this contest would play itself out in arenas that ranged from the intensely local to the national and the global. At stake was the democratic promise of the New Deal, the fate of black Americans, and the shape of the post–World War II world.[12]

UCAPAWA entered the battle for the South when the Arkansas-based Southern Tenant Farmers Union (STFU) affiliated with the new international union. Organized in 1934 by black and white sharecroppers and tenant farmers under the leadership of storekeepers Clay East and H. L. Mitchell, the STFU focused public attention on the plight of southern farmers. But infighting between Communist Party leaders and the local Socialists who served as the organization's principal administrators, as well as personality and ideological conflicts between Henderson and Mitchell, marred the alliance from the start. The STFU and UCAPAWA also differed over a fundamental issue: whether agricultural workers could best be served by a protest organization or a trade union. Despite its name, the STFU functioned more like the former; it was loosely structured, had an uncertain membership, and depended on outside sources for financial support. Mitchell contended that sharecroppers and tenant farmers were too uneducated to keep records and too poor to pay regular dues. Henderson argued that agricultural workers could be taught the rudimentary procedures for running the locals and that union members had to support their own organization.[13]

Originally, UCAPAWA had focused on migrant workers in California. But employer resistance and the seasonality of farm labor made it virtually impossible to establish permanent, self-supporting locals. Finding itself increasingly rushing to the aid of wildcat strikers who had no chance of winning collective bargaining agreements, UCAPAWA temporarily abandoned its efforts in the fields and focused on the canneries and processing plants, where workers' geographic stability made them better candidates for unionization. "Henderson had a terrific strategy for the union," Elizabeth Sasuly, the union's legislative director, remembered. "He wanted to organize the processing plants as a base for agriculture." By the early 1940s, this strategy had paid off, and UCAPAWA was setting an example for the union movement across the United States. Local 3 represented workers at food processing plants in southern California, a majority of whom were Mexican women. In Camden, New Jersey, UCAPAWA broke through at the fiercely antiunion Campbell's Soup Company. Even in Memphis, Tennessee, one of the South's most staunchly antiunion cities, UCAPAWA Local 19 organized hundreds of low-paid workers—most of whom were black—in dozens of large and small companies.[14]

Although it was still small compared to most AFL and CIO affiliates, UCAPAWA had nonetheless shown that it could organize among the nation's most vulnerable workers. It had also shown that women and minority groups were capable of playing an important role in the labor movement. In fact, the union's active recruitment and promotion of women, as well as blacks, Mexicans, and other ethnic minorities, to positions of leadership was unprecedented among American trade unions. These indigenous leaders were key to the union's success in the canneries, as they would be in the tobacco industry.

UCAPAWA's decision to target tobacco manufacturing workers had multiple roots. Among its charter members were a small number of cigar worker locals in New York and Florida, but the main impetus came from tobacco workers in Richmond, Virginia. In 1937 black stemmery workers struck at a local leaf-processing firm and, with the help of organizers from the Southern Negro Youth Congress, a group led by young radicals who had worked in the campaign to free the Scottsboro Nine, organized an independent Tobacco Stemmers and Laborers Union. Within a few years the union had agreements with a number of the city's smaller firms, and affiliation with the CIO provided the financial support needed to tackle the large manufacturers. The CIO awarded UCAPAWA jurisdiction over tobacco workers, and in 1942 the Tobacco Stemmers and Laborers Union became UCAPAWA Local 24. From this base, the union started organizing among tobacco workers throughout the South.[15]

Building a Social Movement

In the winter of 1942, soon after the United States entered World War II, UCAPAWA organizer Franklin Darnes arrived in Winston-Salem with a few copies of the UCAPAWA News under his arm and plans to "begin building the base for a labor organization." Robert Black recalled how Darnes first made his presence felt. "The guy began to write articles in the public opinion [column]. They were broad articles, about how oppressed the workers were, particularly the blacks, and it would take some person that was organizationally inspired to really read and get out of it what he was saying."[16]

Black himself was one of those "organizationally inspired" readers, and he was one of Darnes's earliest and best recruits. "One Saturday I was sitting on my porch and this guy came down the street," Black remembered. He recalled his exchange with Darnes.

"Where do you work?"

"I work at R. J. Reynolds."

"You're the very man I want to talk with."

"What are you selling?"

"I'm not selling anything but better wages and working conditions."

"He asked if he could talk with me, and I told him yes," Black recalled. "We sat down and spent a couple of hours talking over the possibilities of building a union. And then I gave him the names of other people that I knew."[17]

Other workers responded more coolly to Darnes's entreaties, but he found enough interest to justify renting an office above a bank on Third Street. A few people began meeting there and in one another's homes every other Sunday evening. Soon UCAPAWA formally established a Tobacco Workers Organizing Committee, composed of organizers and rank-and-file workers.[18]

Darnes left for the U.S. Army in the spring, but UCAPAWA sent Harry Koger and William DeBerry, fresh from a successful organizing campaign in Memphis, to replace him, and they used Darnes's contacts to continue the organizing drive. Koger, the son of an Illinois farmer and merchant, had spent his early life as a schoolteacher, preacher, and YMCA secretary. He moved to Texas with his wife, Grace, and their children in 1927 hoping to become a real estate developer. The Depression waylaid the Kogers' plans, and like many Americans they reacted to the collapse of the economy with a mixture of anger and determination. They first encountered the labor movement when they read about a pecan shellers' strike in San Antonio and volunteered to collect food for the Mexican American strikers. Soon afterward UCAPAWA offered Harry Koger a job. He quickly distinguished himself as an organizer of tenant farmers and sharecroppers in East Texas and the Mississippi Delta. By 1943, according to a fellow unionist, he "had faced more than his share of boss-inspired vigilante-ism and . . . seen the inside of a few southern jails."[19]

William DeBerry was born in Memphis in 1911. His father was a fireman, which was a good position for an African American in the Jim Crow South, and DeBerry was able to get a high school education before the onset of the Depression. He played a minor role in the Southern Tenant Farmers Union and then went to work for UCAPAWA when the union began organizing in the Memphis area. DeBerry served as the first president of UCAPAWA Local 19, before being asked to take part in the drive in Winston-Salem.[20]

In addition to being UCAPAWA organizers, both DeBerry and Koger belonged to the People's Institute of Applied Religion, and they drew extensively on its blend of prophetic religion and trade unionism. The organization's founder, the Reverend Claude Williams, was one of a coterie of radicals who surfaced in the South between the world wars, burning with a fierce determination to fight the social and economic injustices they saw around them. He had grown up in the Tennessee hills and established a ministry in Auburntown with his wife, Joyce. The opportunity to study religion with Alva Taylor at Vanderbilt Divinity School opened Williams's eyes to the possibility of using Christianity to combat social ills. The Williamses became increasingly concerned with economic inequality—between blacks and whites, planters and sharecroppers—and their religious message began to focus more on "The Kingdom of God on Earth" than on other-worldly redemption and salvation. After taking a decaying Presbyterian church in Fort Smith, Arkansas, in the early 1930s the couple increasingly moved to the left, as Claude "reread the Bible with new eyes," according to the historian Mark Naison. "He saw the Son of Man as a revolutionary who was continually identified with the extremest victims of society —the poor, the suffering, the exploited. The same was true of virtually all the Old Testament figures who represented the prophetic impulse, from Moses through Amos and Isaiah. Looked at from this perspective, the Bible read as 'the longest continuous record of struggle against oppression that mankind possessed.'"[21]

Such ideas were bound to affront Presbyterian Church leaders, and soon enough the Williamses found themselves dismissed from their post. Rather than seeking another pastorate, they threw themselves into the political and economic struggles of mid-1930s Arkansas, including those waged by the STFU. Asked by unionists to help train black and white labor leaders, Claude developed an approach to labor education that grew directly out of his religious convictions. That approach "was necessitated by the strong religious background of virtually all the participants," Naison observed, "and the fact that the Bible represented virtually the only framework within which they could make sense of their struggles, their setbacks and their aspirations." Williams served a stint as director of Commonwealth College (a residential labor school established by utopian socialists in the 1920s), during which he became embroiled in UCAPAWA's fight with the STFU, and then established the People's Institute of Applied Religion. He and the institute helped inspire some of the STFU's most successful organizers, including the Reverend Owen Whitfield, who, along with his predecessor, John Handcox, brought thousands of Missouri plantation workers into the STFU and then went on to become one of UCAPAWA's most effective leaders.[22]

Williams envisioned the institute as a nonsectarian organization that would train religious leaders to be labor organizers and to lead campaigns against racial discrimination. To communicate with people who could barely read and write, Williams asked an artist to design illustrations depicting Bible stories that seemed to contain revolutionary messages or showing scenes of contemporary struggles accompanied by appropriate Biblical passages. The preachers Williams trained made these illustrations a centerpiece of their organizing campaigns.[23]

In August 1940, UCAPAWA president Donald Henderson asked Williams to conduct an institute in Memphis in conjunction with the union's organizing efforts among cotton and cottonseed processing workers. With the assistance of Henderson, Koger, Whitfield, and others, Williams mixed lectures on religion, labor history, and social issues to create a revival atmosphere for the more than sixty workers and ministers in attendance. Vigilante violence soon forced Williams to leave Memphis, but Whitfield carried on the work of the institute. "I have my charts on the wall here in the hall," he wrote Williams, "and teach them four times a week to four groups of workers from four different plants. There are always ten to fifteen working preachers of different sects, and no end of church officers in the meetings. OH! if our sponsors could see how the common preachers and common people respond to what they call these 'GOSPEL FEASTS' and how they rush up and shake hands and give thanks, and invite me to come to their churches." The institute and the meetings conducted by Whitfield and Koger helped develop strong rank-and-file leadership in Memphis and soon led to the organization of numerous plants in the city and the formation of UCAPAWA Local 19.[24]

In Winston-Salem, DeBerry and Koger applied an organizing strategy similar to the one they had developed in Memphis. Soon after he arrived, DeBerry began making contact with black ministers. Common sense dictated his decision, but embedded in this approach was a strategic understanding of the centrality of the church and the importance of its leaders within the black community. DeBerry described his method: "Many times I walked into churches all over the South and put down five or ten dollars in the plate, or maybe go and talk with the minister. We didn't talk too much about labor business, but he knew who I was. We'd feel one another out. He'd say, 'Brother DeBerry, come down to service Sunday and worship with us.' After the service he'd say, 'I've got somebody I want you to meet.' I could reach all of those people, otherwise I wouldn't have a chance." DeBerry made the rounds of black churches in Winston-Salem, contacting Frank O'Neal, R. M. Pitts,

Thomas Kilgore, Jerry Drayton, and many others. Their support—or at least their promises of neutrality—would be crucial to the organizing drive.[25]

One minister who responded enthusiastically to DeBerry's message was the Reverend Edward Gholson, pastor of Holy Trinity Baptist Church. A Virginia native, graduate of Temple University, and prolific author of religious and inspirational books, Gholson enjoyed a reputation as a forceful advocate of civil rights. He sponsored a week-long institute led by Claude Williams and later convened a series of meetings at his church. Selected black ministers attended, many of whom were also workers in the tobacco factories.[26]

Aquilla Hairston, a Reynolds worker and an ordained Baptist minister without a church, was among them. Hairston, who eventually became an outspoken opponent of the union, provided an affidavit in 1944 that, despite its critical viewpoint, conveys some of the flavor of the sessions. "Rev. Gholson," he recalled, "would take up the first thirty or forty minutes with talking about how labor was oppressed by capital and said that people were talking bad about communism, that communism didn't mean anything except dividing up everything like they did in Russia and that was why the white folks were against Communism." Then Williams spoke, drawing on familiar Old and New Testament stories. "Some of the references were to the Children of Israel in bondage from Exodus," Hairston continued. "One was to where Jesus was in the synagogue on the Sabbath Day and opened the book and read, 'The Spirit of the Lord is upon me because He hath anointed me to preach the Gospel to the poor.' . . . At the end of these meetings Rev. Gholson would always make an appeal for us to join the CIO and during the classes on several occasions, William DeBerry was given time to make a speech in which he urged us to join the CIO."[27]

The Reverend Owen Whitfield presented a well-publicized series of talks before Baptist congregants that ended with an appearance before the Ministerial Alliance. Such gatherings highlighted the importance of the free public spaces created by the black churches. Here ministers, workers, and organizers talked openly and honestly about tactics for change. Here too was forged the relationship among trade unions, black freedom struggles, and prophetic Christianity that defined civil rights activism among working-class blacks in the 1940s.[28]

Important as it was, gaining the backing of prominent men such as Gholson was only a first step; to succeed, the union would have to attract rank-and-file workers. As with most social movements, the organizing campaign started small. A nucleus of about two dozen activists provided the crucial leadership. Who were these early recruits? How did they get involved? Why were they willing to take risks when so many others would not?

Eddie Gallimore was one of Franklin Darnes's first initiates, and he turned out to be a miracle worker. Gallimore had been a charter member and officer of TWIU Local 224. Once he signed on with UCAPAWA, he helped develop a core group of unionists, first by bringing in his wife, Leanna, and then by reaching into his social networks and recruiting Theodosia Simpson. "Eddie and my husband were very good friends," Simpson remembered, "and Eddie said one Sunday, 'Why don't you go with me to a meeting?' I discussed it with my husband. He belonged to the AFL in the plant where he worked; he was familiar with the union. He told me it was okay for me to go ahead and join." Included in the group of young couples with whom the Simpsons and the Gallimores socialized were Bill and Ann Anderson, and they too became active members and highly effective organizers.[29]

The union's goals of higher wages, better working conditions, and equal rights made eminent sense to Simpson. Forced by the Depression to leave college and go to work at Reynolds, she had to put aside her dream of becoming a teacher, but she still had ambitions that could not be achieved as a minimum-wage factory worker. She resented how the poorly educated foremen ridiculed her for reading the newspaper at lunch. She was furious when nurses attributed every illness a black woman complained of to venereal disease. Simpson had no illusions about "white supremacy"; she knew she was more capable than those supposed betters she dealt with every day. Even the subforeman, who had little education, recognized her talents. He told her one day, "You don't need to be here; you need to be [a secretary] over at the Reynolds Building."[30]

Robert Black was another friend of Eddie Gallimore, a member of TWIU Local 224, and one of Darnes's early contacts. Black was a bit older than other members of this core group, and as we have seen, he was motivated by a long-standing indignation at the injustices of southern society, including the repression of textile workers in Gastonia. In small ways, he and his family had long worked for change. His mother had joined an unemployed council in the 1930s. A brief sojourn in Baltimore in the mid-thirties had exposed him to the possibility of greater personal freedom and a higher standard of living. There he had also seen the benefits that came with unionization. Others looked to Black for leadership not only because of his dignity and wisdom but also because of his sociability and lanky good looks. He was a familiar figure on the baseball fields, at the checker corners, and in the pool rooms of black Winston-Salem. Although he did not consider himself much of a singer, Black participated in quartets and choral groups. "I had friendly relations with hundreds of people on a social basis, in church activities and recreation," he acknowledged, "mostly men, but with a lot of women."[31]

Evander Rogers and Alexander "Rock Hill" Woods knew Black in the factory and on the baseball diamond, and Rogers and Black also played checkers together. An acquaintance of all these men was William "Bro" Malone, who grew up next door to Black and worked in Number 97 with Gallimore. All became active in the union drive. Willie Grier was another early recruit. A 1930 high school graduate, he deeply resented the lack of opportunity available to African Americans and had vowed to find a way to better his condition.[32]

Two of the most effective TWOC members belonged to the Reverend R. M. Pitts's Shiloh Baptist Church. John Tomlim, who worked in Number 8 Machine Room, had come to Winston-Salem from his native Philadelphia as a young man. An accomplished musician, he had extensive contacts in the black community, serving as music director of Shiloh Baptist Church and director of the YMCA glee club. He was also an officer in the Camel Elks Lodge 1021.[33]

Velma Hopkins exemplified the leadership roles played by both working- and middle-class women in the black community. Described by many people as a model club woman, Hopkins combined her roles as a mother, wife, worker, and community member. "My training, I guess, came from being a mother and working in the [Shiloh Baptist] church and in the school," she said. "I'd always participated in PTAs. And I was head of an organization in the church [the Galaxy Club]. I got lots of my training from my pastor too."[34]

These rank-and-file leaders represented a generation of articulate, aspiring, and relatively well educated black workers. Most had come of age in the early 1930s. Segregation, discrimination, and depression had combined to limit their prospects severely, but the stirring rhetoric, if not always the actual policies, of the New Deal whetted their appetites for greater social and economic opportunities. Denied jobs commensurate with their training, intelligence, and ability, they sought ways to challenge the restrictions of Jim Crow. In a war-driven economy, they knew that despite persistent discrimination, there were job opportunities in other cities, North and South, and they were self-confident and mobile enough to try to take advantage of them, if need be.

Organizers spent hours knocking on doors and distributing leaflets around the plants. Koger, DeBerry, and the other UCAPAWA organizers who helped out on the campaign became familiar figures to thousands of Reynolds employees as they stood at the factory gates day after day. Although the Wagner Act prohibited employers from firing workers for union activity, supervisors had many ways of intimidating potential union members. Some workers took the leaflets and a few stopped to talk to the organizers, but most feared for their jobs, and at first the hours spent on the streets outside the plant gates, at all times of day and in all kinds of weather, netted few recruits. Still, the presence of the UCAPAWA organizers served an important symbolic purpose. It said to workers: the union is here, it is here to stay, it has the right to challenge the company on its own ground, and you have a right to participate if you so choose.[35]

The more determined early unionists were meeting openly by the summer of 1942. "We began to have discussions on Sunday afternoons after church," Black remembered. "Some weeks we'd have eighteen or twenty, but most times it was just this old faithful eight or ten. The organizers would instruct us how you go about building a union. DeBerry would sit in the meetings with us and we would always have broad discussions about how unions were built, how they were operated. It was a slow process, but we never gave up the idea of building a union. We rented a little union hall, and we would publicize in the newspaper about these meetings and who was elected to serve in certain capacities. And the company's executives would read it and laugh about it because they didn't see how we were ever going to get the workers together to build a union."[36]

Management's false confidence, along with the umbrella of federal protection—however tenuous and far away it might seem—allowed black workers room to maneuver. The NLRB's reinstatement of Ruel White, the local TWIU leader who had been fired during the organizing campaign of 1938–41, may have made officials cautious about interfering with union activity. In any event, management's hands-off policy and workers' dogged determination created a space in which ideas and organization could develop.[37]

The workers' regular meetings with UCAPAWA organizers served a dual educational purpose. Organizers transmitted the knowledge and experience they had gained in the labor movement; workers, in turn, taught them about life in the factory and in Winston-Salem. The meetings mixed practical training with discussions of labor's role in American history and workers' struggles in other industries. Darnes, DeBerry, and Koger also offered a critique of capitalism and white supremacy that melded the class-based messages of Marxism with the prophetic vision of the Bible. This critique had an enormous appeal because it resonated with black workers' culture and experience even as it elevated the collective efforts of Winston-Salem workers to national and international significance.

Koger and DeBerry believed and taught that unionization was largely a matter of self-organization. UCAPAWA could provide the framework and certain resources and the organizers could act as facilitators, but the core group of local unionists

Left to right: UCAPAWA organizers Harry Koger, Barney Henley, William DeBerry, and D. S. Upchurch (*UCAPAWA News*)

had to convince their fellow workers of the need for organization. To this end, rank-and-filers formed a Volunteer Service Club to sponsor "cottage meetings," arrange entertainment for union gatherings, and staff the union hall. DeBerry and Koger brought the idea of cottage meetings with them from Memphis. One of the organizers (or occasionally one of the more experienced recruits) would go to someone's home to talk about the union with a few workers invited by the host. Secrecy was one advantage of this strategy; the ability to have frank, in-depth discussions with a group of workers was another.[38]

The Volunteer Service Club also drew on Winston-Salem's rich musical traditions, especially on its popular choral clubs, to stamp the union drive as the workers' own. Among the TWOC's early converts were members of the Smith Choral Club, one of the city's best-known singing groups. Theodosia Simpson's husband, Buck, was a long-time member, and he and three others formed a quartet to sing at union gatherings. A Reynolds worker named Coy Ledford came up with the idea of having the quartet record union songs to be played at workers' homes. This innovative use of record-making technology allowed them to spread the union message unobserved. Like the cottage meetings, the records protected fearful workers from prying eyes.[39]

The quartet performed gospel tunes and CIO standards, but, like the choral clubs more generally, it also drew on popular musical traditions, including seemingly unpromising tunes such as Stephen Foster's nostalgic "Old Black Joe."

> Gone are the days when the boss had all the say,
> Gone are the days when we worked for meager pay.
>
> How does it come? Do you really want to know?
> We hear the workers' voices calling "CIO."

Such cultural improvisations, which combined sacred and secular traditions with popular music, simultaneously claimed the imprimatur of Christianity and softened the radical implications of the union's rhetoric for fearful listeners. It also subverted the racist overtones of popular music, giving a critical, antiracist edge to pro-union messages.[40]

Person-to-person contacts, combined with cottage meetings and occasional gatherings of larger groups in churches or fraternal halls, proved to be the most effective method of recruitment in the long months leading up to the Reynolds walkout. The Volunteer Service Club sponsored informal recruitment contests that were won by Ada Byrd, the team of Bill and Ann Anderson, and Eddie Gallimore. In addition to using their social contacts, club members tapped into the informal work groups in their departments. Factory-based birthday clubs, flower clubs, and reading groups, for example, could essentially be recruited as a bloc. Using these and other means, the core group of eight to ten recruits had persuaded a few hundred Reynolds workers to sign union cards by the spring of 1943.[41]

The union's influence in the factories extended well beyond its card-carrying members. Equally critical to the TWOC's ultimate success was the example that union-minded workers set for others in their departments. Robert Black never won the Volunteer Service Club's competition for recruiting the most new members, but he constantly talked union with the other men in his department and his friends on the street. "Those people in Reynolds knew us," he explained, "because we would pin them down during lunchtime and on the weekends and even in the plant about trying to intensify and build up a resistance in there."[42]

As the TWOC gradually created a base of support among workers, activists began to explore the limits of the possible in the factory and in the community. They started, as successful advocates of change often must, to test prevailing expectations in small but portentous ways. They had to be careful to make their points without getting themselves fired or landing in jail. Defeat would only reinforce fear and pessimism. Growing frustrated with the slow place of recruitment in her department, Theodosia Simpson devised a clever way to get her message across. "The organizers gave us cards and I would go back to my department and try to get these people to join," she remembered. "Oh, my God, the resistance that we ran up against. We wore uniforms that buttoned down the front. One day I tore all the buttons off my dress, and buttoned it up with union buttons and went to work like that. The foreman didn't know what to do about it. So he just asked if I would go home and change uniforms please, and he paid me for the time I was gone.

"Then a memo came out the next day. No pins in your clothes. No pins, no earrings, no rings but your wedding ring. They were afraid this stuff would get into the tobacco. That was the excuse they gave. After that I was able to get a few people to sign up, when they saw that I didn't get fired for it. That's why we had a nucleus in Number 65. But they were afraid for even the person on their machine to know that they had done it."[43]

Simpson's supervisor retaliated, but his response paled in comparison to her imaginative display of her convictions. Perhaps he felt stymied by the Wagner Act's prohibition against intimidation of union members. Perhaps his relationship with Theodosia Simpson warranted this mild response. Perhaps he was simply frustrated by the fact that he could not ask her to remove the buttons without taking off her dress. In any case, she gave him little choice but to concede the temporary attenuation of his authority.

The TWOC deliberately violated traditional patterns of racial behavior outside the workplace as well. The Volunteer Service Club, for example, spearheaded a countermovement to the white monopoly on voluntarism and philanthropy. The TWOC conducted well-publicized war bond drives. Club members, much like ward politicians, helped elderly citizens file claims for old-age assistance and consulted with government officials to ensure that the claimants received adequate relief. A meeting in the Forsyth County Courthouse with a representative of the North Carolina Office of Price Administration, a federal agency charged with rationing goods and keeping down wartime inflation, announced a communitywide campaign to ensure local merchants' compliance with price controls.[44]

Such working-class intrusions into public life were virtually unheard of in southern cities. At one level, the TWOC's actions were a logical extension both of the self-help spirit of the black community and of the long tradition of brokering for white-controlled social services. But they also represented a response to the culture of civic participation unleashed during the New Deal. Making demands on the state more far-reaching than those that the South's black citizens had ever been able to make before, union organizers projected a vision of social democracy that would grow more and more radical in the closing years of the war.[45]

White southerners, on the other hand, reacted to black assertiveness with a paranoia reminiscent of the rape scares that had fueled the white supremacy campaigns. Encountering insults and violence, black soldiers stationed in North Carolina's training camps clashed with white citizens and police. Rumors that black men were arming themselves for a postwar Armageddon and that black women were forming "Eleanor Clubs" determined to put "every white woman in her own kitchen by Christmas" swept through the region. These mounting racial tensions were by no means limited to the South. They echoed through the halls of Congress and burst into riots in northern cities. No less a figure than FBI director J. Edgar Hoover wrote to the head of the Selective Service warning that black men might attack white women left alone when their husbands went to war.[46]

Clearly, most white Americans saw no problem in fighting for democracy while 10 percent of the nation's population lacked basic civil rights. It was not enough to point out the contradictions, to remind the country that full participation of blacks in the war effort required freedom at home. Every inch of ground would be contested and hard-won. African Americans would have to fight for a chance to face the Germans and Japanese on the battlefield. They would have to fight for a chance to weld the rivets on the planes and ships needed to stop Axis advances. They would have to fight for the democratic freedoms the nation had supposedly gone to war to protect. And they would have to link their struggles to those of other oppressed people in the nation and around the world.

In that spirit, TWOC leaders began publicly to condemn the fundamental injustices of Jim Crow. In the fall of 1942, Harry Koger drew attention to the plight of local blacks who had been recruited by the U.S. Employment Service to work at a cannery in Maryland. Returning workers told Koger of "peonage" conditions: wages after deductions amounted to a few cents an hour; women had to stand in water for hours peeling tomatoes; foremen refused to let workers use the toilets and drew guns on those who tried to leave. Koger's call for a federal investigation and the workers' vivid affidavits received extensive coverage in the local press, exposing a common but generally ignored abuse of seasonal workers.[47]

The union's most significant intervention in public affairs occurred it when took up the cause of William Mason Wellman, the brother of Volunteer Service Club member Hunter Wellman, who was sentenced to die for raping an elderly white woman in Iredell County in 1942. The victim picked him out of a police lineup, although Wellman claimed—and others eventually corroborated his story—that he was hundreds of miles away at Ft. Belvoir, Virginia, when the crime took place. TWOC members, led by Koger and DeBerry, mounted a vigorous campaign to save Wellman's life, coordinating their efforts with those of the black Ministerial Alliance. Koger played an important role in publicizing the case. He talked to newspaper reporters, contacted union groups in other parts of the country, and attended a meeting with Governor J. M. Broughton, while DeBerry and the Volunteer Service Club members gathered more than 2,000 signatures on a petition to the governor for clemency.[48]

Alerted by the TWOC and fearing "bloodshed at home," prominent white liberals based at the University of North Carolina, including the regional sociologists Guy B. Johnson and Howard Odum, the playwright Paul Green, and the president of the university, Frank Porter Graham, supported the Wellman defense. The Southern Conference for Human Welfare and other progressive regional and national groups joined the union-led effort as well. Charles Houston, the NAACP's chief legal counsel, and the chief architect of its southern strategy, seized the opportunity to push the central message of the Double V campaign. Writing to Governor Broughton, he warned that "the Wellman case had serious and widespread implications for good and evil in the war effort. The granting to Wellman of a complete and generous opportunity to establish his innocence will bulwark the confidence of the Negro people in the sincerity of our war aims and thus strengthen the unity of all Americans."[49]

The evidence of Wellman's innocence proved overwhelming, and in April 1943 Governor Broughton pardoned him. At a time when black assertiveness was stoking whites' racial and sexual fears, Wellman could have easily joined the long line of black suspects who had died at the hands of vigilante and state-sponsored violence over the years. Instead, a coalition generated by workers had saved an innocent man's life. This was tangible evidence of what a worker-based social movement could do.[50]

Bolstered by this victory against a legal system that often victimized rather than protected black citizens, union leaders moved to take on the electoral system. In the spring of 1943, DeBerry, Whitfield, and Gallimore helped to organize a Citizens' Committee aimed at building on the earlier efforts of black ministers, getting out the black vote, and backing a black candidate for the Board of Aldermen. The Reverend Edward Gholson, a strong TWOC supporter from the start, agreed to run. Because so few African Americans were registered, Gholson stood no chance of beating his white opponents. But victory was not the point; his candidacy was intended both to continue the struggle against disfranchisement and to demonstrate that the union could be at the forefront of that struggle. The last-minute candidacy of Dr. H. T. Allen, sponsored by the Civic League on Negro Affairs, complicated the process, and neither man garnered enough votes to defeat the white candidates. Still, their willingness to step forward was a portent of political initiatives to come.[51]

The Volunteer Service Club, the protest against peonage, the Wellman defense, and the Gholson candidacy were all aimed at the political and economic mobilization of black workers. But almost from the start, Koger had begun to make contacts with union-minded whites as well, particularly those who had been active in earlier AFL drives. Koger enlisted the aid of the North Carolina CIO director, E. L. Sandefur, who was a resident of Winston-Salem and a former AFL official. Sandefur wrote to Clark Sheppard and other former TWIU leaders asking them to lend support to the CIO drive. When Frank Hargrove replaced Koger as chairman of the TWOC in January 1943, part of his responsibility was to intensify this effort.[52]

Born and raised in Arkansas, Hargrove had become involved in the labor movement in Nashville, where he and Ed McCrea organized a union at the tool handle factory where they worked. "We learned our trade unionism together," McCrea recalled. "We organized the first state CIO Council. I had enough influence to get UCAPAWA to put him on as an organizer in Memphis." Hargrove also worked for a brief time with William DeBerry in Memphis before coming to Winston-Salem.[53]

One of Hargrove's first contacts was with Crawford Shelton, a white TWIU activist. "The AF of L had tried, and tried, and tried to organize and they couldn't," Shelton remembered. After the TWIU's failure to win an NLRB election, Shelton sought out the CIO. "I called E. L. Sandefur and he brought [Hargrove] up to my house one night. Never had much to say. He left and I told my wife, I says, 'If they gonna put him in as an organizer, we'll never go nowhere.' Next day he come by his self. It wasn't the same man. He come and meant business and they went right at it." Part of Hargrove's reticence involved the TWOC's distrust of Sandefur, who, at least to local tobacco workers, seemed to be more concerned with his social standing in the white community than with organizing workers. This was the first but not the last sign of tension between UCAPAWA and the state CIO.[54]

Black and white TWOC members met separately during the organizing campaign, but Hargrove reported regularly to the Volunteer Service Committee on his contacts with Clark Sheppard, Crawford Shelton, and the others. At the time, Theodosia Simpson felt optimistic about the prospects of building an interracial union. "We really thought we were going to be able to do it. Knowing that we had strength in the stemmeries, we felt sure that Sheppard and Shelton were going to be able to do more than what they were really able to do at Number 12. We hoped that if we got a good showing of white workers from the cigarette plants, it would have been an easy matter to get the black cigarette plants to come over."[55]

By May of 1943, the prospects at Reynolds looked promising enough for UCAPAWA president Donald Henderson to come to Winston-Salem to launch an intensive organizing drive. On Sunday, May 30, the TWOC held its largest meeting to date, an interracial victory rally at the Mt. Calvary Holiness Church. UCAPAWA vice president Owen Whitfield spoke to more than 350 workers about the need to maintain interracial unity in the war against fascism and stressed the vital role the CIO played in making the Four Freedoms—freedom of speech, freedom of worship, freedom from want, and freedom from fear—a reality for blacks. Local representatives of the Office of Price Administration and the U.S. Employment Service shared the platform with the Soul Stirring Gospel Singers.[56]

As spring gave way to summer, the TWOC still lacked anything like the critical mass needed to put serious pressure on the company. But the UCAPAWA organizers and the small group of rank-and-file workers they had recruited were slowly making headway. Membership had reached the point at which it was possible to establish informal workers' committees in some plants and departments. To increase communication and highlight specific grievances, the TWOC began putting out a shop paper. "There was no discouragement," Robert Black remembered, "because most of the members of this Volunteer Committee recognized what a tough job lay ahead."[57]

By the summer of 1943, the transformations wrought by the Depression and the New Deal had combined with the militancy of organized labor and political radicals to create a national climate increasingly supportive of working-class organization. The interventions of federal agencies on the side of workers and minority groups, limited as they were, had tempered the power of local elites. Taken together, these developments had enhanced black workers' political leverage, even as the patriotic egalitarianism unleashed by the government's wartime propaganda machine called into question the legitimacy of segregation and provided them with a moral justification for action.[58]

Meanwhile, the war had pulled the United States out of the doldrums of a decade-long depression. The economy was booming, in the South as in the rest of the nation. Black workers, helped by the economic upswing, the imposition of a minimum wage, and overtime at factories that were running around the clock, enjoyed a higher standard of living than most had ever known. Labor shortages and new jobs in war plants gave them unprecedented confidence.

Critical to the TWOC's chances were the thousands of African Americans whose personal experiences in the factory and in the community predisposed them to rebel against the company's policies. Individuals, of course, experienced the deprivations and degradations of life under Jim Crow in unique ways, and they attributed their misfortunes to a combination of factors, ranging from their own failings to the greed of their employers. But most African Americans saw the society in which they lived as essentially unjust and, at the end of the 1930s, many believed that they had a right and duty to resist those injustices. These convictions had deep roots in African American history and culture. But the social learning that had occurred in Winston-Salem over the previous decades placed a special stamp on how these particular men and women thought, how they behaved, and how they felt about the possibilities for change. Their classrooms were the workplace, neighborhood, home, church, and social clubs; their teachers were family, friends, bosses, AFL organizers, and, for the past two years, the idealistic, hard-driving paladins representing the CIO.

Winston-Salem's black community stood at its peak of organizational readiness. More than five decades of sustained population growth had produced one of the most concentrated urban black populations in the South. Urbanization had created deplorable living conditions for many people, but it also encouraged the dense social networks necessary for collective action. More black men and women had entered the industrial workforce than ever before—albeit at jobs that paid little and offered few chances for advancement—thus limiting the dependency and insecurity that could flow from domestic and casual labor. Reynolds's consolidation of its manufacturing operations in downtown Winston-Salem intensified working-class cohesion. Numerous religious, educational, civic, and social institutions (many of which had counted workers as leaders) had been sniping at Jim Crow for years and, in the process, cultivating their members' political skills. The TWOC's efforts had heightened the community's indignation at racial injustice and alerted people to the possibilities for change.

The black community as a whole, moreover, was less internally divided than most, both because of segregation, which weighed on all alike, and because of the extent and nature of industrialization, which drew such large numbers of blacks into the blue-collar working class. There were fault lines aplenty, and political solidarity would have to be created and re-created, never simply assumed. Yet the nature of the churches, where the preachers themselves were often tobacco workers, and the demographics of the city, which meant that the black middle class depended heavily on a working-class constituency, ensured that working-class voices would resonate more powerfully than in most southern communities.[59]

The position of women contributed to possibilities for collective action. The availability of factory jobs enhanced women's ability to support themselves and to raise families on their own, as well as to contribute to the family wage economy and to community life. Black women, moreover, were more likely to graduate from high school than black men, and by the 1940s, Winston-Salem was home to a cohort of self-supporting, self-confident, sophisticated working-class women confined to factory work but ready to grasp the new opportunities opened by the war. The large proportion of women in the tobacco plants ensured that, under the right circumstances, the leadership styles of such women would reinforce the connections among community, workplace, and union that could transform a union organizing campaign into a social movement.

Neither the window of opportunity opened by World War II nor the presence of thousands of disaffected black workers was sufficient to spark a rebellion. Some organizational structure had to link the aspirations of individuals with the potential for social action. In Winston-Salem the TWOC served as the incubator of protest. The movement had started when a small but critical group of workers, aided by a few organizers and with the backing of a national union, had imagined that they, along with others, could wrest a more equitable share of wealth and power from the mighty Reynolds Tobacco Company. This talented and committed group of rank-and-file leaders had educated themselves in the principles of trade unionism and had acquired a bag of analytic tools—a hybridized race and class analysis based on Marxist, Afro-Christian, anticolonialist, and social democratic thought—that helped them to understand the world they sought to change. Although their base remained small, the actions and examples of these leaders influenced thousands of others whose perspectives and structural situation disposed them to support the union movement. The TWOC had transformed an opportunity into a possibility through painstaking one-on-one recruitment combined with public challenges to the status quo.[60]

There were, to be sure, numerous reasons to doubt the TWOC's chance of success. Workers could expect the support of the black community, yet there were sectors of the black middle class who had long been skeptical of unions and who were deeply committed to strategies of race solidarity, uplift, and negotiation. Although a small contingent of white workers had embraced the CIO, the limited participation of whites certainly undermined the union's potential. Still, the size and strategic placement of the black workforce gave unionists the power to confront the company even without broad white support. Reynolds Tobacco Company remained a formidable foe, having staved off every attempt at labor organization during the preceding twenty years. But the times seemed ripe for insurgency, and workers had organized to grasp the opportunity open to them. On June 17, 1943, Theodosia Simpson and the 200 women in Plant Number 65 stopped work, striking the match that started the flame.

CHAPTER SEVEN

A Dream Come True

On June 23, 1943, a committee of Reynolds workers prepared to sit down with management in the presence of a member of the U.S. Conciliation Service to voice complaints that for years had gone unheard. Robert Black had looked forward to this moment for a long, long time. "There was a pool room right on the corner opposite the Reynolds main office," he remembered. "They had a railing that people called the 'buzzard's roost.' I'd go there Saturday mornings and sit on that rail and just look up from the ground level to the top of the Reynolds Building. I said to myself many times, 'I want to live to see a day when something will come to Winston-Salem that will enable us to bring that big giant down to earth, down on a level with the workers.' It looked impossible that we would ever be able to do it. [After we built the union] I told people that instead of them feeling that I had done something to help them, they had helped me make a dream come true."[1]

To end the walkout, Black and John Whitaker had reached an agreement promising to "cooperate fully" in bringing about a settlement of differences that would be "mutually satisfactory to both sides." Whitaker had signed reluctantly and belatedly, but he had signed. Now it was Wednesday morning and time for those negotiations to begin. Had the giant really come down to earth? Would management sit at the bargaining table "on a level with the workers"? Had a dream come true?

Negotiation

The heat and humidity of the previous few weeks showed no signs of abating that day. Throughout dozens of plants the foremen and superintendents stood by, ready to begin operations. At 7:30 A.M. the whistle blew. It was time to start work. The stemmeries had been closed since Friday, so the manufacturing departments had no tobacco to process, leaving most white workers idle for the day. In the stemmeries it was business as usual—the pungent smell of tobacco, the noise, heat, and dust. Outwardly, nothing in the plant had changed. But the thousands of black workers who only a week before had dared not mention the word "union" now had an air of defiance about them. The foremen had little to say. Word had come from the Reynolds Building to "take it easy." Theodosia Simpson remembered the atmosphere in Number 65. "The people didn't try to take advantage of what was happening by not working. Actually I think the guy got better work from the people after he lightened up. The boxes weren't as heavy. One girl who had been in the union all along told me she tried him out. She wasn't sick, but she told him she had to go to the nurse. 'By all means go,' he said. The nurse kept her down there a long time. 'How do you feel now? Do you think you're able to work?' 'No, I just don't feel like working.' 'Well, go home.' "[2]

While everyone else waited to see what would happen, the workers' committee prepared for its meeting with management. Robert Black had warned Whitaker the previous day that the TWOC was "not going to play around with the company. We're going to start ironing out these grievances and we expect the company to bargain in good faith. If there's any foot dragging, we're going to pull those workers out of the plant." But John Whitaker remained a reluctant negotiator. In the past, he had generally refused to meet with groups of workers, preferring one-on-one discussions with disgruntled employees. And he continued to insist that the company's policies were fair and just. Robert Black remembered pressing the point in the discussions that ended the walkout. " 'Mr. Whitaker, you continue to tell the members of our committee that these conditions doesn't exist in the plants, that you know your supervisors, you know that no male foreman goes into a rest room and opens the door of a woman's rest facility and calls them by name.' I said, 'Now I'll tell you what. Those conditions exist out there, and you say if they do you want to correct them. So why wait until there has been an election? Let's go to work on these things now.' "[3]

Albert Cuthrell operated the Number 3 elevator in the Reynolds Building, the company headquarters in downtown Winston-Salem. One of a handful of black men who represented the company to the public, he had been at that post since the building opened in 1929, and he knew the name, floor, and office number of virtually everyone who worked there. He had had few black riders during those years, so he must have been astonished when ninety members of the workers' committee filled the lobby shortly before 11:00 A.M. The committee had expanded almost threefold overnight as rank-and-file leaders eagerly came forward and workers in virtually every department elected representatives to present their grievances.[4]

The lobby radiated the wealth and self-confidence of a hugely successful corporation. The European marble and polished brass that dominated the art deco interior contrasted sharply with the wood frames and tin roofs of workers' homes. But this aura of power did not intimidate committee members. Velma Hopkins, with the bravado that characterized all her confrontations with management, remembered the disturbance their presence in the tenth-floor conference room caused: "All of us went in there and were sitting in those big black chairs and the bosses got scared and run. They were afraid of black people. Their nerves could not allow them to meet with more than ten black people without an attorney." Such a boisterous invasion of the company's inner sanctum testified to the workers' soaring confidence even as it upset the conventions of Jim Crow.[5]

Commissioner Goodrick announced that the committee was too large for meaningful discussions, so during the lunch break the workers adjourned to the Reverend Frank O'Neal's Union Mission Holy Church and winnowed their number down to forty. By the time they returned, management had moved the gathering from company headquarters to the tin box plant; the next morning, it was moved to the tinfoil plant. Reynolds had closed both facilities because of shortages of metal during the war. The company cited lack of adequate space as the reason for the moves, but union members suspected the company had other motives. "Most of us could come by the overpasses [that connected the buildings]," Robert Black observed. "By holding these meetings in this tinfoil plant, the public wouldn't see the negotiating committee entering the company's premises. The company was embarrassed. A group of workers was forcing the big R. J. Reynolds Tobacco Company to enter into grievance negotiations."[6]

The streets of downtown Winston-Salem served as a large public theater. Everyone had a role to play, from the corporate executives who made a point of walking to work each morning to the shoeshine boys who set up business in the same location day after day. People noticed anything out of the ordinary. If startling enough, the disruption of routine could become a topic of communitywide conversation. The walkouts of the previous week had already interrupted the predictable rhythms of daily activity; the sight of black workers gathering outside the Reynolds Building each morning could only further damage the company's standing in the community's eyes. Reynolds had real clout, but the company's domination of local affairs was based partly on its seeming invincibility.

Confusion, caused partly by the move from place to place and partly by an unexpected break in the workers' ranks, marked the first day's session. Frank O'Neal described what happened when representatives began to talk about conditions in their departments. "We finally got to a preacher, Reverend Hairston. He got up and said, 'Gentlemen, I'm going to tell you about my department. We don't have no grievances. We get along just fine.'" The workers were "incensed," O'Neal recalled. "Those people was touching each other and looking at each other and saying, 'Man, what you want to say that for.'" As soon as the meeting concluded, Robert Black, Velma Hopkins, Theodosia Simpson, and Eddie Gallimore rushed over to the Number 256 Press Room to find out whether Aquilla Hairston really represented the men there. The press room workers said they had not elected Hairston, but rather John Mitchell, to whom they had given a long list of grievances.[7]

It is difficult to say what Hairston intended by his actions. Although not a TWOC member at the time, he was familiar with the organizing drive and had been present at some of the meetings in Holy Trinity Baptist Church where William DeBerry spoke. He claimed to have been selected by workers in Number 256. But during the process of reducing the committee, Robert Black recalled, "several questioned Hairston's right to be on the committee at which time Hairston replied by saying 'he was on the committee at the request of Mr. Whitaker—and Mr. Whitaker had said for him to get on the committee and stay there.'" Hairston may well have been one of John Whitaker's "plants" in the factory.[8]

Whatever his motives, Hairston's statements brought down a storm of opposition. After all, a major goal of the union was to put an end to the system of favoritism that Hairston seemed to represent. For years, a few black workers had benefited from the personal bonds they had established with supervisors and managers. As picks and spies, they secured a modicum of protection against the arbitrariness of factory life. But organization threatened to deprive them of special privileges, giving all workers the security that in the past only a few could enjoy.

According to an affidavit given by Hairston a year later, the men in Number 256 confronted him the next morning. "Before work started," Hairston recounted, "a group of twenty-five or thirty workers gathered around me and started talking about what someone had said I had said at a previous committee meeting. The statements were untrue and I told them so but they threatened to beat me to death, kill me and many other threats of physical violence. . . . The threats became so real that I quit work about eight or eight thirty that morning." Frank O'Neal confirmed that the workers meant business. "Those Negroes went and got their guns and went over to his house and shot all through the windows. Reynolds had to get him out of town. They were going to kill him. He got out of town for about four weeks. He was assistant pastor of Velma Hopkins' church. When he came back they told him, 'No sir, you're not coming back here. We don't want a traitor like you.'" Group sanctions against racial betrayal, even violent ones, were by no means unusual in the polarized environment of the Jim Crow South. The rigid racial and class segregation that was the basis of that world could tolerate few apostates.[9]

With Hairston gone, the committee finally got down to work. On Thursday morning, company representatives and conciliators took their seats behind a table at the front of a room in the tinfoil plant. Surrounding them in a semicircle sat the workers' committee. Once again male leaders came to the fore, as thirty-two men and six women represented the thousands of black workers at Reynolds. Some were chosen because of their long association with the TWOC; they had been the first to join and to spread the idea of unionization to others. Other members of the committee had not been active in the organizing campaign but were "natural leaders" who had won the respect and trust of their fellow workers long before. From this committee would come many of the key figures in the union.[10]

The Reverend Carnell Bonaparte, an employee in the Turkish leaf division, offered the benediction, and Commissioner Goodrick and North Carolina labor commissioner Frank Crane provided a structure for the discussion. One by one, committee members proceeded to explain the problems in their departments. It was no easy task. Some complaints grew out of the recent speed-up, but many had persisted for years. A few petitioners sought mercy for a particular employee (a worker who had lost a hand in the Number 8 Machine Room wanted "a job where he is better fitted"), but most raised concerns that were widely felt. A lifetime of emotion came out in each report. The picture of life in the factories that emerged stood in sharp contrast to the one painted by company executives.[11]

Not surprisingly, wages and working conditions dominated the agenda. How much were people to be paid? How long and how hard would they have to work? What would be done about illness and injuries? And what was to be the nature of the supervision? These were the stock-in-trade issues of trade unionism. But class-based dissatisfactions were compounded and occasionally fused with race- and gender-based grievances. Women's demands for privacy, for instance, cut as deep as any bread-and-butter request.[12]

Money was one issue everyone had in common, and the conference first took up the issue of wage adjustments. In every department workers wanted more compensation for their labor. Most representatives called for a seventy-five-cent minimum wage (the federally mandated minimum stood at forty cents), to be applied regardless of position and length of service. The amount of the increase indicated not only the workers' feelings that they were grossly underpaid, but also their opposition to the company's policy of paying employees doing the same job at different rates. Generally wage rates did not reflect any measurable difference in the abilities or performance of workers but were used by the foremen to reward cooperation and maintain divisions between workers. Standardization would not only be fair, it would also take power away from the foremen and promote unity among the workers.

As galling as low wages was the company's practice of classifying almost all black workers as unskilled labor. The tradition had tangled roots, reflecting both an economic calculus and a social prejudice, and had little to do with the experience and training needed to perform most jobs. The mores of Jim Crow dictated that black workers occupy the bottom rungs of the occupational ladder. To admit that blacks were in fact skilled workers would upset the racial hierarchies that helped keep white and black workers apart. When the tobacco manufacturing industry emerged in the late nineteenth century, employers had not considered blacks capable of working with machines. In fact, many of the skilled positions in the tobacco industry had long been held by blacks. But the practice of typing jobs by race had solidified as whites came into the industry in increasing numbers and were channeled by management into the "skilled" positions.

Labeling the work blacks did as "unskilled" also helped to justify the low wages the company paid its black workforce. Equating the skills required by factory jobs with those associated with household and agricultural labor kept the wages of all black workers at the bottom of the scale. Since blacks were excluded from textile work as well as from most craft, clerical, and professional opportunities, they could not use mobility within the labor market to bargain for higher wages on the farm or in private homes, public laundries, or factories.[13]

Two groups voiced particular displeasure at the lack of skilled designations for black workers. Stemming machine operators resented the fact that they had not been upgraded when the technology of stemming changed in the mid-1930s. The white women who ran the cigarette-making machines had long been classified as skilled workers, so why not black women who also operated machinery? Theodosia Simpson brought this request from every stemmery. An equally obvious case of discrimination involved the men who made chewing tobacco. These workers could trace their craft back to colonial times, and the twists and lumps they made required a speed and dexterity that few people possessed. They too asked to be classified as skilled workers.

In a few instances, workers directly challenged blatant racial discrimination.

Lum Bell and his fellow "colored firemen" requested wages equal to those of whites who performed the same job. Robert Parker and the men in Numbers 8 and 256 Press Rooms demanded "consideration for colored workers in granting promotions." But for most jobs, segregation by race was so rigid and so deeply entrenched that black workers sought only improvements in the race-typed positions they already held, not full integration on the factory floor. To ask for more was not only beyond the bounds of the possible, it would also doom any hope of attracting white workers to the union.[14]

On the second day of negotiations, representatives turned to working conditions. A frequent complaint involved the company's callous attitude toward workers' health. With the death of James McCardell, the issue had become more urgent than ever. Theodosia Simpson recalled the existing policy. There was a nurse in each plant, and "if you had a headache, she had aspirin. If it was something more than that you had to go to her to allow you to go home or see the company doctor. You were never sick as far as they were concerned." "I had a kidney ailment," Simpson continued. "And I went to the nurse and she sent me over to the medical department in the big office. The first thing they wanted to do was get blood. You had to go to the company and get a blood test like you had syphilis or some kind of venereal disease. I told them that I had already been to my doctor and I had kidney stones. No, they're going to get this blood. I've got bad veins. It takes a good person to draw blood from me. She stuck me about nine times until my arm was hurting so bad. When she finally did get blood she was looking away talking and it dripped all over the floor. I wouldn't let her stick me no more. So I went to my doctor that same evening and he wrote these letters and from then on I didn't have to go back up there. If I'd go to the nurse and say I was sick, I got to go home. You had to do things like that. They didn't care."[15]

The frequent complaints about the white nurses spoke to the formidable barriers to gender solidarity that racism created in the plant. White women in their white, starched uniforms were everything that black women were not. They were professionals; they had the respect of white men. When Ruby Jones had a run-in with her foreman and he demanded to know what she expected of him, she replied, "I want your respect. That's all I ask. I want you to be treating me like the nurse, because you don't know nothing about me but a decent woman." The culture of professionalization, as well as the split image that associated black women with disease and promiscuity, encouraged white nurses to identify more with the company than with the workers and to treat blacks, male and female, with a striking lack of regard.[16]

Some demands seemed so reasonable that the company made immediate changes in its policies. Willie Grier pointed out that requiring all handlers to report to work at 5:00 A.M. to open the hogsheads so that tobacco would be ready when the rest of the workers arrived at 7:30 meant that many workers had to take cabs rather than the bus to work, which ate up a large chunk of that day's pay. Reynolds agreed to add extra workers so that those in this situation could come in a half-hour later. Frank Patterson, who worked in the Truck and Storage Department, pointed out another hardship that could be easily corrected. Since trucks usually had only one seat, and most truck drivers were white, blacks rode in the back of the truck. For Patterson and the men who worked with him that was a fact of life; what they found intolerable was that they had to ride in the open even in the rain. In response to their complaint, the company eventually added covers to the backs of the trucks. Such changes did nothing to erase racial boundaries, but they did signal a concession to African Americans' desire to be treated with at least a minimum of consideration.[17]

Many grievances revolved around the women's restrooms. These areas differed from factory to factory, but most simply provided a hanger for a change of clothes and a few toilets. Almost everyone wanted larger areas for dressing. At the beginning and end of the shift, women had to wait in line or crowd into the closet-like spaces. Privacy, however, was the main issue. Women on the fifth floor in Number 43 asked to "be further away from men." In Number 256 they demanded curtains on the dressing room windows. "The foremen would come in the dressing room where the women were," Ruby Jones remembered. "Come in there, and you had your clothes off. Come in the toilet!" Women in every department demanded an end to such insults.[18]

Men and women alike wanted freedom from the petty rules through which the company tried to control their every move. Frank O'Neal's requests were typical: "Employees should be granted the privilege of talking to others when necessary." "Every worker wants to take Doctor's prescribed medicine without first going to the Company nurse." "Every worker wants to be excused or allowed to go the lavatory when necessary."[19]

On Friday afternoon the workers' committee completed the presentation of its grievances, and the conference adjourned for the weekend. Over two-and-a-half days, the workers had calmly and methodically challenged Reynolds's personnel policies. Although they had not directly questioned the race and gender segregation that was at the heart of so many of their problems, they left no doubt about the depth of their dissatisfaction with the conditions under which they labored.

On Monday company officials got a chance to respond. Couching his appeal in the language of a shared Protestant faith (with flourishes of industrial relations jargon), John Whitaker spent three-quarters of an hour trying to counter the image of factory life presented by the workers and reassert a perspective in which workers identified with the company and looked to management to resolve problems through personal—and paternalistic—means. "As I see it," he began, "the handling of grievances is a matter of common sense. Confidence and cooperation must be inspired. Goodwill and respect must be inspired. They cannot be compelled. So if there is any bitterness or ill will or hatred in your hearts drive it out— get rid of it—as Reverend Bonaparte petitioned in his prayer this morning." He asked that workers "always remember that whatever helps the Company helps you and whatever hurts the Company hurts you. We are one big family trying to stay ahead of our competitors who are always trying to sell our customers a better plug, or a better cigarette, or a better smoking tobacco."[20]

The company, Whitaker continued, had obligations to three groups of people: customers, employees, and stockholders. Management's task was to see to the details of day-to-day operations and ensure the well-being and satisfaction of each group. The company had introduced a variety of services to its employees over the years, and Whitaker claimed that it paid the best wages in the industry. "This proves to you—it must prove to you—a genuine wholehearted interest on the part of the Company in its employees; a desire on the part of the Company to make the lives of its employees more secure."[21]

In addition to material benefits, the company had concerned itself with "mental wages." Whitaker repeated for the committee some remarks he had made to his supervisors a few months before.

> For most employees an occasional pat on the back is essential to bring out the best that's in him. You might call these pats on the back mental wages. . . . Cash wages keep the body and soul together—yes—but mental wages spur the worker on, keeps him on his toes, makes him proud of his job, puts a smile where a frown was and generally lifts him a little higher in his efforts to please.
> . . . Let us realize that the human side of business is becoming increasingly important each day. . . . I believe that successful management from "now on out"— to use a Negro expression—is going to depend more and more upon the management of men.

These observations, Whitaker concluded, "show the attitude of management in the matter of human relations, and it is management's desire that these points be carried out by its supervisory forces."[22]

"Nobody believed that," Theodosia Simpson remembered. "If he sent that memorandum or if he talked to his foremen like that he should have seen that it was done or got rid of the foremen. We all realized that the only reason we were there was to make a profit for the company and they were going to do everything they could to dog us and get more." A devoted churchgoer herself, Simpson was especially annoyed by Whitaker's use of the language of Christian benevolence. "Like so many people, black folks believe in God, and they believe in goodwill. They believed at that time in trying to get along. That's the point Whitaker tried to drive home to us. He tried to appeal to that side of us more than sitting down and saying, 'Well, this is what we'll give you and this is what we won't give you.' He entered all this religious stuff every chance he got. Whitaker was prejudiced and tried to cover it up with this religious stuff. The foremen just didn't give a damn. Knowing Whitaker, it's hard to determine whether he actually knew this stuff or they were keeping it away from him. To hear him talk you would think he was God's right hand. He intended to treat everybody right. There was no wrong in him. But to go back into the plant and see what was going on, you wondered."[23]

In the end, Whitaker neither confirmed nor denied the existence of the hundreds of grievances painstakingly detailed by the workers' committee. He simply promised to have management "study and analyze" their complaints. Rather than dirty his hands with the mess of human conflict, he recited an unconvincing litany about the company's "sincere, genuine, whole-hearted, and everyday interest" in its employees.[24]

By the time the negotiations concluded, the workers' initial optimism had been tempered with the recognition that until they had a legally recognized union, the company was not going to give much ground. Still, the meetings with management represented a psychological and rhetorical victory. After all, the company had made some concessions. Reynolds had been forced to justify itself and acknowledge the humanity of its black workers. And a federal conciliator had been there, writing down all the grievances, witnessing the workers' version of life at Reynolds.[25]

Unionists' morale got a boost a few days later when a committee of white workers chaired by Clark Sheppard, a former TWIU member and now a TWOC supporter, presented their grievances to the company. The committee had been hastily assembled by the union to show the company that whites also had complaints and that the TWOC was an interracial organization. Although the white workers' grievances paled in numbers or seriousness to the hundreds of complaints by blacks, they went to the heart of injustices that affected all workers in the plants and were strategically designed to draw more white workers into the union. The committee championed the right of newly hired workers to a speedy probationary period, after which they would be paid the going wage. Like many manufacturers, Reynolds often kept new employees, black and white, in a state of limbo for months, only to dismiss them and hire a fresh contingent of workers. In addition, the committee charged that these newly hired employees were given work assignments that should be filled by long-time employees. Like blacks, white committee members wanted a hiring and job assignment system governed by seniority, not the caprice of foremen and superintendents.[26]

As the workers' committees concluded their meetings with the company, UCAPAWA formally requested an NLRB election. Almost immediately the TWIU-AFL announced the beginning of an "intensive organizing drive" at the Reynolds plant and asked to be included on the ballot. Embarrassed by UCAPAWA's success, AFL president William Green sent one of his top aides to direct the campaign and poured thousands of dollars and dozens of organizers into the Twin City. The TWIU could count on the remnants of the local it had established in 1939, but many of the most dedicated workers had already switched to UCAPAWA. With thousands of blacks in the CIO union, the AFL had a tough road ahead.[27]

The TWIU strategy became clear as the company and the unions began jockeying over the terms of an election. Agreement on an appropriate bargaining unit proved the major sticking point. Controversies over the definition of bargaining units for NLRB elections had erupted periodically since the inception of the Wagner Act. During congressional debates on the legislation, supporters insisted that employers, employees, and unions were too self-interested to make such decisions and that an impartial agency should act in the best interest of the majority of workers. The AFL opposed giving the NLRB responsibility in this area, preferring instead to allow unions or groups of workers who petitioned the board for elections to define their own bargaining units. This strategy was in keeping with the craft orientation of most AFL affiliates. The CIO, based on the principle of industrial unionism, supported units that encompassed all workers and preferred that the composition of these units be determined by the NLRB.[28]

After the passage of the Wagner Act, NLRB members continued to debate the law's intent. Did the board have the authority to shape the bargaining unit in order to achieve an ideal system of industrial relations, or should it, as one member argued, follow "established custom and practice as embodied in collective bargaining agreements"? If the board did have such power, should it be used to "establish collective bargaining on the widest possible basis," or should smaller groups of workers have the right to "self-determination"? By 1943, changes in the NLRB's membership produced a solution whereby customary practice prevailed in situations where collective bargaining already existed; in other cases, the board followed what seemed to be the desire of the majority of the workers.[29]

In 1943, as in 1941, the TWIU wrote off the stemmeries and requested a single bargaining unit limited to workers in the cigarette factories. The TWOC, on the other hand, asked that all production workers—black and white—be included in a single bargaining unit. The company argued for two separate bargaining units, one for prefabrication workers, most of whom were black, and another for manufacturing workers, a small majority of whom were white.[30]

This controversy posed an immediate threat to hopes for a speedy election. The NLRB field examiner advised the TWOC that a decision through normal channels could take from six to eight months. Union organizers knew that some workers, frustrated by meetings with the company that had produced few tangible results, were threatening another walkout. Fearing that another strike would jeopardize its whole campaign, the TWOC consented to the company's proposal in return for the guarantee of an early election. The AFL joined in the agreement. The NLRB chose August 3 and 4 for the vote. Unit I was to consist of all employees engaged in prefabrication of leaf tobacco. Unit II would include all manufacturing workers. The stage was set for one of the most hotly contested NLRB elections of the 1940s.[31]

A War of Words

Not since the late nineteenth century had there been such an open public challenge to the status quo in Winston-Salem. Protests during the intervening years had been short-lived. No counterforce was able to stimulate widespread public discussion about the social, political, and economic hierarchies that had solidified in Winston-Salem after the turn of the century. The rapid organization of Reynolds workers in 1943 ended that uneasy quiet. For the next seven years, Winston-Salem witnessed an open, vigorous, and often acrimonious debate about the merit and meaning of class and racial (and sometimes gender) arrangements. In the newspapers, on street corners, on the radio, and in homes throughout the city, residents listened to the contending parties, considered the issues, and took sides. Charges of Communist domination commingled with threats of racial violence and assertions of working-class solidarity. The dialogue was unrestrained and unpredictable. "We never knew what to expect in the next morning's *Journal*," remembered Theodosia Simpson. "We'd get up real early to find the newspaper and see what was in there."[32]

The conflict between the company and the union and the war of words that accompanied it exposed deep-seated tensions within Winston-Salem and across the South. Both sides aimed to sway public opinion, and their pronouncements therefore must be carefully interpreted; at stake were the hearts and minds of thousands of loyalists as well as numerous fence sitters. Still, the novelty of public conversations about the rights and responsibilities of black workers in this segregated company town, and the suddenness and intensity of the engagement, imparted a rare frankness and spontaneity to the debate.

The management of Reynolds Tobacco Company and the workers in the TWOC were the principal players in this emerging drama, but dozens of groups and individuals played supporting roles. The company maintained that it was a fair and even generous employer that paid prevailing wages and had voluntarily established a generous benefits program. Executives insisted that there was no justification for strikes, negotiations, or organization because they could be trusted to keep the best interests of their employees as well as their stockholders in mind. Union supporters, on the other hand, portrayed themselves as the victims of a greedy, ruthless corporation that dominated the life of the community, rewarded its officers and stockholders handsomely, and played a major role in institutionalizing white supremacy.

From the start, the TWIU directed its attacks against the CIO, not the company, and fashioned its appeal to whites, not blacks. Calling itself the "only real tobacco workers' union," the AFL affiliate painted the TWOC as an organization of "Bean Pickers, Cucumber Growers, and Cotton Planters," a pejorative reference to UCA-PAWA's beginnings among agricultural workers. Claiming the allegiance of three-quarters of the company's white workers, the TWIU made little attempt to lure black supporters. Instead, it admonished black workers for "being misled, misguided, and being made victims of vicious propaganda, false rumor and deliberate misrepresentation." AFL organizers claimed that the CIO had won black workers' allegiance by promising "social equality in Winston-Salem," the replacement of "white foremen with colored foremen," and "a new world for the colored worker." Such efforts "to change the economic, political or religious life of a community" were "Pipe Dreams," the TWIU claimed, and "would create racial hatred, confusion and chaos." If black workers wanted to pursue their interests as workers rather than the will-o'-the-wisp of social equality, TWIU leaflets argued, they should abandon the CIO and join with the white workers in the AFL.[33]

The TWIU developed a racially divisive campaign in hopes of gaining the support of white workers and possibly winning the election in Unit II. The emerging rivalry between the two unions also contributed to the vehemence of the TWIU's attacks. The TWIU did have strong claims to being the one union in the country exclusively devoted to organizing tobacco workers. Since the late nineteenth century it had represented thousands of workers at dozens of tobacco firms, including Reynolds for a short time after World War I. But the union's record in Winston-Salem was decidedly uneven. Black workers in particular had reason to distrust the AFL affiliate. Not only had the TWIU failed to appeal to blacks in its earlier, abortive organizing campaigns, but where it had successfully negotiated contracts—as at Winston-Salem's Brown & Williamson Tobacco Company and Taylor Brothers—it had established segregated locals and denied blacks any voice in union affairs. UCAPAWA, moreover, had begun making inroads among the TWIU's membership nationwide, most recently at plants owned by P. Lorillard in Ohio and American Tobacco Company in Pennsylvania.

But more than jurisdictional jealousy motivated the TWIU's attacks. Many AFL unions felt intense animosity toward the CIO, particularly toward left-led unions such as UCAPAWA, and that animosity grew more bitter every year, as the newer organization increased its membership and power in national affairs. The TWIU also resented UCAPAWA's ability to mobilize thousands of black workers. After all, the AFL had all but written these workers off in earlier campaigns, reasoning that they were too frightened to be a force for organization. Underlying the rivalry between the TWIU and UCAPAWA, moreover, were fundamental differences regarding the goals of organization. While one sought the betterment of wages and working conditions for its members, the other sought that and more, working for the empowerment of unionists in the political and social life of the community as well as in the workplace.[34]

As the time for the election approached, the TWIU played what it thought was its trump card in its campaign to demonize the CIO. "ARE THE COMMUNISTS ATTEMPTING TO ORGANIZE R. J. REYNOLDS CO?" asked an advertisement in the *Winston-Salem Journal*. As evidence that the answer might be yes, organizers pointed to a notice in the *UCAPAWA News* urging members to write to Soviet citizens praising their struggle against fascism. The letter-writing campaign was sponsored by the National Council of American Soviet Friendship. TWOC representatives responded with a list of eminently respectable council sponsors and statements by President Roosevelt and AFL president William Green extending support for the Soviet war effort. "Does this make F.D.R. a Communist?" they asked. "We haven't changed our minds!" the AFL rebutted. "We say the Cannery Workers Union, C.I.O., reeks with advocates of the Communist doctrine. If this be libel—See Us! We invite investigation of the charge." The issue went no further, but another log had been added to a smoldering fire. The Communist question would flare again a few years later, but in the midst of a war in which the Soviet Union was an American ally, the charges had little effect.[35]

Since the union had limited support even among the white workers, and therefore little chance of winning an election, TWIU officials concentrated their efforts, as they had in the past, on organizing the company. They hoped to instill enough fear about the prospects of a CIO victory in the company, the white workers, and the white middle class to force Reynolds to negotiate with the TWIU in the manufacturing departments. "I believe that deep down within the R. J. R. Company," said a TWIU official, "they had rather deal with the Tobacco Workers' International Union than with any other organization." The TWIU had used similar strategies to get union label and closed shop agreements with other tobacco firms. But now, under the provisions of the Wagner Act, the union would have to win an election, and that would require the votes of workers. "UNIONS NOW CONTROL A STRONG MAJORITY!" read one advertisement aimed primarily at undecided white workers. "CHOOSE YOUR SIDE—WHAT WILL IT BE?" In other words, unionization was inevitable; if white workers wanted a voice and if the company wanted to deal with a responsible organization, both had better support the AFL. Whatever the TWIU's motivations, its attacks on the CIO proved a windfall for the company, which had to maintain a low profile before the election in accordance with national labor law.[36]

An even more serious challenge to the unionization effort came from a small but vocal group of "colored leaders." On July 10, six black business and professional men expressed their concern to the *Journal* about the "followers of John L. Lewis and William Green." It did not make sense, they said, to believe that union leaders "are more interested in the welfare of the colored people of Winston-Salem than are the leaders of industry. . . . Everyone . . . knows that every door in the Reynolds Building has always been open to any citizen without regard to race—whether employees or public-spirited individuals—to discuss problems of employment, problems of betterment and progress and uplift." Lauding the company's treatment of black workers, they declared, "We would not speak one word begrudging to members of our race the best possible wages and working conditions. But if we want to be fair and honest about the matter, we will have to admit that the fairest wages and working conditions for us in the entire tobacco industry are to be found in the Reynolds Tobacco Company."[37]

The men who signed this letter represented a cross-section of Winston-Salem's black business and professional elite. Clark Brown had moved to Winston-Salem in the early 1930s after graduating from City College in New York City. He owned a funeral home, was active in the state funeral directors association, and served on the boards of a variety of local social and civic organizations, including the Negro Division of the Community Chest and the Young Negro Democratic Club of Forsyth County. Dr. A. H. Ray, a local physician, acted as medical advisor to the Safe Bus Company and to Winston-Salem State Teachers College. The Reverend A. H. McDaniel, a native of South Carolina, had studied at the University of Chicago and the Hood Theological Seminary in Salisbury. He had come to Winston-Salem in 1933 to pastor the Union Baptist Church. Jack Atkins was the son of Simon Atkins, founder of Winston-Salem State Teachers College; from his position as secretary, he virtually ran the school. He was also the only African American on the local draft board. The Reverend G. J. Thomas headed the Wentz Memorial Congregational Church. N. M. Mock ran a grocery store in the black community.[38]

Recognizing the interconnectedness of life under Jim Crow, these "colored leaders" understood that the workers' challenge threatened the whole structure of race and class relations in the Twin City, and they feared what might result. "Colored employees," they argued, "face more than the problem of collective bargaining. They also face the larger problem of race relations. . . . No formula for solving this problem has yet been found to equal that of good will, friendly understanding, and mutual respect and co-operation between the races. . . . There is no proof that we cannot continue to make progress through that policy." Goodwill had long been the watchword among spokesmen for the black community. Jack Atkins's father, for example, had passed the torch to his sons after a lifetime of winning white support for his endeavors through a skillful blend of flattery and guile. To such men, Winston-Salem, for all its faults, was a haven that provided economic opportunity for aspiring African Americans and an atmosphere of relative racial peace and tolerance. Implicit in their broadside against the union was their fear that black workers were abandoning the prudent counsel of mediators such as themselves and demanding rights rather than relying on the time-tested strategy of elite-led negotiations within the bounds of Jim Crow.[39]

In Winston-Salem, power resided with an especially small network of white men, and they wielded it through highly personalistic channels. Individual power brokers conferred privileges on selected members of an even smaller, and equally tight-knit, black elite. In the city, as in the factory, the white industrialists had their "picks" and "pets" through whom they dispensed charity and favors. They put up money for churches, schools, community centers, parks, and hospitals. In return they obtained information not only about the needs of the black community but also about potential troublemakers. More important, they gained a public show of support for the racial status quo. If successful, UCAPAWA's brand of civil rights unionism posed a fundamental threat to that system of personalism and patronage, in and out of the factory. Direct working-class action not only threatened the tenuous position of race leaders as go-betweens and spokesmen in a carefully calibrated system of racial control, it could also backfire, causing whites to withdraw their support for schools, hospitals, and other agencies serving the black community.[40]

Reynolds workers responded with indignation to the statement of the "colored leaders," and their many letters to the *Journal* suggested that the cleavages within the African American community that had opened with the great migration to the city during and after World War I had been exacerbated and reshaped by the UCAPAWA organizing drive. Mabel Jessup expressed the feelings of many workers:

> How could anyone who does not work in the factory and knows nothing of the conditions under which others work expect to make sense of what workers do?
>
> All that our leaders know is the fact that they get their money from the labor of the colored people of Winston-Salem. They do not have to work from 7:30 A.M. to 5 P.M. for a minimum of 40 cents an hour.
>
> Our leaders can work on the same basis as any other race, in their particular branch of duty or business. They always look clean and refreshed at the end of the hottest day, because they work in very pleasant environments. But the employees in many of the factories work in tobacco dust and by not having adequate facilities for washing themselves in the factories, make very poor and repulsive appearances on the streets and buses at the end of a day's work.
>
> As for the hospital and recreational centers, we deserve them. Have not the colored people of Winston-Salem helped to make R. J. Reynolds Tobacco Company the great manufacturing plant that it is today? Have not many of our people worked long hours for low wages, and for many years before R. J. Reynolds Tobacco Company "used their money for any such humanitarian purposes?"
>
> I have worked in the factory, and all I ask of our leaders is that they obtain a job in one of the factories as a laborer, and work two weeks. Then write what they think.[41]

Jessup demolished the notion of an automatically unified and undifferentiated black community and exposed the lived realities of class distinctions. In the years after disfranchisement, members of the black middle class had been forced to accept what Simon Atkins called "voluntary segregation," invest in institution building, and cultivate the help and protection of powerful white men. Yoking their own success to the progress of the race, they reached out a helping hand to the black masses. Even as they did so, however, black elites elaborated class differences, and they never doubted that those differences—in education, occupation, and deportment—gave them the right and the obligation to lead. Now Mabel Jessup and her coworkers were transforming the meaning of difference, tracing class markers not to individual exertion and free choice but to structural conditions that benefited some at the expense of others. They were also laying claim not to "humanitarian" aid but to the fruits of their own labor and to the right to speak for themselves. "You do not live like us; how could you expect to understand us?" Jessup asked. By emphasizing the class lines that white supremacists refused to acknowledge but that were well understood within the black community, Jessup stripped her "betters" of a claim to leadership based on the natural solidarity of caste. One group of union members put the matter even more boldly: "We feel that we are the leaders instead of you."[42]

Such a statement would have been unthinkable—or at least unprintable—in Simon Atkins's day. As the fate of the trade union movement and the fate of the black freedom movement became increasingly entwined, however, new definitions of "leadership" emerged and new leaders stepped to the fore. These new leaders came, most significantly, from what Atkins had called the "submerged element," the vast army of the working poor. But UCAPAWA was part of a larger movement that included significant sectors of the black middle class as well. These men and women believed wholeheartedly in unionization as the key to overcoming black poverty and powerlessness or saw the CIO as a radical front that would afford them opportunities to carve out new leadership strategies behind the lines.[43]

The peculiarities of Jim Crow thus encouraged entrenched leaders to defend the racial status quo while simultaneously ensuring that new leaders and new strategies could emerge with changes in the political terrain. Because they lacked access to capital, even black elites built their lives on a precarious material base. The middle class of teachers, nurses, clerks, part-time ministers, and small business owners barely eked out a living, and they pivoted between the elites and the poor they served and from whom they had often emerged. Moreover, the line between the respectable working class and the middle and upper classes was always more porous in the black community than it was among whites. This nebulousness could cut two ways. Black opponents of unionization in Winston-Salem refused to acknowledge the class basis of workers' protest, insisting that workers' aspirations be subsumed under the larger problem of race relations. Members of the black middle class who were less directly dependent on whites and had a weaker material stake in the status quo, on the other hand, linked their fate to the fortunes of the poor. From the moment UCAPAWA organizers arrived in Winston-Salem, they looked not only to workers but also to such possible allies within the black middle class.[44]

Foremost among these union allies were three groups of younger ministers. The first consisted of men such as Frank O'Neal of the Union Mission Holy Church, who pastored small churches in poor neighborhoods while working in the tobacco plants themselves. The second was made up of dissenters such as Edward Gholson of the Holy Trinity Baptist Church, who held full-time positions in larger, mainstream churches with congregations that included large numbers of tobacco workers. The third group had recently arrived in the city and had no ties to the Old Guard and no allegiance to what Simon Atkins had proudly called the "Columbian Heights Method." These men were already using their pulpits to speak out on racial issues. Now, as their working-class parishioners forcefully shifted the terms of public debate, their voices were amplified, and they began to lambaste not only the injustices perpetrated by whites but also the "danger of false leadership" and the assumptions and strategies of the black elite. "We have had these kind of leaders," wrote James S. Blaine, pastor of the Metropolitan Community Church, founder of the Colored Improvement League, and member of the local NAACP, "and they have always stood in the way of racial progress. These leaders have been chosen for us. They have always told us what the white people want, but somehow or other they are peculiarly silent on what we want. They fail to speak for the race, and white people usually feel that they interpret the will of their people because they tell them what they like to hear. In this they not only deceive their own people, but the white people as well."[45]

Louis E. Austin, editor of Durham's *Carolina Times*, a militant black newspaper that was avidly read in Winston-Salem, attacked the Twin City's black leaders with even less restraint. Since the mid-1920s Austin had upheld the motto of his paper, "The truth unbridled," by pressuring the Durham city government to provide services to blacks, registering black voters, running for office himself, and generally functioning as a "fearless editor" who had the nerve to call "white people big apes and fools." As the political terrain shifted to the left in the 1930s and 1940s, Austin allied himself with the Southern Front, mincing no words in his support for the New Deal, the CIO, and the militant elements within the NAACP. The Winston-Salem leaders' broadside against UCAPAWA, Austin wrote, was "a stab in the back, inflicted upon its victims for the sole and selfish purpose of aiding these belly crawlers into the good graces of the Reynolds Tobacco Company." Honing in on the element of secrecy and self-interest that shadowed behind-the-scenes diplomacy, Austin went on to suggest that the city's black citizens "ought to find out about [the] frequent visits, private conferences and confidential telephone conversations in which Negroes of their city have time and time again been sold down the river for the purpose of raising the stock of one man or a small group of men.... The time has come for Negroes in Winston-Salem to select their own leaders and not permit them to be hand-picked, or to be placed at the mercy of self-appointed leaders."[46]

The problem of "false leadership" was not unique to Winston-Salem, Austin observed. Throughout the South there had emerged a "set of puppet leaders" who were "fed a few political crumbs" and had become "drunk with the fumes of power which they sniff in the confines of their white masters' office." But, he continued, "the Negro had arrived at the place in the South and the nation when a few buildings belatedly given Negro colleges and the glorification of one or two carefully selected Negroes, will no longer satisfy him. He wants all the rights received by any other citizen and no power on earth is going to stop him from using every peaceful means at his command to obtain them."[47]

Austin's indictment reflected a broader debate about ideology and strategy kindled by the civil rights unionism of the 1940s. Such debates had always gone on within the black community, where racial solidarity by no means precluded sharp political conflicts and disagreements, but they had seldom erupted into *white* public view since the turn-of-the-century clashes between Booker T. Washington and W. E. B. Du Bois and the subsequent exclusion of African Americans from political life.[48]

In Winston-Salem this uproar had immediate repercussions for some of the union's opponents, who were not only subject to white pressure but also dependent on a black clientele. Shurley Brown reminded the "leaders" that "if they are to stay in business their support will come from the Negro workers of Winston-Salem." This was not an idle threat; it soon became clear that the newly politicized black working class could use its economic leverage against the union's opponents in the black community. After this exchange of letters appeared in the newspaper, union members organized a boycott against N. M. Mock's store, workers left the churches of A. H. McDaniel and G. J. Thomas, and a family removed a body from Clark Brown's funeral home. Such actions may have drawn on collective memory, for a similar boycott had taken place in 1919 when several merchants in the black community had spoken out against the TWIU.[49]

With racial unity cracking and open conflict raging between the AFL and CIO, a group calling itself "Satisfied Reynolds Employees" joined the chorus. Composed almost entirely of whites in the manufacturing division, the group urged other workers to vote for "no union," rather than for either the TWIU or UCAPAWA. Its newspaper and radio advertisements argued that Reynolds employees already enjoyed the benefits the unions were promising, and more:

> Working conditions are the best in the industry.
> Workers are protected by a generous Company Insurance Plan.
> Wholesome, attractive Grade "A" Cafeterias available to all.
> Best obtainable Toilet and Bath Facilities for every one.[50]

This ad appeared in the *Journal* accompanied by familiar company graphics, including a pack of Camels, prompting unionists to suspect the involvement of company supervisors. "Satisfied Reynolds Employees," moreover, were suspiciously active within the plants, and both the AFL and the CIO charged that the "no union" forces were given free access to the company's facilities to solicit votes and monies to be used against the unions, and that foremen and other supervisors encouraged their efforts. A similar "no union" movement had appeared in 1941 when the AFL asked for an election, and NLRB investigators determined that a few lower-level supervisory personnel had instigated that whole campaign. The NLRB later drew the same conclusions about the 1943 activities when it investigated UCAPAWA's charges of unfair labor practices against Reynolds.[51]

Supervisory officials undoubtedly played an important role in the "no union" campaign, but a substantial number of rank-and-file workers did oppose unionization. Among them were Hobart Johnson, a white worker in the machine shop at Reynolds. Johnson came from Yadkin County, where his parents and their fifteen children farmed one hundred acres of land. After marrying in 1915, he moved to Winston-Salem, worked at the Salem Ironworks, and then took a job at Reynolds. He stayed with the company for over forty-three years. Machinists made more money than the average worker, and Johnson supplemented his wages by working for many years in an uptown clothing store on Saturdays. In 1928 he began buying Reynolds stock, a decision that would make him a millionaire by the 1980s when Reynolds became the object of a corporate takeover.[52]

In language that echoed John Whitaker's address to the workers' committee, Johnson invoked a family metaphor to defend the policies of the company. "Here there is a feeling of cooperation and working together among us," he wrote to the *Journal*, "through which we are united rather than each individual working for himself alone. We believe in ourselves, our fellow men, and our company, its good name is our good name. Directors with sound judgment and just determination are our superiors—that in itself gives us a feeling of security." Johnson's identification with his "betters" helped to make him one of those rare workers who did achieve upward mobility through hard work, luck, deference, and loyalty.[53]

Blanche Fishel's rationale for her opposition to unionization sprang from resignation rather than ambition. She remembered being approached about joining the union. "I told them, 'I come down here and asked for this job. They told me how much they'd give me, and I took it and went. That's the way I've always done. That's the way I'm going to do. I'm not going to tell them what they've got to give me. These people own this place, and they know what they can pay you and what they can't. I'm not going to try and do that.' But lawd, some of them just thought they could just take over everything."[54]

As in the case of the "colored leaders," the daily experiences of white workers set them apart from working-class blacks. Did Hobart Johnson or Blanche Fishel have foremen who opened their toilet stalls, called out their given names, and told them to get back to work? Who among the "satisfied" labored, sweaty and stoop-shouldered, in the priming rooms day after day? Mabel Jessup's admonition could be rephrased to apply to many of the white workers: "Come and work where I work, under the conditions I endure, and then see what you have to say. Try to support a family on the average black workers' wage and see how much is left over to buy Reynolds stock."

The appearance of the "Satisfied Reynolds Employees" prompted the TWOC to step up its recruitment of white workers. It was unlikely that workers like Johnson and Fishel could be persuaded to join the CIO, but there were nearly 4,000 white workers at Reynolds, and they were not all of one mind. A small but determined group of white workers, most of whom had been involved in earlier AFL campaigns, had already come out for the CIO, and they played a critical role by bringing in their friends, neighbors, and family members.

In the last few weeks before the election, dozens of union organizers and sympathizers streamed into Winston-Salem. Clara Hutchinson, a white textile worker from Roanoke, Virginia, spearheaded the operation. She became a familiar figure at the plant gates, handing out leaflets and talking with workers. She and other women union members met threats and innuendos from the "no union" forces. But they offered the best hope of appealing to white women workers, who seemed at the time more open to unionization than white men. In another attempt to appeal to whites, the union brought in Karen Morely, a minor Hollywood star and supporter of numerous Popular Front causes, who spoke to a special rally for workers in the cigarette manufacturing plants.[55]

After a month of extraordinary public and private maneuvering, the time came for Reynolds workers to vote. At 8:00 A.M. on Tuesday, August 3, 1943, stemmery workers in Numbers 256, 65, and 60 began to cast their ballots. They had been the catalyst that brought the workers together and the staunchest supporters of the union drive. For black workers who for generations had been denied the right to participate in local, state, and national elections, the opportunity held a special meaning. Most were exercising their political rights as citizens of the United States for the first time in their lives. Voting continued in Unit I, the prefabrication division, until 4:30 P.M. and was described as "very heavy and very orderly." Workers in the manufacturing departments, Unit II, took their turn at the ballot box the next day.[56]

By early Wednesday evening, workers tense with anticipation and excitement had gathered downtown to await the results. Vote counting began at about 8:30 P.M., as an NLRB examiner dumped the ballots into a huge vat at the Number 8 lunchroom. Shortly after 9:30, he announced the results from Unit I. The vote represented an overwhelming victory for the TWOC. Of the 3,883 ballots cast, 3,598 were for the CIO, 20 for the AFL, and 236 for neither union.

Attention turned to the counting in Unit II. Over a hundred union officials, poll watchers, and company representatives crowded into the lunchroom, while a throng of workers waited outside the building. The CIO and "neither union" ran neck and neck. The suspense resembled that surrounding the judging of a close championship boxing match as the four counters gave their totals to the NLRB official. The CIO and "neither union" each recorded pluralities at two counting tables. The final tabulations indicated a narrow, twenty-eight-vote margin for "neither union." UCAPAWA president Donald Henderson requested a recount. The final count of the 5,865 votes cast gave 2,856 to "neither union" and 2,829 to the CIO; the AFL received only 115 votes. The TWOC failed to win a majority in Unit II, but a runoff would provide another opportunity.[57]

All sides filed protests with the NLRB. Reynolds contended that an NLRB telegram questioning the legality of John Whitaker's letter to the workers had been given widespread publicity and had "misrepresented the attitude" of the company. The TWIU declared that the company had intimidated and coerced workers. At issue was the company's relationship with the "Satisfied Reynolds Employees" who organized the "neither union" vote. The TWIU charged that this group had the "assistance and consent" of foremen and supervisors and that much of its activity took place on company property and on company time. UCAPAWA joined in protesting the intimidation of workers by company supervisors and members of the "neither union" group. Given the unlikelihood of a speedy resolution of these administrative disputes, UCAPAWA decided to challenge the creation of separate bargaining units and ask the NLRB to place all production and maintenance workers in a single unit.[58]

As the TWOC awaited the results of an NLRB inquiry, a wave of recruits from the independent leaf houses bolstered the union's presence in the community. The leaf houses in Winston-Salem and throughout the Southeast functioned much like the prefabrication division at Reynolds. Workers, virtually all of whom were African American and the majority of whom were women, prepared green leaf tobacco (tobacco that had been recently harvested and cured) for storage and eventually for sale. Some of this product went to smaller manufacturing firms, some to Reynolds and the other tobacco giants, and some to foreign companies. Conditions in the leaf houses were, if anything, worse than those at the Reynolds plants. The work was seasonal, which made it impractical to install stemming machines, so most of it was done by hand. The season could last anywhere from five to nine months.

Once workers had processed the summer's harvest, they were simply laid off. Because of the perishable nature of the crop, leaf houses enjoyed a fourteen-week exemption from the minimum wage and maximum hour provisions of the Fair Labor Standards Act, and it was not uncommon for workers to put in fifty-five to sixty hours a week at straight time. Wages in the leaf houses were lower than wages for similar work in the manufacturing plants, although the Winston-Salem-based firms paid wages approximating those in Reynolds's stemmeries.[59]

Winston-Salem was home to three independent leaf dealers: Piedmont Leaf Tobacco Company, Winston Leaf Tobacco and Storage Company, and Export Leaf Tobacco Company. Both Piedmont and Winston were locally owned companies, while Export was a subsidiary of British-American Tobacco Company. On Monday morning, August 9, a few days after the Reynolds election, several hundred stemmers at Winston Leaf walked off their jobs. Following the lead of friends and neighbors who worked at Reynolds, a majority of the workers signed union cards, enabling the TWOC to request an NLRB election. The Conciliation Service arranged a meeting that produced a quick agreement for a consent election, and the workers returned to their jobs.[60]

The TWOC had little difficulty signing up workers at Piedmont and Export after it had secured an election at Winston. Union members in both plants presented membership cards to organizer Frank Hargrove, who immediately requested elections at each company. The leaf houses were in no position to fight the TWOC. The union had already secured membership cards from the vast majority of workers. More important in the owners' minds was the serious shortage of stemmers in the Winston-Salem area in the summer of 1943. With shipments of tobacco arriving daily, the leaf houses could not risk a prolonged strike at their busiest time of year. The NLRB conducted elections at the three leaf houses during the last week of August, and the TWOC won hands down.[61]

With the addition of over 2,000 leaf house workers to the union, the TWOC became an even more powerful and visible presence in Winston-Salem. The mass meetings, which began during the sit-down strike at Reynolds, were now regular Sunday afternoon events. Unable to afford extensive newspaper and radio advertising, the TWOC used these gatherings to communicate with union members and the larger black community. The Sunday meetings also helped to forge and maintain unity. Praying, singing, and testifying in the hot summer sun, workers renewed their pledge to one another in an atmosphere that resembled a religious revival. Such events sent a message to the white community, and perhaps also to the black middle class: black workers were determined to be visible and vocal participants in the city's civic life.[62]

"A Contract to Protect Our People"

On September 3, the director of the Fifth Region of the NLRB voided the election results at Reynolds, citing the protests of all parties involved. This ruling formally returned the situation to where it stood after the work stoppage in June. There was no agreement on the appropriate bargaining unit, the union did not legally represent the workers, and no contract governed relations between the company and workers inside the factories. But union members had not been waiting for legal confirmation to test their newly won strength. According to Robert Black, the TWOC viewed the document John Whitaker signed to end the June walkout as a "contract to protect our people," and it had begun at once to create its own representative structures. This was a brilliant movement-building strategy, as important as any other organizing tactic.[63]

"We started holding membership meetings to allow workers to elect representatives," Black recalled. "We didn't go in and dictate to those people who to select. We asked them to select someone that they thought would give the best representation. I said, 'Don't ask me to pick them because I may pick the wrong person. You have observed these people, you know their general character. The burden is on you.' Then the stewards would select chief stewards to be over each plant. The chief steward had the right—we exercised this right, we didn't have it included in the document—that if any problems arose the chief steward would discuss it with the worker and the foreman." By the beginning of September, 175 shop stewards were busy recording in writing precise accounts of complaints and, especially, information on wages. In the departments where the union had its greatest strength, these stewards pressed for resolution of grievances.[64]

The TWOC also began collecting dues, the lifeblood of any voluntary association. Without a dues checkoff, Black recalled, "we had to do it in the plant, and that was hard on us." The foremen threatened to fire stewards who collected money during working hours, but they did so with ease because "everybody was so proud of the union." Taking up her post in the ladies' dressing room every Friday as soon as the pay wagon came through, Velma Hopkins pocketed the dues of the women in her department and carried them straight to the union office.[65]

While workers built a union from within, supervisors tried to recoup their near-dictatorial power, triggering a series of skirmishes on the shop floor. Press room workers, for instance, staged a wildcat strike after a shop steward was fired for refusing to accept increased production quotas. Such incidents involved more than mere pre-election maneuvering by the union. Workers and their elected representatives had already begun contending for power on the shop floor. They were not waiting for governmental approval to select their shop stewards, and they were not waiting to challenge the foremen's control.[66]

With the August elections set aside, the TWOC petitioned for a new vote with a single bargaining unit. At the NLRB hearing on September 17, Reynolds argued that tobacco manufacturing naturally divided the workforce into two distinct groups. UCAPAWA attorney Harold Cammer contended that such a division was "without any significance whatever as far as the labor relations, the community of interest, and the problems of all the workers of the company" was concerned. "The record shows that this is a well-integrated, well coordinated business, run here in Winston-Salem." The effect of two bargaining units "would be a thinly disguised and effective segregation of a large section of the Negro workers from the rest of the workers, in spite of the fact that there is no difference in their problems, or in their relations towards the company. . . . So I say that the reason the company wants two units is to destroy unionization among the workers."[67]

On October 13 the NLRB issued a decision supporting each of the union's requests. The board concluded that "a plant-wide unit is the appropriate bargaining unit for the Company's employees at Winston-Salem." It also excluded head inspectors from the bargaining unit and included seasonal workers. It ordered an election within thirty days.[68]

With the single bargaining unit ordered by the NLRB virtually guaranteeing a TWOC victory, anti-CIO forces increased the scope of their attacks. The company's strategy borrowed heavily from the "Mohawk Valley formula," devised by Remington Rand in the mid-1930s and widely promoted by the National Association of Manufacturers. The plan was designed for breaking strikes, but several of its techniques had also proved useful in derailing organizing campaigns. These included labeling union organizers as outside agitators, forming a "Citizens Committee" of "bankers, real estate owners, and businessmen" to oppose the union, and organizing a group of "loyal employees."[69]

As soon as the NLRB announced its decision, over 500 supporters of the "no union" position met to formalize their organization. Calling themselves the R. J. Reynolds Employees Association, they hired a local attorney, John J. Ingle. Although the association's expressed purpose was to keep unions out of the Reynolds factories, it set itself up as a rival labor organization and asked the NLRB for a place on the ballot. The group's leaders came mostly from the ranks of lower-level supervisors and included more men than women. But the association was not all white, and Robert Black's memory of the most notorious black member suggests how persistent ties between patrons and their retainers could be. "They had this one poor Negro guy there," Black remembered. "Of course, he turned out to be a real company stooge. They elected him vice-president of the Reynolds Employees' Association. His name was Jasper Redd. He killed a man way back years ago, and old man Whitaker and those got together and used their influence through the court and got him out, and they made a real Uncle Tom out of him about that. A real Uncle Tom."[70]

The NLRB quickly denied the association's request for a place on the ballot, reasoning that the goal of the group was to have no union representation and that a simple "no union" vote guaranteed that right. On November 4, the Employees Association went into federal court to seek a restraining order against the NLRB on the grounds that the board "acted unlawfully by refusing to give the employees an opportunity to vote for a labor organization other than the C.I.O." The judge issued an order restraining the NLRB from holding the election and scheduled a court hearing for November 9.[71]

Faced with these delays, union leaders reassessed their strategies. On Saturday morning, November 6, the shop stewards council and the departmental committees met with TWOC officials and UCAPAWA officers who were in town for a Sunday rally in anticipation of the election. The discussion was lively, with the stewards emphasizing the workers' impatience and warning that further delays would mean more work stoppages. "It is obvious," a spokesman for the group said, "that the sudden incorporation of the no union–company group into an 'independent union' was simply a turnabout in order to put itself on the ballot and thereby attempt to delay the process of a democratic election. So, we say, put the Employees Association on the ballot and let the Reynolds workers give the answer."[72]

With the "loyal employees" group in place, Reynolds quickly turned to the formation of a citizens committee that could directly attack the union. Alarmed at what the *Journal* called "the apparent attempt of outside C.I.O. organizers to foment racial prejudice and strife," members of Winston-Salem's white civic clubs had invited Employees Association attorney Ingle to address their luncheon meeting on October 26 at the Robert E. Lee Hotel. After Ingle's speech, the group adopted a resolution condemning the efforts of the CIO and calling for the organization of an Emergency Citizens Committee to help defeat the union.[73]

A resolution adopted at the meeting and given prominent placement by the *Journal* claimed that "there has heretofore existed a splendid and mutually helpful relation between the white and colored races in Winston-Salem; and . . . there has heretofore existed a splendid spirit of understanding and co-operation between labor and the employers of labor in Winston-Salem." Echoing the charges of the "colored leaders" as well as the pervasive antiunion rhetoric of the day, the resolution claimed that "self-seeking representatives of the CIO . . . from outside the State" had stirred up the "colored employees" so that the union could collect "more than $500,000 in one year."[74]

Robert M. Hanes, president of Wachovia Bank and Trust Company, assumed the chairmanship of the Emergency Citizens Committee and named a group of businessmen to join him. Among those selected were *Journal* editor Santford Martin. In an editorial the next day, Martin praised the action of the civic groups and looked to the committee "to furnish the leadership necessary to preserve and extend the good relations that have existed between the races for a long time."[75]

Angered by the committee's action and the *Journal*'s support, CIO regional director E. L. Sandefur wrote to Martin. "There is not the least basis," he said, "for the falsehood that the CIO has engaged in stirring up racial strife or discord. . . . It is silly to think that any union could succeed in organizing workers by creating racial differences or misunderstandings. On the contrary, it is of utmost importance that we have racial understanding and harmony before we can hope to achieve unity which is unionism. . . . As a matter of cold fact, the only attempts to stir up any racial misunderstanding about which we have the slightest knowledge have been made by the 'Civic' clubs and the crusading lawyer for the Employees Association." Sandefur went on to argue that such public appeals were signs of desperation. Unable to influence workers' votes, the company and the Employees Association had turned to "the big industrial interests" and the local press, which was "owned or controlled by the great combine." Sandefur charged the company and its minions with raising the "bloody flag" of racial strife in an attempt to derail the union drive.[76]

Reynolds certainly played a role in formulating the Citizens Committee's strategy. Indeed, the NLRB later charged the company with "causing, instigating, sponsoring, assisting, and supporting" the committee. In any case, it is inconceivable that members of Winston-Salem's white elite, which included Reynolds officials, did not discuss these matters over the dinner table, at the country club bar, and on the church steps. As Jonathan Daniels observed, they were all guarding the same gold mine. Still, not everyone shared in the bounty, and not everyone saw the unionization of tobacco workers as a direct personal threat. Indeed, that was the committee's purpose: to persuade the unconvinced that UCAPAWA might turn their world upside down.[77]

The committee directed its message first and foremost to members of the white middle class. Many, of course, benefited directly from the company's stock dividends and had a stake in keeping wages low and profits high. Many more benefited indirectly. The depressed wage scale for black workers made it possible for white families of modest means to employ domestic servants. But just as important as economic interests were shared assumptions about personal service, deference, and racial hierarchy. The maids, gardeners, and manual laborers whom most middle-class whites encountered day to day were the relatives or neighbors of tobacco workers or were seasonal tobacco workers themselves. What white employer wanted to find himself or herself "negotiating" with the servants? Who wanted to imagine that a Robert Black or a Theodosia Simpson might suddenly emerge from the faceless crowd?[78]

Such possibilities were not far-fetched. Since the beginning of the economic upturn associated with World War II, black female household workers in Winston-Salem and across the South had sought to raise their wages, reduce their hours, and gain more respect from their employers. They were aided and inspired in their efforts by the availability of war jobs that paid their husbands higher wages and sometimes provided opportunities for them as well.[79]

The Emergency Citizens Committee had two goals: First, it aimed at reinforcing racial solidarity. Second, and more obliquely, it hoped to convince whites to use their influence with the blacks who worked in their homes. To this end, it combined self-interest with appeals to peer pressure and subtle intimidation. Members of the white middle class who aspired to promotion within one of the city's major firms, hoped to operate a small business successfully, or sought membership in a country club or a position of influence in any of the city's many civic and social organizations had to be mindful of the economic and social power of the elite. As committee members circulated petitions at their offices, clubs, and churches, it would have been difficult, if not impossible, for such people to refuse to sign. As a result, the signers represented a cross-section of Winston-Salem's middle class, although Reynolds employees, who formed the largest battalion in that bourgeois army, were carefully excluded to avoid the appearance of company interference in the election. The list included virtually all the officers of all the banks in town; the owners of many small businesses; resident managers for insurance companies, trucking firms, and oil companies; and no fewer than sixty doctors. No influential whites spoke out in behalf of the union or against the committee. And some housewives apparently did try to convince their domestic workers to tell their husbands "not to mess with that union."[80]

White workers constituted a potentially more problematic target group. They had responded to union appeals in the past; only two years earlier the TWIU had counted over 2,000 members. And some white workers had been supporting the TWOC from the outset. In order to appeal to white working men and women, it was crucial for the committee to paint the issues in racial rather than economic terms, to represent the CIO not as a threat to profitability but as a threat to white privilege. If the racial divisions among workers that Reynolds had done so much to encourage were successfully bridged by the union, the company could not withstand the tide of organization.

A third, and even more unreliable group—from the point of view of the company and the committee—was the black middle class. The paternalism of the Reynolds clan had limited the influence of the black middle class in Winston-Salem, in contrast to cities such as Durham, where the success of the black-owned North Carolina Mutual Life Insurance Company and the laissez-faire attitude of the city's white elite had encouraged the rise of a sizable, cohesive black middle class that consistently opposed unionization of the city's tobacco workers. To be sure, a few professionals and business leaders had already lent their support to the company, but to little effect. And a significant number of ministers, whose influence far outweighed that wielded by small business owners, had proved impervious to company pressure and had given the union strong material and moral support.[81]

The Reverend Frank O'Neal was a case in point. O'Neal's skill at making twists of chewing tobacco had earned him the distinction of being the highest paid black worker in the Reynolds plant. Although he was not particularly active in the early organizing drive, he had thrown in his lot with the union and served on the workers' negotiating committee—apparently much to John Whitaker's surprise. "Bumgardner and Whitaker called me up at home and said, 'Reverend O'Neal, what in the world are you doing.' They had gotten a job for my son and had offered my wife a job and they reminded me about it. I said, 'I appreciate what you all have done for me, but let me say this to you. I don't know whether you all realize this or not, but I'm a Negro. I'm a Negro preacher. I preach to Negro people. I've got to live with my people.' 'What can the union do for you that we can't do?' they asked. I said, 'They can do for all the people. I'm for all the working people. I know you have picked people here and there to do little favors for. Fine. We appreciate that. But there comes a time when we've got to be together. We all got to hang together or get hung together.'"

"He thought he could use me," O'Neal continued, "but he couldn't do it. I didn't care no more about the Reynolds Tobacco Company than I did the devil. I knew how they were doing my people because during the Depression that Reynolds Tobacco Company cleared $30 million profit when the people were starving, standing in bread lines and soups lines. We remembered all of that."[82]

Confronted with such expressions of solidarity, the committee relied on a combination of flattery, co-optation, and fear. First, it broke precedent by doing what no white civic group had done before: it invited "colored citizens interested in the future welfare of Winston-Salem and the preservation of harmonious relations be-

Reverend Frank O'Neal (Parker-Condax; *The Worker's Voice*)

tween the races" to make up fully half its members. Participation in such a group would lend conservative black leaders legitimacy and prestige, the committee reasoned. It would also offer antiunion forces in the black community an alternative avenue for pursuing racial progress and create the illusion of an interracial movement against the CIO. Second, the committee threatened that what the white elite had given it could take away. "Splendid and mutually helpful" relations between the races, it warned, could give way to "riots and bloodshed."[83] On one level, such references addressed white fears of black violence. But they were also aimed at the black middle class and at the key players in the unfolding drama: the black Reynolds workers who had already indicated their commitment in the August elections. Experience had taught that when racial violence came to a southern city, the victims were usually black, not white.

A different kind of threat appeared in two full-page advertisements in the Sunday *Journal and Sentinel*, addressing the "Negro Citizens of Winston-Salem Who Believe in Homes, Schools, Churches and Hospitals." Photographs of Booker T. Washington and George Washington Carver appeared alongside a reprint of a *Journal* editorial enumerating the dollar value of the city's investment in the black community between 1920 and 1940. The committee reminded readers that during the previous twenty years, the citizens of Winston-Salem had voluntarily spent more than $3 million "for the direct benefit of our Negro people." To make sure that black readers understood the point, the advertisement concluded: "The Hospitals, the Schools, the Churches, the playgrounds, the Health Department, and the recreational facilities of Winston-Salem, the best in the entire South, are not the result of any trading—not the result of any demands." "Will this growth continue?" "It's up to you."[84]

At quitting time on December 1, just before the election, the company made a similar appeal. As workers filed out of the plants, foremen handed them a letter from William Neal Reynolds. "Will," as he was known around Winston-Salem, was the brother of R. J. Reynolds and a past chairman of the board of directors. He had retired to Florida, where he raced horses, but he remained a symbolic link with the company's legendary founder. The photograph that accompanied the letter depicted an elderly gentleman in white hat and suit with a rather stern expression on his face. "This letter is sent to you at the request of the Citizens Emergency Committee," he began. "I don't see you as often as I used to, but I think about you a lot. Recently I have been worried about you and when I think of that great body of you, who have remained loyal to the principles we all worked so hard for, I conclude that some of your folks have allowed themselves to be misled." Driving home the

Vivian Bruce (Stone's Studio)

message of the committee, he concluded: "After all these years of working together and solving all our problems by understanding and cooperation, I just can't believe our folks will permit outside interests to come among us and, by creating hatreds through false statements and promises, tear down this house of protection which has taken us generations to build. I have too much faith in the power of RIGHT to believe that."[85]

Frank O'Neal remembered the workers' reactions. "When we organized our union, the company put out Will Reynolds's statement with his picture on it. They put out thousands and thousands of these bills all around telling us not to join the union. The folks just took them and tore them up and threw them all over the streets. The workers answered him back. The union sent him a copy of the bills we wrote. We told him, 'Look here, you're enjoying a comfortable life now. We've been suffering under Reynolds Tobacco Company for these forty, fifty, sixty years. We want better working conditions and more money and we had to organize to get it.

You just stay down there in Florida and tend your horses. We'll stay here and tend to the business of Reynolds Tobacco Company.'"[86]

And tend to business they did. By the time election day rolled around, the jokes and stories making the rounds foretold a CIO victory. An Employees Association member asked CIO stalwart Vivian Bruce whether she had heard of "the CIO's funeral." Bruce replied, "There isn't enough room in all of Winston-Salem to bury the CIO, nor enough no-Union–Company-Union stooges for flower girls." Another association member in Number 12 offered to bet $700 that the CIO would lose. When some TWOC members raised the stakes, he had second thoughts. "Well, I'll see about getting the money, but mind, the bet is that the CIO will not win by more than two to one."[87]

As it turned out, he lost that bet too. After months of delay, workers finally cast their ballots on December 16 and 17. A few hours after the polls closed, an NLRB representative announced the results: the CIO received 6,833 votes, the Employees Association, 3,175.[88]

CHAPTER EIGHT

Like Being Reconstructed

Ruby Jones exemplified as well as anyone the enormous release of intelligence and ingenuity the workers' movement in Winston-Salem brought about. The daughter of a railway worker, Jones learned the value of organization at an early age. "My daddy was a labor organizer," she recalled. "I was borned up in a labor union home." A smart and articulate student, Ruby could well have followed in the footsteps of her mother, a country schoolteacher. But she aspired even higher. "In my life, there isn't but one thing that I ever wanted to be, and that was a lawyer. Because I understand people, and I can talk to a person. I've got that instinct. I can tell when a person's telling a lie or when he's not. I didn't want to be no teacher or no nurse; I wanted to be a lawyer."

Jim Crow blocked the path to her dreams. Like Theodosia Simpson, Ruby found herself routed down a different road, one that ended at the "Colored" entrance to the Number 60 stemmery. "I had to quit after two years of college [at Winston-Salem State] to help my mother," she recalled. "I know I didn't get there, but I'd have been some damn good lawyer." Instead of defending clients before a judge and jury, she spent forty-one years in the factories of the R. J. Reynolds Tobacco Company. It was bad enough to work day after day in those "terrible conditions," but Jones especially hated the demeaning treatment of black women by the foremen and the way Jim Crow reinforced that second-class citizenship. "You worked like a dog and then was talked to like a dog. We didn't get no recognition or be treated as human beings 'till that union came in there. Some stores you couldn't go in. You couldn't eat at places. You couldn't vote. You had to take what the other people give you. So that's the reason I say it was just like being reconstructed."[1]

Critical to the process of "reconstruction" was the new system of federally sanctioned collective bargaining that emerged from the creative interaction between New Deal liberals, the left, and the CIO. Through the 1920s, government action had, more often than not, spelled disaster for workers' struggles. Court injunctions against picketing and boycotts squelched numerous organizing drives. Employers often deployed police, National Guardsmen, and even federal troops to break strikes and destroy unions. But the role of the federal government had changed dramatically during the Great Depression. From the first days of the work stoppage in Winston Salem, the U.S. Conciliation Service had been on hand to help settle the dispute. The NLRB's close supervision of the election, along with its refusal to divide the workforce into two separate bargaining units, proved crucial to the union's victory. Contract negotiations, in turn, would be shaped by the National War Labor Board (NWLB), which President Roosevelt established by executive order on January 12, 1942, in order to stabilize labor-management relations and assure continuous production after the Japanese attack on Pearl Harbor.[2]

Unlike the NLRB, which could only oversee elections and certify unions, the National War Labor Board had power to adjudicate disputes that interfered with the war effort and ruled on wages, hours, and other points of disagreement, thus ensuring that election victories actually led to binding union contracts. The board became, in effect, the administrator of a national system of compulsory arbitration. Aimed not at empowering workers but at ensuring production during the emergency of war, the NWLB had an enormous impact on the lives of working Americans and long-lasting implications for postwar labor-management relations.[3]

The First Contract

A month after the TWOC's historic victory on December 17, 1943, the NLRB certified UCAPAWA as the bargaining agent for all Reynolds manufacturing employees in Winston-Salem. A hastily called meeting of the informal, self-initiated shop stewards council already operating in the plants recognized the momentous achievement of certification with "such applause as had never been heard before." With the sound of clapping still ringing in their ears, the stewards moved quickly to the business at hand. Increasingly schooled in the ways of trade unionism, they knew that certification was not the end of the process. Reynolds had to concede the results of the election, accept the NLRB's decision to certify the union, and then enter into collective bargaining. John Ingle, attorney for the antiunion Employees Association, hoped that the company would contest the proceedings and drag the issue before the federal courts. But Reynolds did not adopt this strategy; instead, it agreed to recognize the union and begin contract negotiations. While negotiating was one thing and signing a contract quite another, the decision meant admitting at least a temporary defeat. John Whitaker may have believed, as management had in 1919, that it was prudent to wait until after the war ended to challenge the union.[4]

A poem by Theodosia Simpson trenchantly stated the workers' analysis of the situation:

> With the Stewards and leaders of TWOC
> We'll talk to Reynolds (in his misery);
> He won't want to recognize us, I know,
> But the NLRB says he must do so.
> We'll talk of grievances, also the pay,
> These bad conditions will be changed, I'll say,
> Then after things are agreed upon, fine as wine,
> We'll ask them to sign on the dotted line.[5]

The extraordinary conversation Simpson celebrated opened at 10:00 A.M. on February 8 in the Reynolds Building. On the company side sat John Whitaker, Edgar Bumgardner, and Judge Clayton Moore. Union members on the negotiating committee included white workers Crawford Shelton, Vivian Bruce, S. B. Templeton, Henry Cofer, and Verna Dixon and black workers Robert Black, Velma Hopkins, Caroline Clark, John Tomlin, and William Malone. Theodosia Simpson, who had come out of the plant to work for the union, represented UCAPAWA along with international representatives Frank Hargrove and Clara Hutchinson.[6] The negotiating committee personified the remarkable changes that had taken place in the factories over the past year. Black unionists sat down with white unionists, men beside women, skilled workers next to unskilled. These workers, most of whom had little education, were now negotiating with the most powerful men in one of America's most powerful companies.

The group first took up UCAPAWA's demand to reinstate forty-two workers who had been fired for union activity. Complaints dated back to the election campaign, but union officials charged that more recent firings showed continued company harassment. Management representatives refused to budge. Whitaker claimed that supervisors had legitimate reasons for the firings that had nothing to do with the union. Besides, Reynolds viewed its right to hire and fire as sacrosanct. "In our attempt to settle reinstatement," reported Frank Hargrove, "the biggest obstacle is the old paternalistic policy of the Company. Never before have they run into employees questioning the 'rightness' of the supervisory forces!"[7]

Reynolds's complaints that some of the fired workers had overstepped their rights under the National Labor Relations Act undoubtedly contained a grain of truth. Newly selected shop stewards had much to learn about how to pursue shop floor democracy while adhering to complex labor regulations, and much to teach their fellow workers. But foremen were equally unschooled in the new procedures and, more important, deeply resistant to the whole enterprise on which they were embarked. After much discussion and the possibility of a full-scale NLRB investigation—the TWOC had filed charges of unfair labor practices with the board in January—the parties reached an agreement on all but nine cases. Reynolds agreed to reinstate eighteen workers, while the union withdrew its complaints in what it termed sixteen "weak cases." The union forwarded the nine unresolved cases to the NLRB for investigation.[8]

Just as the company feared, this sign that the union had the clout to put fired workers back on their jobs buoyed unionists' spirits. Lulu Wilson was one of those who won reinstatement, and once she returned to work she was "eating, sleeping, talking and singing CIO." For years the power of Reynolds to deny a livelihood to anyone who bucked the system had loomed large in the lives of workers in Winston-Salem. "Some of my fellow workers told me that I would never go to work for the Company again," recounted William Myers, "but now I'm thankful to say that through the good old CIO, I'm back at work again. Anyone who thinks and says the CIO is not a worthwhile organization, just see me and I can convince you differently."[9]

With the compromise on fired workers out of the way, contract negotiations began in earnest. But if union negotiators thought that other issues could be as easily resolved, they were quickly disappointed. Frank Hargrove told the UCAPAWA News that the company's opening proposal was "fit only for a museum of antiques." Indeed, the parties were so far apart that UCAPAWA immediately appealed to the U.S. Conciliation Service to intervene. After four days of meetings, the conciliator assigned to the case reported that the "parties involved are deadlocked on all issues and points of any consequence . . . from the preamble to the termination clause . . . in this the first contract they have attempted to negotiate."[10]

Part of the problem was that Reynolds officials had spent the previous nine months fighting unionization and had made no effort to find creative solutions to the workers' complaints. Factory supervisors had received little or no instruction on how to deal with the newly empowered workers. The union, on the other hand, had been preparing its case for months: gathering information on wages and working conditions, establishing its leadership cadre within the plants, and studying provisions in other collective bargaining agreements. Not surprisingly, given the gap between the company's foot-dragging and lack of preparation and the union's well-planned eagerness to push ahead, the negotiations got nowhere. Finally the Conciliation Service concluded that only the National War Labor Board could settle the dispute. Accordingly, it convinced both parties to sign a contract dealing only with those matters on which they could agree and then to abide by the rulings of the NWLB on everything else—including such key issues as wages, union security, dues checkoff, vacations, and top seniority for shop stewards.[11]

On April 13, 1944, John Whitaker signed the company's first union contract in over twenty years. Although key issues remained unresolved, the contract represented a milestone for Reynolds workers. Seniority replaced the arbitrary decisions of foremen as the primary consideration in layoffs, recalls, and promotions within each department. A woman who desired a leave of absence to have a baby could stay out for one year and still retain her seniority. A letter from a family physician could overrule the medical department in case of sickness. Most important, a four-step grievance procedure brought Reynolds workers within the NLRB's system of industrial jurisprudence.[12]

One issue was conspicuous by its absence: the seniority clause was effective by department only, rather than division- or plantwide. The union had not even raised the question of plantwide seniority. To do so would have challenged the pattern of racial segregation by departments and the taboo against the promotion of blacks to semisupervisory positions over whites. The possibility of building an interracial union might be foreclosed if white workers saw the union as a direct threat to their interests. Fearing white backlash and confident that more white workers would join once the union demonstrated the advantage of solidarity across the color line, union negotiators decided not to force the issue. They had little choice in the matter, but the failure to win a plantwide seniority system would prove to be a serious weakness, which the company would exploit to full advantage in later years.

The arbitration of the many issues that remained unresolved began with a public hearing before a panel of the Fourth Regional War Labor Board at 10:00 A.M. on May 31. Union and company representatives took their places in front of the judges' bench. Donald Henderson, UCAPAWA president, and Elizabeth Sasuly, the union's legislative director, presented the case along with Frank Hargrove. Judge Clayton Moore headed Reynolds's legal team. Additional company and union officials, curious townspeople, and numerous workers—black and white, men and women, pro- and antiunion—filled the seats and lined the walls. At stake were thousands, perhaps millions of dollars in wages and benefits that Reynolds executives had successfully avoided sharing with their workers. Each party hoped to make a case for its position and influence the decisions of the panel. To company officials, having to testify at the hearings must have been particularly galling. For over fifty years Reynolds had run its business largely behind closed doors. The issues themselves seemed mundane: wages, vacations, seniority, and union security. Hundreds of other NWLB panels would consider similar disputes. But to the participants—company and union alike—the hearings were serious business and the outcome by no means clear. And the issues in question were suffused not only with economic but with political and cultural significance.[13]

Vacations were a case in point. While workers sweated day and night during the hot, humid summer months, the Winston-Salem elite moved en masse to summer homes in the mountains around Roaring Gap, taking their maids, chauffeurs, and cooks with them. Reynolds had instituted a vacation plan to provide "periods of rest and recreation" in the midst of the 1940 TWIU campaign. Although a progressive measure by the standards of southern industry, the plan provided only for one week of paid vacation at Christmas, when the company closed the plants for cleaning and retooling, and even that applied only to employees who had completed two years of continuous service before the first day of that year. Workers who had completed five years received an additional week off. The union's representatives proposed a plan that would give workers a real vacation, "not time off when the company needs to overhaul its plants." Pressed during contract negotiations to allow employees more vacation time and the opportunity to take it whenever they wanted, the company, Robert Black remembered, "jumped sky-high." "They'd say, 'Who is going to pay a worker to go out of town and have fun and come back, and we've got to pay him while he's gone.' They said they'd never heard of such a thing."[14]

The outward appearance of "sweet reasonableness" that marked the start of negotiations turned acrimonious as the hearing took up UCAPAWA's request for a union shop and mandatory checkoff of dues. Labor and management had fought about these issues since the early nineteenth century. Unionists maintained that the closed shop, in which membership in the union was a condition of employment, or the union shop, where workers were obligated to join the union after being hired, offered organized workers their only protection against antiunion employers and economic downturns. They also argued that workers who enjoyed the benefits of a union contract should contribute to the union's support; there should be no "free riders." Employers claimed that such arrangements violated the rights of individual workers, who should be free to choose whether or not they wanted to belong to a union. Wartime conditions complicated the debate, for CIO unions feared that the new workers flooding into the mass production industries, many of whom had recently migrated from rural areas with no tradition of trade unionism, would see little reason to join unions that had given the federal government the right to set wages and had signed no-strike pledges for the duration of the war.[15]

The National War Labor Board sought to break the logjam by adopting "maintenance of membership" as a compromise between the open and closed shop. This plan did not require nonmembers to join the union, but those who did had to maintain their membership in the union for the life of the contract as a condition of employment in the company. The board justified maintenance of membership in light of the unions' agreement to refrain from strikes during the war and because government controls limited wage increases.[16]

Although the board seems never to have provided for a union shop where none existed before, Donald Henderson requested a union shop at Reynolds. "An unbroken string of antiunion activity" by the company, the union president said in an hour-long address to the panel, had forced "upon the union a constant struggle to maintain itself." Over the years, Reynolds had resisted numerous attempts by its employees to organize and had a record "few firms can duplicate in successful union-busting." In the wake of the organizing campaign of 1943, Henderson charged, the company had stepped up pressures against union members in the factory and had given tacit support to the Employees Association. In addition, Henderson supplied evidence that the Emergency Citizens Committee had attempted to "drum up sentiment against the CIO and provoke race disturbances" and claimed that the company had a hand in this campaign. Only if the union's existence was removed from the sphere of conflict would it be possible "to establish a bona fide collective bargaining relationship."[17]

Reynolds officials questioned the authority of the board to grant maintenance of membership, much less the union shop. After denying the union's charges of intimidation and discrimination, the company's lawyers charged that, in fact, UCAPAWA, not the company, was the "irresponsible" party in the case. The company produced newspaper reports and signed statements that tied union leaders to the 1943 sit-down strikes and to other work stoppages during the past year, in violation of the NWLB's requirement of strict adherence to the no-strike pledge. Reynolds lawyers also introduced a report by the House Committee on Un-American Activities branding UCAPAWA "an irresponsible union."[18]

The charge of "irresponsibility" was crucial to the company's case. The NWLB's central purpose was to preserve wartime stability in labor-management relations. It would not use its power in behalf of a union that did not observe the no-strike pledge and demonstrate its commitment to cooperating with management in order to maintain the high levels of production the war required. UCAPAWA, in turn, had to prove that the company was responsible both for fomenting the previous year's ongoing strife and for stonewalling on contract negotiations.[19]

But more was at stake for each party than the necessity of framing the issues in ways that would prove convincing to the NWLB. Since the early days of slavery, African Americans had been branded by southern whites as irrational and dependent and therefore incapable of citizenship. Reynolds executives—and southern elites more generally—saw themselves as the keepers of order and their business practices as the engine both of riches for themselves and of rational economic progress for the region. Now, as black workers and white bosses met face to face in a bid for power on the shop floor and in the community, they spoke a familiar language of order and rationality. The union did so in part by accusing the company of violating the spirit of the law by using "union-busting" tactics behind the scenes. But mainly it marshaled evidence of how the company's routine operations created turmoil rather than good order in its plans. The company, on the other hand, resorted to accusations that spoke directly to reigning assumptions about the characteristics that made blacks unfit for equal participation in civic life.

Midway through the hearings, Reynolds asked the panel to hear approximately twenty affidavits, many of which painted black workers in a lurid light. Printed in the *Journal,* these tales of petty personal disputes, name-calling, threats of violence, and charged sexuality evoked the Dickensian world imagined by the white middle class. Edna Foy's testimony was typical. She had written a letter to the editor of the *Journal* before the election commenting on the good relations between the company and the union. Shortly after that, she claimed, "Pearl Landingham came to me in the café. She said, 'Edna, you had better be careful. These South Carolina Negroes will kill you. They'll cut your heart out. They'll shoot your head off.' . . . On two occasions I received telephone calls . . . they told me that I had gone against my color and that I had better be careful." An affidavit by Neil Branon, a white worker, relayed secondhand that Clark Sheppard had "cursed and abused" Eva Blevins when Blevins threatened to quit the CIO. Sallie Palmer claimed that Evander Rogers told her "the 'butchers' were going to get me" if she failed to support the union.[20]

Supervisory personnel had drummed up some of these accusations and actually wrote a number of the documents. Company attorneys, for instance, read an affidavit from Janie Hunt alleging that union members had threatened to whip her if she bought a drink off the company milk truck. Hunt, a union stalwart, said in a counterstatement that the event described never happened; her foreman had tricked her into signing what she thought was a job reassignment form.[21]

In other cases, however, the affidavits reflected real tensions behind the scenes. It should not be surprising that there were dissenters. The thousands of men and women who worked in the factories had been forced to devise their own survival strategies, and many were loath to risk something new. The company's system of labor discipline, which rested on favoritism, arbitrary punishments, and the extensive use of spies, cultivated a climate of conflict and distrust among the workers that the union could not easily overcome. Given the demands and risks of unionization, it was perhaps inevitable that differences of opinion and commitment would be fought out on the street, within families, and in churches in intense and personal ways.

The company's use of these affidavits, along with the unusually detailed coverage the *Journal* gave them, appealed to white middle- and upper-class prejudices about working people, black and white, which the newspaper abetted in its limited coverage of working-class life. Like the *Journal*'s distorted treatment of criminal activities in the black community, the affidavits depicted a population in need of control. In its presentation to the NWLB panel, the company contended that the union was fomenting chaos, suggesting that only a return to traditional, personalistic discipline would ensure productivity, civic order, and labor peace.[22]

The fireworks died down as the panel turned to the seemingly more straightforward matter of wages, although even this bread-and-butter issue was sometimes couched in the language of order versus disorder. The union had two goals. The first was to raise the workers' standard of living through higher minimum wages and a general wage increase; the second was to reduce intraplant and intrajob inequalities by securing length-of-service rather than merit wage increases.[23]

Federal regulations set the terms of the debate. The NWLB elaborated its position in the famous "Little Steel formula," the wartime wage policy that Theodosia Simpson had evoked so effectively in her confrontation with John Whitaker during the 1943 sit-down strike. The formula limited across-the-board wage increases to 15 percent of the wage prevailing on January 1, 1941, but since it applied only to dispute cases, it had little effect on the problem of rising inflation. In the fall, Congress and the president extended the NLRB's jurisdiction to include all wage increases.[24]

Stabilizing wages did not mean freezing wages, however, and the board had considerable leeway in carrying out the president's program. Wage increases were permissible to "eliminate substandards of living, to correct gross inequities, or to aid in the effective prosecution of the war." These loopholes proved vital to low-wage workers, but as inflation intensified, Congress curbed the board's discretionary powers. By 1943 rising prices had seriously undermined the standard of living of American workers, and the CIO began to withdraw its support of the president's stabilization program. At its annual convention in November, the CIO decided to seek general wage increases in excess of the Little Steel formula.[25]

With the CIO's new policy in mind, Donald Henderson presented the union's request to the NWLB panel. He asked it to recommend a sixty-cent minimum wage throughout the plants and a general increase for all workers, although the proposed across-the-board increase exceeded the bounds of the Little Steel formula. In insisting on an increase in the minimum wage, Henderson reminded the panel of the board's mandate to eliminate "substandards of living." He presented evidence to show that the average tobacco worker's income fell below even a maintenance-level budget and that the rise in the cost of living far exceeded the 15 percent accounted for in the Little Steel formula. Henderson cited a Bureau of Labor Statistics study calculating that in June 1943, a manual worker's family required $1,624.65 a year to maintain itself at a minimum subsistence level. Reynolds workers brought home an average annual income of $1,144. At least 2,500 employees, mostly black women, made considerably less.[26]

In addition to higher wages, workers wanted to put an end to what Henderson described as "a situation of complete chaos . . . with respect to the Company's wage structure." "No circumstance can be more destructive of morale in a plant," he claimed, than "arbitrary inequalities in wage rates for workers performing the same job." Indeed, the company's records showed that workers doing the same job were paid at as many as fifteen different wage rates. The union also charged that job classifications were a shambles and that people working side by side on the same task were often classified differently and assigned different rates of pay.[27]

Foremen had long used their discretionary power to play one worker off against another, and workers deeply resented this practice. "Within this ill-defined hodge-podge," the union contended, "the Company grants what it terms 'merit increases' which serve only to create further inequities." The fact that the company provided no information on how workers might qualify for merit increases furthered infuriated union members. To remedy this situation, the TWOC proposed simplifying and consolidating the numerous job classifications within a new wage structure. The union also asked that automatic length of service increases replace merit increases.[28]

Company attorneys attacked the entire package of union requests. Above all, they argued that UCAPAWA was attempting to break the Little Steel formula: "Every demand the union has made would require a drastic revision in the War Labor Board policy. It would be disastrous to the wage stabilization program. It would involve millions and millions of dollars. None of these requests can be granted within the Board's policy."[29]

The NWLB panel released its report on August 4, 1944. It offered concessions to both the union and the company, but the real victors were Reynolds's employees, who gained rights and benefits already extended to millions of other American workers. The panel followed the NWLB's standard policy on vacations, granting one week's vacation with pay after one year and two weeks after five years. For the first time, seasonal workers shared in the vacation plan as well. The union security issue proved more complicated. The panel concluded that both sides had been guilty of improper behavior but attributed the "friction . . . to the newness of the collective bargaining relationship, complicated by the large number involved and by the heavy proportion of negroes, whose experience in collective bargaining is still to be gained for the most part." The fact that the company was equally inexperienced and actually contemptuous of the process escaped the panelists, as did the fact that black workers had become quite sophisticated in their use of federal labor law. In keeping with NWLB policy, the panel denied the TWOC's request for a union shop but did recommend a maintenance of membership provision and a voluntary checkoff.

The panel took seriously the union's claim that tobacco workers desperately needed a general wage increase and that the wage structure was "chaotic." In no case, however, was it willing to grant the entire increase requested by the union. It established new minimum rates for each job and granted retroactive across-the-board increases, with the lowest-paid workers receiving the highest raises.[30]

On October 18, 1944, the War Labor Board for the Fourth Region approved the recommendations of the panel. UCAPAWA chartered United Tobacco Workers Union, Local 22, and Local 22, with its 14,000 members, took its place as the international's largest and most dynamic outpost in the South. Soon afterward, UCAPAWA changed its own name to Food, Tobacco, Agricultural, and Allied Workers of America (FTA) to reflect the growing importance of tobacco workers in its ranks.[31]

For over a year the two sides had fought bitterly, the company to maintain what it saw as its right to determine the conditions and rewards of employment in its factories and the union to give workers a voice through collective bargaining. In the middle were the various agencies of the federal government—the NLRB, the Conciliation Service, and the NWLB. These agencies had a powerful impact on the style and substance of labor-management relations in Winston-Salem. When the negotiations began eight months earlier, the company and the union were "so far apart on so many matters" that they could barely agree on the issues for negotiation. By the end, Reynolds had been forced to adhere to national standards.[32]

Shop Floor Democracy

Union recognition, increased wages, paid holidays, and seniority rights—all represented accomplishments for Reynolds workers. Still to be achieved, however, was the workers' most cherished objective, a more democratic workplace. The company, the union, and the federal government had established the framework for a radically new system of industrial relations, but the effectiveness of the system would depend on the workers' resolve. Above all, it would be up to the shop stewards, operating through a formal grievance procedure, to realize the democratic potential of contractual rights. Reynolds had not given up its "right to manage": it retained "the exclusive power to hire, promote, fire for just cause, and maintain and schedule production." But now management did not have the final say on all these matters; workers could contest management decisions they viewed as unjust.[33]

Although the CIO's shop steward system went hand in hand with a formal grievance procedure, each had its own ancestry. One thread of the shop steward system, moreover, reached back to the syndicalist impulse of the early twentieth century. Syndicalists stressed the need for direct action at the point of production, such as strikes, slowdowns, and sabotage, to uphold workers' rights. This vision of workers' control contrasted sharply with the traditional trade unionism advocated by the AFL, where business agents and other union staff members, not workers, bargained with management. During the heyday of this first wave of the struggle for workplace democracy, syndicalist workers' councils exercised remarkable influence. The brutal suppression of radicalism during and after World War I curtailed such militant activism, but the tradition lived on in a few industries, unions, and political groups.[34]

The more recent lineage of the shop steward system began with the employer-sponsored employee representation plans that emerged from the welfare capitalist programs of the 1910s and 1920s or were rushed into existence after the passage of the NIRA and the burst of union organization that followed. Hoping to deflect the impulse toward self-organization, corporations created "workers' councils" and company unions that were designed to co-opt potential leaders and control the expression of workers' aspirations. Such schemes had unintended consequences, for they recognized shop floor leaders and gave them a chance to meet together. As these representatives confronted management resistance to workers' demands, many became union activists and adapted the representative structure to their own needs.[35]

The grievance procedure had an altogether different history, but it too became a defining feature of early CIO contracts. As president of the Amalgamated Clothing and Textile Workers Union, Sidney Hillman pioneered the use of a legal/constitutional apparatus for settling shop floor disputes in the years after World War I. Like other reformers, Hillman saw harmonizing labor-management relations as the key to providing stability in labor-intensive and highly competitive industries. Shop committees, with the assistance of business agents and union officers, cooperated with management to establish "work rules, standards of performance, disciplinary procedures, and new codes of shop floor behavior." Any disputes the parties could not resolve went to an industrywide arbitration board.[36]

Early CIO contracts borrowed heavily from these somewhat contradictory traditions, creating a hybrid structure that affirmed workers' power on the shop floor while at the same time institutionalizing a system of rules within the factory. In the auto, steel, rubber, and electrical industries, shop committees, like earlier syndicalist workers' councils, became the organizational base for many industrial unions. Formal grievance procedures, on the other hand, were inimical to the direct action favored by syndicalists. Indeed, they lay at the heart of the bureaucratic system that protected workers from the abuses of management, while at the same time limiting their ability to resort to slowdowns, wildcat strikes, and other spontaneous forms of protest and control.[37]

At Reynolds, the shop steward system emerged from the bottom up. The TWOC drive, modeled on earlier CIO campaigns, had relied heavily on worker organizers. They, in turn, had intervened openly in shop floor conflicts as a way of recruiting members. Theodosia Simpson's leadership of the sit-down in 1943 was a dramatic and consequential example of such shop floor actions.

During the subsequent contract negotiations and NWLB hearings, the union fought hard to obtain official recognition of the shop steward system, top seniority for stewards, and the right to determine the appropriate number of stewards. Reynolds conceded the implementation of the shop steward system and did not contest the union's demand for top seniority, which was designed to protect shop floor leaders from discrimination. But it refused to grant the union sole right to determine the number of stewards, claiming that too many stewards only produced confusion. In one case, the company reported, "four shop stewards took up the same grievance with the foreman at different times the same day and each had a different idea of what he thought should be done." The TWOC refused to give in on this issue because the accessibility and effectiveness of its shop stewards had been so vital to its success. Over the course of the previous year, workers had elected stewards wherever they felt a need for representation. The TWOC's proposal thus represented, in effect, a ratification of self-initiated shop floor practices and an affirmation of union democracy. Indeed, that was the crux of the matter: the company had a valid interest in rationalizing the shop steward structure, but its obduracy on the issue had less to do with rationalization (which its own system of foremen did not promote) than with a desire to undermine the shop stewards' role and hence the union's democratic identity. Here again, the company's charges of chaos and confusion masked concerns about power.[38]

In the end, the NWLB panel resorted to stopgap measures when it designated the appropriate number of stewards. It recommended that the two parties negotiate the placement of one hundred stewards for a trial period of four months. If after that time either side was unhappy with the arrangement, the NWLB would appoint an arbitrator to fix the number.[39]

The grievance procedure, according to Theodosia Simpson, was "the most important part of any contract." And it took its meaning from the context in which it appeared. Among workers who had the skills, organizational clout, and community support to exercise shop floor control, it could certainly serve management interests and dampen union militance. But in Winston-Salem, it did much more than provide a defensive, quasi-judicial apparatus for resolving workplace conflict. It also created a framework in which the union could carry forward a process of movement building, both by constantly renegotiating the fine points of the collective bargaining agreement and by solidifying its members' loyalty and attracting new support. Despite the usual evocations of labor-management harmony—goals both the workers and the union genuinely desired—FTA, like most left-led unions, believed that the relationship between workers and management was an inherently adversarial one, a view shared by most of Reynolds's black workers. Conflict, therefore, was an ongoing feature of the workplace and generated continual negotiations between the company and its workforce. Accustomed to relying on racial etiquette, paternalism, personalism, and covert forms of resistance to resolve such conflicts, managers and workers alike had to learn a new language of rights and obligations and new, formal ways of resolving the daily frictions on the shop floor.[40]

Ruby Jones understood the momentous change that had taken place. Not long after she had been elected a shop steward, her foreman confronted her about her new role.

"Ruby," he said, "why are you sticking your neck out? These people come around here and talk about you."

"Well, that's all right. I don't care if they do. I'm helping myself, because I'm not going back yonder."

"I've been in this business longer that you have. I've been a foreman thirty years."

"I beg your pardon, Mr. Lawson. You've only been a *foreman* six months. Don't count the time you chain-ganged them lines out there."[41]

Union activists at Reynolds quickly made the shop steward system the crucible of democratic activity in the workplace. Its strength depended on the abilities of individual stewards, the rank-and-file leaders who were the union's most direct link to workers and management alike. "The most important people in the plants were the shop stewards," said Velma Hopkins. Ruby Jones thought "the steward was more important than the union, because you're in there to carry out the contract."[42]

Many stewards had emerged informally in the heady days before certification; union procedures now required that they stand for election. Not every choice was a wise one. Before unionization, rank-and-file leaders operated in a personalistic manner, much like the foremen, and not everyone could make the transition to the new system with its written rules and formal codes of behavior. Workers sometimes elected the most popular person in the department rather than someone who had the fortitude to buck supervisors and settle difficult conflicts among workers. Some stewards simply did not have the necessary time to devote to union activities. Others lacked the literacy skills to keep up with the required paperwork. From time to time, workers or the union had to intervene to discipline or remove ineffective shop floor leaders. This was particularly true in the case of stewards who did not understand the terms of the contract, missed too many meetings, or developed overly friendly or antagonistic relationships with the foremen. Union officials, however, could not be too heavy-handed in their interventions. They wanted to operate democratically, and stewards had their own power bases in the plants. All in all, the stewards constituted a remarkable cadre of militant shop floor leaders who were committed to using the grievance procedure as a means of strengthening the union and challenging employers' power rather than entrenching themselves in lower-level bureaucratic positions.[43]

The grievance procedure involved a mandatory four-step process that lay at the center of the NWLB's system of industrial jurisprudence. When a dispute arose, the worker first took up his or her complaint with a foreman, either alone or through a union representative. If the decision did not prove satisfactory to the worker, the steward put the complaint in writing and submitted it to the plant superintendent, who discussed the problem with the worker and/or the chief shop steward. In cases where the worker remained dissatisfied, the personnel manager reviewed the grievance with a representative of the union. In the fourth stage, a company-union grievance committee discussed the matter. If the grievance committee could not agree, the company and the union and, if necessary, the U.S. Conciliation Service selected an arbitration panel to settle the dispute.[44]

This system mirrored the company's supervisory structure. Robert Black remembered, "We told the company that our stewards are the same thing to the workers as your foremen are to the company." At the third stage, a union staffer became the counterpart of the personnel manager. Most remarkably, the fourth stage brought together the top rank-and-file leaders—Velma Hopkins, Robert Black, and Clark Sheppard—with representatives of top management, usually John Whitaker, Judge Moore, and Ed Bumgardner. Only at the final stage, with arbitration, did the matter move out of the local union's hands.[45]

Both the company and the union had an investment in settling grievances at the first stage. For one thing, there was much more leeway in interpreting the contract and working out creative solutions when the discussion took place between two individuals. More important, settlement at this stage gave the worker immediate satisfaction and allowed others to see the union in operation. The company, on the other hand, wanted to avoid the taint of having to negotiate with the union grievance committee or submit to federal arbitration. In departments with well-trained, militant stewards, few grievances ever went past the first stage. The steward knew the contract and had explained its provisions to the workers, and the foremen stayed in line. "You couldn't bring a grievance out of the departments where the most militant stewards worked," Black recalled. "If some worker in there felt that he had a grievance, the company put pressure on those foremen to settle it right there. They wouldn't allow those foremen to be brought before the union representative on the top grievance committee."[46]

In the first months of the contract, the union faced the thorny problem of figuring out exactly what constituted a legitimate grievance. Although management had told the foremen to go easy, the dynamics of shop floor life did not change overnight; in a sense, the wrangling had just begun. One woman called Robert Black at home at night.

"I've got a grievance and I want to come to the union office in the morning and explain it."

"What is your grievance?"

"My foreman keeps looking at me."

"What is he saying?"

"He's not saying anything, I just don't want him to look at me. Don't the union say you can stop a foreman from looking at you?"[47]

There was little the union could do to curtail the sexual gaze of the foreman, but the worker's complaint articulated both long-term resentments and the confidence the union inspired. "We never tried to close the mouths of workers around a grievance," Black continued. "We left the membership free to feel that if there was any kind of problem in his or her respective department to bring it up. We said if you feel you've got a grievance, you are covered under the contract. There was never a feeling that a worker doubted the ability of the union to process and solve their grievances. They never felt they were denied the right to discuss their grievances."[48]

Given such broad parameters and the rancor built up over years, it is not surprising that complaints mushroomed. "Our grievances, I don't know why, [but] they became more once we got the union," Velma Hopkins observed. "In the past," she continued, people had been afraid. Faced with insults and injustices, they opted for self-preservation: "I've got to work. I'm head of a household. I'm feeding children. Even though you ain't making but $9.35, that $9.35 meant survival. And once we got the union, they felt like, well, I've got some protection. I've got somebody that really cares. They didn't feel like it was a little group here and there: It was 10,000 on checkoff, and 10,000 members makes you feel good, you know. You're surrounded. And the grievances became more."[49]

The most common grievances involved disciplinary actions and discharges. Foremen were used to firing workers at will, and they were reluctant to give up that prerogative. The contract upheld the right of management to discharge any employee for "just cause" and included dishonesty, incompetence, inefficiency, insubordination, intoxication, and pilfering among a long list of possible grounds, the bases for which were highly subjective. The first grievance settled under the contract attacked the arbitrary power of the foreman. Orvelle Crowder worked on the loading dock in Number 12. The work load increased one Friday, and Crowder could not keep up. As in the old days, the foreman lost his temper and fired him on the spot. But the shop steward, Gollie Weatherspoon, intervened and went to the superintendent, who put Crowder back on the job on Monday.[50]

Settling grievances in a huge and complex factory environment preoccupied stewards and union officials alike. Stewards often intervened to help individual workers. Ella Marshall, for instance, had a heart condition, and her doctor advised her not to work the night shift. The steward in her department in Number 60, Lola Bates, worked out an arrangement with the superintendent to have Marshall transferred to the day shift until her health improved. But the more aggressive stewards went beyond reacting to individual problems; they used the grievance procedure to address workplace issues that were of general concern. Viola Brown, a shop steward in Number 60, took workers' complaints about excessive heat and lack of ventilation to a second-stage grievance hearing. She and the plant superintendent worked out a plan for correcting some of these conditions. Velma Hopkins and other stewards translated first-stage settlements into improved conditions in the restrooms. Humidifier cleaners worked at night, but the company refused to pay them the four-cent night-shift differential the contract provided. It claimed that the differential applied to second-shift workers, and since there was only one shift of humidifier cleaners, they were not covered under the terms of the contract. The union countered that the extra pay was intended to make up for the hardships of working at night, not just on the second shift. The case went to arbitration and the arbitrator sided with the union.[51]

Disadvantaged by their class, race, and sex in relations with the foremen, black women especially benefited from the power of the collective, the union, and the state, all of which offered not only a means of influencing working conditions but protection against retaliation, sexual exploitation, and physical violence. Velma Hopkins remembered one of the foremen in her department: "Old man Cole. He was tall, looked like a chain gang boss. He went around to where the women were working and they had [overloaded the machine] and the belt had stopped. He told them, 'You get your damn ass up off of that tobacco.' And they came to me crying, and I just went out there and pulled the damn switch and stopped all of it. So when we took it up, I demanded that before we'd go back to work they'd have to move him and he should not be allowed to work over women anymore. They moved him to Number 10 where [there were] nothing but men."[52]

Indeed, far from being subdued by the grievance procedure, Reynolds workers delighted in finding ways of flaunting their newfound power. According to Geneva McClendon, a shop steward in Number 65, "When we got the union over there, well, me being a shop steward, I could take the grievance over to personnel in the Reynolds Building. Before the union, I didn't go over there no way; but after we got the union there I was smoking Lucky Strikes and I'd go over there and lay them on the table so they'd be sure and see them because they couldn't fire me about it then. And Mr. Bumgardner would pull out his Camels and lay them over there [and say], 'Smoke a good cigarette.' I didn't touch them, though; I kept smoking my Luckies."[53]

Local 22 chairman Frank Green relayed a story told him by Moranda Smith, head of the local's education committee and a shop steward in Number 60. "Her foreman was a hot-headed man. One day she raised a grievance with him. I don't know what it was about, and he got all up in the air about it. Moranda told [him], 'I'll tell you what you do. Walk over to the end of the building and spit a spit of your tobacco out of the window and come back and see if in that time you can cool down enough that we can talk reasonably.' And he did it."[54]

An even more dramatic display of workers' influence occurred in October 1945. "They had a German prisoner of war camp in Winston-Salem," Frank Green recalled, "and [the company] hired these prisoners of war to come and work in the plant. They didn't fire anybody for it, but they gave [the regular workers] more difficult jobs" in the nicotine plant. The shop steward filed a grievance, but the superintendent refused to hear it. "All of a sudden in the middle of one afternoon the people start piling in our office, telling me what's happening. They just walked off. And so we very quickly got some placards made up." Within a few hours, the reassigned workers were on the streets around the business district and plant gates with signs protesting the company's action. "A Nazi prisoner took my job at No. 1 leaf house," read one. "We won the war in Germany, but not in Winston-Salem," proclaimed another.

"Mr. Bumgardner called me in," Green continued, "extremely angry." 'What the hell are you doing?' And I told him, 'Well, these people just walked off the job.' He said, 'Don't tell me that.'" Bumgardner could not believe that the workers had acted on their own; from his point of view, it was up to the union not to aid and abet them but to keep them in line. "Pretty soon," Green remembered, "I got a call to come up to Judge Moore's office. He was on one of the top floors in the Reynolds Building. He said, 'What's the problem? Is there anything we can't settle?' I said, 'No, not at all. I don't object to the prisoners of war working for the plant here. I don't want them to take anybody else's job and I don't want any people to be transferred to less desirable jobs. He said, 'Well, that's reasonable. We'll take care of that.' I said, 'Fine.' And that was that."[55]

The fourth-stage meetings, which involved three workers' representatives, three company officials, and the foreman and worker if necessary, could also turn into high drama. Velma Hopkins remembered a grievance hearing involving Whitaker, Bumgardner, and a foreman from Number 12. The foreman had fired a man who worked in the sweating bins, accusing him of spitting in the tobacco. "He's down there with sweat running off of him and he couldn't wear a shirt, and his pants was wet to the bottom, but they said he spit in the tobacco. So I asked them, 'How did you know whether he was sweating or pissing or what?' As wet as he was." As the hearing proceeded, Hopkins challenged not only the supervisor's authority but one of the linchpins in the etiquette of Jim Crow. She took Whitaker aside and requested that he tell the foreman to call the worker "Mister," seeing as how he addressed Whitaker, Bumgardner, and even Hopkins by their titles. Whitaker agreed, and the foreman fumed. "I don't give a damn what you do, I'll never go over there [to grievance meetings] no more," he said as he left the hearing. "I'll never call another nigger Mister." "But he had to call him mister that day," Hopkins said proudly. "We didn't have no more grievances out of there after we made that superintendent call that black man mister."[56]

Of course, it took time to eradicate a culture of fear and a highly personalized system of industrial relations that had evolved over many decades. "We had some black workers that were too timid for one reason or another," Robert Black recalled. "You see, that company had things on a lot of the people that worked in those plants. Some of it was misconduct, and some of it was from probably larceny, when a foreman forgave them. When we would take a worker in that Reynolds building for a grievance, that company would come up with written documents, letters, fifteen and twenty years back, every little thing that he'd ever done and lay it on the table. 'Now you mean this is the kind of worker you're going to represent?' I said, 'We are talking about from the day we got a union contract. Anything that you forgave those people for back there, we are not interested. [We are interested in] what happened from '44 when we signed the contract up till the present day.'" In the old days, Black observed, the company could, in effect, blackmail a worker forever. "Now you'd think if the company carried a bad letter against you for five years, they'd burn it up. Mm-mm. Not them. And files, files on top of files."[57]

Unlike managers at some unionized firms who embraced the grievance procedure as a way to limit shop floor flare-ups, Reynolds officials found little redeeming value in the system of industrial jurisprudence and operated within it only under duress. Charles Wade, who joined the personnel department after the war, felt it was disruptive of the good relations between the company and its workforce. "We had a grievance committee with [the union] for a long time," he recalled, "and it was just completely phony. They'd create these grievances. It took a lot of patience to work through all of those things. The union wanted to keep us involved at the management level so they could demonstrate to the employees what they were doing for them. A lot of times they would bring the employee in, which was a terrible thing for us because we didn't want to take an adversary position against one of our employees, unless the employee was a very active union member, then we really didn't give a damn. You know, I didn't give a damn what we said to them because I felt that they were basically not trying to get along. They were basically trying to organize the rest of the employees. So I didn't spend much time worrying about them."[58]

The union commanded large majorities in the predominately black departments, where the shop steward system and the grievance procedure worked best. The smaller group of white unionists, however, was scattered throughout the factory and thus was subject to constant intimidation by foremen and antiunion Employees Association members. The company fired Eva Blevins, a white packing machine operator in Number 12 and a member of the negotiating team for the first contract, for stealing cigarettes. Velma Hopkins took her grievance up at the third stage. "We hadn't been able to do very much with the whites," she remembered, "so the union officials weren't too interested in it, but I took it up and took it to arbitration." Workers often carried a single cigarette, rather than a pack, with them to work, Hopkins explained. "If you went in there with that cigarette, you'd put it behind your ear because bumping the machines and sweating, the cigarette would get wet. When you hit the door to go down the steps, you'd light your cigarette because you hadn't had one all day. And they got so they were picking up people and saying, 'You stole a cigarette.' Fired, for smoking just one cigarette and it'd be a Camel. And they'd say, 'Well, I carried it in.' They'd say, 'Where's your pack?' And the arbitrator came down, and we found out during that hearing that each cigarette had a date and a number on it of the machine from which it was made. And the arbitrator found that out, and they found out that Eva's cigarette wasn't made on that date and the machine number wasn't her machine, and she got her job back. From that, we made a little break in Number 12."[59]

Since under the collective bargaining agreement Local 22 was legally bound to represent union and non-union workers alike, it found itself taking up grievances of white workers who had been among its most vociferous opponents. Clark Sheppard settled cases for three Reynolds Employee Association members in the first few months of the contract. Robert Black remembered both the special pressures the company sometimes brought to bear on white turncoats and the difficulty of translating even a union success into solid white support. "We sat in on a case [where] the company fired a [white] guy because of absenteeism who had been working for Reynolds for ten or fifteen years. He admitted that he had never joined the union, but he said he wanted to join. He asked Clark Sheppard to file a grievance through the union. We sent the request into Reynolds to have a third stage grievance meeting. They tried to beat the guy down. The foreman jumped on him, wanted to know why he went to the union. The superintendent called him in. They couldn't get him to change his mind. We publicized this nonunion worker's grievance, so the company settled it and put him back to work. They didn't want to make a big fanfare out of it." The aggrieved worker did join the union, but, according to Black, "he never lifted a finger to try to encourage anybody else to join."[60]

The union readily defended workers who had been unjustly dismissed; representing those who deserved to be disciplined by the company was more problematic. In those situations, the shop stewards—and even other union members—did sometimes try, at least behind the scenes, to keep troublemakers in line. "We had one rank-and-filer at 60 Extension," Robert Black recalled, "[who] wouldn't work on Monday. He laid out thirteen Mondays in a row. He'd booze himself off on the weekend. He just wouldn't work. Well, the steward kept bringing him over to the union office, not for us to browbeat him, but to sit down and discuss with him. Finally, the foreman had had enough and fired the worker." The worker's excuse, Black recalled, "was he buried four grandmothers, out of those thirteen weeks. The foreman refused to discuss the grievance, and we went to the superintendent. Well, the foreman had done had it out with the superintendent. Superintendent said, 'I'm not going to even discuss it.' Then we go to the fourth stage, and Whitaker

Chief shop stewards and union officers, ca. 1946 (Collection of author)

brings out this man's record in writing and said, 'How can you honestly go before a board of arbitration and try to defend a person with a record like this?' We said to him that this person is a member of our union, and he has all the rights that any other member of our union has, regardless as to his absentee record or anything involving that. So we are going to arbitrate this case with a strong feeling that the arbitrator's decision just might be that this man is entitled to be reinstated. Of course, among ourselves, we never admitted it, but, you know, we knew he was going to lose. So the arbitrator's decision was that the company had investigated and found out that out of all these grandmothers that this guy had claimed that he attended the funerals for, that only one of his real grandmothers was dead. And [the company] had all this in the record.

"And you know that guy went back among the people over there in that plant and lambasted the union. He'd come up to the union office sometimes half drunk and stand downstairs there and cuss me and Slim Sheppard and Velma out. 'Damn union ain't no good. Taking people's money and then won't do nothing for them,' and all this. And the members got together and they called a meeting."

The workers appealed to the union not to carry the man's case forward because they had worked with him and knew that the company was right. "Now, the guy was a good union member. He paid his dues and he'd come to meetings, but he just wouldn't work. So the workers said to him, 'With enough members like you, you would wreck the union because you are causing suspicions to be thrown on a lot of other people who have legitimate grievances.' But it didn't bother us. It's just one of those things. Out of a large number of people like that, that had never been in a union before, you would expect to find a few people [like him] among the large membership."[61]

Industrial Jurisprudence

In the end, the intervention of the federal government dramatically altered labor-management relations at Reynolds. Without the assistance of the Conciliation Service, the NLRB, and the NWLB, the resolution of the conflict between unionists and the company would have been very different. The federal intervention in Winston-Salem imposed an overall structure and elaborated particular policies that reflected the generalized state of labor management relations in the United States.

These institutional developments bestowed a complex legacy on American workers. Looking back from the vantage point of the 1970s, when the mainstream labor movement had become increasingly hidebound and bureaucratized, labor historians began to argue that, for labor, the bargain had not been worth the price. They saw World War II as the fateful moment when the militant workers' movement of the 1930s tied its fortunes to the Democratic Party and to a potentially enervating system of legalistic, top-down state regulation. Submission to federal arbitration procedures made trade unions dangerously dependent on the party in power: when antiunion forces gained ascendancy, government regulation spelled disaster. Moreover, legal procedures that made eminent sense during a period of depression and world war had unintended consequences in a postwar atmosphere of peace, prosperity, and deepening conservatism. This new bureaucracy encouraged trade unions to put their needs for survival and security above their commitment to organizing the unorganized and forwarding the goals of equality and democracy within their own ranks, on the shop floor, and in the larger world.

In hindsight, that critique is telling. But the suggestion that labor could or should have resisted federal intervention applies mainly to male industrial workers in the North and West, whose claim to specialized skills gave them some control over the pace of production and for whom rank-and-file militancy, expressed in work slowdowns, wildcat strikes, and other methods, offered a realistic means of countering employers' power.

From the perspective of the South, and especially southern black workers, a federally imposed system of what came to be known as "industrial jurisprudence" was quite simply indispensable. Localism and personalism, in the workplace and in the community, lay at the heart of owners' power. Tobacco manufacturers viewed their black workforce through the prism of servitude. They saw employees less as workers with labor power to sell than as dependents at their beck and call. Supervisors treated blacks with an arbitrary mix of harshness and benevolence that drew on regional traditions of race relations. Black workers, moreover, had been excluded from the political process and subjected not to an evenhanded rule of law but to a capricious and often violent combination of legal and extralegal repression. For them, industrial jurisprudence was anything but a legalistic barrier to militancy. In the context of the times, it offered their only conceivable route to power. It positioned them, not as the South's "white man's burden"—an unruly, backward, servant population that had to be controlled and gradually uplifted—but as worker-citizens who were partners in producing the goods on which a war for democracy, at home and abroad, depended. In Winston Salem, they would use this new industrial rule of law to fashion their own version of representative government on the factory floor and to extend that experience of citizenship into the larger polity.

A *Pittsburgh Courier* correspondent caught the spirit of the moment when he visited Winston-Salem in 1944. "I was aware of a growing solidarity and intelligent mass action that will mean the dawn of a New Day in the South," he wrote. "One cannot visit Winston-Salem and mingle with the thousands of workers without sensing a revolution in thought and action. If there is a 'New' Negro, he is to be found in the ranks of the labor movement." But that "New Negro" meant something quite different to the white community than to blacks. And the revolution in thought and action that had transformed Winston Salem's black community still faced formidable barriers on the ground.[62]

CHAPTER NINE

In Dreams Begin Responsibilities

The fall of 1944 found Local 22 at a critical juncture. In any social movement, the transition from initial mobilization to institutionalization is fraught with both hope and danger. The structures that emerge from the inaugural battles must be strong enough to withstand the coming reaction, yet flexible enough to permit experimentation with new forms of social relations. The movement in Winston-Salem rested on a solid foundation. It commanded the loyalty of thousands of workers and the support of much of the black community. At its helm stood a remarkable group of indigenous leaders, and FTA provided critical staff support. To be sure, most white workers remained indifferent or hostile to the union's entreaties. Rank-and-filers, many of whom could barely read or write, would have to acquire new skills in order to function effectively as union members, and even TWOC veterans had much to learn as they steered their way through a maze of labor laws and political pressures. The task now was to create a firm, resilient organizational scaffolding while at the same time sustaining the momentum of a workers' movement. To that end, Local 22 launched a multipronged effort to develop the leaders, programs, and policies that would make it an effective voice for the workers' aspirations and a vehicle for democratic social change.

Creating a Union Culture

Shortly after the conclusion of the NWLB hearings, the international union appointed temporary officers for Local 22 with the approval of the shop stewards council. Frank Green, a twenty-three-year-old North Carolina native, a graduate of the University of North Carolina, and an FTA international representative in Charleston, South Carolina, replaced Frank Hargrove as chairman and director of the 10,000-member local, now the largest in the union. As a student, Green had been a member of the Young Communist League and the American People's Mobilization and had helped to organize a CIO union of janitors and laundry workers at the university. Upon graduation in 1942, he took a job with the federal government in Washington and became an active member of the Federation of Architects, Engineers, Chemists, and Technicians. FTA recruited him in 1944. "They were looking for someone to assign in the South," he remembered, "and they also wanted someone with a southern accent." Robert Black and Evan Blakely, a white worker in Number 12 and an early union supporter, served as vice chairmen.[1]

An executive board, consisting of all the officers and representatives of the international, oversaw the week-to-week operations of the union, but the force and character of the movement emanated from the men and women who made the daily trek up Third, Fourth, and Fifth Streets to their jobs in the factory. Rank-and-filers voiced their opinions in a number of forums, ranging from the annual election of union officers and the membership's ratification of the collective bargaining agreement (which had to be renegotiated every year) to departmental meetings and shop stewards councils. Hundreds also participated in the organizational life of the union as officers and members of committees on education, organizing, veterans affairs, welfare, and political action, as well as various subcommittees, each with its own complement of officers, meetings, and projects.[2]

During the organizing drive, the dense social networks within departments had proven to be the union's most important avenue for recruitment, and departmental gatherings, which functioned much like town meetings, represented union democracy in its most direct form. Twice a month, about half an hour after the end of the day and night shifts, workers from each department met in the union hall. They began with a prayer, a song, and a report from one of the union officers or staff members. After that the group took up the workers' questions and comments about conditions in the plants, "the attitude of the bosses," or anything else on their minds. "People talked freely about their problems," Velma Hopkins remembered about her departmental meetings, "because there wasn't nobody there but Number 256. We hashed it out with 256. You didn't have Number 12 or some other plant, be-

Frank Green (Parker-
Condax)

cause they might have the same problems but you might not feel free to talk in front of the people from Number 12."[3]

The shop stewards councils—one for Reynolds, one for the leaf houses, and one joining the two—symbolized the emergence of extradepartmental solidarities and served as the union's central legislative and policy-making bodies. The joint council of 200 members was the union's most dynamic assemblage. It met two or more times a month, initially at the Union Mission Holy Church and later at the union hall, always starting with prayer and song. Frank Green thought these were "the most important meetings held in the union [because these] were the day-to-day leaders of the union." The agenda varied from meeting to meeting, depending on what issues were critical at the time. When Green was chairman, he remembered, "We would have an open floor discussion for any steward to raise any question they wanted to." Many questions had to do with interpretations of the contract, and Green would offer his opinion. Soon the stewards were talking to each other. "One person might have one particular problem and somebody else who'd faced the same kind of problem and solved it in a certain way" would respond.[4]

The union hall became the hub for all of these activities. During the organizing drive, the TWOC had rented two offices in downtown Winston-Salem, one for white workers and one for black workers. By the summer of 1944, the union had out-grown those spaces, as well as some of the vulnerability that made separate offices necessary, so it moved to larger, integrated quarters. Situated across the street from the county courthouse with a direct view of the statue of the Confederate soldier and one block south of the Reynolds Building, the union headquarters served as a concrete embodiment of the workers' newfound power. One of the few racially integrated meeting spaces in town, the union hall stood as a challenge to the formal and informal strictures of Jim Crow. Each day when the shift changed, hundreds of men and women headed out the factory gates and walked up the hill to *their* office at 247 ½ North Main Street. The new offices also served as the center of an expanding array of cultural and educational activities. Chief among these was a "broad educational program" launched by the union on April 22, 1944.[5]

Workers' education had a long tradition in the South, and by the 1940s it had helped to produce a network of left-wing intellectuals eager to lend Local 22 their support. The industrial department of the YWCA was the first to address the social and educational needs of the South's growing class of wage workers. Beginning in the early 1920s, both black and white women benefited from YWCA programs that ranged from home economics and Bible study to courses in economics, history, and public speaking. Despite the dependence of community YWCAS on support from women whose husbands often formed the local business elite, the industrial secretaries introduced many workers to the principles of trade unionism and the ideal of cross-class solidarity among women.

The Southern Summer School for Women Workers in Industry grew out of this more radical wing of the YWCA movement and constituted the region's first residential workers' education program. Founded by Louise Leonard McLaren and Lois McDonald in 1927, the school held six-week sessions that sought to arm women with the confidence and knowledge that would enable them to participate fully in the southern labor movement. Bowing to the realities of segregation, the school was for whites only, but it challenged students' racial assumptions and stressed black and white workers' commonalities. The school's approach reflected the socialist perspectives of the its founders, and after the CIO's successful entry into the South, it allied itself closely with organized labor. Men joined, and the residential format gave way to short courses and weekend conferences. Well into the 1940s, when Brownie Lee Jones took over as director and focused especially on racial issues, the renamed Southern School for Workers remained an important source of instruction and inspiration for the region's workers.[6]

The other notable center of workers' education was the Highlander Folk School in Monteagle, Tennessee. Myles Horton and Don West, both Christian radicals, founded the school in 1932, modeling its programs on the Danish folk schools and paying careful attention to the particular needs of the South's poor and working people. As with the Southern Summer School, until 1944 only whites attended Highlander's residential sessions, but its staff was committed to a vision of a pluralistic, democratic society and to overcoming the prejudices of white workers. Horton and others frequently left Monteagle to work with biracial unions, and the addition to the staff of Zilphia Johnson Horton, who used music to break down racial barriers, helped to broaden the cultural appeal of the school. Hundreds of new unionists—including, especially after 1944, many black and white FTA members—made their way to the Tennessee mountains, and Highlander alumni furnished the southern labor movement with many effective grassroots leaders.[7]

This workers education network linked Local 22 members to the southern labor movement more generally. In the summer of 1944, two black women, Martha Moses and Lucy Mae Peoples, represented Local 22 at the Southern School for Workers' Fifth Annual Workers Education Conference in Richmond, Virginia. One-third of the 120 participants were African Americans. The session topics— "Labor and Community," "Next Steps in Eliminating the Poll Tax," "War Labor Board Policies"—aimed at alerting the South's newly organized workers to the fact that the fortunes of labor would be determined as much by regional and national politics as by collective bargaining and at driving home the point that only a truly biracial labor movement had a prayer of success.[8]

A few months later, the school's director, Brownie Lee Jones, led a special leadership training school for FTA in Winston-Salem that was attended by representatives of locals from across the South and by twenty-one members of Local 22. Sessions covered everything from demonstrations on how to use a mimeograph machine to the CIO's battle to defeat reactionary southern congressmen and revive the labor-based New Deal coalition.[9]

Workers from Winston-Salem continued to attend such residential programs and conferences, but Local 22 needed hundreds of rank-and-file leaders, and like many CIO unions, it moved quickly to develop its own extensive, in-house programs. In the days before the Wagner Act, the CIO, and the NWLB, a union official, called a business agent, with occasional help from the international office, could handle most of the chores associated with negotiating a contract, collecting dues, and other administrative matters. In fact, many AFL unions made no effort to involve the membership in the practical business of the organization. But FTA was dedicated not just to representing the bread-and-butter interests of its members but to building a democratic social movement, and that entailed promoting both men and women, blacks and whites, Reynolds employees and leaf house workers into positions of authority. Local 22 thus did double duty as a trade union and as a laboratory for the practice of participatory democracy.[10]

As soon as the ink had dried on its contract with Reynolds, Local 22 hired Eleanore Hoagland as its full-time educational director. Hoagland's husband, William Binkley, was a veteran of radical politics in the area: he had worked for the Trade Union Unity League, defied the efforts of Winston-Salem's Board of Aldermen to keep Communist organizers out of the city, and run for Congress on the Communist Party ticket. Like the leaders of the Southern Summer School, Hoagland had received her political education from the YWCA. A native of Chicago, she earned a bachelor's degree in social science from Northwestern University and did graduate work at Northwestern and the University of Chicago before serving as a YWCA industrial secretary for twelve years, first in Indiana and later in New Orleans. Like many industrial secretaries, Hoagland moved steadily to the left and felt increasingly constrained by the compromises her YWCA job required; she eventually took a position in the educational department of the International Ladies Garment Workers Union in Chicago. Moving to New Orleans, she married Binkley, who had become the Communist Party's district organizer, and in the early 1940s the couple returned to North Carolina to take over his family's farm. Each had played a minor role in the TWOC organizing drive, and Hoagland's extensive background in workers' education and left-wing connections made her a perfect person to head the union's effort.[11]

Hoagland wasted no time getting started, and by early summer the education department was "in a whirl of work and activity." She began by addressing the high level of illiteracy among workers, a task that spoke volumes about the system of racial oppression the union had to combat. Blaming themselves rather than the injuries perpetrated by poverty and discrimination, many unionists tried to conceal their inability to read and write. "A worker came to me," Hoagland recalled, "and gave me a letter and asked what did I think of it. After a while I realized he wanted me to read it for him. He couldn't read." For those who needed immediate help writing letters or preparing grievance slips, the union offered an "Aid in Writing" class. Hoagland remembered that "it was very hard to find materials for adult education," especially ones that spoke to African Americans' experiences. FTA Local 26 in Suffolk, Virginia, contacted faculty members at Hampton Institute, a historically black college, who provided the union with teaching materials. The Southern

Eleanore Hoagland
(*UCAPAWA News*)

School for Workers also helped, and director Brownie Lee Jones called for unions, departments of education, and community groups to go beyond such programs to develop a more broad-based "attack on illiteracy in the South."[12]

The education department's newspaper, *The Worker's Voice,* provided a means of communication between the union and the workers and encouraged the workers' growing sense of themselves as citizens of a wider world. The *Winston-Salem Journal,* published by Gordon Gray, barely recognized the existence of the city's working-class population. Workers, black and white, made news largely as victims or perpetrators of criminal activity or as servants retiring from loyal service to a prominent white family. The *Journal* did devote a page to "Negro News" on Sundays, but it carried mostly stories about the middle class, although given the relative fluidity of black community life, workers might appear there in their roles as choral group organizers, church members, and the like. *The Worker's Voice,* by contrast, featured workers and assumed their right to a voice on domestic and international issues as well as union affairs.

Local 22 also broadcast a weekly radio show on station WAIR. The national radio networks ignored African American listeners while attracting large audiences with programs like *Amos 'n' Andy* that used African America characters for comic effect. In Winston-Salem, however, the sheer size of the black population translated into consumer power, and local stations (even those owned by the same men who ran the factories and published the antiunion *Winston-Salem Journal*) were remarkably open to broadcasting union news. The relative openness of a powerful new medium, the need to fill up the airwaves, and the eagerness with which black and white workers joined the listening audience all helped to make radio a key means by which the union spoke to its members and conveyed its political views to the public at large. Radio also furnished one of the chief venues—an alternative public space— in which the town's citizens could comprehend and debate the larger issues that the struggle for unionization brought into high relief.[13]

In part because of Eleanore Hoagland's special commitment to women workers and in part because of black women's traditional role as teachers and lay church leaders, the educational department quickly became the center of women's activities in the union. Those activities, in turn, often became the springboard by which women emerged as rank-and-file leaders and as the union's most effective political educators. Moranda Smith, one of Local 22's most eloquent and beloved representatives, was a case in point.[14]

A native of Dunbar, South Carolina, Smith moved with her family to Winston-Salem in 1920 when she was five years old. She began working at Reynolds in 1933 after graduating from high school at the age of eighteen. "She was like hundreds of other people," Robert Black recalled. "She was convinced that Reynolds was a big giant and that nobody was going to be able to ever pin a contract to him. At the beginning of the union, Moranda was working in the same department where my sister was working and when they made the decision that they was going to close the plant and all the people in the plant was told that at a certain time we're going to pull the switches and turn off these machines, Moranda stayed on her machine." Lonnie Nesmith remembered that "it took a long time before we could convert her. She was stubborn. It was in her, but we just couldn't get her to move. But when she moved and got the wheel turned, you couldn't stop her." According to Black, "she began to attend meetings and, somehow, somebody got over the importance to Moranda to become an outspoken person in her department. Through the education committee Moranda developed. She was just as strong a leader in the union after she had got a hold of herself as she was against the union in the early stages."[15]

Moranda Smith (Collection of author)

Eleanore Hoagland remembered that Smith "came by every day after work to talk and read." She had just had a baby, and "she wanted her child to have things that she didn't have." In informal as well as formal ways, Hoagland became one of Smith's mentors. Hoagland remembered, for example, that she "left her appointment book out for Moranda to see as a way of teaching her how to do things." Having benefited from the education department's various programs, Smith began devoting her time to helping others. In November 1945 the workers elected her to chair the education committee.[16]

Union leadership training in Hoagland's hands aimed not only at developing administrative skills, but at political education on a grander scale. With the aid of Rosalie Green, whose husband was Frank Green, director of Local 22, Hoagland offered classes on labor history, black history, and current events. These classes introduced workers who had been denied self-governance for generations to the nitty-gritty operations of City Hall, the statehouse, Congress, and beyond. That alone had radical implications, as blacks nationwide were gaining a leverage at the ballot box they had never had before. But Local 22 went beyond the regional and national levels, joining the fate of workers in Winston Salem to that of their counterparts around the world and of blacks throughout the African diaspora.[17]

As the war progressed, it not only transformed the domestic landscape, it brought to the fore the links between race relations at home and colonial exploitation abroad. Rooted in the cross-fertilization between leftist and Pan African movements after the Russian Revolution, popular anticolonialism flowered during and after World War II, spurred on by the Italian invasion of Ethiopia in 1935, the postwar creation of the United Nations as a forum for adjudicating international conflicts and addressing oppression on a worldwide scale, and the emergence of colonial liberation movements in India, Asia, and Africa. This critique of imperialism was embraced by the black press and by mainstream black leaders such as Walter White of the NAACP and Mary McLeod Bethune of the National Council of Negro Women as well as by leftists such as W. E. B. Du Bois, A. Philip Randolph, and Paul Robeson, the internationally acclaimed singer and Shakespearean actor. The protest against Western indifference to the fascist attack on Ethiopia, in particular, marked a watershed because, as Robeson put it, it exposed "the parallel between [black American] interests and those of oppressed peoples abroad." In leader-ship classes and departmental meetings, in union publications and in the black press, Local 22 members saw their own movement linked to a global struggle for democracy.[18]

Along with classes on political issues, the education department offered lessons in labor and black history that emphasized the story of African American resistance to domestic oppression. Winston-Salem's black churches and schools had long used Emancipation Day as a moment of celebration and reflection. Building on that keen historical consciousness, the union invited Herbert Aptheker, one of his generation's most prolific scholars of African American history and a prominent member of the Central Committee of the Communist Party, to speak to Local 22 members during Negro History Week. Aptheker's book, *American Negro Slave Revolts*, published in 1943, was a favorite among union members, and shortly after his appearance, *The Worker's Voice* published an article on Denmark Vesey, who led one of the South's most spectacular slave revolts. Leaf house workers made presentations and led discussions on the life of Harriet Tubman, who escaped from slavery and then made daring forays into the South to guide dozens of slaves to freedom.[19]

The education department's library became a special point of pride. Hoagland stocked novels, biographies, and poetry as well as books on labor history, black history, and current events. She also made an assortment of labor newspapers available—the *FTA News*, the *CIO News*, and the *Daily Worker*—along with dozens of booklets with instructions on how workers could become better union members. According to Hoagland, a batch of pamphlets on political and international affairs would arrive on Friday and be "completely sold out by Saturday afternoon." The demand grew so great that the education committee had to set up borrowing procedures and fine delinquent readers. "You know, at that little library the city had for us, you couldn't find any books on Negro history," Viola Brown, chair of the shop stewards council, remembered. "They didn't have books by Aptheker, DuBois, or Frederick Douglass. But we had them at our library."[20]

Hoagland, Robert Black remembered, "drawed in a lot of people, male and female, who attended her classes. She discussed different phases of the union, how to handle grievances, how to perform as shop stewards. It really spurred the rank and file leadership to become more militant. She had large attendance in her classes. The membership, through Eleanore's educational classes—I'm sure she didn't go all out [with Marxist ideas]. But the understanding that she was able to instill in the rank-and-file membership caused them to become more militant. They began to look around and make suggestions and give ideas as to what they thought would strengthen the organization. Eleanore, in the membership meetings, in the educational report, she would always point out something pertaining to politics, the records of the congressmen, what the board of aldermen and the city administration were doing or what should be done. She continued to develop the thinking of the rank-and-file." Hoagland was amazed by the eagerness of her students. "They wanted to learn everything in one meeting," she remembered.[21]

Schooled in a workers' education movement that saw sports as a means of fostering teamwork, discipline, and self-respect and anxious to make Local 22 integral to local community life, Hoagland put almost as much energy into social and recreational activities as into education. Despite meager funding, athletic competition was central to the life of black high schools and colleges. Rivalries with neighboring football, basketball, and baseball teams drew hundreds of spectators and received regular coverage in the *Journal*'s weekly "Negro News" page. But college was the privilege of a special few, and many workers never completed high school, so for most working people—especially for African Americans, who were excluded from most textile and hosiery teams—recreation remained informal, a matter of pickup games in dusty lots rather than formal team competition. In this as in other public services, blacks had to fall back on their own resources and ingenuities. The city and the YMCA/YWCA sponsored a few organized recreational activities for African Americans, but never enough to meet the demand. A 1947 Urban League

The CIO Tigers, Local 22's hard-hitting baseball team (*FTA News*)

study found drastic inequalities in the recreational facilities in the city. Whites had access to twenty-seven baseball diamonds; blacks had eight. The city maintained four swimming pools for whites, but only one for blacks.[22]

Nevertheless, sports, which linked mind and body, individual achievement and community spirit, provided one of the few arenas in which both white and black workers could express their talents and achieve public renown. Local 22's recreation program became a major attraction for participants and fans alike. A union athletic committee organized a swimming class at the black City Park pool and launched an ambitious program of women's softball. Within a few weeks, a league with six teams and ninety players had sprung to life. The Winston-Salem Recreation Department cooperated with Local 22, allowing the women to use the field and showers at City Park, which were normally restricted to men's baseball teams. An all-union team competed in the all-black city league in 1946. Baseball was a particular passion for many male unionists, and they flocked to a new CIO league. The first summer almost one hundred players participated on the nine teams. Local 22 sponsored a baseball team, the CIO Tigers, in the all-black city league; the team won the championship in 1946. A committee of male workers also organized a checker tournament, where enthusiasts like Robert Black established bragging rights among union members.[23]

Music, too, became a central ingredient in the life of the union. African American music had always had an oppositional cast. Antebellum spirituals had revolved around the hope for release from bondage, and work songs helped to counter the soul-destroying pace of work in the tobacco plants. In the 1930s and 1940s, white vernacular performers as well as black blues musicians and gospel quartets carried on this protest tradition. The Popular Front played an important role in disseminating a regional music of "release, redemption, and revolt." Two white Kentucky women, Aunt Molley Jackson and Sarah Ogan Gunning, preserved the terror and pathos of the Depression-era mining wars in powerful songs. Margaret Larkin, a pioneering folklorist who championed new voices on the left, carried the songs of textile worker Ella May Wiggins from Gastonia to New York and helped to convince left cultural critics of the aesthetic and political value of the unadorned Appalachian style. John Hammond, who covered the Scottsboro trials in 1933 and published a host of union newspapers, recruited Piedmont blues musicians for Popular Front concerts and rallies. As World War II approached, Winston-Salem's black singing groups increasingly included James Weldon Johnson's "Lift Every Voice and Sing," known as the "Negro national anthem," in their repertoires. Paul Robeson in particular symbolized the links between the left and black popular culture. Projecting a vision of a prosperous America unmarred by divisions of race and class, his version of Earl Robinson's "Ballad for Americans" became the hymn of the left in the thirties and forties.[24]

The Communist Party, influenced by Robeson and other black leaders, encouraged cultural exchange between whites and blacks and exhorted whites to acknowledge blacks' contribution to the nation's heritage. This support was of inestimable value during an era when even white liberals often saw black culture as a pathological reaction to oppression. The Party, by contrast, drove home the point that the "distinctive culture of blacks contributed to much that was vital and original in American life."[25]

Southern leftists, whether Christian radicals, trade unionists, independents, socialists, or Communists, were deeply affected by and instrumental in creating this cultural milieu. Claude Williams, the white preacher from Arkansas whose radical interpretation of the Bible infused UCAPAWA's tobacco organizing campaigns, and John Handcox, a black sharecropper from Missouri, turned spirituals into labor songs for the Southern Tenant Farmers Union. "Roll the Union On" and "No More Mourning"—both of which became favorites of Local 22—were first sung at meetings in the rural areas of Missouri and Arkansas. At a UCAPAWA leadership training school in Memphis in 1940, a black sharecropper transformed the hymn "Gospel Train" into "Union Train." Zilphia Horton of Highlander Folk School, along with Woody Guthrie, the Oklahoma Dust Bowl balladeer, Pete Seeger, a radical folklorist who helped spark the left-wing folk revival of the thirties and forties, and the Almanac Singers carried this protest music throughout the region and the nation.[26]

Drawing on a tradition of labor songs that dated back to the nineteenth century as well as on these Depression-era developments, the CIO gave music pride of place in its organizing activities. Even CIO president John L. Lewis, who personally preferred "high culture," acknowledged what popular culture could do: "A singing army is a winning army, and a singing labor movement cannot be defeated. . . . The fact that a man sings shows that his spirit is still free and searching, and such a spirit will not submit to servitude. When hundreds of men and women in a labor union sing together, their individual longing for dignity and freedom are bound into an irrepressible force. Workers who hesitate are swept into the movement, and before all these determined marchers, united by their purpose and their singing, the citadels of oppression crumble and surrender."[27]

In Winston-Salem, that "irrepressible force" began when the Smith Choral Club sang at cottage meetings during the initial organizing drive and a Reynolds worker made union records for workers to listen to surreptitiously at home. Every meeting— from departmental gatherings to shop stewards councils to the largest mass rally— opened with a prayer and a hymn. Theodosia Simpson led the first mass meeting in 1943 in the singing of "Do Lord, Remember Me." This spiritual became something of a theme song for the union. As workers learned the words to labor songs, their voices simultaneously praised the Lord and condemned the bosses. Throughout the 1940s, Winston-Salem workers performed at international union conventions, giving delegates a taste of the spirit and culture of southern tobacco workers.

Over the years Zilphia Horton, Woody Guthrie, Pete Seeger, and Paul Robeson made pilgrimages to Local 22. Robeson became an especially beloved figure. A Phi Beta Kappa graduate and All-American football player at Rutgers University, Robeson was fluent in dozens of languages and dialects. He had appeared on stages and in meeting places throughout Europe, Asia, Africa, and North America. He could truly be called a "citizen of the world."[28]

Beginning in the late 1930s, Robeson had moved increasingly to the left. An ardent socialist, antifascist, and internationalist, he refused to see assimilation as the answer to African Americans' problems; he praised black culture and raised the spiritual to the level of the European operas he also sang. The son of slaves, he embraced the struggles of southern workers as his own. Throughout the life of Local 22, Robeson appeared in Winston Salem at critical junctures, investing events in North Carolina with world-historical meaning and linking local people to the global liberation movement of which he was a leading symbol.[29]

Left to right: Bea McCrea, Moranda Smith, [unknown], Theodosia Simpson, and Velma Hopkins singing for the 1946 FTA convention (Parker-Condax)

While these performers brought music from elsewhere, they also learned from Winston-Salem workers, whose songs in turn became part of the protest tradition. Members of Local 22 adapted the music of "Solidarity Forever" for a picket line favorite, "'T' Stands for Tobacco." Perhaps the most famous protest song of the twentieth century, "We Shall Overcome," emerged from a situation very much like that in Winston-Salem. In 1945, black workers in FTA Local 15 struck the American Tobacco Company in Charleston, South Carolina. One of the traditional hymns they adapted was "I Will Overcome." As with most folk songs, no one wrote out the words and music, and no one put his or her name on a song sheet. One Charleston worker even speculated that organizers from Local 22 had brought the song to town when they came to help with the organizing campaigns. Whatever its origin, "I Will Overcome" became a Local 15 favorite. While attending workshops at Highlander, two strike participants, Anna Lee Bonneau and Evelyn Risher, taught the song to Zilphia Horton, who, along with Pete Seeger and Highlander's Guy Carawan, spread it among labor and civil rights activists across the country.[30]

Just as important as the blues allegories of "imprisonment, exploitation, and Jim Crow" and the labor songs "zippered" into religious and popular tunes were the hymns themselves. The hymns and spirituals that resounded at every meeting gave unionization a transcendent meaning, likening it to the prophetic tradition of black churches. Workers who might have been ill at ease in a traditional union meeting could feel at home in a meeting that resembled a Sunday service. In addition to the ability to heal a broken heart, lessen the burdens of work, and smooth the way for the life hereafter, song had the power to sting the meanest foe and, through call and response, to make each individual singer part of the group. These overlapping musical genres produced the soundtrack of black labor activism, and taken together, they forwarded the "laboring of American culture" by infusing popular musical forms with the sensibility of the black working class.[31]

"You've Got to Organize Continuously"

Workers' education, music, and recreation all sustained the workers' movement. Equally important was the need to reach those who remained outside the union fold. Most workers who had supported the TWOC became active members of Local 22, but hundreds of others, after having voted for the union, still had not signed membership cards or begun paying dues. The union needed their money, of course, but more important, it needed their support in the factory and their participation in union affairs.

There were also the 3,000 workers who had voted for the Employees Association to consider. What role, if any, could they be expected to play? Most were whites whose racial prejudices, combined with pressure from the company, made them unlikely candidates for membership. But the union could not give up on them, for both practical and ideological reasons. Local 22 had to have at least some white support in order to maintain its numerical majority, and white unionists were anxious to recruit their fellow workers in order to combat their own isolation and gain support in the white community. Beyond that, while black FTA activists invoked an ethic of racial pride and solidarity, they also maintained interracialism as an article of faith. Influenced in part by the teachings of the black church, which held fast to the hope that whites would cast off the sin of racism and embrace the brotherhood of all people, in part by the secular radicalism of a left-led union, and in part by popular anticolonialism, both FTA organizers and local black and white leaders were committed to breaking down the barriers to class solidarity that white supremacy had created and reinforced. With time, they believed, white workers could and would come to see that their interests lay in class-based alliances, not in loyalty to Reynolds, and put the benefits of organization ahead of those that whiteness conferred.

Local 22's experience gave substance to these hopes. After all, Clark Sheppard, Etta Hobson, and a few hundred other white workers had found the courage to buck the company and openly throw in their lot with a black-led union at a time when its success was by no means assured. As the union proved its staying power and its ability to improve the lives of whites and blacks alike, there was every reason to believe that this circle of white supporters would expand.

Unionists, moreover, could look to other models of success. The West Virginia and Tennessee coalfields, the Louisiana docks, the Birmingham mining district, and the timberlands of East Texas had all sustained interracial unions at the beginning of the twentieth-century. In Memphis, Norfolk, Richmond, Atlanta, Birmingham, and New Orleans, the CIO's policy of nondiscrimination was again, however slowly, opening the door to an interracial movement.[32]

To be sure, racial divisions had historically been a rock on which southern union campaigns had faltered, especially in those few industries that employed both black and white workers. And Local 22 leaders were keenly aware of the difficulties ahead. Ironically, FTA's very success among blacks posed problems for organizing whites. Like all social movements, the union depended on personal networks and shared cultural symbols. It had gone to great lengths to cast the issues it raised in class rather than racial terms; still, there was no denying the union's opposition to racial discrimination or the centrality of the black church in mobilizing black workers. Segregation was such an effective means of maintaining the economic status quo precisely because it seemed to promise white workers protection from black competition; it had effectively cut white and black workers off from each other. The union would have to build cultural, institutional, and personal bridges across the racial divide. It would have to convince white workers that white supremacy offered only false promises—that the chimera of white privilege was not worth the trade-off of poverty and powerlessness, the scourge of the South's workers, white and black alike.

Local 22 would also have to overcome the nexus of sex and race that had twisted through the turn-of-the century white supremacy campaign and remained an undercurrent of everyday race relations. Interactions between white women and black men could still lead to false rape charges, lynchings, and—more common now—the court-sponsored railroading of blacks. An incident could occur out of the blue and mesmerize a whole community.

The union had found itself embroiled in just such an explosive situation as the NWLB adjudicated the details of the 1944 contract between Reynolds and Local 22. On the last day of the hearings, a shouting match broke out between union leaders and white workers in the Employees Association that resulted in the police charging TWOC organizer William DeBerry with assaulting a white woman. The prospect of a headline proclaiming "WHITE WOMAN ATTACKED BY BLACK UNION ORGANIZER" was a union's worse nightmare and could have been a bonanza to those who all along had predicted that FTA's "race mixing" would lead to violence and violation.

That morning's testimony had heightened tensions between association members and union supporters. Louise Johnson, a fifteen-year Reynolds veteran, was among the small group of white workers who had originally supported the TWOC, but she had quit the union shortly after the election. In an affidavit read by company attorneys at the hearing, she charged that, after she withdrew, "a number of threats were made against me. Vivian Bruce, who acted as secretary of C.I.O. meetings, threatened to throw me out of the window of the factory." Johnson claimed that Frank Hargrove had told her, "'When we get our contract with your company, we will make it so hot for you at the factory that you will quit the R. J. Reynolds Tobacco Company.'"[33]

When the hearings adjourned for the noon recess, Johnson remained seated in the jury box talking with other association members. In later court testimony she recounted her confrontation with DeBerry. "I came down out of the jury box . . . [with] my back to the Courtroom" and started talking to R. T. Hauser, another association member. At that point, Johnson claimed, DeBerry "came up and slapped me and grabbed my skirt and pulled it. I kind of turned and looked up, it scared me so, and when I did, he was just standing there with his hands clenched, and gritting his teeth. He seemed awfully mad. . . . When [he] did that, Mr. Hauser spoke up and said, 'You keep your hands and your eyes off her.'"[34]

William DeBerry's account of the events differed substantially. He claimed that he was conferring with UCAPAWA legislative director Elizabeth Sasuly and other union members when "I heard a lady's voice . . . say something about 'them damn leaders' and what she would do when she got on the stand to testify against the CIO. When I looked around, Mr. Hauser said, 'Keep your damn eyes off that woman.' I said, 'What did you say?' He said, 'Keep your damn eyes off that woman.' I said, 'Are you crazy?' At that time Garfield Wilson [a black union activist] walked up and Mr. Hauser said, 'You, too.' Garfield said, 'Me what?' Mr. Hauser said, 'Keep your damn eyes off that woman, you black s.o.b.'s.' Garfield jerked his glasses off and said, 'You are another one.' That is all that was said." Union leaders quickly separated DeBerry and Wilson from the association members, the courtroom cleared, and the afternoon session continued. After the panel adjourned, Johnson went to the police station and filed a complaint charging that DeBerry "had slapped or pushed her" during the recess of the NWLB hearings. She claimed that she had not cried out in the courtroom because she was scared and had not reported the matter immediately because she did not know where to go. The police charged DeBerry with assault and issued a warrant for his arrest.[35]

Given the circumstances, Johnson's account was implausible. No black man, especially one with the political savvy of William DeBerry, would have slapped a white woman in a crowded courtroom. One possible scenario is that Johnson, Hauser, and the other association members decided during lunch to add a few details to a verbal exchange and swear out a warrant against DeBerry for assaulting a woman. Such a ploy was entirely in keeping with the tenor of the association's and the company's attacks on the union. When the TWOC looked into the accusations made in the affidavits produced by Reynolds, a number of workers claimed that the incidents had been fabricated by company personnel and that they had signed the affidavits at the instruction of their foreman without knowing their contents. Both Hauser and Johnson knew how badly such charges could taint the union cause.

On the other hand, it is possible that in the heat of the moment Louise Johnson actually believed that William DeBerry had slapped her. The angry verbal exchange that DeBerry and other union leaders described undoubtedly took place. Feelings were at a high pitch as a result of the affidavits read by the company attorney that morning, and serious altercations between blacks and whites always held the potential for physical violence. Johnson, moreover, may have had reason to be particularly susceptible to exaggerating the details of her confrontation with union leaders. In her affidavit she claimed that she just "didn't like their policies." But she may have had, or thought she had, a more personal grievance against union officials. An FBI report claimed she gave John Whitaker an affidavit "alleging moral misconduct" on the part of Frank Hargrove and Donald Henderson.[36]

In any case, in joining the union Johnson had broken powerful, anxiety-causing taboos. Her brief sojourn in Local 22 brought her into social contact not only with local black men but with white and black international union leaders, and for her these interactions may have carried a frightening sexual charge. She certainly came under intense pressure from supervisors, other white workers, and her own friends and family to abandon such a controversial cause.

Like many who repent the evils of their former ways, Johnson became fervent in her antiunionism. She not only left the union, she joined the Employees Association and took a personal interest in its charges against the union, going so far as to provide an affidavit and attend the NWLB hearings. If DeBerry was right, she also initiated the confrontation with her comments about the "damn [union] leaders."

The warrant for DeBerry's arrest demonstrated the persistent link between racial and sexual phobias and how those fears could be mobilized to undermine interracial movements. Yet the fact that Louise Johnson and the other Employees Association members looked to the courts for redress also indicated how much things had changed since the days of the white supremacy campaign. Hundreds of black men had died in the South without the benefit of a trial for allegedly committing crimes no worse than DeBerry's purported assault. And the fact that R. J. Hauser would let Garfield Wilson call him an "s.o.b." without immediately striking back would have been unthinkable in earlier times and in other places.

Writing about notions of justice in the nineteenth-century South, the historian Edward Ayers observes: "When black gestures signaled flagrant contempt, many white southern men literally knew no way to react other than with violence. If a black man insulted a white man and the white man did not strike back immediately, he had, in his own eyes and the eyes of his peers, no honor left to lose." That code of behavior was still in force in much of the South in 1944. What constrained Hauser? Self-interest, perhaps: he was certainly outnumbered by union members at the time. The new status and power of black workers, a transformation that surely fed his antiunionism, might have inhibited him as well. But Hauser's constraint was also an indication of the increasing desire and ability of the state, particularly in urban areas, to control and contain the violent behavior it had sanctioned in the past.[37]

Nevertheless, DeBerry and union leaders had reason to take the incident very seriously. The whole thing "caught us all by surprise," DeBerry remembered, "We didn't know what was going on. Frank Hargrove said, 'Bill, go to Philadelphia until we can find out what the hell's going on and what we can do.'" Union officials feared that DeBerry's life might be in danger. Lynch law might have been largely a thing of the past in North Carolina in the 1940s, but the memories of "mobocracy" remained vividly alive.[38]

DeBerry left but returned a week later and turned himself in to police. "I'd never been arrested a day in my life," he remembered. "They fingerprinted me, mugged me, measured me, and I don't know what-all. They took me to the jail. There were some prisoners in there that knew me; everybody knew me. They said, 'Brother DeBerry, what you doing in here?' Well, I just couldn't say nothing." Evan Blakely, a white worker and TWOC member, soon arrived to post DeBerry's bail. "When I walked out down the street," DeBerry continued, "there were two plainclothes po-

William DeBerry (*UCAPAWA News*)

licemen in front of me and two in back, and I was in the middle, walking as though I was John Dillinger. People were looking out of office windows at me. I got calls. They'd threaten me. And I mentioned it to the workers, and they took turns walking around my house with shotguns and pistols."[39]

A few days before DeBerry went to trial, the *Journal* reprinted an editorial from a South Carolina newspaper offering "Advice to Colored People of the South." The editorial acknowledged that conditions for African Americans had improved during the New Deal and World War II, but it warned that they should neither take such advances for granted nor use their newfound leverage to "stir up trouble." After all, the economic bloom of the war would fade, jobs would once again be scarce, and wages would fall. Frightfully similar to the warning issued by Winston Democrats during the white supremacy campaign, the editorial continued: "The boss man who has jobs to offer will hire the people he can depend on. He will re-member these times, and he will ask: 'How did you act when times were good?'" More generally, communities would punish people who pressed too hard for change. "Any person, white or black, who starts conflicts or tries to stir up trouble is a public enemy," the editorial concluded. Perhaps William DeBerry's allusion to feeling like John Dillinger, "Public Enemy No. 1," was not so farfetched. In any event, he and the leaders of UCAPAWA had been duly warned.[40]

When DeBerry appeared in municipal court on July 7, the judge found him guilty of assaulting a woman and sentenced him to thirty days at hard labor. De-fense attorneys appealed, and on July 13 the case came before the Forsyth Superior Court. William DeBerry and Louise Johnson stuck to their earlier stories, as did all of the witnesses. But rather than confine the trial to the charges against DeBerry, Solicitor Erle McMichael used the occasion to paint the union as a vehicle for black social equality. Like the Emergency Citizens Committee and the Reynolds Employ-ees Association, McMichael sought to racialize the unionization effort, obscuring its economic goals and its challenge to class as well as race relations and thus un-dermining its potential appeal to white workers.[41]

John Erle McMichael was a solid member of the Winston-Salem elite. His father had been a successful lawyer. After serving in World War I and taking a law degree at the University of North Carolina, McMichael returned to set up a practice in the Twin City. He spent most of his career as an officer of the court, first as a clerk, then as assistant solicitor, and later, beginning in 1937, as solicitor of the Superior Court. He belonged to both the Twin City and Forsyth County Country Clubs (although not to the more prestigious Old Town club). During his tenure in the solicitor's office, McMichael had earned the special enmity of black citizens. Robert Black re-membered McMichael's reputation and his courtroom manner. "He was real reb-bish. He would stand up in court and call you a big nappy-headed nigger."[42]

Rather than trying to uncover the facts of the case against DeBerry, McMichael asked repeated questions about the interracial practices of the union. His point seemed to be that these breaches of southern etiquette had stilled DeBerry's fear and allowed his rapacious instincts to emerge. "You call Mrs. Sasuly [UCAPAWA's white legislative director] 'sister' at the hearings all the time?" McMichael asked De-Berry. "Yes, sir, but I don't put my hands on her," DeBerry retorted. When UCA-PAWA's field representative, Clara Hutchinson, who was white, took the stand, McMichael's main concern was whether she had been "hauling Negroes to the polls" during the Democratic primary that spring. He also questioned her about referring to DeBerry as "Mister DeBerry" and "Bill." According to the UCAPAWA

News, McMichael became "hysterically lyrical" during the trial as he recounted all that had been "'done for the niggers'" in Winston-Salem.

The point McMichael tried to drive home to the jury was that the union was an incubator of revolt against southern racial mores, nurturing dangerous visions of social equality between blacks and whites. The familiarity between DeBerry and the white female unionists was a breach of racial rules that opened the door to sexual aggression. Louise Johnson's testimony mobilized those sexual fears. In her initial statement to the police, she had claimed that DeBerry "slapped or pushed her"; by the time the case came to court she added the incendiary charges that he "grabbed her buttocks," tried to pull her skirt, and "leered."

The jury needed only twenty minutes to return a guilty verdict, despite the conflicting testimony. All-white juries rarely doubted the word of a white woman against a black man. The judge increased DeBerry's sentence to sixty days on the road. Again, DeBerry's lawyers appealed.[43]

UCAPAWA established a defense committee to raise money for legal fees. This was no Scottsboro case, but a small, articulate group of liberals, laborites, and civil rights activists could be counted on for support. A national campaign generated contributions from workers throughout the country. Union attorneys appealed to the North Carolina Supreme Court, which heard the case in December 1944. It reversed the decision of the lower court on the grounds that since the alleged assault occurred on federal property, state and municipal authorities had no right to arrest and prosecute DeBerry.[44]

The accusations against William DeBerry represented the culmination of a year-long campaign waged by Reynolds Tobacco Company, the Emergency Citizens Committee, and the Employees Association to discredit and destroy the unionization campaign. They also underscored one of the greatest difficulties the new local would continue to face: recruiting white members in the face both of overwhelming cultural barriers and sexualized racial fears and of opponents' attempts to exploit those barriers and fears to the hilt. Still, the outcome of the case offered cause for hope. The case would never have arisen and played out as it had if white workers were a monolith. Louise Johnson had, after all, originally cast her lot with UCAPAWA, and some white unionists had sided with DeBerry. One had even posted his bail. In an industry dominated by blacks, the union's survival required only a solid minority of intrepid white support. Moreover, the mobilization of the black community, the watchful eye of federal officials, and the commitment of officialdom to

Velma Hopkins (*FTA News*)

replacing the sledgehammer of lynching with more subtle mechanisms of white power ensured that DeBerry would walk away relatively unscathed.

In the months and years that followed, attracting white members became a major battlefront in Local 22's struggle both for institutional survival and for political and cultural clout. From the outset, the union sought to overcome the barriers to white participation by endorsing a biracial leadership structure and enlisting white organizers to make direct appeals to white workers. In the spring of 1945, it hired Gene Pratt, a Forsyth County native and the former president of AFL Local 178 at Brown & Williamson. It was risky to hire an official of a union that had so strongly opposed the CIO, and in the end the decision proved disastrous. But Pratt made a strong public case for his decision to join the CIO. "The CIO is more progressive than the AFL," he said, "and better qualified to meet the demands of the post war era. Knowing that the CIO does not tolerate discrimination makes me proud to become a part of this wonderful organization."[45]

The union also recruited white organizers from within the rank and file. Spencer Long worked in the carpenters shop at Reynolds; in June 1946 he took a three-month leave of absence to join the staff of Local 22 as an organizer. Also a native of Forsyth County, Long had not been among the early white recruits but had joined FTA sometime in 1945. His job was to bring in the skilled workers—electricians, plumbers, and carpenters. He apparently had some success in meeting with workers and even signed up a small number, but the usual response to his inquiries seems to have been, "We'll think about it."[46]

In the summer of 1945, workers formed a committee of volunteer organizers to consolidate the union's support in both white and black departments where membership remained low; the committee sponsored a contest with prizes for the person who brought in the most new members. The final two weeks of the contest coincided with the fifteen-day "escape" period mandated by the union's collective bargaining agreement. From July 16 through July 30, any member could withdraw from the union and "escape" the dues checkoff for the following year. After that, union members had to remain in good standing or lose their jobs. The antiunion Employees Association used the occasion to pass out hundreds of escape cards in the factory. In turn, volunteer organizers intensified their campaign to help workers "escape from the clutches of the boss." Four thousand workers, most of whom were black, turned out for a rally that capped the organizing drive.[47]

Soon afterward the union established a permanent Organizing Committee with Velma Hopkins at its helm. Her outgoing personality, her fearlessness, her firm base in Shiloh Baptist Church, and her connections throughout the black community made her a perfect choice for the job. She also epitomized the democratic leadership style that did so much to secure workers' loyalty and to give rank-and-file members a sense of ownership and responsibility. As Hopkins explained it, "I know my limitations and I surround myself with people that I can designate to be sure it's carried out. If you can't do that you're not an organizer."[48]

Most of the committee's efforts focused on the year-round workers at Reynolds, but the seasonal employees in the leaf houses at Reynolds, Piedmont, Winston, and Export offered a fertile field for recruits as well. In August 1945 the opening of the tobacco market signaled the beginning of the green leaf season in the industry, and hundreds of seasonal workers began lining up outside the employment offices at Reynolds and the other leaf houses. "Armed to the teeth with application cards and pencils . . . organizers talked unionism and signed the workers as fast as they were hired." Frustrated with the union's success, Reynolds started holding the newly hired workers in the employment office until there was a sizable group. "Then," according to *The Worker's Voice*, "they would send the whole gang out in a bunch, led by a company guard" and march "them all the way from the employment office to No. 64, like prisoners." Undeterred, "the union workers joined right in with them and talked as they walked, and practically everybody signed up anyhow, despite the guard." At Winston Leaf, workers already had what amounted to a closed shop. The company allowed the union to set up a table in the factory; before the ink dried on their employment forms, the workers had joined the union. These efforts brought over 1,600 new members into the union during the late summer of 1945.[49]

CHAPTER TEN

There Was Nothing in the City That Didn't Concern the Tobacco Union

When CIO organizers first arrived in Winston-Salem in 1941, Robert Black was a lanky young baseball player who could barely imagine that a trade union might some day bring "that big giant," R. J. Reynolds, "down to earth." By the end of the war, Black not only stood at the helm of the South's largest black-led local, he also found himself at the epicenter of a political struggle that turned on the enfranchisement and mobilization of the South's black and white poor. Local 22 had never limited itself to workplace demands. Even before it gained recognition, it had taken up broader civic issues, supporting the federal government's wartime price controls, helping to defend William Wellman against a death sentence on a false rape charge, backing a black candidate for the Board of Alderman, and joining forces with the city's dynamic young ministers to help blacks register to vote. Once established, the union put voting rights and education for active citizenship at the top of its agenda. This linkage between union building and social transformation propelled Local 22 beyond the bounds of conventional trade unionism. As Black recalled, "After we built our union, we told the people that just to build a union is not going to solve all of our problems. We have got to get control of the election system and get people in public office. . . . If you are going to defeat these people, not only do you do it across the negotiating table in the R. J. Reynolds Building, but you go to the city hall, you elect people down there that's going to be favorable and sympathetic and represent the best interest of the working class."[1]

The CIO had spearheaded labor's national political offensive by forming a semi-autonomous Political Action Committee (CIO-PAC) in the summer of 1943. Led by Sidney Hillman, CIO-PAC sought to mobilize militant unionists behind a strengthened postwar state in which the federal government would intervene in the economy to ensure full employment and stable prices, provide health and unemployment insurance and social security for all citizens, guarantee a role for labor in economic planning, protect black civil rights, and cooperate with its wartime allies to ensure world peace. CIO-PAC aimed to work from the local level up, not only to support the interests of labor but also to overcome the effective disfranchisement of thousands of poor and minority citizens throughout the country and thereby reinvigorate American political life, just as it had already tried to democratize economic life.[2]

By 1944 the Democratic Party stood at a crossroads. How could it hold the allegiance of black voters, the most steadfast supporters of progressive reform, while accommodating its white supremacist southern wing? While President Roosevelt vacillated, progressive labor leaders, the southern liberals and radicals who made up the Southern Front, and left-leaning New Dealers nationwide increasingly agreed that the party could not satisfy both constituencies. With Vice President Henry Agard Wallace as their chief national political spokesperson and CIO-PAC in the lead, these progressives were determined to bring an end to nearly a half century of black disfranchisement by registering large numbers of black voters and then mobilizing them to vote for pro-labor New Deal candidates in the upcoming congressional campaign. Their ultimate goal was to realign the party around its northern and southern left wings.[3]

Taking its cue from CIO-PAC, Local 22 formed its own Political Action Committee (PAC) in the spring of 1944 and threw itself into the congressional campaign. The impetus sprang from a variety of sources: the return of black soldiers who, having fought for democracy abroad, were not about to bow to Jim Crow's humiliations at home; black women's experience both as workers in a booming wartime economy and as increasingly seasoned union leaders; the NAACP's first major legal victory in the Supreme Court's 1944 decision to outlaw the white primary in *Smith v. Allwright*; and the determination of the CIO to protect its wartime gains from the alliance of Republicans, business lobbies, and conservative southern Democrats that was determined to take back Congress and reverse what it saw as the Roosevelt revolution.[4]

Communist Party organizers, who became increasingly active in Winston-Salem after the war, helped to sharpen local unionists' perception of the links between workplace democracy, social welfare, and black civil rights. At the same time, the Party's presence heightened an already volatile situation. When government controls and the no-strike pledge ended with the close of the war, thousands of workers walked out nationwide, frustrated by years of wage controls and escalating inflation, but also inspired by the promise that peace would bring the industrial and economic democracy of their dreams. In some cases, these were "forced strikes"; flexing their corporate muscle, companies balked at contract negotiations, pressing unions into confrontations that hurt their public image, exposed them to red-baiting, and stoked the conservative backlash that had also gained force during the war. Steering their way through this maelstrom, guided by their own strong internal compasses but also caught up in the high-stakes euphoria of the left at this critical watershed in history, Robert Black, Moranda Smith, Theodosia Simpson, and others found themselves not only fighting to make Local 22 a prime mover in the city's political life but speaking for a national labor-based civil rights movement.

Civic Unionism and Civil Rights

The 1944 election in the Fifth Congressional District had special significance for Local 22. The Democratic incumbent, John Folger, a small-town lawyer/politician, had been a strong supporter of the New Deal and organized labor. Along with his brother, Alonzo Dillard Folger, he had engineered the rise of the Democratic Party in traditionally Republican Surry County. John Folger served as mayor of Mt. Airy, state representative, and state senator before succeeding Alonzo as a U.S. congressman in 1941. Over the years Folger won the loyalty of the white farmers who predominated in the once-Populist strongholds of the northern Piedmont. At the same time, he used his tight control of the "courthouse gang" to establish a smooth-running political machine. Folger's opponent in 1944 was a Winston-Salem Republican, John J. Ingle, who served as the crusading counsel of the Reynolds Employees Association. Predictably, Ingle attacked the CIO-PAC's endorsement of Folger and accused him of being a pawn of Sidney Hillman and "C.I.O. agents from Winston-Salem."[5]

John Folger was no one's pawn. His deep-rooted, Populist-tinged liberalism made him a strong proponent of progressive social policy. In the North Carolina legislature, he championed the extension and reform of the state education system. As a congressman, he helped to push through a bill setting up a federal school lunch program that included equal funding for black schools in the South. Folger also voted against the Smith-Connally War Labor Disputes Act, an effort to drive unions out of national politics by prohibiting them from making political contributions.[6]

In preparation for the race, FTA's Washington representative, Elizabeth Sasuly, came down to help plan a voter registration drive. She carried with her the paraphernalia of CIO-PAC's innovative media and educational campaign: posters, leaflets, and the usual how-to-do-it guides with titles such as *What Every Canvasser Should Know, The CIO Political Action Radio Handbook*, and a *Speaker's Manual.* She also brought special literature targeting women and African Americans; most striking was *The Negro in 1944*, a thirty-three-page publication filled with photographs that featured ordinary black citizens, often in integrated settings. Such materials contained a powerful message. They pictured black workers as they saw themselves: as citizens in a pluralistic society rather than as problems or pathological types. They also summoned both black and white workers to participation in a new kind of labor movement, one that included the diverse labor force that actually inhabited the country's factories and mills.[7] "It didn't take much more than getting them started," Sasuly remembered, "and then they were more than capable of doing it under their own power. They didn't need to have their hands held once they got the idea. They were most apt pupils, if you could even call them pupils. All they needed was to be set off and then they were going."[8]

Local 22's efforts relied on the same vibrant networks and growing organizational skills that had powered its earlier organizing and voter registration campaigns. "We urged the crippled and the blind, everyone that could read or write to go to the polls," Robert Black recalled. PAC members opened a booth at the black county fair, recorded spots for broadcast on the local radio station, and distributed leaflets at the plant gates. Going door to door in their neighborhoods, buttonholing workers during lunch breaks, speaking up during church meetings, and sponsoring citizenship classes on the U.S. and North Carolina constitutions, unionists encouraged their friends and neighbors not only to stand up against trickery and intimidation but to overcome the insidious, internal barriers created by generations of political exclusion.[9]

Velma Hopkins and J. H. R. Gleaves explained just how this culture of exclusion worked. Hopkins was one of the few Local 22 activists who, with the help of a black doctor, had registered to vote before the union arrived. Yet the habits of Jim Crow kept even her away from the polls. "I didn't take registration seriously until the union came in and we began to talk about PAC and the importance of voting," Hopkins recalled. "The union taught us what each segment of government meant; what the aldermen and county commissioners controlled. We'd never heard nothing about them because they were all white." Gleaves was a small business owner who had been active in the voting rights movement since the late 1930s. He pointed out that even in the midst of a war for democracy, registrars were still arbitrarily declaring that "some high school and college graduates . . . who can read and write the Constitution, not only in the English language, but often in several other languages" were not qualified to vote.[10]

The union's tactics included effective negotiating as well as voter registration. For example, when Local 22 leaders held a public meeting with the county election board chairman to seek his cooperation in getting eligible voters on the books, he not only assured them that he supported the right of every "eligible" voter to register, he promised to look into the possibility of sending registrars to the union hall—an extraordinary reflection of the clout and credibility Local 22 had acquired. Even the Reynolds Tobacco Company bowed to the force of the workers' desire to vote. According to Robert Black, the company gave voters "time off to go to the polls with no loss of pay for the first time in the history of North Carolina."[11]

Even so, individual registrars continued to reject qualified black voters. As Eleanore Hoagland remembered it, "People met in the union hall and went to where the registrar was en masse." This show of collective force turned the tables on registrars who had long intimidated black voters; it yielded what the *Winston-Salem Journal* described as "record registration by Forsyth County citizens."[12]

On November 7, the voters of the Fifth District returned John Folger to Congress and helped keep Franklin Roosevelt in the White House. Nationally, the CIO-PAC claimed a large share of the credit for enabling the Democratic Party to hold its own in the Senate and gain twenty seats in the House. Black workers in Winston-Salem, a large majority of whom had never voted before, had their first taste of successful political campaigning. The next month Robert Black told delegates to the FTA national convention in Philadelphia that Local 22 was responsible for 30 percent of the Democratic vote in Forsyth County.[13]

As it turned out, Roosevelt's reelection to a fourth term was a bittersweet victory. At the Democratic convention in Chicago, a showdown between the two wings of the party over Roosevelt's running mate ended in defeat for Henry Wallace, who had the wholehearted support of CIO-PAC and of black leaders. With Roosevelt's acquiescence, the nomination went to a relatively unknown senator from Missouri, Harry Truman, who had backed New Deal programs but whose roots lay in the party's conservative wing. Less noted, but equally portentous, was the effort of blacks representing South Carolina's newly organized Progressive Democratic Party to challenge the seating of "Regulars," who had barred black voters from the Democratic Party primary in defiance of *Smith v. Allwright*. The convention disqualified the Progressive Democratic Party, but its very presence symbolized the breadth and depth of black political mobilization.[14]

The significance of Truman's selection became clear by late spring. As the day shift made its way to the factory gates on the morning of April 13, 1945, union leaders greeted them with sad faces and a special edition of *The Worker's Voice* with the headline, "President Roosevelt Is Dead." Echoing the sentiments of the Double V campaign, the paper exhorted: "We must resolve to carry through to victorious conclusion the war—the complete defeat of the fascist forces in the world—and build a permanent and lasting peace that the Brotherhood of Man may be realized in this world." The one-page edition concluded with a warning that placed the union campaign in Winston-Salem within the long sweep of the black freedom struggle. "History must not be allowed to repeat itself," the paper warned. "We cannot allow the traitors to triumph as they did in the tragic period following the death of another great leader—Abraham Lincoln."[15]

Soon after Truman took office, the Axis forces in Europe conceded defeat, and his decision to drop the atomic bomb on Hiroshima and Nagasaki ensured the Japanese surrender on August 14. The war was over, but the battle over the shape of the postwar world had only begun. As Winston-Salem celebrated the Allied victory and veterans began streaming back to town, Local 22 leaders looked ahead optimistically to what they hoped would be an expansion of democracy comparable to the changes that followed the Civil War.

Renewing its contract with Reynolds in the summer of 1945, Local 22 turned to the key legislative debate of the summer: a bill to establish a postwar full employment policy. Federal initiatives established by Roosevelt assisted defense contractors in converting to peacetime production but left workers to fend for themselves as layoffs mounted, wages declined, and returning soldiers pushed blacks and women out of their toeholds in industry. Staff members from Highlander Folk School led day- and night-shift workers in discussions of the bill; the shop stewards council voted to telegraph the union's support; and a general membership meeting passed a motion to inform North Carolina's senators of the union's position. The veterans' committee also sent messages urging the establishment of a permanent Fair Employment Practices Committee, the passage of a bill on federal unemployment compensation, and the improvement of conditions in veterans' hospitals. Over the next few years, local workers continued to flood Congress with telegrams and postcards urging support for pro-labor, civil rights, and consumer protection legislation.[16]

The threat to abolish the Office of Price Administration, which had been critical in keeping workers' incomes from being undercut by inflation, generated hundreds of letters, including many by friends and neighbors of Mattie Liles, a Piedmont Leaf worker who spent two days going door to door in her neighborhood asking people to write to Washington. Other union members brought up the issue during church meetings. Local 22's Janie Wilson won a prize in an FTA News–sponsored contest for her letter to North Carolina senator Clyde Hoey on the need to protect workers through price controls. Velma Hopkins represented FTA at a Washington conference on the issue. She detailed her expenditures from weekly earnings that averaged $17 to $18. "You can see," she told the conference, "that my pay check is spent each week for only the barest necessities of life. My budget makes no allowance for clothing, recreation, or emergencies."[17]

FTA's Elizabeth Sasuly made sure that the voices of Local 22's most articulate leaders were heard at the highest levels of government. In November, Christine Gardner, a seasonal worker at Piedmont Leaf and a Local 22 member, traveled to Washington to address a Senate Education and Labor subcommittee considering a new minimum wage. The mother of three children described the difficulty she and her husband had making ends meet on a combined income of less than $40 a week. "My husband and I have been married 10 years," she testified, "during which time he has never had a suit of clothes. His greatest ambition is to buy for me a Christmas present, and for himself a complete set of clothes." An interracial committee of male veterans from Local 22 boarded a plane on the morning of March 26, 1946, bound for the capital, where they met with President Truman to urge him to back the sixty-five-cent minimum wage bill.[18]

Theodosia Simpson and Clark Sheppard joined the parade to Capitol Hill, testifying before the House Ways and Means Committee against a proposed national sales tax. Both detailed the inadequacies of their current incomes and the hardships additional taxes would impose. Sheppard had grown up in committee chairman Robert Doughton's hometown, a fact that prompted a warning from another committee member: "[Doughton] keeps pretty good track of you. You want to behave yourself, because he is watching you all the time." Simpson's testimony drew this response from one of the congressmen: "I would like to say that the little colored girl who addressed us a while ago made a very fine statement."[19]

In the end, the Democratic Congress scuttled nearly every item on labor's agenda. A filibuster by southern congressmen defeated attempts to create a permanent FEPC, which would have posed a serious challenge to a regional economy that depended on systematic discrimination. Truman finally signed an Employment Act, but it was a pale imitation of the original. "We were kicked in the teeth by Congress," one CIO official concluded.[20]

This pessimistic assessment, however, obscures the meaning of this legislative

Elizabeth Sasuly
(*UCAPAWA News*)

offensive at the local level. Winston-Salem workers, black and white, neither expected immediate victory nor despaired at setbacks. Meeting with the president, lobbying representatives and senators, and dashing off telegrams to Washington were heady experiences for workers who had been excluded from politics at any level. Moreover, these ventures carried a powerful symbolic punch. Every delegation Local 22 sent to Capitol Hill was made up of blacks and whites, men and women. The photographs in the *FTA News* and *The Worker's Voice* documenting these excursions pictured unionists working side by side for a common cause. These defiant images countered the aura of naturalness and inevitability that surrounded segregation, suggesting instead that interracial activities were not only possible, but a postwar fact of life.

The institutionalization of segregation had allowed whites to live in a "racial dream world" based on the belief that blacks were satisfied with their place at the bottom of a harmonious social world. By the end of World War II, much of the white South was awakening from that dream. In Winston-Salem, black activists—

Members of Local 22's delegation to the Sixth FTA International Convention in Philadelphia, 1947. *Front row, left to right:* Cora Lee, Clark Sheppard, Theodosia Simpson, Vivian Bruce, Frank O'Neal, Moranda Smith, and Mattie Demore. *Back row, left to right:* Thomas Jackson, John Henry Minor, Spencer Long, Ed McCrea, Velma Hopkins, Luke Landreth, Robert "Chick" Black, Christine Gardner, and Viola Brown. (*The Worker's Voice*)

and working-class activists at that—seemed to be everywhere: moderating discussions on the radio, appearing before congressional committees, commenting on national affairs in the newspaper, reporting to the ministerial alliance. To be sure, their visibility inflamed the opposition, and among some whites it stoked what amounted to a siege mentality. It also upset settled hierarchies within the black community. A small but vocal element of the black middle class had always opposed unionization, and some continued to find the new assertiveness of working people unsettling. Clark Brown, a local funeral home director, was still writing to the *Journal* in the fall of 1944 about the "outsiders" who would "destroy the past and present progress" of friendly race relations. But even these opponents—both white and black—had to acknowledge the union's vocal concern with civic affairs, its growing credibility with much of the black middle class, and its ability to mobilize the political energies of the workers who made up the vast majority of the city's black population.[21]

The revitalization of the NAACP was a case in point. The civil rights group had chartered a local chapter in 1918, but when field secretary Madison Jones visited in 1941 the branch had only eleven members. "The national program of the NAACP was one thing," Robert Black felt, "but the local program of the NAACP was another. The NAACP had a program of militancy among blacks, but on a local basis we had a guy serving as president who didn't plan any militant activities that was going to advance the cause of blacks, such as registering, voting and getting people elected to the city council. They didn't sponsor those kinds of programs."[22]

That changed quickly when Local 22 decided to spearhead a membership campaign for the branch. "We saw the need of strengthening the NAACP," Black remembered, "not to dominate it with our members, but to build it. Because that was the political arm of the blacks, short of our union. By building and getting our members to support these organizations, it gave us extra strength in our community." As tobacco workers poured in, the local branch exploded in size. In 1946 Madison Jones returned to the Twin City to speak at an "NAACP Mass Meeting." Robert Black joined a lawyer, a minister, and a businessman on the program to make an appeal for new members. Within a few months, membership had reached 1,918, and the city boasted the largest NAACP chapter in North Carolina.[23]

The Winston-Salem chapter paced the NAACP's wartime growth across the South, which was carried forward by Ella Baker, a native of rural North Carolina whose organizing strategies were based on the belief that ordinary people could act effectively in their own behalf. Baker played a key role in convincing southern activists that what had been a northern-based, top-down organization did indeed have a grassroots "program of militancy among blacks." Under her vigorous direction, the number of NAACP branches in North Carolina more than doubled between 1941 and 1945. Nationwide, membership grew tenfold, and three-quarters of the new branches sprouted below the Mason-Dixon line. By the end of the war, the NAACP claimed 156,000 members in the region.[24]

Running for Congress

In the spring of 1946, Local 22 again threw itself into congressional politics on the side of John Folger, who was running against Winston-Salem industrialist Thurmond Chatham, the candidate of Fifth District conservatives. The son of a textile manufacturer and Democratic Party leader from Elkin, Chatham represented the second generation of the powerful industrial/banker elite that had emerged in Piedmont towns after the Civil War. Like his contemporaries among Winston-Salem's leading families, Chatham inherited substantial wealth and was groomed to take his place as a leader of the community. He had attended Woodberry Forest, the University of North Carolina, and Yale University. After serving in World War I, he married Lucy Hodgin Hanes of the Winston-Salem textile family; they settled in a mansion on Stratford Road, near the Twin City's other richest citizens, and also maintained a large farm in Elkin and a summer home in Roaring Gap. At first Chatham supervised his family's local mill operations, but after his father died he took charge of the corporation and made Chatham blankets one of the state's most successful products.[25]

Following a stint in the navy during World War II, Chatham returned home to hear his name mentioned as a possible candidate for Congress. His only experience in public office consisted of four years of service on the Forsyth County Board of Commissioners. But in that position he had gained a reputation as an outspoken opponent of FDR and the New Deal. Despite his Democratic Party membership, he had joined the Liberty League, an anti–New Deal business lobby, in 1934, and he supported Republican presidential candidates in 1936 and 1940. Chatham later claimed that he had been reluctant to reenter political life after the war, but the strike wave during the winter of 1945–46 changed his mind. He placed much of the blame for the unrest on Congress. "Unless we get enough people in Washington with some backbone," he wrote one supporter, "we are in mortal danger of losing in peace what we have gained by winning the war." He chose as his campaign slogan, "More business in government and less government in business." Chatham was well known and well connected, and he could count on virtually unlimited financial contributions. With such a challenger, Folger faced a strong possibility of defeat. The incumbent hesitated, but when liberal Democrats expressed their support, he decided to join the race.[26]

Folger's campaign represented an attempt to keep the New Deal alive. He lambasted Chatham's membership in the Liberty League. Why, Folger asked, had Chatham opposed FDR and the New Deal? "Roosevelt was responsible for the eight-hour day, time-and-a-half for overtime, Social Security, old age pensions, and a fair and square deal for farmers, merchants, schoolteachers, and the little businessman." Absent from this list was one key player in the New Deal coalition: organized labor. Folger's district contained two of the major centers of union strength in the South, Winston-Salem and Leaksville-Spray, where the CIO's Textile Workers Union had a contract at Marshall Field, and he depended heavily on union votes. By 1946, however, conservatives were whipping up antilabor sentiment by claiming that CIO-PAC was Communist inspired. Folger deplored the excesses of anti-Communism at home and abroad. He had opposed changing the special committee chaired by Senator Martin Dies, which since 1938 had been making sweeping accusations of pro-Communist disloyalty against labor unions and New Deal agencies, into a permanent House Committee on Un-American Activities (HUAC), and he would become a strong critic of the support for right-wing dictatorships that U.S. competition for global influence entailed. Yet he felt compelled to downplay his trade union support. When he received the endorsement of the textile workers' union, he responded only that the workers were entitled to vote for whomever they wished and then announced that he would not accept contributions from CIO-PAC. Sensitive to Folger's vulnerability, Local 22 did not officially endorse him, but behind the scenes its PAC did everything possible to ensure his victory.[27]

Local 22's interest in the upcoming primary was not limited to the Folger campaign. It also channeled its energies into two other races, one for the post of district solicitor, the state's chief prosecutor, where the incumbent was J. Erle McMichael, the man who had prosecuted William DeBerry, and the other the last-minute candidacy of Gene Pratt, Local 22's business agent, for a seat in the North Carolina legislature.[28]

Setting up an elaborate political structure with precinct workers and captains, holding special voting classes, and contacting schools, ministers, and a local black newspaper, Local 22 concentrated especially on the returning veterans. At a veterans' conference convened by the union in February, 300 former servicemen voted to ask the Board of Elections to register without further questioning any veteran who presented his discharge papers. "Registrars in the past," they argued, "have questioned at length citizens who have attempted to register—even college graduates—and made registration difficult. The feeling of the conference was that veterans should not be required to go through that time-wasting, grueling performance, and that their service in the armed forces qualifies them to vote."[29]

At a political rally a few days before the election, union members heard a spirited discussion of the issues raised in the primary contest. In a scene more reminiscent of the Fusionist campaigns of the 1890s than of twentieth-century Democratic primaries, Reidsville attorney and University of North Carolina trustee William Dalton attacked Thurmond Chatham as a candidate of big business. Sharing the platform with Dalton were Gene Pratt; Louis Austin, editor of the *Carolina Times*; Local 22 director Philip Koritz; and Robert Black. Austin stressed the importance of each attempt to register, even if it brought "again and again the embarrassment" of being denied the right to vote. "Only at the ballot box," he told his listeners, "does the worker, teacher, [and] lawyer have equal power—one vote." Pratt outlined a platform that included repeal of the state sales tax, improvement of school facilities, better highways for farmers, and a state medical care and housing program. The rally received extensive coverage in the local press. Both the *Journal* and the

Sentinel reported the speakers' comments in detail, along with a photograph show-ing Dalton, arm raised, with Robert Black sitting nearby.[30]

The next day, speaking before the Elkin Lions Club, Chatham launched a full-scale assault on the CIO and its support of Folger. In language as rancorous as any used in the white supremacy campaigns, but with the specter of Communism join-ing the more familiar bogies of race and class insurrection, he characterized the CIO as a "wrecking crew that is laboring to reduce this country of modern liberal free-dom to the medieval slavery of Russia." John Folger, Chatham said, was submitting to men "who would bring all the wheels of industry to a halt, array neighbor against neighbor, class against class . . . and even in our Southland, race against race. . . . The working people of the South," Chatham concluded, "must free them-selves from the communistic party-line ward-heelers and their legislative associates that have led this nation to the very brink of disaster." Afraid that his fulminations against the CIO might not have much effect in rural areas, Chatham then played the race card even more forcefully: "A vote for Mr. Folger," he claimed, "is a vote against racial segregation." Chatham's supporters, supposedly without his knowledge, also made the rounds of country stores in the district with photographs showing whites and blacks together on stage at the Folger rally.[31]

When officials tallied the ballots in May, Chatham emerged with a plurality, but because of a third candidate he did not garner the needed majority. Forsyth County went solidly for Chatham, except in the precincts of East Winston-Salem, where the hundreds of newly registered black voters saved Folger from defeat. These same precincts also gave Local 22's business agent, Gene Pratt, overwhelming support, although he lost his bid for the state legislature. Folger called for a runoff, and both sides geared up for a final confrontation.[32]

Unluckily for Folger, the race reached its climax just as the time came for Local 22 to enter its annual contract negotiations with Reynolds. Sensing advantage in the gathering clouds of political reaction, Reynolds balked, compelling the union to file strike notices with the NLRB. Although the parties managed to come to an agreement at the last moment, Thurmond Chatham seized this opportunity to un-dermine the union's claim to have the welfare of all working people at heart. Ap-pealing to the fears of the rural voters who held the balance of power in the Fifth District, he warned that a strike at the beginning of the tobacco market would mean "disaster to the farmer. I want to repeat to you that I am against these threats and that I will fight openly to see that all farm products are allowed to flow freely through free markets so that the whole year's work of the farmer may not be lost on account of C.I.O. action." Identifying himself with his rural constituents, he emphasized that his Klondike Farm was home to one of the finest Guernsey cattle herds in the United States and that he was a member of the National Grange and a former president of the North Carolina Dairyman's Association.[33]

In fact, it was Folger, not Chatham, who had built his political career on the support of small farmers, and he had no intention of conceding that constituency. Local 22 director Philip Koritz led the counterattack: "If Mr. Chatham were the farmer he claims to be, he'd know that the tobacco marketing season in this area begins about the end of September. . . . Surely no farmer in this area took seriously the charge that a strike in July would mean disaster. . . . Maybe if Mr. Chatham got behind a plow in a tobacco field, he'd learn these things." In an advertisement that ran the day before the election in both the *Journal* and the *Sentinel*, Local 22 denounced Chatham's attacks as "a clear attempt to divide the people and to pit the farmer against the worker." The union reminded tobacco farmers that they too were being exploited by Reynolds. The company's conviction for antitrust violations showed that its monopolistic practices deprived farmers of a fair price for their crops. Workers were simply trying to get a "fair settlement through the process of collective bargaining. . . . Workers' and farmers' problems are similar and by working together we can raise the standard of living for ourselves and our families."[34]

Folger's appeals to farmers relied in part on his record as a supporter of New Deal agricultural programs and in part on rural residents' resentment of the wealth and privilege of gentleman farmers like Chatham. In a series of public addresses during the last few weeks of the campaign, Folger and his supporters attacked "Tory-minded Democrats" who sided with reactionary Republicans. "I propose to be fair to the wealthy and the poor alike," Folger announced, "but I confess that as heretofore my watchful eye will be looking out for the farmer, the small businessman, and the man, either in a white collar or overalls, who works for a living."[35]

A large voter turnout, almost unheard of in second primaries, propelled Folger to victory. Black and white union voters in Forsyth and Rockingham Counties in combination with farmers throughout the district provided his winning margin. An updated version of Populism seemed to ride again, overcoming the rhetoric of race and the tensions between the countryside and the city with a victorious appeal to class commonalities.[36]

Black voter registration campaigns also made impressive gains in Georgia and South Carolina that year, and liberal candidates scored victories in key races across the South. Nationally, however, Republicans swept into Congress. This stunning achievement in an off-year election, which gave the party control of both the House and Senate, would put labor on the defensive and help make anti-Communism the core issue not only of the Republican resurgence but of Democratic Party politics.[37]

By the time the dust settled on the November elections, moreover, it was becoming clear not only that the Truman administration would fail to expand New Deal social policies but that its chief commitment was to an aggressive Cold War against the Soviet Union. In March 1946 Truman joined Winston Churchill on the podium for a speech in which the former British prime minister called for an aggressive anti-Soviet Anglo-American military alliance. Truman backed away when Churchill's proposal met strong opposition from a wide variety of groups, including black activists and journalists, who saw it as a betrayal of the United Nations and a call for the revitalization of British imperialism, as well as the general public, which feared atomic warfare and continued to share Roosevelt's optimism about the possibility of U.S.-Soviet cooperation. The following fall, Henry Wallace, whom Truman had named secretary of commerce and who was the last of the New Dealers in his cabinet, went public with his opposition to such a manichean approach to foreign policy, which he believed encouraged neocolonialism abroad and stirred up hatred and hysteria at home. Within days of the speech, Truman forced Wallace to resign. With Wallace out of the way and James Byrnes, a conservative Democrat from South Carolina, as his secretary of state, Truman moved quickly to "scare the hell out of the American people" and win support for the "Truman Doctrine," which made containing the Soviet Union the federal government's No. 1 priority. That project would have a fatal impact on the fortunes of the labor-led civil rights movement. But for the moment even such portentous changes in the national political climate did little to diminish Local 22's economic and political momentum.[38]

The Communist Party

Registering voters, lobbying Congress, and supporting candidates were the core activities of American politics, and Local 22 members, who had been denied these basic rights of citizenship, embraced them with gusto. Adding an extra dimension to this civic unionism, however, was the increasing radicalization of many of the union's leaders and some rank-and-file activists, a process abetted—although not by any means caused—by their contact with the ideas and members of the Communist Party.

After its initial foray into the Twin City in the wake of the 1929 textile strikes, the Party had met with quick repression and largely faded from view. It made itself felt again in the early 1940s with the arrival of UCAPAWA organizers, some of whom were Party members and some of whom were independent leftists who had been schooled in a political culture strongly influenced by Communist views on race, class, and international affairs. Yet Party members among the organizers "stuck strictly to the union policy," Robert Black recalled, discussing their political views with only a few of the most trusted rank-and-file leaders.[39]

Those discussions made a strong impression on men and women who harbored few illusions about American democracy, had a keen sense of the courage and persistence that organizing required, and were willing to take their friends where they found them. "My first knowledge of the presence of the Party in Winston-Salem," Black remembered, "was after we had the major work stoppage [in 1943]. [William] DeBerry was working as the representative of UCAPAWA in the Winston-Salem area. After the big strike, DeBerry said to me, 'Black, I'd like to have a man-to-man talk with you.' He didn't name the Party as such, but he just said, 'The time has come when we need to develop more militant leaders in order to cope with this organizing situation. I have been asked to talk with you and some of the others.' [He] never asked me to join the Party, but he did illustrate to me that through the work of the Party was the only hope we had of developing the militant type of leadership that would stand the test in an organizing drive against companies like R. J. Reynolds. I'm sure he had [made contacts with other people]." In discussions with this small group of natural leaders, DeBerry emphasized the class dimensions of black oppression and the role of a disciplined, assertive vanguard in overcoming the fears of the rank and file, the most powerful weapon in the company's arsenal.[40]

"With all due respect to the organizing drive in Winston-Salem," Black reflected, "had not we had the help that we got, I don't believe that the union would have stuck together. I think the presence of these people prior to the strike and in the early stages of the union . . . helped us piece together the militant rank-and-filers that stood the test. I could tell the difference in the militancy of people like Theodosia and Velma, [and Frank] O'Neal [who] began to show this added determination. By me being familiar with their day-by-day actions, the strong determination and advanced development began to show. I knew at the beginning of the drive and at eight months or a year later, it was there, the stronger determination. Had not we had those kind of people who were able to stand together, I don't think we would have been able to hang on."[41]

The Party's local influence increased in 1944 with the addition of Eleanore Hoagland as head of labor education and Frank Green as director of Local 22. Hoagland had been active on the left since at least the late 1930s, and her husband, William Binkley, had been a Party member since the late 1920s; he had risen to the post of district organizer in New Orleans and been elected to the Party's national committee in the late 1930s. Hoagland was a highly qualified labor educator, and

Green satisfied the union's need for a native North Carolinian to help minimize the cries of "outsider." But Don Henderson and the FTA leadership also trusted them because of their left-wing political credentials. Each combined dedication to trade unionism with a radical analysis of social ills, and their presence undoubtedly drew more local leaders into the Party's orbit.[42]

By the summer of 1945, an informer, apparently working with the union, was furnishing the FBI with information on Communist activities within Local 22. In one report, the informer enclosed a list of union officers and Reynolds shop stewards, with an asterisk beside the names of "known members or sympathizers," a designation that included most of the union leaders, black and white, as well as a number of influential stewards. The informer provided few details about their activities, other than to say that they had "indicated a pronounced sympathy for the CPA and in most cases are subscribers to the *Daily Worker*." What the informer meant by "pronounced sympathy" is anyone's guess. And reading or even subscribing to the *Daily Worker* at that time was not uncommon for members of left-led unions. It could always be found scattered on a table in the Local 22 library along with black newspapers, the FTA *News*, and the CIO *News*. FBI agents were notoriously unreliable, often exaggerating their own importance by claiming to find "reds" everywhere. Still, although none of Local 22's activists openly declared their Party membership, it is clear that during this period many joined Marxist discussion groups and developed ties to the Party. Some, including Robert Black, quite likely became members.[43]

The winter of 1945–46 marked a shift in the mood and tactics of the American Communist Party. The Party had supported the war, the CIO, and the New Deal wholeheartedly. In 1944, at the height of the U.S.-Soviet alliance and the Party's political acceptability, chairman Earl Browder had gone so far as to dissolve the Communist Party altogether, reestablishing it as a more moderate and reformist Communist Political Association (CPA) in hopes of becoming a legitimate voice on the left of American politics. FBI informants reported that Robert Black, Etta Hobson, and other members of Local 22 attended regional meetings where this change was discussed and embraced. Browder's approach, which lent legitimacy to Party members who were searching for what would later be called the "American Road to Socialism," was enormously popular. A year later, however, a pronouncement from Moscow suggesting that Browder's promotion of "Americanization" had gone too far caused an uproar at Party headquarters in New York. Browder refused to recant; an old rival, William Z. Foster, took over as chairman, and the Party leadership reversed course, dissolving the CPA and reconstituting the Communist Party. The reconstituted Party continued the Popular Front policy of cooperating with the CIO and trying to keep the Truman administration loyal to the New Deal. But under Foster, its focus shifted to emphasizing "the individual role of the Party," and its rhetoric hardened.[44]

Although more a matter of tone than of substance, this change signaled what would become a crippling detour away from the task of creating a "stable, ongoing, genuinely democratic socialist movement" and toward a vision of eventual class struggle along lines derived from the Bolshevik experience. Individuals in the Communist movement, however, did not necessarily move in lockstep with the Party line. Many veterans returned from their military experience with a vision of postwar possibilities that combined socialism with a passionate belief in American democracy. And seasoned trade unionists often continued to be less concerned about abstract doctrine than about workers' aspirations.[45]

Under Browder, the Party had paid less attention to recruiting members than to forwarding the goals of Popular Front organizations. The new emphasis on Party building depended on recruitment, with a special emphasis on workers, young people, veterans, and blacks. The South, where union membership had swelled during the war and where a labor-led political offensive was in full swing, seemed to offer an especially fertile field, and Party organizers were eager to root their efforts in the struggles of black industrial workers in such centers as Birmingham, Atlanta, Memphis, Richmond, and Winston-Salem. The national office listed only fifty-three members in both Carolinas at the end of 1945. A significant number of those were probably in Winston-Salem, and the city's black workers presented the perfect opportunity to test the new approach to Party building.[46]

In the early part of 1946, Alice Burke, head of the Party in Virginia and the Carolinas, asked Anne Mathews to assume the duties of a Party organizer in Winston-Salem. Mathews had joined the Party in 1937 in New York City while a member of the CIO's Office Workers Union. After a stint working for UCAPAWA in Florida, she became the secretary of Local 22 in the summer of 1945. In most unions with a strong Party presence, Party "fractions" met separately to study, discuss union and Party issues, and hammer out strategies. Mathews's primary responsibility as Party organizer was to develop such an organizational structure for the handful of local members.[47]

This potentially sectarian effort, however, was counterbalanced by the arrival of Sam Hall, the new district organizer for the Communist Party in North and South Carolina, toward the end of May 1946. Described by the *Journal* as "a short, chubby, soft-spoken man who has been fashioned by nature more in the mold of a young businessman than anything else," the thirty-six-year-old native of Alabama drew on his experience as a journalist and navy officer as he sought to build the Party in the two states. Unlike most Party leaders in the South, Hall assumed a high profile that was due at least in part to his ebullient personality but was also in line with the Party's new emphasis on playing an independent, public role. He placed ads in local newspapers, appeared on radio programs, gave interviews to the press, and spoke before civic groups. All of these activities were intended to refute the image of Communists as secretive outsiders, and thereby aid in the recruitment of new members.[48]

Hall's actions highlighted one of the Party's central dilemmas. When the Party first emerged after World War I, the threat of deportation and criminal prosecution made secrecy essential. But even during the 1930s and 1940s, when Communists were at the peak of their influence and the number of people working with them in pursuit of common goals swelled, individuals who openly declared their membership risked losing their credibility and their jobs. In the South, where extralegal violence as well as official repression flourished and freedom of speech for radicals was virtually nonexistent, the risks were even greater. Labor organizers might choose not to divulge their Party membership because they were more concerned about promoting workers' welfare under existing conditions than about the long-term goal of building a class-conscious Communist movement and believed that discretion made them more effective at their jobs. "We didn't go out and shout from the rooftops whether we was party members or not," one union president explained. "But on the other hand—in the shop there was nobody that paid any attention to the union had any doubt in their mind who was Communist and who wasn't." For all these reasons, as well as a more problematic cult of secrecy, Party members commonly kept quiet about their affiliation. Some worked under assumed names and lied outright. Despite calls from the Party's New York office for public disclosure of membership, the California activist Jessica Mitford remembered that the Party "was a strange mixture of openness and secrecy" during this period.[49]

Under Hall's leadership, the Party in Winston-Salem undertook an intensive membership drive, capped by a meeting in mid-June 1946 at Frank O'Neal's Union Mission Holy Church. The gathering's goals were twofold: first, to expose a diverse group of community members to the Party's ideals, and second, to reach beyond the Local 22 leadership to bring more rank-and-file workers into the Party's fold. Robert Black described the occasion: "The meeting was organized by the Party. They invited people from the Negro community, Negro civic leaders. There was no one from the local union that was told about the meeting, from my knowledge, [until] two hours before the meeting was scheduled. Then someone came in and issued the order that as soon as we closed the office, we had a special meeting at Reverend O'Neal's church. There was nothing said about who was invited to the meeting so we took it for granted that it was restricted to the local leadership and membership [of the Party]. When we arrived at Reverend O'Neal's church, here was C. C. Kellum [head of the NAACP] and J. H. R. Gleaves, who was president of the Progressive Civic League there in Winston, and many other local Negro leaders and people from the community who were not affiliated with our union." "During the course of this meeting," Black remembered, "without any knowledge from the leadership of the local union, names were called and people were asked to stand up and identify [themselves] with the Party. People's names were called and these people that were from the community began to make notes of these things."[50]

Approximately sixty-five rank-and-file workers joined the Party during the meeting. "They did recruit a lot of people," Black recalled, "because [workers] felt that if it was good for the leaders, then it was good for the members." He remembered that Willie Grier, Local 22 treasurer, "was approached at this meeting. He said, 'I'll wait awhile.' As far as I know, Willie never signed a Party card, but he said, 'I'll support the program.' Of course he was critical of the way the meeting was planned and by having individuals to stand up. He said, 'I don't think it helped our local union any, by doing this out in the open, unless there had been prior discussion and agreement.' And there were several other people who criticized the manner in which the meeting was organized. I sat in one or more meetings within a few weeks after this meeting where certain criticisms were raised about having these people to get up and testify before people who were not even members of the union as to their role and activities in the party organization."[51]

In principle and in some contexts, overcoming the Party's sometimes damaging addiction to secrecy may have been an admirable goal. But the decision to expose local union leaders without their consent illustrated both the recklessness of some Party leaders and the undemocratic ways in which a Party dedicated to "democratic centralism" sometimes behaved. The response at the meeting, on the other hand, testifies to the appeal of the Party's commitment to African Americans and to the mood of possibility that characterized this highly fraught postwar moment.

By the end of 1946, the Party membership rolls in Winston-Salem reached approximately 150, a large majority of whom were African American tobacco workers, including a large number of union shop stewards. The first North Carolina Communist Party convention held in six years took place in Winston-Salem that year. Communist activist Junius Scales remembered that the letter summoning him to the meeting arrived by mail, something that would have been "unthinkable" before the war. Like other young white radicals, Scales also remembered being awed by the charisma and sophistication of the rank and file leaders of Local 22. An FBI informer reported that the convention elected Sam Hall as chairman, Christine

Gardner, a leaf house worker and Local 22 member, as secretary, and Anne Mathews as treasurer. The district committee included Ed McCrea, Moranda Smith, Sam Hall, Christine Gardner, Junius Scales, and Hardy Scott, an organizer for the International Fur and Leather Workers Union. The Winston-Salem chapter of the Party met not long afterward and elected officers. These included Robert Lathan, Jason Hawkins, Anne Mathews, and Viola Brown, who was in charge of *Daily Worker* sales. All were active members of Local 22.[52]

From the summer of 1946 through the spring of 1947, Winston-Salem saw a flurry of Party activity, much of which centered on the union hall. An upsurge in lynching and other racially motivated violence and an attempted revitalization of the Ku Klux Klan seemed to portend a campaign of terror like the one that had followed World War I. In response, activists circulated a petition in the name of the Party, calling on President Truman to use the power of the federal government to stop vigilante violence in the South. The petition garnered 4,000 signatures, and the *Daily Worker* claimed that there was "no hesitation on the part of workers to sign a petition bearing the name of the Communist Party." At the same time, full-page advertisements, complete with subscription forms for the *Daily Worker*, began appearing in North Carolina's leading newspapers. These appeals combined a tough denunciation of Jim Crow with a "people's program" that included a state minimum wage, repeal of segregation laws, higher salaries for public school teachers, and abolition of the state sales tax. Like the Fusionists of 1896, Party activists sought to counter the appeals to racism on which southern conservatives based their antilabor, anti–New Deal campaigns with a platform of taxation and social spending that benefited ordinary North Carolinians and challenged the banker-planter-industrialist domination of the state's economic and political affairs.[53]

As the Cold War intensified, Party members on Local 22's executive board also backed resolutions denouncing Truman's "get tough" stance toward the Soviet Union and condemning what they saw as Anglo-American imperialism. During the war, while support for the Allied alliance with the Soviet Union was at its height, such pro-Soviet sentiments had seemed unremarkable. During the summer of 1944, for instance, Theodosia Simpson had sent a letter to a worker in the Soviet Union. Describing herself and her job, Simpson told her counterpart about the union's contribution to Roosevelt's Win the War program. Blithely ignoring the charge of "godlessness" that had always animated anti-Communist sentiment, she concluded, "We are all praying for the Almighty to help the Allies and give them the power to win this war and the peace." Simpson's letter found its way to a woman worker in a vitamin processing plant. The worker wrote back, describing the horrors of the Nazi invasion and the self-sacrificing efforts of the Soviet workers and soldiers to turn back the Germans. But by 1947, when Local 22 called the Truman Plan "the first step in a world-wide campaign of American imperialism," it found itself well to the left not only of American popular opinion but of the CIO. Such resolutions did not necessarily misrepresent the opinions of union members; black workers in particular displayed a great deal of interest in international issues and identified with anticolonial struggles around the world. But what one former Party member called the "resolution bit"—offering messages of solidarity and pronouncements on foreign policy issues—could also disintegrate into public posturing that was ineffective and distracting at best and self-destructive at worst, mainly because it lent substance to the charge that the union was slavishly following the Party line.[54]

Sales of the *Daily Worker* became an important indicator of the movement's success and a key responsibility of any Party member. Beginning in the mid-1930s, the *Daily Worker* tried to appeal to a broader readership with a sports page, movie reviews, and extensive coverage of black music. Local 22 gave Sam Hall its membership list to use in a direct appeal for subscriptions to workers in Winston-Salem. These efforts garnered results, as subscriptions to the *Daily Worker* in North Carolina increased from 5 to 350 between June and September 1946, 325 of which went to Winston-Salem. Ed McCrea remembered that "in Winston-Salem there was one shop steward who sold 200 *Daily Worker*s in his department. He had them delivered right down there in the department."[55]

By the fall of 1946, Party membership in the city had grown large enough to support an organizational structure that closely resembled those in large northern cities. Party officials assigned members to one of eight clubs, each of which elected its own officers and a representative to the city committee. The Winston-Salem chapter also had a Trade Union Committee composed of organizers from the various unions and rank-and-file leaders.[56]

Individual clubs consisted of anywhere from ten to twenty members and took their names from African American and Communist leaders: Crispus Attucks, the African American Revolutionary War hero; Benjamin Davis, the Communist councilman from New York; William Z. Foster, who succeeded Earl Browder as chairman of the Party; Sojourner Truth, the feminist abolitionist; and Paul Robeson, the world-famous actor and singer who had become a spokesman for labor, civil rights, and left-wing causes. Although the majority of those who joined were African American, most of the clubs appear to have had at least a few white members, some of whom were in leadership positions in Local 22.

The clubs functioned as discussion groups that met every week or two, primarily for educational purposes and usually in someone's home. Occasional public meetings, usually held during the visit of some national leader, brought the entire membership together, along with sympathizers and other unionists, but there was little interaction among clubs. Anne Mathews described a gathering of the Crispus Atticus club to which she was assigned: "There was usually a typical agenda which consisted of checking up on dues payments and attendance of the members; checking up on whether any subscriptions to the *Daily Worker* had been sold, or how many papers, *Sunday Worker* papers, had been sold of the previous issue; discussing any recruits; and of course, a certain portion of the meeting was set aside for educational study. Sometimes the educational study might consist of a particular phase of Marxist theory or it might concern itself with any current piece of legislation, whether it was concerning trade-unions or the poll-tax bill, or some other such piece of legislation."[57]

When Junius Scales became chairman of the Party in the Carolinas, he had a chance to sit in on club meetings. "The clubs were usually based on areas of the factory that they worked in," he remembered. "There were a few clubs that weren't Reynolds workers, they were former Reynolds or something. They focused on city problems. Of course there was nothing in the city that didn't concern the tobacco union."

"They were led by the club chairman," Scales continued. "It would most likely be somebody who was not in a union role, people who had shown a good deal of astuteness and dependability and were not overwhelmingly burdened with union tasks. Nearly all the club leaders were workers. They were elected in the clubs and I thought the members showed very good judgment. It was very democratically done. One of the things we emphasized was the need for the union to be run democratically."

"Most of the points on the agenda were matters of working in the union," Scales remembered, "or how to put the struggles of the union in a more political context. That's what we tried to contribute to. There would always be some educational portion of the meeting which would try to put local problems in an international context. Fortunately, it seems to me a lot of them had their feet on the ground and when they weren't hooplaahing for the Soviet Union, which we didn't always do, it did tend to broaden their horizons a lot, especially on international and certainly national politics."[58]

That broadening included participation in an internationalist subculture of Communist and Communist-led organizations. Moranda Smith, Christine Gardner, Roy Lingle, and Bea McCrea attended a Party training school in Beacon, New York. Etta Hobson, Vivian Bruce, Pinkey Gwyn, John Henry Minor, and Theodosia Simpson traveled to a meeting of the Southern Negro Youth Congress in Columbia, South Carolina, in the fall of 1946, where Simpson was elected to the SNYC's executive board, an honor that constituted important recognition for the union, for women, and for Simpson. Crawford Shelton and Jason Hawkins ventured to Detroit for a National Negro Labor Congress meeting. Leading Party figures also traveled to Winston-Salem to meet with local members, among them two southerners who rose to prominence in the Party. One was Harry Winston, a black Mississippian who became a pioneer in the movement to aid African nations struggling for independence; in 1947 Winston went to jail for five years under the Smith Act, a 1940 law that made it a crime to teach, advocate, or encourage the overthrow of the U.S. government and one of anti-Communism's chief weapons after the war. The other was Robert Minor, a white political cartoonist from San Antonio who became editor of the *Daily Worker* and a close ally of Earl Browder.[59]

This period of intense activity, in which the Party sought to build a base in Winston-Salem and other southern industrial centers, lasted for no more than a year, from the arrival of the expansive Sam Hall until 1947, when Local 22 found itself locked in a fateful conflict with the Reynolds Company in which red-baiting would play a defining role. What was perhaps most remarkable about this period of interaction was that, even at its height, Party interests and orthodoxy usually took a back seat to the needs of the union and the culture of the black working class. To be sure, given the overlap between union leaders and Party activists at both the local and national level, Party concerns affected the functioning of Local 22, and Party affiliation could serve as a means of gaining influence in the union. But it is equally true that civil rights unionism dominated the activities of the local Party. Even the district organizers devoted the vast majority of their time and energy to union building and voting activism. Sam Hall, for instance, was as committed to forwarding the shared goals of a broad political coalition as any Popular Front radical, and his policy of openness, however problematic, could be seen as an exemplary attempt to widen democratic discourse by asserting the voice of the left into public affairs.[60]

In the arena of culture, the workers' sensibility predominated. For a critical group of local leaders, the millennialism of the black church, with its faith in a future in which justice would prevail, meshed seamlessly with the utopian vision of a classless, raceless society. "We used to hold our Communist Party meetings in Reverend O'Neal's church," Anne Mathews recalled. "The interesting thing was that those meetings were never started without a prayer. I couldn't help but think that these people looked on the Communist Party not so much as a political party but as an organization that was going to help them better their lives. And so we realized that you didn't have a meeting of a whole group of black people and discuss serious affairs of their lives without asking God's help." To orthodox Marxists, religion might be the "opiate of the masses." On the ground, it was the sine qua non of a workers' movement.[61]

Local 22 leaders like Robert Black had no doubt that Party activists were critical to Local 22's success. This was so for reasons both simple and profound. First, the Party provided man- and womanpower: competent, militant allies who usually saw themselves as unionists first and Communists second and who were willing to put their lives and livelihoods on the line. Second, it combined the ideal and practice of interracialism with a commitment to the black freedom struggle. In Winston-Salem and elsewhere, Party members created an "oasis of genuine interracialism" where African American culture was treasured, blacks and whites worked and socialized together, and the "Negro problem" was transformed into the problem of how white racism could be overcome. "Here was an outfit that put its money where its mouth was," Junius Scales explained. "It really meant business on racism." Finally, the Party helped to counter the psychological onslaught of racism by linking the experiences of black Americans to those of other oppressed people and to the cause of the international working class. Scales remembered that the "top leaders [of Local 22] had such inquiring minds that they just soaked up all the educational efforts that were directed at them. The party's program had an explanation of events locally, nationally, and worldwide which substantiated everything they had felt instinctively from their experience. It was right in their guts." Through precept and example, the Party thus offered a reason to hope that workers could be the generative force in a broad-based radical movement and that—despite the phobias spawned by white supremacists, despite the powers arrayed against them—black and white together could some day overcome.[62]

CHAPTER ELEVEN

It Wasn't Just Wages We Wanted, but Freedom

In the turbulent aftermath of the war, Local 22 found itself facing a threat more subtle and insidious than any it had encountered before: the seemingly impersonal and implacable attrition wrought by automation. Winston-Salem unionists responded not by trimming their sails, but with renewed militancy. They could not foresee the future, and what loomed largest in their eyes was the explosion of trade union membership in the South from 3 million in 1933 to 14 million in 1945. Black workers especially had proven to be eager and steadfast recruits. In 1935, 150,000 of the region's black workers had been union members; by the war's end, that number stood at an astounding 1.25 million. After the war Local 22, like other fledgling unions across the country, was in no mood for compromise. Joining the strike wave of 1945–46, the city's independent leaf house workers managed to weather an outbreak of violence that in other parts of the country threatened to destroy labor's post–World War II gains. That success encouraged local activists to take on an even bigger challenge: organizing the unorganized in the tobacco belt of eastern North Carolina and exporting civil rights unionism to their counterparts in the most repressive area of the state.[1]

Mechanization

Reynolds workers always welcomed the Christmas season. The company closed the plants for the week, giving its employees time to rest and visit with family and friends. The 1945 holiday was especially joyful. The war had ended four months earlier, soldiers continued to arrive daily at the bus and train depots, and the shelves in the stores gradually filled with items that had been in short supply.

The factory district was busier than usual that year. Mechanics and construction workers always stayed on the job through the holiday week, since the company traditionally used the Christmas shutdown to clean and repair old machinery. But this time workers were doing more than the normal maintenance; they were ripping out the stemming machines in Number 60 and replacing them with a new "strip preparation department" designed to speed up the production process and reduce the number of workers.

No process in tobacco manufacturing better reflected the antebellum origins and the racialized labor system of the industry than stemming. The development of the cigarette-making machine had revolutionized the industry in the 1880s, but it was harder to invent a machine that could separate the fragile leaf from the woody stem. Owners also had less incentive to develop new technology for the stemmeries, for the abundant supply of low-wage black labor easily kept the manufacturing division supplied. Reynolds had installed some primitive stemming machines in 1913, but certain kinds of tobacco continued to require the careful touch of human hands. In 1935, 1,565 women still stripped the leaves under the watchful eye of a foreman, as their counterparts had done for generations, while 2,750 worked on stemming machines.[2]

During the mid-1930s, Reynolds began experimenting with a pneumatic technique for separating the stem from the leaf. Toward the end of the war the company opened its first strip preparation department. The process used a series of machines to remove the stem, first by softening and then by "thrashing" the tobacco. Reynolds installed the first complete strip preparation unit in October 1944. Forty machine tenders handled the work that 250 hand and machine stemmers had previously done.[3]

Management's decision to retool the stemmeries had multiple roots. A desire for greater speed and efficiency certainly motivated the long search for a mechanical method to separate the stem from the tobacco leaf. The pneumatic process increased the rate at which the leaf could be produced, saved on floor space, improved the quality of the strips, and reduced the amount of dust in the air. This new technology also dramatically reduced the number of stemmers employed as well as the level of skill required to operate the machinery in the stemmeries. Although Reynolds, like all other tobacco manufacturers, treated stemmers as unskilled laborers, in fact both hand and machine stemming required a relatively high degree of experience and expertise. The new machine embodied the deftness that women stemmers had developed over the years. Company officials also saw mechanization as a way to reduce labor costs in the stemmeries, which had increased substantially over the previous decade. Minimum wage rates imposed by the NIRA and the FLSA had been the first inducements to replace workers with machines; the higher labor costs that came with unionization had been the final straw.[4]

When the plants reopened after the 1945 Christmas holiday, Number 60 had been converted to a strip preparation department. The company "no longer needed" 300 of the approximately 600 women stemmers who worked there before the holiday. Fifty women received transfers to other stemming departments, and officials said the rest could find seasonal work in the firm's leaf houses, where wages were lower and workers received fewer benefits. "Reynolds went after the stemmery divisions because that's where the strength of our union was," Robert Black observed. "That's where the union actually sprung from, was from the stemmery. And they figured if they could intimidate the workers in those divisions enough and cut down on the numbers, that they could probably frighten the members out of supporting the union."[5]

At the insistence of union officials, the company promised that all transfers and layoffs would conform to the seniority provisions of the collective bargaining agreement and that it would give discharged workers first crack at any new jobs that opened up in the stemmeries or leaf houses. But seniority applied only to individual departments; it was neither divisionwide nor companywide. Because the union had not been able to challenge the racial and sexual divisions of work, displaced black women, no matter how long they had been with the company or how skilled they were, had no claim to jobs in other areas of the factory.[6]

Local 22 responded by confronting the seniority issue, at first indirectly and then head-on. It refused to accept the logic of technological progress as a cover for manipulating the workforce to the company's advantage. Instead, it offered its own two-part proposal. In the short run, it suggested that the company institute a "share-the-work plan" under which all workers in the affected departments would stay on the job but work fewer hours. To make up for wages lost under the scheme, the union would request partial unemployment compensation. In the long run, it argued, the company should shorten the workday. In a series of membership meetings, workers put forth a demand that had been commonplace during the Depression but that the mainstream labor movement abandoned after World War II: they called for a thirty-hour work week for forty hours' pay. "The machine must be controlled and not be used to enslave people," argued Local 22's newspaper, the *Worker's Voice*. "Labor-saving machinery must be just that—and the time saved from work be used to enrich our lives with more time for recreation, education and the enjoyment of the finer things of life."[7]

Philip Koritz, who took over as director of Local 22 in January 1946, when Frank Green became FTA's Southeast regional director, elaborated on the union's rationale. A "30 for 40 plan" avoided pitting the unemployed against secure unionized workers; it positioned the union as a vehicle not only for fattening workers' pocketbooks but for transforming everyday life; and it symbolized the union's identity as a militant, class-conscious organization even as it sought to rationalize labor-management relations, which was itself a radical departure in the context of southern labor and race relations.[8]

Tentatively, the union broached an even more radical alternative: the absorption of stemmery workers into the general factory population. Production was booming, and Reynolds could easily place the redundant stemmers in other parts of the main factory. But such a strategy would mean putting blacks on "white" jobs or integrating black women into all-white departments. The company was unwilling to do either. Reynolds had already established the precedent of an all-black cigarette department. Why not "start operating the cigarette floor at 97, which has been down because of the manpower shortage?" the union asked. "This would create enough jobs for all laid off." In fact, the company had a chance to do just that a few years later when it established a cigarette department to produce a new brand, Cavalier. A "Brief History" of Local 22, written by staff members in 1951, claimed that the company "transformed a stemmery which employed some 800 Negro women into a cigarette manufacturing department. The company refused to transfer the women into the new job classification, cried that such action would lead to integration in the departments and whipped up this feeling among the white workers. It then laid off the Negro women and hired hundreds of new, young white workers."[9]

Ironically, "sharing the work in bad times" had served for years as the Reynolds version of "unemployment insurance." In a 1938 article in *Fortune*, the company bragged that it had not laid off a worker in twelve years; what it meant was that during lags in production, it shortened workers' hours and cut their pay. But circumstances were different now. Workers were no longer supplicants, begging for handouts. They were making demands, and the company would not consider sharing the work, let alone accepting a "30 for 40" plan.[10]

Ignoring the union's proposals, Reynolds announced an additional layoff of 500 stemmers at Number 60 Extension and 200 stemmers at Number 65 on March 7,

1946. Again, seniority determined who stayed on the job, but because the company's leaf houses had closed for the season, few workers found jobs in other departments. Over the next two years, Reynolds reduced the number of employees in the stemming department to 1,415, down from 4,315 in 1935 and 3,533 in 1945.[11]

Julia Leach, who worked as a machine feeder in Number 60 and was "cut off" in early 1946, remembered the pain hidden in those numbers. "They came around and said everybody what hadn't worked fifteen years, they were going to lay them off. Most of us my age had worked twelve or thirteen years. They were remodeling Number 60, putting in new machines. We didn't ever get to go back to see how the machines looked. They put us over there in Number 60 Extension, and we worked up there at night. They came by one night and told us that was our last night, and if we were interested in seasonal work we could go up to the employment office." For the next forty years, Leach worked in the leaf houses from July through September. Since leaf house workers were not eligible for unemployment insurance (one of the many ways in which welfare programs discriminated against black workers), she supported herself with household jobs during the rest of the year, an outcome that demonstrated how Reynolds's policies worked not only to enrich the corporation but to supply white households with cheap domestic labor.[12]

Even as they scrambled to support themselves, unemployed stemmers refused to sever their ties to Local 22. They formed a parallel organization within the union with their own committees and officers. Then they took to the streets with their share-the-work plan. Calling themselves "distributors of information," they appeared around the plants and courthouse square, armed with signs and leaflets. They were not opposed to the new machinery, they told people, but they did not believe it should be "used to starve the people and cause a hardship on the community."[13]

Over the course of the summer, Reynolds made two additional moves that reduced the power of black women workers. First, it hired whites for seasonal jobs that had traditionally gone to blacks. It could do so because layoffs in defense industries and the return of veterans created a large pool of white workers willing to take any position they could find. Second, it began moving its redrying operations out of Winston-Salem, reducing the number of seasonal jobs altogether.[14]

The layoffs in the stemmeries had a devastating effect on the union. Not only did they immediately eliminate many of its loyal supporters, but they also portended broader changes in the postwar world. During the ensuing decades, other firms followed Reynolds's lead, automating their production processes and relocating their plants outside of the nation's urban centers. Seeking lower taxes, reduced labor costs, and weakened or no unions, manufacturers throughout the country embraced automation and suburbanization. African Americans, who were disproportionately confined to unskilled jobs and penned in central cities by residential segregation, would find themselves relegated to a no man's land of jobless, bombedout ghettos while industries fled to the suburbs with white ethnic workers in tow.[15]

The Leaf House Strike

Despite these developments, Local 22 moved forward with a confidence that had grown steadily during the war. Reynolds was raking in huge profits. Now it was once again time for contract negotiations, and like workers across the country, Winston-Salem unionists were determined to counter the effects of inflation and the end of price controls. They were already in the midst of what proved to be a successful political offensive, as they sought to register black voters and return John Folger to Congress. Responding to the layoffs in the stemmeries and recalcitrance among the independent leaf house owners, Local 22 took up the cause of its most vulnerable members more forcefully than ever before.[16]

Negotiations with Reynolds began on May 14, 1946, only two weeks before the expiration of the contract. The union negotiating committee presented requests designed to reduce some of the racial inequalities in the wage structure and bring Reynolds's wages and benefits more in line with those of other major corporations. It also included the most daring demand Local 22 had made to date: a companywide seniority system that, if implemented, would prevent the company from using automation in the stemmeries to wipe out a whole category of workers. Such a system would virtually eliminate the sexual and racial division of labor. The company refused to meet any of the union's demands. It proposed no general wage increases and demanded an open shop. Most important, it adamantly opposed the union's request for companywide seniority, and foremen used the issue to the company's advantage, frightening white workers with visions of white women working side by side with black men and women or, worse, being supervised by black men.[17]

Local 22 director Phil Koritz reluctantly notified the U.S. Labor Department of the union's determination to strike if an agreement was not reached by July 15. U.S. Conciliation Service commissioners arrived in Winston-Salem on July 1 and began chipping away at the areas of disagreement. Both sides were anxious to work out a bargain. The company could not afford a strike with the tobacco markets so close to opening. The union still had contracts to negotiate at the leaf houses, and Congressman John Folger's opponents were using the threat of a strike to undermine his support among rural voters. After a twelve-hour meeting, the negotiators and conciliators emerged with a settlement that in many ways represented a victory for Local 22. Workers won wage increases. The company promised to continue main

Philip Koritz (*The Worker's Voice*)

tenance of membership and dues checkoff and instituted a system of grading man-ufacturing jobs that finally brought an end to the foremen's ability to use arbitrary raises to play workers off against one another. Hailing the agreement, Koritz said, "Not only will the Reynolds workers benefit from this increase, but the farmers in this entire area, as well as the merchants and other businessmen of Winston-Salem, will be materially affected by this increase in the purchasing power of the company's employees."[18]

Negotiations with the independent leaf houses did not proceed as smoothly. The owners of Piedmont Leaf and Winston Leaf seemed poised for a test of strength. Local 22's contracts expired on July 22, and talks had progressed so slowly that the union filed strike notices with the U.S. Department of Labor in June. It continued to negotiate with Export Leaf, whose absentee owners had proved relatively coop-erative in the past. At each of the three leaf houses, a cadre of militant union lead-ers had emerged over the past three years. Previously overshadowed by their coun-terparts at Reynolds, they now moved to the forefront of the tobacco workers' struggle.[19]

On Monday morning, July 22, 1946, about 300 members of Local 22 set up a picket line in front of Piedmont's plants on Fourth Street. Approximately thirty-five workers walked out, but later that week the company was to begin hiring the 800 or so people who would be needed for the season, and the strike was sure to spread. Four days later, 750 workers walked off their jobs at Winston Leaf. With the opening of the Georgia tobacco markets, the Piedmont and Winston warehouses would soon be full of tobacco. The companies had picked a bad time to test the union's resolve.

In rejecting the union's proposal, the leaf houses claimed that significant wage increases would make them unable to compete with their nonunionized counterparts in eastern North Carolina, and they adamantly opposed granting a union shop, despite the fact that well over 90 percent of the employees at both companies were union members. Phil Koritz believed that the owners' defiance stemmed in part from racial prejudice. Owners deeply resented the gains the union had won for black workers, whom they viewed as little more than servants. Union leaders also believed that Reynolds may have encouraged the leaf houses to take a tough stand as a way of testing Local 22's ability to hold its membership together.[20]

On July 31, Export Leaf broke ranks with the other leaf houses, negotiating a contract that included unprecedented gains for Local 22. Union members felt confident that Piedmont and Winston would eventually agree to similar terms. But by the first week of August, no settlement was in sight, so the union set up relief committees to aid those out of work. The Reverend Frank O'Neal offered his Union Mission Holy Church as the strike headquarters, and the union opened storefront relief centers near each plant.[21]

Neither FTA nor Local 22 had deep pockets, so strikers looked to the black community to make up for lost wages, sending out canvassers to request contributions from businesses and individuals. Although the community generally supported the workers, some merchants refused to donate to the relief fund or to extend credit to strikers. A few complained to the city police that strikers had threatened to boycott their stores if they failed to ante up. Cleverly manipulating the law, Police Chief John Gold informed the union that canvassing was in violation of a city ordinance that required all solicitors for religious or charitable purposes to obtain permits from the Police Department. Not just the organization, but each individual canvasser had to apply for a permit, supply extensive references, and submit to a background check.[22]

In the meantime, strikers marched in two-hour shifts, drawing crowds of people downtown. In an effort to elicit sympathy from the white community, the union took out newspaper ads featuring photographs of the dilapidated houses many leaf house workers lived in with captions that read: "Would you like to live here? Would you like to raise a family on $15 a week?" Underscoring both the ravages of inflation and the leaf workers' poverty, one picket sign proclaimed: "Fatback 75 cents, Our Labor 50 cents."[23]

Pickets at Piedmont Leaf, 1946 (Forsyth County Public Library Photograph Collection)

The strike dragged on through the first weeks of August. On two occasions the police broke the picket lines at Piedmont and Winston to allow construction trucks onto company grounds, even though another, unpicketed entrance was supposed to be used for such purposes. Finally, on Friday, August 23, 1946, Local 22 found itself caught up in the violence that was erupting around the country in the aftermath of the war.[24]

Each side disputed the circumstances of the confrontation. In the months following the strike, through two court trials and in numerous statements to the press, picketers and union supporters presented one version of events, police and opponents of the union another. The official police version went like this: On the afternoon in question, Chief Gold and a contingent of a dozen policemen arrived at the main gate of Piedmont Leaf, an area usually patrolled by two officers. They had been notified that a contractor wished to bring a steam shovel onto the grounds, and they anticipated trouble. Shortly after the police arrived, a truck pulled up to the entrance. The Reverend John Wesley Bee, a Baptist minister and captain of the pickets, approached the driver and "asked him not to break the picket line, stating that the picketers would leave for the day at 5 p.m." Police asked the driver if he wanted to go in. He said yes. Chief Gold claimed that officers asked the crowd to move, to which they responded, "No, No, No!" The police then plunged into the crowd to clear a path for the truck and immediately arrested two women who stood in their way. The strikers fought back. According to the *Journal* reporter, "The ensuing minutes were an uproar of shouting and clamoring, curses and threats, flying fists and kicking feet as the police went grimly about their business."[25]

Bee and other union members denied that they had defied the police orders and testified that picketers, most of whom were black women, had not been given adequate time to move. Strikers, Bee said, were still marching and chanting when Chief Gold, billy club in hand, pushed through the picket line and the police began making arrests. The police first attacked Betty Keels Williams. She testified that "Chief Gold ran in with a stick in one hand and [was] just hitting us, [shouting] 'Get back out of the way and let the truck in.'" According to Williams, "So many of us was in the picket line marching, I couldn't get back." Gold pushed Williams in the chest and she stumbled, dropping the $2.40 she had in her dress pocket. One of the other officers then grabbed her and placed her under arrest. "I said, 'Wait and let me get my money. I haven't did anything.' He says, 'If you dropped anything it is nothing but a penny. Come on.' He had my arm, twisting it, and he was squeezing it and when he got me about to the car, he turned me loose."[26]

Margaret DeGraffenreid, another picketer, fared much worse. She was twenty-two years old, the mother of one child and pregnant with another. A native of Rock Hill, South Carolina, she had come to Winston-Salem shortly before the start of the war. She was supporting her mother and father in addition to herself and her child. Police officers claimed that DeGraffenreid had refused to move out of the way of the truck and then resisted arrest. She "was pulling back and scuffling," according to Captain R. C. Barlow. It took four officers three or four minutes to get her into the car, he said. Officer Hillary Ledwell testified that "DeGraffenreid seemed hysterical. . . . She was fighting and hollering." The *Journal* printed a photograph of DeGraffenreid being put into the police car with the caption, "Police Take Hysterical Striker to Jail."[27]

DeGraffenreid told a different story. "The officers snatched me out of the picket line," she testified, "and didn't give me a chance to walk. They snatched me . . . drug me on down . . . and throwed me in the car." She said one policeman hit her with his club, another shut the door on her arm, while a third grabbed her around the stomach and pulled her into the car. On the way into City Hall, she continued, one of the officers pushed her down on the sidewalk and, as she tried to get up, called her a "black cow." In the elevator "a heavy-built officer. . . . slapped her as hard as he could," and when he threw her into the cell she hit the back of her head.[28]

Margaret DeGraffenreid being forced into police car, 1946 (Courtesy of Forsyth County Public Library Photograph Collection)

Phil Koritz arrived on the scene shortly after the first arrests. By that time the streets were full of people on their way to work at Reynolds. Koritz conferred with the picket captains and then began making his way to the union office so that he could post bail for the arrested strikers. At the same time, Cal Jones, a black Reynolds employee, walked toward the picketers, and officers moved in and arrested him. Jones struggled, causing one officer to trip and fall. At that point, Koritz pushed his way through the crowd. The police claimed that Koritz screamed to the crowd, "Don't let them take that man." According to Koritz, the statement was more like, "Why don't you give him a break? He's not a striker, he's a Reynolds worker." An officer then told him to mind his own business, Koritz said, and raised a billy club. Koritz grabbed the club and scuffled with police, but he too was overcome and quickly rushed off in a police car. Koritz reported that on the way to the police station the officer told him, "Why don't you go back where you came from, you damned kike?"

The melee continued, and the police claimed that the crowd, which had swelled to several thousand with the addition of the Reynolds workers, assaulted several officers. One woman supposedly attacked a policeman with a badge snatched from a fallen officer's shirt. People flung bricks at the squad cars. "The mob howled, jeered and taunted," reported the *Journal*, "as the police attempted to keep the moving hundreds herded on or close to the sidewalk and suppress further violence." Following the police cars to the county jail, the crowd stood outside shouting for the strikers' release.[29]

The *Journal* portrayed the conflict as a major riot, focusing especially on the race, sex, and ethnicity of the alleged perpetrators. The on-the-scene report of staff writer Ted Thompson, for instance, began this way: "Swift-moving mob violence late yesterday tore asunder the atmosphere of peaceable picketing which had prevailed for a month at the strike-bound plant of the Piedmont Leaf Tobacco Company." Thompson's report described "hand-to-hand fighting" between police and "the throng of more than 3,000 Negroes. . . . Hysterical . . . shrieking" women attacked police with "flying fists" and "kicking feet."

A front-page editorial in the *Journal* defended the police actions. "The differences between civilization and barbarism can be summed up in the word—LAW. No single issue among men transcends in importance the necessity to settle our differences by Law. Any other method destroys not only the immediate issue but also all gains of the past, and the future to come. Thus, the *Journal* joins with all sincere Americans in support of Law and the officers charged with its enforcement."[30]

To the strikers and their supporters, the police were not the upholders of civilization or a system of justice, but violent enforcers of a socially sanctioned system of inequality and injustice. Working-class blacks suffered daily at the hands of the Winston-Salem police force, which was no better or worse than the police in other southern cities. In this case, unionists believed, the police had intervened on the side of the company in an effort to provoke the workers and break the strike.

At police headquarters, Chief Gold called for reinforcements from the state highway patrol and alerted Governor Gregg Cherry about the situation. Koritz and Gene Pratt told Gold that they would go back and try to calm things down if all the arrested picketers were released. Gold and Governor Cherry conferred again, and Koritz assured the governor that he would handle the situation. Finally the police chief released all of the prisoners, and Koritz went back to the scene and convinced the people to go home.[31]

Union leaders called a meeting at Shiloh Baptist Church that night, and Koritz tried to persuade the furious workers that their only chance of success lay in tenacious, peaceful picketing. Returning in full force the next morning, the strikers channeled their anger into determined marching and ringing song. But if union leaders thought that conciliation would buy them leniency from local officials, they were wrong.

On September 4, the defendants appeared in Winston-Salem Municipal Court. Both the prosecution and the defense presented a stream of witnesses, who proffered conflicting versions of the events at Piedmont Leaf. The judge found Koritz, Jones, DeGraffenreid, and Williams guilty of resisting arrest. Koritz and Jones received sentences of six and eight months of hard labor on the chain gang, DeGraffenreid got three months at the county farm, and Williams received a thirty-day suspended sentence. The other cases were thrown out for lack of evidence. On appeal, Betty Williams won release, but Koritz and Jones received even harsher punishment. The *Journal* praised the "stiff, unconditional sentences. . . . The Municipal Court . . . has demonstrated in forceful manner the determination of the local courts to discourage mob violence and the reign of chaos and anarchy in community life." *The Worker's Voice*, on the other hand, reported that "the courtroom was crowded with workers who got a liberal education on how 'justice' works in local courts when workers and their organizations are concerned."[32]

Winston-Salem's black citizens saw the trials as anything but just. Some white readers of the *Journal*'s coverage were skeptical as well. Minnie Myers Cook, a white housewife, wrote to the editor of the *Journal* in response to an article alleging Communist involvement in Winston-Salem's labor troubles. Cook was dismayed by the article's allegations but had an analysis of the problem that would become increasingly common as the Cold War affected America's treatment of its black population. "Hunger," she said, "is a fertile soil for seeds of friendship, whether it be from democracy or communism. If we don't want seeds of communism to take root and grow in Winston-Salem, we must be mighty sure that no one is hungry." The contrast between the condition of the leaf house workers and the local social elite, said Cook, was symptomatic of the contradictions that made the United States vulnerable to Soviet propaganda. "It seems so strange that people who live so near each other live so differently. In the same newspaper you will read of the continual holiday at Roaring Gap, where expenses are the least thing thought of and on another page you will see pictures of strikers walking all day back and forth in the hot sun trying to get a few pennies raise in wages. . . . I know these people are mostly Negroes," Cook concluded, "but their little children are as near to them as mine are to me, and their little stomachs get just as empty and like to be filled just as well."[33]

Elizabeth Harvey, a leaf house worker, expressed appreciation for Cook's "words of sympathy." "We haven't been offered a decent living wage. While some can go on vacations, fishing trips, and a general good time, we struggle for a mere existence.

. . . We have to pay the same price for food and other incidentals. These industrialists have money to do anything with. Why not pay their laborers enough, that they and their children will at least not be hungry?"[34]

Far from being deterred by the specter of violence or the heavy hand of the law, the strikers redoubled their efforts to connect with the larger movement of which they were a part. They solicited financial support from unions across the country. They called on local farmers and businessmen to "urge these companies to move from their stubborn and unreasonable position of disregard for the workers, farmers, and the community." With the opening of the Winston-Salem tobacco market only a few days away, the North Carolina Farm Bureau responded by bringing pressure on the companies to settle the leaf house strike.[35]

In the face of this pragmatic worker-farmer alliance, the companies signaled their willingness to negotiate. The union withdrew its demand for a union shop, and both sides compromised on wages. On September 22, 1946, the two parties signed a contract that contained one significant new feature: seasonal workers gained three paid holidays a year—July 4, Labor Day, and Christmas—a privilege they had never enjoyed before.[36]

Operation Dixie

No sooner had Winston-Salem's leaf house workers settled their own strike than they began to look outward, to the plight of their unorganized counterparts in eastern North Carolina, whose low wages not only caused immense local suffering but threatened to undercut the position of tobacco workers everywhere. The "new Bright Belt," as it was called, stretched 150 miles across the coastal plain. By the 1930s, towns such as Rocky Mount, Kinston, Oxford, Wilson, and Greenville had established themselves as busy tobacco marketing and warehousing centers.[37]

Thousands of African American workers, over 75 percent of whom were women, found seasonal employment in the leaf houses from late summer to early winter. Even by the low standards of leaf houses, wages and working conditions in North Carolina were dreadful. Companies took full advantage of the exemptions that southern congressmen had managed to write into the Fair Labor Standards Act, crowding the lion's share of the season's work into the fourteen weeks during which they were exempt from paying time-and-half for overtime. The drive system was in full force, with foremen pushing workers to do as much as they physically could. "The boss would curse all day long," one worker remembered. "No name was too dirty for them."[38]

According to Louis Austin of the *Carolina Times*, eastern North Carolina harbored the state's most vicious sharecropping system, its most disgraceful criminal justice system as far as blacks were concerned, its deepest poverty, and its least independent black middle class. It's "what's considered the black belt," observed Ed McCrea, "and it's more reactionary than probably any other part of the South."[39]

The Great Depression had driven thousands of small farmers off the land, and World War II had upset the balance of race relations "Down East" as surely as it did in Piedmont cities. In the aftermath of Pearl Harbor, three of the country's largest military bases were established in the region. Newly minted soldiers from all over the country filled the streets, and white officials complained that the northerners among them refused to obey segregation laws. Young people jumped at jobs in defense plants, ventured across the border to Norfolk, Virginia, or headed north to Baltimore. In rural counties where simply joining the NAACP could still bring retribution, hundreds showed up for meetings in churches, lodges, and homes. Such assertiveness alarmed the region's white population, and the reborn Ku Klux Klan launched a wave of terror. Kidnappings, shootings, and whippings resulted in felony indictments against more than sixty Klansmen, including the police chief of Tabor City. When the war ended, black and white soldiers returned home to an atmosphere tense with the mingling of hope and fear.[40]

In the late spring of 1946, FTA stepped into this volatile situation. Women in the leaf houses had benefited relatively little from war-born prosperity. Yet they, as much as anyone, had been touched by rising expectations, broader horizons, and the rhetoric of the New Deal and the war. At the urging of Winston-Salem unionists, Frank Green, who had just taken over as FTA's Southeast regional director and opened an office in Raleigh, began to investigate their situation. Appalled by what he learned but convinced that the leaf houses were ripe for organization, Green convinced national FTA leaders to undertake a campaign to bring the gains won by Local 22 to workers across the state. Robert Lathan, who had emerged as a key leader of the leaf house workers in Winston-Salem, joined Green and started making contacts in the east.[41]

Two months later the CIO announced plans for Operation Dixie, a million-dollar southern organizing campaign. Despite the strategic importance of the South and the upsurge of union membership during World War II, the federation had made no concerted effort to conquer the region. By the end of the war, however, it could not avoid facing the threat that such a reservoir of cheap labor posed to northern unions.

Just as pressing was the ever-growing threat posed by antiunion southern congressmen. At the peak of the New Deal, northern blacks, labor, and liberal Democrats had joined forces to pass pro-labor legislation over southern opposition. Even

so, Bourbon Democrats had succeeded in denying these new protections to agricultural and domestic workers—still a major sector of the southern workforce—
and thus ensuring a steady supply of captive low-wage labor for their farms and
factories. Desperate for better-paying industrial jobs, these workers formed a reserve army of labor that undermined not just northern unions but every attempt
to organize southern workers. Now southern congressmen, in league with resur-
gent Republicans, were poised to roll back labor's gains. They had already defeated
labor's efforts to institute a full employment plan and a permanent FEPC. Their ultimate goal was no less than repeal of the Wagner Act or, barring that, amending it
so as to dismantle the system of industrial jurisprudence that ensured workers'
right to organize.[42]

Operation Dixie aimed to put 200 organizers in the field with orders to "organize everything in sight." Couched as a "Holy Crusade," the campaign promised to
accomplish on a regionwide scale what Local 22 was doing in Winston-Salem: rally
workers in an assault on the bastions of privilege in the workplace, at the ballot
box, and in the community at large. The timing seemed extraordinarily propitious,
given the rise of unionization in the South during the war. Even the president of
the National Association of Manufacturers "predicted success for the C.I.O.'s
efforts to organize the South."[43]

From the outset, however, there were signs that behind the CIO's crusading rhetoric lay conflicting tactics, goals, and values. If the protection of northern labor was
the CIO's main motivation, how would that affect its approach to organizing in
the South? If the campaign's primary goals were economic, what would happen to
the political ambitions of CIO-PAC? What role would left-wing unions play? Would
the CIO seek to expand its enclaves of biracial, civil rights–oriented, civic unionism
or would it stick to safer channels and bread-and-butter issues? CIO president
Philip Murray's appointment of the conservative unionists Van A. Bittner and
George Baldanzi to lead the offensive intensified the concerns of some FTA officials,
who feared that Operation Dixie might turn newly established locals over to less
radical unions rather than to FTA. Nevertheless, at the urging of president Donald
Henderson, the FTA decided to fold the leaf house campaign into the larger effort.[44]

Within weeks after Operation Dixie was announced, William Green, president
of the AFL, told southern delegates gathered in Asheville, North Carolina, that his
federation was also "launching a crusade to organize the unorganized workers of
the South." George Meany, the AFL's secretary-treasurer, foresaw a battle against
two groups: "representatives of entrenched capital" and Communists, "parading
and preaching under the banner and name of the C.I.O." Both leaders predicted
that the AFL would be able to exploit employers' fears and recruit one million new

members. "Grow and cooperate with us," Green told southern industrialists, "or fight for your life against Communist forces." With this encouragement, the TWIU quickly entered the fray in eastern North Carolina, signing sweetheart deals with two leaf houses in Wilson, neither of which involved an NLRB election.[45]

A few weeks later, Robert Black arrived in Greenville, armed only with the name of a local minister who operated a small dry cleaning business in town. The minister introduced him to a neighbor, the thirty-five-year-old Cornelius Simmons, who worked at Imperial Leaf but had seen the benefits of unionization during a wartime job in New York. Encouraged by Black's tale of FTA's success at Reynolds and the Winston-Salem leaf houses, Simmons agreed to introduce him to friends at work who had been quietly agitating for better working conditions. Soon Black had the names of workers at other firms, and together he and Simmons built a volunteer organizing committee.[46]

Word of the organizing drive spread rapidly in the black community. Some of the workers the committee approached were too frightened to respond. Annie Little, who became chair of the committee at Export Leaf, recalled the initial reaction of the workers at her plant. "Most of them did not believe what we were saying [about the benefits of the union], but we kept trying to convince them. . . . [W]e never convinced some of them because Mr. Charlie didn't want no labor union in their plants." Others, however, were "glad to get out from under that whip." Soon there were additional committees at Greenville Leaf, Person-Garrett, and E. B. Ficklen. As in Winston-Salem, cottage meetings in workers' homes proved critical. Momentum began to build, and soon organizers were signing up hundreds of new members. Within less than two months, the CIO petitioned the NLRB for elections.[47]

The afternoon before the first ever NLRB-sponsored election in Greenville, a local radio station broadcast speeches by a black doctor, a minister, and an undertaker urging workers to vote against the union. The three men "attended the mass meeting the union organized on the eve of the election," Robert Black recalled. "They were not invited, but they came in to . . . browbeat the workers. . . . The church was packed, people sitting in the windows, no air conditioning. Three carloads of police and deputy sheriffs and a couple of the owners of the plants sitting out on the lawn, right where they could hear everything. . . . They had amplifiers all out in the yard and you couldn't see the church for the people."[48]

Cornelius Simmons chaired the meeting and invited the three men to present their case. Dr. James Battle, Simmons remembered, "got up and told the workers about how good Mr. Garrett, one of the leaf house owners, and the [white] people had been to them." Addressing a room full of women, most of whom combined seasonal work in the leaf houses with household service, the doctor acted as if he were talking only to blue-collar men. "'You know,' he said, 'in the winter when there is no work going on here and if you happen to need five dollars, you can always go to Mr. Garrett and get it. If your wife works [in white homes] the wife will give them one of their dresses or slips to help them out some.'"

Battle had badly misjudged his audience. Not only were women leaf house workers unlikely to appreciate such an appeal, but their husbands were equally insulted. As soon as the doctor had finished, Cornelius Simmons took the stage. "You are my family doctor and every time I call you the first thing you want to know is if I have any money. Suppose I say yes and come on up and after you have given me service I give you one of my wife's old slips for your pay, how would that suit you?"[49]

Then Robert Black jumped in. He had done some research on likely opponents of the union among black professionals. "This doctor was a sitting duck," he remembered. "On a hot day in August, this Dr. [Battle] walked into Greenville with a suitcase in his hand. Didn't own a car and knew very little about medicine. [Now] he was living in a big house up on the hill, his wife was driving a Cadillac and he had a Lincoln, and they had a maid in the house. [During the meeting, Battle] told about the times he used to visit the homes of those tobacco workers and they didn't have the money to pay him in full and he took what they had. But he didn't tell them that he kept gouging until he gouged out the rest."

Speaking directly to the women workers who filled the pews, Black said, "'When you went to work in the bossman's kitchen, at the end of the day they would probably give you seventy-five cents and the husband would offer you a couple of old pair of pants that had patches on the seat and the wife would give you a bowl of cold cabbage or whatever you had had that was left over to carry home to feed your family. And that was just about your day's pay. So I want to make a suggestion: when one of you all get sick call Dr. [Battle] and after he has given you his pills and sawed on your bones, go in your pantry and give him a pair of your husband's old pants, be sure they have patches on them, and give him a bowl of soup or whatever you had planned to have for dinner as his pay. That's what he's telling you to continue to take and he's praising the people that's continuing to enslave you.'"[50]

As the doctor quietly slid out the rear door, state CIO director William Smith stood up to address the crowd. He "let the workers know that they weren't alone," Black remembered, "that they had this big nationwide organization there. It gave strength to people to know this. They felt like for the first time that we have something here that we can stick our teeth in." As in Winston-Salem, a broad base of support from the African American community, which included many ministers and, especially in Greenville and Rocky Mount, the recently activated branches of the NAACP, quickly muted the few oppositional voices.[51]

While Robert Black, Cornelius Simmons, Annie Little, and others built an organization in Greenville, FTA organizers and rank-and-file activists crisscrossed the state signing up workers and establishing organizing committees in dozens of other communities. Ed McCrea remembered some of the difficulties. "At that time, it was a very dangerous job. The black organizers had a hard time finding some place to eat. They had to live out of people's homes. They couldn't go to a hotel. They couldn't find a restaurant to eat in if they were traveling, and if you're a white and a black traveling together, you weren't going to split up. Usually what we did was just stop somewhere on the roadside, and the white guy would go and get something to eat and bring it out and then eat in the car."[52]

Marie Jackson, who worked at Winston Leaf, volunteered to help the drive. "Local 22 would pay your transportation and a little money for food," she remembered. "The people in the various places agreed that we could stay at their house." Bouncing "around in the Greyhound Bus in the back," she moved from town to town. Workers in the smaller plants were the hardest to organize, she remembered. "They were afraid. You're talking about their bread. Although it was bits and pieces of crumbs, that was all they had."

When workers drew back in fear, Jackson had a simple but powerful response: "'You've just got to make it up in your own mind. Do you want to work under these conditions? Do you want to work for forty cents an hour the rest of your life? Do you want your children and your grandchildren to come up under these same conditions? There's got to be a better way. Other people are doing it. Why not you? You're just as good as anybody else. But it's going to mean some sacrifice. Yeah, somebody may lose their job. Somebody may lose their life.'"[53]

Such dangers did not deter John Pease, an Oxford man who had seen his share of violence. He burned with the memory of white vigilantes lynching three men in front of the Export Leaf plant in the 1920s. Pease had worked briefly at a local factory organized by the United Furniture Workers, and after he transferred to Export, he started talking union. Robert Lathan found him, and with a few other workers they began meeting secretly to plan a campaign. A month later they had enough recruits to hold a rally for 200–300 people at a local church. Pease observed shortly afterward, "It wasn't just wages we wanted, but freedom."[54]

The desire for wages *and* freedom swept more and more people into the union, and by the end of the summer, FTA organizers had signed up workers in over sixty-six plants. At that point, FTA passed along the authorization cards and $1 initiation fees to CIO officials, who requested elections in twenty-eight plants where the union represented a majority of the workers. "They were fast elections," Ed McCrea remembered. "The board cooperated because they knew it was a short season, and they speeded up the elections. They were held in pretty rapid-fire order. It was a tremendous drive, and it was very rapid. We just swept the whole area, and all the elections were overwhelming, hardly any votes against the union." By the end of November 1946, FTA had defeated the AFL in twenty-five elections, covering close to 8,000 eastern North Carolina workers, in Greenville, Oxford, Rocky Mount, Henderson, Smithfield, Kinston, Goldsboro, and Lumberton.[55]

This outpouring of support continued as FTA began the difficult process of negotiating contracts without the help of the now defunct National War Labor Board. Frank Green described the atmosphere. "I remember in Henderson, North Carolina, going up there for a meeting. And I went to a lady's house who was chairman of the union. We're meeting in the church there, and she says fine, come on. So we walked down the street together and she just calls out as we pass every house, come on, we're going to the union meeting. And by the time we got to the church, there were a hundred people walking down the street. You know, just a feeling of cooperation. Really of love, concern for each other. I didn't know everybody's name, but she did. By the time you got there, you got a hundred people following you down the street. They felt they were free. They knew that their history had been slavery and they knew that since the end of chattel slavery they still were not free. And now for the first time in their lives, they had a chance, they saw a way out." "We'd go down there to negotiate," Robert Black recalled, "and those people would be at the plant waiting for the negotiating committee an hour or more before the time. You didn't have to go around pulling them out of bed. They realized that they had something."[56]

"In the course of negotiations a couple of times," Ed McCrea remembered, "we had to have stoppages that covered the whole belt. [We had to] make the companies realize how serious we were, so they'd [quit] stalling on negotiations. A couple of times we'd just have a ten or fifteen minute stoppage, but that cost them a lot of money because that tobacco was burning up in the drying kilns, and that's where they couldn't afford to have a stoppage. We never had a strike. We wouldn't have tried to have a strike because just to have those little stoppages would kill them in that short season. As a result, they signed up pretty rapidly, and we got some things that they never had before."[57]

Frank Green explained how this tactic worked in a particularly difficult case. "We were just getting nowhere. We decided the only way we could make any progress was to show them that we could stop the operation any time we wanted to. So, we had our signs. In the middle of our negotiations, Bob Lathan would go out to get a drink of water from the water cooler—he had to drink from the colored fountain, of course. [If] he leaned over and just took one big sip of water, things were progressing. If he took one sip, and then raised his head, and then took another sip, that's the sign that things were not progressing and we needed to let them know. One of the maintenance people was to get word of this, but we had the plant one hundred percent organized and we could do things like this. So, this maintenance worker walks through the floor and this is just one great big building. He walks through the floor with a hand saw. If he has this saw down in his hand, things are progressing. If it's up on his shoulder, things are not progressing. So, Bob goes out and takes two sips. About five minutes later, the maintenance worker walks through the plant with his saw on his shoulder. Everybody stops work. The leaf starts running off the end of the belt. The foreman had to shut the machines down. Somebody come running, [yelling], 'What the hell's going on?' I said, 'I'm not sure what's going on. I really believe the people are not satisfied with the progress that we are making.'"[58]

In the end, the contracts brought eastern North Carolina leaf house workers in line with their counterparts in Winston-Salem. It was impractical to set up separate locals in each small plant or town, so FTA opted to bring all organized eastern North Carolina leaf house workers into an amalgamated local—Local 10, which prided itself on being "the baby sister of Local 22." Workers got a ten-cent wage increase, and companies agreed not to request the fourteen-week exemption. At Imperial in Greenville, workers won a week's vacation with pay and improvements in factory conditions that had been willfully insulting and demoralizing. "Instead of sitting on a stack of tobacco to eat," Cornelius Simmons remembered, "we got a dining room. We got coolers rather than a nail keg with water in it." At Oxford's Export Leaf, management provided clean restrooms and soap for the first time. There were other, less tangible gains as well. Frank Green explained: "Bob Lathan and I negotiated [a contract], and they had a secretary there who transcribed word for word everything that was said. And they sent it to me to approve and send back. Every place they had what Lathan said, they had 'Lathan.' Everybody else was 'Mr.' except Lathan. He was just Lathan. So, I would not sign it until they added Mr. in front of the Lathan all the way through."[59]

From the outset, Local 22 activists had conceived of their mission in eastern North Carolina as more than a unionization campaign. To be sure, their first goal was to organize enough workers to win an NLRB election and develop the rank-and-file leadership that could sustain a union. But as in Winston-Salem, they also wanted to mobilize leaf house workers and other African Americans to fight for political power and civil rights. Couching their aims as "full respect for the workers' rights as citizens," they mounted a challenge that struck at the core of a social system that had changed remarkably little from the turn of the century until World War II.[60]

From their base in Local 10, Frank Green, rank-and-file activists from Winston-Salem, and local leaf house workers now moved to challenge Jim Crow in ways large and small. The effort was as daunting as their first one-on-one contacts and secret meetings had been. Their first step was to create a Local 10 Political Action Committee, modeled on the one formed by the national CIO in 1943 and by Local 22 a year later. Each city, in turn, created its own committee, usually led by someone who had proven his or her mettle in the organizing campaign. When the North Carolina CIO-PAC held its convention in 1947, Local 10 sent delegates from Goldsboro, Greenville, Henderson, Kinston, Lumberton, Oxford, Rocky Mount, Smithfield, and Wilson—more than any other union local in the state.

According to Cornelius Simmons, Greenville's PAC was especially adept at mobilizing new networks of support, overcoming the literacy requirements that kept so many blacks off the voter registration books, and using the black vote against the more egregious white officials. "After we got the union in there we started educating people," he remembered. But before union members tried to register, Simmons called for help. FTA sent Laurent Franz, who was studying law at Duke and, like an increasing number of Duke and University of North Carolina students, volunteering for FTA. Simmons "took him down there and introduced him to the registrar and told him he was a lawyer. That scared them so bad." Franz began accompanying union members when they went to register, and the registrar evidently passed the word to let them sign up. "They were standing at the precincts begging people to come in," Annie Little remembered. "We just loaded the places up and they got on the books." According to Simmons, that political beachhead made a difference. Over the next few years, "we got rid of a judge there who was real nasty. We changed a lot of the aldermen and got a different chief of police."[61]

Returning veterans, some of whom sought jobs in the leaf houses and many of whom were the husbands and sons of leaf house workers, gave Local 10 union strong support. "We found that none of the discharged [black] veterans were getting the severance pay that they were entitled to," Ed McCrea remembered. "[This was] for accumulated leave time, which amounted to thousands of dollars. . . . They couldn't collect it because all the postmasters had orders—where they got the orders, I don't know whether it was from the state or the Ku Klux Klan or what it was—but none of them would give them forms to fill out to apply for the GI accumulated time." McCrea wrote to Elizabeth Sasuly, FTA's Washington representative.

She went to the Veterans Administration, "and all of a sudden all these veterans were told to come in and apply for their accumulated pay. This was something that all the people of the black community in every town knew that we did that. We had a tremendous favorable response, and the veterans, man, they'd do anything to help us."[62]

By any measure, FTA's eastern North Carolina drive was among the most successful of Operative Dixie's endeavors. In his president's report to the 1947 FTA convention, Donald Henderson observed: "It cannot be emphasized too much that the Southern Drive is more than a mere organizing campaign. It is in fact a social revolution." A social revolution, however, was not what CIO leaders had in mind, and while they were pleased with the success of the leaf house drive, they did little to support it and viewed it less as a jewel in their crown than as a liability.[63]

For one thing, CIO officials saw white textile workers as the key to organizing the South, not only because textiles were the region's largest single industry, employing 25 percent of the region's industrial workforce, but also because the textile unions were Operation Dixie's largest financial backers. Assuming as they did that white textile workers were irredeemably racist and that they would respond only to the most cautious and narrowly defined appeals, Operation Dixie's leaders took pains to play down the CIO's strength in the black community, hired few black organizers, and avoided any linkage between unionization and civil rights. Moreover, neither CIO president Philip Murray nor Operation Dixie directors Bittner and Baldanzi, both of whom were resolute anti-Communists, acknowledged how important left-wing organizers had been to the CIO's earlier success. As a result of their abhorrence of the left and their assumptions about the South's rock-solid conservatism, they sought to distance themselves from the men and women who helped to build many of the region's most dynamic unions. Finally, despite the centrality of politics to labor's postwar agenda, the CIO did everything in its power to portray Operation Dixie as a "purely organizational campaign," even going so far as to refuse support from the Southern Conference for Human Welfare and ordering its staff to sever their ties to CIO-PAC, the spearhead of the CIO's political operations.[64]

All of these policies, which the historian Robert Zieger summarizes as the "privileging of textiles, the marginalization of the left, and the relegation of blacks to a subsidiary role," as well as a focus on the workplace rather than the community, played themselves out beneath the surface of the FTA's leaf house drive. The director of Operation Dixie in North Carolina was William Smith, a Californian with little knowledge of southern industry or workers, and he put Elijah Jackson, one of the few African Americans in the state CIO office, in charge of the organizing drive. Smith was supportive of FTA's campaign—which was technically under his jurisdiction—but, in line with the overall drive, he focused on the textile industry, especially on a doomed effort to organize Cannon Mills in Kannapolis, a huge, tightly controlled enterprise, legendary for its imperviousness to unions. According to Ed McCrea, Jackson, too, put his energies elsewhere. Operation Dixie "didn't provide really any manpower or any energy" in the leaf house campaign.[65]

Equally grating was Operation Dixie's effort to dampen the union's civil rights appeals. When Local 22's perennial competitor, the TWIU, sent organizers into eastern North Carolina, FTA responded by criticizing the AFL union's policy of maintaining segregated locals. One leaflet in particular drew William Smith's ire. It summarized a recent NLRB ruling against the TWIU disallowing the establishment of a segregated black local at a plant in Richmond and asked, "Does This Look Like Democracy in the American Federation of Labor?" Smith strenuously objected to the leaflet and wrote to Frank Green requesting "that this leaflet be suspended and not distributed." Smith claimed that the leaflet raised "a negro nationalistic approach which could easily be dangerous to us" and that such appeals were unnecessary given the success of the leaf house drive. What concerned him most was that "this material could very easily boomerang on us and be used by the AFL against us . . . in the textile industry."[66]

Such worries were perfectly understandable, especially in a region where labor faced so much hostility, key industries were so competitive, and evidence of racist reaction abounded. Yet, in the end, it was Operation Dixie's decision to play by the rules—and not the antiracist stance of left-led unions—that boomeranged. The CIO's attempts to disguise rather than exploit its political progressivism did nothing to prevent its enemies in the AFL and among employers from attacking its organizers as communistic race-mixers. Nor did its decision to ignore food processing, lumber, and transportation—all industries that employed a biracial workforce and in which black workers especially had responded enthusiastically to unionization—pay off in the textile industry. Even among white textile workers, the CIO's strategy proved self-defeating. Inexperienced male organizers made little headway in an industry where half the workers were women, and textile workers failed to respond to bread-and-butter appeals not because they were intrinsically passive or hostile to unionization, but because they had endured a series of earlier, crushing defeats, their standard of living had risen significantly, and many of their grievances revolved around less tangible issues of respect and working conditions. In North Carolina the Cannon Mills campaign failed miserably, and by the end of the year organizing efforts were faltering across the region. The CIO did not officially disband the southern organizing drive until 1953, but it was already clear that neither the CIO nor the AFL would achieve the ambitious goals they had set for themselves in the spring of 1946.[67]

CHAPTER TWELVE

Fighting the Fire

Nineteen forty-seven opened with Local 22 fresh from its success among leaf house workers and at the height of its prestige in the international union. It had weathered anti-Communist attacks and technological attrition. Having registered hundreds of workers, it was now prepared to take on City Hall. Within five months, a cross-class, biracial coalition with labor at its core would succeed in electing to the Winston-Salem Board of Aldermen the first African American to win office against a white opponent in the South since the turn-of-the-century disfranchisement campaigns.

That challenge to white supremacy transpired on the cusp of a prolonged strike that revealed both the union's broad support in the black community and the ominous intensification of the Cold War. Over Local 22's political and economic ambitions also hung the shadow of the Taft-Hartley Act. These developments, together with the growing rifts within the CIO, threatened to dismantle the system of industrial jurisprudence on which the union depended, isolate it from its liberal anti-Communist allies, and scuttle the Southern Front of which it was a part. An equally serious threat came from the union's local antagonists, who combined red-baiting with the more subtle, and equally effective, tactics of electoral manipulation and co-optation. By the summer of 1947 the union and its opponents were in a standoff, with Taft-Hartley set to go into effect in September and Local 22 weakened but by no means conceding defeat.

Local Politics

In January 1947 the Food and Tobacco Workers Union elected Moranda Smith to its executive committee, making her the first African American woman in the country to hold such a post. It was a singular honor, and one that signaled FTA's commitment to promoting women and minorities into positions of authority. Smith's election also recognized both Local 22's position as the international's prize local and Smith's special gifts—as a mesmerizing public speaker, a forceful negotiator, and an intensely dedicated trade unionist. Less than three months later, she was speeding to Washington to help defend FTA, and the labor movement generally, against what threatened to be the worst setback since the CIO burst upon the scene in the 1930s.[1]

Corporations and conservative politicians had been attempting to repeal or gut what they saw as the pro-labor Wagner Act since the late 1930s. The Republican sweep in the congressional elections of 1946, together with the antiunion sentiment stirred by the strike wave of 1945–46, gave them the opening they needed. Behind this drive to dismantle the New Deal dispensation in labor affairs lay one of the largest and most expensive lobbying and public relations campaigns in legislative history. Initiated by the National Association of Manufacturers, this campaign centered on a step-by-step plan for shifting the focus of federal labor law from protecting labor's right to organize to strengthening employers' ability to resist unionization.[2]

On March 25, Moranda Smith and FTA president Donald Henderson appeared before the Senate Labor Committee chaired by Ohio senator Robert A. Taft to explain the international union's opposition to the proposed legislation. Henderson spoke at length, but when Moranda Smith asked for time to explain how the law would affect workers, Taft brusquely informed her, "You have exactly two minutes." Smith's statement, which she had to summarize rather than read in full, was an eloquent expression of the ideals of civil rights unionism and of the deeply personal meaning that Local 22 had for many of its members: "Every human being longs for a life made happy with freedom and security," she said. "Through our union, my fellow workers and I have made the first steps toward that kind of life. . . . [The] union opened our eyes and put gladness in our hearts. It has given us strength and hope. We love our union. [It] gives us a chance to plan our lives, to provide education for our children, to keep up our strength and health and energy, to develop our understanding and citizenship." But, she warned, "there are bills before this committee designed to weaken our organization, to make it helpless, to keep it from continuing to build and carry us onward. . . . Weakening the bargaining power of unions . . . is absolutely and directly equivalent to lowering the living standards and the citizenship standards of the nation."[3]

Unionists' efforts were no match for the hostility of congressmen bent on halting the march of labor. On May 14, 1947, Congress passed the Labor-Management Relations Act of 1947, popularly known as the Taft-Hartley Act, a grab bag of provisions, many of which drew directly on a "Declaration of Principles" formulated by the National Association of Manufacturers in 1946. The law prohibited unions from contributing to political campaigns; expanded employers' ability to dissuade workers from joining unions; allowed employers to charge unions with unfair labor practices, bring decertification proceedings, delay elections, and in other ways string out negotiations; put the internal workings of unions under closer scrutiny; removed antiunion citizens' committees from the NLRB's jurisdiction; and generally augmented employers' power, undermined unions' economic and political clout, and bogged the NLRB down in a morass of legalistic proceedings. Of most immediate significance for Local 22, Taft-Hartley required union officers seeking access to NLRB services to file affidavits declaring that they were not members of the Communist Party, and it allowed states to write their own laws governing union security and gave those laws precedence over federal regulations. Anxious to maintain labor's electoral support and convinced that Taft-Hartley went too far, President Truman refused to ratify the measure. Undeterred, proponents began marshaling the votes to override the president's veto.[4]

Early in 1947, even before Taft-Hartley made its way through Congress, North Carolina legislators jumped aboard what would become a "right-to-work" bandwagon, introducing a bill that outlawed not only the closed shop, but also the union shop, maintenance of membership, and the dues checkoff. When the proposal went before a House committee, Local 22's cochairs Robert Black and Clark Sheppard joined a biracial group of fifteen Winston-Salem union leaders that attended the hearings in Raleigh. Although the committee did not hear testimony from the Winston-Salem delegation, Black told the *Journal* that, like other union men, he considered the law a "labor busting technique" that would result in greater, not less, labor militancy. If legislators were really concerned about the "right to work," Sheppard suggested, they should pass legislation guaranteeing every worker a job.[5]

Unionists were not alone in their condemnation of right-to-work legislation. The *News and Observer*, a ringleader in the turn-of-the-century white supremacy campaigns but by the mid-1940s one of the main voices of liberalism in North Carolina, editorialized against the bill, calling it "foolish and dangerous." The editorial continued, "Despite all of the mealy-mouthed protestations about 'the right to work,' the bill is nothing more or less than a part of a campaign to destroy unions." Publisher Jonathan Daniels attacked the legislation as a tool of Wall Street monopolists. Despite these protests, conservatives had firm control of the General Assembly, and the bill passed both the House and Senate on voice votes.[6]

Following the lead of state and national legislators, Winston-Salem Democrats looked to legislative maneuvers to halt the threat posed by blacks and labor to their half-century stranglehold on power. In so doing, however, they encountered more effective resistance than that offered by opponents of the Taft-Hartley Act and state right-to-work legislation. In fact, by the spring of 1947, they found themselves witnessing a display of unity not seen since the Fusionist victories of the 1890s, as Winston-Salem's black and white unionists joined civil rights activists in a coalition that set its sights on City Hall.

That cross-class, biracial labor alliance had coalesced six months earlier during a walkout by workers in the city's commercial laundries that followed hard on the heels of the uprising of the leaf house workers in Winston-Salem and eastern North Carolina. Organized by the International Fur and Leather Workers Union, another of the CIO's left-led unions, the strikers, a large majority of whom were African American women, were among the city's lowest paid workers. Moreover, they were exempt from the Wagner Act, and therefore could not look to the NLRB for help in bringing the companies to the bargaining table. Yet in October 1946 they had dared to walk out in a bid for union recognition, higher wages, and safer working conditions.[7]

To their aid came a United Citizens Committee made up of representatives of what one newspaper termed "Union and Negro organizations." Local 22 and the Transport Workers Union, which had organized drivers at the black-owned Safe Bus Company, supplied the bulk of the committee's union supporters, but white workers from the furniture and electrical workers' unions also contributed. Most impressive was the array of backers from the black community. The NAACP, the National Negro Congress, the Negro Chamber of Commerce, the barbers' and beauticians' associations, the Ministerial Alliance, and the American Veterans' Committee all sent representatives, many of whom were younger leaders who would be at the forefront of civil rights agitation in the following decades. At the committee's urging, black churches "adopted strikers," and individuals contributed groceries and money to the union's soup kitchen. The strike dragged on for months and ended without a contract, but in the months to come, the United Citizens Committee would help propel workers and African Americans toward their most direct and successful foray into electoral politics since the turn of the century.[8]

Alarmed by these events, stung by the defeat of their own Thurmond Chatham in 1946, and fearful that increased voter registration might enable blacks to control at least one of the city's eight wards, the Winston-Salem Democratic Executive Committee, the behind-the-scenes power broker in local politics, formulated a plan for diluting blacks' potential electoral clout. In December 1946 the committee petitioned the Board of Aldermen to modify the existing ward system, recommending that aldermen be elected in citywide elections. Such at-large elections would become a common ploy after 1965 as other southern cities sought to circumvent the effects of the Voting Rights Act and stunt the growth of black political power. Winston-Salem's black leaders immediately requested a hearing and privately voiced strong opposition to the measure. In a surprise move, the Board of Aldermen's Ordinance Committee rejected the Democratic committee's request for a citywide election. Anticipating a line of thinking that would become increasingly influential in the following years, the *Journal* editorialized that token black representation in local government would "give Winston-Salem a position of leadership in the South in making democracy work so well that no alien 'ism' could thrive in the community."[9]

At the same time, the Board of Aldermen approved an increase in the number of precincts, establishing two that were almost entirely inhabited by blacks. The board's purpose was to speed up voting and prevent the mingling of whites and blacks at the polls, but the United Citizens Committee saw the decision as the perfect opportunity to end discriminatory registration procedures and quickly gathered 1,500 signatures on a petition requesting black registrars in the new precincts. In the debate that followed the presentation of the petition before the board, committee spokesmen exchanged heated words with the aldermen and with Irving Carlyle, the city attorney. "We see those who are white, who can scarcely make their alphabet, get on the books," said one speaker, "while some of us have to write the whole constitution." The discussion heated up as C. C. Kellum, president of the NAACP, told the board that a "top official of the city" opposed the petition because he believed that incompetent black registrars would put unqualified voters on the books. Carlyle admitted to being the official in question but claimed that experience was the deciding factor in choosing registrars. "This is a process of evolution. It can't be done overnight. . . . I say a definite step is being taken by this board to grant to the Negro fair representation." The board was willing to appoint two black election judges, he continued, which would give them experience, and "in due time they would be qualified" to become registrars. When questioned about the qualifications of the registrars currently serving in the black precincts, an alderman said he "believed" one of the men had been a judge or "worked around the polling places." To this, Local 22 representative Velma Hopkins replied, "There are lots of us who have worked around the polling places. . . . Is that the qualification you need?" In the end, the Board of Aldermen rejected the petition, approving an all-white list of registrars and agreeing only to designate two blacks as election judges.[10]

Despite this disappointment, activists were convinced that enough people had managed to register over the previous few years to give the African American community a real chance to put one of its own on the Board of Aldermen in the May 1947 election. But who? Union leaders were anxious to solidify the cross-class alliance that Local 22 would need for the inevitable contract battle it would face shortly after the election. That alliance could draw on a fund of racial solidarity, but it also required diplomacy and hard work. It depended on the continued ability of Local 22 to mobilize large numbers of working-class voters and to attract the support of sectors of the black middle class that remained, at heart, wedded to a politics of uplift and diplomacy. Moreover, anti-Communism loomed on the horizon, pitting the NAACP against more radical groups and threatening to frighten the union's backers away. "We knew that if we didn't have somebody that everyone agreed on, that is, the middle class and the union," Ed McCrea remembered, "that the company would put enough people in that race to split the vote and we wouldn't get anybody elected. We had some people in the local who wanted to run, and, sure, they might have been elected, but it wouldn't have unified the community. It would have split the community wide open."[11]

Jason Hawkins, a shop steward at Reynolds and chairman of the Local 22 PAC, was one of the unionists who wanted to run, but, as Robert Black remembered, "we knew that the middle-class Negro would not go all out and support an ordinary worker. They suggested several people, like C. C. Kellum, who was president of the NAACP." Ed McCrea sat in on the discussions. "I didn't care who we got," he remembered, "just so they were black, just so the workers could express themselves and make things change. I knew we couldn't do it without the middle class. We would have been red-baited and [that would have] split up and divided the community so bad." William DeBerry, now working for the CIO, came back to Winston-Salem to consult with the union leaders. "I had never been a politician," he remembered, "but I knew one thing: anybody that ran had to be almost pure, because being black he was automatically on the outside." DeBerry still had good connections in the black community, and he spoke with some potential candidates, looking above all for someone who "had a clean slate."[12]

The union finally settled on the Reverend Kenneth R. Williams as the candidate best able to unite the black community. Williams was a solid, middle-class native of Winston-Salem. After graduating from Columbian Heights High School, he went to Atlanta's Morehouse College and then to Boston University for his master's degree. Returning from Boston in 1936, he took a job as chaplain and instructor in history at Winston-Salem Teachers College. The next year he also accepted a position as pastor of the First Institutionalist Baptist Church. After a stint as a chaplain in the army during the war, he returned to his positions in Winston-Salem. Despite his active public life, Williams "had no idea of becoming a politician. That's just one of the things that didn't interest me at all," he recalled. Friends encouraged him to enter the aldermen's race that spring, and, reluctantly, he agreed. "My interest," he said, "was in getting into office to prove that such a thing could work. I was conscious of the fact that there was a great deal that needed to be done and that I could be the catalyst to get it done."[13]

The union's decision to push Williams's candidacy exemplified Local 22's characteristic blend of pragmatism, autonomy, and what Robert Black would have called "advanced" left thinking. Determined to take advantage of local openings, buttressed by a loyal constituency, and guided by indigenous leaders who combined native intelligence, a long process of social learning, and experience in the school of hard knocks, the union saw itself simultaneously as part of a larger social movement and as a responsible, independent actor on a local stage.

Southern CIO leaders, on the other hand, voiced strenuous objections to the campaign on the grounds that a black victory would alienate white textile workers, the primary targets of Operation Dixie. "During our campaign in the 1947 city election," McCrea recalled, "Elizabeth Sasuly informed me that the CIO-PAC had an argumentative day-long session in Washington about Local 22's supporting a black City Council candidate." Not long after that, the southeastern director of the CIO-PAC came to Winston-Salem. "He argued that a black's election would cause a mean white backlash and 'a river of blood in the South' that would set labor back twenty years," McCrea remembered. "I told him that it was that kind of mentality that already held labor back twenty years." Robert Black later testified that CIO officials told him, "The time is not ripe to elect a negro, and you will get no support from national CIO; in fact, we will go all out to defeat you."[14]

Some national Communist leaders, oblivious to the blend of class-consciousness and racial solidarity on which Local 22 depended, also opposed the involvement of local Party members in Williams's campaign. As Junius Scales remembered it, "There were some has-been black leaders [from New York] who thought we were dead wrong in supporting Kenneth Williams for the Board of Aldermen. One of the arguments was that we are a proletarian party, we can't be spending our time and energies fooling around with the black bourgeoisie, trying to promote them to the front. The idea of unity in the black community didn't seem important to them; they were textbook reds."[15]

The all-important registration for the 1947 Democratic primary took place April 4–12. All prospective voters had to register because when the aldermen redrew the precinct lines, they purged the registration books, a tactic often used in later years to frustrate black political aspirations. "We tried to get the registrars to come to the churches and the recreation centers," Robert Black recalled, "to make it more convenient for the people. But the city refused to do that. We had to see to it that the people were able to get to their respective place of registration." Registration was slow at first, but on the last two days it surged dramatically. The Third Ward registered the largest number of voters, with the two black precincts leading the way. Although the registrars signed up qualified persons, they made their displeasure known. "You niggers can register," one man told Velma Hopkins, "but you're not going to have a nigger. We're not ready for a nigger to be elected to office."[16]

The Saturday before the election, the United Labor Committee held a political rally at the Forsyth County Courthouse that attracted close to 500 people. The committee had been formed in January to fight the right-to-work bill. In an unprecedented display of unity, local representatives of the AFL, the CIO, and the railroad brotherhoods appeared together on the stage. What had brought them all there, despite state CIO leaders' misgivings, was the legislative attack on the labor movement, both in Raleigh and in Washington. An AFL representative praised the gathering: "For once, we've got all labor sitting together and thinking the same thing at the same time." He wondered if the right-to-work movement might have been a "blessing in disguise."[17]

At the rally, men and women, blacks and whites condemned the recent passage of what they called the "anti-labor bill" and disparaged the representatives who voted for it, in particular state senator Gordon Gray, publisher of the *Journal* and the *Sentinel*. Speakers' comments and the United Labor Committee's campaign literature blamed "monopoly corporations" for the high prices that they claimed threatened a new depression. "Only labor . . . can battle the greed of corporations and uphold wages and buying power." The 250 people seated and standing in the courtroom, along with the 200 or so listening over loudspeakers outside, heard Spencer Long, a white officer in Local 22, offer a plea for cross-class, interracial unity. "May we work harder in organizing the working people of this country, by unitedly pushing together a program to allow every man, woman and child to see the value of all humanity working together in fellowship — one with the other, as

Reverend Kenneth R. Williams (Winston-Salem State University Archives)

God has commanded." At the end of the rally, the United Labor Committee announced its support for the Reverend Kenneth Williams in the Third Ward.[18]

Although he undoubtedly realized that he had no chance of winning without the votes of Local 22 members, like John Folger before him, Williams distanced himself from the union. A radio talk over wsjs the night before the election set the tone for his campaign: "I have no desire to set one class of our population against another class. I have made no binding commitment to any group or individual. . . . I have no interest in any political theories or ideologies designed to overthrow democracy. . . . I am convinced that our political salvation, and the salvation of the world rests in our return to the political theories of Thomas Jefferson, founder of America's Democratic Party. I believe in rule by the people, all of the people." Williams's campaign stressed the need for improvements in public services for the black community. He called for better schools and recreational facilities for citizens of the Third Ward, as well as for improvements in housing and street repair.[19]

Because Williams's agenda dovetailed with the goals of civic unionism, "there was plenty of enthusiasm" for the election, Robert Black recalled. "On Sunday, it was publicized from the pulpits on the importance of people getting out to vote. The whole black community involved itself in guaranteeing his election. We had a coordinated committee city-wide. On the day of the election we had so much unity city-wide that the owners of the Safe Bus Company ran their buses hauling people to the polls, the Camel City Cab sent their cabs out hauling people to the polls. We had a united front in Winston-Salem that was second to none. We had each registered voter's name on the voters list. We had people who would carry those sheets block by block and check out whether the people had voted and those who had not voted by 4:00 on election day, people in cars would go to these people's homes and contact them personally and drive them to and from the polling place. Our union gave the leadership to these efforts of guaranteeing that people on the books got out to vote."[20]

In the Third Ward, Williams handily defeated his opponents. Although registration in the two predominantly black precincts outnumbered that in the white precincts by only a few hundred, Williams had well over 1,000 more votes than his closest rival. Most black voters, it seemed, had marked their ballots for one candidate only, rather than the two who were to be nominated from that ward. This practice, known as "single shot" voting, withheld votes from other contestants so as not to dilute the black vote. This tactic was particularly effective because there were five white candidates in the Third Ward.[21]

Kenneth Williams's victory in the Democratic primary on April 22 was tantamount to election and represented a critical turning point in the history of the modern civil rights movement. For the first time since blacks were driven from politics at end of the nineteenth century, an African American had triumphed in a race against a white opponent in the South. Ed McCrea remembered that when Williams took office after the May 6 general election, it "really solidified the black community" and served as an example for blacks in other southern communities. "The next year it just spread like wildfire," McCrea recalled. That November, members of FTA Local 26 were instrumental in the election of an African American to the board of supervisors in Nansemond County, Virginia. And in 1951 voters in nearby Greensboro elected a black city councilman.[22]

The 1947 Strike

Unionists reveled in Kenneth Williams's victory. But the celebrations were short-lived as Local 22 turned its attention to what were bound to be tough negotiations for a new contract with Reynolds. A special contract preparations committee made sure that every member had "full opportunity to make known what they want in the new contract." The uncertainty created by the antilabor legislation wending its way through Congress made it all the more critical that Local 22 leaders maintain close contact with the rank and file.[23]

A few days before negotiations began, union officials briefed the *Journal* on their demands. Citing a rapid rise in the cost of living that had cut the real wages of Reynolds workers over the past year, Local 22 asked for an across-the-board wage increase with a new minimum wage of ninety cents. Such a raise was possible, FTA claimed, because Reynolds was in the midst of one of the most profitable periods in its history. Profits before taxes in 1946 had been $28 million, and FTA officials projected that they would be even higher in 1947. To limit the impact of layoffs, the union wanted a clause that would establish a joint union-company conference to consider alternatives to dismissal. As in past negotiations, it requested a union shop, which the company had always opposed.[24]

The union formally submitted its proposals to the company in an all-day meeting on April 4, 1947. After weeks of delay, Reynolds refused Local 22's request for an across-the-board hourly raise, offering a 7 percent increase instead. The actual value of the company's proposal fell far short of what the union felt was necessary to maintain the standard of living won in previous contracts. Even worse, a percentage increase benefited the highest paid workers the most, widening the gap between the non-union white workers at the top and the black union members at the bottom of the wage hierarchy.[25]

On Sunday afternoon, April 27, over 4,000 workers gathered on the grounds of the Woodland Avenue School to hear the negotiating committee's report on the status of the talks. Ed McCrea told the assembly that the antiunion climate in the nation had made Reynolds "tougher than ever" during negotiations. Negotiators had agreed to reduce their wage proposals to an increase of fifteen cents an hour, the amount recently won by workers in the automobile industry. Even with this concession, McCrea remained pessimistic about the chances of the company accepting the union's offer. "I think we are going to have to fight," he said. The negotiating committee recommended a strike unless the company was willing to compromise. After further discussion, Robert Black asked for a show of hands on the committee's recommendation to strike. Thousands of arms, most black but some white, shot up into the air. "The only way R. J. Reynolds can avoid trouble," declared Black, "is to give a 15 cent wage increase."[26]

Negotiations continued throughout the day on Wednesday, April 30. At 11:00 P.M. the company presented its final offer. The union negotiating committee continued to confer, but picket captains for the seventy-three gates of the Reynolds complex gathered at the union hall as the deadline neared. A few minutes before midnight, black workers in Number 12 walked out prematurely. Back at the Reynolds Building, union negotiators met with company officials one last time, but no settlement was forthcoming.

Emerging from the Reynolds Building, Donald Henderson addressed the press. "The R. J. Reynolds Tobacco Company has brought on this strike by their flat refusal to make an acceptable offer to the workers in their plants. . . . The increase in food costs in Winston-Salem is the second highest of all U.S. cities. Reynolds workers simply can't live on such wages. Winston-Salem merchants and neighboring farmers can't prosper on such low buying power. . . . R. J. Reynolds has chosen to ignore the needs of the workers and of the community. The company has chosen to force a strike." Reynolds officials argued that the union's insistence on a union shop and a dues checkoff was "one of the main reasons" for the failure to reach an agreement. "The company's position," said Judge Clayton Moore, "was that it could not make a contract carrying provisions clearly designed to evade" North Carolina law.[27]

Picket captains and strikers immediately went into action, marching back and forth across the street from the Reynolds Building with placards in hand and voices raised in song. At little-used entrances only a few pickets appeared, but at the main gates hundreds of striking workers made their presence known. In the street under the windows to Number 12, strikers called to their fellow workers to "come on out." By morning, the Employees Association was out in force as well, distributing leaflets saying: "We will Work! We will not strike! We can carry on! We can carry on easily! The CIO will lose and we will become the bargaining agents."[28]

The excitement of the strike drew hundreds of people downtown. Picket captains and police alike had a difficult time controlling the crowds that swelled onto the streets. Police officers, stationed at every gate, went on twelve-hour shifts. Radio cars patrolled the industrial district; even the state police had a force of plainclothesmen on hand. But picketing proceeded in an orderly manner, and Chief John Gold reported no serious disturbances.

Shortly after the morning shift began, the company told reporters that approximately one-half of its 10,000 employees were on strike, and that all but 150 of the strikers were black. It was clear that production had not come to a standstill as it had in 1943, primarily because blacks now made up a smaller percentage of the workforce than they had five years before. Still, internal documents reported that production was "severely handicapped." The smoking tobacco division, which re-

Picketers during Local 22's 1947 strike (Courtesy of the *Winston-Salem Journal*)

lied almost exclusively on black labor, effectively shut down for the duration of the strike, and the chewing tobacco division also experienced serious disruptions.[29]

A Reynolds foreman, E. T. "Jazz" Isley, described the company's efforts to keep the prefabrication departments in operation by resorting to a strategy it always held in reserve: ignoring the race- and sex-typing of jobs that it had established and usually enforced. Suddenly, no one was above the most menial job. "Even the foremen went to work as cuspidor cleaners and just everything," Isley recalled. "These old white foremen would be the cuspidor men. Now that looked kind of odd. See, they volunteered. I was working in the plant office when the strike came along and I volunteered. I went down there and did a hard labor job. Anything to keep going. We had enough company pride."

Company officials, Isley said, "had to have the Camel cigarette because that was their bread and butter. When these black people struck, [the supervisors] went over to these plug places where the white girls worked and they got those girls to come over [to the stemmeries] every morning. They'd go over yonder and get those white girls out of another plant and march in here in the morning to take the black people's place. They'd have a police escort and they'd come and get them at four o'clock in the afternoon and take 'em back. They did that thing what the colored women had been doing and they kept running."[30]

The cigarette-making departments were less affected by the walkout. But the absence of a few hundred white machine tenders and virtually all of the blacks who moved the tobacco and cleaned the plants seriously disrupted production. With black workers on the picket lines, white women took over many of their jobs. "I fed hoppers and pushed tubs, that's what the colored men done most of the time," Ellen Marsh recalled. "They didn't push us too hard. They was glad to get us to work anywhere."[31]

Facing the monumental task of persuading white workers to join the strike, the union tried to drive home the message that the privileges of whiteness were illusory and contingent. Contacts in the plants had reported a great deal of confusion and dissatisfaction as whites tried to cover blacks' jobs, and the union hoped that some of the nonstriking workers would recognize their powerlessness, question their loyalty to the company, and rethink their decision to cross the picket lines. "Did they tell you before the strike that you would have to operate a stemming machine?" a leaflet read. "Did they say you would have to work in the bulk room? Did they say you would have to roll barrels?" There were signs that the strategy might work. On the second night of the strike, two white women who worked as packing machine inspectors told a radio audience they had decided to join the strike when the foreman took them off their regular machines. They also said they supported the union's demand for a fifteen-cent wage increase.[32]

By the weekend, offers of support began pouring in from local ministers and other FTA locals. Despite the tensions that had surfaced during Operation Dixie, the state CIO closed ranks as well. North Carolina CIO director William Smith quickly formed a fund-raising committee that included leaders of all the state's CIO unions. Talking with an Associated Press reporter, Smith emphasized that the outcome of the conflict in Winston-Salem was "of paramount importance to the entire labor movement." Ed McCrea told a mass meeting: "We have entered one of the most important struggles in the history of the labor movement in the South."[33]

The energy and exuberance of the strikers impressed even the most seasoned union veteran. Ed McCrea remembered "the tremendous surge of enthusiasm by these workers. It was almost like they broke out of jail. When they came out of that plant it was like being released from prison." Initially at least, workers relished the freedom from the daily grind of the factory. Leon Edwards had been in the thick of things during the 1943 sit-down, but he had especially fond memories of 1947. "That was about one of the best times I ever had in my life. I'd go down there and

White strikers led by Clark Sheppard and Etta Hobson, 1947 (Courtesy of the *Winston-Salem Journal*)

march and make my three hours; I'd have me a gal and [be] gone. I'd be over to High Point, Greensboro, or anywhere. Havin' a good time." Others went fishing, worked in their gardens, or relaxed on their porches discussing the day's events.[34]

Tempered by years of institution building and political action, the strikers had no trouble mixing joie de vivre with disciplined organization. "The strike was so well organized," McCrea remembered. "That's one thing that the black people had learned from their church organization was how to organize. They'd delegate authority. They know exactly how they are going to move. Everybody had a certain amount of service on the picket line every day and all the picket captains had a record, they had captains on over them, and they turned their records in every day, and that's how people got food and relief. And everybody did their picket duty."[35]

Broad-based support from the African American community buttressed the solidarity on the picket lines. Almost to a person, the city's ministers supported the strike, in contrast to 1943 when many clergymen had remained on the sidelines. The Interdenominational Ministerial Alliance sent a letter to the *Journal* asserting that the strikers' actions were "within the limits of our spiritual concern in the welfare of humanity."

Greetings in the name of our Lord and Savior, Jesus Christ: We the spiritual leaders of our people, having full knowledge of their economic status, feel called upon to make the following statement based upon the information which we have received: That the workers of the R. J. Reynolds Tobacco Company are asking for an increase of 15 cents per hour, which increase seems reasonable in the light of the high cost of food, clothes, rent and other necessary commodities: That all people are entitled to a wage that will give security physically, intellectually and morally: That an early settlement of this strike will be most beneficial to the industrial life of our city and the community in general.[36]

Such support proved crucial as the strike entered its second full week, and Local 22 had to begin providing relief to the workers. Reynolds always held back a week's pay, so workers had been able to get by for the first week. But since most people lived from paycheck to paycheck, the lack of funds that second week had an immediate effect. Neither FTA nor Local 22 had large treasuries to support a prolonged strike. Instead, the union drew on African American self-help strategies developed during decades of poverty and intermittent employment. The union set up four soup kitchens to help ensure that workers had at least one good meal a day, using both money from the general strike fund and food donated by local merchants. Churches, recruited by the Interdenominational Ministerial Alliance, helped by taking turns serving meals to strikers and their families. Families pooled resources; neighbors helped neighbors.[37]

The union might have been able to feed workers with donations from the community, but rent payments required cold hard cash. The Winston-Salem Board of Realtors warned city residents early on that rents would continue to be collected during the strike. By the end of the second week, the local rent control board reported an increase in eviction notices. The union developed two strategies to forestall evictions. First, it provided money for those most in need. Second, it took their case directly to the landlords. "Reynolds's whole effort was to drive these people in debt," Robert Black observed. "We had a committee that visited landlords who were threatening to evict people from their premises. We told them point blank, 'If you evict these people no one else is going to move into your houses.' We worked out a [deal] on automobiles as well. We didn't let our people, like some towns during the course of a strike, lose everything they had. We had committees that worked on that. It was effective."[38]

The black community showed its support on the picket lines as well as in the soup kitchens. Shoe repair stores offered to resole striking workers' shoes. One morning over 200 barbers and beauticians joined strikers on the picket lines and promised free hair styling and haircuts for the duration of the strike. "Those barbers said to us," recalled Robert Black, "'All of you people that patronize one barber shop or another, come get your needs taken care of if you don't ever pay. Don't wear long hair just because you haven't got the money to pay barber fees.' That's the kind of relation we had in the black community."[39]

The next day proved even more exciting, as 400 uniformed veterans took over the lines. "That wasn't too long after World War II," Ed McCrea remembered, "and we had a whole lot of veterans. We must have had a battalion. 'Milky' Gold was the police chief. I called Milky up and said, 'We want to have a veterans' parade. How do we get this permit?' He says, 'Naw, you can't have one.' I said, 'We're going to have one anyway. You're not going to arrest all of these veterans.' We gathered them all up; we must have had five or six hundred of them. They all came in their uniforms, well not fully. There had to be something a little different. You weren't allowed to wear your full uniform. They looked like a regular military force. We had sergeants."[40]

The group gathered at union headquarters and planned to march en masse to the central factory area. In anticipation, a crowd of curiosity seekers and strikers lined the streets of courthouse square, alerting police to the planned demonstration. Quickly, police cars, motorcycles, and foot patrolmen rushed into the area to direct traffic and handle the crowds. Police Chief Gold arrived on the scene and advised union officials and veterans that the demonstration violated the law requiring parade permits.[41]

The veterans agreed to divide into small groups as they took up positions on the picket line. "I had already planned it and talked to some of the people about it," recalled Ed McCrea. "We had platoons of twenty already picked out. That's normally what a platoon is. And black people can sure march. It was just like the army pouring out. They'd all line up—Hut, Hut—and they'd go off." At 10:00 A.M., in groups of twenty to twenty-five, the veterans—many in uniforms with campaign ribbons and battle decorations—filled the streets. "The people over there in the Reynolds Building were all looking out the windows; they thought they had been invaded," McCrea remembered. Picket signs read "From the firing line to the picket line" and "We fought together in the foxholes, why not here?" Haywood Davenport, a winner of the Purple Heart who served thirty-six months in Europe during the war, told the *Daily Worker*: "We learned how to stand up and take it when the going was toughest. We're not going to give up the fight for a decent life now. R. J. Reynolds can't beat us where the Nazis couldn't."[42]

Looking back on the events of the strike, participants remembered especially the singing that filled the air day and night. The union maintained picket lines twenty-four hours a day at all seventy-three gates. "You'd go to sleep with the music and wake up in the morning with it," Bea McCrea remembered. "You can't realize what it was like unless you were there," recalled Ed McCrea. "Those plants were all concentrated uptown. With that many people singing it just engulf[ed] the whole town. You could hear it all over town. They had some tremendous singers. Every picket captain pretty near was a song leader."[43]

Gospel hymns and spirituals were the strikers' favorites. But they also knew all the union standards—"Union Train," "Roll the Union On," and "Which Side Are You On"—many of which had come out of the struggles of black southern workers and farmers. And as they had in 1943, they adapted them to local circumstances. "'T' Stands for Tobacco," sung to the tune of "Solidarity Forever," was a favorite during the 1947 strike.

> T stands for Tobacco, all over the U.S.A.;
> W stands for Workers who work for little pay;
> U stands for Union and Solidarity;
> The Tobacco Workers Union will fight for you and me.

Music provided a pace and rhythm for the marching, as well as a distraction from sore feet. It knew no boundaries. No one could escape it (much like the sounds and smells of the tobacco factories); it claimed the whole downtown. The gospel songs, especially, served as a shield against violence by scabs or the police. They also functioned as a collective prayer, asking for God's help—"Do Lord, Remember Me."

"When we went into negotiations with Reynolds Tobacco Company, we negotiated on the ground floor in one of their meeting rooms which was right on the street level and right across from one of the main plants," Ed McCrea remembered. "And we had to have all the windows open because it was the summer time. It was hot and we didn't have any air conditioning in the building. So we talked to the pickets and we arranged to have them, while we were in negotiations, to sing low on the picket line for fifty minutes and then just sing as loud as they could for ten minutes, which meant, of course, we just had to stop negotiations for ten minutes out of every hour. It rattled the hell out of the company. They couldn't do anything about it. We just had to stop negotiating, that's all." The singing so unnerved one white worker in the Reynolds Building that she threw a paperweight out the window at the pickets. "She said the singing was driving her crazy," remembered Velma Hopkins. "'Just stop them from singing.'"[44]

The resolve of the black workers appeared unshakable, but by the second week, signs of defections among the white workers increased. According to an account of

Factory superintendent observing picket lines during the 1947 strike (Courtesy of the *Winston-Salem Journal*)

the strike prepared by the union in the early 1950s, Reynolds tried to widen this gap with explicitly racist appeals. "[The company] called meetings in the plants where in some cases entire departments of white workers were refusing to work. High officials of the company charged that the strike was not over wages and working conditions but over the Union's demands to integrate Negro and white workers in all departments. Demagogically, they declared . . . 'This company is run by white Southern gentlemen and we will close down before we will see n——r men working side by side with white women, drinking from the same fountain.' "[45] A friend of Lucy Randolph Mason, the former general secretary of the National Consumers' League who was serving as a roving ambassador for the CIO, reported that a rumor had been circulating through white working-class neighborhoods claiming that "the workers aren't really striking for the 15 cent raise or any other professed purpose; what they really want is equal toilet rights."[46]

To keep production going, Reynolds began hiring white replacement workers to take over some of the operations usually performed by blacks. Luther Ranson got his foot in the door at Reynolds on May 12. "The reason I got my job [was] because

Reynolds was replacing the striking employees," he recalled. "At the time they hired me, I think it's fairly safe to say, they hired the largest group of people at one time—I'm talking about over a period of a few weeks or a few months. The year that I went there, they hired more people in that group than they've ever hired before or after." Ranson got assigned to the casing and cutting department in Number 97. "Oh, very hot and humid. No air conditioning anywhere. Open windows, you know, hot air blowing. Just like a steam room, and in these two departments most everything was steam operated. See, your steam would condition your tobacco. Yeah, it was hot, very hot, but we knew no different. We thought, you know, this is it. But it was certainly a privilege even to get on at Reynolds Tobacco Company. You know, I was happy. They didn't come hunt for me. I asked for a job and they gave it to me."

"They hired me to go to work, and I didn't separate no job, whether it was black or white. I didn't know the difference. The supervisor said, 'You get up yonder and do that.' I got up there and done it. Made no difference." The picket line posed no problem for people like Ranson, who had no industrial experience and were desperate for work. "We walked right around and go around them or go through them, and go right on upstairs and go to work. You see, North Carolina gives you the right to work, and that was one privilege we had. We'd double up and do two or three people's jobs, you know, until they replaced them, you know, with new employees."[47]

Realizing that it could not prevent Reynolds from maintaining production, however limited, and that the company was willing to absorb substantial financial loses, Local 22 and FTA officials began requesting support from political groups and labor organizations throughout the country. Traveling to Philadelphia, Floree Baity appealed for the food and money that could keep the company from starving the strikers into surrender. Robert Black and a white shop steward named Glenn Jonas journeyed to Detroit to address Local 600 of the United Auto Workers. As Black remembered it, the CIO council in Detroit arranged for them to speak to "all the workers in the area, Local 600 of the automobile workers union, the Cadillac workers, the clothing workers, and all of the other big CIO locals in Detroit. They passed resolutions in their meetings and began sending weekly donations to support the strike. They offered to assign members from their staff to come in and recruit the white workers and show them the need of supporting the strike." Local 600 also donated $50 a week to the union's relief fund and voted to boycott all Reynolds products. An FTA representative in California, Dixie Tiller, reported that when he told the Los Angeles CIO council of the Reynolds strike, "hundreds of packs of Camels went sailing out the windows." "200,000 C.I.O. members in Los Angeles will not buy Camels," he told Reynolds strikers. "Keep me advised because our workers like Camels, but until they pay a fair wage, no Camels."[48]

During the first two weeks of the strike, coverage in the *Journal* and *Sentinel* remained relatively evenhanded, but as the strike wore on, the newspapers dropped any semblance of neutrality. The *Journal* began to feature isolated incidents, particularly alleged threats against nonstriking workers, that evoked the association of blacks with crime and unions with violence. The *Sentinel*, for instance, reported a stabbing on the picket line that had no connection to the strike but grew out of a personal feud. In a front-page article headlined "Threatening Letters Received by Reynolds Tobacco Workers," Braxton Harriston reported that two of his tires had been slashed after someone had called his home trying to get him to stay off the job. A member of the R. J. Reynolds Employees Association found a rock thrown through her window with a note saying, "You are working." One man said a group of blacks had stoned his house. Another woman said she had received a letter telling her to stay away from the plant or "take what's coming." But the victims in each of these alleged incidents were blacks, not, as the newspaper implied, whites. According to Robert Black, efforts to stir up fears of interracial violence were "just a lot of company propaganda. The same thing that they tried to do to the workers in Gastonia, they started violence down there in order to take the people's mind off of the real issues."[49]

Exposé

The context of the strike changed dramatically on Monday, May 19, 1947, four days after the Taft-Hartley Act passed Congress and two days before Truman's veto. That morning the *Journal* charged in a front-page story that "the Communist Party has captured Local 22 . . . lock, stock and barrel." Statements by three former officials of the union—all white—accompanied articles written by the executive editor, Leon Dure Jr., and staff writer and one-time FBI investigator Chester Davis. Former Local 22 business agent Eugene Pratt and organizer Spencer Long provided affidavits, but Anne Mathews offered the most damaging testimony. A past secretary for Local 22 and former treasurer of the Communist Party in Winston-Salem, Mathews gave the *Journal* a detailed account of her experiences as a trade unionist and Party member in New York, Florida, and North Carolina. Most important, she identified many Local 22 leaders as members of the Party.[50]

Eugene Pratt had begun assisting the newspaper with its investigations weeks before Mathews came forward. Born in 1909 in St. Louis, Missouri, Gene Pratt had moved with his parents to Forsyth County and eventually settled in Pfafftown, a village near Winston-Salem. He went to work for Brown & Williamson Tobacco Company in the early 1930s, becoming president of Local 178 of the AFL's Tobacco Workers International Union and chairman of the Winston-Salem AFL Central Labor Union. He joined Local 22 as business agent in May 1945. At the time, Pratt praised the CIO's program, which he said was "constructive, democratic, and definitely in the interest of the working man." He also applauded the CIO's stance against discrimination.[51]

Pratt's statement to the *Journal*, however, conveyed a different motivation for his switch from the AFL to the CIO. When he joined the Local 22 staff, he told Chester Davis, he knew about FTA's "reputation as a Communist-dominated labor organization. . . . I was told that if I had any chance to clean out the local, rid it of its left-wing element, that I would have to bore from within and bore harder than the communists. That was my intention when I joined." By the summer of 1946, Pratt said, Communists were making little effort to hide their involvement in the local. He complained to various union officials, but nothing was done. Pratt did not believe the 1947 strike was "Communist inspired," but he had become convinced that militant Party members were preventing a settlement and using tactics that might "lead to trouble and possibly to race rioting."[52]

Pratt and Spencer Long had first taken their concerns to Police Chief John Gold when union leaders decided to go ahead with the veterans' march despite being refused a permit by the police. Gold, in turn, arranged a meeting with Leon Dure and Chester Davis. The union officials were ready to make their charges of Communist involvement public. But since such rumors about Local 22 had long been circulating to little effect, Dure suggested that it might be more damaging to the union if the CIO could be convinced to intervene and "clean up" the situation. To that end, he accompanied Long and Pratt to Washington to confer with CIO president Philip Murray.[53]

There was no love lost between Murray and FTA. Throughout his tenure the CIO president had often clashed with the left-led unions, and he especially detested Donald Henderson because of his well-known membership in the Communist Party and his tendency to lecture his colleagues on matters of political and racial practice. Nevertheless, he was convinced that strident anti-Communism played into the hands of labor's enemies. Murray shared many of the core values that animated the Popular Front, including the hope for continued cooperation between the United States and the Soviet Union, and he was committed to maintaining the CIO as an inclusive federation of politically diverse industrial unions. Truman's decision to devote his administration to a militantly anti-Soviet foreign policy posed a fatal challenge to Murray's ecumenical approach. Increasingly tying its fortunes to the Democratic Party, the CIO would soon redefine itself as an exponent of a new liberal anti-Communist consensus. But in the spring of 1947, this shift had only begun, and Murray was unwilling to sanction an outright assault on the federation's left wing. Consequently, he reminded his interlocutors that the CIO was a confederation of unions and that there was little he could do. He suggested they talk with FTA president Donald Henderson, who came to Washington from Philadelphia but refused to intervene.[54]

When Dure, Long, and Pratt returned from Washington, Chester Davis felt that the newspaper still did not have "enough to go with a story." Pratt, however, had a plan. He knew that Anne Mathews was vulnerable to pressure. Determined to make her an accomplice in exposing Local 22, he told the newspaper's reporters, "I know somebody you can get."[55]

Born into an Irish working-class family in Newark, New Jersey, in 1908, Mathews had attended local Catholic schools before going to Drake Business School in New York City. While working as a secretary at Columbia Pictures, she joined Local 16 of the United Office and Professional Workers Union, CIO. Three months later, in August 1937, she also became a member of the Communist Party. She had come into contact with many Communists in her Greenwich Village neighborhood, but developments in Europe had been equally important in shaping her political consciousness.[56]

In January 1943, after the death of her mother, Mathews took a "chance" and moved to Orlando, Florida, as secretary for a new UCAPAWA organizing campaign. Later that year she assumed the post of business agent for a local in Jacksonville, Florida. The international union transferred her to Winston-Salem in July 1945, to help Local 22 service its membership. Once again she did double duty, working long hours for the union and, with the reconstitution of the Communist Party in 1946, as city organizer and later as district treasurer of the Party. At some point Mathews also became romantically involved with Gene Pratt.

Mathews apparently came under intense scrutiny from some of the black women in the Party after they discovered she was pregnant. "They wanted to know what that was all about, and I told them it was none of their business. You see, you had to be like Caesar's wife—above reproach—as a member of the Communist Party because you were representing the Party." Mathews resented these women for "sitting in judgment on me" in part because sexual affairs among union people were not unusual, in Winston-Salem or elsewhere. She also believed that she was being singled out because she was white. "I suppose the way they looked at it, everybody expected the blacks to do it, but no one expected the whites to do it," and so her behavior could have special repercussions, especially among white workers. Above all,

Mathews resented the double standard that condemned her while tolerating the behavior of union leaders like Donald Henderson, who was known as a drinker and a womanizer.[57]

In January 1947 Mathews took a leave of absence for "maternity reasons." She also decided to give up her Party work. "You see," she said, "I was going to have a baby. And in the years that I'd been in the Communist Party, I had seen the lives of so many children ruined because their mothers and their fathers were so tied up in the Communist Party that these kids were always having to be looked after by somebody else. And I thought to myself, well, damn it to hell, if I've gotten to this age [39], and I've gone through nine months of this, I'm certainly not going to have a baby and walk out and leave it. So as far as I'm concerned, the most important thing in my life is my child."[58]

Once Pratt told the *Journal* that he thought Anne Mathews would be willing to talk to them, Chester Davis took the lead in securing her story. Davis had grown up in Montana and then moved to Washington, D.C., where his father served as a top administrator in the Agricultural Adjustment Administration during the early days of the New Deal. He graduated from Georgetown University and Harvard Law School, but rather than practice law he went to work for the FBI. After assignments in Norfolk and Charlotte, he had been transferred to Winston-Salem, where he served as a resident agent with Chief Gold. Among his duties was keeping track of the Communist Party activists who surfaced from time to time. Prior to the organization of Local 22, Davis received a transfer to Texas to be near his wife's family, but he returned to Winston-Salem after the war, when *Journal* publisher Gordon Gray offered him a job working for the newspaper. "I was told by Gray and others that the reason they wanted me was that they were having a hell of a time covering this labor story. The company took a no comment stand on everything, and the union talked freely with the reporters. And I suspect that the reporters might have had a predilection toward the union. To the Reynolds people, the stories seemed loaded in favor of the union. They told me what they wanted was an investigative background to balance this. I suspect that they also wanted my FBI background and knowledge." Although he had no prior newspaper experience, Davis became a feature writer for the *Journal* in 1946. Among his first assignments was a series of full-page articles on the Communist Party that drew heavily on confidential FBI files.[59]

When Pratt invited Davis to meet Anne Mathews, he leaped at the chance. "She was very, very reluctant to talk to me," Davis recalled. "She was in a hell of an emotional bind. But she gave me the story. Then we had it in spades. Here we had what the FBI didn't know. They caught a woman on the rebound, she was resentful of the way the union had treated her and I guess in love with Pratt and Pratt was putting the heat on her."[60]

"It was Chester Davis who did the questioning," Mathews remembered, "and it took them a long time to convince me. But since I had made up my mind not to go back to the union, I just decided the hell with it. So I just sat down and said, 'You ask the questions.' I volunteered absolutely nothing. He asked me a question, I answered it. And if he didn't ask a complete question, I didn't give him a complete answer." From Mathews's answers Davis prepared a statement that she signed. The *Journal* printed it along with the testimony of Pratt and Long with banner headlines on May 19.[61]

Mathews's statement consisted of a brief history of her own activities in the Party, the development of the Winston-Salem chapter, and the names of Local 22 activists whom she claimed were Communist Party members. She singled out the various international representatives of FTA who had passed through Winston-Salem during the past few years but said they had not been particularly active in Party affairs. "The real active Communist Party leaders within the union," she claimed, "were those which came to the union out of the leaf house and out of the Reynolds plants." These allegedly included Theodosia Simpson, Velma Hopkins, Viola Brown, Moranda Smith, Christine Gardner, Robert Black, Clark Sheppard, John Henry Miller, Jethro Dunlap, and Vivian Bruce. Although Mathews believed that these people had not always acted in the best interests of the workers because "they mixed party and union policies," her primary criticism was reserved for Velma Hopkins, Moranda Smith, and Phil Koritz, whose "inflammatory tactics" had isolated "the union from the community and one section of the union from another." But it was their personalities, as much as their politics, that Mathews deplored. "In my feeling, they would have done this whether they had been members of the Communist Party or not. Their attitude alienated white workers in the union and possibly prevented other white workers from joining the union."[62]

Anne Mathews's disclosure was the smoking gun the *Journal* had been looking for. Without it, Davis remembered, "we didn't have a good story, particularly in the situation we were in. We were in a vulnerable situation. Here we're pulling Reynolds chestnuts out of the fire and our paper is owned by the Reynolds family in effect. We were braced for the kickback that came."[63]

Despite the sensationalist tone of the exposé, Mathews's confession did little more than identify union leaders as Party members. Her only criticism, then or later, was that some of them mistreated her regarding her pregnancy and that a few had been "inflammatory." It was up to the *Journal* to make a case as to why the presence of Party members in Local 22 was a serious threat to the community. And here it drew heavily on the demonization of the Party by the FBI.[64]

Central to this demonization was the presumed association between blacks, violence, and Communism. Executive editor Leon Dure drew a direct connection between the presence of the Communist Party and the upheaval that had taken place in Winston-Salem in the past year.

> Such an identity of interest and viewpoint on the part of Local 22 and the Communist Party unmasks much of the labor disturbance of the last year, including both the violence in the leafhouse strikes of last Summer and the wave of threats and lawlessness in the background of the present Reynolds strike. [The] first precept of the Communist Party is the necessity for creating class hatred as a preliminary to violence and finally chaos—after which the "dictatorship of the proletariat" might be imposed. Any instrument available—and a young, inexperienced labor union is virtually a "natural"—may be used to that end.[65]

Staff writer Chester Davis took up where Dure left off. He acknowledged that some people believed that Reynolds was "willing to run the risks of a prolonged, dangerous strike in an effort to rid the plants of organized labor," but he found no evidence that that was the case. There was, on the other hand, "impressive evidence" that Local 22 was governed by "irresponsible leadership." (Davis saw Gene Pratt, by contrast, as a responsible union leader, although he was a married man who had seduced a union colleague who was also his secretary, gotten her pregnant, pressured her into informing on her former friends and colleagues, and then abandoned her.) Davis accepted the statement of Long and Pratt that the strike was neither "Communist inspired" nor the "result of any calculated policy on the part of the leadership of Local 22." This concession, of course, completely undermined Dure's argument. But ignoring that contradiction, Davis went on to argue that "loose-witted ideologies" had made Local 22 leaders "over-aggressive" and "irresponsible" and encouraged them to move from "peaceful picketing to open rioting." Davis claimed, for instance, that Local 22 leaders were "passing the word along that the police are tools of the Reynolds Tobacco Company and not public servants. Should that idea filter through the ranks to the men on the picket line, the peaceful, well-organized files of psalm-singing pickets can very quickly rupture into unorganized violence."[66]

Local 22's press release that Monday afternoon labeled the exposé a "red-baiting attempt to stir up hysteria and violence. . . . No attacks on the leadership of Local 22 can hide the fact that the strike had been conducted in complete peace and order. . . . By the gains that have been made in wages and conditions since the union was organized, and by the management of this strike, the union has demonstrated that its leadership is responsible and competent." Both the company and the *Journal*, the statement continued, "have failed in all three of their aims: to provoke violence, to confuse the wage issue in the strike, and to divide the workers and their community support."[67]

One worker who was not confused was Mrs. M. B. Wallace. In a letter to the *Journal*, she made clear why she had spent hours on the picket line: "We struck for a better wage." The money she took home every week was not enough to pay her bills or give her mother the medical care she needed. "A lot of rumors are going around saying Communists are dominating the strikers. It isn't the Communists that dominate the strikers, but the 5½ cents the company offered the workers."[68]

On the following Sunday evening, radio station WTOB presented a roundtable discussion titled "Communism in Action." Chester Davis appeared along with two WTOB employees; all three had worked as special agents for the FBI. They began by reciting a litany on Communism perfected by FBI director J. Edgar Hoover that would, by the 1950s, become a popular article of faith: Communists are committed to the overthrow of capitalism by any means necessary, including violent revolution; Communists are not friends of the working people, but are only using unions for their own political ends; and Communists owe their first allegiance to the Soviet Union. The speakers warned that the Party's use of deceit and trickery had made it difficult to identify the enemy within. "Communists do not look any different from any other average American," Davis told listeners. "The Communist might be a truck driver, white collar government worker, milk man, office worker, union employee, or most any other ordinary fellow." Communist Party district organizer Sam Hall was a case in point. His "softly Southern rather than foreign" accent made him appear to be an average person, rather than the leader of the Party in the Carolinas. Although its numbers might be small, Davis reminded the radio audience, the Communist Party was "numerically stronger in the United States today than when [it] seized the Russian government." There was one Communist for every 2,277 persons in Russia in 1917, while in the United States in 1947, there was one for every 1,814.[69]

Sam Hall replied to these depictions of Communism on the front page of the *Journal* and over WSJS radio. Attacking Dure's claims as a "bunch of overworked lies," Hall argued that the Communist Party did not "advocate the use of force and violence to overthrow this government." To the contrary, he insisted, "we have proved our devotion to democracy by fighting to defend and extend it." Hall described the Party's efforts to end the poll tax, its support for an antilynching bill, and its demands for relief and unemployment insurance during the Depression. "While we support every progressive measure which can in any way benefit the people under our present capitalist system," he continued, "we Communists are firmly convinced that the ills of modern society stem from the monopoly owner-ship of our industrial wealth by a handful of multimillionaires and billionaires who exercise autocratic power greater than the kings of old." Socialism—"the pub-lic ownership and operation of the great industries of our nation under a govern-ment of the common people"—was the only remedy for these ills. "Our aims are for a better life for the people, for the greatest good for the greatest number. We strive to end discrimination and inequality in order that people will be more united. This is part of our universal conception of the real brotherhood of man." When asked by the radio moderator whether American Communists "advocated imposing the Russian system in this country," Hall replied that "the road to social-ism in this country will be prospected and cleared by the millions of democratic Americans who will learn to seek it."[70]

Headlines such as "Exposé of 'Commie' Unionists, Undenied in Countercharges, Prompts Hopes for Settlement" revealed the *Journal*'s belief that it would force the union to settle the strike quickly—and on the company's terms. As it turned out, the newspaper's charges failed to bring Local 22 back to the bargaining table on bended knee. In retrospect, even Chester Davis realized that the exposé "wasn't going to have any effect on the workers around here. It was a way for the R. J. Reyn-olds Tobacco Company to get rid of that union." Referring to Taft-Hartley's require-ment that union officers sign anti-Communist affidavits, Davis explained: "The law had been passed that if your union was Communist dominated you did not have to sign the contract with them. . . . And so, when they got the evidence that was it. They didn't have to get up and prove that [Communists] were undermining the workers or anything else because the union was running just as well with the Communists in control. The chances are it was probably being run better, you see. So Reynolds was not concerned about whether the Communist propaganda was undermining their workers. . . . It was just that this was a way to get the union off their backs. When they discovered that . . . the majority of the executive board, the man that was at the head of the union, and the people on the staff and so many others were members of the Communist Party, that was all they needed because the law was right behind them. Before that time, I don't think it would have made a bit of difference because then it would have been up to the membership of the union to get rid of the Communists. It was their problem. But the law had been changed so that industry was told that the law doesn't require you to sign a contract with a union that is Communist dominated. And so that's all that they needed."[71]

In any case, unionists were not the newspaper's only audience, perhaps not even its primary one. The *Journal*'s revelations also aimed at mobilizing opposition to the union among whites, middle-class blacks, and organized labor. The all-white local post of the Veterans of Foreign Wars adopted a resolution calling for a grand jury investigation of Communist activities and retained an attorney to help prosecute Party members under a recently passed law that required propaganda agencies to register with the state. Strikers complained that Wachovia Bank was making it difficult for them to withdraw money from savings accounts, and that local insurance companies were refusing to extend them loans on their life insurance policies. North Carolina's two senators called for an investigation by the House Committee on Un-American Activities.[72]

The reaction in the black community and among CIO officials was more restrained. The Tuesday after the revelations, J. H. R. Gleaves of the Progressive Civic League presented a petition to the Board of Aldermen signed by 3,854 people asking that the board help negotiate a "fair and just settlement" in the strike. A day later the United Citizens Committee, led by the Reverend R. M. Pitts, met at the black YMCA. With representatives of Local 22 present, the committee discussed the strike and the charges by the *Journal*. It issued a statement supporting the strikers, but Pitts also appointed a committee to investigate the charges of Communist domination of Local 22. When asked for a statement on the disclosures, North Carolina CIO director William Smith said that while he opposed any Communist interference in the affairs of the CIO, "the strike of the Reynolds workers in Winston-Salem had nothing to do with the Communist Party and . . . any attempt on the part of outsiders to make it appear so [was] misleading. . . . The national C.I.O. is supporting the strike 100 per cent and is backing the workers of the local union in their fight for decent wages."[73]

Nevertheless, charges of Communist domination made it increasingly difficult to raise money for strike support, particularly from southern liberals. Karl Korstad, who, as a young veteran, had organized support for striking workers at the American Tobacco Company in Charleston, South Carolina, and then become a business agent for Local 19 in Memphis, helped to raise funds for Local 22. He approached labor supporters in New York and Washington but could inspire nothing like the interest that the Charleston strike had stirred. FTA and Local 22 asked Virginia Durr, a founding member of the Southern Conference for Human Welfare, vice president of the National Committee to Abolish the Poll Tax, and one of the best connected of the Washington-based southern liberals, to form a national relief committee similar to the one that had been so effective in the Charleston battle. But even she had a difficult time rousing the troops.[74]

Among those whom Durr asked to serve on the relief committee was Nelle Morton, executive secretary of the Fellowship of Southern Churchmen, a group of liberal ministers and lay people with offices in Chapel Hill. Her response illustrates how anti-Communist liberals often framed their concerns. Before agreeing to Durr's request, Morton and three ministers from Chapel Hill ventured to Winston-Salem for a day of "fact-finding." They met with a reporter from the *Journal*, Police Chief Gold, some local ministers, strikers, and union officials from Local 22 and FTA. "Try as we may through excellent sources," Morton reported, "we could not see one representative from management. . . . Our feeling from the day's experience is that the Christian is placed in an almost impossible position—a dilemma." The union, she believed, was clearly in the right in demanding higher wages, given the workers' needs and Reynolds's profitability. She also faulted the *Journal* for failing to publish the union's demands or to clarify the real issues behind the strike. "The communist story broke at such an opportune time that it is quite evident it is a weapon of management to break the Union. . . . Successfully it has clouded the issue of the strike and is affecting appeals for funds." On the other hand, Morton felt that the "communist leadership" prevented her group from getting the workers' story. They met with Local 22 cochairman Clark Sheppard, but before they knew what was happening, Ed McCrea, representing FTA, "sat down by Sheppard, took the ball and clearly and keenly told us of the Union, the strike, issues involved, management proposals. Sheppard nodded and joined in with monosyllables. Ed . . . is reputed to be a communist" (as was Sheppard, she might have mentioned). Although the strikers' cause was just and their needs real, Morton hesitated "to cooperate in appealing for funds because of the hands through which those funds will be administered."[75]

Morton wrote to a number of liberals and labor leaders for advice. Franz Daniel, the CIO director in South Carolina, a graduate of Union Theological Seminary who had gotten his start in the labor movement through the Highlander Folk School in 1930s, replied that he was "supporting the strike both as a matter of personal opinion and as a matter of union policy." He advised that the fellowship issue an appeal for funds, while at the same time "calling attention to the charges of communist domination." Barney Taylor, the southern representative for the Americans for Democratic Action, an influential anti-Communist pressure group created by former socialists in the 1940s, advised Morton to ignore the strike. "The strike is probably already lost," he told her. "I do not believe it possible for you to aid the strikers without strengthening FTA, which is the same thing as strengthening the Communist Party. I believe that no union is better than a Communist controlled and operated union. I realize that I have ignored the human needs of the people themselves—that I have also ignored the unquestionable fact that Reynolds is a bad employer, but as a unionist, I believe there are some things worse than temporary sufferings and reactionary bosses." Taylor did not specify what things could be worse or how temporary the suffering and the reaction might be.[76]

A committee headed by Clark Foreman, president of the Southern Conference for Human Welfare, on the other hand, enthusiastically supported the union and the strike. Foreman, along with David Jones, president of Bennett College for black women in Greensboro, and Jennings Perry, a columnist for the Popular Front tabloid *PM* and a former editor for the *Nashville Banner*, went to Winston-Salem at the request of FTA president Donald Henderson. After interviewing the mayor, chief of police, ministers, and other citizens, the trio concluded that the strike was not "Communist inspired" but rather the result of justifiable economic demands by the workers. Their report surveyed the many contributions the union had made to Winston-Salem, not the least of which was the election of Kenneth Williams, and concluded: "Those who would attribute such developments to 'Communism' well might reflect that in doing so they are telling millions of people that their only hope of democracy and prosperity lies with the Communist Party. The makers of this report believe that what has been achieved in Winston-Salem is wholesome, American, and wholly in keeping with our Constitutional aims and national traditions."[77]

Aubrey Williams, editor and publisher of the *Southern Farmer* and former head of the National Youth Administration, also traveled to Winston-Salem to offer support. Strong unions, Williams told a Local 22 gathering, were the pillars of postwar prosperity. "Higher wages made possible through unions increase the purchasing power in the community where the workers are employed. This means more money for the farmer, for the preacher, the teacher, and white collar workers."[78]

Local 22 members themselves showed no signs of losing heart. At a mass meeting on the Sunday after the Communist exposé story appeared, Jethro Dunlap, cochairman of the strike committee, told the strikers to "put the *Journal* and *Sentinel* in the background; pay no attention to the headlines . . . they are only trying to divide us so they can conquer us. . . . The leaders in Local 22 are outstanding men and women and we are going to follow them. We are going to follow them if they are red, white or blue." In an effort to turn the table on the *Journal*'s charge of potential violence, Ed McCrea introduced a resolution protesting against lynchings in the South. "Lynchings or attempted lynchings are a cancer to the entire community. They are a form of lawlessness which plays into the hands of monopoly inter-

Workers celebrate the end of the 1947 strike (Courtesy of the *Winston-Salem Journal*)

ests who for the sake of bigger profits try to suppress the striving workers, farmers, and small shopkeepers for better living standards." At another rally, the Reverend Walter Young of the Hanes ME Church exhorted the crowd: "We are in this fight to win. Oh, Lord, some may have to die. But we your children, will march forward to victory. We are not walking through the fire. We are fighting the fire."[79]

The standoff lasted until the end of May, when each side, for its own reasons, decided to resume talks. Local workers were suffering from lost income, despite community support, and FTA, as a small international made up of low-wage workers, did not have deep pockets, even for such a critical struggle. Unable to resume full production, the company was also sustaining significant losses; at the same time, it was confident of its bargaining position. Finally, after weeks of proposals and counterproposals, the parties reached an agreement, subject to ratification by a union membership meeting scheduled for Sunday evening, June 8, at the Southside Baseball Park.[80]

As twilight approached on the appointed day, thousands of members of Local 22 lined up outside the ballpark. Union marshals moved up and down the lines reminding people that they had to have their membership cards to be admitted. A

Journal reporter who was allowed into the park once the program began said that "order was maintained at all times," despite the fact that it was one of the largest crowds ever gathered in Winston-Salem and there were no policemen on the grounds. On a makeshift platform behind home plate, officials of Local 22 and FTA sat ready to make their reports. The meeting opened as always with a song—"Lord I Want to Be a Christian"—and a prayer. Donald Henderson outlined the contents of the agreement, and members of the negotiating committee explained how they had arrived at the results. Then there was a show of hands—it seemed as if everyone was ready to go back to work.[81]

After the meeting, the negotiators returned to the Reynolds Building to sign a new contract. It was to be the last time the management of Reynolds would sit down with workers to agree on conditions affecting employment in the factories. The company agreed to a voluntary dues checkoff and to a wage package that averaged about twelve cents an hour, significantly below the fifteen cents that had been the union's bottom line. On balance, the agreement fell far short of the demands the workers had made six weeks before.[82]

Local 22 leaders viewed the outcome with mixed feelings. They could take justifiable pride in the fact that they had won a contract in the midst of an anti-Communist firestorm. But the union had not been able to halt production at the Reynolds plants completely, and the company had extracted more concessions than it had ever managed before. Most important, while the strikers had attracted significant support from the black community, from other unionists across the country, and from the most steadfast members of the left-liberal Southern Front coalition, FTA had also seen defections among its old allies—a flight from the left-led unions that signaled a collapse of the progressive coalition on which Local 22's long-term success depended. Straggling back into factories at the end of the summer, Winston-Salem's tobacco workers faced the future with unbroken spirits but with the sobering realization that they could no longer count either on federal intervention or on the broad-based labor mobilization of which they had been a part. The political terrain had shifted, and they would have to survive and move forward on uncertain ground.

CHAPTER THIRTEEN

Jim Crow Must Go

On Monday morning, June 9, 1947, for the first time in almost six weeks, thousands of black workers made their way through the gates of the giant Reynolds factories. Initially, confusion reigned. The union contract directed all strikers to report to their superintendents or foremen. If their jobs were still available, they could go back to work. Those not needed immediately would form a pool and return to the plant according to seniority. But much had changed during the previous thirty-eight days. In some departments white workers now performed jobs that blacks had been doing for decades. Hundreds of new faces peered out from behind machines. Would they remain there, or would the strikers return to their old jobs? The company had used the strike to mechanize certain operations. What would happen to people who had been replaced by machines?

Within a few days many strikers were laboring at the old routines, but hundreds of others lingered anxiously at home or gathered in worried circles near the factory gates. The union charged the company with wholesale violations of the settlement. Local 22 officials contended that management had agreed to staff all jobs according to strict seniority. Reynolds countered that seniority provisions applied only *among* strikers.[1]

Restaffing the plants was bound to be complicated, particularly with the addition of approximately 700 strikebreakers. But there was a measure of vindictiveness in the employment office's decisions. Ed McCrea felt that "the company particularly wanted to see the white workers suffer as an example to the others. They tried all forms of humiliation to force them to beg for their jobs back." As of June 21, 481 strikers who had reported to work had not been rehired, and one group of fifty-six workers remained out of work for almost three months, resulting in lingering feelings of bitterness toward the union as well as Reynolds. The workers went so far as to hire a lawyer and individually file unfair labor practice charges against the company. McCrea had to convince them to stick with the union's efforts to enforce the terms of the contract. FTA put pressure on Reynolds by printing 10,000 brochures featuring the personal histories of some of the white strikers and threatening a nationwide boycott of the company's products. The company finally put the workers back on the job at the end of September as production increased and as college students hired during the strike returned to school.[2]

Even as strikers went back to their jobs, relief funds continued to be desperately needed, both for the unemployed and for those who were employed but had not yet received a paycheck. The hand-to-mouth existence of most Reynolds employees had seriously weakened the bargaining position of the union and caused serious hardships among the strikers. The soup kitchen and commissary stayed open, and appeals went out to other unions as well as to liberal and left-wing supporters. The black community remained the union's major source of help.[3]

The relief effort concluded with an event that offered powerful evidence of Local 22's importance to the labor left and to Winston-Salem's African American community. The boiling sun hung over the grounds of the Woodland Avenue School as thousands of people gathered one late June afternoon for another mass meeting. But this Sunday was special: the famed African American singer, actor, and political activist Paul Robeson had come to help raise money for the union. People began arriving several hours early, bringing chairs to reserve the shady places under the trees that ringed the playground. Most stood, with hats in place and fans moving back and forth, fighting the heat. Hundreds more rested on nearby church steps and front porches. A late start allowed workers the chance to sing their own familiar songs, but it was Robeson's massive bass voice that the people had come to hear.[4]

Standing between the two giant oak trees on the north side of the grounds, Robeson directly addressed recent charges that he was a Communist sympathizer. "If fighting for the Negro people and their trade-union brothers, if fighting for democracy and the welfare of my people, if that makes me the subversive that they're talking about in Congress, if that makes me a 'red' then so be it." "The crowd roared approval," reported the *Journal.*[5]

Robeson began his concert with "Water Boy." Junius Scales, who had taken a group of students from the University of North Carolina to the rally, remembered the scene: "As Robeson held the incredibly low final note of 'Water Boy' like a pedal point on a great organ, a Negro worker next to me stood openmouthed and unbreathing until the sound died away; then he slapped his knee in ecstasy, shouting out, 'Gah-ahd DAMN!' while tears coursed down his face." Robeson dedicated "Joe Hill" to the "great struggle" of the workers in Winston-Salem. He entertained the audience with folk songs from France and England and delivered messages of support from "friends around the world." "Scandalize My Name" and "Swing Low, Sweet Chariot" followed, but workers called especially for "Ol' Man River," and Robeson ended his program with the most popular of his recorded spirituals.[6]

Pausing between songs, Robeson spoke eloquently of what had brought him to North Carolina. "If anyone wants to know why I'm singing for tobacco workers, [it is because] I cannot forget my father who was born a slave in the tobacco country at Rocky Mount, North Carolina. . . . I have come back to my people, and I am fighting not as an artist, but as one of you." An untiring champion of human rights everywhere, this popular and international figure had returned to home ground. It was an unforgettable moment, but the dark clouds that appeared on the horizon as Robeson's concert came to a close were a portent of the stormy days that lay ahead. The next three years would be among the most contentious in Winston-Salem's history.[7]

The HUAC Hearings

The settlement of the strike did nothing to dampen the rhetorical attack on Local 22, which continued to revolve around charges of Communist domination. The stage was set at the national level, not only by the anti-Communist provisions of the Taft-Hartley Act but by the Truman administration. In January the Republican leadership in Congress had set forth a sweeping plan to purge Communists and their allies from unions, the motion picture industry, educational institutions, and the remnants of the New Deal agencies. Two months later, Truman preempted the political advantages the Republicans hoped to accrue by announcing his own program of loyalty oaths for federal employees. That program legitimized the charge that Communist Party members had infiltrated the federal government, that the Party was primarily an agent of a foreign power, and that anyone associated with it posed a serious threat to national security. At the same time, it had a chilling effect on criticisms of Truman's foreign policy, which was based on the premise that the containment of Soviet power—and not, as progressives would have it, the strengthening of the United Nations, the promotion of anticolonial movements, and the pursuit of democracy and freedom from want worldwide—should be the nation's major postwar goal.[8]

Reflecting, as well as influencing, this emerging anti-Communist consensus, the city's industrialists and journalists felt genuine antipathy toward the goals and tactics of the Communist movement. But Winston-Salem's red scare was not simply a local manifestation of Cold War ideology. It represented a concerted effort to break the union and discourage demands for systemic change. Attacks on the concrete goals of the workers' movement seemed only to strengthen the union's standing in the black community. Corporate anti-Communists thus sought to undermine the union's legitimacy as a vehicle for workers' discontent by linking demands for racial and economic justice to Soviet-sponsored subversion. Tactically, anti-Communists hoped to drive a wedge between union leaders and the rank and file, divide the union from the black middle class, and frighten white workers and liberals. Anti-Communism also allowed Winston-Salem industrialists to tie local issues to a snowballing national attack on progressive forces and to use the power of the state, embodied by the House Committee on Un-American Activities and the FBI, in the same way that the union had drawn on the National War Labor Board.[9]

On June 19, 1947, the day after the strike ended, the *Journal* threatened the officers of Local 22 with the provisions of the Taft-Hartley bill, then awaiting action by President Truman. Following former FBI agent Chester Davis's advice on redbaiting, the *Journal* ran the headline, "Labor Bill Forces 'Commies' to Quit Party or Lose Jobs, Posing Problem for Local 22." Equating the Communist Party with the Ku Klux Klan, the *Journal* predicted that by requiring all union officers to sign affidavits swearing that they were not Party members, the bill would "knock the props from under the 'invisible empire' of communism in the Carolinas, since the leadership of both the party and the United Tobacco Workers in these two states have been identified by the *Journal and Sentinel* as one and the same." The paper reminded union leaders that if they swore falsely on the non-Communist affidavits, "the F.B.I., with its voluminous files on Communists throughout the nation, would be given carte blanche to enter a situation it long had chafed to bring into the open."[10]

That same week in Washington, a subcommittee of HUAC authorized a full investigation of Local 22 at the behest both of North Carolina's two senators and of Herbert Bonner, a four-term congressman from eastern North Carolina and a member of HUAC, who had asked his colleagues to investigate the allegations of Party influence in the union after the *Journal* published its exposé a month before. Richard M. Nixon, an ambitious freshman representative from California, saw Winston-Salem as the "first test case" of the anti-Communist provisions of the Taft-Hartley

Act, which had passed over the president's veto on June 23 and was set to go into effect in September. But HUAC actually had the whole Southern Front in its sights. A few days later the *Journal* featured a HUAC report claiming that the Southern Conference for Human Welfare was "perhaps the most deviously camouflaged Communist front organization." The editors underscored charges against University of North Carolina president Frank Porter Graham and SCHW president Clark Foreman, noting in particular Foreman's recent visit to Winston-Salem to conduct an investigation on behalf of Local 22. HUAC's accusations provided ammunition to the SCHW's detractors, although the committee did not go so far as to hold hearings on the likes of Frank Graham (although he was, it said, "one of those liberals who show a predilection for affiliation to various Communist-inspired front organizations"). FTA, on the other hand, was an easy target. The committee subpoenaed Local 22 cochairmen Robert Black and Clark Sheppard and international representative Ed McCrea, as well as Anne Mathews, Gene Pratt, and Spencer Long. On July 12, the former colleagues found themselves on the witness stand in a congressional hearing room, face to face in the glare of a spotlight that cast them as characters in a protracted and costly national morality play.[11]

Before they departed for Washington, Black and Sheppard had issued a statement that put the issues in bold relief:

> It is a personal outrage to us, and a grave warning of danger to the civil liberties of all Americans, that we can be seized and forced to submit to insults and questioning because we have dared to stand up for a better living and the financial security of millions of working Americans, and have challenged the right of a few people to have immense wealth and power at the expense of hardship and injustice for thousands of others. Hundreds of Winston-Salem workers know us personally, and know for themselves that these have been our policies. If these things be "un-American," God help America. The power of the wealthy to persecute the poor is not democracy. It is fascism.[12]

In Washington, Anne Mathews led the parade to the witness chair. Expanding on her earlier revelations to the *Journal,* she told of her experiences in the Party and provided additional details on day-to-day activities in Winston-Salem. Again she named names, this time implicating Junius Scales, head of the Party in Chapel Hill. Gene Pratt and Spencer Long mostly reiterated points made in the *Journal* exposé.

Robert Black testified next. Black, Clark Sheppard, and Ed McCrea had arrived in Washington a few days before the hearing to confer with other union leaders about what tactics to pursue with the committee. FTA had retained David Rein of the Washington firm of Greenberg, Forer & Rein to represent Black, Sheppard, and

McCrea. But Rein was busy elsewhere, defending German-born Communist Gerhart Eisler on perjury charges (a fact that HUAC investigator Robert Stripling made sure committee members knew), so Joseph Forer took his place. After a few perfunctory questions, Stripling performed the HUAC's ritualistic chant.

"Mr. Black, are you now or have you ever been a member of the Communist Party?"

"Not knowing the definition of the Communist Party," Black responded, "I am just a worker—I would have to decline to answer that; it may tend to incriminate me."[13]

The answer infuriated Herbert Bonner. He repeated the question, and Black gave the same reply. "You know what I am asking you," Bonner shot back, "and you can answer the question if you want to answer the question. . . . Your plea of ignorance doesn't go very far with me. You convict yourself in my mind. You don't want to defend yourself." Resorting to racist stereotypes, Bonner continued, "You are the first man of your race that I ever saw that couldn't—that didn't have the cleverness to defend himself on the witness stand. Most of the time your people are the cleverest people in the world on the witness stand—smart."[14]

Congressman Bonner was less openly contemptuous of Ed McCrea. A World War I veteran himself, he couldn't help admiring the Distinguished Flying Cross and the Purple Heart that McCrea had won as an aerial machine gunner during the war. But Bonner grew impatient as McCrea repeatedly invoked the Fifth Amendment when asked about his participation in the Communist Party. Clark Sheppard followed suit, and the committee quickly dismissed the union leaders.[15]

The trio's decision to invoke the Fifth Amendment, the constitutional protection against self-incrimination, was a strategic move designed by their attorneys, Forer and Rein, to prevent them from being held in contempt of Congress. Earlier witnesses before HUAC who had refused to cooperate with the committee or answer specific questions had invoked their free speech rights under the First Amendment. They were promptly cited for contempt of Congress.[16]

The *Journal* relished the national attention given to the charges of Mathews, Pratt, and Long. No new evidence appeared, yet the paper argued that the fact that the witnesses had testified under oath before a committee of the U.S. Congress bore out the charges of Communist control of Local 22. Although the intent of the Fifth Amendment was otherwise, the *Journal* interpreted the refusal of the three representatives of the union to answer questions "as a clear, if indirect, admission of the charges." "Had these men been non-Communists and leaders opposed to Communist domination of the union it is difficult to believe they would have failed" to answer the committee's questions.[17]

When the union leaders returned home, they faced a different kind of grilling. "When we came back to Winston," Robert Black remembered, "I had hundreds of people look me in the face and ask me, 'Why didn't you tell us that you were a member of the Party?' I said, 'Who told you that I was?' 'The paper said so.' I said, 'Hell, the paper and their supporters are the ones who have tried to destroy our union.' Some of them would go so far as to ask me, 'Well are you?' I said, 'Well what do you think? You know of my work here in the union and my stand on a better life and an organized effort on the part of the workers. Now you judge between that and what the newspaper wrote.'"[18]

Black's refusal to acknowledge his Party membership, then or ever, was far from unusual. In the deepening chill of the Cold War, open membership anywhere, but especially in the South, entailed huge risks, as illustrated by the experience of Junius Scales, who "went public" when he heard on the radio that he had been named before HUAC as a Party member. It was a step he had been contemplating, and dreading, for sometime. He had just finished his B.A. in comparative literature at the University of North Carolina and begun graduate work in history, convinced that he could make himself "more politically useful" by deepening his understanding of the American past but also anxious to pursue an academic career. As a member of a well-known North Carolina family and a married veteran, he hoped that he could humanize the image of the Communist Party and help to stem the tide of anti-Communism locally by giving the Party a public face. It was, as it turned out, a vain and even naive gesture: Scales's announcement created a firestorm that engulfed him and his family, jeopardized his friends, and ended his plans for a scholarly career. It also alienated liberal allies who had known and respected him all his life. Many, it seemed, blamed him more for announcing his affiliation than for his beliefs; almost everyone preferred public silence and personal discretion.[19]

Workers' apparent acceptance of Black's response to their queries reflected a different experience and sounded a somewhat different theme. They were curious about, but not shocked by, the HUAC revelations; the *Journal* had been waving the bloody shirt of anti-Communism since the first days of organization in 1943. For years, Communism had been used as a catch-all denunciation for any challenge to Jim Crow. Moreover, many union leaders had already been identified by the Party itself during the infamous membership drives of the previous summer. If Robert Black was a Communist Party member, his coworkers seemed to feel, he was also —and more important—a friend, a neighbor, an exemplary trade unionist, and a militant race leader. They were willing to leave it at that.

All in all, Ed McCrea thought the hearings did little to diminish the union leaders' standing among the rank and file. "As far as the [black] workers were concerned, we were being attacked by people they knew weren't their friends, and it kind of made us heroes in a way. Because when we walked around the plant, I had people come up and slap me on the back and say, 'Boy, we're sure proud of you.' As far as the white workers, I don't think it really had much effect on them. They'd heard so much of this stuff before anyway. It was drummed in day after day."[20]

But the HUAC hearings and the anti-Communist juggernaut they represented had serious repercussions for Local 22. Even rank-and-file unionists not identified as Party members faced grilling from their supervisors. Ruby Jones remembered an encounter she had with the personnel director, Ed Bumgardner. Her typically astute analysis told the whole story.

"Ruby, I heard a bad report about you. I heard you were a communist."

"You did?"

"Yeah, I didn't say it was so, but I heard about it."

"Where did you get that story from?"

"Well, are you?"

"No, I'm an American. Maybe the definition used by the person who told you I was a communist was not the definition in the Webster's Dictionary. It's you people's definition."

"What's the difference?"

"Well, I'll tell you your definition of being a communist. When you get tired of being oppressed and treated like a dog and rise up and do something about it, you're called a communist."[21]

Just as the sit-down in the Reynolds stemmeries in 1943 had sparked a frank, wide-ranging dialogue about the meaning of trade unionism and the rights of black workers, the *Journal* exposé and the HUAC hearings in the summer of 1947 plunged local people into a heated debate over the relationship between anti-Communism and race in the postwar era. From such conversations, which were bubbling up in various forms throughout the country, emerged the outlines both of a forceful argument for black civil rights—an argument so persuasive, in fact, that even devout segregationists could not ignore it altogether—and a regional version of liberal anti-Communism, the ideological consensus that would dominate discussions not only of race but of class and gender in the decades to come.[22]

Throughout the summer and fall, the Elks Club, the Chamber of Commerce, and other white civic groups devoted themselves to parsing the red menace. William J. Casey of the Research Board of America, who went on to become head of the Central Intelligence Agency under President Ronald Reagan, presided over a multimedia evening at the Chamber of Commerce that began with the showing of *Deadline for Action*, a movie on the postwar economy made by the left-led United Electrical Workers. Such films, Casey said, "were powerful propaganda weapons" that Communists used to "intensify their constant effort to squeeze as much chaos as they can out of high prices and strikes and our other troubles." Casey called on local businessmen to combat Communist claims that American corporations were making "fantastic profits" and therefore had the ability to pay higher wages. He brought along his own movie, *Crossroads of America*, which acknowledged such problems as slums and high prices but emphasized that capitalism, not Communism, was the solution.[23]

Chester Davis also offered advice on how to deploy anti-Communist rhetoric more effectively. Davis had spearheaded the *Journal*'s red-baiting campaign against Local 22 and had made no effort to investigate or understand the causes of workers' discontents. But he counseled against undiscriminating, extremist tactics. Equating liberalism with Communism in the form of "unfounded name calling" and "red baiting" only played into the hands of the Communists, he told members of the Rotary Club. Such practices had allowed Communists in Winston-Salem to condition the workers against attacks on the Local 22 leadership. Driving the Communist Party underground by passing restrictive legislation, moreover, would only aid their cause. The best way to deal with Communists was "to keep them out in the open and continually try to improve the [capitalist] system."[24]

In a more simplistic vein, the *Journal* ran an editorial titled "A Striking Contrast of Two Ways of Life," which reprinted a chart from an AFL publication comparing life in a "Democracy" with that under "Communism." In a democracy, "everyone has basic rights and freedoms guaranteed," while under Communism, "everyone is subservient to 14 Politburo dictators." In the Soviet Union everything was dominated by the state; in the United States anyone could "start any kind of business" or "own a home, farm, or business." As a result, democracies had "high standards of living" while Communism produced "miserable living standards." "In the face of these facts," the *Journal* concluded, "it is difficult to see how any American citizen could wish to swap our way of life for the Russian way. For in doing so, we would not only be trading liberty for slavery, but we would also be swapping wealth for poverty."[25]

Beginning in 1946, civil rights liberals such as the NAACP's Walter White had begun to argue that international criticism of American racism undermined the United States in its struggle against the Soviet Union. A sharp departure at the time (White had previously combined criticism of the Communist Party with anticolonialism and opposition to Truman's hard-line prosecution of the Cold War), this strategy shrewdly highlighted the contradictions between American aspirations to moral leadership of the "free world" and its treatment of African Americans at home. "The American Dilemma" was the term that the Swedish economist Gunnar Myrdal used to describe this glaring discrepancy. His book by that name, published in 1944, helped to break the Popular Front's linkage of race to economics and to the history of slavery and colonial exploitation. Instead, liberals increasingly figured racism as a moral or psychological problem confined primarily to the backward South, an aberration from the "American Creed."[26]

Responding to the *Journal*'s juxtaposition of "two ways of life," Bessie H. Allen, a civic leader and wife of a local black physician, demonstrated just how telling this contrast between promise and reality could be. If the *Journal*'s facts were "real and true," Allen wrote, she too would wonder why an American might choose Communism.

> I am not well enough versed in Russian communism to question the stated facts on it, but I am an American Negro citizen, and I can, without hesitancy, say that the information given on democracy in the United States is truly a farce. . . . To say democracy in the United States and have listed under it such things as (1) no arrest without warrant, no arbitrary seizure of person or property or search of homes, trial by jury guaranteed; (2) freedom to seek truth in schools, universities; (3) free elections, candidates nominated in primary elections or conventions of parties; (4) worker is free to choose job and change job, and (5) high living standard, is really a farce to the Negroes of America and we too are citizens.

"No," Allen concluded, "we may not want to swap this for communism as Russians know it, but we are constantly longing, searching, and working for that proposed democracy which has been 'guaranteed' by the United States Constitution for lo, these many years."[27]

In the midst of this discussion, a Committee on Civil Rights appointed by President Truman issued *To Secure These Rights*, a report that many white southerners saw as an ideological bombshell. Truman had appointed the committee in part as a means of maintaining his support among urban blacks and labor. But he was also responding to the initiatives of civil rights liberals who had begun to draw links between the Cold War and the need for antidiscrimination measures. *To Secure These Rights* reflected the transitional moment in which it took form. In a reprise of the Southern Front's political perspective, it tied together issues of region, class, and race, tracing the South's problems to its status as a producer of raw materials and proposing economic measures designed to lift all boats. Alongside this argument, honed throughout the 1930s by southern intellectuals and activists, ran a more recent international rationale. In America's quest for moral leadership in the postwar world, the committee said, "our domestic civil rights shortcomings are a serious obstacle. . . . The United States is not so strong, the final triumph of the democratic ideal is not so inevitable that we can ignore what the world thinks of us or our record." The committee called for a range of measures, including an end to segregation in the military, abolition of the poll tax, legislation to prevent discrimination in voter registration, and an antilynching law. It also condemned segregation in general terms, without suggesting how it might be brought to an end.[28]

Receptive as they might have been to the version of anti-Communism represented by William Casey and Chester Davis, Winston-Salem leaders were far from prepared to accept the presidential committee's more far-reaching conclusions. While they were beginning to understand just how difficult it would be to join in the celebration of American democracy while denying the "basic rights and freedoms" of the country's black citizens and to glimpse the necessity of accommodating at least some of the demands of African Americans, that did not mean they were prepared to sacrifice segregation on the altar of Cold War politics.

The Civil Rights Committee's suggestions, the *Journal* argued, were "utterly impractical and impossible in the South." Ending segregation was "a revolutionary step" that would bring about "social chaos" and "precipitate internecine strife." "The Better Way . . . to promote friendlier relations and greater cooperation between the white and Negro races," the *Journal* countered, was a variation on the solution that had been hammered into place at the turn of the century by Governor Charles B. Aycock, one of the architects of segregation in North Carolina. In fact, the *Journal* quoted extensively from Aycock's infamous address to the Negro State Fair in which he laid out the need for separate racial worlds: "What you wish, what you need, more than recognition by the President or other people in authority," Aycock had said, "is the establishment among yourselves of a society founded upon culture, intelligence and virtue and in no w[ay] dependent upon those of a different race." Whites were willing to assist that effort, Aycock had assured his listeners, but "it is absolutely necessary that each race should remain distinct, and have a society of its own. Inside of your own race you can grow as large and broad and high as God permits, with the aid, the sympathy, and the encouragement of your white neighbors. . . . [B]ut all of them in the South will insist that you accomplish this high end without social intermingling."[29]

Members of the local chapter of Alpha Kappa Alpha, a black sorority, took strong exception to the *Journal*'s stance. "The time is now for the elimination of segregation and discrimination," they wrote. "The inconsistencies of those who speak vehemently on the one hand against Communists, Fascists, . . . and other 'un-

Americans' and yet propose a society within a society to keep each race distinct is almost unbelievable in a supposedly intelligent people. Insert the word 'Aryan' into your editorials and then they would be in complete accordance with Hitler's doctrines." The sorority was particularly offended by the mantra of separate but equal.

> These mythical equal systems are at best a pitiful and truly tragic attempt at fooling yourselves. We are not being deceived. We know that our schools, employment opportunities, trials by white juries, and scores of other rights are not equal to yours. Separate they are, but not equal. . . . You seem to think that minorities are standing outside the fence (which you built) "rending their garments," clamoring to be considered socially acceptable by some superior white race. Nothing is further from the truth. As human beings, citizens of this country, we were born with the same rights as yours. Of these rights you have deprived us.

The sorority's rebuttal reflected the momentum of African American protest during the 1940s: forced by Jim Crow to build vibrant and ultimately resistant communities and institutions, blacks of all classes and political persuasions were now demanding an end to segregation.[30]

Recruiting White Workers

As industrialists maneuvered to contain social change, Local 22 embarked on its most extensive campaign to attract white members. Soon after the 1947 Reynolds strike ended, FTA leaders realized that "there was less than a year to do something with white workers, or the whole thing was in trouble." At the time, they felt very confident about their chances. Even the failure of all but a few hundred whites to honor the picket lines during the 1947 strike had not shaken union officials' belief that white workers were "very sympathetic with the black strikers," or at least "not really antagonistic." There had been few confrontations on the picket lines, and black workers reported getting occasional financial help from whites who stayed in the plants. "We felt," Ed McCrea remembered, "that the white workers were ripe to be organized. We had a good selling point [in that] they had already seen what the black workers could do by themselves. The company couldn't beat them."[31]

Up to that point, Local 22 had had little success in expanding beyond its small circle of dedicated white recruits: only a few hundred were on the checkoff at any one time. The ideological power of racism, the pressure of job competition, and the company's divide-and-conquer strategies kept most whites away. The hiring of Gene Pratt in 1945 helped with recruitment, particularly among men in the construction departments. The union added white workers to the local's executive board, and Spencer Long came out of the plant to join the organizing staff.[32]

Sometime after this, probably in 1946, some of these new recruits raised the possibility of creating a separate FTA local for the cigarette departments, claiming that this would make it easier to recruit white workers. On the one hand, this was evidence that there was substantial support among whites for unionization. Such a move would perhaps have made it more palatable for the many "unofficial" FTA supporters in the plants to come out in the open. On the other hand, the creation of a separate white local was anathema to everything Local 22 and FTA stood for, and Robert Black remembered that both the national and local leadership immediately rejected the idea. Not only was it reminiscent of the Jim Crow locals set up by the AFL, but it was yet another example of the deep-seated unwillingness of whites to participate in a black-led organization. The unwillingness of FTA officials to go along with this plan probably contributed to the decision by Gene Pratt and Spencer Long to renounce the union in the midst of the 1947 strike.[33]

In the fall of 1947, FTA launched an intensive campaign among the white workers led by three crack organizers with a strong record of success among southern white workers. Jack Frye, a business agent for FTA Local 75 in Houston, led the effort. Joining him were Fred Less and Mary Lou Koger, whose father, Harry Koger, had helped organize Local 22. Although Frye, Less, and Koger kept in close contact with Local 22 officials, they were to have a free hand in planning the drive, to be known as the FTA Reynolds Campaign, and controlled their own budget and bank account. "It was explained to the black leaders and members," Frye remembered, "as being a special campaign to organize the white workers." The plan was to concentrate on the cigarette-making and packing departments, and the organizing strategy was similar to that used in 1943 among black workers. "It was house to house to start with, trying to build up small groups within those departments," Frye recalled.[34]

Ed McCrea explained the campaign's strategy regarding acknowledgment of union membership. "They would sign up these workers with the understanding that their name wouldn't be put in on a check-off until they had enough workers in that particular department to protect the ones that were on check-off. . . . We planned that we'd take some kind of grievance action in a department when we had enough workers and . . . [had the] backing of the workers in that department. It'd be something that we would fix up and everybody would back. It would organize the department. After all, that's really the basic way to organize a plant. In fact, that's what organized the workers to start with in Reynolds, was grievances. And we had a contract and we had grievance procedures, and we began to use the grievance procedure. Wherever we could get union members who were on check-off to take up grievances through the contract we did, which had never been done before for white workers, really, on any large scale.

"We were getting people to secretly take [a leaflet] into the plant and leave it." McCrea explained. "And after we'd get something going we then would try to get them to do things on grievances informally, maybe two of them talk to the foreman or something, but not claiming to do it as a union or not really wanting them to get the idea it was the union too quick. But [the supervisors] sure got it, and there was an awful lot of tale-bearing and gossiping. You were always hearing from these people about those you couldn't trust that would carry tales to the foreman, and some of the stuff would go back for years, the knowledge about who was married to who [and so forth]. . . . There was all kinds of men-women alliances in the factory. It's a very complex society in those big factories, and it goes out into the countryside and it goes for generations."[35]

Indeed, Reynolds's policy of hiring family and friends of people already on the payroll contributed to the dense kinship networks in the plants. Many factory hands had met their spouses at work, further tightening bonds among white workers. As was the case among blacks in the prefabrication departments, the person on the next cigarette-making or packing machine might be a member of one's extended family, church, fraternal organization, or car pool. A white worker who stepped forward as a unionist might face conflict with family and friends. The favoritism and informal spy system that permeated the factories complicated such relationships, all the more so because white workers—unlike blacks—were often related to their supervisors by kinship or friendship.

Still, Frye and his associates began to make some inroads. "We found young people, generally in their twenties, thirties," Frye recalled, "who were forthright and intelligent. They were very receptive. They didn't have the ingrained fear as much as the older ones did, partly, I think, because they didn't realize what they were up against. And the people there are more class-conscious than anywhere I ever lived. They know which side is which and they don't have any illusions that they'll ever get to be a boss or an owner of a business. So we would get their participation and they were very interested in how things worked and what we could do about it."[36]

"We were putting out a paper," Frye explained, "that was aimed at the white workers, a four-page offset called the *Reynolds Organizer*. It was like a shop paper, set up in columns, and most of the inside was pictures. All of us had cameras, and we took pictures of these white workers. There was a lot of interest in it. Then

FTA president Donald Henderson meeting with white unionists in Winston-Salem, ca. 1948 (*FTA News*)

there'd be a lot of short stories about grievances and wages." "It was very popular with the workers, union and nonunion," McCrea remembered. "Everybody wanted to see if they had their name in it." A regular column by "Snoop and Scoop" provided information about births, illnesses, and marriages but also fingered the more egregious violators of the ethics of fair play:

> Did you hear about the blonde in 97 who made line girl in ten months?
> Sam Davis, noted Ass'n stooge and contract violator has even stooped to slandering young girls in trying to keep the A-2 workers scared.
> Some people wonder how George Lackey operates his two cigarette machines as he does so much visiting all over the floor.
> Why doesn't the company ease up and let the nurses act more human—especially with the girls when they aren't feeling so good.[37]

"Snoop and Scoop" paid particular attention to the interests of women, and the photographs were overwhelmingly of young women workers, perhaps because the union assumed that they, like the young veterans, would be more receptive than older workers. Looking back on the experiences, Mary Lou Koger wondered how realistic that approach had been. "I couldn't get over the fact that there were so many women who went with the foremen and the supervisors in the plant. Of course, they wouldn't join. I always wondered, are these foremen unmarried or are these women going with them to keep their job? There was that kind of talk."[38]

Organizers felt that younger, city-dwelling workers might be responsive to the union message and tried to offer them an alternative social environment similar to the one Local 22 had supported among blacks. "The first thing along the line of making it a little social," Frye recalled, "we set up a club room upstairs in a building a block or two from the union hall. We had a jukebox there and coffee and cold drinks. We had a group coming there when they got off the 4-to-12 shift, and some in the afternoon before going to work."

"Then we had dances at the union hall," Frye continued. "They were surprisingly well attended. The union hall was full of white people, probably for the first time in history." The officers of the union, both black and white, took the opportunity to "stand around and talk to people." These Saturday night dances drew big crowds. Square dancing, complete with a string band made up of workers, competed with jitterbugging to the latest songs on the jukebox, appealing to older and younger workers alike. For the first time, FTA was paying attention to the culture of white workers. The music, dancing, and socializing helped to make the union part of everyday life, just as hymns and prayers had melded the sacred with the secular when Local 22 began to build an alternative public culture among blacks.[39]

There was, however, a critical difference: black cultural events might have had the *effect* of excluding whites, but these whites-only dances in the union hall of a predominantly black union were explicitly segregated. Some members told Frye they did not want "black people's money paying for entertaining these white people that won't even pay dues to the union." "It really is a Jim Crow dance," Frye admitted. "I'm not trying to pretend that it's not. But it's a way of trying to reach these people." By and large, Frye recalled, "the black people understood it perfectly well."[40]

One person who did not understand was the famed folk singer Woody Guthrie. FTA brought Guthrie to Winston-Salem for a few days in December 1947 to entertain and talk with white workers. Guthrie behaved oddly, often disappearing for hours at a time. Organizers attributed his conduct to alcohol, but he was probably also suffering from the effects of his undiagnosed Huntington's chorea. Guthrie played the first night for the black membership of Local 22, and the next night he attended and sang at a dance for white workers. One month later he skewered the union in the labor press. Writing for the *Worker Magazine,* he titled the article, "A Minstrel in Tobacco-land," with a subheading that read, "Down in Winston-Salem way the union's fighting to organize. But it would go faster if all colors of feet would dance together." Lambasting the union's policy of holding separate dances,

Guthrie also claimed that staff members had prevented him from putting new lyrics to "You Gotta Go Down and Join the Union" when he sang the song on the union's weekly radio program:

All colors of hands gonna work together
All colors of hands gonna laugh and shine
All colors of feet gonna dance together
When I bring my CIO to Caroline, Caroline.[41]

Notwithstanding such criticisms, FTA forged ahead not only with day-to-day organizing, but with two "concentration drives." On these occasions Frye called on all the available white FTA organizers in the region as well as people from the CIO office in Charlotte. John Ramsay, director of community relations for the CIO and its liaison to the churches, met with local religious leaders during the first drive and addressed the rally that climaxed the campaign. "There is one God, one Father, and one creation," he told the crowd that packed the Forsyth County Courthouse, "and we're all a part of it." That unity was the heart of Christianity, Ramsay continued. "Men and women who have a vision of great unity . . . are those who built the union."[42]

These efforts brought new workers into the union camp and buoyed the morale of members and organizers alike. "There were several times during the first eight months when we really thought we had it going," Frye remembered. "You could feel the potential in the groups we concentrated on. One of the CIO organizers was a guy named Deneen who had been regional director in Texas when I had been there before the war. He was sure we were going to hit, he had that feeling. And I had it myself. I thought it was going to be a big fight but that we'd make it."

"After we would get something going," Frye recalled, "we would try to get them to do something on grievances informally; maybe two of them talk to the foreman but not doing it as a union. But what happened repeatedly is that before it got to the point where we were strong enough to start talking openly on grievances, something would happen. They'd get on to it and they'd break it up. It happened repeatedly. So much pressure would be put on the key people that they couldn't take it."

"I had great expectations of a guy who lived five houses down the block from me," Frye continued. "He was a Navy veteran and a key guy for a whole floor in one of those departments. His wife worked there, too, and I thought it was going great. One night he came to my house about midnight, said they were threatening his wife and she was crying all the time. He said, 'You couldn't even understand it unless you lived all your life in this town. When I see you tomorrow, I'm not going to speak to you.' And that was the end of him."[43]

Since the beginning of the union drive in 1943, Reynolds supervisors and Employees Association members had continuously raised the linked bugaboos of racial mingling and violence. "The company preached to that white worker," Robert Black observed. "They would take them in the office, they would hold group meetings with them in their homes, the white preacher was advising the people: 'You'd better stay out of that union. They're going to turn that thing into open violence. You're going to have to eat and sleep with them black men, your wife and daughter.' "[44]

Encouraged by the company, antiunion workers used ostracism to enforce white racial solidarity. According to Luther Ranson, a white worker hired during the strike, "The general feeling was that the white wasn't supposed to belong to it, and if you did, you was kindly put over in a group by yourself. I was in the [Reynolds Employees Association]. It was kind of a sideline, something to take the attention off of the union people. We were dedicated and we were against the union. I worked freely against [the union]. Anywhere I could go and speak against it. That was my prerogative, you know. Supervision would tell me, 'Anywhere you can go and speak against it,' you know. We felt that nobody should be against Reynolds Tobacco Company, and if they were, we kindly disassociated ourselves with them."[45]

The company and the Employees Association kept up the pressure on white unionists and any suspected sympathizers. But as in the past, the shop floor was not the only forum in which Reynolds and Local 22 competed for workers' loyalty. During the spring of 1948, the battle moved into the public arena, as Local 22 opened its campaign for the annual renegotiation of the contract with Reynolds, which expired in May. This time, many of demands focused on bread-and-butter issues that were of concern to white as well as black workers.

A full-page advertisement in the *Journal* listed the issues being discussed by the membership. Foremost among them were a general wage increase, a better vacation plan, the end of the fourteen-week exemption period for seasonal workers, and plantwide seniority to protect stemmery workers against unemployment because of mechanization.[46]

Four times in the past, local unionists, bolstered by FTA representatives, had held their own at the negotiating table, each time gaining new benefits for their members, augmenting their leverage on the shop floor, and building their political base. This time, however, Local 22 was hamstrung in a way it had never been before: after the passage of the Taft-Hartley Act in June 1947, FTA officials had refused to sign the required anti-Communist affidavits and thus forfeited the all-important services of the NLRB.

Both CIO and AFL officials had been outraged by the affidavits provision, which infringed on their civil liberties and put Communists and non-Communists alike in an untenable position. Non-Communists who signed reinforced the implication that while employers and their agents had no need to swear allegiance to their country, unionists were uniquely suspect. Party members who did so could be prosecuted for perjury. Union leaders who refused to sign lost the right to appeal to the NLRB to investigate allegations of unfair labor practices, conduct elections, and force companies to bargain in good faith. They also opened their organizations to raiding by other unions or decertification proceedings by employers. Initially, most international leaders—including CIO president Philip Murray—stood on principle, and the left-led unions urged the federation to wage an all-out fight for repeal, shun the vastly weakened NLRB, and rely on solid organization and the support of the rank and file. The CIO leadership, however, was unwilling to risk mass demonstrations, and within months most of the federation's international unions had capitulated. FTA, along with the Mine, Mill, and Smelter Workers, the United Electrical Workers, and other left-led unions, refused to comply. That decision meant that when Local 22's contracts expired the union would have to rely entirely on its own clout to bring Reynolds and the independent leaf houses to the bargaining table.[47]

In February 1948, Local 22's worst fears came true. Reynolds formally announced that after April 30 it would no longer recognize or bargain collectively with the union. The company said that, based on the checkoff records supplied by the union and "other information," it did not believe that Local 22 represented a majority of the workers in its plants. It filed a decertification petition with the NLRB and asked the board to hold a new election to determine whether the union still represented a majority of workers.[48]

Knowing that unless FTA officials signed the Taft-Hartley affidavits, the NLRB would not investigate the company's allegations or hold a new election, Local 22 suggested an alternative. "We are ready," the union said, "to submit to an election conducted by any impartial local group, such as the ministers of Winston-Salem. But we will not ensnare the Reynolds workers in the legal entanglements of the Taft-Hartley Labor Law."[49]

In hindsight, most Local 22 leaders saw FTA's failure to sign the Taft-Hartley affidavits as a strategic blunder. Workers lost the limited protections provided by the NLRB, and Reynolds had more ammunition in its battle to get rid of the union. But even had FTA signed the affidavits, it is doubtful that the union would have been able to renegotiate a contract in 1948. As the 1947 strike had proved, black workers did not have the power to close down the plant, and the federal government was now on the side of the company. This was made clear in a report by the U.S. Congress's Joint Committee on Labor-Management Relations released in March 1948. The committee had been created by the Taft-Hartley Act to study and report on the status of labor-management relations; a major portion of its report consisted of seven plant studies, including one of Reynolds Tobacco Company.

Two members of the committee's staff conducted the investigation, supposedly gathering information from the company, the police, the union, and nonunion Reynolds employees. But in fact the report read like a press release from the Emergency Citizens Committee or the Reynolds Employees Association. The committee sent copies of the report to Donald Henderson and John Whitaker for comment and suggestions prior to its release. John Whitaker corrected the spelling of a few names and suggested changing a sentence so as not to imply that the company had charged that the 1947 strike was Communist inspired. Donald Henderson, on the other hand, called the report "open union busting" by the committee and a "perversion of the dignity and integrity of the Senate."[50]

CIO president Philip Murray sent an equally angry reply to the committee.

This Report . . . deeply disturbs me. It would be alarming coming at any time and from any committee because the working people of this Nation have a right to be treated fairly by their elected representatives. However, I am particularly troubled by the release of this Report at this time for the release comes at precisely the moment when the R. J. Reynolds Company is apparently preparing to renew its historic anti-union policies. Nothing could more effectively further the present attempts of the Company to disavow the bargaining agent selected by its employees and to repudiate the collective bargaining process than the present Report.[51]

Local 22 prepared an extensive rebuttal. The union was particularly critical of the report's depictions of black workers and the black community. The descriptions of early organizing activities were "lies," the union said. "They are complete fabrications, and the whole chronology of organizing, the tactics used, and the events which led to success, are deliberately falsified. . . . Church services were not the pro-union rallies described. At hours other than services, the union members met in church buildings for business and classes, simply because no other meeting place was available in the city, so great was the pressure brought to bear against the union."[52]

Despite Reynolds's continued insistence that it had no "moral responsibility" to bargain with Local 22, the union prepared a set of contract demands and sought to rally its members. Robert Black told the crowd at a Sunday afternoon membership meeting in early April to keep on fighting. "We didn't build a union over five years just to see it torn down." On Friday afternoon, April 30, 1948, the streets around the Reynolds building swelled with people as the shift changed. A few minutes after 5:00 P.M., a committee from Local 22 entered the offices of Vice President John C. Whitaker carrying a list of contract demands. They came in "unannounced, without an appointment," Whitaker remembered, and he refused to receive their demands. Down below, at the corner of Fourth and Church Streets, near the entrance to the employment office, hundreds of union members formed a circle, chanting "We want a contract" and waving placards that read "Reynolds Has Got It, Reynolds Can Pay It," "Quit Stalling, Meet With the Union Committee," and "In Unity There Is Strength." Summarily dismissed, the committee members left the building. As they came out onto the street, the marchers began singing "Solidarity Forever."[53]

On Sunday afternoon Local 22 met to decide on the next step. Workers were apprehensive as they gathered on the grounds of the Woodland Avenue School. For the first time in four years they had no contract. Robert Black opened the meeting and quickly got to the point: "Where do we go from here?" No one had easy answers. Ed McCrea told the crowd that FTA "recommends that you continue to build your union. Fight for unity until the workers are like a sea that will engulf the company's opposition." The workers adopted a resolution authorizing the executive board to do whatever was necessary to win a contract. The Reverend Frank O'Neal thanked the members for that vote of confidence and, in perhaps the most prescient message of the day, said, "As we retreat, we still fight." The organizing committee made plans to collect dues directly from the workers and announced a series of membership meetings to work out ways to conduct union business in the absence of a contract.[54]

Despite the failure to secure a new contract, the campaign to bring in additional white members continued through the summer of 1948. Jack Frye and his organizing staff continued to visit workers in their homes, to hand out leaflets at the plant gates, and to put out a weekly newspaper. But in the end, the drive could never attract the white workers who could be the nucleus of a volunteer organizing committee. And, as blacks had learned in 1943, only workers could really organize other workers. "We put on a good campaign," Frye recalled, "and in fact I'd say that's the best organizing campaign I ever put on in my life. Some of the best ones are the ones you lose. That's the ones you have to work the hardest at."[55]

The union's inability to bring in more whites not only weakened its position vis à vis the company but also exacerbated tensions within the leadership of Local 22. Union leaders' attitudes were complicated. The large black majority in the wartime plants had given many unionists a false sense of security. In some quarters, the overwhelming vote for the CIO in 1943 led to a belief that the union did not need white support.

In the postwar period, the Communist Party's ongoing internal campaign against white chauvinism, what one union official called "the dancing madness of the time," may well have reinforced this stance. The Party, as Junius Scales explained it, had long held that membership for whites "carried with it the obligation to rid oneself of all the traces of anti-Negro prejudice which were bound to persist where racism was both enshrined in the law and embedded in social custom." In the South especially, this policy meant that white workers had to unlearn a lifetime of ingrained habits in order to treat their black comrades with respect. This exemplary attack on racism, however, could sometimes turn into a self-destructive heresy hunt in which charges of white chauvinism, which inevitably contained some grain of truth, were used to "disarm and paralyze" the most well-meaning white members.[56]

Local 22 apparently escaped the worst excesses of this campaign, which intensified at the end of 1949, but the inward-turning aspect of the Party's quest for ideological purity still made itself felt. Frustrated by the difficulties of organizing white workers and influenced by the strands of black nationalism that mixed with class-conscious interracialism in Local 22's political thought, some Local 22 leaders did find themselves thinking "to hell with the whites"—an attitude that, however understandable, undermined the union's ability to go after white members with a whole heart.[57]

Jack Frye explained the tightrope he had to walk. "We were always under pressure," he recalled, "probably more from outside political sources, Party sources, about pushing the ideas or the ideology of, I think they called it then, the Negro Liberation Movement. There was pressure to be up front about dealing with the issues of segregation, and I tried to make it into a positive thing. I remember spending a lot of time once on a fairly long piece . . . about Robeson and the Negro Liberation Movement and its importance as a source of power that helped the union and blacks and whites both in the union. Anyway, I wouldn't say that we did anything in dealing with the black-white issue or Negro Liberation or any of the rest of that that was not pretty good trade unionism. But there was pressure from an ideological point of view to do more, and I, of course, being primarily a trade unionist, was feeling the pressure, and I was agreeing that the issues had to be dealt with, that you couldn't duck them. If the fact that you represented those 5,000 blacks there was a disadvantage, why, you were lost."[58]

An incident that occurred in the spring of 1948 indicated the depth of black workers' frustration and the internal tensions that increasingly beset the union. Frye kept checkoff authorization cards signed by white workers but did not turn them in to the company. Workers paid their dues directly to him, with the expectation that their names would be kept secret until there were enough white workers enrolled to give them real protection. Velma Hopkins, chair of the Local 22 organizing committee, opposed the separate organizing drive and resented the protection it gave white workers. "Velma went in and got the cards out of Jack's desk and sent them in," Ed McCrea explained, "because it was considered white chauvinism not to put them on the checkoff. As soon as she did that they broke that whole thing up, they transferred [the union members] all over the plants. With that kind of thing going on it was really difficult to get anything accomplished as far as the white workers were concerned. Because . . . the main way to win the white workers was to fight for their economic rights to begin with and then get them involved. That's the way you get white workers involved."[59]

The question remains, Was there really any potential for bringing a significant number of white workers into the union? Or was racial prejudice and company pressure just too powerful? Organizing industrial workers was never easy, even during the heyday of the CIO. This was especially true in the South and in industries where employers could use race and gender to divide workers. In fact, most unionization campaigns failed to solidify what in many cases were majority desires for unionization. Workers generally were unwilling to take the risk and step forward.

Jack Frye and his staff and most of the other leaders of Local 22 saw real possibilities. In fact, among whites in 1948, there was probably as much outright support for unionization as there had been among blacks in 1943. But turning potential into actuality requires some transformative moment, like the death of James McCardell in 1943, to galvanize that support. Nothing like that happened among whites in this postwar era, in part because Reynolds kept such a close watch on its employees and worked on so many fronts to keep white workers out of the union.

The Progressive Party Campaign

Both the HUAC investigation and Local 22's inability to renew its contract in the spring of 1948 reflected profound changes in the political and cultural atmosphere. At the local level, labor's political initiatives had paid off spectacularly—in the election of Kenneth Williams to the Board of Aldermen, the unprecedented interracial cooperation symbolized by the United Citizens Committee, and the cross-class solidarity of the black community. National politics were another story. The corporate offensive against labor, the electorate's rightward political shift, and the Republican takeover of Congress had forced the CIO into a defensive position. In the meantime, Truman's prosecution of the Cold War and his refusal to aggressively pursue either progressive social programs or black civil rights (the recommendations of his Civil Rights Committee notwithstanding) convinced many on the left that they could no longer look to the Democratic Party for leadership on either the domestic or international front.

Increasingly, they turned to Henry Wallace, a forceful spokesman for expanding and internationalizing the New Deal and ushering in the "century of the common man." A politician of rare breadth and intelligence, Wallace came from a line of midwestern agrarian intellectuals and reformers whose roots stretched back to the Populist insurgency and the abolitionist movement. First as Roosevelt's secretary of agriculture and then as vice president, he had cast the meaning of the New Deal as a search for economic democracy. Wallace had allied himself with the rising tide of liberalism in the South, and more than any other national political figure, he saw democratizing the region as the key to national progress and racial equality as critical to democratic reform. Consequently, the leading figures of the Southern Front were among his most ardent backers. These stands earned him the growing enmity of the Democratic Party machinery, which torpedoed his bid for a second term as vice president in 1944, despite strong support among rank-and-file Democrats throughout the country. As Truman's secretary of commerce, Wallace had been the only member of the cabinet to speak out against the president's get-tough policy toward the Soviet Union. When he made his views public in the fall of 1946, Truman had forced him to resign.[60]

In December 1947 Wallace announced that he would run for president on the ticket of the newly formed Progressive Party. That decision brought the deep conflicts in the labor movement to the surface, precipitating an ideological split that would have far-reaching reverberations. The clash came to a head when the CIO's executive board met in January 1948. On one side stood Philip Murray and his allies, who saw support for a third party as an invitation to Republican victory and believed that support for Truman was labor's best hope for maintaining a place in a ruling coalition. They were also enraged by the actions of the Communist Party's central committee, which abandoned its policy of cooperating with the Democrats and pressed the leaders of the left-led unions to back the third-party effort. On the other side stood those who saw in the Wallace campaign an opportunity for rejuvenating an industrial union project that had lost its militant edge, becoming an appendage to the Democratic Party and a hostage to Truman's foreign policy. They urged the board to reaffirm the autonomy of each union to make its own decisions in political matters. In the end, the executive board voted to maintain an officially nonpartisan position, which in practice meant strong-arming dissidents into supporting the Democratic Party candidate.[61]

Ignoring the CIO's directives, FTA's executive board quickly endorsed Wallace, one of only five CIO unions to do so. Delegates to a January meeting of FTA's Southeast regional council in Suffolk, Virginia, affirmed the international's action, denouncing "the evil coalition that now runs the Congress and the Government in Washington and in the states" and asking union members to help get the Progressive Party on the ballot in the South. The executive board of Local 22 held discussion meetings with workers and made a similar announcement, lambasting the Democrats and Republicans as parties of "Wall Street" that stood for "high prices, low wages, and war-talk abroad. . . . Another depression and another war are being prepared by those who are looting the American economy and attempting to loot the people of the world."[62]

Unlike other unions that endorsed Wallace but did little to promote his candidacy, Local 22 members were among the Progressive Party's most ardent supporters. A Wallace for President Committee formed in Forsyth County in late February. Local 22 provided the major push, but the committee included representatives from other unions and a number of nonunion activists from the African American community, including C. C. Kellum, president of the local NAACP, J. H. R. Gleaves of the Progressive Civic League, and the Reverend Kelley Goodwin—all veterans of the coalition that had elected Kenneth Williams.[63]

The campaign went into full swing at the end of April 1948, when the first statewide convention took place in Winston-Salem, an indication of the city's status as the center of progressive activism in the state. Virginia Foster Durr, who was a leading member of the SCHW and the wife of former Federal Communications Commissioner Clifford Durr, gave the main address at a dinner the night before the convention. Over 450 people attended the event at the Oasis Club, which the *Journal* reported "was unsegregated, as have been other meetings of the new third party." This disregard for one of Jim Crow's most powerful taboos was sure to offend the paper's white readership as much as any political positions the convention might adopt.[64]

The next day the 217 convention delegates, convening at an empty tobacco warehouse, went about the business of establishing a political party, agreeing on a platform, and making the necessary plans to get on the ballot in November. The convention named Mary Price of Greensboro as party chairman, United Furniture

Workers organizer Mike Ross as secretary, and a St. Augustine's College professor, Tinsley Spraggins, as treasurer. After some heated debate on socialized medicine, the death penalty for lynchers, and a one-time bonus for all veterans, the delegates adopted what the *News and Observer* called "the most liberal political platform ever to come out of this state." Among other things it called for an antilynching bill, an end to racial segregation and discrimination, and abolition of the atomic bomb.[65]

In an effort to link the Wallace campaign to an earlier third party effort and to combat the historical amnesia imposed by white supremacists, Mike Ross spoke to the convention about his recent study of the history of the Populist Party. "Probably the greatest political falsehood peddled to the people in North Carolina," he declared, "is that the Democratic Party has held constant sway here, without challenge, for the last 60 years, and that consequently nothing can be done to advance the people's interests except through the Democratic Party." He reminded his audience that they were heirs to "a strong movement of progressive forces" that had remained active in North Carolina after the triumph of white supremacy and the Populists' defeat: the small farmers who supported Socialist Party candidate Eugene Debs, liberals such as University of North Carolina president Frank Porter Graham, former gubernatorial candidate Ralph McDonald, State Supreme Court Chief Justice Walter Clark, and the textile workers who organized in the 1930s. Ross ended by presenting charter memberships in the Progressive Party to two former Populists, a grand symbolic gesture that tied the past to the present and positioned the Progressive Party campaign as an attempt to overthrow the white supremacist settlement of 1898.[66]

Idaho senator Glen H. Taylor, the Progressive Party's vice presidential candidate, reiterated the party's goals in an afternoon address. When the senator, a former actor and "singing cowboy" who had won his first political office in 1944, entered the Liberty Warehouse, a crowd of over 2,500, a large majority of whom were Local 22 members, greeted him with "thunderous applause." Taylor, a consistent foe of Truman's foreign and domestic policies, blasted the threat to world peace by "a small clique of bankers, big corporate executives, and militarists who are determined to run the country for their own power rather than the welfare of the people." The senator reiterated his commitment to a civil rights program to end segregation and discrimination. "Jim Crow Has Got To Go," he told his appreciative audience, repeating a favorite slogan of the Wallace Clubs.[67]

The campaign of the Wallacites befuddled, as well as angered, not only the CIO leadership but most New Dealers even as it attracted the enthusiastic backing of many southern white liberals and African Americans. These supporters did not necessarily expect to win the White House, and they were keenly aware of the fear that a third party would siphon off enough votes to ensure a Republican victory. They were convinced, however, that loyalty to a party that had largely abandoned New Deal efforts to restructure the South's economy and ensure blacks' civil rights would do nothing to forward a progressive agenda. The Progressive Party campaign, moreover, offered an unprecedented opportunity to articulate a radical challenge to white supremacy, in both its economic and racial dimensions. By joining what came to be called "Gideon's Army," Wallace supporters hoped to push the Democratic Party to the left and refocus and revitalize the Southern Front.

The Progressive Party also offered an unprecedented opportunity for women's political participation. Although North Carolina women wielded political influence of various kinds both before and after the ratification of the Nineteenth Amendment, this was a more visible foray into the world of electoral politics. Bucking the tide of postwar gender stereotypes, which restricted women to the roles of mothers and homemakers, Mary Price and her female colleagues were breaking new ground. The Progressive Party did not articulate a feminist politics or champion women's causes, yet the very fact that a woman occupied the top spot in the party organization and that African American women workers were prominent in the leadership challenged white male prerogatives.[68]

In Henry Wallace the Southern Front seemed to have found the perfect standard-bearer. Certainly no national political figure spoke more clearly or more forcefully for the core issues around which the South's progressive coalition had united. In a 1947 address to Alpha Phi Alpha, a national African American fraternity, Wallace made his position clear: "Today we must act upon the . . . fundamental premise that a strong and democratic America cannot be built while the one-third of our people who live in the South, Negroes and whites, alike remain the common victims of an oppressive economic, political, and social system. . . . The problems of the Negro people lie at the very heart of the problem of the South; and the problems of the South are basic to the critical problems of our entire nation." Wallace went on to analyze the causes of the South's problems. "The cancerous disease of race hate, which bears so heavily upon Negro citizens, and at the same time drags the masses of southern white citizens into the common quagmire of poverty and ignorance and political servitude, is not an isolated problem to be attacked completely apart from our other national problems. It is part of an ever more dominant philosophy of dollars above men, of property values over human values. The Jim Crow system pays handsome profits to a small number of men in positions of economic and political power. Jim Crow divides white and Negro for the profit of the few."[69]

The Wallace campaign generated enthusiasm among college students, African Americans, and unionists across North Carolina. But North Carolina law imposed serious obstacles to the third-party effort. To get on the ballot for state and federal elections, a political party had to present a petition to the state board of elections ninety days before the election with the signatures of 10,000 registered voters. This was a formidable task in itself, but in March the board adopted even more restrictive regulations. Using a provision of the law that required all signatories to affiliate with the new party and vote for it in the coming election, the board ruled that petitioners could not vote in the primaries of any other party. This measure prohibited petitioners from participating in the Democratic primary that took place in May, the only significant election for state and local officials.[70]

On primary day in 1948, Progressive Party workers were at the polls asking people not to vote so that they might be eligible to sign a petition to get the party on the November ballot. The primary that year was not as critical as it had been in 1946. Congressman John Folger had decided against running for reelection, and Thurmond Chatham had no serious opposition. Still, even though there were no progressives or blacks on the ballot, staying away from the polls was not an easy decision for African American citizens who had worked so hard over the previous decade to register and vote in the all-important Democratic primary. A group of Baptist ministers wrote to the *Journal* warning blacks who signed Progressive Party petitions that they were forfeiting their right to participate in the Democratic primary. "Notwithstanding the imperfections of the present existing parties," the letter said, "the Democratic Party will, in all probability, continue to be the dominant party in North Carolina; and to sever our connection with said party is equivalent to political suicide." Despite such warnings, the Progressive Party was effective in keeping African Americans from voting in the Democratic primary.[71]

In June, Paul Robeson returned to Winston-Salem, this time in his role as cochairman of the National Wallace for President Committee. A racially mixed audience at Pepper's Warehouse heard Robeson, Mary Price, and Clark Foreman, former head of the SCHW and the treasurer of the Progressive Party, blast the Republicans and Democrats for their lack of commitment to peace and civil rights. After a night of speech-making, Robeson hit the streets at 6:30 A.M. to sing for the workers as they made their way into the factories. "We had Paul Robeson singing in the street with the loudspeaker on top of my car," remembered Jack Frye, "holding his ears with both hands to keep the noise out."[72]

With the struggle for union recognition at Reynolds on hold in the summer of 1948, Local 22 intensified its involvement in the Progressive Party. "It was a good thing that we hoped would help us in the union," Jack Frye remembered. "It was very stimulating, and my recollection is that the white workers were receptive. While there was always a virulent opposition, there was also a lot of latent support.

We did a lot of work signing people up in the textile towns and those little company towns all around. I think that the whole black membership signed the petitions" to get the party on the ballot.[73]

In the midst of the Progressive campaign in North Carolina, Mary Price was charged before HUAC with being a Communist Party operative. The youngest daughter of a "dyed-in-the-wool" Democrat who grew tobacco and served as superintendent of roads in Rockingham County, Price grew up in Greensboro and attended the Woman's College there before receiving a degree in journalism at the University of North Carolina at Chapel Hill. After working briefly for a newspaper, she moved to New York and became private secretary to the columnist Walter Lippman. After the war she returned to the South as executive secretary of the Committee for North Carolina of the SCHW. When Wallace announced his candidacy, Price helped to form the state's Progressive Party.[74]

Testifying before HUAC on the Communist infiltration of the United States government, Elizabeth Bentley, the first of a series of former Party members who became professional witnesses, claimed that while Price was working for Lippman, she had supplied Bentley with documents taken from Lippman's files. Price refused to respond to Bentley's charges, saying only that she was "like most Southerners . . . a natural born liberal . . . just in the last couple of years I've gotten to be boiling mad." Recent discoveries in the archives of the former Soviet Union substantiate Bentley's testimony: for a short period during the war, Price apparently did pass documents from Lippman's files as well as from a friend who worked for the U.S. government.[75]

Ignoring such attacks, the Wallace campaign planned a swing through the South to take its message to the people. At the Democratic Party convention Truman had moved to undermine Wallace's appeal by adding a civil rights plank to his platform, prompting a walkout by southern Democrats and the formation of a States' Rights Party. Taken together, the Progressive Party's position on segregation and the fulmination of the "Dixiecrats" charged the political atmosphere. Wallace began his southern tour by defying Virginia's compulsory segregation laws in Richmond, Norfolk, and Suffolk. When the Washington Duke Hotel in Durham refused to accommodate the party's black staff members, Mary Price canceled the reservations and announced that Wallace and Clark Foreman would stay at the home of Mr. and Mrs. G. W. Logan. The Logans owned a theater and doughnut shop in the black business district known as Hayti and had been active in the Progressive Party. Wallace's black secretary, Viola Scott, was to stay with the *Carolina Times* editor,

Louis Austin, while the rest of the group, including folksinger Pete Seeger, reserved rooms at the black-owned Biltmore Hotel.[76]

Wallace's visit to Durham coincided with the North Carolina Progressive Party's nominating convention. His speech was planned as the highlight of the closing session. The meeting began at 10:00 A.M. on Sunday, August 29, as 200 delegates gathered at the Regal Theater. After a short religious service, Local 22's Velma Hopkins presided over the adoption of the rules for the convention, followed by various committee reports. That afternoon the delegates moved to the City Armory to nominate candidates for state and local offices. Mary Price received the gubernatorial nomination; the convention chose a white portrait painter, Kenneth Harris of Wrightsville Beach, to run for lieutenant governor, and C. O. Pearson, a black attorney from Durham, as the candidate for attorney general. The *Durham Sun* commented that this was "probably the first time since 'reconstruction days' that a Negro had appeared on a general election ballot."[77]

When Henry Wallace arrived in Durham that evening, he held a press conference at Progressive Party headquarters and attended a fund-raising dinner at the Algonquin Club, a black social club in Durham. Meanwhile, an audience of between 1,500 and 2,000 people, composed of equal numbers of blacks and whites, jammed the armory for Wallace's public speech. Shortly after the session opened, a group of twenty young white men carrying anti-Wallace placards blaring "Wallace, Alligator Bait" and "Send Wallace Back to Russia" marched down the aisle and out of the building. When the protesters tried to get back in, some young Progressive Party members got up to stop them, and a fight broke out. FTA organizer Jack Frye remembered the incident. "Since we were young and white, we had the physical job of putting them out. That was fun. I enjoyed that. It was the first time I got to take a sock at a couple of those people who were giving us so much trouble. I actually connected with a couple of them." National Guardsmen and Durham police on the scene quickly intervened. A correspondent for the *Baltimore Afro-American* reported that when the scuffle ended, "several persons lay cold upon the floor. The picket signs were torn to bits, and the 'rebels' were pushed out the side door. . . . About half of the persons at the convention were colored and they seemed to be contented in sitting back and letting the 'white folks fight it out among themselves.'"[78]

Wallace entered the armory through a side door, led by a National Guardsman with a drawn .45-caliber revolver. A most unusual introduction, Wallace noted. The candidate began a prepared address that focused on the economic problems of the South. He proposed a $4 billion aid program for southern industry and agriculture. As he spoke, a small group of hecklers scattered throughout the armory began whistling and shouting, "We Want Thurmond," a reference to Dixiecrat candidate Strom Thurmond. After a string of firecrackers, which some thought were gunshots, went off, Wallace broke from his prepared speech and told the protesters, "I will not be intimidated. . . . I can stand here just as long as you can yell. . . . A small group of demonstrators cannot down the Progressive Party." Afterward, he spent a quiet night at the Logans' home before heading out on a whirlwind speaking tour of Piedmont North Carolina.[79]

An early morning stop in Chapel Hill went according to plan, but when the Wallace motorcade entered Burlington shortly after noon an angry crowd greeted the candidate. Before he could begin speaking, spectators hurled eggs and tomatoes at Wallace and his party, including Mary Price. Wallace's aides got him back to the car before any serious violence happened, but in Greensboro they met the same response.

A twenty-car motorcade arrived in Winston-Salem at close to 5:00 P.M. It was too late for Wallace to take his place on the street outside the Reynolds factories to talk with workers as they left the plant. Given the events of the day, it was probably just as well. Some of the party stopped at the Robert E. Lee Hotel. On a previous trip to Winston-Salem as vice president, Wallace had been the houseguest of R. J. Reynolds Jr., but this time he made his way into the black community, to the home of Carl H. Russell, an undertaker.[80]

A large crowd began gathering in the early evening at the Southside ballpark to hear Wallace speak. The police on hand made no attempt to segregate the early arrivals, who found seats in the sheltered grandstand, but for the most part blacks and whites confined themselves to different areas of the stadium. Observers estimated that as many as 6,000 people were in attendance, roughly 40 percent of whom were white. Shortly before the start of the program, a heavy rain began to fall. Coats and umbrellas came out of the crowd for the speakers on the platform. Floodlights exploded and fell to the ground and were quickly turned off. Pete Seeger announced a delay in the beginning of the program, but stayed to entertain the crowd with his banjo and songs.

The audience had a difficult time hearing Seeger, as a group of approximately 200 young white men kept up a steady roar. "Wallace opponents in the audience seemed to know no end to different methods of protesting the proceedings," a *Journal* reporter observed. "Rebel yells, catcalls, boos, woody woodpecker noises came frequently. Much of the time the booers could not hear what they were protesting. Sometimes a group of youths would take a loud note and yell and hold it for several seconds. They kept up a fire of comments, evidently considered humorous by those who made them." When Seeger began singing "God Bless America" the audience joined him, but "the rowdy youths warbled in the wrong places and purposefully sang off key."

The invocation and singing of the "Star Spangled Banner" temporarily quieted the hecklers, but the noise grew louder as Progressive Party candidates began to speak. By the time Clark Foreman addressed the gathering, it was almost impossible to hear. When the clamor subsided for a moment Foreman told the troublemakers: "We will not be frightened. You can call us black, you can call us red, but you cannot call us yellow." Foreman instructed the black women ushers to take up a collection, while Seeger and the audience sang hymns. Seeger changed the words of the popular hymn "Farther Along We'll Know All About It" to "Farther along they'll know all about it," and Wallace supporters directed their voices toward the protesters.

When Henry Wallace appeared the boos reached a crescendo, but the cheers of hundreds of Progressive Party supporters soon drowned them out. After he recognized the importance of Local 22, hecklers chanted "Down with Wallace" and pounded their feet. The candidate had to stop, but his supporters responded with an even louder chant, "We Want Wallace." Chief of Police John Gold finally moved into the demonstrators and asked them to be quiet, and the noise subsided enough for Wallace to finish his talk.[81]

Miraculously, no fights broke out between Wallace's supporters and the hecklers. The preponderance of black faces may have tempered the actions of the white rowdies (no eggs or tomatoes appeared during the evening), and there were a number of police and Progressive Party marshals patrolling the stands. But it was primarily the forbearance of the white and black Wallace supporters that kept the situation from getting out of hand. Even so, Chief Gold had the temerity to tell the *Journal* that "some of the booing and hollering was started by persons who have been identified to us as members of the Communist Party."[82]

Local reactions to Wallace's visit were predictably mixed. The *Journal* railed against the "bankrupt, irresponsible leadership" of the Progressive Party and Wallace's disregard for the social customs of his host town. The fact that the candidate's actual hosts were blacks and whites for whom segregation had ceased to be customary was lost on the editorial writers. "Mr. Wallace himself was largely responsible for the demonstrations against him," said the editor. Nevertheless, the paper denounced the behavior of the crowds as "unworthy of North Carolina." Progressive Party representatives called the actions a "disgrace to the State," saying the violence was in no way spontaneous, but "the work of an organized Klan-minded minority."[83]

Many citizens wrote to complain about the treatment Wallace had received.

Latta B. Ratledge, a white tobacco farmer from Mocksville, attended the speech at the Southside Park. He blamed the police for the lack of order. "Those who had a right to put a stop to the hecklers failed to do so. If all those officers could not stop those hecklers, please tell me what they would do if a real riot were to break out." Ratledge admonished people who sent prayers and dollars to help blacks in Africa and then had their Christianity upset when Henry Wallace dined with a black family.[84]

Virginia Sturgis drew her philosophy from the Gospel of Matthew: "But many that are first shall be last; and the last shall be first" (Matt. 19:30). "God does not intend for the Negro to always stay at the bottom," Sturgis told *Journal* readers. "I think the biggest trouble is that the white people of the South are afraid that if Mr. Wallace is elected President, the Negro will be able to advance more and stop being worked and treated as an animal." She urged blacks to "unite and work together" and asked whites to join with them in support of Wallace. "All we need is courage and grit and we will come out victorious."[85]

The unity Virginia Sturgis sought was not to be. Shortly before the November election, Winston-Salem alderman Kenneth Williams, Progressive Civic League president J. H. R. Gleaves, and former Local 22 PAC chairman Jason Hawkins formed the Negro Democratic Club. Gleaves lambasted Local 22 a few days later for using the Progressive Party to lead blacks to what he said was a "dead-end destination. Why not help elect them [local officials] instead of leading our people for your selfish ends — to nowhere." Alarmed by public opinion polls that showed Republican presidential candidate Thomas Dewey in the lead, many Wallace supporters defected to Truman and the Democrats on election day, choosing to cast a vote that counted rather than one that expressed their political views. Wallace received 1,157,063 votes nationally; in North Carolina, he received about 4,000, and in Forsyth County, 701.[86]

No one expected Progressive Party candidates to be serious contenders for public office. The point of the campaign all along had been to raise issues and temper the conservative swing of the Democratic Party. The final vote tallies, however, were a major disappointment: Progressives did not come close to duplicating the success of their Populist forebears. But the campaign had momentarily opened up the political process in North Carolina. The third-party campaign stimulated voter registration in urban centers, small towns, and rural areas across the state. It placed blacks and women on the ballot for state and local offices and forced a real political dialogue that included issues of war, economics, and race. Just as important, the campaign audaciously defied segregation statutes throughout the state.[87]

For Winston-Salem unionists, the real tragedy of the Progressive Party campaign was not the small number of ballots cast, but the damage done to their fragile alliances with the CIO and the local black middle-class. Neither Philip Murray nor Kenneth Williams ever forgave FTA and Local 22 for joining Gideon's Army. However much they might have supported key party policies on the economy, foreign policy, and civil rights, Murray and Williams saw this push to the left, in the face of such powerful conservative reaction, as foolhardy.

CHAPTER FOURTEEN

If You Beat the White Man at One Trick, He Will Try Another

Many of Local 22's critics assumed that the Progressive Party debacle had dealt the union its death blow. By the end of 1948, with no contract at Reynolds, the third party in ruins, and the coalition that had elected Kenneth Williams unraveling, Local 22's "influence among the Negro population," claimed the *Journal*, "had diminished to almost nothing." Union activists saw things differently. Their alliance with the black middle class had always been strategic and uneasy, and they were convinced that, despite the loss of their contract, they could still count on the support of the rank and file. They could not help but be sobered by the Progressive Party's defeat at the polls, but that repudiation did not cancel out the confirming aspects of their involvement in the party's extraordinary North Carolina campaign. A major national figure had allied himself—in person, in the South, and at significant personal risk—with the most far-reaching goals of the Southern Front. Local 22 leaders had crisscrossed the state as central players in a national political campaign. Now, ignoring its political obituaries, Local 22 moved to win back bargaining rights at Reynolds and press its demands for more comprehensive social welfare provisions. Its organizing platform included a number of labor's most expansive bread-and-butter demands: a thirty-six-cent wage increase, thirty hours' work for forty hours' pay, and $100-a-month pensions for workers with twenty years' experience. It also contained an ambitious social agenda: the repeal of the Taft-Hartley Act, the return of price controls, the enactment of civil rights legislation, the development of low-income housing, and the dismissal of "generals and other brass hats and Wall Street men" from Truman's administration.[1]

Taking on City Hall

Three years earlier, in 1945, when Reynolds ripped out the stemming machines in Plant Number 60 during Christmas week, Local 22 had offered two proposals that, if implemented, would have substantially altered the quality of workers' lives: a shorter work day and a system of plantwide seniority that would have required the integration of black women into white-coded jobs. Neither of these proposals was taken seriously by the company, and the union was unable to prevent Reynolds from mechanizing the prefabrication processes, laying off black women, and hiring white workers to run the new machines. In mid-February 1948, the company had laid off an additional 150 workers in the stemmery division. As in the past, the re- ductions were carried out according to seniority in conformity with the collective bargaining agreement. Nevertheless, because postwar mechanization had already cut so deeply into the labor force, a number of the laid-off workers had fifteen years' experience. Combined with the annual furlough of leaf house workers, these new dismissals meant that black working-class neighborhoods were filled with households facing the winter with no pay checks coming in.[2]

The plight of the unemployed intensified when Reynolds exercised a loophole in the 1947 revision of the state's unemployment compensation law (which it had un- doubtedly helped to write) to deprive its seasonal workers of benefits. Under the terms of the revision, seasonal workers could claim up to sixteen weeks compensa- tion, but only during the period when they would normally be employed. Reynolds was one of the few tobacco manufacturing firms in the state that chose to define its season as less than the entire year, thus reducing the company's contribution to the compensation pool. Since Reynolds's "season" ran only from August through Feb- ruary, its workers could collect no compensation from March through July when they were out of work. Local 22 estimated the tax savings to Reynolds at $25,000 to $30,000 per year, and the cost in lost compensation to workers at over $300,000. Reynolds never had to defend this policy, so it is difficult to know what the com- pany's rationale might have been. Tax savings were no doubt a concern, but per- haps as important was the message the policy sent to rebellious black workers. The decision not to allow seasonal workers to collect unemployment served as one more way of demonstrating Reynolds's power while at the same time forcing hun- dreds of workers into the city's low-wage labor pool.[3]

Soon after the layoffs, the union had invited representatives of public and private welfare agencies to participate in a discussion of the unemployment problem and outlined a "program of community action" that included a local Fair Employment Practices Committee to help increase job opportunities for blacks, more relief from state and county governments, the rehiring of laid-off workers by Reynolds, and consideration of the problem by the Board of Aldermen. Unemployment, the union insisted, was "the responsibility of the whole community."[4]

On February 20, 1948, a delegation of black women affected by the layoff filled the council chambers in City Hall. The situation was desperate, for many had "no heat, no food, and no shelter." They asked the aldermen to set up an unemployment committee to help find additional funds and jobs for those affected and to conduct an extensive study of the problem. Local officials had never considered black unemployment a serious issue; after all, it helped keep wages down and ensured an adequate supply of labor for the city's homes and factories. The union wanted precise numbers, an examination of trends, a record of relief and welfare programs, and proposals for alleviating the problem.[5]

Local 22 also called for "immediate steps to enlarge city public works employment." Drawing inspiration from the New Deal public works programs, the union suggested that the city set up sewing room projects, add janitors and cafeteria workers in the schools, repair public buildings, and launch a citywide cleanup program to spruce up streets, backyards, and vacant lots, particularly those in black neighborhoods. The proposal called for an increase in relief and welfare funds, with monies coming from sales tax surpluses and increased taxation of "those with the greatest ability to pay." It also demanded that the aldermen take steps to "correct unfair employment practices" by asking local industries to employ African Americans in a broader range of jobs.[6]

The Board of Aldermen responded with a callous dismissal of what even the State Employment Service recognized as a serious problem. The aldermen contended that unemployment was at a normal level and that "seasonal unemployment among the negro women in the leaf processing part of the tobacco industry is as old as the industry itself." These women, moreover, had "husbands, children, and other members of their families employed at regular year-round jobs and seek seasonal employment merely as a means of obtaining surplus income for the family group."[7]

The board also rejected the union's proposals for a public jobs program and an increase in funds for welfare and relief, calling both fiscally irresponsible. The aldermen liked the idea of vocational education but had a limited vision of what that would mean. There was a "large latent demand for trained workers in the household service field," the aldermen noted, which could absorb much of the black un-employment. "It is believed that the current wage rates being paid for this service would increase substantially provided that those offering themselves for this work were properly trained in cleaning, modern dietetic cooking, laundering, elementary nursing, and other household work." It was, of course, precisely this channeling of black women into household and agricultural labor that the union was trying to change.[8]

A year later, by the end of February 1949, an estimated 3,300 people were unemployed in Winston-Salem, less than half of whom were eligible for unemployment compensation. Local welfare agencies found themselves overwhelmed by requests for assistance. The Forsyth County Welfare Department said that budgetary constraints had forced it to limit itself to aiding "unemployables." The director of the Salvation Army, whose agency provided assistance only to transients, told the *Journal* "that public house-to-house begging is greater that at any time in the past five years."[9]

In March 1949 the state legislature began considering the changes in the unemployment compensation law made in 1947, and unionists took the opportunity to try to close the loophole that allowed Reynolds to exclude leaf house workers. An FTA committee representing Local 22 and Local 10 met with the Employment Security Commission, and some fifteen workers appeared at an evening session of a joint Senate-House committee, describing the hardships of unemployment to the assembled lawmakers. Among the witnesses was Eliza Black Warren, Robert Black's mother, a small, gray-haired women who had helped organize an unemployed council in Winston-Salem in the 1930s.[10]

Local 22 also took the matter before the Board of Aldermen, again asking the city fathers to adopt a resolution requesting that Reynolds withdraw its seasonal exemption. The meeting quickly turned into a confrontation between Kenneth Williams and Robert Black, with Williams accusing the union of misleading unemployed workers and putting him on the spot. "I want to let these people know right now that this is a thing that we (the Board of Aldermen) do not control," Williams told Black. "You brought these people down here under the impression that we could get that money for them. If we don't, you tell them that we didn't do what we can do. . . . I am interested in these people. Local 22 said I did nothing for them. What I want to know is what can I do? You people say that we control the matter of unemployment compensation. If that were possible, I'm sure we all would say give those workers the money. But all that originates in Raleigh."[11]

All the union was asking, replied Black, was "that the Mayor and the Board strongly recommend to the R. J. Reynolds Company that they withdraw this seasonal pursuit. . . . There's been no accusation and there will be none that you can get this money. But if you all would use your influence it might help." Still on the defensive, Williams drew a strained analogy between his own situation and that of the leaf house workers. "I want to get this good and straight," he said pointing a finger a Black. "I teach school. I work nine months. I'm a seasonal worker, but I get no unemployment compensation." Finally Williams spoke directly to the point. "What right," he asked, "has the Board to meddle in the affairs of the R. J. Reynolds Tobacco Company, or Hanes Knitting Company, or any other private company? This is a governmental body. Somebody has misled you. This Board of Aldermen has no authority." Black repeated his request. "We only ask this board to use your influence to get the R. J. Reynolds Company to withdraw the seasonal exemption." After further discussion, which included stories of "families without funds, homes and hopes of employment," one of the unemployed women stood up to lambaste Williams for comparing his situation as a college professor and an alderman to the plight of women who could barely put food on their tables for five months out of the year.[12]

As the ranks of the unemployed continued to grow, the following spring a committee of black women unionists petitioned the board to "take immediate action." Blending workplace and consumer demands, they asked Reynolds and the city to provide "$100 a month pensions to workers after [they were] 60 years [old]"; "stop the speed-ups and stretch-outs"; cut back to thirty-five hours' work for forty hours' pay; create more jobs by building additional public housing, municipal day nurseries, schools, and hospitals; and increase public welfare spending. The mayor dismissed the women's demands, accusing them of being misled by Communists who were only trying to "stir up disagreement and disorganize our community."[13]

In the end, the union made little headway in its effort to win increased unemployment compensation and open municipal jobs to African Americans. Industrialists simply had too much at stake to compromise. The political economy of white supremacy demanded the maintenance of a pool of low-wage workers as well as a racially segregated job structure.

In its fight for slum clearance and public housing, on the other hand, Local 22's challenge to local government enjoyed some success. Deplorable, substandard housing, from the tenements of urban centers to the sharecropper shacks of the rural South, was a perennial problem in twentieth-century America. Yet prior to the New Deal, policy makers largely ignored the housing needs of poor citizens, in part because of opposition from private developers and real estate interests. During the Depression, Congress realized the need for an effective national housing policy. Although the National Housing Act and the newly created Federal Housing Authority were aimed mainly at reforming the banking and mortgage systems, providing low-term loans to homeowners, and stimulating employment in the construction industry, they did make some federal funds available for slum clearance and public housing projects.[14]

In 1935 Winston-Salem had applied for and won tentative approval of a $1 million public housing project for blacks as part of a slum clearance program. The Board of Aldermen, however, gave in to pressure from "real estate dealers, the building and loan men and the owners of cheap rental properties" and scuttled the proposal. In 1941 a less ambitious project won approval "under the enthusiastic prodding" of Mayor Richard Reynolds, heir to the Reynolds Tobacco Company fortune, but the war intervened to stop all non-defense-related federal housing programs.[15]

President Truman fought hard for funds for slum clearance, redevelopment, and public housing in his legislative packages, but the anti–public housing lobby, made up of realtors, construction firms, and conservatives in Congress, stymied these efforts. Public pressure for federal intervention intensified as millions of Americans found themselves living in substandard housing after the war. Congress finally passed the Housing Act of 1949 and committed the federal government to providing funds to local municipalities for low-cost housing.[16]

Winston-Salem's housing was among the worst in the urban South. Between 1940 and 1949, only 656 new houses became available to blacks, and few of those were rental units. This shortage of new housing, compounded by the ongoing deterioration of old dwellings and the negligence of slumlords, created shockingly bad housing conditions in low-income black neighborhoods. Wage gains had allowed some workers to move out of the worst slums, but they had few places to go given residential segregation and the extreme shortage of decent housing for blacks at any price. Many still lived in places like Monkey Bottom, where overcrowding, raw sewage, and rat paths were a way of life.[17]

In the summer of 1948, the *Journal* ran a series of articles with graphic photographs of the conditions in many black neighborhoods. Photograph after photograph showed boarded-up community toilets, some meant to serve up to fifty people, with captions explaining that "ditches and spaces between the houses serve[d] the purpose instead." Although appalled at the conditions they saw, newspaper reporters and government officials seemed not to notice the human suffering that resulted; their only real concern appeared to be the threat that such conditions posed to the larger, and implicitly white, community. These slums were "breeding places for disease, vice, and other evils," the *Journal* observed.[18]

Not surprisingly, the paper's investigation coincided with a polio epidemic in neighboring Guilford County. There was speculation at the time that the polio virus might be spread by flies that had come in contact with raw sewage. "If we create or tolerate breeding places for disease through unsanitary housing conditions," the *Journal* editorialized, "carriers from those breeding places spread through all the community and imperil the health of all." Concern focused especially on the black women living in these neighborhoods who did laundry for white families. City officials observed a clothesline " 'hanging over a filthy ditch. On that line were children's clothes that were going to Ardmore and Buena Vista [two white neighborhoods].' " The city's short-run solution was to force the owners of rental property to repair existing toilets, while at the same time pushing ahead with a slum clearance and redevelopment plan.[19]

Local 22 commended the city's efforts and the following year released the results of a union survey of 294 black workers' homes. Only 13 of the homes had hot running water; 151 families used outdoor toilets, and almost all reported their houses were in bad condition. Robert Lathan said, "People talk of slums and slum clearance, but very few who don't live in these areas understand what poor housing means in terms of inconvenience and actual suffering." Lathan called for a "broad public housing, slum clearance program." Unlike city officials who feared contamination, Local 22 emphasized the need to provide "decent homes" for workers.[20]

In contrast to its stand on unemployment, the Board of Aldermen decided it had a right to intervene in the housing crisis and requested federal aid. The *Journal* provided the rationale: "The vast majority of the people of Winston-Salem want to see an end of the slum areas. They believe that the community should put local democracy in action to see that these blights upon the life and progress of the community are removed and the underprivileged people who live in these ramshackle 'shacks' and tenements given an opportunity to rear their families in clean, wholesome surroundings. They want to see an end of the crime, illiteracy, vice, and communism, which are bred in these dirty hovels. They believe that local democracy and community decency go hand in hand."[21]

When Congress authorized new funds for public housing, the mayor reconstituted the city housing authority and began campaigning for federal funds. The Board of Aldermen approved an application by the Winston-Salem Housing Authority requesting $270,000 from the Public Housing Administration to build 1,200 housing units over the next two years.[22]

In the rush to secure public housing, one crucial issue escaped official notice:

contractors in Winston-Salem were ready and willing to build houses for working-class clients. But even the most modest dwellings rented for $30 a month, two or three times what many people could afford to pay. Since the majority of people living in the slums worked in the tobacco industry, the obvious alternative to public housing was higher wages. During the 1947 strike, the union had repeatedly stressed the economic benefits to the whole community of better pay for workers. It made a similar point in discussions of unemployment. But Reynolds preferred piecemeal handouts or government subsidies to a more equitable distribution of its enormous wealth. As Velma Hopkins put it, "Who built these great factories here? . . . We did—our mothers and fathers did, working here for 10 or 15 cents an hour. That's why we are uneducated and living in slums. They talk about slums. Who's living in these slums? R. J. Reynolds workers are living there."[23]

In any case, for workers the more critical short-term issue was the maintenance of rent controls. In supporting public housing, the Board of Realtors had requested an end to rent controls in Winston-Salem so that property owners could make enough money to justify improving their properties. Local 22 immediately began organizing to prevent the lifting of controls. Membership meetings took up the issue, and union members conducted an informal survey among hundreds of residents. At the end of December, the union presented the Board of Aldermen a petition opposing the removal of rent control with over 2,000 signatures. When the matter came up before the board, those who opposed the lifting of controls came out in such numbers that the meeting had to be moved from the aldermen's chambers to the city courtroom.[24]

The Metamorphosis of White Supremacy

Such confrontations between the working-class citizens of Winston-Salem and the Board of Aldermen were unheard of before the organization of Local 22. *Journal* staff writer Marie Belk covered the labor beat in town, and her stories on Local 22 were evenhanded in comparison to the attacks from the paper's editorial page. Belk observed a "revolution in the attitude" of local citizens toward the city government, for which she gave Local 22 partial credit. Board meetings had become forums for public debate, a far cry from the old days when decisions were made without public participation. The result, Belk said, was greater democracy in Winston-Salem's civic life.[25]

But containment, not democracy, was the goal of Winston-Salem's business and political leaders. The successful mobilization of the city's African American community had sent tremors through the white neighborhoods of West Winston. The initial response had been to deny that any problems existed, blame outside agitators for the conflagrations, and fight the workers head-on. But such tactics only seemed to strengthen the union's standing with its membership and within the black community. Once it became clear that change was inevitable, white civic leaders attempted to steer it into channels of their own.

Their late-nineteenth-century predecessors had blamed the excesses of democracy for what they saw as the threat of "Negro rule" and responded by remaking the entire political and social order. White supremacy at midcentury required a lighter touch. In response to reformers' efforts, North Carolina had abolished the poll tax, the U.S. Supreme Court had declared the white primary unconstitutional, and civility had replaced official violence. As Reynolds executives moved to limit unionists' power in the plants, white civic leaders looked to undermine the influence of black workers in the city.

This midcentury metamorphosis of white supremacy was sophisticated and deliberate. It aimed to moderate some of the more restrictive and discriminatory aspects of Jim Crow while retaining the fundamental inequalities of the system and avoiding any real social change. White power brokers began by appropriating the mantle of race relations reform in partnership with a select group of middle-class black leaders. Next, they sought to transfer much of the power of local government from elected officials to an appointed committee and a hired administrator. Finally, they maneuvered to dilute the voting strength of blacks by annexing white suburbs and gerrymandering the ward structure so that black voters would be unable to elect an additional alderman.

In a move first suggested by the Emergency Citizens Committee in 1943, business leaders began to forge a highly selective interracial alliance with an agenda of piecemeal change. For help they turned to the National Urban League. Founded in 1911, the Urban League was an interracial social welfare organization that sought to ameliorate some of the worst conditions of African American city life. The league was less politically engaged than the NAACP, but its local affiliates exercised a great deal of autonomy and were deeply involved in the affairs of many urban black communities. During World War II there had been talk in Winston-Salem as well as at the league's headquarters in New York about establishing an affiliate in the Twin City. Local 22's success had frightened white community leaders and stalled those discussions. In 1945 league officials again sought to open a beachhead in Winston-Salem by suggesting that the city participate in its recently established Community Relations Project (CRP). This time the city fathers were receptive, even enthusiastic about the plan.[26]

Funded by the General Education Board of the Rockefeller Foundation, the

CRP's goal was "to assist local community leadership in improving race relations and Negro welfare by removing the causes of racial tensions." Leaders in a troubled community had to request a survey of local conditions and, if their request was granted, to establish an advisory board to assist Urban League officials. A team headed by Dr. Warren Banner, a noted black sociologist and director of the CRP, would then conduct a month-long survey and present the results to the members of the advisory board, which would agree upon a set of problems in consultation with the CRP. Finally, specialists in health, housing, family and child welfare, recreation, and labor and industrial relations would develop specific recommendations for addressing those problems.[27]

James G. Hanes, as president of the Chamber of Commerce, and Caroline Wagner, executive secretary of the Community Council, invited an Urban League representative to meet with "Negro and white business men and prominent leaders of the community" in January 1946 to discuss the possibility of a CRP survey. Despite earlier fears among whites that the Urban League might be too radical, the representative "found no opposition and the fullest cooperation and interest in the Project."[28]

In April Dr. Banner held a follow-up meeting, this time with a committee established to prepare a CRP application. The committee included John C. Whitaker of Reynolds Tobacco Company, Gordon Gray, publisher of the *Journal*, James Hanes, and Carlyle Bethel of Wachovia Bank. No blacks were asked to serve. Although Banner assured the group that the purpose of the CRP was to avoid racial "conflict and conflagration," he faced "a very frank question and discussion period." Chairman Carlyle Bethel wanted to know what position the survey would take on school segregation and separate seating on buses. Banner had heard the question many times before. "We work within the framework of what is," he replied. "We have to accept the local pattern, or we could not work in Florida, South Carolina, Georgia and other southern states." He assured the committee that the CRP was "a community organization project only, and that it was not concerned with such social action as the revision of laws." Uplift, not social change, would be the order of the day.[29]

Equally sensitive was the issue of labor unions. Bethel read part of the CRP's report on Gary, Indiana, which stressed the importance of greater black participation in the United Steel Workers Union. Just the mention of unions caused consternation, and James Hanes reminded Banner that "we don't want anyone to come in and create a disturbance." Banner reassured them that Gary was an entirely different situation because, he said, it was a "one-company town" where the CIO was very powerful.[30]

Gordon Gray wondered "what would happen if the industrial relations man on the survey staff came here and recommended unionization to a committee made up predominantly of industrialists who did not believe in unions." Banner told Gray that in circumstances where unions discriminated against blacks, the CRP tried to find ways to improve relations between black and white workers. But the project did "not get into the controversy of whether Negroes should or should not belong to unions." "Then you never advocate union or non-union?" inquired committee member James Hanes. "Never," replied Banner. Gray, however, still worried that a labor member of the advisory committee might raise such issues. Hanes assured him that "we would not pick a labor leader for the committee unless he was also a good citizen."[31]

Reassured, the committee voted to apply for a CRP survey, provided that Banner supervise the project. The Urban League approved the application, and James Hanes accepted appointment as chairman of the local advisory board. As a former mayor of Winston-Salem, long-time chairman of the local county commissioners, and president of Hanes Hosiery, Hanes was Winston-Salem's premier civic and industrial leader. He had also been a member of the Emergency Citizens Committee. The sixty-one-member interracial advisory board, with forty-one whites and twenty blacks, read like a Who's Who of Winston-Salem white society. It included the city's most prominent businessmen, professionals, heads of women's organizations, clergymen, and directors of local welfare agencies. The African American representatives were equally well known. Among them were Daniel Andrews, president of the Negro Chamber of Commerce; Clark Brown, funeral home director; John Carter, principal of Atkins High School; Laura Fox, secretary of YWCA; insurance executive George Hill; Carl Russell, publisher of the *People's Spokesman*; and the Reverend Kenneth Williams. Not surprisingly, the list included no representatives from Local 22, although the union was at the height of its power and influence at the time of the study. The lone labor representative was E. L. Sandefur, the former state director of the CIO, who later became an outspoken foe of the tobacco workers' union, and even he was soon dropped from the board.[32]

Banner and an associate at the Urban League conducted a preliminary survey in November and December of 1946 and identified many issues that cried out for action. Using census data, municipal records, questionnaires sent to businesses and social agencies, and interviews with a wide range of community leaders, the Urban League researchers prepared reports on housing, employment, unions, crime, welfare, race relations, and a variety of other topics. Recommendations included increased public spending in health, education, and recreation; improved job opportunities for blacks in the public and private sectors; and the inclusion of blacks on local decision-making bodies. The *Journal* called the final report, issued in November 1947, "the blueprint for better community relations."[33]

In October 1948 the CRP acquired permanent funding and hired a full-time black field secretary, Harry Alston, a social worker with experience in other Urban League locations. Alston's job was, according to James Hanes, "to work among the Negro groups with the idea of developing a greater Christian leadership within his race and of promoting and pushing an ever-improving interracial relationship in Winston-Salem." By 1949, the CRP could boast of some progress. Alston reported in January that he had taken a number of small steps to improve race relations. Social service organizations added blacks to their staffs and boards, the police department hired additional black officers, and traditionally white federal and municipal agencies found employment for a few black workers.[34]

Support for the CRP represented an attempt by Winston-Salem's industrial oligarchy to recapture the high ground on race relations and delegitimize the workers' movement. The CRP assumed that money for racial betterment would come from white philanthropists, that it would be funneled through organizations controlled by white citizens, and that it would be used for projects that would not challenge existing class relations. Although black middle-class leaders had no role in the decision to bring in the CRP, their participation was vital to its success. Many welcomed the opportunity to meet and discuss community issues with their white counterparts and to find solutions to problems that affected so many of their race. No doubt some of the group's black members shared the belief of the white power brokers that gradualism offered the best solution to the problems of race relations. They may also have welcomed the opportunity to distance themselves from the union, whose success and continued demand for immediate reform threatened both their social position and their role as mediators between industrialists and the African American community.

The selection of the CRP advisory board made clear which leaders of the black community Hanes and his fellow industrialists were willing to recognize and constituted a direct rebuff to unionists who had been elected to their positions by thousands of black citizens. Not only did the project exclude representatives of the city's predominant African American organization, it included many of the very people who had attacked the CIO in 1943. Most questions of concern to workers— wages, benefits, working conditions, shop-floor democracy—received no mention.

This effort to promote carefully selected middle-class black leaders had an obvious political intent. But the attributes of leadership were infused with class considerations as well. The city's white elite still believed deeply in Governor Aycock's prescription of separate worlds for blacks and whites and shared his conviction that African American culture was deeply inferior to that of whites. As blacks became more civilized, the reasoning went, their society would increasingly resemble that of whites. One important indicator of black advancement would be its replication of the hierarchies of white society. Whites therefore saw working-class leadership within the black community as a sign of immaturity. The fact that much of that leadership was self-educated and female only compounded their negative assessment. If blacks were to be integrated into the public life of the community, middle-class men were their proper representatives.

By improving opportunities and conditions for African Americans and developing an alternative leadership cadre in the black community, white leaders maneuvered to maintain white supremacy. As during the Populist era, they also moved to restructure government so that the state would be less vulnerable to demands from a revitalized citizenry. Control of the state, particularly its policing, taxing, and regulating functions had been crucial to the ability of the industrial oligarchy to maintain tight control. Local 22's mobilization of African Americans and the emergence of white working class insurgents threatened that rule. This worker-based movement had put two members on the eight-person Board of Aldermen and actually had the numerical strength to control the board. Equally threatening was the fact that the union was making demands on the state, both to provide greater resources and services to underserved communities and to intervene in the economy.

In 1946, as chairman of the county commissioners, James Hanes had spearheaded the creation of a Committee of 100, a group of business and professional men who would patrol the halls of government in order to ensure greater efficiency and better financial planning. The inclusion of a few small business owners and professionals, including two African Americans, helped broaden the group's base and deflect attention from its domination by the bankers and industrialists who ran the town. Hanes had gotten the idea from the head of a similar committee in Philadelphia. There, ward-based politicians rooted in the city's ethnic communities controlled municipal government. Concerned about the presence of "inefficient (and dishonest) public servants," the Philadelphia committee provided instruction, oversight, and pressure to assure good government. In addressing the first meeting of the Winston-Salem committee, the visitor from Philadelphia acknowledged that the local situation was quite different but urged the group to carry on. "You don't have too much to cure," he said, "but you may have an awful lot to prevent as time goes on." Local 22 director Philip Koritz lambasted the committee as a group "who wish to control every process of a supposedly democratic city and county government." This "super-government," he told the *Sentinel*, would take power out of the hands of the electorate and put it in the hands of a small group of lawyers and businessmen.[35]

Over the next few years, the Committee of 100 conducted numerous studies of city issues and forwarded recommendations to the Board of Aldermen. Its first proposal urged the board to abandon deficit financing in favor of a balanced budget and raise local property taxes in an effort to pay off the accumulated city debt. During the 1920s, Winston-Salem had borrowed millions of dollars to upgrade its physical facilities. When the loans came due in the 1930s, depleted financial reserves made it impossible to pay off the notes. Rather than increase property taxes, which were among the lowest in the state, the city kept refinancing the loans; by the end of World War II, a significant portion of the city's revenues were going to pay off this debt. A disproportionate share of these past revenues had been spent on buildings and services for white citizens. Having provoked a fiscal crisis by their profligate spending and miserly taxation, whites now pleaded poverty as black citizens began to demand their rightful share of city services.[36]

The committee did recommend some increases in municipal spending. But rather than address the significant racial inequalities in schools, recreational facilities, and city services, it recommended increasing the size and budget of the police department and increasing wages for municipal employees. Low salaries had in fact contributed to a shrinking supply of well-qualified police officers, but the committee emphasized a different problem: "Labor unrest in the form of strikes," it argued, "had vastly increased the demands on police agencies," and "the postwar rise in crime rates put additional demands on the hard pressed police." Wage increases might also undermine the appeal of the United Public Workers of America–CIO, which was trying to organize municipal workers.[37]

When the committee pressured the Board of Aldermen to approve a bond referendum to expand the city's water supply, Local 22's shop stewards council articulated an alternative vision of how taxation and spending should be applied. "We hope that the present issues will arouse all citizens to take a more active interest in management of local affairs, and that a general overhaul of our financial structure will result, in which those groups and individuals who have profited most and are best able to pay will assume the responsibility in taxes proportionate to their means and adequate to the city's needs."[38]

The Committee of 100's most far-reaching recommendation was its call in the fall of 1947 for a city manager form of government for Winston-Salem. Under the existing mayor-council form, the Board of Aldermen established policy and the mayor oversaw day-to-day operations. The committee's plan called for a full-time professional city manager to become the city's chief administrator, with the board still setting policy.[39]

Growing towns like Winston-Salem certainly needed an efficiently managed municipal government, and the manager form was a step in that direction. But removing the day-to-day control of city government from the hands of the board minimized the power and influence of individual aldermen, just as blacks and white workers gained representation on the board for the first time. Kenneth Williams and Fred Denny, a representative from the white working-class Salem ward, might have had their differences with Local 22, but both were committed to pushing for expanded city services to the black and working-class communities.

For this reason, Local 22 members saw the city manager plan as a direct political threat. An issue of the union's weekly newsletter questioned the timing of the proposal: "Why, we should ask ourselves, has this big drive for a city manager come up, just when working people have begun getting a voice in city affairs?" The answer, the union believed, was that "for many years, politicians and big shots in Winston-Salem have looked on the city government as their private chicken-house. But recently the working people of the city have been moving toward getting a proper voice in city affairs. . . . The city manager plan looks like an effort by the big shots to get the chickens out of the hen-house before we get there."[40]

The shop stewards council discussed the measure and issued a statement urging citizens to vote against it. It argued that the plan was "a move toward getting full control of the city's affairs out of the hands of our elected Aldermen and Mayor, and centralized under the direction of one man who is not politically responsible to the city's voters. We consider that such a change is dangerous and undemocratic and also provides an opportunity for buck-passing and evasion of issues by elected city officials. The control of the city's affairs should be kept as closely as possible in the hands of the voters and the elected representatives who are directly responsible to them." When the plan came up for a public referendum, it passed by a small margin, in part because the union lacked the time and resources to get out a large vote.[41]

The removal of governmental functions from democratic scrutiny helped to prevent the unraveling of white supremacy, but further measures were needed to prevent blacks and working-class whites from gaining the political leverage that would enable them to challenge the extralegal influence of groups like the Community

Relations Project and the Committee of 100. For this, political leaders looked to two methods for diluting the black vote. The first was annexation. The second was gerrymandering, a favorite ploy of their nineteenth-century predecessors.[42]

To be sure, the annexation of white suburbs was a way to increase the city's tax base and population (city boosters were trying to reach the 100,000 mark for the 1950 census), but the addition of over 5,000 middle- and upper-class whites would also help offset black voting strength in the city. The problem was that under North Carolina law annexation had to be approved by a majority vote both of city residents and of those living in the affected areas, and here Democrats ran into the unintended consequences of their own elite rule. Although African Americans had been the primary target of disfranchisement in the early twentieth century, poor whites had been effectively denied the ballot at the same time. The narrowing of political discourse by the 1920s, particularly at the local level, had reduced politics to a game played by the local elite, with the occasional gadfly lawyer allowed to participate. As a result, voter participation rates were appallingly low. The early turnout for the vote on annexation was so small that the Junior Chamber of Commerce began calling local civic club members reminding them to vote. "If everybody votes," noted a Junior Chamber of Commerce member, "we will get the right decisions. If few vote, we won't." "Everybody" referred to whites, of course; the "few" were black voters. In fact, blacks made up 45 percent of the population, and if they registered and voted in mass, they might gain even more power than their numbers warranted. The annexation proposal passed, but just barely. Alarmed by the closeness of the outcome, city officials turned quickly to a "ward-splitting" plan that opponents called "discriminatory" and "gerrymandering of the rankest kind."[43]

After Kenneth Williams's election in 1947, local Democratic leaders had publicly expressed support for increased black participation in city government, asserting that it was yet another indicator of North Carolina's progressive approach to race relations. Simultaneously, the executive committee of the city's Democratic Party moved to replace the Twin City's four two-member wards with eight single-member wards. The new boundary lines would concentrate blacks in east Winston-Salem in one ward, thus assuring them a representative on the Board of Aldermen, while others would become a powerless minority in white-dominated wards.[44]

Black citizens expressed outrage. Kenneth Williams convened a meeting of the Piedmont Democratic Club, formed just before the 1948 presidential election to counter the influence of the Progressive Party and win black support for Democratic candidates. Although most of those present opposed the ward-splitting plan, Williams listed the pros and cons and reminded club members that the proposal would give blacks complete control of one ward, with registrars, judges, membership on the Democratic Executive Committee, and a guaranteed seat on the Board of Aldermen.

To Progressive Civic League president J. H. R. Gleaves, the proposal was "nothing more than segregating so Negroes can do what they want in a small way." Astutely sizing up the situation, he continued: "My experience in the South is that if you beat the white man at one trick, he will try another. And that's what they're getting ready to try." Other civic league members also condemned the plan, saying that it would limit a group that comprised well over one-third of the city's population to one out of eight representatives. The club delegated a committee to appear before the Board of Aldermen when the matter came up for discussion.[45]

The board considered the Democrats' ward-splitting plan at its first meeting in 1949. A parade of representatives from predominantly black organizations—the Ministerial Alliance, the Piedmont Democratic Club, Local 22, the Progressive Civic League, the Progressive Party, and the Baptist Ministers Conference—spoke in opposition. Their presence demonstrated the remarkable politicization of the black community over the previous decade. J. F. Lewis of the Piedmont Democratic Club charged that the constitutional rights of African Americans would be violated "by this type of gerrymandering" because the proposal would set "definite limits of political and civic participation on the part of the Negro." He estimated that roughly three-fourths of the black population had been placed in the new South Third Ward. The Reverend James S. Blaine, representing the Ministerial Alliance, said that "the splitting of the Third Ward as proposed would forever destroy the hope of our colored population for sharing a fair and just participation in our City's government." The Baptist Ministers Conference spokesman, the Reverend Kelley Goodwin, complained that no blacks in the Third Ward had been consulted about the proposal. Countering popular depictions of civil rights advocates as agents of subversion, he reminded the aldermen: "We are not aliens, we are citizens. We are not invaders, we are citizens."[46]

Although most opponents of the ward-splitting plan favored retention of the old system, representatives from Local 22, always in the vanguard, went further, suggesting that the number of aldermen be expanded to fifteen to coincide with the precincts used in state and national elections, an arrangement that more nearly approximated the one man, one vote principle. Speaking for the union, Robert Black told the aldermen that "the people of Winston-Salem have complained for a long time about the peculiar and confusing election set-up, with conflicting precincts and polling places for different elections." The union's plan, he said, was "the genuine way to get broader and more direct representation for all the citizens. . . .

The proposal of the Democratic Executive Committee would do nothing but block the growing influence of workers and small businessmen and tighten the present industrial control over the city affairs." Moranda Smith and Velma Hopkins were the only women to address the meeting, an indication of Local 22's promotion of women leaders. Smith criticized the proposal and lectured the board that "the only way to have real democracy in Winston-Salem is not to discriminate and not to segregate, but to work for all people, regardless of their race, creed, or color."[47]

Kenneth Williams had the difficult task of trying to convince his fellow aldermen that the plan was not in the city's best interest. He did so by resorting to the argument that was becoming a common refrain among liberal civil rights and labor leaders: that moderate reform was the only alternative to more radical social change. "We have set up here a situation that is hand-made for people who have foreign political beliefs and want to take advantage of Negroes," Williams told the aldermen. "We were hoping to get the negro vote behind the Democratic Party, and I still think we can, but I personally don't think it is much of a reward for the way some of us worked to see the negro vote for the Democratic Party, when there was a great possibility that the whole thing could have gone otherwise in the last national election."[48]

Anxious to avoid additional debate, the ward-splitting plan's sponsors asked for an immediate vote on the measure. Williams and City Attorney Irving Carlyle exchanged heated words about this departure from the customary practice of voting on a resolution only after discussion in committee. The aldermen, the city attorney, and the mayor, ever vigilant in the fight against subversion of the democratic process in other organizations, pushed through a motion to consider the proposal without further discussion. The vote was six to two in favor of the plan.[49]

Ignoring the extensive political involvement of African Americans in late-nineteenth-century Winston-Salem, one alderman boasted that the plan was "one of the most liberal and far-reaching steps that the Negro race had ever received in the South." No other southern city had gone so far as to guarantee black representation. The *Journal* too saw the proposal as "a great step forward." Chiding Williams and other "Negro leaders," the editors assured them that when they understood the "true nature and full scope and significance of the program," they would come around.[50]

Black citizens were not the only ones who saw the ward-splitting plan less as a sign of progress than as an effort to limit the growing influence of black and white working-class voters. At the next month's Board of Aldermen meeting, a representative of the Sun-Waugh Men's Civic Club requested that the proposed South Salem Ward be split into two wards to give residents of that part of town adequate representation. This largely white working-class area had a population almost equal to that in the South Third Ward and was therefore equally underrepresented.[51]

Ignoring these pleas, when Forsyth County representatives presented the proposal to the North Carolina legislature, which had final jurisdiction over local affairs, they included additional measures to restrict the franchise in Winston-Salem. Despite the Progressive Party's limited success, members of the Forsyth County delegation were taking no chances that a future challenge to the two-party system (in reality, of course, a one-party system) might succeed. They included a provision raising the petition requirements for independent candidates from 10 to 25 percent of the voters for that office in the past election. An even more draconian measure, designed to make it more difficult for potential voters to register, reduced the number of days registrars were on duty from ten to two and required registration books to be open only two Saturdays during the registration period, instead of every day.[52]

The same groups that had opposed the gerrymandering proposal before the Board of Aldermen pleaded with state legislators to defeat the bill. But the recommendations of the mayor and city attorney carried the day. In the House the bill passed by a vote of 118 to 6. The *Journal* reported that the nays were the result of "horse play—the favorite House practice of a few shouted votes against the bill just for the sake of being funny." What was an occasion for "horse play" in the all-white legislature was a serious defeat for the black citizens of Winston-Salem, who watched as the door to political empowerment, pushed open with such effort, slammed shut. Over the next seventeen years, the Board of Aldermen never included more than one member who represented the interests of the black community. Although back voters continued to register and vote, they found their influence in local government tightly constrained. Gerrymandering, the annexation of affluent white suburbs but not black ones, the adoption of the city manager form of government, and continued restrictions on registration cut short a struggle for full civic participation that aimed not only at reenfranchising blacks but at putting both class- and civil rights-based issues at the center of the Democratic Party agenda.[53]

Human Relations Techniques

With the termination of the collective bargaining agreement on April 30, 1948, Reynolds had moved to consolidate its control over the workforce. Although the formal grievance procedure had come to an end, the company feared, with justification, that the shop stewards would continue to exercise informal power on the plant floor. To limit their effectiveness, it began quietly transferring the more active stewards to other departments. Geneva McClendon, who quit rather than accept a transfer, described what happened. "After the union lost the contract, I went to work one morning—it was right after Labor Day, the day after Labor Day—and, as I say, I was working in the stemming division. And when I walked in the room that morning, they didn't send me back to my same job, they sent me to a plant called Number 38. And when I walked in this big huge room and there was a huge pipe that came down from the center of the building. Tobacco would drop down real hard. Everybody had their nose tied up and that dust was just flying every which way. And I looked in and I didn't see anything but shop stewards. This was the worst place you could work. When I saw there wasn't nothing in there but shop stewards, I turned around and said to the foreman, I said, 'This is the only place you got for me to work?' He said, 'Yes.' I said, 'Well, I don't want it.' Now Reynolds was a funny plant. They would fire you at the drop of a hat, but they didn't want you to quit. And the superintendent at that time told me if I would work that job that day, that he would let me pick my job the next day. Well, I didn't, but somehow I believe he'd have kept his word."[54]

Even as it worked to undermine shop floor leaders, Reynolds pushed to incorporate union initiatives into company policy. Over the life of four contracts, Local 22 had established new expectations of compensation, new definitions of workers' rights, and new procedures for handling conflicts. Even without a contract, these norms could not be changed overnight. Moreover, like the leaders of many of the nation's non-union firms, John Whitaker had come to realize that wage, benefit, grievance, and seniority policies introduced by collective bargaining could benefit the company by lessening the union's appeal. Despite the obituaries for the union in the *Journal* and Reynolds's official pronouncements, Whitaker also realized that Local 22 remained a powerful adversary in and out of the factory. The company sought to win back the support of its union-minded employees and elicit appreciation for the benefits the company bestowed. Guided by its own tradition of paternalism and inspired by a postwar resurgence of welfare capitalism spearheaded by the National Association of Manufacturers, Reynolds introduced wage increases, improved medical benefits, and a reorganized employment office. The company had held firm on wages during the 1947 strike and had repeatedly resisted union demands to reopen wage talks during the final contract. But as soon as the union was out of the way, it granted a general wage increase.[55]

Reynolds also unveiled an improved hospitalization plan that included partial coverage for employees' families. The *Journal* portrayed the innovation as "one of many programs inaugurated by enlightened and liberal employers to minister to the health, recreational, economic and other needs of their workers in this State." In a classic statement of welfare capitalism, the editorial continued, "There exists a growing spirit of mutual co-operation and strengthening of the 'family group' feeling which links everybody in a given plant from president to the humblest over-all worker in a common bond. The spirit is brought about by the sharing of benefits and the sharing of effort in the interests of the whole industrial 'family.' "[56]

As one of the patriarchs of that industrial family and the effective heir of R. J. Reynolds, John Whitaker had been trying for years to persuade superintendents and foremen to abandon the harsh "drive" system of factory discipline, but he had faced stiff resistance from both the board of directors and the supervisors. The workers' determined efforts to replace an arbitrary, personalistic style of labor-management relations with one based on a rational system of "industrial jurispru-dence" had confirmed the need for reform. Implicitly responding to this pressure, Whitaker professionalized his supervisory staff. In 1946 he introduced a *Management Information Bulletin* to instruct foremen in the proper ways to handle dis-putes. A few years later, the company began hiring college graduates into the super-visory ranks. In 1947 Reynolds officials guided the formation of the Winston-Salem Supervisor's Association to promote the professional development and enhance the status of the supervisory forces in the city's major industries.[57]

By then the board of directors had signed off on something that Whitaker had been advocating for almost thirty years: a plan to consolidate the company's cha-otic benefits and employment operations in a single, modern personnel office. Charles Wade, as administrative secretary to the board's Personnel Committee, be-came the de facto head of the new department in the spring of 1948 and took over as personnel manager the next year. A native of Morehead City, Wade had begun working at Reynolds in 1938 after graduating from Duke University with a degree in labor relations and personnel management. Wade's "benevolent style" con-trasted sharply with that of the bombastic Ed Bumgardner, and he put into place a systematic personnel policy based on the therapeutic "human relations" model in which he had been trained.[58]

Improved wage and benefits packages and more sophisticated personnel policies coupled with efforts to undermine shop floor leaders were common features of postwar management strategies. More unusual was Reynolds's intervention in the moral and spiritual lives of its workers. Southern textile magnates were notorious for their control of mill churches and their use of ministers as antiunion mouth-pieces. During the labor conflicts of the 1930s and in Operation Dixie, mill-sponsored screeds like the *Militant Truth* and the *Trumpet* had circulated particularly vicious forms of racism, anti-Semitism, and anti-Communism couched in the rhetoric of evangelicalism. Neither John Whitaker nor Reynolds board chairman James Gray was inclined to such shrillness, which would, in any case, have been counterproductive among black workers. But Whitaker was a devout Episcopalian, and from the beginning of his dealings with Local 22 he had often resorted to moral or psychological appeals. With the union now on the defensive, he returned to that strategy, putting R. J. Reynolds in the forefront of an alliance between business and religion that would have major ramifications in the decades to come.[59]

The key figure in this alliance was Norman Vincent Peale, one of the mid–twentieth century's most influential religious personalities. By 1944, Peale had built a vast religious empire, using pioneering communications techniques to saturate the country with his books, sermons, and direct mailings. The major link in this network was *Guideposts*, a compact, inspirational monthly modeled after *Reader's Digest*, which combined anti-Communism with the gospel of "practical Christianity."[60]

Peale's most influential book, *The Power of Positive Thinking*, topped the bestseller list in 1952. It held that "the answer to people's troubles lay within themselves, in the divine energy stored within the unconscious, which they had only to tap into through prayer and positive thinking." Peale saw his message as a means of preserving traditional American values and returning the country to a simpler time. In fact, it forwarded a distinctly modern therapeutic culture based not on traditional communities but on the plastic, psychological self. His combination of therapeutic evangelicalism (a counseling clinic was the centerpiece of his New York ministry), cutting-edge communications technologies, and conservative politics would saturate the 1950s and reemerge spectacularly in the 1970s, when the religious right burst upon the American political scene.[61]

Peale was especially eager to build an alliance with the business community, and from the outset *Guideposts* depended on the support of industrialists, who distributed free copies to their workers and sometimes to neighboring school districts. The star performer in this group was R. J. Reynolds. Attracted to Peale's message and anxious to direct attention away from the conflicts that had wracked the company throughout the war, Whitaker and James Gray began sending copies of *Guideposts* to the homes of all supervisors in the fall of 1947. In January 1949 Whitaker helped bring Peale to Winston-Salem. Speaking to an audience that included the mayor and more than 500 members of Winston-Salem's all-white, all-male civic organizations, Peale touted *Guideposts* as a vehicle of religious awakening that would simultaneously "save American freedom" and cure modern psychological ills. At the end of Peale's address, John Whitaker rose to announce that henceforth Reynolds would send the monthly magazine to all 12,000 regular Reynolds employees, a practice the company continued for many years at a cost of $25,000 annually. *Guidepost* officials estimated that someone received the publication in every other home in the city. Nowhere else in the country did the monthly enjoy such broad circulation.[62]

Whitaker had begun at least a year earlier to search for even more direct ways of affecting employees' personal lives. In the fall of 1949, he found the person he was looking for: a white Methodist minister, the Reverend Clifford H. Peace, whom he hired to serve as an "industrial chaplain" in the plant. This move received wide publicity in the national press. Taking credit not only for the benefits the company provided to its workers but for all those the union had so painstakingly extracted, Whitaker told a writer for the *American Magazine* that while the company had long offered high wages, vacations, and other material benefits, he had become increasingly convinced that it should also attend to workers' spiritual needs. Lacking "a basic faith to give meaning and purpose to their lives," he argued, they engaged in destructive behavior both on and off the job. What they needed to cure these symptoms of "misery and heartsickness" was "Christianity with Its Sleeves Rolled Up."[63]

Clifford Peace seemed to be the perfect man for the job. He had grown up on a tobacco farm near High Point, North Carolina, graduated from High Point College, and attended divinity school at Duke University, working in the Durham tobacco factories to pay his way through school. After distinguished service as a chaplain in the army air force and a term as a pastor in western North Carolina, Peace was persuaded by Whitaker to give up his pastorate and take on this novel role. He began his duties by meeting every supervisor and worker in Reynolds's maze of plants and then settled into a routine of individual counseling and in-house prayer meetings. At his request, the company built a small chapel beside his office.[64]

On the surface, Peace's job looked relatively straightforward. People sought his counsel, and he responded to a long litany of marital difficulties, family tensions, and alcohol-related problems with a combination of psychology and admonitions based on Christian faith. Like Norman Vincent Peale, Peace saw such problems not as social issues but as manifestations of an individual "emotional sickness" endemic to modern life. He was quite aware of the ambiguities of his position and sought to distance himself from supervisors who had responded to workers' problems—scrapes with the law, threatening landlords, sick children, and the like—by doing favors, playing favorites, and taking advantage of the people who were thus in their debt. Peace assured the press that anything an employee told him would be held in confidence; he had, moreover, insisted on the company's promise that he could "follow his conscience when counseling an employee even when his opinion ran counter to that of management." By all reports, he kept his word and was a sensitive and circumspect advisor. Blanche Fishel visited him "once or twice" and remembered that in addition to talking to people in his office, he often toured the plants "to see these people that would be in different kinds of trouble."[65]

Nevertheless, the chaplain's presence carried a political lesson. Black workers, along with some whites, had embraced collective action in addition to calling on the help of God and individual determination. They had also created an elaborate shop stewards system that allowed them to share their problems with one another. Norman Vincent Peale and Clifford Peace, by contrast, preached a gospel that downplayed group solidarity, communication, and effort in the name of self-improvement and the "power of positive thinking." Praising Reynolds's innovative venture, the *Journal* made the point clear: the new counselor was expected to restore a sense of a "community of interest" to industrial relationships and to demonstrate that "the world cannot be made right by organization." And Reynolds was happy to report that labor turnover, absenteeism, accidents, and other thorns in management's side diminished after Peace arrived.[66]

Peace's appointment also represented management's clear assertion that religion and unionization did not mix. Since 1943, opponents of Local 22 had argued that the union had co-opted black ministers, both those, like Frank O'Neal, who worked in the plants and those, like R. M. Pitts, who did not. These militant church leaders had helped to organize workers and spoke out against Jim Crow. A racial moderate who would participate in interracial forums in the 1950s, Peace kept careful track of the race and sex of the employees who sought him out and published case histories, protected by pseudonyms, that always included stories of blacks and whites alike. But he made little headway with the eighty black ministers he found working in the plants. They were, Whitaker noted, " 'quite a power' in the corporation and community," and they viewed Peace with suspicion. Peace courted them dutifully, but he also spoke out, at least implicitly, against the activism of the black church, arguing, as Reynolds did, for ministerial neutrality.[67]

Peace's efforts had mixed results. Many workers were devout Christians, and, reflecting a nationwide trend, local religious activities and church membership had grown dramatically after the end of the war. Reynolds had a long tradition of in-plant prayer services, conducted by workers themselves during breaks or between shifts, and Peace reported that these increased in number after he came, among blacks as well as whites. Not surprisingly, the chaplain also noted that he had "brought more solace to his white charges than to the colored cohorts." At a time when African Americans made up approximately half of the workforce, Peace reported that only seventy blacks, as opposed to 451 whites, consulted him over a two-and-a-half-year period.[68]

When Clifford Peace arrived in Winston-Salem in the fall of 1949, the plants were buzzing with the charges and countercharges of a hard-fought, three-way organizing drive. White workers, bruised by poverty and the perpetual crises of working-class life, not to mention the specific anxieties of Cold War America, may well have welcomed Peace's reassurances. But the city's black workers had not given up on collective solutions.

CHAPTER FIFTEEN

Trust the Bridge That Carried Us Over

As the ward-splitting controversy wound to an end in the early months of 1949, Local 22 focused once again on the workplace. Knowing that the union remained hamstrung by the FTA's refusal to sign the Taft-Hartley affidavits and its loss of NLRB protection, Reynolds had refused to negotiate when its contract expired in 1948. As Local 22 prepared to try to win back its bargaining rights, the company took pains to stand above the fray, quietly reaping the benefits both of the CIO's internecine conflicts and of anti-Communist hysteria, which peaked in the wake of the Wallace presidential campaign.

At first, Local 22 watched helplessly as its old rival, the TWIU-AFL, as well as a tiny CIO union, the United Transport Service Employees (UTSE), stepped forward to try to fill the institutional void. It finally reentered the contest in August 1949 when FTA officials signed the non-Communist affidavits. In so doing, it precipitated an extraordinary confrontation between one of the last vigorous outposts of a waning Southern Front and the emergent Cold War political culture. "Trust the Bridge That Carried Us Over" was the slogan Local 22 used to mobilize workers to reject the entreaties of the TWIU and UTSE as well as the attacks on FTA. Ironically, it became the clarion call of R. J. Reynolds as well, as it fought one more time for the hearts and minds of the workers.

The 1949 Organizing Campaign

In the spring of 1949, organizers for both the TWIU and UTSE began converging on Winston-Salem. Local 22 still lacked NLRB standing, which meant that it could count only on the loyalty of its constituency to stave off these competitors and bring Reynolds back to the bargaining table. The rivalry between Local 22 and the TWIU was longstanding. The presence of a raiding CIO union, on the other hand, signaled a drastic change in the labor movement and in the political climate generally.

Throughout the CIO's history, it had accommodated a wide range of political views. FTA had always stood firmly on the federation's left wing, along with the Mine, Mill, and Smelter Workers, which also managed to form biracial locals in the Jim Crow South, and the much more powerful United Electrical Workers Union. There had been recurrent tensions between the left and the federation's more conservative unions, especially those that represented workers from Eastern Europe, whose hatred of the Soviet Union was reinforced by the growing anti-Communism of the Catholic Church, as well as with some national officials, who saw the leftists as too ideological, too tied to the Soviet Union, and too uncompromising in their promotion of black civil rights. But until 1947, a broad center-left consensus reigned, and, at least in principle, the CIO was united behind FDR's vision of world peace based on the continuation of the United States's wartime collaboration with the Soviet Union as well as a renewal and expansion of the New Deal. The mounting antagonism between the two superpowers, however, dragged the federation into the international arena, bringing its factional rifts into sharp relief. The Progressive Party campaign dealt the CIO's fragile unity a final blow. In its wake, the CIO's executive board moved not only to curb the political autonomy that international unions and even locals had always enjoyed but also to isolate and undermine the left-wing unions. It did so chiefly by insinuating unions sympathetic to the national CIO leadership into election campaigns where rival organizations competed for representation, even if the raiding unions had little affinity with the workers involved.[1]

Virtually since its inception as UCAPAWA, FTA had been a thorn in the side of the national CIO leadership. William Smith, director of the North Carolina CIO, had had run-ins with Local 22 over the leaf house workers' drive during Operation Dixie, and he had become even more critical when the union channeled its resources into the Progressive Party campaign. Seizing the chance to oust the FTA's leading local, he asked CIO officials to support an organizing drive in Winston-Salem led by UTSE, a small, mostly African American union whose membership consisted primarily of "red caps," baggage handlers at the nation's railway stations and airline terminals.[2]

UTSE's president, Willard Townsend, the first black member of the CIO's executive board, had attended college in Canada, helped to organize the union as an AFL affiliate while working as a red cap in Chicago, and then brought UTSE into the CIO in 1942. Townsend's contribution to Rayford Logan's *What the Negro Wants* (1944) was an eloquent statement of the social democratic vision that animated the Popular Front coalition. His willingness to participate in this raid on FTA, a union that exemplified so many of his stated ideals, suggests just how polarized the political climate had become. It also suggests how destructive the CIO's policy could be, since no matter how the election turned out there was virtually no chance that this small red caps' union could effectively represent FTA's constituency of food and agricultural workers.[3]

The corruption of CIO policy was revealed in other ways as well. Just before the UTSE drive began, Robert Black got a summons to meet William Smith in Charlotte. Black believed that "Bill Smith and the Reynolds Tobacco personnel had worked this deal up" to persuade him to leave FTA and help to bring Reynolds workers into UTSE. " 'We'll put you on the organizing payroll of the Southern Organizing Drive [Operation Dixie] at a fancy sum of money,' " Black remembered Smith saying, " 'and all we want you to do is just to go back to Winston-Salem to that executive board meeting and announce to all the board members that Local 22 is corrupt, the international union is corrupt, and that you are taking a walk and you are appealing to everyone else who is an honest trade unionist to get up and take a walk with you. There'll be a person in that meeting that will have $750 in cash money, and in thirty minutes after you leave that meeting that person will contact you. Now that money will be for you and your family until we can work out the details. You've got a job on the Southern Organizing Drive. You can report to me here in Charlotte. We'll assign you out of town until the wind blows over.' "

Black was noncommittal, but he returned to Winston-Salem and discussed what had happened with FTA and Local 22 officials. With their encouragement, he got up at the beginning of the Local 22 executive board meeting and said that he had an announcement to make. Instead of denouncing FTA, he told the officers and stewards about the offer. When he finished, "one of the real honest trade unionists got up and said, 'Well, Brother Black, I want to tell you something. Had you gone along with that scheme, I personally would have killed you. After we have gone this far, I personally would have killed you. You never would have been able to walk the streets in Winston-Salem.' "[4]

Unable to persuade Black to join forces with UTSE, Willard Townsend selected Frank Hargrove, a white CIO organizer, to head the drive in Winston-Salem. It was a good choice. Hargrove was a former FTA representative who had played a central role in the initial organizing campaign at Reynolds in 1943 and served as the first director of Local 22. According to one of his CIO colleagues, Hargrove's disillusionment with FTA began when Frank Green replaced him in Winston-Salem in 1945. Green, a young white North Carolinian, got the job, Hargrove felt, because of his Communist Party connections, not his trade union experience. Nevertheless, Hargrove had left amicably for another FTA assignment, and he was still well known and liked by many of the workers. William Smith also assigned Elijah Jackson, a black state CIO official who had been nominally in charge of the eastern North Carolina leaf house drive, to the UTSE staff, and he promised the "entire facilities" of the state organization to aid in the campaign.[5]

Hargrove honed in immediately on FTA's refusal to sign the non-Communist affidavits required by the Taft-Hartley Act. "Had the FTA complied with the terms of the act two years ago," he pointed out, "it is quite possible it might be the bargaining agent for the Reynolds workers today. But it elected to follow the political line of the Communist Party rather than protect the economic rights and the welfare of its members. It should have protected the people in spite of the fact that it didn't like the new labor law. Thus the R. J. Reynolds workers were tossed to the wolves so that a few top officers of the FTA could make the newspaper headlines and conform to the policies and dictates of the American Communist Party."[6]

Hargrove was right in one sense: FTA's refusal to sign the affidavits was Local 22's Achilles' heel, and in retrospect many local FTA activists saw it as a strategic blunder. In one stroke it deprived Local 22 of its federal allies, confirmed the worst suspicions of its anti-Communist detractors, frightened away white workers, and confused black supporters, some of whom even signed petitions to allow UTSE and the TWIU to come in rather than be left with no representation whatsoever. At the same time, coming from a former friend, Hargrove's attack seemed to be a stab in the back. Even staunch anti-Communists like Philip Murray had initially refused to sign the affidavits; the left-led unions had banked on CIO-led protests to repeal the law, and leftists on the FTA executive committee (whether or not they were Party members) had good reason to see their refusal to sign as principled trade unionism, however much it may also have reflected the stance of the Communist Party. Moreover, Hargrove must have known that UTSE had neither the time nor the resources—nor, very likely, the know-how—to build an organization among tobacco workers. This was a raid by one CIO union on another, designed more to destroy one of the federation's largest and most dynamic black-led locals than to establish a viable alternative union.

Having failed in its attempt to persuade rank-and-file leaders like Robert Black to abandon FTA, UTSE's best hope was to target "opinion makers" who might persuade the workers to support an alternative CIO union. "In order to offset the disruption caused by FTA during past years," wrote William Smith, "we have to do a public relations job." Following a strategy that had become a centerpiece of Operation Dixie, Smith requested that the CIO send in Ruth Gettinger, a white public relations specialist, "to arrange meetings with the colored ministers and the white ministers for us." Gettinger spent considerable time in Winston-Salem over the next few months, meeting with ministers, civic leaders, and governmental administrators. "I have been concentrating on interviews with the city governing board and other city fathers," she reported. "I have a few others to see and then I want to see some more ministers *and also some of the workers*."[7]

While UTSE looked to civic leaders, the TWIU concentrated on white workers. The AFL affiliate had maintained a low profile in Winston-Salem since its decisive defeat in the 1943 election, servicing its locals at Brown & Williamson, but doing little else. Now it brought in a large staff of organizers—as many as thirty to forty at one time—to concentrate on the white workers who were becoming an increasingly large percentage of the workforce at Reynolds. As in the past, the union announced that it would follow "the Southern tradition" of maintaining separate locals for blacks and whites. By July 1949, TWIU representatives were so confident of their efforts—or perhaps so sure that Reynolds would view them as the lesser of three evils—that they asked the company for recognition as the workers' bargaining agent. When the company quickly rejected that proposal, the TWIU presented the NLRB with authorization cards from over 30 percent of the workers and petitioned for an election.[8]

At the same time, FTA announced that its officials would comply with the Taft-Hartley Act and sign the anti-Communist affidavits. It had little choice. Few of its locals had the economic muscle to win contracts with no federal protection, and raids by the AFL and CIO unions were taking a devastating toll. To avoid signing, Donald Henderson resigned his post as FTA president and became the union's national administrative director. The NLRB, however, refused to accept affidavits from other union officers as long as Henderson remained on the staff. Finally, Henderson admitted that he had once been a member of the Communist Party and signed an affidavit. The NLRB then recognized FTA as a legitimate union under the terms of the Taft-Hartley Act, and the international committed itself to an intensive drive to regain bargaining rights in Winston-Salem.[9]

In mid-October, NLRB officials arrived in Winston-Salem to conduct hearings in preparation for an election, and Local 22 began its campaign in earnest. Within a few weeks, however, FTA found itself facing not only a CIO-backed raid on its most important southern local but the threat of expulsion from the federation. At the CIO's October convention in Cleveland, Philip Murray and his allies asked delegates to authorize changes in the federation's constitution allowing the executive board to refuse to seat Communist Party members and to expel any affiliate deemed to have followed policies directed toward achievement of the Party's "program" or "purposes." The resolutions passed over bitter resistance from the left-led unions, and the CIO brought charges against FTA and eleven other unions (including two that had already left in protest) and prepared to hold "trials" demonstrating a "systematic pattern of pro-Soviet behavior" on the part of the accused members.[10]

Throughout the fall and winter, Reynolds officials stood on the sidelines and watched the battle unfold as Local 22, backed by a besieged and weakened international, exchanged charges with its two rivals over the radio, in the newspaper, and on the streets around the factories. In early November Neil Hickey, head of the International Woodworkers Union in North Carolina, replaced Frank Hargrove as director of the UTSE drive. Hickey, a native of Butte, Montana, and a thirty-four-year veteran of the labor movement, followed a simple plan: UTSE would claim the mantle of the CIO, present an organizing platform very similar to Local 22's, and brandish the charge of Communist domination, citing the CIO's charges against FTA. He broadcast his message in a series of hard-hitting weekly radio programs claiming that workers had four choices in the upcoming election: the insecurity of no union, a Communist-led union, the "aging, crafty A.F. of L. soft-living bureaucrats," or UTSE-CIO.[11]

UTSE's campaign devolved, in large part, into a battle for history. At its heart lay two conflicting narratives about the rise and fall of Local 22 and, beyond that, about the evolution of the CIO. The anti-FTA narrative began in 1943 when, seemingly out of nowhere, the CIO arrived in Winston-Salem and built Local 22. "It was the talk of Winston-Salem. Thousands of workers attended mass meetings. . . . Local plant leaders learned how to make their union work for them." The union "won the support of many public spirited citizens outside the plant." Then, "in late 1944, FTA . . . sent in new representatives [a reference to Local 22 directors Frank Green and Philip Koritz] who believed more in the program of the Communist Party than in the CIO." They recruited local leaders into the Communist Party, which took control of the union; those "who opposed the communists were pushed aside." The story then jumped to a national stage, where "the communist bloc in the CIO," declining to go along with majority rule, refused to sign the anti-Communist affidavits and endorsed the Progressive Party. When Local 22's contract expired in 1948, Reynolds refused to negotiate with the union, not because

Congress had passed the Taft-Hartley Act over the vociferous objections of the CIO; not because FTA officials, having refused to sign the affidavits required by that law, as had others in and out of the Party, lost the services of a government agency financed by FTA members' tax dollars; not because R. J. Reynolds, exploiting that political advantage, refused to bargain in good faith; and not because it was virtually impossible for unskilled workers in industries like tobacco processing to win contracts unless the NLRB stepped in to hold elections. Rather, according to this narrative, the union lost its contract in 1948 and "was unable to do anything about it" because workers had "lost their enthusiasm for FTA because of its communist policy."[12]

It was true that FTA officials had assigned Frank Green and Philip Koritz to Local 22 in part because of their political affiliations and that a number of local leaders had either joined or allied themselves with the Communist Party. But Frank Hargrove's departure had not spelled the end of the Golden Age of the CIO in Winston-Salem; it occurred at the beginning of Local 22's heyday. That institutional flowering and political expansion flowed directly from the efforts of local people, drawing strategically on a range of resources and allies, including the Communist Party, and guided by a shrewd sense of strategy and an expansive vision of a democratic future. An identity-making process of collective action, made meaningful both by past experience and by exposure to the core of beliefs that animated the Southern Front, had created a tenacious sense of ownership: Local 22 was the workers' invention, their vehicle, the product of their sentiments and aspirations. And even in 1949, after seemingly overwhelming setbacks and attacks, after one obituary after the other, Local 22's leaders were confident that the majority of the workers still felt that commitment—so confident that they had entered a three-way race against two old antagonists, TWIU and R. J. Reynolds, and a new foe, their own national industrial federation, even while still burdened with the incubus of the unsigned Taft-Hartley affidavits. What UTSE did not allege was that Local 22's record in the factory or the community demonstrated anything but militant, civil rights–oriented trade unionism. Nor did UTSE seriously present itself as a plausible vehicle for tobacco workers' ambitions. Its leaflets, newspaper ads, and radio programs barely mentioned its own name; instead, they asked workers to vote for the CIO. And they offered a program that paralleled Local 22's point for point, even down to the union's slum clearance program.[13]

Like this local struggle, the CIO's expulsion of the left-led unions turned on conflicting readings of history. In the months leading up to the FTA's trial by a panel of CIO executive board members, the CIO's research department pored through the *Daily Worker* and the *FTA News*, cobbling together parallel statements on political issues.[14] In accordance with the federation's revised constitution, the executive board charged FTA with forwarding the interests of the Communist Party rather than those of the CIO. "The Communist Party in America," the trial committee argued, "is part of the world-wide Communist movement which seeks to organize workers into unions in various countries to spearhead a revolution for the establishment of a proletarian dictatorship. The first such dictatorship was established in Russia, and the entire movement is primarily dedicated to protecting and preserving this dictatorship." Although the Party "sought to rationalize its program in terms of the needs of American labor," it was doing do so only in order to defend the Soviet Union. The evidence consisted primarily of FTA's criticisms of Truman's foreign policies. The charges also mentioned the union's support for Henry Wallace as an "additional link" that helped to prove its adherence to the Party line. The only charge related to FTA's trade union record was that it had lost members over the previous few years. FTA's membership *had* declined, but the charge of underperformance failed either to take account of its commitment to organizing the most vulnerable of workers or to demonstrate that the CIO's mainstream internationals could or would do better.[15]

Local workers, including people like Robert Black, Velma Hopkins, and Moranda Smith, disappeared in this rewriting of history, subsumed by the assumption that outsiders—FTA and Communist Party officials—had, after the glory days of 1943, called the shots. Speaking to a small group of CIO union directors in January 1950, George Baldanzi, who was still serving as director of the CIO's faltering Operation Dixie and as vice president of the Textile Workers Union, made explicit what more diplomatic spokesmen implied. FTA, he said, was preying upon the "ignorance and prejudice" of blacks by telling them that only the Communists would fight their battles. "I am convinced," Baldanzi continued, "that 85 percent of the people in Winston-Salem who think they are Communists don't know the difference between communism and rheumatism." In a reprise of Operation Dixie's main grievance against Local 22—that it had stirred up whites' racial feelings by recruiting blacks too aggressively and pushing black civil rights—Baldanzi concluded with the claim that FTA had "done more harm than the KKK itself."[16]

"Trust the Bridge That Carried Us Over," Local 22's slogan throughout the 1949 campaign, encapsulated its defense: the union embodied workers' aspirations and its record justified the workers' trust. A political cartoon printed in numerous union leaflets and publications graphically depicted that message, which was packed with Afro-Christian allusions. It shows three bridges spanning a deep river gorge. Two muscular male workers in overalls climb up from the foreground. With the black worker in the lead, they approach the edge of the gorge. On the other side lies a union contract. A rickety, wooden bridge labeled AFL stands upstream, with a sign marked "Condemned" hanging on the entrance. "My grandfather fell thru the first one," says the black worker, referring to the ill-fated efforts of the segregated TWIU to organize Reynolds. Farther downstream an uncovered plank, marked only with the letters UTSE, juts out across the ravine, held up only by balloons labeled "False Promises." An "Unsafe" sign warns away potential users. "The second one won't even reach the other side," observes the worker. Directly in front of the men stands a sturdy brick structure with protective walls on either side. The path down the middle reads "Local 22 FTA." "Negro-White Unity" is emblazoned on one wall, "$50,000,000 Won" on the other. The two workers agree on which route to take over the modern version of the River Jordan: that offered by a solidly built interracial local. "The third is strong—Trust the Bridge That Carried Us Over!"[17]

Throughout the campaign, Local 22 sounded the themes of interracial unity. And no one addressed them with more conviction than Robert Black. Having entered the factories as a young boy in 1913, he had seen one union campaign after the other falter on the rock of racial divisions. "Reynolds," he said in a radio broadcast, "has tried to keep us from realizing that our economic problems are the same and that only through our united strength ... will we be able to win in our struggle. In recent years," he continued, "we, you and I, the Negro and white workers of Reynolds, began to build this kind of unity. And though our beginnings were small to be sure, in a short five years we have been able to win holidays and vacations with pay, job security, a shop steward system that won justice for hundreds of aggrieved workers and decent treatment for all, and fifty million dollars in wage increases." TWIU and UTSE were splitting the workers and playing "directly into the hands of the company," he argued. The AFL had "only contempt for the Negro workers" and would set up a segregated local; UTSE was a "catch-all union for Negro workers" that made no effort to organize whites. "I, as a Negro worker," Black continued, "am just as opposed to an all-Negro union as I am to an all-white union where the companies hire both Negro and white workers. . . . I am for the only kind of a union which can defeat R. J. Reynolds—a union of Negro-white unity, with both white and Negro leadership."[18]

The bridge to a contract, however, was blocked not just by rival unions but by charges of Communist domination that Local 22 could not ignore. It could hardly deny that many FTA leaders and rank-and-file activists were or had been members of the Communist Party: Anne Mathews had named names, and Donald Henderson had recently admitted being a Party member. But local activists could not pub-

Local 22 and FTA officials confer during 1950 election campaign. *Left to right:* Robert Black, John Tisa, Robert Lathan, and Donald Henderson. (*FTA News*)

licly admit their Party affiliations without paying what they saw as an intolerable price. Since 1947, witnesses called before HUAC had found themselves fired, blacklisted, and worse, whether they cited the Fifth Amendment and invoked their right to remain silent or answered "Yes" to the dreaded question, "Are you or have you ever been a member of the Communist Party?" Beginning in 1949, high-level Party members went to trial under the Smith Act of 1940, which made "advocating the violent overthrow of the government" a federal offense. A bill outlawing the Communist Party was pending before the North Carolina legislature.[19]

In the end, Local 22 leaders responded with silence, deflection, and assertions about the democratic nature of their union. Many unionists—Party and non-Party members alike—kept silent throughout their lives, motivated by a variety of beliefs and fears: the knowledge that to come forward now would be suicidal for the union; devotion to the principles of free speech and association; fear for themselves and their families; reluctance to implicate others; embarrassment born of defeat and the drumbeat of red-baiting; or, perhaps most important, the conviction that, whatever their degree of involvement with the Party, Local 22 had been a democratic workers' movement and they had in fact been good trade unionists above all.

Usually, they tried to frame the issue as a red herring, a strategy that continued to resonate for many southerners, given how often and indiscriminately the Communist epithet had been hurled at any hint of reform. Robert Lathan took that approach. A leaf house worker who at the outset of his involvement could barely read and write, Lathan had attended Party schools and, in part as a consequence, became an international vice president of FTA. "Red-baiting means yelling 'Communist!,'" he told a radio audience. "Local 22 demands 26½ cents, that's why they call us Communist. . . . Local 22 fights against the Taft-Hartley Law, fights for a $1.00 minimum wage, fights for civil rights, fights to expand social security, fights for a medical and health insurance program, fights against high taxes for workers, fights for aid to education, that's why they call us Communist."[20]

Local 22's treasurer, Willie Grier, who does not seem to have been a Party member, tried to counter the persistent charge that left-led unions were undemocratic and dishonest because they were secretly dominated by Communists by describing his own contrary experience. "For four years," he said, "I had the privilege of serving the workers in Reynolds and our union . . . as an officer. During these years I attended almost every meeting of the officers and executive board of Local 22. I went to the meetings of the shop stewards councils—and the departmental meetings. You might say I was on the inside of Local 22 all during that time. I know, from my own experience, just how we, the workers ran our union. . . . I signed every check that was written in Local 22 for four years. I, a Negro worker, signed them. And right next to my signature was the name of the financial secretary, a white worker. To me that was a symbol of Local 22, because that is what it takes to make a union good and strong. . . . It takes the signatures and support of all workers. . . . In Local 22 we knew that next to unity, the most important key to strength is democracy. Don't let anyone fool you. We, the workers, ran Local 22. We had real democracy in Local 22. . . . Maybe, sometimes, if you were like me, after you had sat in a meeting two hours after work when you were tired, you felt we had too much democracy! But, of course, you can't have too much democracy. Those meetings made us strong."[21]

Defending itself before the CIO tribunal, FTA took a similar tack. It made no effort to dispute the parallels between its pronouncements on political issues and those of the Communist Party, claiming only that it had a right to political expression. But it did deny the charge that it had followed the "policies and programs" of the Communist Party rather than the "objectives of the CIO Constitution." Centering its defense on its democratic structure and its record of pursuing the interests of American workers, FTA relied heavily on presentations by rank-and-file leaders, including Robert Black. These witnesses detailed numerous ways in which CIO officials had interfered with the democratic rights of FTA and its locals, including CIO-PAC's effort to prevent Local 22 from backing Kenneth Williams in his historic bid for a seat on the Winston-Salem Board of Aldermen in 1947 and from endorsing of the Progressive Party in 1948.[22]

Ironically, even as Local 22 was defending its participation in the Southern Front alliance that elected Williams, the alliance itself lay in tatters. At the national level, the deepening divisions between liberals and leftists in the civil rights, anticolonial, and labor movements had emerged in full force during the Progressive Party campaign. Locally, Kenneth Williams, Progressive Civic League president J. H. R. Gleaves, and others had lambasted Local 22 for leading black voters into a "dead-end destination." Now, as the Reynolds campaign reached into the early months of 1950, that parting of ways stood out in sharp relief.[23]

To bolster UTSE's appeal in the black community, union president Willard Townsend called on his friend Mary McLeod Bethune. As the founder and former president of Bethune-Cookman College, director of black affairs in the National Youth Administration, and long-time president of the National Council of Negro Women, Bethune had ties to Franklin and Eleanor Roosevelt and was one of the most influential black leaders in the United States. In 1946 she had appeared with Paul Robeson at a Madison Square Garden rally of "anti-imperialist and democratic forces" opposed to Truman's foreign policies.[24] That same year, she visited Winston-Salem as part of a membership drive for the SCHW. Like Walter White of the NAACP and others, however, she had made an abrupt turn after 1947, allying herself with the Truman administration and combining the fight against racial discrimination with fervent anti-Communism. Appearing in Winston-Salem with Townsend and Kenneth Williams on a program attacking FTA, Bethune praised the city's workers for joining the CIO but admonished them for permitting "their organization to fall into the hands of a small group of political carpet-baggers . . . somewhere along the road."[25]

Local 22 countered with a statement by Charlotte Hawkins Brown, a veteran of many of the same women's organizations through which Bethune had risen and one of North Carolina's most influential black women leaders. The founder of Palmer Memorial Institute in nearby Sedalia, Brown had been active in the SCHW and its affiliate, the Committee for North Carolina. There she had met the impressive women leaders of Local 22, who asked her to come to Winston-Salem to help counter the impact of her long-time ally. She too spoke at a rally, ending with a very different admonition, based on an alternative reading of history: "Trust the Bridge That Carried You Over."[26]

Kenneth Williams's growing hostility toward Local 22 was the most serious manifestation of the collapse of the Southern Front. The alderman owed his position, and thus his ability to influence local affairs, to Local 22 and the thousands of black workers who had voted for him. The CIO-PAC had registered the voters and organized his campaign, even writing some of his campaign speeches. The union had backed Williams, a middle-class minister and college professor, rather than a working-class candidate in order to ensure solidarity within the African American community. Williams's relationship with the union had been brittle from the start, however, and he was determined to chart an independent course. In his role as the city's only elected black official, he took on the time-honored role of mediator between the black community and the white elite in Winston-Salem. On issues such as public housing, gerrymandering, and black representation on the police force, he had supported the union's position. But when the union asked the Board of Aldermen to pressure Reynolds to pay into the unemployment compensation pool, Williams had refused.

In the spring of 1949, just before FTA signed the Taft-Hartley affidavits and entered the organizing campaign, Williams had come up for reelection. This time Local 22 activists were divided over how to respond. Some thought a working man should step forward, and Local 22 treasurer Willie Grier threw his hat in the ring. Grier and Williams had been high school friends, and both had worked during the summer at Reynolds, but after graduation their lives had unfolded very differently. Grier went to work full-time at Reynolds in 1930 and married in 1933. During the Depression, he joined what he ruefully called the "Peanut Club," a group of men who economized by eating nothing but peanuts for lunch. Williams, whose father had been a minister and whose stepfather was a doctor, went to Morehouse College in Atlanta. He and Grier crossed paths again when Williams, like many sons of the black middle class, did time back at Reynolds after graduating from college. But Williams soon entered graduate school at Boston University, while Willie Grier matriculated at Reynolds Tobacco Company. One of the union's early supporters, Grier became a shop steward and then treasurer of Local 22. He also served on the board of deacons at the Mount Zion Baptist Church, became a thirty-second degree Mason and a Shriner, and belonged to the NAACP.

Although Grier was as solid a working-class candidate as the city could produce, his candidacy created divisions that suggested just how complex local political affiliations could be. The Communist Party's city committee apparently supported Williams, while Local 22 activists, including those who were Party members, were

Willie Grier campaign card (Collection of author)

convinced that Grier was "a great guy and . . . felt it's time to get a worker in there. We had enough ministers." Robert Black and Velma Hopkins, one Party member remembered, "were just adamant about that. 'It's time. We're big enough and we're strong enough and it's time for us to run a worker.'" Bob Lathan, on the other hand, "was against it, I remember. He said 'This is leftism; we want to build unity in the community; this is adventurism.'" In the end, the two groups found themselves "on the street on the same day handing out different leaflets."[27]

Willie Grier's candidacy brought Kenneth Williams a surprise supporter. Thurmond Chatham, the newly elected representative from the Fifth Congressional District and a long-time foe of Local 22, made an unannounced visit to a Williams rally a few days before the election. He told the crowd, "The only man I'm supporting in this election is this man here, Kenneth Williams. . . . My friends are going to be working for him and I want you to work for him, too." While black workers struggled hard to develop coalitions with white workers, middle-class blacks and whites seemed to be building a strategic alliance overnight.[28]

In the mayor's race, Local 22 activists united around a gadfly named Marshall Kurfees, who was running against the second-term incumbent, George D. Lentz. Kurfees came from a poor white family and had little education, but his opposition to the monied interests of the city won him significant support. In a major upset, Kurfees won the Democratic nomination for mayor, "a surprising victory of labor, poor whites, and local malcontents over the establishment," noted a Winston-Salem historian. Willie Grier was less fortunate. With Local 22 divided, many black workers stuck with Kenneth Williams, who won by a large margin.[29]

The Final Vote

From October 1949 to February 1950, Winston-Salem unionists had waited for the results of the NLRB's hearings. Bogged down by the bureaucratic complications imposed by the Taft-Hartley Act and by the loss of the vigor and clarity of purpose that had marked its prewar deliberations, the NLRB had dragged its feet. Finally, in February, it scheduled an election for the week of March 5. It also issued two rulings that had critical significance for Local 22: it included departmental inspectors in the bargaining unit but excluded approximately 1,000 seasonal workers.[30]

After months of campaigning, it was time to vote. Balloting began at 8:00 A.M. on March 8 at eleven voting places throughout the plants. Over 9,000 employees were eligible to vote. NLRB officials believed that it was the largest election conducted in the South since the passage of the Taft-Hartley Act. Just as in 1943, a crowd gathered at the company's cafeteria across the street from the Reynolds Building shortly after the polls closed at 10:00 P.M. NLRB officials began counting the ballots shortly before midnight. At 1:15 A.M. they announced the results: "no union," 3,426; FTA, 3,323; TWIU, 1,514; UTSE, 541.[31]

Virtually every observer west of Main Street had written off Local 22, and most had expected Reynolds workers to reject unionization altogether. Instead, FTA held on to its core constituency and captured a majority of the pro-union votes, while over 60 percent of the workers voted for some form of representation. The NLRB promptly scheduled a runoff election between FTA and "no union" for March 23.

Over the next two weeks, as it struggled to hold on, Local 22 faced a firestorm of criticism, the most damaging of which came from members of the black middle class. Kenneth Williams acknowledged Local 22's clout, pernicious though it might be, even as he emphasized outside influences, adopted the apocalyptic language of embattled anti-Communism, and positioned himself as the only legitimate spokesman for the black community. Supporting a Board of Alderman resolution, he condemned the "communistic" leaders of Local 22 as "detrimental" to the workers and the community and "injurious to the welfare" of the country. "I do not hold the masses of workers responsible. They have been fed a line, a dangerous line. And will be fed an even more dangerous one if this thing isn't stopped." "As a friend of the workers," Williams concluded, "and as one who has the welfare of Winston-Salem at heart, I ask the people of Winston-Salem to come to their senses and send the Communists away for good."[32]

It is not hard to understand why Williams took this stand. A few months earlier, the Soviet Union had detonated an atomic bomb. The Korean War loomed on the horizon. Senator Joseph McCarthy had just announced the hearings on Communist influence in the federal government that would push the red scare to its all-time height. Leaders such as Walter White and Mary McLeod Bethune had committed the mainstream civil rights movement to an anti-Communist strategy. In the meantime, local elites had made only a tenuous commitment to reform. Even as they offered a program for improving race relations, they insisted that segregation was inviolate and moved to curb black political power. Williams himself had watched helplessly as the Democratic Executive Committee and the Board of Aldermen gerrymandered the wards to prevent the election of an additional black aldermen. The choice, from his point of view, was between making an alliance with whites who might support advances that posed no threat to the economic order or watching from the sidelines as the civil rights project was torpedoed by the forces of right-wing reaction. Moreover, Williams shared the prevailing Cold War consensus and, at least in retrospect, saw Local 22's leaders as talented but uneducated workers who had been "trained" by FTA and the Communist Party and were incapable of independent thought. He was not willing to trust the political future of the black community to them. In any case, he had no choice but to take a side; in the early months of 1950, there could be no neutral ground. The vast majority of black workers had voted to put their trust in Local 22. Williams chose to help Reynolds end an era of unionization.

The newly elected mayor, Marshall Kurfees, whom Local 22 had supported, also used his influence to encourage a "no union" vote. It was he who had introduced the anti-Communist resolution to the Board of Alderman, and in the days before the election, he spoke out on station WSJS. He did not oppose "labor organizations who believe in our American way of life," he said, only those that were "communistically controlled."[33]

The mayor and aldermen received formidable reinforcements. A group of twelve black ministers adopted a resolution asking the mayor to appoint a committee "to work out some means of ridding this community of elements suspected of being subversive." The Reverend Jerry Drayton, who went on to become one of the leaders of the city's civil rights movement over the next ten years, told the group that Local 22 had created "confusion" and even "chaos" in Winston-Salem.[34]

This last round of criticism of the union came mostly from black middle-class spokesmen who had the most to lose, or the least to gain, by the organization of the Winston-Salem working class. But there were ordinary workers, black and white, who also spoke out against Local 22. Aime Bazinet had been a shop steward in Number 12. As one of the few white workers willing to participate openly in the union, he had taken his share of abuse from supervisors and other workers. He had also been among those who had suffered from Reynolds's refusal to rehire strikers promptly in the wake of the 1947 walk-out. On the night that the alderman denounced Local 22, Bazinet spoke at a meeting organized by the Reynolds Employees Association. He told the fifty night-shift workers that union leaders had not done enough to help strikers in 1947, insinuating that they had allowed workers to suffer in order to generate propaganda for the *Daily Worker*. It was shortly after that, he said, that he realized that they were Communists, told his foreman, and was "weaned from the union." Not long afterward, the company had promoted him to inspector.[35]

Loyal employees wrote numerous letters to the *Journal* urging the defeat of Local 22. Almost all declared their opposition to Communism and belief in a "Free America." But perhaps more striking was their commitment to Reynolds Tobacco Company. "I believe in my Company and its products," wrote one worker, "and I believe their welfare is my welfare, and I am not alone believing this." Another writer claimed that "there had never been a company in the history of the world that had done more to build a community and to help improve living standards of community and employee than Reynolds Tobacco Company." Jewel Blum wondered, "Why not trust our employers? They are the ones to whom we look for our money with which to buy our food, fuel and clothing, and to spend in any way in which we choose. We wouldn't want to bite the hand that feeds us, would we?" The Reynolds Employees Association had a hand in orchestrating this letter-writing campaign. But the letters also reflected a growing unease on the part of even union sympathizers toward Local 22's strident attacks on the company.[36]

Once more, Local 22 responded by stressing its record and its commitment to democracy. "No few individuals run our union," read one statement signed by 217 Reynolds workers. "We who are workers in the plants have always made the decisions which have brought millions of dollars to the workers and the entire community. That is why the Reynolds Company hates and fears us." Reynolds worker Johnsie Saunders dismissed the charges made by Alderman Williams. "He's for himself just as other white collared men are," she said. "We are not thinking about communism. We want better wages and decent working conditions just as you do Mr. Williams. . . . But I noticed when the colored man got a chance to express his opinions and ask for what he wanted he is communistic. We have worked hard to build up the big man's industry for nothing in return. We are used to hard knocks and promises, and if we lived by the big man's promises it won't hurt us to try others."[37]

Thursday, March 23, 1950, was election day at Reynolds. Kenneth Williams proclaimed it the most important day in the city's history. Even those not directly involved felt drawn in. The *Journal* carried news stories, letters to the editor, an edi-

Moranda Smith (Collection
of author)

torial, and advertisements devoted to the election. As people throughout the city
prepared for work that morning they could hear the voice of Mayor Kurfees over
the radio telling Reynolds workers to vote "no union." "Let's drive Stalin's little
songbirds from our doorsteps," he said.[38]

The voting ended at 10:00 P.M., and people again crowded into the cafeteria. First
one side and then the other took the lead. At 12:30 A.M. the NLRB official announced
the result. FTA led with 4,426 votes; 4,383 voted for "no union." FTA had challenged
134 votes that remained outstanding, charging that they had been cast by "foremen,
petty supervisors, and others not eligible to vote." The outcome depended on those
contested votes.[39]

Each side reacted cautiously. Reynolds personnel director Charles Wade said the
company would have no comment until the NLRB announced the final results. The
Journal hoped the vote would go against FTA, leading "to a far more wholesome situation in the industrial life of Winston-Salem." The union urged workers to prepare for contract negotiations. At the same time, it filed objections to the election,
charging that the company encouraged ineligible voters to cast ballots, the NLRB

failed to provide safeguards against fraudulent voting, and the mayor and alder-men interfered with the election.[40]

On Wednesday night, April 12, a group of union and Party activists met at the home of Moranda Smith. Suddenly, in the midst of a debate with Velma Hopkins over a point of strategy, Smith suffered a stroke. She died shortly afterward at the Katherine Bitting Reynolds Memorial Hospital; she was only thirty-four years old. Velma Hopkins was inconsolable. Smith's friends were convinced that she had been killed by the stress of the election campaign, combined with the extraordinary leadership responsibilities she had assumed. Ruby Jones had spoken with Smith not long before her death. "She'd been to the doctor," Jones remembered, "and the doctor told her she'd have to ease up. She said, 'Ruby, there ain't no easing up to come. I went this far, I'm going on.'"[41]

Smith's death was a devastating blow to the union and to the thousands of work-ers whom she represented—first as director of Local 22's educational committee, then as the first black woman on an international union's executive board, and finally as FTA's regional director. Thousands gathered to pay their respects at the Groler AME Zion Church. Even the *Journal* reported that "it was one of the largest crowds ever to assemble for a funeral here." The sanctuary filled with people, and loudspeakers were set up outside to accommodate the crowd. The gathering was a witness to the love and respect Smith commanded.[42]

The funeral also demonstrated the breadth and biracial nature of the movement that had supported her. The mourners included her family, her minister, friends from her church and neighborhood, and local and international union leaders. Donald Henderson came from union headquarters in Philadelphia. And Paul Robeson, on the verge of being stripped of his passport and officially declared "un-American" by the United States government, interrupted his own battles to be on hand. But what was perhaps most unprecedented, in this segregated town, was the makeup of the pallbearers, honorary pallbearers, and flower-bearers. They in-cluded a mixture of black and white, male and female, young and old.

Representatives of FTA and Local 22 spoke, and the Reverend Hunter Bess deliv-ered the eulogy. Then Paul Robeson addressed the mourners. "It is hard to believe that this person who has given so much to the Negro worker is gone. Yet there are thousands of us to carry on her labor. Her name will remain deep in the hearts, not of Negro people, but all people. She is a symbol of the best in the land. Winston-Salem will give her the greatest victory. Her name will remain a part of the city. She is a symbol of the dignity of full expression as human beings. We must dedicate ourselves to the struggle as she did—to see that this will be a bounteous, peaceful world in which all people can walk in full human dignity." As Robeson sang "Swing Low, Sweet Chariot," black and white pallbearers carried Moranda Smith's body down the aisle.[43]

EPILOGUE

The NLRB investigated FTA's charges of widespread voting irregularities in the March run-off election but found no wrongdoing and counted all 134 challenged ballots. Local 22 lost the election to "no union" by sixty-six votes. The *Journal* welcomed the NLRB's decision and hoped for a return to the "peaceful and co-operative . . . interracial relations" of the pre-union era. Reynolds began firing key rank-and-file union leaders still in the plants while simultaneously issuing an across-the-board pay raise of six cents an hour. For the first time in the company's history, it gave black workers the same wage increase as whites.[1]

In a last-ditch effort to keep FTA alive, Donald Henderson arranged a merger with two left-wing unions based in New York to form the Distributive, Processing, and Office Workers of America (DPOWA), which held its founding convention in New York City in early October 1950. As they had done so many times over the past seven years, Local 22 leaders made their way north in search of allies. Despite everything, hope still propelled them. An indomitable belief in themselves and their movement constituted both their armor of survival and the chief weapon on which they relied. The troops, after all, had not deserted: the vast majority of black workers had reaffirmed their support for Local 22. Fifty more white votes would have spelled victory.[2]

Robert Black, Velma Hopkins, and Robert Lathan addressed the DPOWA convention, reminding delegates that the South remained the critical battlefield in the fight for a social democratic society. Southern manufacturers and politicians had led the opposition to social welfare programs, supported Taft-Hartley, and spear-headed the revival of HUAC. Defeating these "reactionary Congressmen," Velma Hopkins told the delegates, was in the interest of all workers, black and white, North and South. "Let no one be fooled," Robert Black said. "No union anywhere will be safe, and there will be no security nor civil rights for anyone so long as millions of Southern workers, and particularly the 9 million Negro workers of the South, remain unorganized." In response, DPOWA dispatched two of its top officials to work with the local organizing committee. But the new union's leaders soon decided that neither their resources nor the local situation justified a full-scale drive and withdrew their support. By the fall of 1951, the decade-long struggle to unionize Reynolds had come to an end.[3]

Velma Hopkins, Robert Black, and other leading activists never again worked in the Reynolds plants: a vigilant blacklist saw to that. But the company maintained many of the wage standards, benefit provisions, and seniority policies negotiated during the union era. It also further modernized its personnel department, rationalized procedures for hiring, firing, and evaluating employees, and upgraded its supervisory force by weeding out old-timers and replacing them with college-educated foremen and, in a few cases, promoting black foremen in all-black departments. To forestall union activity, Reynolds kept wages slightly ahead of those paid by its unionized competitors. In 1961, under pressure from the federal government, the company reluctantly integrated the cigarette manufacturing departments at Whitaker Park, its new production facilities on the outskirts of town.[4]

Local 22 disappeared from Winston-Salem's political and economic life, NAACP membership in the city declined to less than 500 in the early 1950s, and civic decision-making once again moved behind closed doors. When grievances arose from the black community, a group of ministers met quietly with James Hanes to seek a compromise. A few phone calls by the white industrialist, for instance, led to the desegregation of the bus system in 1958. Chamber of Commerce publicists boasted of enlightened race relations, and not entirely without reason: because of the pressure created by long years of worker mobilization, blacks continued to register and vote in relatively high numbers, consistently returning a single African American representative to the Board of Aldermen. Moreover, by responding to black protest with a program of gradual, carefully managed change, white power brokers guaranteed that the city would not become a hotbed of "massive resistance" to integration. Within three years after the *Brown v. Board of Education* decision struck down segregation in the public schools, officials initiated the token integration of R. J. Reynolds High School without incident. In a few more years, other public institutions, such as the libraries, the municipal golf course, the coliseum, and the police and fire departments, admitted blacks as well.[5]

Throughout the 1950s, Winston-Salem continued to enjoy a reputation as an island of racial peace. But when the student sit-ins began at the end of the decade, a new generation of civil rights activists stepped forward to shatter that image. On February 8, 1960, only a week after the famous Woolworth sit-ins in nearby Greensboro, demonstrators filled Winston-Salem's segregated lunch counters, and the voices of black protest reverberated again through the city's streets. College and high school students predominated on the picket lines and in new protest organizations such as the Commandoes, an NAACP youth group, and a local branch of the Congress of Racial Equality, which challenged the politics of gradualism as practiced both by white paternalists and by the black community's middle-class leaders. By 1964, these protests had broken the color line at most retail stores, hotels, and restaurants.

The subsequent freedom struggle in Winston-Salem followed what became a familiar trajectory. Demands for greater school desegregation and job creation for blacks fell on deaf ears. The anger and frustration of young blacks led to rioting in 1967 and a burst of nationalist-tinged radicalism. The demobilization of the protest movement and years of trench warfare in the city council followed.[6]

The political career of Larry Little, the son of Reynolds workers who had been members of Local 22, highlights both the success of the young activists and the differences between them and their predecessors. Little moved from leadership of the North Carolina Black Panther Party in 1969 to city alderman in 1977. But because he and his peers lacked the backing of a national, interracial, mass-based institution such as FTA, they could not restore crucial issues of economic security and workplace democracy to the political agenda in Winston-Salem, nor, given the political context, could they link black aspirations with a resonant and expansive vision of a social democratic society.[7]

The rise and fall of civil rights unionism left an ambiguous legacy. Throughout the 1940s, it was a primary, though by no means the only, vehicle for African American mobilization against racial discrimination and second-class citizenship. The half a million black workers who joined the ranks of organized labor were in the vanguard of a broad movement for social change, and they had important allies among middle-class African Americans and white radicals and liberals. Mass protests and organized pressure contributed to important victories at the federal level, including the creation of the FEPC, the Supreme Court's decision in *Smith v. All-wright*, and Truman's decision to desegregate the armed forces. For the first time since the turn of the century, southern blacks in large numbers registered to vote, and a few won local political office.[8]

Yet for all these accomplishments, the movement never realized its potential. The Cold War, the metamorphosis of white supremacy, the containment of the trade union movement, and the fracturing of the political left all helped to derail civil rights unionism and the broader insurgency of which it was a part. The first casualties were the tens of thousands of workers, including the members of Local 22, who lost their union representation. Many were affiliated with left-led unions, but the postwar reaction wiped out weaker AFL and CIO locals as well.[9]

The purge of left activists also deprived labor of its most effective organizers, men and women who were dedicated to organizing the millions of workers who remained outside the house of labor. Southerners constituted the largest bloc of these potential recruits, both those who moved north and west in the great postwar migration and those who stayed behind. But there were also clerical workers, agricultural laborers, and government employees who might well have constituted the next wave of unionization had the left-led organizing surge of the thirties and forties continued. Stripped of the activists who were most committed to eliminating discrimination and most capable of appealing to a multicultural workforce, unions in the postwar period often stood in opposition to the civil rights and women's movements. As their strongholds in heavy industry dwindled, the service sector grew, and the workforce became increasingly diverse, these blue-collar institutions proved ill-equipped to respond to new challenges.[10]

The political spectrum narrowed disastrously as well. Driven out of labor and civil rights organizations, black working-class radicals and their white allies— Communist and non-Communists alike—found themselves engulfed in another wave of anti-Communist furor, led this time by Senator Joseph McCarthy. FTA officials Donald Henderson and Ed McCrea were called to testify before a Senate subcommittee in 1953. In 1956 a House subcommittee put Viola Brown, a former chair of Local 22's shop stewards council, on the witness stand, along with a number of the white student activists who had aided the workers' movement in Winston-Salem. Karl Korstad, who had been FTA's Southeast regional director and an organizer for Local 22 in 1949 and 1950, appeared in 1958 before the last of the HUAC investigations of southern activists of the 1940s. Such people became liabilities to the new movement. Throughout the 1960s, the FBI and white supremacist groups kept up a drumbeat of pressure by taking every opportunity to tar a new generation of activists, including Martin Luther King Jr., with the brush of "un-Americanism."[11]

This red scare provided strident white supremacists with a new language of de-monization. "Red" supplemented "nigger" as the rallying cry of those who sought to maintain the racial status quo. State and local prohibitions on "subversive" or-ganizations became the twentieth century's black codes. Few southern liberals, let alone radicals, survived the "redwashing" they received as white supremacists used anti-Communism to frighten and delegitimate both black and white leaders, leav-ing a leadership vacuum that in many places could only be filled by more cautious elements.

None of this quelled the ferment among African Americans nor prevented the second wave of protest against Jim Crow from becoming a powerful force. But it did narrow the range of ideas and leaders on which the movement could draw. Within the civil rights movement, the absence of radical, union-based leaders and institutions marginalized economic concerns. Activists' demands for income redis-tribution and workplace security simply did not have the resonance they once had. The black challenge of the 1950s and 1960s came to be understood as a single-issue attack on Jim Crow and not as a more broad-based critique of racial capitalism.[12]

The losses of the 1940s severed institutional links as well. The demise of the Southern Conference for Human Welfare left the South without a dynamic cross-class, interracial organization that could temper the influence of white suprema-cists. The Southern Negro Youth Congress, which served as a training ground for militant college-educated young activists, had disappeared by the time the next generation created the Student Non-Violent Coordinating Committee. At the na-tional level, a number of groups that had been instrumental in the fight for racial justice fell by the wayside as well. The Civil Rights Congress held out until 1956, fo-cusing attention on the injustices of the southern legal system, including a number of celebrated cases in North Carolina. The loss of these organizations meant that the New Left, which emerged on the heels of the civil rights movement, could not easily learn from the accomplishments and failures of the Old. The possibilities for open, intergenerational dialogue were foreclosed by the silencing of an older gen-eration of activists who had looked to unions as their movement's critical base.[13]

Some links between the civil rights unionism of the 1940s and the movement of the 1950s and 1960s did manage to survive. Larry Little's parents and others like them influenced the youthful protesters of the 1960s, and, here and there, first-wave activists walked the front lines of the later movement. In Winston-Salem, Velma Hopkins accompanied the first black student when the city desegregated its schools in 1957. Elsewhere, veterans of the struggles of the 1930s and 1940s re-emerged to lead local movements as well. E. D. Nixon, a member of the Brother-hood of Sleeping Car Porters, used his union experience to help organize the

Montgomery bus boycott. Coleman Young, a United Auto Workers and Progressive Party activist, won election to the Michigan legislature in 1962 and became mayor of Detroit in 1973.[14]

The civil rights movement's success in liberating the South from the albatross of segregation transformed the region profoundly. Local struggles and federal legislation opened the doors to voting booths, and blacks held more and more offices in the last decades of the twentieth century. One racial barrier after another fell. Although blacks and whites still occupy different worlds at home and in church, they mingle in work and commerce in ways that few could have imagined forty years ago.

The southern economy improved dramatically as well. State and local officials took the lead in the "selling of the South," providing tax incentives and subsidies for northern and foreign corporations and promoting the region's cheap labor. By the end of the twentieth century, the Sunbelt, roughly the southern United States stretching from North Carolina to California, had become the nation's economic powerhouse. Per capita income in the states of the old Confederacy neared the national average. Job growth was higher than in any other part of the country. Capital investment set records year after year.[15]

A closer look, however, reveals old patterns beneath the shiny patina of prosperity. Despite increased prosperity in urban areas, the southern countryside has languished. Eastern North Carolina, for instance, although only a short drive from the affluent Research Triangle area of Raleigh, Durham, and Chapel Hill, suffers from unemployment and poverty rates ten times greater than those of that mecca of technology, medicine, and higher education. Even in metropolitan areas, it is the largely white suburbs and not the more racially diverse city centers that have prospered. The downtowns of Durham, Greensboro, and Winston-Salem have had to fight to keep from becoming ghost towns. Race is still the great divide. Discrimination, unequal educational funding, and strident antiunionism have kept African American workers trapped in the least skilled and lowest paying jobs. Well over half of all African Americans working in the private sector are confined to the three lowest job classifications. Poverty remains a fact of life for most black workers, with roughly a quarter of all Africans Americans living below the poverty line. Social welfare benefits do little to ameliorate such conditions, for southern states rank at the bottom in nearly all categories of social spending. Poor blacks are doubly segregated— from whites and from the black middle class, which profited most from the civil rights revolution.[16]

It could be argued, moreover, that Sunbelt prosperity illustrates mainly the speed with which capital can now be transferred from one place to another in a global economy. No longer tied to the land, tethered to mill villages, or closed off by a separate regional labor market, workers too have become infinitely movable. This free flow of people and money has made the South a "conservative capitalist's dream come true." That same freedom, however, means that the investments that have been attracted by low-cost non-union labor, cheap land, and low taxes can also flow to the even more inviting Third World.[17]

The political structure of racial capitalism has proven to be remarkably resilient as well. In the two decades after passage of the Voting Rights Act, African Americans gained unprecedented access to the political system in the South. But since the early 1990s, state legislatures and the courts have nullified many of these gains. Challenges to minority opportunity districts, the revival of at-large elections, and efforts to end federal supervision of elections are all pursued in the name of "colorblind" justice. The fact that the party of Lincoln is leading these efforts to dilute black political influence indicates the continuities beneath seemingly dramatic change. The Democratic Party's domination of the South, which in turn gave southern legislators disproportionate power in Congress, was one of the pillars of white supremacy. But that power also rested on strategic alliances with the national Republican Party. As newly enfranchised African Americans registered Democratic, Republicans capitalized on the disaffection of conservative whites. This "southern strategy" has enabled Republicans to dominate politics in much of the region, representing the interests both of formerly Democratic white southerners and of long-time Republican transplants from the North, who have turned the growing suburbs around southern cities into reliable bastions of economic, if not always social, conservatism.[18]

At century's end, the South and the nation have yet to erase the color line, have yet to extend democratic citizenship to the workplace, have yet to attend to the basic health, education, and welfare needs of vulnerable citizens, have yet to create a truly participatory political system. Despite the enormous changes of the past fifty years, to which the black freedom struggle contributed mightily, the persistence of the past is everywhere apparent. Perhaps only when another generation of activists refashions the dreams of the 1940s to fit the contours of the new century will the legacy of racial capitalism be laid to rest.

NOTES

Abbreviations

BOA	Board of Aldermen Records, Hall of Records, Winston-Salem, N.C.
CIOSTO	CIO Secretary-Treasurer Office Records, Archives of Labor History and Urban Affairs, Walter Reuther Library, Wayne State University, Detroit, Mich.
DW	*Daily Worker*
FBIHQ	FBI Headquarters File 100-930 ("Charlotte, N.C."), Box 1178, Military Intelligence Division Files, Records of the Army Staff (Record Group 319), National Archives and Records Administration, Washington National Records Center, Suitland, Md.
FMCS	Records of the Federal Mediation and Conciliation Service (Record Group 280), Dispute Case Files 1913–48, National Archives, Washington, D.C.
J&S	*Winston-Salem Journal and Sentinel*
LRP	Leonard Rappaport Papers, Southern Historical Collection, University of North Carolina at Chapel Hill
MHR	M. H. Ross Collection, Southern Historical Collection, University of North Carolina at Chapel Hill
N&O	*News and Observer*
NLRB	Records of the National Labor Relations Board (Record Group 25), National Archives, Washington, D.C.
NRA	Records of the National Recovery Administration (Record Group 9), National Archives, College Park, Md.
NWLB	Records of the National War Labor Board (World War II) (Record Group 202), Dispute Case Files, Region IV, 111-7701 D, National Archives, Washington, D.C.
ODP	Congress of Industrial Organizations, Organizing Committee, North Carolina Papers, 1909–57 (Operation Dixie), Manuscripts Department, William R. Perkins Library, Duke University, Durham, N.C.
RBP	Ralph Bunche Papers, Schomburg Center for Research in Black Culture, New York Public Library, New York, N.Y.
TCS	*Twin City Sentinel*
TW	*The Tobacco Worker*

TWIU   Tobacco Workers International Union Records, Special Collections Division, Hornbake Library, University of Maryland, College Park, Md.

TWV   *The Tobacco Worker's Voice*

UR   *Union-Republican*

UV   *Union Voice*

WSC   *Winston-Salem Chronicle*

WSJ   *Winston-Salem Journal*

Introduction

1. Previous accounts of the events in Winston-Salem can be found in Lerner, *Black Women*, 265–74; Philip S. Foner, *Organized Labor*, 281–82; Barthwell, "Trade Unionism"; Craig T. Jones, "Communism, Rheumatism, and Cigarettes"; and Robert Korstad, "Daybreak of Freedom." On the importance of local activists, see Chafe, *Civilities and Civil Rights*; Lipsitz, *Life in the Struggle*; and Dittmer, *Local People*.

2. The most complete history of R. J. Reynolds Tobacco Company is Tilley, *R. J. Reynolds*.

3. The term tobacco "mule" is from Tursi, *Winston-Salem*, 174. Moranda Smith's story can be found in *UV*, June 3 and 17, 1951.

4. Rosemary Feurer uses the term "civic unionism" to describe the perspective of William Sentner, a United Electrical Workers Union official in St. Louis. Feurer, "William Sentner."

5. Among recent studies of African American women workers are Leslie Brown, "Common Spaces, Separate Lives"; Hunter, *To 'Joy My Freedom*; and Clark-Lewis, *Living In, Living Out*.

6. Robert Black interviews, December 28, 1976, and August 3, 1981. Studies of the FTA include Ruiz, *Cannery Women, Cannery Lives*; Honey, *Southern Labor*; Karl Korstad, "Black and White Together"; and Nelson-Cisneros, "UCAPAWA and Chicanos."

7. Among the works that address the importance of the South to national politics in the World War II era are Sullivan, *Days of Hope*; Michael Goldfield, *Color of Politics*, 231–61; Michael K. Brown, *Race, Money*, 99–134; and Katznelson, Geiger, and Kryder, "Limiting Liberalism."

8. This paragraph is drawn from Korstad and Lichtenstein, "Opportunities Found and Lost," 786–88. There we sought to draw attention to the working-class-led civil rights movement of the 1940s as a step in the reframing of twentieth-century American history. The article has been cited extensively in support of wide-ranging reinterpretations of the period. Criticism of our analysis has been concerned primarily with the commitment of the CIO to racial equality. But our argument, and the argument of this book, was not that the CIO wholeheartedly supported black rights, but that working-class blacks, through their participation in the labor movement, were in the vanguard of civil rights efforts in the 1940s. For discussion of this argument, see Richard H. King, *Civil Rights*, 3–4; Bruce Nelson, "Organized Labor"; Forbath, "Caste, Class"; and Michael Goldfield, *Color of Politics*. For other examples of civil rights unionism and appreciations of the central role played by black workers and the CIO in the 1940s civil rights movement, see Townsend, "One American Problem," 183; Moon, *Balance of Power*, 141; Mason, *To Win These Rights*, 30; Duberman, *Paul Robeson*, 310; Honey, *Southern Labor*; Halpern, "The CIO and the Limits"; Feurer, "William Sentner"; Stepan-Norris and Zeitlin, *Talking Union*; and Bruce Nelson, *Divided We Stand*.

9. The literature on the CIO is voluminous. Among the works that I have drawn on for

this study are Filippelli and McColloch, *Cold War in the Working Class*; Steven Fraser, *Labor Will Rule*; Friedlander, *Emergence of a UAW Local*; Gerstle, *Working-Class Americanism*; Michael Goldfield, "Race and the CIO"; Rosswurm, *CIO's Left-Led Unions*; Gabin, *Feminism in the Labor Movement*; Griffith, *Crisis of American Labor*; Halpern, *Down on the Killing Floor*; Honey, *Southern Labor*; Roger Horowitz, "*Negro and White*"; Nelson Lichtenstein, *Labor's War at Home* and *The Most Dangerous Man*; Bruce Nelson, *Workers on the Waterfront*; Stepan-Norris and Zeitlin, *Talking Union*; and Zieger, *CIO*.

10. Alex Lichtenstein, in a review of Patricia Sullivan's book *Days of Hope*, uses the term "Southern Front" to describe this coalition. Alex Lichtenstein, "Cold War and the 'Negro Question,'" 186. Accounts of the coalition include Sullivan, *Days of Hope*; Egerton, *Speak Now against the Day*; and Reed, *Simple Decency*.

11. On the role of the Communist Party in tying events in the United States to international struggles, see Von Eschen, *Race against Empire*.

12. Important recent works on the white supremacy campaigns include Gilmore, *Gender and Jim Crow*; Greenwood, *Bittersweet Legacy*; Cecelski and Tyson, *Democracy Betrayed*; Kantrowitz, *Ben Tillman*; William Cohen, *At Freedom's Edge*; and Michael Goldfield, *Color of Politics*, 30–31. The term "racial capitalism" is from Robinson, *Black Marxism*.

13. "Reactionary revolution" is from Kousser, *Shaping of Southern Politics*, 261. The South as "the Nation's No. 1 economic problem" is from Carlton and Coclanis, *Confronting Southern Poverty*, 42. This analysis is drawn from Griffin and Korstad, "Class as Race and Gender," 447.

14. Goodwyn, *Breaking the Barrier*, xxii.

15. On the reluctance of Reynolds officials to release Tilley's manuscript, see *WSJ*, March 19, 1969.

16. Woodward, *Strange Career*, xvi; Caute, *Great Fear*. On the role that anti-Communism and McCarthyism played in silencing a generation of activists, see Schrecker, *Many Are the Crimes*; Lerner, *Fireweed*; and Daniel Horowitz, *Betty Friedan*, among others. In an effort to recover this history I have been involved with William Chafe and Raymond Gavins in directing the project "Behind the Veil: Documenting African American Life in the Jim Crow South" at the Center for Documentary Studies at Duke University.

An energetic new scholarship on African American life during the Jim Crow era is beginning to emerge. See James D. Anderson, *Education of Blacks in the South*; Leslie Brown, "Common Spaces, Separate Lives"; Gaines, *Uplifting the Race*; Gilmore, *Gender and Jim Crow*; Grossman, *Land of Hope*; Higginbotham, *Righteous Discontent*; Honey, *Black Workers Remember*; Hunter, *To 'Joy My Freedom*; Kelley, *Hammer and Hoe* and *Race Rebels*; Earl Lewis, *In Their Own Interests*; Litwack, *Trouble in Mind*; McMillen, *Dark Journey*; O'Brien, *Color of the Law*; Rymer, *American Beach*; Shaw, "*What a Women Ought to Be*"; Trotter, *Coal, Class, and Color*; and White, *Too Heavy a Load*.

17. The literature on social movements is extensive. An excellent synthesis of this literature, and one that I have drawn on extensively, is McAdam, McCarthy, and Zald, "Social Movements." See also McAdam, Tarrow, and Tilley, *Dynamics of Contention*; Tarrow, *Power in Movement*; and Chong, *Collective Action*.

18. Scholarship critical of federal intervention includes Nelson Lichtenstein, "Industrial Democracy"; Atleson, *Labor and the Wartime State*; Stone, "Post-War Paradigm"; Klare, "Labor Law as Ideology"; and Halpern, *Down on the Killing Floor*. An interesting critique of this literature is found in Brody, "Workplace Contractualism," and Dubofsky, *State and*

Labor. A recent book that addresses these issues from a somewhat different perspective is Kryder, *Divided Arsenal*. For the importance of public participation in the creation and administration of labor law and the role of women in this process, see Storrs, *Civilizing Capitalism*

19. For this broad definition, see Denning, *Cultural Front*. Denning calls the period the "Age of the CIO" (21–38). Studies that emphasize the influence of the Soviet Union on American Communism include Theodore Draper, *American Communism*; Howe and Coser, *American Communist Party*; Klehr, *Communist Cadre* and *Heyday of American Communism*; Klehr and Haynes, *American Communist Movement*; and Kraditor, *"Jimmy Higgins."* Other histories of the Communist movement, many of which focus on specific communities or particular industries, see the Party as part of an American radical tradition. These include Barrett, *William Z. Foster*; Cochran, *Labor and Communism*; Freeman, *In Transit*; Feurer, "William Sentner"; Gornick, *Romance of American Communism*; Halpern, *Down on the Killing Floor*; Honey, *Southern Labor*; Roger Horowitz, "Negro and White"; Hutchinson, *Blacks and Reds*; Isserman, *Which Side Were You On?*; Johanningsmeier, *Forging American Communism*; Keeran, *Communist Party and the Auto Workers Unions*; Kelley, *Hammer and Hoe*; Kimeldorf, *Reds or Rackets?*; Karl Korstad, "Black and White Together"; Earl Lewis, *In Their Own Interests*; Alex Lichtenstein, "'Scientific Unionism'"; Lieberman, *"My Song Is My Weapon"*; Naison, *Communists in Harlem*; Painter, *Narrative of Hosea Hudson*; Pintzuk, *Reds, Racial Justice*; Rosswurm, "Introduction"; Scales and Nickson, *Cause at Heart*; Schatz, *Electrical Workers*; Schrecker, *Many Are the Crimes*; Stepan-Norris and Zeitlin, *Talking Union*; Von Eschen, *Race against Empire*; and Zahavi, *Workers, Managers*, "Fighting Left-Wing Unionism," "Passionate Commitments," and "'Who's Going to Dance?.'"

20. *WSJ*, May 19, 1947.

21. Scholars have thoroughly documented and analyzed the postwar business offensive, and this book benefits from their insights. Among the works that have been most useful are Howell John Harris, *Right to Manage*; Fones-Wolf, *Selling Free Enterprise*; Jacoby, *Modern Manors*; and Nelson Lichtenstein, "Great Expectations" and "From Corporatism to Collective Bargaining." Reynolds's antiunion strategy was so comprehensive that it might well be labeled the "R. J. Reynolds formula," an update on the "Mohawk Valley formula" initiated by Remington Rand in the 1930s and promoted by the National Association of Manufacturers. On the Mohawk Valley formula, see "In the Matter of Remington Rand," Case No. C-145 (March 13, 1937), in National Labor Relations Board, *Decisions and Orders*, vol. 2 (1936–37), 626–27, and Irving A. Bernstein, *Turbulent Years*, 478–80. For a fresh interpretation of the postwar settlement, see David M. Anderson, "Battle for Main Street U.S.A."

22. Scholars have focused little attention on the role of white moderates in restructuring white supremacy after World War II. Exceptions are Chafe, *Civilities and Civil Rights*, 15–97; Dunbar, *Against the Grain*, 192–258; Egerton, *Speak Now against the Day*, 345–513; and Anders Walker, "Legislating Virtue."

23. For an excellent analysis of McCarthyism, see Schrecker, *Many Are the Crimes*. Studies that analyze the impact of anti-Communism on the labor and civil rights movement include Honey, *Southern Labor*; Denning, *Cultural Front*; and Levenstein, *Communism, Anti-Communism, and the CIO*. On Henry Wallace and the challenge to Luce, see Norman D. Markowitz, *Rise and Fall of the People's Century*.

24. For examples of the negative effects of federal policy on labor, see Hahamovitch, *Fruits of Their Labor*, and Irons, *Testing the New Deal*.

25. Michael K. Brown, *Race, Money*; Nelson Lichtenstein, "From Corporatism to Collective Bargaining."

26. Recent discussions of interracial unions in the South are Honey, *Southern Labor*; Kelly, *Race, Class, and Power*; Arnesen, "'Like Banquo's Ghost'"; Letwin, *Challenge of Interracial Unionism*; and Stein, *Running Steel*.

27. First quote is from Simon, *Fabric of Defeat*, 8. Second quote is from Gordon, "Race and Family," B4. See also Arnesen, "Up from Exclusion."

28. For an example of efforts to combine "union power" and "social power" in the 1960s, see Fink and Greenberg, *Upheaval in the Quiet Zone*, 181–208.

29. Daniel Horowitz, *Betty Friedan*; Michael Goldfield, *Color of Politics*; Carlton, "Revolution from Above"; Zieger, *CIO*; Jacoby, *Modern Manors*.

Chapter 1

1. The high temperature on June 7 was 98 degrees. The average temperature of the two weeks prior to June 17 was over 85; the lows had been only a few degrees below 70. *WSJ*, June 7–17, 1943.

2. See Mezerik, "Dixie," 448, for a vivid description of black and white entrances at a factory in Birmingham, Alabama.

3. *WSJ*, June 17, 1943.

4. John Whitaker was born on August 7, 1891. His father was a prominent local tobacco manufacturer. His mother, Anna Bitting, also came from an established local family, and her sister married William Neal Reynolds, R. J. Reynolds's younger brother. *J&S*, January 31, 1960; Tilley, *R. J. Reynolds*, 24, 329, 519.

5. Theodosia Gaither Simpson Phelps was born on April 2, 1919, in Winston-Salem. She graduated from Atkins High School in 1934 at the age of fifteen and spent one year at Winston-Salem State Teachers College. Theodosia Phelps interview, April 17, 1979; *UCAPAWA News*, December 1, 1944; and "Witness to the Resurrection for Mrs. Theodosia G. Gaither Simpson Phelps," July 7, 1988, original funeral announcement in author's possession.

6. See Tilley, *R. J. Reynolds*, 237–42, 485–88, for background on the stemming process at Reynolds.

7. "Preliminary Statement of the Union," [1944], Exhibits, Company and Union, 17, NWLB; Theodosia Phelps interview, June 1, 1978.

8. On the beginning of the TWOC, see Geneva McClendon interview; Theodosia Phelps, Robert Black, and Karl Korstad interview; and *FTA News*, December 1, 1944.

9. Geneva McClendon interview; Affidavit of Geneva K. McClendon, Bessie A. Phillips, and Juanita Puryear, [1944], Transcript of Hearings, pt. 2, NWLB.

10. Theodosia Phelps interview, June 1, 1978; Geneva McClendon interview.

11. Leon Edwards interview.

12. Geneva McClendon interview; Affidavit of McClendon, Phillips and Puryear, NWLB.

13. Leon Edwards interview; Theodosia Phelps interview, June 1, 1978. The supervisor acknowledged that McCardell had been ill, but he claimed that McCardell refused to leave his job. Tilley, *R. J. Reynolds*, 378.

14. Tilley, *R. J. Reynolds*, 378, 565; Affidavit of McClendon, Phillips, and Puryear, NWLB; "Remarks of John C. Whitaker before Negro Committee Representing Negro Employees," June 28, 1943, Case No. 300/9086, FMCS.

15. Theodosia Phelps interview, June 1, 1978.

16. Leon Edwards interview.

17. Theodosia Phelps interview, June 1, 1978; *WSJ*, June 18, 1943.

18. Geneva McClendon interview.

19. "Remarks of John C. Whitaker before Negro Committee," FMCS.

20. Ibid.; Theodosia Phelps interview, June 1, 1978. This speech, while not a verbatim account of Whitaker's remarks, draws on other speeches he gave at this time, and it is faithful to the descriptions given by workers who were present.

21. Theodosia Phelps interview, April 17, 1979; Theodosia Phelps, Robert Black, and Karl Korstad interview.

22. Theodosia Phelps interview, June 1, 1978.

23. Ibid. The "Little Steel formula" was the method used by the National War Labor Board to determine wage increases during World War II. The formula limited increases to 15 percent of the existing wage on January 1, 1941. See Zieger, *CIO*, 168–69. Symbolically at least, Simpson's challenge fused the opportunities that had conditioned the possibility of the protest with the workers' anger. She had appropriated the power of the federal government and the political possibilities of a decade of social change for the workers in Winston-Salem.

McAdam, "Recruitment," 70, discusses the importance of "biographical availability," or "the absence of personal constraints that may increase the costs and risks of movement participation." Simpson was young, had no children, and had a husband with a full-time job. She was also aware, as were many of the young black workers, that there were jobs available elsewhere. Within a year, Ann and Bill Anderson, Eddie Gallimore, and Simpson's husband, Buck, had gone to Detroit to work. Theodosia Phelps and Karl Korstad interview.

24. Theodosia Phelps interview, June 1, 1978.

25. "Remarks of John C. Whitaker before Negro Committee," FMCS.

26. Theodosia Phelps interview, April 17, 1979; Geneva McClendon interview.

27. Theodosia Phelps interview, April 17, 1979; Theodosia Phelps, Robert Black, and Karl Korstad interview; *WSJ*, June 19, 1943. On the no-strike pledge, see Zieger, *CIO*, and Nelson Lichtenstein, *Labor's War at Home*.

28. Theodosia Phelps, Robert Black, and Karl Korstad interview.

29. Ibid.

30. Theodosia Phelps interviews, June 1, 1978, and April 17, 1979. On the importance of courage in social protest, see Sparks, "Dissident Citizenship." On the strike wave in 1943, see Nelson Lichtenstein, *Labor's War at Home*, 127–35, 152–56.

31. Theodosia Phelps interview, June 1, 1978.

32. *WSJ*, June 18, 1943.

33. Robert Black and Ruby Jones interview.

34. Theodosia Phelps, Robert Black, and Karl Korstad interview; Leon Edwards interview. Mack Dyson, president of UCAPAWA Local 19 in Memphis, was a similar type of rank-and-file leader. See Honey, *Southern Labor*, 126, and Karl Korstad, "Black and White Together," 76–77. Calling on male spokesmen was not unusual among civil rights activists. See, for instance, Robnett, *How Long?*, 41–44.

35. Robert Black interview, October 7, 1977.

36. Theodosia Phelps, Robert Black, and Karl Korstad interview.

37. Robert Black interviews, June 1, 1976, and October 7, 1977.

38. Robert Black interview, January 2, 1981.

39. Robert Black interview, June 1, 1976; Theodosia Phelps, Robert Black, and Karl Korstad interview; *WSJ*, June 19, 1943; Affidavit of R. F. Hamrick, June 16, 1944, Transcript of Hearings, pt. 2, NWLB. Frank Hargrove reported that the entire workforce in Number 60, Number 60 Extension, and Number 64 walked out on Friday.

40. *TCS*, June 18, 1943; *UCAPAWA NEWS*, July 15, 1943; Theodosia Phelps, Robert Black, and Karl Korstad interview. Quote is from Theodosia Phelps interview, June 1, 1978.

41. Willie Grier interview; Theodosia Phelps, Robert Black, and Karl Korstad interview.

42. Theodosia Phelps interview, June 1, 1978.

43. Robert Black interview, June 1, 1976; Theodosia Phelps, Robert Black, and Karl Korstad interview. *UCAPAWA News*, July 1, 1943, reported that "workers flocked into the union since the outbreak of stoppages." The July 15, 1943, edition claimed that during the walkout 2,000 people per day signed union cards.

44. Leon Edwards interview. For a discussion of how a sudden event can cause people to act, see McAdam, McCarthy, and Zald, "Social Movements," 706.

45. Theodosia Phelps, Robert Black, and Karl Korstad interview; Theodosia Phelps interview, April 17, 1979.

46. Theodosia Phelps, Robert Black, and Karl Korstad interview. On the Detroit "riot," see Widick, *Detroit*, 99–112.

47. Theodosia Phelps, Robert Black, and Karl Korstad interview.

48. Ibid. Selected were Robert Black, Lola Love, William Malone, Estelle Howard, Mary Fare, Martha Penn, Willie L. Grier, Minnie Austin, Eddie Gallimore, Anne Austin, and Andrew Thacker. *TCS*, June 21, 1943.

49. *WSJ*, June 20, 1943; *TCS*, June 21, 1943.

50. Robert Black interview, April 8, 1979. On the importance of social learning in developing strategy, see Goodwyn, *Breaking the Barrier*, xxvi.

51. Robert Black interview, April 8, 1979.

52. Geneva McClendon interview.

53. Ibid.; Robert Black interview, March 3, 1988. Pitts was a native of Newberry County, South Carolina, and had taught school and pastored a number of churches in the surrounding counties before moving to Winston-Salem in 1933. "Dr. Pitts," 4–9.

54. Robert Black interview, March 3, 1988.

55. Theodosia Phelps interview, June 1, 1978.

56. *TCS*, June 21, 1943.

57. Theodosia Phelps interviews, June 1, 1978, and April 17, 1979; Theodosia Phelps, Robert Black, and Karl Korstad interview.

58. Theodosia Phelps, Robert Black, and Karl Korstad interview.

59. Robert Black and Ruby Jones interview. Workers often made references to slavery in the interviews I conducted. Such language, which was undoubtedly common at the time, provided a frame for the interpretation of workers' grievances. See McAdam, McCarthy, and Zald, "Social Movements," 713–14.

60. Theodosia Phelps, Robert Black, and Karl Korstad interview.

61. *WSJ*, June 21, 1943. Closing down the plants leads to a new vision of what might be possible. See McAdam, McCarthy, and Zald, "Social Movements," 713, for a discussion of cognitive liberation.

62. Robert Black interview, April 8, 1979; Theodosia Phelps, Robert Black, and Karl Korstad interview.

63. "Total Employees R. J. Reynolds Tobacco Company," [1943], Case No. 300/9086, FMCS; Robert Black interview, March 3, 1988.

64. Lonnie Nesmith interview, undated.

65. *WSJ*, June 22, 1943; *TCS*, June 21–23, 1943.

66. R. W. Goodrick, "Progress Report," June 21, 1943, Case No. 300/9086, FMCS; Affidavit of various members of the workers committee, June 22, 1944, Transcript of Hearings, pt. 2, NWLB.

67. Robert Black interview, April 8, 1979. See Chapters 5 and 6 for a discussion of anti-union activity at Reynolds prior to 1943.

68. Robert Black interview, March 3, 1988; *WSJ*, June 22, 1943.

69. Robert Black interview, March 3, 1988; *WSJ*, June 22, 1943.

70. Robert Black interview, June 1, 1976.

71. Theodosia Phelps, Robert Black, and Karl Korstad interview.

72. Ibid.; Robert Black interview, June 1, 1976; *WSJ*, June 22, 1943.

73. The analysis that follows owes a great deal to my collaboration with Larry Griffin. See Griffin and Korstad, "Class as Race and Gender" and "Historical Inference."

74. *WSJ*, June 18, 1943.

75. This analysis draws on the social movements literature described in McAdam, McCarthy, and Zald, "Social Movements."

76. It seems less likely that tears would have triggered men to organize a sit-down strike. Men did not normally display their emotions by crying, and they were not especially socialized to respond empathetically. In fact, crying was considered a sign of weakness. But they did respond positively to the women's willingness to stand up to the boss, an action they could more readily identify as "manly." It was not tears but defiance that evoked their response. For an interesting discussion of male work culture, see Montgomery, *Workers' Control*, 9–31.

77. Theodosia Phelps, Robert Black, and Karl Korstad interview.

78. Even here the issues were not so cut and dried. Theodosia Simpson remembered that someone in the group of women she had first consulted had "snitched" to the subforeman, Will, who, whether out of stupidity or concern for the women, told the cleaning woman that he knew about the planned sit-down (he probably even told some of the workers). This still allowed them to surprise the supervisors after lunch. Theodosia Phelps interview, April 17, 1979.

79. Robert Black interview, December 28, 1976.

80. This allows the workers to "aggregate their individual beliefs." See McAdam, McCarthy, and Zald, "Social Movements," 714.

Chapter 2

1. Two excellent studies of the antebellum economy in Salem and Winston are Sensbach, *Separate Canaan*, and Shirley, *From Congregation Town*. Other histories of Winston-Salem and Forsyth County are Fries, Wright, and Hendricks, *Forsyth*, and Tursi, *Winston-Salem*. On economic development in postbellum North Carolina, see Tilley, *Bright-Tobacco Industry*; Escott, *Many Excellent People*; Janiewski, *Sisterhood Denied*, 8–26, 67–76; Laura F. Edwards, *Gendered Strife*; and Billings, *Planters and the Making of a "New South."*

2. Shirley, *From Congregation Town*, 60–93.

3. An overview of antebellum tobacco manufacturing is found in Robert, *Story of Tobacco*, 3–112. The early days of the postbellum period are discussed in Tilley, *Bright-Tobacco Industry*, 123–54; Janiewski, *Sisterhood Denied*, 10–18; and Robert, *Story of Tobacco*, 115–21.

4. Carlton, "Revolution from Above," 461–67. Quote is on 462. A discussion of the nineteenth-century textile industry in North Carolina can be found in Hall et al., *Like a Family*, 24–31, and Beatty, *Alamance*.

5. Quote is from Tilley, *R. J. Reynolds*, 24. Background on Reynolds's move to Winston is also found in Shirley, *From Congregation Town*, 146–47. For additional background on the history of the Reynolds family, see Tilley, *Reynolds Homestead* and *R. J. Reynolds*, 29–92; Carlton, "Revolution from Above," 464–65; and Burrough and Helyar, *Barbarians at the Gate*, 42.

6. U.S. Department of Commerce, Bureau of the Census, *Twelfth Census, 1900*, 289. On the economic growth of Winston, see Shirley, *From Congregation Town*, 144–71.

7. See Hall et al., *Like a Family*, 24–43, on the textile industry, and Shirley, *From Congregation Town*, 193–99, on tobacco.

8. Tilley, *R. J. Reynolds*, 36–40; Shirley, *From Congregation Town*, 201–2.

9. Shirley, *From Congregation Town*, 193, 197.

10. Ibid., 172–233.

11. Tilley, *Bright-Tobacco Industry*, 594; Carlton, "Revolution from Above," 465; Chandler, *Visible Hand*, 290–92, 382–91.

12. Tilley, *R. J. Reynolds*, 95–128.

13. Ibid., 108–10.

14. The development of Price Albert is discussed in ibid., 160. On the role of the modern advertising agency, see Lears, *Fables of Abundance*, 93–94. For increases in the production of Prince Albert, see Burrough and Helyar, *Barbarians at the Gate*, 43–44.

15. On the breakup of the Trust, see Tennant, *American Cigarette Industry*, 57–66. On the Times Square advertisement, see Burrough and Helyar, *Barbarians at the Gate*, 44–45.

16. Tilley, *R. J. Reynolds*, 188–91.

17. Hale, *Making Whiteness*, 170; Jane Webb Smith, *Smoke Signals*, 21. See, generally, Lears, *Fables of Abundance*, 93–98, 181–83 ("magical regeneration" is on 57).

18. Robert, *Story of Tobacco*, 230; Tilley, *R. J. Reynolds*, 219, 321; Cox, *Caste, Class, and Race*, 41, 66.

19. Tilley, *R. J. Reynolds*, 332; Tise, *Building and Architecture*, 43–44.

20. "Camels," 45; Cox, *Caste, Class, and Race*, 100–115; Tennant, *American Cigarette Industry*, 237–45; Tilley, *R. J. Reynolds*, 262–66. The New Jersey plant evidently closed after the employees went on strike. See E. L. Crouch to E. Lewis Evans, May 3, 1927, II/8, TWIU.

21. Tursi, *Winston-Salem*, 196–97; Cox, *Caste, Class, and Race*, 100–115; Tilley, *R. J. Reynolds*, 68.

22. Carlton, "Revolution from Above," 466.

23. Daniels, *Tar Heels*, 157–59 (quote is on 158).

24. The oligopolistic character of cigarette manufacturing is described in Raymond M. Jones, *Strategic Management*, 9.

25. On the democratic character of North Carolina's political system, see Kousser, *Shaping of Southern Politics*, 183, and Escott, *Many Excellent People*, 181. On the role of African Amer-

ican women in late-nineteenth-century political life, see Elsa Barkley Brown, "Negotiating and Transforming," and Laura F. Edwards, *Gendered Strife*. On the Republican Party in Winston, see Shirley, *From Congregation Town*, 223.

26. Steelman, "Progressive Era," 66, and Escott, *Many Excellent People*, 195. Shirley, *From Congregation Town*, 218–23, describes the activities of the Knights in Winston. Valuable discussions of the Knights in Richmond, Virginia, are Fink, *Workingmen's Democracy*, 149–77, and Rachleff, *Black Labor in the South*, 109–201. See McLaurin, *Knights of Labor*, for a regionwide focus. On the general strike, see Tilley, *R. J. Reynolds*, 38–39.

27. Bertha Hampton Miller, "Blacks in Winston-Salem," 24–25, 31; *UR*, November 3, 10, 1892. See Kousser, *Shaping of Southern Politics*, 187, for sources on the 1889 election law. On post-Reconstruction efforts to curtail black voting in the South, see Rabinowitz, *Race Relations in the Urban South*, 305–28, and Kousser, *Shaping of Southern Politics*, 224–38.

28. On Populism in North Carolina, see Escott, *Many Excellent People*, 241–53. On the Fusionists, see Edmonds, *Negro and Fusion Politics*. On Republicans, see Crow and Durden, *Maverick Republican*. An excellent study of the turn-of-the-century protest tradition in North Carolina is Ross, "Third Party Tradition."

29. Steelman, "Progressive Era," 119–55; Kousser, *Shaping of Southern Politics*, 185–87; Bertha Hampton Miller, "Blacks in Winston-Salem," 32–33; Edmonds, *Negro and Fusion Politics*, 128; Hanchett, *Sorting Out the New South City*, 82.

30. Kousser, *Shaping of Southern Politics*, 187; Bertha Hampton Miller, "Blacks in Winston-Salem," 53.

31. *Winston Free Press*, reprinted in *N&O*, September 22, 1898. Quoted in Gilmore, *Gender and Jim Crow*, 103.

32. *Winston Free Press*, reprinted in *N&O*, September 22, 1898. On the rising tide of segregation and disfranchisement across the South, see Kousser, *Shaping of Southern Politics*, and Litwack, *Trouble in Mind*, 217–46.

33. Kousser, *Shaping of Southern Politics*, 188–95; Gilmore, *Gender and Jim Crow*, 91–118.

34. *Winston Journal*, November 1, 1898.

35. Ibid. A similar statement appeared in Wilmington. See Escott, *Many Excellent People*, 255, and Prather, *We Have Taken a City*, 35. See also Kousser, *Shaping of Southern Politics*, 188–89; Hanchett, *Sorting Out the New South City*, 83–88; Leloudis, *Schooling the New South*, 133–41; Greenwood, *Bittersweet Legacy*, 190; and Honey, "Class, Race, and Power," 165.

36. Hale, *Making Whiteness*, 8; Gilmore, *Gender and Jim Crow*, 82–89.

37. *UR*, September 22 and October 17, 1898. On the Fusionist efforts to hold back the forces of white supremacy, see Kousser, *Shaping of Southern Politics*, 188, especially the extensive footnotes, and Edmonds, *Negro and Fusion Politics*.

38. *UR*, November 11, 1898; Kousser, *Shaping of Southern Politics*, 188; Woodward, *Strange Career*, 80–81.

39. *Charlotte Daily Observer*, June 6, 1900, quoted in Steelman, "Progressive Era," 215. On the disfranchisement amendment, see Gilmore, *Gender and Jim Crow*, 120–26, and Kousser, *Shaping of Southern Politics*, 189–93.

40. *UR*, July 26, 1900. The 1900 vote totals are found in ibid. and Bertha Hampton Miller, "Blacks in Winston-Salem," 68. On the limitation of local democracy, see Kousser, *Shaping of Southern Politics*, 190, and Escott, *Many Excellent People*, 258–59.

41. *UR*, November 6, 1902.

42. *Winston Journal*, July 10 and August 3, 1900. "Reactionary revolution" is from Kousser,

Shaping of Southern Politics, 261. Turn-of-the-century white supremacists were a polyglot group, and there was a great deal of variation among states in the legal prescriptions and social practices they followed. South Carolina's Ben Tillman, for example, saw the world much differently than tobacco manufacturers in Winston-Salem did. See Kantrowitz, *Ben Tillman*.

43. See Kousser, *Shaping of Southern Politics*, 250–57, and Escott, *Many Excellent People*, 259–60, for discussions of the nondemocratic impulses of white supremacists. By seeing gender and race as biologically based traits rather than socially constructed phenomena, white supremacists attempted to make their position at the top of the social and political hierarchy unassailable. On the fear of interracial sexuality, see Gilmore, *Gender and Jim Crow*, 68–72, and Kantrowitz, *Ben Tillman*, 163.

44. On the use of Jim Crow statutes to restrain what many whites saw as a new generation of blacks who refused to accept customary subordination, see Litwack, *Trouble in Mind*, 229–38, and Cell, *Highest Stage of White Supremacy*, 134–35, 143. Legal statutes gave white elites the police power to keep blacks subordinated on the land and to control the increasing number of black migrants to the cities. See discussion on urbanization and race relations in Cell, *Highest Stage of White Supremacy*, 131–35; Gilmore, *Gender and Jim Crow*, 96; and Hale, *Making Whiteness*, 284. On the need to keep blacks in the state, see Greenwood, *Bittersweet Legacy*, 217. On black men's sexual appetite, see Hall, *Revolt against Chivalry*, and Gilmore, *Gender and Jim Crow*, 94–99. On disease, see Hunter, *To 'Joy My Freedom*, 187–218. On Southern Progressives' association of segregation with progress, see Link, *Paradox of Southern Progressivism*, 63–70.

45. The seminal work defining the Jim Crow era is Woodward, *Strange Career*. A useful review of the importance of that work is Rabinowitz, "More Than the Woodward Thesis"; see also Woodward, "Strange Career Critics." Barbara Fields and Karen Fields made the important distinction between Jim Crow and segregation. Fields and Fields, "Remarks." It is interesting to note, however, that according to Woodward, segregation on railroads applied only to first-class coaches until the end of the century (*Strange Career*, 24).

46. On the importance of invented tradition, see Woodward, *Strange Career*, and Bishir, "Landmarks of Power." Unfortunately, political activists and historians have not been immune to this static interpretation of race relations.

47. Leloudis, *Schooling the New South*, 137. See also Cell, *Highest Stage of White Supremacy*, 121, and Escott, *Many Excellent People*, 260. On the implications of segregation for white class relations, see Woodward, *Strange Career*, 97–109; Gilmore, *Gender and Jim Crow*, 117–18; and Hale, *Making Whiteness*, 284–85. This is not to say that all that poor and middling whites received for their support of white supremacy was the right to drink out of the same courthouse water fountain as the judge or to attend separate schools from blacks. There were many privileges, such as better jobs and preferred housing space, and some opportunities for civic participation.

48. On the policing aspects of Jim Crow statues, see Litwack, *Trouble in Mind*, 229–38. On the economic importance of black labor, see Janiewski, "Southern Honor," 81.

49. Lichtenstein and Harris, *Industrial Democracy*, 1–16; William Cohen, *At Freedom's Edge*, 201–311.

50. One notable exception was a South Carolina law passed in 1915 mandating racial segregation in textile mills. Hall et al., *Like a Family*, 66.

51. Kousser, *Shaping of Southern Politics*, 73–80. It is important to remember that while there were general features of disfranchisement throughout the South, each state was

unique. In North Carolina, for instance, the white primary was not a major disfranchising device, at least relative to the rest of the South, and it had been abandoned statewide before *Smith v. Allwright*, the Supreme Court case that outlawed the white primary. North Carolina was also closer to being a two-party state than states in the Deep South. There was an active Republican Party, especially in the western counties, and it was not totally lily white. Key, *Southern Politics*, 205–28, 620.

52. On the limitations of Progessivism in alleviating the socioeconomic problems of whites and blacks, see Leloudis, *Schooling the New South*, 177–228, and Link, *Paradox of Southern Progressivism*. On the effects of segregation on white workers' wages, see Gavin Wright, *Old South, New South*, 124–97, and Wood, *Southern Capitalism*.

53. "The status quo of about 1890 tended toward segregation, single-party hegemony, a concentration of power in the hands of upper-class whites. By 1910, these tendencies were hardened into fundamental legal postulates of the society. To put it differently, folkways became stateways, with all the psychological power of legality and the social power of enforceability now behind them. When the federal courts and Congress refused to overturn segregation and discriminatory voting laws, the new system gained the added buttress of constitutionality." Kousser, *Shaping of Southern Politics*, 262.

54. See Hale, *Making Whiteness*, and Ritterhouse, "Learning Race."

55. Bishir, "Landmarks of Power."

Chapter 3

1. Winston-Salem was the largest city in North Carolina in 1920, but Charlotte outdistanced it soon thereafter. By the end of the 1920s, Forsyth County could boast of having a higher per capita income and more value added through manufacturing than any other county in the state. The Twin City was by far the leading industrial city in North Carolina and the third in the South, ranking behind only Baltimore and Richmond, another tobacco manufacturing center. Tursi, *Winston-Salem*, 170; Winston-Salem Chamber of Commerce, *Unit on City Government*; James Howell Smith, *Industry and Commerce*, 30–32.

2. Tursi, *Winston-Salem*, 169–74; James Howell Smith, *Industry and Commerce*, 14–15, 24; Fries, Wright, and Hendricks, *Forsyth*, 228–55.

3. Quotes are from Daniels, *Tar Heels*, 169, 166. On the first families of Winston-Salem, see ibid., 159; MacNeill, "The Town," 101; Paxton Davis, *Being a Boy*, 31; and Ladd, *Negro Political Leadership*, 51.

4. Key, *Southern Politics*, 211.

5. Tise, *Government*, 48. On James Hanes's political career, see *WSJ*, May 3, 1921; *Thursday*, July 18, 1940; and Linn, *People Named Hanes*, 169. On Robert Hanes, see ibid., 183. On James Gray, see Linn, *Gray Family*, 112.

6. On Furnifold Simmons, see Simmons, *F. M. Simmons*, and Tilley, *R. J. Reynolds*, 136. In the 1904 governor's race, the Winston group successfully supported one of their own, local lawyer and white supremacist politico Robert Glenn, against Simmons's candidate. Tise, *Government*, 46. On O. Max Gardner, see Morrison, *Governor O. Max Gardner*, 43. Clay Williams's involvement with the National Industrial Recovery Board is described in Abrams, *Conservative Constraints*, 165, 167. On Dick Reynolds's appointment, see *Thursday*, September 26, 1940.

7. The quote is from Tise, *Building and Architecture*, 38. The homes of the rich are described in Tursi, *Winston-Salem*, 183; Taylor, *From Frontier to Factory*, 39; and *WSJ*, April 24, 1938. Two streetcar developments, Winston's West End and Salem's Washington Park, anticipated the move to the suburbs. Fries, Wright, and Hendricks, *Forsyth*, 205–6. An excellent study of urban and suburban development in Charlotte is Hanchett, *Sorting Out the New South City*.

8. On Reynolda, see Margaret Supplee Smith, "Reynolda," and Mayer, *Reynolda*. Will Reynolds's estate attracted notoriety in the 1960s when civil rights activists successfully challenged Reynolds's will, which had designated Tanglewood as a park for the "white citizens" of Forsyth County. Fries, Wright, and Hendricks, *Forsyth*, 293. On Hanes, see Linn, *People Named Hanes*, 171. On Whitaker, see *WSJ*, January 31, 1960. The history of Roaring Gap can be found in Noel, Wilson, and Wilson, *Roaring Gap*, and Young, *Morobullia*, 68–71.

9. Daniels, *Tar Heels*, 167; Winston-Salem Chamber of Commerce, *Directory, Twin-City Club*; Taylor, *From Frontier to Factory*, 187; Young, *Morobullia*, 100.

10. Ties to the University of North Carolina at Chapel Hill can be found in the biographies of each man in Powell, *Dictionary of North Carolina Biography*. For an interesting discussion of the tension between different factions at the university, see Zogry, *University's Living Room*, 72–76.

11. First quote is from Tursi, *Winston-Salem*, 197. Second quote is from Wilhelmina Jackson, "Memo on Winston-Salem," 3–4, box 36, folder 4, RBP.

12. Information on Katharine Reynolds and Kate Reynolds is found in Tursi, *Winston-Salem*, 190–91 (first quotes are on 195). Second quote is from Smith and Wilson, *North Carolina Women*, 210. R. J. Reynolds bought the Plaza Hotel at Chestnut and Third Streets, remodeled it, and named it the Reynolds Inn. Tursi, *Winston-Salem*, 190.

13. On the black exodus during the Great Migration, see Grossman, *Land of Hope*, and Harrison, *Black Exodus*.

14. Robert Black interview, August 24, 1984.

15. Ibid.

16. Robert Black, Janie Black, Viola Brown, and Karl Korstad interview.

17. Ibid.

18. Ibid.

19. This comparison is to cities over 50,000. Charleston and Montgomery had 44 percent blacks, and no manufacturing center was even close. The biggest upsurge came between 1900 and 1920, when the number of blacks in Winston-Salem shot up by 128 percent. By contrast, Atlanta's black population grew only by 76 percent in the same period. In Birmingham, 31 percent of blacks were industrial workers; in Memphis, 47 percent. Even tobacco cities had smaller industrial proletariats—in Richmond the figure was 40 percent. U.S. Department of Commerce, Bureau of the Census, *Sixteenth Census, 1940: Population, Characteristics*, pt. 1, 331 (Birmingham); pt. 2, 374 (Winston-Salem); pt. 6, 716 (Memphis); pt. 7, 281 (Richmond).

20. Ladd, *Negro Political Leadership*, 52 n. 1. A description of the various tobacco firms in Winston-Salem is found in *Tobacco*, March 25, 1943. On the development of the tobacco industry in Winston-Salem and other North Carolina cities, see Lemert, *Tobacco Manufacturing Industry*.

21. The male-female sex ratio in North Carolina urban areas in 1930 was 85.3, and in rural areas 98.1. Leslie Brown, "Common Spaces, Separate Lives," 339. In Winston-Salem in 1940,

the sex ratio was 86.5. In 1940, 19,314 black women lived in Winston-Salem, compared to 16,704 black men. U.S. Department of Commerce, Bureau of the Census, *Sixteenth Census, 1940: Population, Characteristics*, pt. 5, 401–2.

22. Charles S. Johnson, "The Tobacco Worker," 1935, 269, box 62, folder 39, NRA. Of the 9,339 black women wage earners in the city, 3,672 worked as operatives, mostly in the to-bacco industry, while 2,443 listed their occupation as "domestic service worker." Another 826 were laborers or general service workers; 347 were professional or semiprofessional workers —far more than black men. Only 89 were clerical, sales, and kindred workers—far fewer than black men. U.S. Department of Commerce, Bureau of the Census, *Sixteenth Census, 1940: Population, Characteristics*, pt. 5, 401–2.

23. Trotter, *Black Milwaukee*, 39–79; Earl Lewis, *In Their Own Interests*, 3–4; Opperman, *Winston-Salem's African-American Neighborhoods*, 21; Ladd, *Negro Political Leadership*, 153.

24. James Howell Smith, *Industry and Commerce*, 22–23; Baxter Holman interview.

25. James Howell Smith, *Industry and Commerce*, 23–25; Hall et al., *Like a Family*, 218–19.

26. Claude V. Dunnagan, "I Know My Machine," 545, folder 15, LRP; Blanche Fishel inter-view. See story in *WSJ*, May 10, 1950, on a mechanic at Reynolds who farmed twenty-two acres in Pfafftown.

27. See Gutman, *Work, Culture, and Society*, 15, for an argument about how the differential timing of proletarianization among industrial workers forestalls the development of a sin-gular working class and in fact contributes to fragmentation.

28. Opperman, *Winston-Salem's African-American Neighborhoods*, 15. The exact location of Monkey Bottom is in dispute. Opperman (36) claims it was a neighborhood in the Pond, but *WSC*, February 24, 1979, 13, locates it southeast of the factory district.

29. Opperman, *Winston-Salem's African-American Neighborhoods*; Bertha Hampton Miller, "Blacks in Winston-Salem," 116–36.

30. Bertha Hampton Miller, "Blacks in Winston-Salem," 36, 123. The U.S. Supreme Court consistently struck down such housing ordinances on the grounds that they violated the due process clause of the Fourteenth Amendment. The North Carolina court invalidated the Winston law on narrower grounds, but the effect was the same. See Charles S. Johnson, *Pat-terns of Negro Segregation*, 173–76.

31. *Thursday*, May 22, 1941. On the process of black integration of white neighborhoods in Detroit, see Sugrue, *Origins of the Urban Crisis*, 181–207.

32. First quote is from Fields and Fields, "Remarks." Second quote is from Geneva Mc-Clendon interview.

33. Theodosia Phelps interview, April 17, 1979.

34. Ibid.

35. Robert Black interview, August 24, 1984.

36. Greenwood, *Bittersweet Legacy*, 77, 88.

37. On Atkins, see Newbold, *Five North Carolina Negro Educators*, and Caldwell, *History of the American Negro*, 167–72. On the growth of the nineteenth-century African American community in Winston and Salem, see Bertha Hampton Miller, "Blacks in Winston-Salem," 6–17; Brownlee, *Winston-Salem*, 49; and U.S. Department of Commerce, Bureau of the Cen-sus, *Twelfth Census, 1900*, table 23. See Greenwood, *Bittersweet Legacy*, and Gilmore, *Gender and Jim Crow*, 1–59, on African American community-building in Charlotte and other North Carolina cities. On the role of educators, see Fairclough, *Teaching Equality*, 77.

38. For a description of North Carolina's racial paternalism, see Key, *Southern Politics*, 205–28. For a critique of Key, see Chafe, *Civilities and Civil Rights*, 1–55.

39. *Booker T. Washington Papers*, 458–59; Tursi, *Winston-Salem*, 136.

40. *WSJ*, February 10, 1929.

41. Ibid. See Leslie Brown, "Common Spaces, Separate Lives," for more examples of the black middle class's response to migration, noting especially the concern about women's morality.

42. Ladd, *Negro Political Leadership*, 115–16; Gilmore, *Gender and Jim Crow*, 186.

43. See Charles S. Johnson, *Patterns of Negro Segregation*, 231–43; Stein, *World of Marcus Garvey*; Kelley, *Hammer and Hoe*; Lincoln and Mamiya, *Black Church*, 123–25; Gaines, *Uplifting the Race*; Gilmore, *Gender and Jim Crow*; Leslie Brown, "Common Spaces, Separate Lives"; O'Brien, *Color of the Law*; James Howell Smith, *Industry and Commerce*, 183; White, *Too Heavy a Load*, 92–108; and Ramsey, "More Than the Three R's." See the photographs in Tursi, *Winston-Salem*, 178, of the Depot School, where most of the teachers are women, and of Slater Academy, where most of the students are women. In 1940 the census classified fewer than 10 percent of gainfully employed blacks as professionals, semiprofessionals, or proprietors, the occupations that whites considered middle class. U.S. Department of Commerce, Bureau of the Census, *Sixteenth Census, 1940: Population, Characteristics*, pt. 5, 401–2.

44. On black businessmen, see Tursi, *Winston-Salem*, 147. On the important role of black businesses, see *J&S*, April 24, 1938; *WSC*, February 10, 1979, 7; Earl Lewis, *In Their Own Interests*, 38–46; Bertha Hampton Miller, "Blacks in Winston-Salem," 97–110; and O'Brien, *Color of the Law*. For contrasting views, see Stein, *World of Marcus Garvey*, and Rymer, *American Beach*.

45. Tursi, *Winston-Salem*, 134.

46. Ibid., 174–77.

47. Weare, *Black Business*; Bertha Hampton Miller, "Blacks in Winston-Salem," 99–103. The city's only black-owned bank, Forsyth Savings and Trust, opened in 1907 but did not enjoy the longevity of Winston Mutual. A victim of the Depression, the bank sold its assets to the white-owned Wachovia Bank and Trust Company. Ibid., 103–4.

48. Fries, Wright, and Hendricks, *Forsyth*, 206; Tursi, *Winston-Salem*, 184; Opperman, *Winston-Salem's African-American Neighborhoods*, 19–48.

49. Theodosia Phelps, Robert Black, and Karl Korstad interview. In 1940 over 85 percent of all nonwhites occupied rental units. Fifty percent of whites were renters as well. U.S. Department of Commerce, Bureau of the Census, *Sixteenth Census, 1940: Housing*, 400. Dr. W. H. Goler, a black physician, owned a number of rental homes along Patterson Avenue. See Fries, Wright, and Hendricks, *Forsyth*, 265–66, and Bertha Hampton Miller, "Blacks in Winston-Salem," 122. Charles Jones was perhaps the most successful African American real estate developer in Winston-Salem. See "Charles Henry Jones," *Who's Who*. Opperman, *Winston-Salem's African-American Neighborhoods*, 22, mentions Jerry L. Newton and Newton Brothers Real Estate as managers of properties in Happy Hill.

50. Theodosia Phelps, Robert Black, and Karl Korstad interview.

51. Geneva McClendon interview; Robert Black interview, June 1, 1976.

52. Robert Black interview, June 1, 1976.

53. Gilmore, *Gender and Jim Crow*, 147–50; Link, *Paradox of Southern Progressivism*.

54. *WSC*, February 24, 1979; Bertha Hampton Miller, "Blacks in Winston-Salem," 161.

55. On Reynolds High School, see Wellman and Tise, *Education*, 42–43. On the other white and black schools, see Bertha Hampton Miller, "Blacks in Winston-Salem," 150; Tise, *Government*, 40; Winston-Salem School Board, *Education for Citizenship*; and Koos, "Our Schools Today," 3–6.

56. Robert Black interview, June 1, 1976.

57. Bertha Hampton Miller, "Blacks in Winston-Salem," 137. See also Thomas, "Wound of My People," and Beardsley, *History of Neglect*.

58. Thomas, "Wound of My People."

59. Grimes, "Kate B. Reynolds Memorial Hospital."

60. Theodosia Phelps, Robert Black, and Karl Korstad interview.

61. Larkins, *Negro Population*, 50.

62. Quote is from Best, "Breaking the Gender Barrier," 151. See also Earl Lewis, *In Their Own Interests*, 70–71, and Leslie Brown, "Common Spaces, Separate Lives."

63. Opperman, *Winston-Salem's African-American Neighborhoods*, 7; Tise, *Churches*, 36.

64. Bertha Hampton Miller, "Blacks in Winston-Salem," 152; Gilkes, "Together"; Best, "Breaking the Gender Barrier." The Wentz Memorial Congregation Church operated a kindergarten, nursery school, and employment bureau in the basement of the church. *WSJ*, April 24, 1938.

65. On the role of middle-class black men in church generally, see Higginbotham, *Righteous Discontent*, 207–8. On the role of working-class black women in Winston-Salem, see Velma Hopkins interview; Larkins, *Negro Population*, 44; and *WSJ*, October 1 and 29, 1939.

66. Quotes are from Lincoln and Mamiya, *Black Church*, 205–6. See also Bertha Hampton Miller, "Blacks in Winston-Salem," 176, and Higginbotham, *Righteous Discontent*, 12.

67. Sheer numbers created numerous opportunities for leadership. Fraternal and sororal orders, which offered aid in sickness and death, included Sons and Daughters of Peace, Independent Order of St. Luke, the Eastern Star, and Households of Ruth. Clark, "Report of the Field Services," 24, and *WSC*, February 17, 1979. Service and social clubs included the Don't Be Idle Club, the United Butlers Club, the Junior Civic League, and the Cotillion Literary Club. *WSC*, February 24 and March 3, 1979.

68. "Moral panics" is from Carby, "Policing the Black Woman's Body," 739. Second quote is from "Industrial Movement among Colored Women," November 1918, 1, YWCA National Board Papers, Sophia Smith Collection, Smith College, Northampton, Mass.

69. Sidney Royal interview; Theodosia Phelps interview, June 1, 1978; Geneva McClendon interview.

70. See Cripps, *Making Movies Black*, and Hunter, *To 'Joy My Freedom*, 160–61.

71. *Thursday*, May 16, 1940; *WSC*, February 24, 1979.

72. Bastin, *Red River Blues*.

73. Savage, *Broadcasting Freedom*, 6–9. Blacks had virtually no influence on national radio broadcasting, which dominated the airwaves, but by mixing extensive local programming with NBC offerings, WSJS offered blacks what would become in the 1940s a critical political voice. By focusing on national broadcasting, Savage may underestimate black access to the airwaves in this period. WSJS was owned by the *Winston-Salem Journal*, which was in turn controlled by Reynolds, but blacks made up almost half the population and half the consumers to which advertisers appealed. See "Sign of Welcome." On the importance of radio to working-class populations, see Grundy, "'We Always Tried to Be Good People,'" and Hall et al., *Like a Family*, 258–62.

74. Robert Black interview, August 24, 1984.

75. This is not to imply that household workers were any less capable of organization than factory workers. See Hunter, *To 'Joy My Freedom.*

76. Theodosia Phelps interview, June 1, 1978.

77. Robert Black interview, August 24, 1984.

Chapter 4

1. Tilley, *R. J. Reynolds*, provides an excellent examination of the non-labor-related challenges facing Reynolds in these years. On Reynolds's collusion with other manufacturers, see Raymond M. Jones, *Strategic Management*, 9–11.

2. The best contemporary description of the production process in tobacco manufacturing is Lemert, *Tobacco Manufacturing Industry.* Alfred Chandler discusses the development of continuous-process cigarette manufacturing. Chandler, *Visible Hand*, 249–50. The phrase "money-making place" is from Nettie Carter interview.

3. Milkman, *Gender at Work*, 7–8; Gavin Wright, *Old South, New South*, 156–58. On the division of labor in the antebellum tobacco industry, see Robert S. Starobin, *Industrial Slavery*, 17; Robert, *Story of Tobacco*, 86–92; and Rachleff, *Black Labor in the South*, 6–8.

4. See Tilley, *Bright-Tobacco Industry*, 490–521, for an overview of the introduction of whites into the tobacco industry. For a general discussion of the division of labor in the tobacco and textile industries, see Janiewski, "Southern Honor," 77–88, and Hall et al., *Like a Family*, 65–77.

5. As Charles Johnson put it, many whites came to believe that blacks were "mentally, culturally, and temperamentally ill-adapted to work with machinery." Charles S. Johnson, *Patterns of Negro Segregation*, 89. "Hopelessly petrified" were the words Donald Dewey used to describe the racial division of labor in unionized tobacco factories in the 1940s. Dewey, "Negro Employment," 290. See also Johnson, *Patterns of Negro Segregation*, 100–103, and the testimony of Edgar Bumgardner, "Official Report of the Proceedings before the NLRB," September 17–18, 1943, 67–77, 5-R-1356, Transcripts and Exhibits No. 6173, NLRB.

6. First quote is from Dewey, "Negro Employment," 284. "Mule" quote is from Hurston, *Their Eyes Were Watching God*, xxii. See also Yaeger, *Dirt and Desire*, and Hunter, *To 'Joy My Freedom*, 187–218.

7. Charles S. Johnson, *Patterns of Negro Segregation*, 99; testimony of Edgar Bumgardner, NLRB. A 1932 survey by the U.S. Department of Labor's Women's Bureau found that less than 1 percent of white women in Winston-Salem and Durham worked in leaf departments, while almost 98 percent of black women worked there. Manning and Byrne, *Effects on Women.* See also Northrup, *Organized Labor and the Negro*, 104.

8. Northrup, "Negro in the Tobacco Industry," 4–5. Workers had some influence on the assignment of jobs; there were a few walkouts around the turn of the century over demands that whites be given black jobs. Tilley, *Bright-Tobacco Industry*, 625.

9. Donald Dewey observed that "Southern employers, whatever their personal outlook on race relations, do not view their firms as the chosen instruments of white supremacy; and they are not without the power to seek a better factor combination by altering the racial division of labor within their organizations." Dewey, "Negro Employment," 281. On Reynolds's alternations of the racial division of labor, see Kaufman, *Challenge and Change*, 70–71, and Charles S. Johnson, "The Tobacco Worker," 1935, 308–12, box 62, folder 39, NRA. Reynolds

added another cigarette department staffed by blacks in 1929. See E. L. Crouch to E. Lewis Evans, August 10, 1929, II/13, TWIU. On the use of the division of labor to divide workers, see Michael Goldfield, *Color of Politics*, 14–15, and Cliff Brown, "The Role of Employers."

10. Johnson, "The Tobacco Worker," 131–32, NRA. See also testimony of Bumgardner, 120, NLRB.

11. "$57,000,000 Worth," 100. See a similar assessment in Charles S. Johnson, *Patterns of Negro Segregation*, 99, and Gordon, Edwards, and Reich, *Segmented Work*, 141–43. Over time, of course, whites and blacks, men and women, acquired the experience and training that justified their placement in certain jobs. But with a few exceptions, there was nothing in the capacities of particular groups of workers that would have prevented a total restructuring of the division of labor.

12. First quote is from Johnson, "The Tobacco Worker," 308, NRA. Second quote is from Blanche Fishel interview. Whites also served as "weigh men" in the hand stemming departments, and blacks felt the employers used whites to cheat them. Johnson, "The Tobacco Worker," 311, NRA. See also Lucy Bowles and Jim Stine interviews. Ernest Tilley recalled that white men and women predominated in the manufacturing departments in the smoking division, "but the Negroes swept the floors and done what we called the 'heavy work.'" Ernest Tilley interview. A white worker interviewed by the WPA commented on his work in the leaf house: "One good thing, most of the heavy, dirty work is done by Negroes." Claude V. Dunnagan, "I Know My Machine," 534, LRP.

13. Johnson, "The Tobacco Worker," 309, NRA.

14. Cooper, *Once a Cigar Maker*, 104–7 and 137–39; Kaufman, *Challenge and Change*, 11–23.

15. Strikes and organizing campaigns at tobacco factories around the country led to TWIU contracts with most major manufacturers. Kaufman, *Challenge and Change*, 53–55. See also Troxell, "Labor in the Tobacco Industry," 168–70; Northrup, *Organized Labor and the Negro*, 110; and Tilley, *Bright-Tobacco Industry*, 625.

16. Quote is from Hall et al., *Like a Family*, 187. Also see *TW* 23 (April 1919): 8–13, and Tilley, *R. J. Reynolds*, 256–57. The AFL soon began publishing a local newspaper, the *Labor Leader*, and was able to hold an interracial rally at the county courthouse in support of the TWIU. Tilley, *Bright-Tobacco Industry*, 260.

17. Kaufman, *Challenge and Change*, 44–51. On the racial policies of the Knights of Labor, see Rachleff, *Black Labor in the South*, 109–201, and Fink, *Workingmen's Democracy*, 149–77.

18. *TW* 23 (April 1919): 11–12. For similar attitudes, see Meier and Rudwick, "Attitudes of Negro Leaders," 39–41; Letwin, *Challenge of Interracial Unionism*; Kelley, *Hammer and Hoe*; Leslie Brown, "Common Spaces, Separate Lives"; and Kelly, *Race, Class, and Power*. Reynolds might have instigated Hill's action. See Tilley's report of a Reynolds official's letter on industrial democracy sent to Simon Atkins. Tilley, *R. J. Reynolds*, 634.

19. *TW* 24 (June 1919): 8. On consumerist strategies, see Kelley, *Race Rebels*, 55–75; Lizabeth Cohen, *Making a New Deal*; Frank, *Purchasing Power*; Newman, "Forgotten Fifteen Million"; and Weems, *Desegregating the Dollar*.

20. Tilley, *R. J. Reynolds*, 634 n. 117 (first quote), 260 (second quote).

21. Tilley, *Bright-Tobacco Industry*, 261–62; *TW* 23 (October 1919): 5. A contract negotiated the following spring extended these benefits until April 1921.

22. Tilley, *R. J. Reynolds*, 252–53, 260–62; Troxell, "Labor in the Tobacco Industry," 174–75.

Quote is from the *Textile Worker*, June 1928, 295. Although not involved, Robert Black remembered the events of 1919. See Robert Black interview, June 1, 1976.

23. On welfare capitalism in the 1920s, see Zahavi, *Workers, Managers*, 37–125; Halpern, *Down on the Killing Floor*, 76–95; Jacoby, *Modern Manors*, 11–34; and Daniel Nelson, *Management and Workers*, 140–62.

24. *J&S*, January 31, 1960; Tilley, *R. J. Reynolds*, 258.

25. See Tilley, *R. J. Reynolds*, 144–54, 248–49, for a description of life in the factories before World War I. On management, see Richard Edwards, *Contested Terrain*, 22–36, and Gordon, Edwards, and Reich, *Segmented Work*, 137–38.

26. Tilley, *R. J. Reynolds*, 279.

27. Whitaker is quoted in ibid., 274.

28. Tilley, *R. J. Reynolds*, 273–80. Quote is on 279. For evidence that children still worked in the factories, see Hazel Jones interview.

29. Tilley, *R. J. Reynolds*, 266.

30. Johnson, "The Tobacco Worker," 264, NRA.

31. Ibid., 266.

32. Ibid., 265.

33. Ibid., 268; Theodosia Phelps interview, June 1, 1978; Wardell Boulware interview.

34. Johnson, "The Tobacco Worker," 269, NRA. On Winston-Salem's sex ratio in 1940, see Chapter 3, note 21.

35. Dunnagan, "I Know My Machine," 544, LRP.

36. Willie Grier interview; Robert Black and Ruby Jones interview.

37. Viola Brown and Julia Leach interview.

38. Ibid.

39. Lonnie Nesmith interview, undated. See also Robert Black interview, June 1, 1976.

40. Robert Black and Ruby Jones interview.

41. Johnson, "The Tobacco Worker," 290 and 305, NRA. A graphic map in the gadfly weekly *Thursday* showed the concentration of tuberculosis deaths in poor black neighborhoods of East Winston. *Thursday*, February 13, 1941. See Hunter, *To 'Joy My Freedom*, 187–218, for a discussion of tuberculosis among blacks in Georgia. See Beverly Jones, "Race, Sex, and Class," 445, for evidence of high death rates from tuberculosis among black female tobacco workers in Durham.

42. Johnson, "The Tobacco Worker," 290, NRA; Robert Black and Ruby Jones interview; Beverly Jones, "Race, Sex, and Class," 444–45.

43. Testimony of Bumgardner, 160, NLRB; *WSC*, February 10, 1979, 8. See also Dewey, "Negro Employment," 283.

44. Robert Black interview, June 1, 1976; Robert Black and Ruby Jones interview; Johnson, "The Tobacco Worker," 290, NRA; Tilley, *R. J. Reynolds*, 272.

45. Johnson, "The Tobacco Worker," 292, NRA. The "drive system" predominated in early-twentieth-century corporations and remained the predominate method of labor discipline in the prefabrication departments at Reynolds until the late 1940s. See Jacoby, *Modern Manors*, 11.

46. Geneva McClendon interview.

47. Theodosia Phelps interview, June 1, 1978.

48. Johnson, "The Tobacco Worker," 291, NRA; Evelyn and Langfell Hairston interview;

Robert Black and Ruby Jones interview. Racial epithets were not limited to the uneducated foremen but came out of the boardroom as well. "'Nigger, take off your hat when you come in this office,' was the standard greeting of [company treasurer] D. Rich to any Negro who might fumble with his ragged hat." Tilley, *R. J. Reynolds*, 242.

49. Robert Black interview, June 1, 1976. By some accounts, these practices were not confined to sadistic supervisors; they came from the company's very top. R. J.'s grandson, Patrick Reynolds, contends that R. J. "used his power as an employer to induce women from the packing floor to come to a back room with him." The younger Reynolds claims that R. J. had a number of illegitimate offspring by both black and white women in Winston. Reynolds and Shachtman, *Gilded Leaf*, 44–45. Similar stories about Durham manufacturers can be found in Janiewski, *Sisterhood Denied*, 97–98. A discussion of sexual harassment as a transaction between men can be found in Hall, "'The Mind That Burns,'" 332.

50. Robert Black and Ruby Jones interview. See also Tilley, *R. J. Reynolds*, 272.

51. Robert Black and Ruby Jones interview.

52. Johnson, "The Tobacco Worker," 293, NRA.

53. Willie Grier interview; Robert Black interview, April 8, 1979.

54. Lonnie Nesmith interview, undated; Johnson, "The Tobacco Worker," 292, NRA.

55. Robert Black, Janie Black, Viola Brown, and Karl Korstad interview; Robert Black interview, March 3, 1988; Johnson, "The Tobacco Worker," 293, NRA. Workers' metaphors of slavery, prison, and the chain gang demonstrate how well they grasped the political linkages between their work and the larger system of racial capitalism. They did not need a history lesson to understand that life in the factory was all too reminiscent of slavery times. Nor did they need a reminder of their perilous status in the new social order; ensnarement in the criminal justice system for even the most minor crime resulted in a quick trip to jail or the road gang.

56. Dunnagan, "I Know My Machine," 537, LRP; Blanche Fishel interview. White women inspectors in the cigarette department complained to Charles Johnson about uncomfortable chairs, the heat, and the strain of lifting trays all day. See Johnson, "The Tobacco Worker," 300–301, NRA.

57. Blanche Fishel interview.

58. James McKensie interview.

59. Robert Black interview, undated.

60. Tilley, *R. J. Reynolds*, 247, 255, 465. "It should be noted that migration itself . . . is a form of protest." Charles S. Johnson, "Social Relations," 347. On Blue Monday, see Theodosia Phelps interview, June 1, 1978. Company officials sought to control absenteeism because it forced them to keep extra people on the payroll to ensure a full crew each day. In 1916, during a severe labor shortage, Reynolds created a bonus plan to cut absenteeism. Employees who worked "regularly" and "faithfully" during the year were to receive two cents for every dollar they earned. The company increased the bonus to four cents the next year, but as wartime demand abated and labor became more plentiful, the bonus was rescinded. Tilley, *R. J. Reynolds*, 253–56.

61. Theodosia Phelps interview, June 1, 1978; Leon Edwards interview.

62. Robert Black interview, December 18, 1976.

63. Willie Grier interview. In addition to paying low wages, foremen looked to wring every cent out of workers, sometimes cheating them out of rightfully earned wages. Take, for example, the company's policy of weighing stems the morning after rather than at the end of

work. Etta Stevenson, a stemmer in Number 256, described the process. "You'd go line up at the barrel to get tobacco, somebody would be there to give it to us in our aprons, and then go back to our benches and stem. They would weigh the stems up every morning and that's what we would get paid for. We'd pack the stems down real tight so it wouldn't dry so it would weight good." Etta Stevenson interview. See also Johnson, "The Tobacco Worker," 114, NRA.

64. Robert Black interview, June 1, 1976; Blanche Fishel interview.

65. Louise Smith, Viola Brown and Sally Mitchell, and Frank Green interviews. Also see Kelley, "'We Are Not What We Seem,'" 88–89.

66. Kelley, "'We Are Not What We Seem,'" 94–95; Charles S. Johnson, *Patterns of Negro Segregation*, 101.

67. Claude V. Dunnagan and Ester Searle Pinnix, "Operator to Organizer," 584–85, folder 16, LRP.

68. Robert, *Story of Tobacco*, 86; Tilley, *Bright-Tobacco Industry*, 318–19; Levine, *Black Culture*, 202–17; Hinson, *Virginia Work Songs*.

69. Hinson, *Virginia Work Songs*.

70. Velma Hopkins interview; *WSJ*, October 1 and 29, 1939.

71. Viola Brown and Julia Leach interview. See also Hazel Jones and Velma Hopkins interviews.

72. Velma Hopkins interview.

Chapter 5

1. Montgomery, *Fall of the House of Labor*, 1–8. Quote is on 8.

2. The TWIU held no conventions between 1900 and 1939. Kaufman, *Challenge and Change*, 79.

3. *The Textile Worker* 16 (August 1928): 294–96 (first quote is on 295); Piedmont Organizing Council, "Resolution," June 24, 1928, Winston-Salem, North Carolina, II/13, TWIU. Second quote is from Robert Black interview, May 1, 1978.

4. Troxell, "Labor in the Tobacco Industry," 177–78; Charles S. Johnson, "The Tobacco Worker," 1935, 283, box 62, folder 39, NRA. Quote is from Willie Grier interview. The 1928 layoffs may be related to installation of the Arenco packer, a high-speed machine that packaged the cigarettes, wrapped the package, and attached the revenue stamps. See Tilley, *R. J. Reynolds*, 344–45; E. L. Crouch to E. Lewis Evans, March 4, 1929, II/13, and Crouch to Evans, December 30, 1930, II/14, TWIU. TWIU organizer E. L. Crouch claimed that the black local was better organized and "bolder" than the white local and may have been willing to force a strike. But the TWIU rarely, if ever, used the strike to organize a plant. Art Shields, "Meet Ed Crouch." See Marshall, *Labor in the South*, 26–27, for a discussion of 1920s antiunionism in the South.

5. Quotes are from *The Textile Worker* 16 (August 1928): 294. See also Kaufman, *Challenge and Change*, 71–72, and G. V. Kite and J. G. Taylor to G. M. Smith, September 7, 1929, in International Brotherhood of Electrical Workers, "Twentieth Biennial Convention," 48–50.

6. E. Lewis Evans to R. E. Lasater, February 14, 1930, II/14, TWIU.

7. Naison, *Communists in Harlem*, 17; Johanningsmeier, *Forging American Communism*, 245.

8. Quotes are from Naison, *Communists in Harlem*, 18. See Record, *Negro and the Commu-*

nist Party, 22, 39–42, 55; Kelley, *Hammer and Hoe*; and Von Eschen, *Race against Empire*, 10. Also see Von Eschen's notes to the larger literature in ibid., 193 nn. 10 and 11. For a revisionist interpretation stressing the middle-class orientation of the Garvey movement, see Stein, *World of Marcus Garvey.*

9. Crouch, "Brief History," 1. On the Loray strike, see Salmond, *Gastonia*, and Tyson, *Radio Free Dixie*, 7. See Haessly, "Mill Mother's Lament," for Ella May Wiggins's welcoming attitude toward blacks.

10. Robert Black interview, March 3, 1988.

11. E. L. Crouch to Lewis Evans, March 11, 1930, II/14, TWIU; "Special Meeting of Negro Departments with Out of Town Comrades," April 5, 1930, fond 515, reel 155, 2023, 7; "Meeting of the Secretariat of Dist. 16," February 3, 1930, "Report of the March 6 Demonstration in Dist. 16," June 30, 1930, and "Dear Comrade," December 1930, reel 162, 2147–48, 30, 10, *Communist Party of the United States of America Papers, Manuscripts Division, Library of Congress, Washington, D.C.* See also various reports in *DW*, March 1, April 12, 26, 29, May 23, and June 4, 1930, and *Southern Worker*, November 11, 1930. A fictional account of Communist agitation in Winston-Salem can be found in James M. Shields, *Just Plain Larnin,'* 209–24. See also Solomon, *Cry Was Unity*, 112, 127, 150, 186.

12. On the unemployed councils, see Naison, *Communists in Harlem*, 34–35; Leab, "'United We Eat,'" 300–315; and Klehr, *Heyday of American Communism*, 49.

13. Robert Black interview, June 1, 1976. Party reports on the unemployed council in Winston-Salem indicated 140 members. "Report of March 6th Demonstration," [1930], fond 515, reel 162, 2148, 1, *Communist Party of the United States of America Papers.* See also Solomon, *Cry Was Unity*, 127.

14. Robert Black interview, June 1, 1976.

15. Crouch, "Brief History," 7.

16. On the Scottsboro case, see Carter, *Scottsboro*, and James Goodman, *Stories of Scottsboro.*

17. Background on the NIRA can be found in Hall et al., *Like a Family*, 289–98, and Storrs, *Civilizing Capitalism*, 91–123.

18. Storrs, *Civilizing Capitalism*, 101.

19. Ibid., 101–11.

20. See National Recovery Administration, *Code of Fair Competition.*

21. Tilley, *R. J. Reynolds*, 265–66; Johnson, "The Tobacco Worker," 281, NRA.

22. Johnson, "The Tobacco Worker," 280, NRA.

23. Anonymous letter, October 25, 1933, 25, Cigarette and Snuff Manufacturing Industry, box 1390, Complaints, NRA.

24. See William Powell Jones, "Cutting through Jim Crow," 130–74, and Irons, *Testing the New Deal*, 63–96, for the negative aspects of the NRA's impact on southern workers.

25. Kaufman, *Challenge and Change*, 79; Sam H. Scott to Samuel L. Evans, June 17, 1939, III/11, TWIU; Johnson, "The Tobacco Worker," 287–89, NRA (quote on 287); Robert Black interview, May 1, 1978; Theodosia Phelps interview, June 1, 1978. Charles Johnson found that both black and white workers gave highly critical accounts of the TWIU locals at Brown & Williamson ("The Tobacco Worker," 287–89, NRA).

26. On the provisions of the Wagner Act, see Tomlins, *State and the Unions*, 132–47.

27. Janiewski, *Sisterhood Denied*, 161–68. Black women in the stemmeries received less support from the TWIU and showed less interest in unionization, and it was not until the 1940s that they won representation. See Fantasia, *Cultures of Solidarity*, 47.

28. Janiewski, *Sisterhood Denied*, 163; Kaufman, *Challenge and Change*, 83–97.

29. First two quotes are from Lewis Evans to Samuel H. Scott, February 18, 1937, and Sam H. Scott to Samuel L. Evans, May 22, 1937, II/54, TWIU. Last two quotes are from E. N. Ellis and R. E. Carn to E. Lewis Evans, July 8, 1939, and Evans to Ed R. Ellis, July 10, 1939, III/11, TWIU. See also Scott to Evans, June 17, 1939, III/11, TWIU. On Evans's attitude, see Kaufman, *Challenge and Change*, 96–97. Under the leadership of Warren Smith (1940–42) the TWIU realized the need to organize black workers, who made up 65 percent of its potential membership, and even in Winston-Salem organizers made efforts to inform the black community about the benefits of organization. After Smith's ouster in 1942 and the CIO's success with blacks, however, the TWIU paid little attention to the needs and concerns of blacks. Kaufman, *Challenge and Change*, 103–5.

30. Johnson, "The Tobacco Worker," 283–84, NRA; Wilhelmina Jackson, "Memo on Winston-Salem," 8–9, box 36, folder 4, RBP. Viola Brown mentions that people were even scared to used the term "union suit" to describe long underwear. Viola Brown and Julia Leach interview.

31. On this change of attitude among blacks, see Von Eschen, *Race against Empire*, 47–54.

32. Storrs, *Civilizing Capitalism*, 186.

33. Ibid., 126 and 313 n. 5.

34. *TW*, March 1941; Sam Scott to Samuel Evans, September 17, 1938, II/55, TWIU; Johnson, "The Tobacco Worker," 283, NRA; "R. J. Reynolds Tobacco Company," July 21, 1941, National Labor Relations Board, *Decisions and Orders*, vol. 7 (1941), 115, 679; National Recovery Administration, *Code of Fair Competition*.

35. *TW*, May 1941.

36. Progress Report, January 29, 1941, Case No. 196/4364, FMCS. A black newspaper, the *Winston-Salem Telegram*, told its readers that "the Negro is far better off with the R. J. R. Company than in any places that have the tobacco union." *Winston-Salem Telegram*, April 1941, clipping in III/31, TWIU.

37. "R. J. Reynolds Tobacco Company," National Labor Relations Board, *Decisions and Orders*, vol. 7 (1941), 115.

38. Theodosia Phelps interview, June 1, 1978. See Robert Black interview, May 1, 1978, for an extended discussion of the racial discrimination by the TWIU.

39. Tise, *Government*, 48.

40. Abrams, *Conservative Constraints*, xiii–xx; Marcello, "Politics of Relief," 18–21.

41. Sullivan, *Days of Hope*, 91; Sitkoff, *A New Deal for Blacks*.

42. Abrams, *Conservative Constraints*, 210–30; *Thursday*, June 27, 1940.

43. Abrams, *Conservative Constraints*, 187; Lewinson, *Race, Class, and Party*, 219. Mabry describes the movement of North Carolina blacks from the Republican to the Democratic Party beginning in the 1920s. See Mabry, *Negro in North Carolina Politics*, 80–81. On the importance of women's suffrage to the black vote, see Gilmore, *Gender and Jim Crow*, 205–24. On North Carolina's abandonment of the poll tax, see Key, *Southern Politics*, 578.

44. Bunche, *Political Status of the Negro*, 477, 482–84; Augustus M. Burns III, "North Carolina and the Negro Dilemma," 202–3.; Mabry, *Negro in North Carolina Politics*, 78–83; Harry J. Walker, "Changes in Race Accommodation," 206–28. Winston-Salem attorney Hosie Price served as head of the state committee in 1939. *J&S*, January 6 and 15, 1939.

45. Lewinson, *Race, Class, and Party*, 219; Robert Black interview, December 28, 1976.

46. George Stoney to Ralph Bunche, July 14, 1940, box 36, folder 4, RBP.

47. *UR*, April 6 and 20, 1939; Stoney to Bunche, July 14, 1940, RBP. For background on Bruce, see *J&S*, April 13, 1941. Local Democrats no doubt used their patronage to secure black votes. Similar instances of vote buying had bloated registration books in both Durham and Raleigh and led to the election of machine candidates. Stoney and Jackson encountered a great deal of resentment toward black ward heelers who did the bidding of whites. Weare, *Black Business*, 242–43. Apparently white Democrats also supported black registration and voting in a number of other North Carolina cities as a means to defeat Republican opponents. See Harry J. Walker, "Changes in Race Accommodation," 186, 188.

48. First quote is from *J&S*, February 3, 1939. Second quote is from Jackson, "Memo on Winston-Salem," 7, RBP. The NAACP also became more active in recruiting members and taking positions on local issues. *J&S*, November 5, 1939.

49. *J&S*, December 10, 1939; Thomas Kilgore interview. Kilgore went on to a distinguished career as a minister and civil rights leader. *New York Times*, February 10, 1998.

50. *J&S*, May 19 and August 11, 1940. The quote is from Jackson, "Memo on Winston-Salem," 17, RBP. See also Bunche, *Political Status of the Negro*, 87.

51. *Thursday*, October 24 and December 5, 1940.

Chapter 6

1. Tyson, *Radio Free Dixie*, 27. On A. Philip Randolph and the March on Washington movement, see Bates, *Pullman Porters*, 148–74.

2. Tyson, *Radio Free Dixie*, 29.

3. Robert Cohen, *When the Old Left Was Young*, xiv. For more on Henderson, see the *New York Times*, April 6, 1932, and Schrecker, *No Ivory Tower*, 45. On UCAPAWA's arrival in Winston-Salem, see Progress Report, January 29, 1941, Case No. 196/4364, FMCS; C. W. Weaver to R. J. Petree, February 18, 1941, III/31, TWIU; and testimony of Robert Black, "Hearings before the Committee to Investigate Charges against the Food, Tobacco, Agricultural, and Allied Workers of America," January 6, 1950, box 109, FTA Hearings, CIOSTO.

4. Jamieson, *Labor Unionism*, 27–29; Henderson, "Rural Masses."

5. Quote is from DPOWA, *Founding Convention*, 14. See also Ruiz, *Cannery Women, Cannery Lives*, 43; Jamieson, *Labor Unionism*, 27; UCAPAWA, *Official Proceedings, 1937* and *Official Proceedings, 1940*.

6. Edwin McCrea interview.

7. On the role of the Communist Party in the CIO, see Stepan-Norris and Zeitlin, "'Who Gets the Bird?,'" and Zieger, *CIO*, 82–83.

8. Most of the 112 organizers initially employed by the CIO to work in the South were native southerners, and they were deeply committed to the region. Sullivan, *Days of Hope*, 95.

9. Edwin McCrea interview. See also Sullivan, *Days of Hope*, 92–93, and Denning, *Cultural Front*, 3–50.

10. "Structure of feeling" is from Denning, *Cultural Front*, 26, quoting Raymond Williams. This structure of feeling, moreover, was not confined to trade unionists, artists, and intellectuals. Indeed, by 1942 Popular Front attitudes had so "impressed themselves on the American people that opinion polls found that 25 percent of the population favored socialism and another 35 percent had an open mind about it." Denning, *Cultural Front*, 4.

11. Sullivan, *Days of Hope*, 84–91.

12. Alex Lichtenstein, "Cold War and the 'Negro Question'"; Sullivan, *Days of Hope*, 7. Much of the thinking of southern activists was summed up in Carlton and Coclanis, *Confronting Southern Poverty*.

13. On the STFU, see Mitchell, *Mean Things Happening*; Thrasher and Wise, "Southern Tenant Farmers' Union," 5–32; and Egerton, *Speak Now against the Day*, 154–58. On the tensions between the STFU and UCAPAWA, see Grubbs, *Cry from Cotton*, 171–79, and Naison, "Southern Tenant Farmers' Union." Mitchell's analysis of the issues can be found in Mitchell, *Mean Things Happening*, 169.

14. Elizabeth Eudy interview, November 1, 1987. On UCAPAWA, see Jamieson, *Labor Unionism*; Ruiz, *Cannery Women, Cannery Lives*; and Honey, *Southern Labor*.

15. Dunbar, *Against the Grain*, 130–35, 164–85. There may have been initial attempts to hire TWIU organizers and raid AFL locals in New York, Florida, and Virginia, but apparently nothing came of it. Kaufman, *Challenge and Change*, 92. UCAPAWA won the right to represent workers at P. Lorillard in Middletown, Ohio, in 1942. Northrup, *Organized Labor and the Negro*, 114–15; Kaufman, *Challenge and Change*, 104. It also organized cigar workers at American Tobacco Company plants in Charleston, South Carolina, and Philadelphia. FTA, *Report of the General Executive Officers*, 10.

16. Robert Black interview, June 1, 1976. Darnes served in the U.S. Army during World War II and returned to Winston-Salem in 1946.

17. Robert Black interviews, June 1, 1976, and March 3, 1988.

18. Robert Black interview, December 28, 1976; DPOWA, "Brief History," 1; *UCAPAWA News*, June 15, July 1, and August 1, 1942.

19. Quote is from "Harry Koger," n.d., box 29, folder 27, International Fur and Leather Workers Union Records, Kheel Center for Labor-Management Documentation and Archives, M. P. Catherwood Library, Cornell University, Ithaca, N.Y. See also Mary Lou Koger Ford, "Biographical Sketch of Harry Koger," original in author's possession; Dickerman and Taylor, *Who's Who in Labor*, 184–85; and Honey, *Southern Labor*, 124–25. On the pecan shellers' strike, see Jamieson, *Labor Unionism*, 278–81.

20. William DeBerry interview.

21. Naison, "Claude and Joyce Williams," 41.

22. Ibid., 44; Jamieson, *Labor Unionism*, 322–23.

23. Naison, "Marxism and Black Radicalism," 46. The strategy Myles Horton used at Highlander was very similar. See Myles Horton, *Long Haul*.

24. Naison, "Claude and Joyce Williams," 47–48 (quote on 48); Honey, *Southern Labor*, 132; Claude Williams to "The Reverend Majority," [1947], box 7, folder 3, Claude Williams Papers, Archives of Labor History and Urban Affairs, Walter Reuther Library, Wayne State University, Detroit, Mich.

25. William DeBerry interview. On the importance of the black church as an organizing base, see McAdam, *Political Process*, 43–44.

26. *J&S*, April 27, 1941; Harry Koger to Claude Williams, November 27, 1942, January 2, 1943, October 25, 1943, box 14, folder 14, CWP. For Gholson's views on Southern race relations, see Gholson, *Negro Looks into the South*.

27. Affidavit of Aquilla Hairston, June 8, 1944, Transcript of Hearings, pt. 2, NWLB.

28. *WSJ*, July 28, 1942.

29. Theodosia Phelps interview, June 1, 1978. Martha Penn and her sister Lola Love (Bates)

were also friends of Eddie Gallimore and were active in the organizing drive. C. W. Weaver to R. J. Petree, February 18, 1941, II/62, TWIU. On the importance of personal relations in recruitment, see McAdam, McCarthy, and Zald, "Social Movements," 708.

30. Theodosia Phelps interview, June 1, 1978.

31. Robert Black interviews, August 3, 1981, and August 24, 1984; testimony of Robert Black, "Hearings before the Committee," 346, CIOSTO.

32. Willie Grier interview; Robert Black interviews, June 1, 1976, and August 24, 1984.

33. *J&S*, January 15, 1939, and June 15, 1941.

34. Velma Hopkins interview; *WSJ*, March 22, 1942.

35. *UCAPAWA News*, July 1, 1942.

36. Robert Black interviews, June 1, 1976, and March 3, 1988; DPOWA, "Brief History," 1.

37. "Statement by Ruel White," [1940], II/64, TWIU.

38. *UCAPAWA News*, July 1, August 1 and 15, 1942; William DeBerry interview; DPOWA, "Brief History," 1.

39. *UCAPAWA News*, July 15, August 15, and November 15, 1942. The CIO was not the only union to utilize black singing groups. During the earlier TWIU drives, these groups regularly performed at mass meetings. At a 1942 rally that included black and white workers, the Acme Quartette, the Daniel Gospel Singers, and the Silvertone and Jubilee Quartettes performed. *TW*, May 1942.

40. Song lyrics from Robert Black interview, March 3, 1988, and *UCAPAWA News*, July 1, 1942. On the role of spiritual music generally in union campaigns, see Lieberman, *"My Song Is My Weapon,"* 30–35, and Lott, "'Seeming Counterfeit.'"

41. *UCAPAWA News*, August 15 and September 15, 1942.

42. Quote is from Robert Black interview, April 8, 1979. See also Robert Black interview, December 28, 1976. These informal recruitment efforts were critical to the union's success in mobilizing people during the sit-down and are an example of "frame-bridging." See Snow et al., "Frame Alignment Processes," 467–68.

43. Theodosia Phelps interview, June 1, 1978. "In practical terms, the organizing dilemma facing would-be activists was quite real: how to perform the acts necessary to encourage workers without undercutting oneself by getting fired and inadvertently proving once again the futility of all such activism." Goodwyn, *Breaking the Barrier*, 137.

44. *UCAPAWA News*, August 1 and 15, and September 15, 1942.

45. Lizabeth Cohen, *Making a New Deal*, 301–13.

46. Tyson, *Radio Free Dixie*, 31–35. On the Eleanor Clubs, see Odum, *Race and the Rumors of Race*.

47. *UCAPAWA News*, December 1, 1942, February 1 and May 1, 1943.

48. *UCAPAWA News*, December 1, 1942, and February 1, 1943. Thanks to Walter Campbell for sharing his research on the Wellman case.

49. First quote is from Jonathan Daniels, quoted in Tyson, *Radio Free Dixie*, 32. Second quote is from Charles H. Houston to J. M. Broughton, December 12, 1942, J. Melville Broughton Papers, North Carolina Division of Archives and History, Raleigh, N.C. The National Federation for Constitutional Liberties also joined the Wellman cause.

50. *UCAPAWA News*, May 1, 1943.

51. Chester Davis reports, April 6, 1943, and August 9, 1943, FBIHQ; Minutes, April 23, 1943, 266, BOA.

52. E. L. Sandefur to Clark Sheppard, [1943], II/11, TWIU.

53. Edwin McCrea interview. For background on Hargrove, see Dickerman and Taylor, *Who's Who in Labor*.

54. Crawford Shelton interview.

55. Theodosia Phelps interview, June 1, 1978.

56. *UCAPAWA News*, April 15 and June 15, 1943.

57. Robert Black interview, March 3, 1988; *UCAPAWA News*, April 15, 1943.

58. Korstad and Lichtenstein, "Opportunities Found and Lost," 787; McAdam, McCarthy, and Zald, "Social Movements," 699–700.

59. The development of black Winston-Salem fits the general pattern of preconditions for collective action. See ibid., 703–4, and McAdam, *Political Process*, 97.

60. The key, according to sociologists Doug McAdam, John D. McCarthy, and Mayer N. Zald, is to comprehend the links between the political and institutional factors favoring organization and the potential that exists within thousands of individuals. They suggest that such linkages can occur in "any small group setting in which processes collectively attributed are combined with rudimentary forms of organization to produce mobilization for collective action." The TWOC functioned as this "micro-mobilization context." McAdam, McCarthy, and Zald, "Social Movements," 709. In the end, however, collective action seldom happens without the painstaking one-on-one recruitment. Goodwyn, *Breaking the Barrier*, 60.

Chapter 7

1. Robert Black interviews, December 28, 1976, and August 3, 1988.

2. Theodosia Phelps interview, June 1, 1978.

3. Robert Black interview, April 8, 1979.

4. Tilley, *R. J. Reynolds*, illustration between 372 and 373; R. W. Goodrick, "Progress Report," June 23, 1943, Case No. 300/9086, FMCS.

5. Velma Hopkins interview.

6. Robert Black interview, April 8, 1979.

7. Frank O'Neal interview; Affidavit of Aquilla Hairston, June 8, 1944, and Affidavit of Robert Black, [1943], Transcript of Hearings, pt. 2, NWLB; Robert Black interview, April 8, 1979.

8. Affidavit of Robert Black, NWLB; Chester Davis interview.

9. Affidavit of Aquilla Hairston, NWLB; Frank O'Neal interview. Hairston apparently had second thoughts about the matter, because later that week he talked with Hopkins about the union, signed an application card, and ultimately paid part of his initiation dues. Affidavit of Velma Hopkins, July 8, 1944, Transcript of Hearings, pt. 2, NWLB.

10. Velma Hopkins interview. For the committee membership, see Goodrick, "Progress Report," June 23, 1943, FMCS.

11. Frank O'Neal interview. The following discussion of the grievance presentation is drawn from Goodrick, "Progress Report," June 23, 1943, FMCS.

12. R. W. Goodrick, "Progress Report," Exhibit F, June 24, 1943, Case No. 300/9086, 3, FMCS.

13. Issues of skill classification were common among black industrial workers. For instance, employees of the Tobacco By-Products Company in Richmond, Virginia, struck in 1938 for recognition as skilled workers. See Augusta V. Jackson, "New Deal," 323.

14. Goodrick, "Progress Report," June 24, 1943, FMCS.

15. Theodosia Phelps interview, April 17, 1979.

16. Ruby Jones interview.

17. Robert Black interview, April 8, 1979; R. W. Goodrick, "Progress Report," Exhibit G, June 24, 1943, Case No. 300/9086, 1, FMCS.

18. Ruby Jones interview. The white foremen were not the only problem. In some of the hand stemming departments the women had to use pitchforks to carry tobacco to their benches. It was a strenuous job, and many women complained; one group asked the company to assign a man to handle the tobacco. But the women in Velma Hopkins's department in Number 256 did not like that idea. They told Robert Black: "You bring a black guy in here and he's going to keep fussing or nagging at the women all the time. We think we'd rather do our own forking." Robert Black interview, April 8, 1979.

19. Goodrick, "Progress Report," Exhibit G, June 24, 1943, FMCS.

20. "Remarks of John C. Whitaker before Negro Committee Representing Negro Employees," June 28, 1943, Case No. 300/9086, 1, FMCS. He did not say the obverse, that whatever hurts you hurts the company, and whatever helps you helps the company.

21. Ibid., 2–5.

22. Ibid., 5–8.

23. Theodosia Phelps interview, June 1, 1978.

24. "Remarks of John C. Whitaker before Negro Committee," FMCS.

25. Frank O'Neal interview.

26. R. W. Goodrick, "Progress Report," Exhibits BB and CC, July 1, 1943, Case No. 300/9086, FMCS.

27. *WSJ*, June 29, 1943; Kaufman, *Challenge and Change*, 107.

28. Tomlins, *State and the Unions*, 148–50, 213–24.

29. Ibid., 216, 217, 221, 229–30.

30. *WSJ*, July 5, 1943.

31. *WSJ*, July 9, 1943.

32. Theodosia Phelps interview, June 1, 1978.

33. *WSJ*, July 4 and 10, 1943.

34. Kaufman, *Challenge and Change*, 83–117.

35. *WSJ*, July 21–23, 1943.

36. Kaufman, *Challenge and Change*, 105 (first quote); *WSJ*, July 16, 1943 (second and third quotes). The TWIU directed the same message to the civic and business community. On July 13 union officials invited business and community leaders to attend a meeting to hear their plea for moderation. *WSJ*, July 16, 1943.

37. *WSJ*, July 11, 12, 1943.

38. Prichard, *Medicine*, 34; *WSJ*, April 24, 1938, September 18, 1949; Theodosia Phelps interview, June 1, 1978. On Atkins, see *J&S*, October 27, 1940, and Leon S. Dure Jr. to Gordon Gray, March 1, 1948, Gordon Gray Papers, Southern Historical Collection, University of North Carolina at Chapel Hill. Thomas Kilgore says that Atkins "was dubbed as a number one Uncle Tom in Winston-Salem by the black people." Thomas Kilgore interview.

39. *WSJ*, July 25, 1943; Philip S. Foner, *Organized Labor*, 216–17. Charles Johnson observed: "The Company has for many years exercised a strong control over the leadership of the Negro community in Winston-Salem. This had been done through a system of strategically distributed benevolence to churches, schools, and other welfare agencies." Johnson and McEntire, "Minority Labor Groups," 381.

40. Myrdal, *An American Dilemma*, 722.

41. *WSJ*, July 14, 1943. Similar sentiments were expressed by W. L. Griffin. See *WSJ*, July 16, 1943.

42. *WSJ*, July 16, 1943.

43. For this phenomena in Durham, see Weare, *Black Business*, 225–27.

44. Gaines, *Uplifting the Race*, 14–15.

45. *WSJ*, July 17, 1943. Interestingly, the Reverend G. J. Thomas, one of the signers of the letter to the *Journal*, had complained a year earlier about "a committee of Negro citizens who had either been appointed, or set themselves up as spokesmen for the race." He was reacting then to the inadequate facilities for blacks at the new bus station that had been approved by such a committee. *WSJ*, September 9, 1942.

46. *Carolina Times*, July 24, 1943. For more on Austin, see Weare, *Black Business*, 225–27, 241–43.

47. *Carolina Times*, July 24, 1943.

48. Myrdal, *An American Dilemma*, 721.

49. *WSJ*, July 26, 1943; Theodosia Phelps interview, June 1, 1978; Robert Black interview, April 17, 1979; Kaufman, *Challenge and Change*, 57. See Charles S. Johnson, *Patterns of Negro Segregation*, 233, for an example of the enforcement of race loyalty.

50. *WSJ*, July 27, 1943. Also see earlier letters to the editor supporting this position. *WSJ*, July 19, 1943.

51. Robert A. Levett to David C. Shaw, August 22, 1944, Formal and Informal Unfair Labor Practices and Representation, Case Files 1935–48, Case: Reynolds, R. J. Tobacco Company, 5-C-1730, (1945), NLRB; Elmer D. Keen to W. M. Aicher, August 7, 1943, and Harold Lane and Donald Henderson to W. M. Aicher, August 9, 1943, Transcripts and Exhibits No. 6173, NLRB.

52. Hobart Johnson interview.

53. *WSJ*, July 19, 1943.

54. Blanche Fishel interview.

55. *WSJ*, July 19, 1943. For more on Morley's work with the Popular Front, see Denning, *Cultural Front*, 155.

56. *WSJ*, August 4, 1943.

57. *WSJ*, August 5, 1943; "Certification of Counting and Tabulating of Ballots, August 4, 1943," Transcripts and Exhibits No. 6173, NLRB.

58. Elmer D. Keen to W. M. Aicher, August 7, 1943, and Harold Lane and Donald Henderson to W. M. Aicher, August 9, 1943, Transcripts and Exhibits No. 6173, NLRB; *WSJ*, August 11, 1943.

59. See Lemert, *Tobacco Manufacturing Industry*.

60. *WSJ*, August 11–13 and 15, 1943.

61. *WSJ*, August 26–28, September 1, 1943.

62. Richard King calls the mass meeting a form of political expression. Richard H. King, *Civil Rights*, 40–42.

63. Robert Black interview, October 7, 1977.

64. Ibid.; Robert Black interview, August 3, 1981; *UCAPAWA News*, September 1, 1943.

65. Robert Black interview, August 3, 1981; Velma Hopkins interview.

66. *WSJ*, October 26, 1943; Levett to Shaw, August 22, 1944, 12–14, NLRB; S. Brewer, "Progress Report," October 27, 1943, Case No. 400/920, FMCS.

67. Transcript, September 17–18, 1943, Transcripts and Exhibits No. 6173, NLRB.

68. "In the Matter of R. J. Reynolds Tobacco Company and Tobacco Workers," Case No. 5-R-1356 (October 13, 1943), in National Labor Relations Board, *Decisions and Orders*, vol. 9 (1943), 1311–323.

69. On the Mohawk Valley formula, see the Introduction, note 21.

70. Levett to Shaw, August 22, 1944, 7–9, NLRB; Robert Black interview, December 28, 1976.

71. *WSJ*, November 6, 1943.

72. *WSJ*, November 7, 1943.

73. *WSJ*, October 27, 1943.

74. Ibid. For an opposing view that equates quiescence to poor race relations, see Charles S. Johnson, "Present Status," 27.

75. *WSJ*, October 27, 1943. The committee was modeled on the citizens' groups organized by corporations during union organizing drives (a model the National Association of Manufacturers helped develop). But in other ways it was a precursor to the white citizens' councils of the 1950s. The difference, of course, was that there were a few blacks on this committee; whites could afford to allow this because the union was not directly raising racial issues.

76. E. L. Sandefur to Santford Martin, November 11, 1943, Santford Martin Papers, Special Collections Department, William R. Perkins Library, Duke University, Durham, N.C.

77. Daniels, *Tar Heels*, 166.

78. Dollard, *Caste and Class*, 97–109.

79. Jacqueline Jones, *Labor of Love*, 235–56.

80. *WSJ*, November 14 and December 5, 1943. Quote is from Robert Black interview, August 3, 1981.

81. Janiewski, *Sisterhood Denied*, 171–72.

82. Frank O'Neal interview.

83. *WSJ*, November 14, 1943.

84. *WSJ*, November 14 and 28, 1943.

85. W. N. Reynolds to Employees of R. J. Reynolds Tobacco Company, n.d., Transcript of Hearings, pt. 2, NWLB.

86. Frank O'Neal interview.

87. *UCAPAWA News*, November 15, 1943.

88. *WSJ*, December 18, 1943.

Chapter 8

1. Robert Black and Ruby Jones interview.

2. National War Labor Board, *Termination Report*.

3. Nelson Lichtenstein, "Industrial Democracy," 524–27; Atleson, *Labor and the Wartime State*, 20–43.

4. *UCAPAWA News*, February 1, 1944.

5. Ibid.

6. *UCAPAWA News*, March 1, 1944.

7. Ibid.

8. Ibid.; *WSJ*, February 29, 1944.

9. *UCAPAWA News*, April 1, 1944.

10. *UCAPAWA News*, March 15, 1943; Ordean Rockey, "Progress Report," March 16, 1944, Case No. 442/392, FMCS.

11. This was standard procedure for the Conciliation Service. See Atleson, *Labor and the Wartime State*, 45. See also Edsforth, *Class Conflict*, 192, for a discussion of a similar situation at General Motors in 1937 after the United Auto Workers organized.

12. "Agreement," April 13, 1944, Case No. 442/392, FMCS.

13. R. W. Goodrick, "Progress Report," April 13, 1944, Case No. 440/392, FMCS; Howell John Harris, *Right to Manage*, 48.

14. "Announcement of Plan for Vacation with Pay," n.d., Exhibits, Company and Union, NWLB; Robert Black interview, June 1, 1976.

15. Rockey, "Progress Report," March 16, 1944, FMCS ("sweet reasonableness"); Nelson Lichtenstein, "Ambiguous Legacy," 217; Reynolds and Killingsworth, "Union Security Issue," 32; Zieger, *CIO*, 145–47. Under the union shop, the employer was free to hire, but the worker was required to join the union after a certain period of time. Gregory and Katz, *Labor and the Law*, 386.

16. National War Labor Board, *Termination Report*, 1:82.

17. "Preliminary Statement of the Union," [1944], Exhibits, Company and Union, 11, NWLB.

18. "Report and Recommendations of Panel in Case No. 111–7701D," [1944], 6–8, NWLB; *WSJ*, June 1, 1944.

19. *WSJ*, June 1 and 21, 1944.

20. Affidavit of Edna Foy, June 8, 1944, Transcript of Hearings, pt. 2, NWLB; *WSJ*, June 21, 1944.

21. Affidavit of Janie Hunt, June 1944, Transcript of Hearings, pt. 2, NWLB.

22. *WSJ*, June 1 and 21, 1944.

23. "Preliminary Statement of the Union," 14, NWLB.

24. Nelson Lichtenstein, "Ambiguous Legacy," 223.

25. National War Labor Board, *Termination Report*, 2:294. For the Little Steel decision, see ibid., 3:288–331. On the CIO's decision to seek general wage increases, see Zieger, *CIO*, 168–70.

26. "Preliminary Statement of the Union," 17, and "Report and Recommendations of Panel," 16, NWLB. The study was of Richmond, Virginia.

27. "Preliminary Statement of the Union," 17, NWLB.

28. Ibid., 14–15. See Nelson Lichtenstein, *Labor's War at Home*, 115–16.

29. "Transcript," June 19–20, 1944, Transcript of Hearings, pt. 2, NWLB.

30. "Report and Recommendations of Panel," NWLB.

31. Regional War Labor Board, Region 4, "In the Matter of R. J. Reynolds Tobacco Company and the Tobacco Workers Organizing Committee, Directive Order," October 18, 1944, NWLB; *UCAPAWA News*, September 15, 1944; *FTA News*, December 15, 1944. The only significant modification of the panel's recommendations called for higher wages: forty-five rather than forty cents per hour as the hiring rate, and slightly higher across-the-board increases. The board ordered the company and the union to "establish through collective bargaining a simplification of the wage structure, a consolidation of job titles, appropriate rate ranges and progression within those ranges." "Directive Order," October 18, 1944, 3, NWLB.

32. Rockey, "Progress Report," March 16, 1944, FMCS.

33. *TWV*, October 1944; "Agreement," April 13, 1944, Case No. 442/392, FMCS. See also

WSJ, October 19, 1944; Atleson, *Labor and the Wartime State*, 90; and Howell John Harris, *Right to Manage.*

34. Montgomery, *Fall of the House of Labor*, 425–64. Some of the craft unions used stewards to police the contract. See Halpern, *Down on the Killing Floor*, 35. James Hinton provides a detailed and engaging examination of the shop stewards movement in Great Britain during World War I. Hinton, *First Shop Stewards' Movement.* See Peck, *Rank-and-File Leader*, 367 n. 20, for a description of how this tradition made its way from Europe to the United States after World War I.

35. Jefferys, *Management and Managed*, 109–18; Peck, *Rank-and-File Leader*, 30.

36. Steven Fraser, *Labor Will Rule*, 225.

37. Peck, *Rank-and-File Leader*, 367; Irving A. Bernstein, *Turbulent Years*, 472, 775–76. Shop stewards were very active in the auto industry, particularly at Chrysler. Edsforth, *Class Conflict*, 177–78, 198–99. In contrast, General Motors' management successfully resisted demands for a shop steward system. Nelson Lichtenstein, *The Most Dangerous Man*, 109.

38. "Transcript," 23, NWLB; "Report and Recommendations of the Panel," 9, NWLB.

39. "Report and Recommendations of the Panel," 9, NWLB.

40. Theodosia Phelps interview, June 1, 1978.

41. Ruby Jones interview.

42. Velma Hopkins interview; Ruby Jones interview. On the critical role of shop stewards, see Edsforth, *Class Conflict*, 199.

43. Robert Black interview, March 4, 1985; *TWV*, June 1945.

44. Lens, "Meaning of the Grievance Procedure."

45. Robert Black interview, March 4, 1985. See Peck, *Rank-and-File Leader*, 33; Nelson Lichtenstein, *The Most Dangerous Man*, 141; and Barbash, *Labor's Grass Roots*, 112–30, for discussions of the role of stewards.

46. Lens, "Meaning of the Grievance Procedure," 717; Robert Black interview, June 1, 1976.

47. Robert Black interview, June 1, 1976.

48. Ibid.

49. Velma Hopkins interview.

50. *UCAPAWA News*, May 1, 15, 1944. Eddie Gallimore, one of the early union leaders, was fired from his job in Number 97, but the union committee convinced management to give him his job back. *TWV*, August 1944.

51. *TWV*, July 1945, June, August, and November 1946, and February 1947. For a discussion of shop floor militancy among packinghouse workers, see Halpern, *Down on the Killing Floor*, 206–18.

52. Velma Hopkins interview.

53. Geneva McClendon interview.

54. Frank Green interview.

55. Ibid.; *FTA News*, November 1, 1945.

56. Velma Hopkins interview.

57. Robert Black interview, December 28, 1976.

58. Charles Wade interview, November 14, 1983.

59. Velma Hopkins interview.

60. *TWV*, October 1944; Robert Black interview, March 4, 1985.

61. Robert Black interview, March 4, 1985.

62. *Pittsburgh Courier*, June 3, 1944.

Chapter 9

1. Frank Green interview; Dickerman and Taylor, *Who's Who in Labor*, 140; Chester Davis report, January 27, 1944, FBIHQ.

2. *WSJ*, September 9, 1944; *UCAPAWA News*, September 15, 1944; *FTA News*, March 1, 1947.

3. Velma Hopkins interview.

4. Frank Green interview.

5. *WSJ*, April 23, 1944.

6. See Frederickson, "Southern Summer School for Women Workers" and "A Place to Speak Our Minds."

7. See Glen, *Highlander*, and Aimee Isgrig Horton, *Highlander Folk School*. Etta Hobson spent a month at Highlander in the summer of 1946. *TWV*, June 1946.

8. "Report-1944" and "Report of the Director, March thru November, 1944," Southern Summer School for Workers, American Labor Education Service Records, Kheel Center for Labor-Management Documentation and Archives, M. P. Catherwood Library, Cornell University, Ithaca, N.Y.; *UCAPAWA News*, August 1, 1944.

9. *UCAPAWA News*, October 15, 1944; "UCAPAWA Southern School, Winston-Salem, North Carolina, September 17–23, 1944," Southern Summer School Records.

10. *UCAPAWA News*, September 1, 1944.

11. Eleanore Binkley interview, August 25, 1990; Chester Davis report, October 20, 1942, 3, FBIHQ; House Committee on Un-American Activities, *Communist Activities in North Carolina*, 3603–14.

12. *UCAPAWA News*, August 1, 1944; *TWV*, November 1945; Eleanore Binkley interview, July 13, 1979; "Report of the Director," Southern Summer School Records.

13. *TWV*, October 1944 and January 1945. On the CIO's use of the radio, see Denning, *Cultural Front*, 73. On the importance of radio to African American protest, see Savage, *Broadcasting Freedom*, and Tyson, *Radio Free Dixie*.

14. On the role of women in labor unions of the World War II era, see Gabin, *Feminism in the Labor Movement*.

15. *FTA News*, April 1950; Robert Black interview, October 7, 1977; Lonnie Nesmith interview, undated.

16. Eleanore Binkley interview, August 25, 1990.

17. *UCAPAWA News*, November 15, 1944. A special eight-week leadership training course took place during the spring of 1945 and included many of the union's most dynamic rank-and-file leaders. *UCAPAWA News*, May 1, 1945.

18. Von Eschen, *Race against Empire*, 1–11, 22–44. Robeson quote is on 11. See also Kelley, *Race Rebels*, 130–32; Naison, *Communists in Harlem*, 138–40, 173–77; and *WSJ*, July 30, 1939, and November 8, 1942.

19. *TWV*, February 1945 and February 1947.

20. *TWV*, April 1945; Viola Brown and Julia Leach interview.

21. Robert Black interview, March 5, 1985; Eleanore Binkley interview, July 13, 1979.

22. Charles S. Johnson, *Patterns of Negro Segregation*, 29–30; *WSJ*, November 15, 1947.

23. *UCAPAWA News*, August 1, 1944; *TWV*, April and November 1945, April 1946.

24. "Release, redemption, and revolt" is from Von Eschen, *Race against Empire*, 1. See also Green, *Only a Miner*, 6, 18, 78, 419; Haessly, "Mill Mother's Lament"; Lieberman, "*My Song Is My Weapon*," 25–49; and Denning, *Cultural Front*, 348–61.

25. Naison, *Communists in Harlem*, 303, 217.

26. Honey, *Southern Labor*, 138–39.

27. Glyn, "Hear the Music Ring," 41.

28. Shirley Graham, *Paul Robeson*.

29. Ibid.; Duberman, *Paul Robeson*.

30. "'T' Stands for Tobacco"; *People's Songs Wordbook No. 1*; Wilson and Ferris, *Encyclopedia of Southern Culture*, 230–31; Reagon, "Songs of the Civil Rights Movement," 75. Daniel Letwin notes that "We Shall Overcome" had even deeper roots. He finds hints that the spiritual "I Will Overcome" was transformed into the movement standard, "*We* Shall Overcome," in the Birmingham coalfields early in the twentieth century and was sung by white and black miners alike. Letwin, *Challenge of Interracial Unionism*, 246 n. 84. See also Lincoln and Mamiya, *Black Church*, 369–70.

31. Denning, *Cultural Front*, 357, 72, xvi.

32. On interracial unionism in the South, see Trotter, *Coal, Class, and Color*; Honey, *Southern Labor*; Arnesen, "'Like Banquo's Ghost'"; Letwin, *Challenge of Interracial Unionism*; Hunter, *To 'Joy My Freedom*; Halpern, "The CIO and the Limits" and "Organized Labor, Black Workers"; Obadele-Starks, *Black Unionism*; and Kelly, *Race, Class, and Power*.

33. Affidavit of Louise Johnson, June 20, 1944, Transcript of Hearings, pt. 2, NWLB.

34. Ibid.

35. *WSJ*, June 21, 1944; William DeBerry interview; "States Evidence," September 12, 1944, Clerk of Forsyth County Superior Court Records, Hall of Records, Winston-Salem, N.C.

36. First quote is from Affidavit of Louise Johnson, NWLB; second quote is from Robert Kinsey report, November 8, 1944, FBIHQ.

37. Ayers, *Vengeance and Justice*, 235; Hall, *Revolt against Chivalry*, 334.

38. William DeBerry interview. See McMillen, *Dark Journey*, 232–33, on the decline of lynching in Mississippi during the 1940s. DeBerry's decision to leave town when confronted with such a charge was not uncommon. See Dollard, *Caste and Class*, 292.

39. William DeBerry interview.

40. *WSJ*, July 4, 1944.

41. William DeBerry interview; *WSJ*, July 7, 1944.

42. *WSJ*, March 3, 1976; *TCS*, March 3, 1976; Robert Black interview, December 28, 1976.

43. *UCAPAWA News*, September 15, 1944; "States Evidence," Clerk of Forsyth County Superior Court Records; *WSJ*, July 15, 1944; Robert Black interview, June 1, 1976; William DeBerry interview.

44. *UCAPAWA News*, September 15, 1944; *State v. William DeBerry*, 224 N.C. 834–37 (Fall term, 1944).

45. *FTA News*, May 15, 1945. Pratt was elected president of TWIU Local 178 in 1942. See *TW*, March 1942. Ed McCrea says that Pratt was hired in part to bring Brown & Williamson workers into the CIO. Edwin McCrea interview. Robert Black confirms this. See Robert Black interview, January 2, 1981. Joe Emmons, a white worker and FTA member at the P. Lorillard plant in Lima, Ohio, joined the staff on February 1945. *FTA News*, March 1, 1945.

46. House Committee on Un-American Activities, *Communism in Labor Unions*, 104–6; "Staff Meeting Minutes," August 28, 1946, series A, folder 1, MHR.

47. For the most part, the organizing committee was an outgrowth of earlier informal groups. Workers themselves had done the bulk of the organizing at Reynolds, and this trend continued. *TWV*, July 16, 1945; *WSJ*, July 14, 1945; *FTA News*, September 1, 1945. A letter from

a Reynolds worker to the NWLB in October asked to be put back on the checkoff. See Mary S. Peay to A. R. Marshall, October 6, 1945, Exhibits, Company and Union, NWLB, and *FTA News*, August 1, 1945.

48. Velma Hopkins interview.

49. *FTA News*, September 1, 1945; *TWV*, August 1945.

Chapter 10

1. Robert Black interview, May 13, 1987.

2. Steven Fraser, *Labor Will Rule*, 503–38.

3. Sullivan, *Days of Hope*, 7–8, 169–92.

4. *Smith v. Allwright*, 321 U.S. 649 (1944).

5. Christian, "Folger-Chatham," 26; biography of Folger in Powell, *Dictionary of North Carolina Biography*, 215; *WSJ*, November 5, 1944.

6. Christian, "Folger-Chatham," 26.

7. Zieger, *CIO*, 185; Gerstle, *Working-Class Americanism*, 289–301; Nelson Lichtenstein, *Labor's War at Home*, 175.

8. Elizabeth Eudy interview, November 1, 1987. See also Gaer, *First Round*.

9. FTA, *Proceedings of the Fifth National Convention*, 17–18.

10. Velma Hopkins interview; *WSJ*, November 14, 1944.

11. *WSJ*, November 26, 1944; FTA, *Proceedings of the Fifth National Convention*, 17–18. On the success of CIO-PAC in national elections, see Steven Fraser, *Labor Will Rule*, 514.

12. "Record registration" is from *WSJ*, October 29, 1944. An article in the *FTA News*, March 1, 1945, claimed that the union helped put 6,000 new people on the registration books.

13. Zieger, *CIO*, 187; FTA, *Proceedings of the Fifth National Convention*, 17–18.

14. Sullivan, *Days of Hope*, 8, 175; Steven Fraser, *Labor Will Rule*, 531.

15. *TWV*, April 13, 1945.

16. Sullivan, *Days of Hope*, 223; *TWV*, August 1944; *UCAPAWA News*, July 15, 1945.

17. *TWV*, May 4, 1945, and July 16, 1945; *UCAPAWA News*, July 1, 1945; *FTA News*, September 1, 1945. Hopkins's quote is from *UCAPAWA News*, May 1, 1944.

18. Gardner quote is from *UCAPAWA News*, December 1, 1944. On veterans' lobby, see *FTA News*, April 15, 1946, and *TWV*, April 1946. See *TWV*, November 1945 and April 1946, for stories of other delegations from Local 22.

19. House Committee on Ways and Means, *Revenue Revisions of 1943*, 986–88 (quotes are on 988); *UCAPAWA News*, November 1, 1943.

20. Zieger, *CIO*, 243–44 (quote on 243).

21. Gilmore, *Gender and Jim Crow*; *WSJ*, October 11, 1944.

22. Robert Black interview, December 28, 1976; "Memorandum for the Report to the Board," February 9, 1942, II, C 141, N.C. State Conference, 1943–45–46, NAACP Papers, Manuscripts Division, Library of Congress, Washington, D.C.; *WSJ*, February 15, 1942.

23. Robert Black interview, December 28, 1976; "Program, NAACP Mass Meeting," February 10, 1946, and Membership Records, [1946], both in II, C 140, Winston-Salem, N.C., 1946–55, NAACP Papers.

24. Tyson, *Radio Free Dixie*, 30; Sullivan, *Days of Hope*, 141–43.

25. Christian, "Folger-Chatham," 28.

26. Ibid., 28–34 (first quote is on 28; second is on 34).

27. *WSJ*, June 6 and 20, 1946; Schrecker, *Many Are the Crimes*, 90–91.

28. *WSJ*, May 20, 1946.

29. "Staff Meeting Minutes," August 28, 1946, series A, folder 1, MHR; *TWV*, March 1946.

30. *WSJ*, May 20, 1946.

31. Quotes are from *WSJ*, May 21, 1946. See also Christian, "Folger-Chatham," 40–41, and H. G. Jones, conversation with the author.

32. *WSJ*, May 26, 1946.

33. *WSJ*, June 19, 1946.

34. *WSJ*, June 20 and 21, 1946.

35. *WSJ*, June 15, 1946. Workers also canvassed in the rural neighborhoods around Winston-Salem. *FTA News*, July 15, 1946, 4.

36. *TWV*, July 1946.

37. Sullivan, *Days of Hope*, 9.

38. Von Eschen, *Race against Empire*, 107.

39. An FBI report from the fall of 1942 reported on six suspected Party members in Winston-Salem who were "presently engaged in no activities beyond reading of party publications." See Chester Davis report, October 20, 1942, FBIHQ. Party members not affiliated with the union lent a hand to the organizing drive. Not long after the UCAPAWA organizing drive began in Winston-Salem in 1942, Bart Logan, district organizer of the Party in North and South Carolina, assigned Dan and Betty Jackson to the tobacco town as "colonizers." Junius Scales interview, April 4, 1987; Scales and Nickson, *Cause at Heart*, 158.

40. Robert Black interviews, June 1, 1976, and May 13, 1987; William DeBerry interview. A similar development of rank-and-file workers took place in Memphis. See Honey, *Southern Labor*, 126.

41. Robert Black interview, May 13, 1987. According to FBI reports, Eddie Gallimore received the *Daily Worker* in 1943. See Robert Black interview, January 2, 1981, and Robert Kinsey report, November 8, 1944, FBIHQ.

42. Kinsey report, November 8, 1944, FBIHQ.

43. Carlton Stuart report, November 13, 1947, FBIHQ; Anne Mathews testimony in House Committee on Un-American Activities, *Communism in Labor Unions*, 65, 72, 81; Robert Black interview, January 2, 1981. It seems that Robert Lathan and Frank Green attended Party training schools during 1945. Mathews named Frank Green, Robert Lathan, Etta Hobson, Clark Sheppard, Robert Black, and Eleanore Hoagland as the only Party members before Sam Hall arrived in 1946.

44. Isserman, *Which Side Were You On?*, 238, 242. Quote is on 238. The FBI reported that "'Robert,' Winston-Salem (Believed to be Robert Black)" and "'Etta' (Hobson)" attended the meeting of the Communist Party USA District 16 in Richmond on July 23, 1944, for the purpose of dissolving the Party. The FBI also reported that Alice Burke, district head of the Party, attended a meeting in Winston-Salem on August 13, 1944, for the purpose of establishing a North Carolina branch of the CPA. A number of Local 22 figures supposedly attended the meetings. Kinsey report, November 8, 1944, FBIHQ.

45. Isserman, *Which Side Were You On?*, 236, 242–43; Scales and Nickson, *Cause at Heart*, 151. For a discussion of the Party's change of course, see Johanningsmeier, *Forging American Communism*, 304–13. On trade unionists' reaction, see John Williamson, "New Organizational Problems," 1115. Ironically, the Party's new strategy dovetailed nicely with the demand

of liberal anti-Communist Arthur Schlesinger Jr. that "communist and fellow travelers . . . stand and be counted." Sullivan, *Days of Hope*, 232.

46. Scales and Nickson, *Cause at Heart*, 149–52.

47. Mathews testimony in House Committee on Un-American Activities, *Communism in Labor Unions*, 64–65; Anne Mathews interview. See also Schrecker, *Many Are the Crimes*, 31.

48. *WSJ*, August 18, 1946; Scales and Nickson, *Cause at Heart*, 162. See profile of Hall in *N&O*, February 21, 1947. For background on Sam Hall, see Kelley, *Hammer and Hoe*, 196, 223–25, and Sylvia Thompson interview.

49. Storrs, *Civilizing Capitalism*, 235, 348 n. 15; Schrecker, *Many Are the Crimes*, 23–26 (first quote is on 26); Mitford, *Fine Old Conflict*, 67 (second quote).

50. Robert Black interview, May 13, 1987. For Anne Mathews's description of the meeting, see Mathews testimony in House Committee on Un-American Activities, *Communism in Labor Unions*, 67–68.

51. Robert Black interview, May 13, 1987.

52. Mathews testimony in House Committee on Un-American Activities, *Communism in Labor Unions*, 71; Scales and Nickson, *Cause at Heart*, 157; Stuart report, November 13, 1947, FBIHQ.

53. On the upsurge of violence, see O'Brien, *Color of the Law*, 1–2. Quotes are from *DW*, September 2, 1946. Selling the *Daily Worker* was one of the membership's major responsibilities. Isserman, *Which Side Were You On?*, 235.

54. On Simpson's letter, see *FTA News*, December 1, 1944. Resolution quote is from *WSJ*, March 16, 1947; "resolution bit" is from Schrecker, *Many Are the Crimes*, 31. See Scales and Nickson, *Cause at Heart*, 205, for an evaluation of the effectiveness of such resolutions. See similar opposition from local TWIU official in *WSJ*, March 19, 1947. Party officials stressed the need for members to take a more active role in speaking out against imperialism and reactionary politics at home. The *Daily Worker* was to be an important medium for this. See John Williamson, "New Organizational Problems."

55. *DW*, September 20, 1946; Edwin McCrea interview. Hosea Hudson also sold the *Daily Worker* in his shop in Birmingham during this period. See Painter, *Narrative of Hosea Hudson*, 311. For background on the *Daily Worker*, see Buhle, "Daily Worker," 174–78.

56. Junius Scales interview, May 2, 1987; Mathews testimony in House Committee on Un-American Activities, *Communism in Labor Unions*, 71. Also see Stuart report, November 13, 1947, FBIHQ. For a description of Communist Party clubs in Detroit, see Stepan-Norris and Zeitlin, *Talking Union*, 157.

57. Mathews testimony in House Committee on Un-American Activities, *Communism in Labor Unions*, 73. Information on the clubs comes from Stuart report, November 13, 1947, FBIHQ; Mitford, *Fine Old Conflict*, 67; Anne Mathews interview; and Bernard Friedland, Junius Scales, and Karl Korstad interview.

58. Junius Scales interview, May 2, 1987.

59. Mathews testimony in House Committee on Un-American Activities, *Communism in Labor Unions*, 72, 78. See also Buhle, "Daily Worker." According to FBI reports, Robert Lathan and another, unnamed person from Winston-Salem attended a Party school in October 1946. Stuart report, November 13, 1947, FBIHQ.

60. See Zieger, *CIO*, 254–55. Zieger's general argument that Party unionists put the USSR at the top of their priorities is not borne out by the record in Winston-Salem.

61. Anne Mathews interview.

62. Schrecker, *Many Are the Crimes*, 31–34 (quote on 33); Bernard Friedland, Junius Scales, and Karl Korstad interview. See also Scales and Nickson, *Cause at Heart*, 201–19.

Chapter 11

1. Zieger, *CIO*, 212–13.

2. Tilley, *R. J. Reynolds*, 237–42.

3. Ibid., 485–86.

4. Retooling the stemmeries was an expensive operation, but one that Reynolds could easily afford. Its net profits for 1945 amounted to almost $20 million. But the company did not finance this retooling out of earnings; it looked to the financial markets instead. In 1945 Reynolds issued $49 million of preferred stock; three years later it sold $60 million of debentures and offered an additional $26 million of preferred stock. Ibid., 556–70.

5. *WSJ*, January 8, 1946; Robert Black interview, March 4, 1985. Tilley alludes to the company's awareness of the impact the layoffs would have on union strength. Tilley, *R. J. Reynolds*, 388.

6. *WSJ*, January 8 and March 8, 1946.

7. *TWV*, January 1946. See Nelson Lichtenstein, *The Most Dangerous Man*, 290, for a discussion of United Auto Workers Local 600's demand for a thirty-hour week and how Walter Reuther rejected such demands as Communist-inspired efforts to subvert Cold War production.

8. Philip Koritz interview.

9. *TWV*, January 1946; DPOWA, "Brief History," 2. The "Brief History" may have referred to Number 1, which was turned into a cigarette plant for the production of Cavaliers. Tilley, *R. J. Reynolds*, 451.

10. "$57,000,000 Worth," 100; "Remarks of John C. Whitaker before Negro Committee Representing Negro Employees," June 28, 1943, 1, Case No. 300/9086, FMCS.

11. Tilley, *R. J. Reynolds*, 485–88.

12. Viola Brown and Julia Leach interview; *WSJ*, March 8, 1946. Louise Smith was in one of the first groups to be laid off. After doing seasonal work at Piedmont Leaf for many years, she had finally been hired at Reynolds in 1943. She managed to get back on the payroll working nights during the summer of 1946, but the next winter she took a job as a domestic for bank president Charles Norfleet, where she remained for many years. Louise Smith interview.

13. *WSJ*, March 29, 1946; *TWV*, April 1946.

14. "Staff Meeting Minutes," August 28, 1946, series A, folder 1, MHR. In February 1946 Reynolds announced plans to build a plant next to North Carolina A&T College in Greensboro. *WSJ*, February 14, 1946.

15. There is extensive literature on the effect of postwar automation on African American workers. See Rifkin, *The End of Work*, 69–80; Gordon, Edwards, and Reich, *Segmented Work*, 165–227; Brecher, "Crisis Economy"; and Sugrue, *Origins of the Urban Crisis*.

16. *TWV*, April 1946.

17. Ibid.; *FTA News*, May 15, 1946.

18. Philip Koritz interview; *WSJ*, June 14 and July 28, 1946.

19. The leaf house companies proposed a two-cent increase in the minimum wage to fifty-

six cents per hour, an offer guaranteed to provoke a strike. Progress Report, July 22, 1946, Case No. 464/953, FMCS. The rank-and-file leaders in the leaf houses were Robert Lathan at Export; Christine Gardner, Clyde Watts, and the Reverend Wesley Bee at Piedmont; and Thomas Jackson, Marie Jackson, and Mildred Gilliam at Winston. Robert Lathan became the chairman of the leaf house council.

20. Philip Koritz interview.

21. Workers at Export Leaf retained their union shop and convinced the company to forgo its right, under the Fair Labor Standards Act, to employ workers for up to fifty-six hours a week for fourteen weeks out of the year without giving them overtime pay. "Synopsis or Brief of Agreement reached 7-31-46," MHR.

22. *WSJ*, August 9, 1946.

23. *WSJ*, August 18, 1946.

24. Clark Sheppard and Robert Black to Friend, September 12, 1946, Case No. 464/951, FMCS.

25. *TCS*, October 16, 1946; *WSJ*, August 25, 1946. Later in court the driver, Frank Reynolds, testified that he had been "willing to wait rather than cause a disturbance." *State v. Philip Milton Koritz*, Spring term, 1947, no. 723, 150, Records of the Supreme Court (Record Group 267), Appellate Jurisdiction Records, National Archives, Washington, D.C.

26. *State v. Koritz*, 104–6. For Bee's testimony, see ibid., 84–88. See also *WSJ*, August 25, 1946.

27. *State v. Koritz*, 56 (Barlow's testimony is on 50–56; Ledwell's is on 56–60); *WSJ*, August 25, 1946.

28. *State v. Koritz*, 106–111, quotes on 108; *WSJ*, August 24, 1946.

29. For Koritz's version of events, see *State v. Koritz*, 125–37. Quotes are on 126–27. For the police perspective, see Chief John M. Gold's testimony, ibid., 141–46, and John M. Gold, "Reply of Winston-Salem Police Department to Charges of Police Attack and Frame-Up against Winston-Salem Tobacco Strikers Made by United Tobacco Workers, Local #22, FTA-CIO," September 23, 1946, box 59, R. Gregg Cherry Papers, North Carolina Division of Archives and History, Raleigh, N.C.

30. *WSJ*, August 24, 1946.

31. *State v. Koritz*, 128. Koritz says that workers came to the police station downtown and shouted and marched. Philip Koritz interview.

32. *WSJ*, September 5 and 6, 1946; *TWV*, September 1946.

33. *WSJ*, September 11, 1946. On the attitude of black Winston-Salem toward the trials, see "Excerpts from a Study of the Economic and Cultural Activities of the Negro People of Winston-Salem, North Carolina, November–December 1946," box 3, folder 89, Gordon Gray Papers, Southern Historical Collection, University of North Carolina at Chapel Hill.

34. *WSJ*, September 13, 1946.

35. *WSJ*, September 15, 1946.

36. *WSJ*, September 22, 1946.

37. Tilley, *Bright-Tobacco Industry*, 141–50; Dunnagan, "The Tobacco Industry," 117; Lemert, *Tobacco Manufacturing Industry*, 5, 10.

38. U.S. Department of Labor, Bureau of Labor Statistics, "Hours and Earnings," 221; *FTA News*, August 15, 1946.

39. *Carolina Times*, January 1, 1950; Edwin McCrea interview.

40. Gavins, "NAACP in North Carolina," 105–13; Tyson, *Radio Free Dixie*, 61.

41. Warlick, "Organization of the Leaf-House Workers," 4; Frank Green interview.

42. There is an extensive literature on Operation Dixie. See Griffith, *Crisis of American Labor*; Honey, *Southern Labor*, 214–44; Michael Goldfield, *Color of Politics*, 240–49; Minchin, *What Do We Need a Union For?*, 26–47; and Zieger, *CIO*, 227–41. Minchin argues that the CIO's motives were primarily economic and not political. Minchin, *What Do We Need a Union For?*, 28–29.

43. Zieger, *CIO*, 231, 233 (first two quotes); Michael Goldfield, *Color of Politics*, 243 (last quote). See also "Labor Drives South." Minchin notes the nation's strong economy, the triumph over fascism, and President Roosevelt's reelection as important confidence boosters for union activists in the South and nationwide. Minchin, *What Do We Need a Union For?*, 27.

44. Karl Korstad, "Black and White Together," 77–79. For descriptions of Baldanzi and Bittner's involvement in Operation Dixie, see Griffith, *Crisis of American Labor*.

45. Southern Labor Conference, "Report and Policy," 2–9. For more on the AFL's response to Operation Dixie, see Honey, *Southern Labor*, 227–28. For more on the TWIU's involvement in eastern North Carolina, see Warlick, "Organization of the Leaf-House Workers."

46. Cornelius Simmons interview; Robert Black interviews, April 29, 1990, and March 3, 1988. See also *UV*, February 11, 1951. The story of the Greenville campaign is told in Windham, "Greenhands." Robert Black roomed with the minister while he was in Greenville. Robert Black interview, August 3, 1981. This was a textbook example of the way the CIO hoped to organize in the South. See Griffith, *Crisis of American Labor*, 68.

47. Cornelius Simmons interview; Annie Little to Lane Windham, July 17, 1990, copy in author's possession. The letter is cited extensively in Windham, "Greenhands."

48. Robert Black interview, August 3, 1981.

49. Cornelius Simmons interview.

50. Robert Black interviews, April 29, 1990, and August 3, 1981. For more background on Battle, see *Carolina Times*, June 20, 1953.

51. Robert Black interview, April 29, 1990.

52. Edwin McCrea interview.

53. Marie Jackson Winston interview.

54. *DW*, January 16, 1947.

55. Edwin McCrea interview.

56. Frank Green interview; Robert Black interview, April 29, 1990.

57. Edwin McCrea interview.

58. Frank Green interview.

59. FTA, *Report of the General Executive Officers*, 8; Cornelius Simmons interview; Frank Green interview.

60. *FTA News*, August 15, 1946.

61. Cornelius Simmons interview; Annie F. Little interview, October 15, 1990. See also *UV*, February 11, 1951.

62. Edwin McCrea interview.

63. Henderson quote is in FTA, *Report of the General Executive Officers*, 39; Ed McCrea and William Smith to Frank Green, October 3, 1946, ODP.

64. U.S. Department of Labor, Bureau of Labor Statistics, *Industry Wage Studies*, 36. "Purely organizational campaign" quote is from Zieger, *CIO*, 233. Minchin describes the CIO's adamant dismissal of local PACs as another reflection of Operation Dixie's funda-

mental economic focus. See Minchin, *What Do We Need a Union For?*, 28–29. For additional information about the impact of the emerging Cold War on the CIO's progressivism, especially in regard to race, see Patton, "CIO and the Search," 5–14, and Honey, *Southern Labor*, 230–33, 236.

65. Zieger, *CIO*, 233; Minchin, *What Do We Need a Union For?*, 27–29; Edwin McCrea interview. Of the various FTA organizers, only Robert Lathan was on the CIO payroll. All the rest were being paid by FTA. Five organizers on the CIO payroll were assigned to the tobacco drive, but none seem to have played a significant role. See "North Carolina Staff as of September 20, 1946," box 88, folder 565, ODP, and "Report of the General Secretary-Treasurer," in Food, Tobacco, Agricultural, and Allied Workers Union, *Report of the General Executive Officers*, 72. Also see Frank Green interview.

66. Smith to Green, ODP. The case was NLRB 5-R-1413. A copy of the leaflet is attached to Warlick, "Organization of the Leaf-House Workers." One of the TWIU officials involved in the case was George Benjamin, an international vice president and the director of the AFL drive in eastern North Carolina.

67. Zieger, *CIO*, 228. See Griffith, *Crisis of American Labor*, 46–61, 109, and Minchin, *What Do We Need a Union For?*, 44–47, 55–62, for judgments of Operation Dixie and discussions of the failed campaign at Cannon Mills. The failure of Operation Dixie has been the subject of much historical debate. Michael Goldfield argues that the CIO's "limited strategic perspective" ensured defeat. Michael Goldfield, *Color of Politics*, 240. Barbara Griffith blames Operation Dixie's defeat in part on the powerful economic, political, and social clout wielded by southern corporations. She also says that the CIO was not ready to deal with the peculiarities of the southern campaign. Griffith, *Crisis of American Labor*, 163–76.

Chapter 12

1. *FTA News*, February 1, 1947.

2. Zieger, *CIO*, 245–46.

3. *FTA News*, April 15, 1947.

4. CIO, *Analysis of the Taft-Hartley Act*; Zieger, *CIO*, 246–47; Tomlins, *State and the Unions*, 282–315; Minchin, *What Do We Need a Union For?*, 32–37. Christopher Tomlins argues that Taft-Hartley was not a significant break with past NLRB policy. Tomlins, *State and the Unions*, 251.

5. *WSJ*, February 23, 1947.

6. *N&O*, February 21 and 22, 1947; *WSJ*, February, 26, 1947. For background on North Carolina politics in the late 1940s, see Pleasants and Burns, *Frank Porter Graham*.

7. *Fur and Leather Worker*, December 1946.

8. *WSJ*, December 10 and 12, 1946. The union called off the strike in early April. *WSJ*, April 7, 1947.

9. *WSJ*, January 8 and 9, 1947.

10. *WSJ*, January 9 and March 19, 1947. The petition requested that Frank K. Thomas, a public school teacher, and E. M. Mitchell, manager of the N.C. Mutual Life Insurance Company, be appointed. In June 1946 J. H. R. Gleaves had written to the *Sentinel* protesting the prejudice of white registrars and asking for all-black precincts with black registrars. *TCS*, June 19, 1946.

11. Edwin McCrea interview.

12. Robert Black interview, May 1, 1978; Edwin McCrea interview; William DeBerry interview.

13. Kenneth Williams interview.

14. Ed McCrea to Bob Korstad, June 22, 1988, original in author's possession; Robert Black testimony, "Hearings before the Committee to Investigate Charges against the Food, Tobacco, Agricultural, and Allied Workers of America," January 6, 1950, box 109, FTA Hearings, CIOSTO.

15. Junius Scales interview, May 2, 1987.

16. Robert Black interview, December 28, 1976; Velma Hopkins interview. For registration figures, see *WSJ*, April 12 and 13, 1947.

17. *WSJ*, April 20, 1947.

18. Ibid.

19. *WSJ*, April 22, 1947.

20. Robert Black interview, May 13, 1987.

21. *WSJ*, April 23, 1947.

22. Edwin McCrea interview; *Norfolk Virginian-Pilot*, November 11, 1947; Chafe, *Civilities and Civil Rights*, 35–37. See Moon, *Balance of Power*, 188, for a similar assessment of Williams's victory.

23. *TWV*, February 1947.

24. *WSJ*, April 3, 1947.

25. *WSJ*, April 24, 1947. For detailed information on the negotiations and the positions of each side, see Progress Reports dated April 22, 26, and May 2, 1947, Case No. 474/565, FMCS.

26. *WSJ*, April 28, 1947.

27. *WSJ*, May 1, 1947; *TCS*, May 1, 1947. Neither the *Journal* nor the *Sentinel* examined the union's charges that postwar inflation had eaten into the real wages of workers in Winston-Salem. But Reynolds's contention that it could not bargain on union security because of the right-to-work law occasioned a front-page story titled "Legal Dilemma Faces Company in Negotiations." *WSJ*, May 1, 1947.

28. *TCS*, May 1, 1947; Reynolds Employees Association leaflet, quoted in Tilley, *R. J. Reynolds*, 396.

29. Tilley, *R. J. Reynolds*, 396.

30. E. T. "Jazz" Isley Jr. interview.

31. Ellen Marsh interview.

32. *WSJ*, May 3, 1947.

33. *WSJ*, May 4 and 5, 1947.

34. Edwin McCrea interview; Leon Edwards interview.

35. Edwin McCrea interview.

36. *WSJ*, May 8, 1947.

37. The union provided over $27,000 in direct relief to workers. United Tobacco Workers, Local 22, FTA-CIO, "Semi-Annual Financial Report," July 15, 1947, series A, folder 1, MHR. On outside donations, see *WSJ*, May 7 and 13, 1947, and *DW*, May 15, 1947.

38. *TCS*, May 9, 1947; United Tobacco Workers, Local 22, "Semi-Annual Financial Report," MHR; Robert Black interview, March 3, 1988.

39. *WSJ*, May 13, 1947; *DW*, May 15, 1947; Robert Black interview, March 3, 1988.

40. Edwin McCrea interview. See also Kelley, " 'We Are Not What We Seem,' " 86.

41. Edwin McCrea interview; *TCS*, May 13, 1947; *WSJ*, May 14, 1947.

42. Edwin McCrea interview; *TCS*, May 13, 1947; *DW*, May 15, 1947.

43. Bea and Edwin McCrea interview. See also Isenberg, "Camel Caravan."

44. Edwin McCrea interview; Velma Hopkins interview. See also *TCS*, May 24, 1947; Levine, *Black Culture*, 203; and Lieberman, *"My Song Is My Weapon."*

45. DPOWA, "Brief History," 5.

46. Ibid; Reba N. Randolph to Lucy Randolph Mason, May 6, 1947, box 5, Lucy Randolph Mason Papers, Manuscripts Department, William R. Perkins Library, Duke University, Durham, N.C.

47. Luther Ranson interview. Reynolds regularly brought high school and college students to work during the summer and was able to use them during the strike. In later court testimony, John Whitaker said that the firm hired a number of students during the strike who were kept on until they returned to school in September, at which point the remaining strikers were rehired. See *WSJ*, May 6, 1948.

48. *WSJ*, May 6, 9, 11, 13, and 16, 1947; *DW*, May 17, 1947; Robert Black interview, March 3, 1988; "Executive Board Meetings, Ford Local 600, UAW-CIO, May 12, 1947, Local 600.," UAW Local 600 Collection, Archives of Labor History and Urban Affairs, Walter Reuther Library, Wayne State University, Detroit, Mich.; *WSJ*, May 5, 1947 (Tiller quote). Hoping that other union men and women would follow these examples, FTA announced plans for a boycott of Reynolds products. President Donald Henderson asked the CIO executive board to recommend a boycott to its 6 million members, but the board delayed action on the recommendation. *TCS*, May 18, 1947; *WSJ*, May 22, 1947.

49. *WSJ*, May 12, 16, 17, and 27, 1947; *TCS*, May 8, 17, and 18, 1947; Robert Black interview, March 3, 1988. The *Sentinel* in particular provided graphic photographs of shot-out windows (see *TCS*, May 8, 1947). Also see the story of the boycott of Camels in black neighborhoods. *TCS*, June 3, 1947.

50. *WSJ*, May 19, 1947.

51. Anne Mathews testimony in House Committee on Un-American Activities, *Communism in Labor Unions*; *TWV*, May 4, 1945; *FTA News*, May 5, 1945.

52. *WSJ*, May 19, 1947. Chester Davis later speculated that Pratt may have been working all along as a plant by John Whitaker. Chester Davis interview.

53. *WSJ*, May 19, 1947. Using company documents, Reynolds Tobacco Company historian Nannie Mae Tilley provided yet another account. According to Tilley, "Pratt, softened by liquid refreshment at a party, began to unburden his conscience." Company officials Edgar Bumgardner and Bailey Lipfert learned of this "confidential information" and "established contacts, gave directions to, and secretly took appropriate steps." Whatever the nature of these "appropriate steps," the *Journal* and the *Sentinel* quickly took over the responsibility of orchestrating an exposé. Tilley, *R. J. Reynolds*, 397.

54. Zieger, *CIO*, 261–67, 283; *WSJ*, May 19, 1947.

55. Chester Davis interview; Anne Mathews interview.

56. Dickerman and Taylor, *Who's Who in Labor*, 226.

57. Anne Mathews interview.

58. *WSJ*, May 20, 1947; Anne Mathews interview.

59. Chester Davis interview; *WSJ*, January 22, 1948.

60. Chester Davis interview.

61. Anne Mathews interview.

62. *WSJ*, May 19, 1947. Mathews fits Victor Navasky's models of both the "informer under duress" and the "truth telling informer." See Navasky, *Naming Names*, 73–77.

63. Chester Davis interview.

64. See Schrecker, *Many Are the Crimes*.

65. *WSJ*, May 19, 1947. This analysis mirrors that of the turn-of-the-century white supremacy campaigns. There it was black political participation that led to violence, insolence, and rape. Here, the Communist Party was responsible for stirring up blacks, which again was leading toward violence.

66. Ibid.

67. *WSJ*, May 20, 1947.

68. *WSJ*, June 9, 1947.

69. *WSJ*, May 26, 1947.

70. *WSJ*, May 25, 1947; *DW*, May 31, 1947.

71. Chester Davis interview.

72. *WSJ*, May 21, 1947; "Evictions," [1947], box 5, file 15, Southern Conference for Human Welfare Collection, Robert Woodruff Library and Archives, Atlanta University.

73. *WSJ*, May 22, 1947.

74. Karl Korstad interviews, August 25, 1987, and December 14, 1980. For more on Durr, see Durr, *Outside the Magic Circle*.

75. Nelle Morton to Dave Burgess, June 1947, 9, 80, Fellowship of Southern Churchmen Papers, Southern Historical Collection, University of North Carolina at Chapel Hill.

76. Franz Daniel to Nellie Morton, June 5, 1947, box 107, ODP; Barney Taylor to Morton, June 9, 1947, box 9, Fellowship of Southern Churchmen Papers.

77. "Report on Strike at R. J. Reynolds Tobacco Company," 4, box 5, folder 15, Southern Conference for Human Welfare Collection, Robert Woodruff Library and Archives, Atlanta University. On *PM*, see Denning, *Cultural Front*, 95, and Buhle, "Daily Worker," 607–8.

78. *WSJ*, June 2, 1947.

79. *WSJ*, May 26, 30, and June 2, 1947; *DW*, June 4, 1947.

80. Progress Report, May 28, 1947, Case No. 474/565, FMCS; *WSJ*, May 27, 1947. See also various reports, *WSJ*, May 28 and 29, 1947.

81. *WSJ*, June 9, 1947.

82. Ibid; D. Yates Heafner, "Final Report," June 10, 1947, Case No. 474/565, and "Progress Report," June 21, 1947, Case No. 474/889, FMCS.

Chapter 13

1. *WSJ*, June 12 and 13, 1947.

2. *WSJ*, June 21, 23, and 28, August 30, September 27, 1947, and May 6, 1948; Progress Report, June 29, 1947, Case No. 474/565, FMCS. McCrea quote is from Ed McCrea to Bob Korstad, June 22, 1988, original in author's possession.

3. *DW*, June 10, 1947.

4. *WSJ*, June 30, 1947. For more on Robeson, see Duberman, *Paul Robeson*.

5. *WSJ*, June 30, 1947.

6. Scales and Nickson, *Cause at Heart*, 182; *WSJ*, June 30, 1947.

7. *WSJ*, June 30 and July 1, 1947; *FTA News*, July 15, 1947. Quote is from *WSJ*, June 30, 1947.

8. Sullivan, *Days of Hope*, 179–80, 225–27, 237–38; Von Eschen, *Race against Empire*, 107–8.

9. Schrecker, *Many Are the Crimes*, 379–83.

10. *WSJ*, June 10, 1947. This was a curious observation given the fact that the *Journal* seemed to have an open pipeline to the FBI thanks to Chester Davis and Police Chief John Gold.

11. Schrecker, *Many Are the Crimes*, 90–91; *WSJ*, June 12, 1947; Sullivan, *Days of Hope*, 243.

12. *WSJ*, July 12, 1947.

13. Anne Mathews, Gene Pratt, Spencer Long, and Robert Black testimony in House Committee on Un-American Activities, *Communism in Labor Unions*, 63–112. Quotes are on 110.

14. Robert Black testimony in ibid., 110.

15. Clark Sheppard and Ed McCrea testimony in ibid., 113–28.

16. HUAC did not begin issuing contempt citations for people taking the Fifth until 1950. See Beck, *Contempt of Congress*, 220. On the Fifth Amendment, see Caute, *Great Fear*, 150–52. Actually, many of the people who invoked the Fifth Amendment before HUAC were not members of the Party and were opposed to Communist domination of the labor movement. See Pollitt, "Fifth Amendment Plea," for an analysis of the motivations of people taking the Fifth.

17. *WSJ*, July 24 and 25, 1947.

18. Robert Black interview, May 13, 1987.

19. Scales and Nickson, *Cause at Heart*, 184–88.

20. Edwin McCrea interview.

21. Robert Black and Ruby Jones interview.

22. The relationship between the Cold War and the advancement of the civil rights agenda is explored in Dudziak, *Cold War Civil Rights*.

23. *WSJ*, October 29 and November 4, 12, and 16, 1947. Quotes are from November 4 issue.

24. *WSJ*, August 13, 1947.

25. *WSJ*, July 19, 1947.

26. Von Eschen, *Race against Empire*, 109–10. See also Myrdal, *An American Dilemma*. Others, of course, have pointed out that racism and inequality were built into American democracy from the beginning—in the Constitution, in republican ideology—and that white freedom was built on slavery. Morgan, *American Slavery*.

27. *WSJ*, July 22, 1947. Not even all whites agreed with the strident anti-Communism of the *Journal*. See letters to the editor, *WSJ*, July 2 and 22, 1947.

28. Von Eschen, *Race against Empire*, 109–12; Walter A. Jackson, *Gunnar Myrdal*, 272–79; President's Committee on Civil Rights, *To Secure These Rights*, 146, 148 (quote is on 166).

29. *WSJ*, October 31 and November 5, 1947. See Wayne Addison Clark, "Analysis of the Relationship," 33, for an excellent discussion of this point of view.

30. *WSJ*, November 11, 1947. The sorority's position is an indication that the black middle class was not a monolith, but a group with internal differences. As individuals and organizations moved toward the push for civil rights, they were more influenced by the left and labor than most historians have supposed.

31. Edwin McCrea interview. Leon Edwards reported that the subforeman in his department had told him after the strike that the union had done "the best damn thing you even did in your life when you came out on that strike." Leon Edwards interview. On white workers at Hanes giving money to black strikers, see Baldanzi's remarks in "CIO International

Executive Board Proceedings," July 7 and 8, 1943, 289–294, box 2, CIO International Board Bound Proceedings, Archives of Labor History and Urban Affairs, Walter Reuther Library, Wayne State University, Detroit, Mich.

32. Edwin McCrea interview.

33. Robert Black interview, December 28, 1976.

34. Jack Frye interview; Edwin McCrea interview; Mary Lou Koger Ford interview; *WSJ*, September 13, 1947.

35. Edwin McCrea interview.

36. Jack Frye interview.

37. Edwin McCrea interview; *Reynolds Organizer*, January 22, 1948.

38. Mary Lou Koger Ford interview. In an effort to bring more white women into the union, FTA recruited Mary Major, an Asheville, North Carolina, native, to be a colonizer in the plants. She got a job as an inspector in the cigarette-making department and had some success getting whites to join the union. The company quickly figured out that she was working for the union and fired her. Although the union won her case in arbitration, the contract soon ran out. See Mary Robertson interview.

39. Jack Frye interview; *FTA News*, February 15, 1948.

40. See story in *FTA News*, February 15, 1948; Jack Frye interview.

41. Guthrie, "A Minstrel."

42. The first drive took place in December 1947. See Karl Korstad to William Smith, November 12, 1947, ODP. The second took place in February 1948. See *WSJ*, February 5 and 15, 1948. Quote is from *WSJ*, February 15, 1948. Jack Frye occasionally took a black minister with him as he made the rounds in the white working-class neighborhoods. Jack Frye interview.

43. Jack Frye interview.

44. Robert Black interview, undated.

45. Luther Ranson interview.

46. *WSJ*, January 4, 1948.

47. Schrecker, "McCarthyism and the Labor Movement," 146–49; Zieger, *CIO*, 247–52. "[The Communist Party's] decision on non-compliance with Taft-Hartley isolated the left unions. . . . The position of FTA's board . . . would never have been upheld in a referendum of the membership. It was disastrous in its propaganda and legal aid to the enemies of the union." Ed McCrea to Bob Korstad, June 22, 1998, original in author's possession.

48. *WSJ*, February 15, 1950.

49. *WSJ*, February 28 and March 5, 1948.

50. Clarke and Fraser, "Plant Study Report"; John C. Whitaker to Senator Joseph H. Ball, February 27, 1948, R. J. Reynolds Tobacco Co.: Company Studied, Records of the Joint Committee on Labor-Management Relations, Records of the Joint Committees of Congress (Record Group 102), National Archives, Washington, D.C.; *WSJ*, March 9, 1948.

51. Philip Murray to Joseph H. Ball, March 10, 1948, R. J. Reynolds Tobacco Co.: Company Studied, Records of the Joint Committee on Labor-Management Relations.

52. Local 22, "Comment and Analysis on Plant Study Report," 3.

53. *WSJ*, April 5 and May 1, 1948.

54. *WSJ*, May 3, 1948.

55. Jack Frye interview.

56. Ed McCrea to Bob Korstad, June 22, 1988, original in author's possession; Scales and Nickson, *Cause at Heart*, 209, 211.

57. Elizabeth Eudy interview, November 1, 1987.

58. Jack Frye interview.

59. Edwin McCrea interview.

60. Henry Wallace, "Century of the Common Man," reprinted in *TWV*, August 1944. See also Blum, *V Was for Victory*, 245, and Sullivan, *Days of Hope*, 175–87.

61. Zieger, *CIO*, 268–77. On Wallace's decision to run for president, see Norman D. Markowitz, *Rise and Fall of the People's Century*, 250–60, and MacDougall, *Gideon's Army*, 224–47. On the Communist Party's support, see Joseph R. Starobin, *American Communism*, 162–77. On labor's position, see MacDougall, *Gideon's Army*, 611–28.

62. *WSJ*, January 19 and 24, 1948.

63. *WSJ*, February 24, 1948; Cochran, *Labor and Communism*, 304; MacDougall, *Gideon's Army*, 714–15.

64. *WSJ*, April 25, 1948. The Progressive Party campaign in North Carolina is discussed in Sullivan, *Days of Hope*, 260–64, and MacDougall, *Gideon's Army*, 732.

65. *N&O*, April 26, 1948. For additional information on Spraggins, see Uesugi, "'Jim Crow Must Go!,'" 37.

66. Ross, "Third Party Tradition," 1; *WSJ*, April 26, 1948.

67. *WSJ*, April 26, 1948.

68. Uesugi, "'Jim Crow Must Go!'" and "Gender, Race, and the Cold War."

69. Wallace, "Ten Extra Years."

70. Uesugi, "'Jim Crow Must Go!,'" 83–84; *N&O*, March 21, 1948.

71. *WSJ*, May 7, 1948. See also reply from Jason Hawkins in *WSJ*, May 9, 1948. For an assertion of this position on the national level, see Plotke, *Building a Democratic Political Order*, 283.

72. *WSJ*, June 22, 1948; Jack Frye interview.

73. Jack Frye interview.

74. Uesugi, "'Jim Crow Must Go!'"

75. *WSJ*, August 1, 1948. See also Bentley, *Out of Bondage*. For the recent discoveries, see Haynes and Klehr, *Venona*, 99–100, 105–6, 112–13, 232, 241, 224–25, 259, and Weinstein and Vassiliev, *Haunted Wood*.

76. See MacDougall, *Gideon's Army*, 707–19, for a blow-by-blow account of Wallace's trip to North Carolina.

77. *Durham Sun*, August 30, 1948.

78. Jack Frye interview; *Afro-American*, September 4, 1948.

79. *Afro-American*, September 4, 1948; *Durham Morning Herald*, August 30, 1948.

80. MacDougall, *Gideon's Army*, 714.

81. *WSJ*, August 31, 1948.

82. MacDougall, *Gideon's Army*, 709, 714; *WSJ*, August 31, 1948.

83. *WSJ*, August 31, September 1 and 5, 1948.

84. *WSJ*, September 17, 1948.

85. Ibid.

86. *WSJ*, September 13, October 20 and 30, and November 4, 1948.

87. MacDougall, *Gideon's Army*, 732–33.

Chapter 14

1. *WSJ*, November 4 and 21, 1948.

2. *WSJ*, February 19, 1948.

3. On Reynolds's decision to define its season from August 1 to February 29, see *WSJ*, February 29, 1948.

4. "Statement and Proposal to Board of Aldermen," February 20, 1948, BOA.

5. *WSJ*, February 21, 1948.

6. "Local 22 Proposals for Action on Unemployment," February 25, 1948, BOA.

7. Minutes, March 18, 1948, BOA. On the state's appraisal of black unemployment, see *WSJ*, February 19, 1948.

8. Minutes, March 18, 1948, BOA.

9. *WSJ*, February 27, 1949.

10. *WSJ*, February 27 and March 7, 1949.

11. *WSJ*, July 16, 1949.

12. Ibid.

13. Minutes, June 2, 1950, BOA.

14. See Willman, *Department of Housing*, and Fish, *Story of Housing*.

15. *WSJ*, November 2, 1949.

16. Michael K. Brown, *Race, Money*, 125–26.

17. *WSJ*, November 3, 1949.

18. *WSJ*, July 8, 1948.

19. *WSJ*, July 9, 10, and 15, 1948.

20. *WSJ*, July 9, August 25, and October 30, 1949; *FTA News*, September 1949.

21. *WSJ*, November 4, 1949. Southern legislators welcomed federal money as long as it did not upset race and labor relations. See Michael K. Brown, *Race, Money*.

22. *WSJ*, July 7 and November 2, 1949.

23. *WSJ*, August 19, 1948.

24. *WSJ*, November 3 and December 22, 1949.

25. *WSJ*, October 12, 1947.

26. Mr. Thomas to Mr. Granger, July 23, 1945, 6/27, National Urban League Papers, Manuscripts Division, Library of Congress, Washington, D.C. On the NUL's activities in the South, see Kerns, "Southern Field"; Weiss, *National Urban League*; and Lasch-Quinn, *Black Neighbors*, 39–42.

27. Fosdick, *Adventure in Giving*, 71. For a brief discussion of the CRP, see Guichard and Brooks, *Blacks in the City*, 313–18.

28. Reginald A. Johnson to Lester B. Granger, January 28, 1946, 6/27, National Urban League Papers.

29. "Committee to Investigate Community Relations Project," Spring 1946, box 6, folder 167, Gordon Gray Papers, Southern Historical Collection, University of North Carolina at Chapel Hill.

30. Minutes, "Meeting of Committee on Community Relations Project," April 13, 1946, box 6, folder 167, Gordon Gray Papers.

31. Ibid.

32. *WSJ*, November 17, 1946. The selection of these particular African Americans and the rejection of the Local 22 leadership was a continuation of the white power structure's unwill-

ingness to acknowledge black leaders who had opinions that differed from theirs. It was only in the mid-1960s that what Ladd calls more "militant" leaders were appointed to the interracial committees. Ladd, *Negro Political Leadership*, 116.

33. *WSJ*, November 16, 1947.

34. *WSJ*, September 18, 1948 (Hanes quote), and January 1, 18, and 21, 1949. The *Journal* saw Alston's hiring as a "pioneering step in race relations." *WSJ*, September 18, 1948. In a similar vein, Gordon Gray suggested to Governor Gregg Cherry that "we ought to think in terms of having a representative of the Negro race on the boards, such as the trustees of our Negro institutions. Of course, I refer particularly to the Winston-Salem Teachers College. I feel the great necessity, especially in view of recent developments in this community, of helping members of the negro race develop competent constructive leadership among their own people." Gordon Gray to R. Gregg Cherry, June 19, 1947, box 48, R. Gregg Cherry Papers, North Carolina Division of Archives and History, Raleigh, N.C.

35. *WSJ*, February 10, 1946; *TCS*, February 13, 1946.

36. Herr, *Winston-Salem*; *WSJ*, September 28, 1947.

37. *WSJ*, September 28, 1947.

38. *WSJ*, October 30, 1947. The committee conducted studies on upgrading the water system, expanding municipal hospitals, and creating ABC (Alcohol Beverage Control) stores to provide additional revenue. While all of these were important community issues, the committee effectively removed the research and planning process from public scrutiny and discussion.

39. *WSJ*, September 28, 1947.

40. *UTW*, October 28, 1947.

41. Ibid.; *WSJ*, October 30, 1947.

42. Kousser, *Colorblind Injustice*, 16, 25–31.

43. *WSJ*, September 22 and December 31, 1948. Despite the efforts of the annexation proponents to get the "right" people out to vote, the final totals showed only 2,571 ballots cast out of a total registration of over 16,000.

44. Kousser, *Colorblind Injustice*, 26–31.

45. *WSJ*, December 31, 1948.

46. Minutes, January 4, 1949, 9–10, BOA.

47. Ibid.

48. Ibid., 19. See Kenneth Williams interview for his analysis of the gerrymandering of the wards in 1949.

49. *WSJ*, January 5, 1948.

50. *WSJ*, January 5 and 6, 1949.

51. Minutes, February 1, 1949, BOA.

52. *WSJ*, February 4, 1949; North Carolina General Assembly, *Session Laws* (1949), chap. 152, 114–28.

53. *WSJ*, February 22, 1949. In nearby Durham, blacks had registered and voted in significant numbers beginning in the late 1930s. But because of the structure of the ward system and at-large voting, it was not until 1956 that an African American was elected to the city council and not until 1967 that a second representative of the black community was elected. Keech, *Impact of Negro Voting*, 47. In the 1950s the North Carolina General Assembly changed the town of Wilson's system from ward to at-large and also outlawed "bullet voting" in fourteen eastern counties. Keech and Sistrom, "North Carolina," 159.

54. Geneva McClendon interview; *FTA News*, May 1948. Viola Brown, former head of the shop stewards council, and Shirley Templeton, a white union activist, were both dismissed at some point in 1948 or 1949. See *WSJ*, April 1, 1949.

55. On Whitaker's reactions to the union's initiatives, see Tilley, *R. J. Reynolds*, 408–14. On raising wages, see Minchin, *What Do We Need a Union For?*, 48–68, and *WSJ*, May 19, 1948.

56. *WSJ*, November 20, 1948.

57. Tilley, *R. J. Reynolds*, 463–64, 455; *WSJ*, November 12, 1948.

58. Tilley, *R. J. Reynolds*, 454–58; "benevolent style" from *WSJ*, October 5, 1980; *N&O*, September 2, 1962.

59. Griffith, *Crisis of American Labor*, 106–22. Tilley, *R. J. Reynolds*, 464, says that Whitaker had a habit of injecting "moralistic statements" in the bulletin sent to supervisors, and that Charles Wade worked to keep them to a minimum.

60. George, *God's Salesman*, 104.

61. Ibid., 112.

62. *WSJ*, January 29, 1949; Tilley, *R. J. Reynolds*, 479; George, *God's Salesman*, 112. The company's hard-bitten foremen, however, seem to have been less than receptive to the message of the free publication that arrived in their mailboxes each month; indeed, there were reports that *Guideposts* was the "subject of facetious remarks" among the supervisory personnel. Tilley, *R. J. Reynolds*, 479.

63. Woodbury, "They Put a Parson," 81–82. According to company records, the hiring of a minister had been under consideration for a number of years. See Tilley, *R. J. Reynolds*, 471–80.

64. Western North Carolina Conference of the Methodist Church, "Journal of the 1967 Session," 319–20; *Tobacco*, May 24, 1951.

65. First quote is from *Tobacco*, May 24, 1951; second quote from Tilley, *R. J. Reynolds*, 471–72; last two quotes from Blanche Fishel interview.

66. Woodbury, "They Put a Parson," 18–19, 81–85; "Yankee-Type Rebels," 17; *WSJ*, September 23, 1949.

67. "Yankee-Type Rebels," 17 (quote); Peace, "Pastoral Care," 16.

68. Fones-Wolf, *Selling Free Enterprise*, 224–25; "Yankee-Type Rebels," 17 (quote).

Chapter 15

1. For the best overview of the CIO's postwar internecine strife, see Zieger, *CIO*, 253–93.

2. Ibid., 283. Discussion of the acrimonious relationship between FTA and state CIO director Smith and the plans for a CIO campaign at Reynolds can be found in *WSJ*, September 5, 24, 26, and December 16, 1948. On the decision to deploy UTSE, see John Yancey to William Smith, July 1 and 14, 1948, and Smith to Yancey, July 16, 1948, Congress of Industrial Organizations, Organizing Committee, North Carolina Papers, 1909–57, Manuscripts Department, William R. Perkins Library, Duke University, Durham, N.C., and Zieger, *CIO*, 283.

3. Townsend, "One American Problem"; *Who's Who*, 498; Zieger, *CIO*, 156. Robert Zieger describes Townsend as a "dutiful CIO loyalist" who by the mid-1950s had lost patience with the CIO's indifference to the plight of African Americans (*CIO*, 348).

4. Robert Black interview, December 28, 1976; Robert Black testimony, "Hearings before the Committee to Investigate Charges against the Food, Tobacco, Agricultural, and Allied

Workers of America," January 6, 1950, box 109, FTA Hearings, CIOSTO, 369–70. See the mention of this story in *WSJ*, December 16, 1948.

5. Neil Hickey, who succeeded Hargrove as director of the UTSE campaign, presented what was undoubtedly Hargrove's assessment of his transfer from Local 22. "In late 1944, FTA International Officers began to revise the program for Local 22. They sent in new representatives and replaced the director with a new one who did not believe in CIO policy, but whose policy was dictated by the communist party." Neil Hickey, "Radio Broadcast-WAIR," November 20, 1949, transcript, series 7, folder 85, ODP. For more on Hargrove's hiring, see Frank Hargrove to Michael Quill, January 28, 1948, John Yancey to Hargrove, October 28, 1948, and William Smith to Nebraska Jones, December 22, 1948, Congress of Industrial Organizations, Organizing Committee, North Carolina Papers. Hargrove left FTA in 1946 to work with another CIO union. See *WSJ*, December 1, 1948.

6. *WSJ*, April 24 and July 14, 1949.

7. William Smith to John Ramsey, March 31, 1949, and Ruth Gettinger to John Ramsey, August 8, 1949, 1566/134, AFL-CIO, Region 8 Papers, Southern Labor Archives, Georgia State University, Atlanta, Ga. Emphasis added.

8. *WSJ*, September 10, 1949. TWIU withdrew its most effective black organizer in July.

9. *WSJ*, July 8, 27, and August 4, 5, 6, 13, and 18, 1949. On the impact of non-Communist affidavits on left-led unions, see Schrecker, "McCarthyism and the Labor Movement," 146–54.

10. Zieger, *CIO*, 286–87 (all quotes); Rosswurm, *CIO's Left-Led Unions*, 1–2.

11. *WSJ*, November 12, 1949.

12. Hickey, "Radio Broadcast," ODP.

13. Ibid.; *WSJ*, November 12, 1949. See Zieger, *CIO*, 254–55, for the record of left-led unions regarding collective bargaining, contract content and administration, internal democracy, and honest governance.

14. Zieger, *CIO*, 287–88.

15. "Report of the Committee to Investigate Charges," 14, CIOSTO. The CIO's expulsion of the left-led unions has received increased attention from historians in recent years. Even those who are highly critical of the left-led unions, such as Robert Zieger, see little to commend in the CIO's actions. Zieger, *CIO*, 287–93. Other scholars see the expulsions as a capitulation to the rising tide of McCarthyism and/or an attempt to find scapegoats for the CIO's failure to repeal Taft-Hartley or to organize the South. See Emspak, "Break-Up of the CIO," 291, 301.

16. *WSJ*, January 8, 1950.

17. The union demanded a twenty-six-and-a-half-cent across-the-board wage increase, retirement pensions at age sixty paid for by the company, a thirty-five-hour work week, and additional vacations and holidays. *Local 22 Organizer*, March 21, 1950. Local union leaders, in conjunction with Bernard Friedland, the new Communist Party district organizer, settled on black-white unity as the theme of the campaign. A reflection in some ways of the Popular Front rhetoric of earlier days, the unity theme also spoke to the heart of the issue in Winston-Salem, the need to bring white and black workers together.

18. *Local 22 Organizer*, February 15, 1950.

19. *WSJ*, February 12, 1949.

20. Robert Lathan radio address, February 14, 1950, 4–5, original transcript in author's possession.

21. Willie L. Grier radio address, February 18, 1950, original transcript in author's posses-

sion. According to Grier, Local 22 followed the "membership line." See a similar description of Local 19 by Ed McCrea in Honey, *Southern Labor*, 265.

22. "Hearings before the Committee," 365–74, CIOSTo.

23. *WSJ*, September 13, October 20 and 30, 1948.

24. Von Eschen, *Race against Empire*, 103–4, argues that the rally represented the apex of the Popular Front movement.

25. *WSJ*, February 5, March 1, 1950 (quote); Scales and Nickson, *Cause at Heart*, 207. For Bethune's biography and her stance on anti-Communism, see Thomas and Smith, *Mary McLeod Bethune*, 267–70, 288–89, and Holt, *Mary McLeod Bethune*.

26. Scales and Nickson, *Cause at Heart*, 207; Sullivan, *Days of Hope*, 206.

27. Bernard Friedland, Junius Scales, and Karl Korstad interview.

28. *WSJ*, May 16, 1949.

29. Tise, *Government*, 49.

30. *WSJ*, February 11, 1950. The records from this election were randomly destroyed by either the NLRB or the National Archives.

31. The TWIU showing was remarkable. It was true that the AFL affiliate had collected over 3,000 signatures authorizing it to request an NLRB election, but many of those signatories were former members of Local 22 who returned to the fold. The TWIU had actually tapped into a core group of whites who desired union representation. Reynolds tried hard to frighten these union-minded whites, firing several activists a few days before the election. The company also allegedly held a meeting of the over 2,000 manufacturing workers who held company stock and offered them a special dividend. Kaufman, *Challenge and Change*, 116–17.

32. *WSJ*, March 18, 1950.

33. *WSJ*, March 22, 1950.

34. *WSJ*, March 23, 1950.

35. For Bazinet's view, see *WSJ*, March 18, 1950.

36. For workers' letters, see *WSJ*, March 16, 1950.

37. *WSJ*, March 22, 1950.

38. *WSJ*, March 23, 1950.

39. Ernest Tilley was one of the workers the union challenged. A third-generation Reynolds employee—his father had been superintendent of the plug department for many years—Tilley worked in the supply department. Ernest Tilley interview.

40. *WSJ*, March 25 and April 6, 1950.

41. *WSJ*, April 17, 1950; Ruby Jones interview.

42. Ibid. The *Journal* estimated the crowd at 3,500; the *FTA News* reported 5,000. *FTA News*, April 1950. Among the various positions Moranda Smith held were member of the Communist Party's National Committee for the Negro Vote; national vice chairman, Civil Rights Congress; and national board member of the Congress of American Women. *DW*, April 14, 17, and 18, 1950.

43. *WSJ*, April 17, 1950.

Epilogue

1. Tilley, *R. J. Reynolds*, 411; *UV*, September 15, 1950; DPOWA, "Brief History."

2. DPOWA, "Brief History."

3. DPOWA, *Founding Convention*, 25, 50, and "Brief History," 8. The extent of AFL and CIO raids on FTA is documented in DPOWA, *Founding Convention*. On the merger, see DPOWA, *Founding Convention*, and Fink and Greenberg, *Upheaval in the Quiet Zone*, 25–26.

4. Tilley, *R. J. Reynolds*, 412–14.

5. For a history of desegregation and the black civil rights movement in Winston-Salem in the 1950s, see Dunston, "Black Struggle for Equality," 61–104.

6. The post-1950s black freedom struggle in Winston-Salem is described in ibid., 105–275. See also Waynick, Brooks, and Pitts, *North Carolina and the Negro*, 180–85.

7. Dunston, "Black Struggle for Equality," 239–45, 262–75.

8. On the accomplishments of the 1940s, see Lawson, *Running for Freedom*, 1–65, and Honey, *Southern Labor*, 280–91.

9. Schrecker, *Many Are the Crimes*, 359–415.

10. David M. Anderson, "Battle for Main Street U.S.A."; Gross, *Broken Promise*; Cobb, *Selling of the South*, 101–5.

11. Schrecker, *Many Are the Crimes*, 389–95.

12. Egerton, *Speak Now against the Day*, 448–60; Branch, *Parting the Waters*, 468–69.

13. Egerton, *Speak Now against the Day*, 553–72.

14. Santino, *Miles of Smiles*, 53–55.

15. Cobb, *Selling of the South*; Gavin Wright, *Old South, New South*, 239–74.

16. Luebke, *Tar Heel Politics*, 58–69.

17. Cobb, "The Sunbelt South," 40.

18. Kousser, *Colorblind Injustice*.

BIBLIOGRAPHY

Manuscript Collections

Atlanta, Georgia
Southern Labor Archives, Georgia State University
    AFL-CIO, Region 8 Papers
Robert Woodruff Library and Archives, Atlanta University
    Southern Conference for Human Welfare Collection

Chapel Hill, North Carolina
Southern Historical Collection, University of North Carolina
    Thurman Chatham Papers
    Fellowship of Southern Churchmen Papers
    Gordon Gray Papers
    James G. Hanes Papers
    Leonard Rappaport Papers
    M. H. Ross Collection
    Southern Tenant Farmers Union Papers

College Park, Maryland
National Archives
    Records of the National Recovery Administration (Record Group 9)
Special Collections Division, Hornbake Library, University of Maryland
    Tobacco Workers International Union Records

Detroit, Michigan
Archives of Labor History and Urban Affairs, Walter Reuther Library,
    Wayne State University
    CIO International Executive Board Bound Proceedings
    CIO Secretary-Treasurer Office Records
    UAW Local 600 Collection
    Claude Williams Papers

Durham, North Carolina
Manuscripts Department, William R. Perkins Library, Duke University
  Arthur Vance Cole Papers
  Congress of Industrial Organizations, Organizing Committee,
    North Carolina Papers, 1909–57 (Operation Dixie)
  Santford Martin Papers
  Lucy Randolph Mason Papers

Ithaca, New York
Kheel Center for Labor-Management Documentation and Archives,
    M. P. Catherwood Library, Cornell University
  International Fur and Leather Workers Union Records
  Southern Summer School for Workers, American Labor Education Service Records

New York, New York
Schomburg Center for Research in Black Culture, New York Public Library
  Ralph Bunche Papers
Tamiment Library, New York University
  Joseph Califf Papers

Raleigh, North Carolina
North Carolina Division of Archives and History
  J. Melville Broughton Papers
  R. Gregg Cherry Papers

Suitland, Maryland
National Archives and Records Administration, Washington National Records Center
  Records of the Army Staff (Record Group 319)
    Military Intelligence Division Files, FBI Headquarters File 100-930
      ("Charlotte, N.C.")

Washington, D.C.
Manuscripts Division, Library of Congress
  Communist Party of the United States of America Papers
  National Association for the Advancement of Colored People Papers
    Group II, C 141, N.C. State Conference, 1943, 1945, 1946
    Group II, C 140, Winston-Salem, N.C., 1946–55
  National Urban League Papers
National Archives
  Records of the Federal Mediation and Conciliation Service (Record Group 280)
    Dispute Case Files 1913–48
  Records of the Joint Committees of Congress (Record Group 102)
    Records of the Joint Committee on Labor-Management Relations (Senate,
      80th Cong.)
  Records of the National Labor Relations Board (Record Group 25)
    Formal and Informal Labor Practices and Representation, Case Files 1935–48
    Transcripts and Exhibits, 1935–48, Transcripts and Exhibits No. 6173

Records of the National War Labor Board (World War II) (Record Group 202)
    Dispute Case Files, Region IV, 111-7701 D
Records of the Supreme Court (Record Group 267)
    Appellate Jurisdiction Records

Winston-Salem, North Carolina
Hall of Records
    Board of Aldermen Records
    Clerk of Forsyth County Superior Court Records

Interviews

Berry, Abner. Interview by Robert Korstad, December 3, 1983, Rocky Mount, North Carolina.

Binkley, Eleanore. Interview by Robert Korstad, July 13, 1979, Winston-Salem, North Carolina.

————. Interview by Robert Korstad, August 25, 1990, Sarasota, Florida.

Black, Robert. Interview by Karl Korstad, undated, Greensboro, North Carolina.

————. Interviews by Robert Korstad, June 1, 1976; December 28, 1976; October 7, 1977; May 1, 1978; April 8, 1979; August 3, 1981; March 4, 1985; May 13, 1987, all in Greensboro, North Carolina.

————. Interview by Craig Jones, January 2, 1981, Greensboro, North Carolina.

————. Interview by Gary Lyons and Robert Korstad, August 24, 1984, Greensboro, North Carolina.

————. Interviews by Chuck Eppinette, March 3 and July 13, 1988, Greensboro, North Carolina.

————. Interview by Lane Windham, April 29, 1990, Greensboro, North Carolina.

Black, Robert, and Ruby Jones. Interview by Robert Korstad, December 28, 1976, Winston-Salem, North Carolina.

Black, Robert, Janie Black, Viola Brown, and Karl Korstad. Interview by Robert Korstad, December 1976, Winston-Salem, North Carolina.

Boulware, Wardell. Interview by Robert Korstad, June 16, 1983, Winston-Salem, North Carolina.

Bowles, Lucy. Interview by Robert Korstad, July 26, 1990, Winston-Salem, North Carolina.

Brice, Mary. Interview by Robert Korstad, July 1, 1985, Winston-Salem, North Carolina.

Brown, Viola, and Julia Leach. Interview by Chuck Eppinette and Robert Korstad, undated, Winston-Salem, North Carolina.

Brown, Viola, and Sally Mitchell. Interview by Robert Korstad, undated, Winston-Salem, North Carolina.

Califf, Joseph. Interview by Robert Korstad, August 24, 1996, Black Mountain, North Carolina.

Carter, Nettie. Interview by Robert Korstad, July 16, 1984, Winston-Salem, North Carolina.

Davis, Chester. Interview by Robert Korstad, May 5, 1988, Winston-Salem, North Carolina.

DeBerry, William. Interview by Will Inman, May 23, 1978, Tucson, Arizona.

East, Bill. Interview by Craig Jones, January 1, 1981, Winston-Salem, North Carolina.

Edwards, Leon. Interview by Chuck Eppinette and Robert Korstad, January 12, 1989, Winston-Salem, North Carolina.

Eudy, Elizabeth. Telephone interviews by Robert Korstad, November 1, 1987, and June 1, 1988, Berkeley, California.

Fishel, Blanche. Interview by Robert Korstad, undated, Washington, North Carolina.

Ford, Mary Lou Koger. Telephone interview by Robert Korstad, March 21, 1991, Iredell, Texas.

Friedland, Bernard, Junius Scales, and Karl Korstad. Interview by Robert Korstad, April 14, 1986, New York, New York.

Frye, Jack. Interview by Karl Korstad, October 16, 1981, Chicago, Illinois.

Goldenstar, Paul. Interview by Lisa Hazirjian, June 17, 1992, Winston-Salem, North Carolina.

Green, Frank. Interview by Robert Korstad, June 3, 1987, Charlotte, North Carolina.

Grier, Willie. Interview by Karl Korstad and Robert Korstad, May 1, 1978, Winston-Salem, North Carolina.

Griffin, Lillian. Interview by Lane Windham, October 15, 1990, Winston-Salem, North Carolina.

Hairston, Evelyn and Langfell. Interview by Robert Korstad, July 17, 1984, Winston-Salem, North Carolina.

Heafner, D. Yates. Interview by Robert Korstad, March 3, 1985, Charlotte, North Carolina.

Holman, Baxter. Interview by Robert Korstad, June 11, 1984, Winston-Salem, North Carolina.

Hopkins, Velma. Interview by Robert Korstad, March 3, 1985, Winston-Salem, North Carolina.

Isley, E. T. "Jazz," Jr. Interview by Lisa Hazirjian, June 13, 1992, Winston-Salem, North Carolina.

Jarvis, Alice. Interview by Robert Korstad, April 25, 1988, Brooklyn, New York.

Johnson, Hobart. Interview by Robert Korstad, July 16, 1990, Winston-Salem, North Carolina.

Jones, Hazel. Interview by Robert Korstad, June 27, 1984, Winston-Salem, North Carolina.

Jones, Ruby. Interview by Robert Korstad, October 2, 1977, Winston-Salem, North Carolina.

Kilgore, Thomas. Interview by Robin Kelly, 1988. Transcript A1713 URL, Department of Special Collections, University of California at Los Angeles.

Koritz, Philip. Interview by Robert Korstad, January 3, 1989, Greensboro, North Carolina.

Korstad, Karl. Interview by Craig Jones, December 1980, Greensboro, North Carolina.

———. Interviews by Robert Korstad, December 14, 1980, and August 25, 1987, Greensboro, North Carolina.

———. Interview by Lane Windham, April 14, 1986, Greensboro, North Carolina.

Kurfees, Marshall. Interview by Robert Korstad, July 1, 1988, Winston-Salem, North Carolina.

Little, Annie F. Interviews by Lane Windham, July 17 and October 15, 1990, Greenville, North Carolina.

Marsh, Ellen. Interview by Lisa Hazirjian, June 2, 1992, Winston-Salem, North Carolina.

Mathews, Anne. Interview by Robert Korstad, February 13, 1986, Winston-Salem, North Carolina.

McClendon, Geneva. Interview by Craig Jones, January 3, 1981, Winston-Salem, North Carolina.

McCrea, Edwin. Interview by Chuck Eppinette and Richard Ward, July 23, 1988, Nashville, Tennessee.

McCrea, Edwin and Bea. Interview by Robert Korstad, undated, Nashville, Tennessee.

McKensie, James. Interview by Lisa Hazirjian, June 10, 1992, Winston-Salem, North Carolina.

Nesbitt, Evelyn. Interview by Robert Korstad, July 13, 1983, Winston-Salem, North Carolina.

Nesmith, Lonnie. Interview by Robert Korstad, undated, Winston-Salem, North Carolina.

———. Interview by Norman Bernstein, January 7, 1998, Winston-Salem, North Carolina.

O'Neal, Frank. Interview by Robert Korstad, November 28, 1979, Hilton Head, South Carolina.

Person, Robert. Interview by Craig Jones, November 9, 1980, Winston-Salem, North Carolina.

Phelps, Theodosia. Interviews by Robert Korstad, June 1, 1978, and April 17, 1979, Winston-Salem, North Carolina.

Phelps, Theodosia, Robert Black, and Karl Korstad. Interview by Robert Korstad, undated, Winston-Salem, North Carolina.

Phelps, Theodosia, and Karl Korstad. Interview by Robert Korstad, undated, Winston-Salem, North Carolina.

Prevard, Inez. Interview by Robert Korstad, July 17, 1984, Winston-Salem, North Carolina.

Ranson, Luther. Interview by Robert Korstad, July 17, 1990, Winston-Salem, North Carolina.

Robertson, Mary. Interview by Jacquelyn Hall, August 13, 1979, Asheville, North Carolina.

Royal, Sidney. Interview by Robert Korstad, June 14, 1983, Winston-Salem, North Carolina.

Salmons, Lee. Interview by Lisa Hazirjian, June 2, 1992, Winston-Salem, North Carolina.

Scales, Junius. Interviews by Robert Korstad, April 4 and May 2, 1987, Chapel Hill, North Carolina.

Scott, Charles, Jr. Interview by Lisa Hazirjian, June 8, 1992, Winston-Salem, North Carolina.

Shelton, Crawford. Interview by Craig Jones, November 7, 1980, Winston-Salem, North Carolina.

Silverman, Robert. Telephone interview by Robert Korstad, April 18, 1998, Greensboro, North Carolina.

Simmons, Cornelius. Interview by Lane Windham, September 2, 1990, Winston-Salem, North Carolina.

Smith, Louise. Interview by Robert Korstad, June 26, 1984, Winston-Salem, North Carolina.

Speaks, Jack. Interview by Lisa Hazirjian, June 5, 1992, Winston-Salem, North Carolina.

Stevenson, Etta. Interview by Robert Korstad, July 7, 1984, Winston-Salem, North Carolina.

Stine, Jim. Interview by Lisa Hazirjian, June 5, 1992, Winston-Salem, North Carolina.

Stine, Katherine. Interview by Lisa Hazirjian, June 8, 1992, Winston-Salem, North arolina.

Thompson, Sylvia. Interview by Robert Korstad and Jacquelyn Hall, May 28, 2000, New York, New York.

Tilley, Ernest Leland. Interview by Lisa Hazirjian, June 10, 1992, Winston-Salem, North Carolina.

Wade, Charles. Interview by Craig Jones, December 29, 1980, Winston-Salem, North Carolina.

————. Interview by Robert Korstad, November 14, 1983, Winston-Salem, North Carolina.

Williams, Kenneth. Interview by Craig Jones, April 2, 1980, Winston-Salem, North Carolina.

Williams, Rebecca. Interview by Robert Korstad, June 27, 1984, Winston-Salem, North Carolina.

Williams, Warren. Interview by Robert Korstad, March 15, 1996, Winston-Salem, North Carolina.

Winston, Marie Jackson. Interview by Lane Windham, September 27, 1990, Winston-Salem, North Carolina.

Wright, Diane. Interview by Lane Windham, September 27, 1990, Winston-Salem, North Carolina.

Newspapers and Periodicals

Carolina Times (Durham), 1937–53

Carolinian, 1946

Chronicle (Winston-Salem), 1979–92

Daily Worker (New York), 1943–50

Fur and Leather Worker (New York), 1946–48

Industrial Leader (Winston-Salem), 1945–46

Journal and Guide (Norfolk, Va.), 1943–44

Labor Defender (Chicago), 1930

Liberator (Boston), 1930

New Herald (Franklin, Pa.), 1971

New Masses (New York), 1943–47

News and Observer (Raleigh), 1936–47

New York Times, 1948

Norfolk Virginian-Pilot, 1947

PM, 1947

Southern Patriot (Atlanta), 1944–50

Southern Worker (Chattanooga/Birmingham), 1930–37

Southern Workman (Hampton, Va.), 1903

Star of Zion (Petersburg, Va.), 1908

Thursday (Winston-Salem), 1940–41

Tobacco (Winston-Salem), 1945–48

The Tobacco Worker, 1919–24, 1940–43

The Tobacco Worker's Voice (Winston-Salem), August 1944–February 1947

Twin City Sentinel (Winston-Salem), 1943–50

UCAPAWA News/FTA News (Philadelphia), 1937–50

Union-Republican (Winston-Salem), 1895–1901, 1911

Union Voice (New York), 1950

United Tobacco Worker/FTA Organizer/Reynolds Organizer/Local 22 Organizer (Winston-Salem), 1947–50

Washington Post, 1947

Winston-Salem Journal, 1940–50

Winston-Salem Journal and Sentinel, 1938–50, 1960
The Worker (New York), 1943–51

Union Publications, Unpublished Pamphlets, and Government Reports

Clark, Ethel Riley. "Report of the Field Services of the Consultant in Social Group Work and Recreation in Winston-Salem, North Carolina, February 9 to March 1, 1947." Community Relations Project, National Urban League, New York, 1947. North Carolina Room, Forsyth County Library, Winston-Salem, N.C.

Clarke, Bert C., and Stewart J. Fraser. "R. J. Reynolds Tobacco Company: Plant Study Report of the Joint Committee on Labor-Management Relations." 1948. North Carolina Collection, University of North Carolina at Chapel Hill.

Communist Party, U.S.A. *What You Should Know about the Communists: Who They Are, What They Believe In, What They Fight For.* New York: Communist Party, U.S.A., 1947.

Congress of Industrial Organizations. *Analysis of the Taft-Hartley Act.* Washington, D.C.: Congress of Industrial Organizations, 1957.

———. *Official Reports on the Expulsion of Communist Dominated Organizations from the CIO.* Washington, D.C.: Congress of Industrial Organizations, 1954.

Crouch, Paul. "Brief History of the Communist Movement in North and South Carolina." 1954. North Carolina Collection, University of North Carolina at Chapel Hill.

Distributive, Processing, and Office Workers of America. "A Brief History of the Organizing Struggles of the Workers in the R. J. Reynolds Plants in Winston-Salem, N.C., since 1942." N.d. [1951]. North Carolina Collection, University of North Carolina at Chapel Hill.

———. *Founding Convention, Distributive, Processing, and Office Workers of America.* New York: Distributive, Processing, and Office Workers of America, 1950.

Food, Tobacco, Agricultural, and Allied Workers Union. *How to Organize a Strike.* Philadelphia: Food, Tobacco, Agricultural, and Allied Workers Union, CIO, 1947.

———. *Outline of a Local Union.* Philadelphia: Food, Tobacco, Agricultural, and Allied Workers Union, CIO, 1947.

———. *Proceedings of the Fifth National Convention of the FTAAWUA.* Philadelphia: Food, Tobacco, Agricultural, and Allied Workers Union, CIO, 1944.

———. *Profits, Prices, and Wages in the Food Industry.* Philadelphia: Food, Tobacco, Agricultural, and Allied Workers Union, CIO, 1947. Industrial Relations Library, Harvard University, Cambridge, Mass.

———. *Report of the General Executive Officers to Food, Tobacco, Agricultural and Allied Workers Union of America, Fifth National Convention.* Philadelphia: Food, Tobacco, Agricultural, and Allied Workers Union, CIO, 1944.

———. *Report of the General Executive Officers to Food, Tobacco, Agricultural and Allied Workers Union of America, Sixth National Convention.* Philadelphia: Food, Tobacco, Agricultural, and Allied Workers Union, CIO, 1947.

———. *Substandard Wages: An Analysis of Their Extent and Effect.* Philadelphia: Food, Tobacco, Agricultural, and Allied Workers Union, CIO, 1946.

———. *Wage Policy Statement, Food, Tobacco, Agricultural and Allied Workers Union.* Philadelphia: Food, Tobacco, Agricultural, and Allied Workers Union, CIO, 1946. Industrial Relations Library, Harvard University, Cambridge, Mass.

―――. *Who's Unamerican!* Philadelphia: Food, Tobacco, Agricultural, and Allied Workers Union, CIO, 1947.

―――. *Your Union: How to Make It Strong.* Philadelphia: Food, Tobacco, Agricultural, and Allied Workers Union, CIO, n.d. [1946].

Herr, Clarence. *Winston-Salem: An Analysis of City Finances.* Winston-Salem: Twin City Sentinel, 1947.

Horton, Zelphia. *Labor Songs.* Atlanta: Textile Workers Union of America, 1939.

International Brotherhood of Electrical Workers. "Twentieth Biennial Convention, International Brotherhood of Electrical Workers." 1929. Copy in author's possession.

Jefferson, Richard R. "Report of the Field Services of the Consultant in Employment, Industrial Relations and Education in Winston-Salem, North Carolina, February 10 to March 1, 1947." Community Relations Project, National Urban League, New York, 1947. North Carolina Room, Forsyth County Library, Winston-Salem, N.C.

Koos, Frank. "Our Schools Today: A Radio Talk." 1930. North Carolina Collection, University of North Carolina at Chapel Hill.

Lawrence, Mary. "Discussion Outline for Classes in Shop Steward Training." Highlander Folk School, Monteagle, Tennessee, 1947. Original in author's possession.

Local 22. "Comment and Analysis on Plant Study Report of the Joint Committee on Labor-Management Relations, Local 22." 1948. North Carolina Collection, University of North Carolina at Chapel Hill.

Manning, Carolyn, and Harriet A. Byrne. *The Effects on Women of Changing Conditions in the Cigar and Cigarette Industries.* Women's Bureau, U.S. Department of Labor, Bulletin, no. 100. Washington, D.C.: GPO, 1932.

National Labor Relations Board. *Decisions and Orders of the National Labor Relations Board.* Vol. 2. Washington, D.C.: GPO, 1936–37.

―――. *Decisions and Orders of the National Labor Relations Board.* Vol. 7. Washington, D.C.: GPO, 1941.

―――. *Decisions and Orders of the National Labor Relations Board.* Vol. 9. Washington, D.C.: GPO, 1943.

―――. *Decisions and Orders of the National Labor Relations Board.* Vol. 14. Washington, D.C.: GPO, 1950.

National Recovery Administration. *Code of Fair Competition for the Cigarette, Snuff, Chewing, and Smoking Tobacco Manufacturing Industry.* Washington, D.C.: GPO, 1935.

National War Labor Board. *Termination Report of the National War Labor Board: Industrial Disputes and Wage Stabilization in Wartime.* Washington, D.C.: GPO, 1949.

North Carolina General Assembly. *Session Laws and Resolutions.* Raleigh: Charlotte Observer Printing House, 1947.

―――. *Session Laws and Resolutions.* Raleigh: Charlotte Observer Printing House, 1949.

Opperman, Langdon. *Winston-Salem's African-American Neighborhoods: 1870–1950.* Winston-Salem: Forsyth County Joint Historic Properties Commission, 1993.

Organization Department, Communist National Committee. *Manual for Community Club Leaders: A Handbook for the Use of Officers and Committees of Communist Community Clubs.* New York: National Committee, Communist Party, 1944.

Patrick, Clarence H. *Lunch Counter Desegregation in Winston-Salem, North Carolina.* Winston-Salem: City of Winston-Salem, 1960. North Carolina Collection, University of North Carolina.

People's Songs Wordbook No. 1. New York: People's Songs, 1947.

Perlman, Jacob. "The Negro in Industry: Earnings and Hours of Negro Workers in Independent Tobacco Stemmeries in 1933 and 1935." *Monthly Labor Review,* May 1937, 1153–72.

Pidgeon, Mary Elizabeth. *Negro Women in Industry in 15 States.* Women's Bureau, U.S. Department of Labor, Bulletin, no. 76. Washington, D.C.: GPO, 1929.

President's Committee on Civil Rights. *To Secure These Rights: The Report of the President's Committee on Civil Rights.* Washington, D.C.: GPO, 1947.

Price, Daniel O. *Changing Characteristics of the Negro Population: A 1960 Census Monograph.* Washington, D.C.: U.S. Department of Commerce, Bureau of the Census, 1969.

R. J. Reynolds Employees Ass. Inc. v. N.L.R.B., et al., 61 F. Supp. 280, 595–601 (U.S. District Court for D.C., Md., N.C., 1943).

R. J. Reynolds Tobacco Company. "Facts about Your Job and Company." Winston-Salem, N.C., 1954.

Ross, Mike. "The Third Party Tradition in North Carolina." Greensboro: Greensboro Public Library, 1947.

"The Sign of Welcome." 1942. Forsyth County Library, Winston-Salem, N.C.

Southern Conference on Race Relations. "A Basis for Inter-Racial Cooperation and Development in the South: A Statement by Southern Negroes." Durham, N.C., 1942. North Carolina Collection, University of North Carolina at Chapel Hill.

Southern Labor Conference. "Report and Policy, Third Biennial Southern Labor Conference." 1946. North Carolina Collection, University of North Carolina at Chapel Hill.

State of North Carolina. "Brief of the State of North Carolina . . . Koritz v. State of North Carolina." 1947. North Carolina Collection, University of North Carolina at Chapel Hill.

State of North Carolina v. William DeBerry, 224 N.C. 834–37 (Fall term, 1944).

State of North Carolina v. Koritz et al., 227 N.C. 552–59.

United Cannery, Agricultural, Packing, and Allied Workers of America. *Official Proceedings, First National Convention, July 9–12, 1937.* Denver: UCAPAWA, 1937.

———. *Official Proceedings, Third Annual Convention, Chicago, Dec. 1940.* Denver: UCAPAWA, 1940.

U.S. Congress. House. Committee on Un-American Activities. *Communist Infiltration and Activities in the South.* 85th Cong., 1st sess. Washington, D.C.: GPO, 1958.

———. *Hearings Regarding Communism in Labor Unions in the United States.* 80th Cong., 1st sess. Washington, D.C.: GPO, 1947.

———. *Hearings Regarding Communism in the District of Columbia, Part 1.* 81st Cong., 1st sess. Washington, D.C.: GPO, 1949.

———. *Hearings Regarding Communist Infiltration of Minority Groups, Part 1.* 81st Cong., 1st sess. Washington, D.C.: GPO, 1949.

———. *Investigation of Communist Activities in the North Carolina Area.* 84th Cong., 2d sess. Washington, D.C.: GPO, 1956.

———. *Investigation of Communist Activities in the Rocky Mountain Area, Part 1.* 84th Cong., 2d sess. Washington, D.C.: GPO, 1956.

———. *Testimony of Paul Crouch.* 81st Cong., 1st sess. Washington, D.C.: GPO, 1949.

———. Committee on Ways and Means. *Hearings on Revenue Revisions of 1943.* 78th Cong., 1st sess. Washington, D.C.: GPO, 1943.

———. Senate. Judiciary Committee. Subcommittee to Investigate the Administration of the Internal Security Act. *Communist Underground Printing Facilities and Illegal Propaganda.* 83d Cong., 1st sess. Washington, D.C.: GPO, 1953.

———. *Subversive Control of Distributive, Processing, and Office Workers of America.* 82d Cong., 1st and 2d sess. Washington, D.C.: GPO, 1952.

U.S. Department of Commerce. Bureau of the Census. *Fifteenth Census of the United States, 1930: Occupation, by States.* Washington, D.C.: GPO, 1930.

———. *Fifteenth Census of the United States, 1930: Population.* Washington, D.C.: GPO, 1930.

———. *Fourteenth Census of the United States, 1920: Population.* Washington, D.C.: GPO, 1920.

———. *Negroes in the United States, 1920–32.* Washington, D.C.: GPO, 1935.

———. *Seventeenth Census of the United States, 1950: Characteristics of the Population.* Washington, D.C.: GPO, 1950.

———. *Seventeenth Census of the United States, 1950: Characteristics of the Population, Statistics for Census Tracts.* Washington, D.C.: GPO, 1950.

———. *Sixteenth Census of the United States, 1940: Housing, Supplement to the First Series, Housing Bulletin, Block Statistics.* Washington, D.C.: GPO, 1941–42.

———. *Sixteenth Census of the United States, 1940: Population, Characteristics of the Population.* Washington, D.C.: GPO, 1940.

———. *Sixteenth Census of the United States, 1940: Population and Housing, Statistics for Census Tracts.* Washington, D.C.: GPO, 1940.

———. *Thirteenth Census of the United States, 1910: Population.* Washington, D.C.: GPO, 1910.

———. *Twelfth Census of the United States, 1900: Population.* Washington, D.C.: GPO, 1900.

U.S. Department of Labor. Bureau of Labor Statistics. "Hours and Earnings of Independent Leaf-Tobacco Dealers." *Monthly Labor Review,* July 1941, 215–21.

———. *Industry Wage Studies: Job Descriptions for Wage Studies, Tobacco.* Washington, D.C.: GPO, 1947.

———. *Labor in the South.* Bulletin, vol. 848. Washington, D.C.: GPO, 1947.

———. *Productivity Trends in the Tobacco Products Industries, 1939–1950.* Washington, D.C.: GPO, 1952.

———. "Seniority Provisions in Union Agreements." *Monthly Labor Review,* May 1941, 1169–77.

———. *Studies of the Effects of the $1 Minimum Wage: Wage Structure, Tobacco Stemming and Redrying, 1955 and 1956.* Washington, D.C.: GPO, 1956.

———. *A Study of Six Occupations in the Cigarette, Smoking Tobacco, and Chewing Tobacco Industries in Virginia and North Carolina, July 1954.* Washington, D.C.: GPO, 1954.

———. *Union Agreements in the Tobacco Industry in Effect, January 1945.* Bulletin, vol. 847. Washington, D.C.: GPO, 1945.

———. *Wages and Hours of Labor in the Cigarette Manufacturing Industry, 1930.* Bulletin, vol. 532. Washington, D.C.: GPO, 1931.

———. *Wage Structure: Cigarettes, Chewing and Smoking Tobacco, and Snuff, 1946.* Washington, D.C.: GPO, 1946.

———. Bureau of National Affairs. *Wage Rates in Union Agreements in Effect, February 1948.* Washington, D.C.: Bureau of National Affairs, 1948.

————. Women's Bureau. *Hours and Earnings in Tobacco Stemmeries*. Washington, D.C.: GPO, 1934.

————. *Negro Women in the Population and in the Labor Force*. Washington, D.C.: GPO, 1966.

————. *Negro Women Workers in 1960*. Washington, D.C.: GPO, 1964.

U.S. Employment Service. Occupational Analysis Unit. *Tobacco in North Carolina: Growing, Marketing, and Processing*. Washington, D.C.: GPO, 1947.

Wallace, Henry. "Ten Extra Years." New York: National Wallace for President Committee, 1947. In possession of author.

Winston-Salem Chamber of Commerce. *Directory, Twin-City Club*. Winston-Salem: Chamber of Commerce, 1926.

————. Publicity Department. *A Unit on City Government*. Winston-Salem: Chamber of Commerce, 1947.

Winston-Salem School Board. *Education for Citizenship through the School Library*. Winston-Salem: Winston-Salem School Board, 1930.

Wrenn, James W. *The Making of a Black Prairie Communist: The Narrative of Abner Berry*. Rocky Mount, N.C.: Abner Berry Freedom Library, 1988.

Articles

"$57,000,000 Worth of Whizz and Whoozle." *Fortune* 18 (August 1938): 25–30, 96–100.

Abrams, Douglas Carl. "Irony of Reform: North Carolina Blacks and the New Deal." *North Carolina Historical Review* 66 (April 1989): 149–78.

Anderson, Karen Tucker. "Last Hired, First Fired: Black Women Workers during World War II." *Journal of American History* 69 (June 1982): 82–97.

Andrew, William D. "Factionalism and Anti-Communism: Ford Local 600." *Labor History* 20 (Spring 1979): 228–55.

Arnesen, Eric. "Following the Color Line of Labor: Black Workers and the Labor Movement before 1930." *Radical History Review* 55 (Winter 1993): 52–87.

————. "'Like Banquo's Ghost, It Will Not Down': The Race Question and the American Railroad Brotherhoods, 1880–1920." *American Historical Review* 99 (December 1994): 1601–33.

————. "Symposium on Halpern and Horowitz: Packinghouse Unionism—Race, Party, and Packinghouse Exceptionalism." *Labor History* 40 (May 1999): 207–15.

————. "Up from Exclusion: Black and White Workers, Race, and the State of Labor History." *Reviews in American History* 26 (March 1998): 146–74.

Atleson, James B. "Wartime Labor Regulation, the Industrial Pluralists, and the Law of Collective Bargaining." In *Industrial Democracy in America: The Ambiguous Promise*, edited by Nelson Lichtenstein and Howell John Harris, 142–75. New York: Cambridge University Press, 1993.

Banner, William M. "Southern Negro Communities." *Phylon* 7 (Summer 1946): 255–59.

Barkin, Solomon. "'Operation Dixie': Two Points of View—*The Crisis of American Labor: Operation Dixie and the Defeat of the CIO* by Barbara S. Griffith." *Labor History* 31 (Summer 1990): 378–85.

Barrett, James R. "Unity and Fragmentation: Class, Race, and Ethnicity on Chicago's South Side, 1900–1922." *Journal of Social History* 18 (Fall 1984): 37–55.

Best, Felton O. "Breaking the Gender Barrier." In *Black Religious Leadership from the Slave Community to the Million Man March: Flames of Fire*, edited by Felton O. Best, 153–68. Lewiston, N.Y.: Edwin Mellon Press, 1998.

Bishir, Catherine W. "Landmarks of Power: Building a Southern Past, 1855–1915." *Southern Cultures* 1, no. 1 (1993): 5–46.

Boyle, Kevin. "'There Are No Union Sorrows That the Union Can't Heal': The Struggle for Racial Equality in the United Auto Workers, 1940–1960." *Labor History* 36 (Winter 1995): 5–23.

Brearley, H. C. "The Negro's New Belligerency." *Phylon* 5 (Fall 1944): 339–45.

Brecher, Jeremy. "Crisis Economy: Born-Again Labor Movement?" *Monthly Review* 35 (March 1984): 1–23.

Brody, David. "The CIO after 50 Years: A Historical Reckoning." *Dissent* 32 (Fall 1985): 456–72.

———. "Workplace Contractualism in Comparative Perspective." In *Industrial Democracy in America: The Ambiguous Promise*, edited by Nelson Lichtenstein and Howell John Harris, 176–205. New York: Cambridge University Press, 1993.

Brown, Cliff. "The Role of Employers in Split Labor Markets: An Event-Structure Analysis of Racial Conflict and AFL Organizing, 1917–1919." *Social Forces* 79 (December 2000): 653–81.

Brown, Elsa Barkley. "Negotiating and Transforming: African American Political Life in the Transition from Slavery to Freedom." *Public Culture* 7 (Fall 1994): 107–46.

———. "Womanist Consciousness: Maggie Lena Walker and the Independent Order of St. Luke." *Signs* 14 (Spring 1989): 610–33.

Brueggemann, John. "The Power and Collapse of Paternalism: The Ford Motor Company and Black Workers, 1937–1941." *Social Problems* 47 (May 2000): 220–40.

Brueggemann, John, and Terry Boswell. "Realizing Solidarity: Sources of Interracial Unionism during the Great Depression." *Work and Occupations* 25 (November 1998): 436–82.

Buhle, Paul. "Daily Worker." In *Encyclopedia of the American Left*, edited by Mari Jo Buhle, Paul Buhle, and Dan Georgakas, 174–78. New York: Oxford University Press, 1998.

Burns, James MacGregor. "Maintenance of Membership: A Study in Administrative States-manship." *Journal of Politics* 10 (February 1948): 101–16.

Burns, Malcolm R. "Economies of Scale in Tobacco Manufacture, 1897–1910." *Journal of Economic History* 42 (June 1983): 461–74.

Butler, W. F., et al. "Simon Atkins." In *Five North Carolina Negro Educators*, edited by N. C. Newbold, 3–32. Chapel Hill: University of North Carolina Press, 1939.

"Camels of Winston-Salem." *Fortune* 3 (January 1931): 45–55.

Campbell, Susan. "'Black Bolsheviks' and Recognition of African-America's Right to Self-Determination by the Communist Party USA." *Science and Society* 58 (Winter 1994–95): 440–70.

Carby, Hazel V. "Policing the Black Woman's Body in an Urban Context." *Critical Inquiry* 18 (Summer 1992): 738–55.

Carlton, David L. "The Revolution from Above: The National Market and the Beginnings of Industrialization in North Carolina." *Journal of American History* 77 (September 1990): 445–75.

Carlton, David L., and Peter A. Coclanis. "Capital Mobilization and Southern Industry,

1880–1905: The Case of the Carolina Piedmont." *Journal of Economic History* 49 (March 1989): 73–94.

Carter, Dan T. "From Segregation to Integration." In *Interpreting Southern History*, edited by John B. Bowles and Evelyn Thomas Nolen, 408–33. Baton Rouge: Louisiana State University Press, 1987.

Christian, Ralph J. "The Folger-Chatham Congressional Primary of 1946." *North Carolina Historical Review* 53 (January 1976): 25–54.

"Christianity on the Job." *Time*, June 4, 1951, 46–50.

"CIO Spurs Negroes in Winston-Salem." In *The Black Worker from the Founding of the CIO to the AFL-CIO Merger, 1936–1955*. Vol. 7 of *The Black Worker: A Documentary History from Colonial Times to the Present*, edited by Philip S. Foner and Ronald L. Lewis, 386–87. Philadelphia: Temple University Press, 1983.

Cobb, James C. "The Sunbelt South: Industrialization in Regional, National, and International Perspective." In *Searching for the Sunbelt: Historical Perspectives on a Region*, edited by Raymond A. Mohl. Knoxville: University of Tennessee Press, 1990.

Cooper, Patricia. "The Faces of Gender: Sex Segregation and Work Relations at Philco, 1928–1938." In *Work Engendered: Toward a New History of American Labor*, edited by Ava Baron, 320–50. Ithaca: Cornell University Press, 1991.

Cooper, Patricia, and Ruth Oldenziel. "Cherished Classifications: Bathrooms and the Construction of Gender/Race on the Pennsylvania Railroad during World War II." *Feminist Studies* 25 (Spring 1999): 7–41.

Cuordileone, K. A. "'Politics in an Age of Anxiety': Cold War Political Culture and the Crisis in American Masculinity, 1949–1960." *Journal of American History* 87 (September 2000): 515–45.

Dalfiume, Richard M. "The 'Forgotten Years' of the Negro Revolution." *Journal of American History* 55 (June 1968): 90–106.

Davin, Eric Leif. "Blue Collar Democracy: Class War and Political Revolution in Western Pennsylvania, 1932–1937." *Pennsylvania History* 67 (Spring 2000): 240–96.

DeFelice, Maxine. "Southern Discomfort." In *Red Diapers: Growing Up in the Communist Left*, edited by Judy Kaplan and Linn Shapiro, 90–94. Urbana: University of Illinois Press, 1998.

De Vyver, Frank T. "The Present Status of Labor Unions in the South—1948." *Southern Economic Journal* 16 (July 1949): 1–22.

Dewey, Donald. "Negro Employment in Southern Industry." *Journal of Political Economy* 60 (August 1952): 279–93.

Dill, Bonnie Thornton. "Race, Class, and Gender: Prospects for an All-Inclusive Sisterhood." *Feminist Studies* 9 (Spring 1983): 131–50.

"Dr. Pitts' 'Help Me Somebody' Theology." *The Expected*, August 1956.

Draper, Alan. "The New Southern Labor History Revisited: The Success of the Mine, Mill, and Smelter Workers Union in Birmingham, 1934–1938." *Journal of Southern History* 62 (February 1996): 87–108.

Dunnagan, M. R. "The Tobacco Industry in North Carolina." *North Carolina Education* 13 (November 1936): 115–19, 134.

Eby, Kermit. "How the CIO Provides Opportunities for Negroes." *Opportunity* 25 (April–June 1947): 104.

Fast, Howard. "Why the Fifth Amendment?" *Masses and Mainstream* 7 (February 1954): 44–50.

Faue, Elizabeth. "'Anti-Heroes of the Working Class': A Response to Bruce Nelson." *International Review of Social History* 41 (December 1996): 375–88.

Fehn, Bruce. "'The Only Hope We Had': United Packinghouse Workers Local 46 and the Struggle for Racial Equality in Waterloo, Iowa, 1948–1960." *Annals of Iowa* 54 (Summer 1995): 185–216.

Feurer, Rosemary. "William Sentner, the UE, and Civic Unionism in St. Louis." In *The CIO's Left-Led Unions*, edited by Steve Rosswurm, 95–117. New Brunswick: Rutgers University Press, 1992.

Fields, Barbara J. "Ideology and Race in American History." In *Region, Race, and Reconstruction: Essays in Honor of C. Vann Woodward*, edited by J. Morgan Kousser and James M. McPherson, 143–77. New York: Oxford University Press, 1982.

———. "Slavery, Race, and Ideology in the United States of America." *New Left Review* 181 (May/June 1990): 95–118.

Finkle, Lee. "The Conservative Aims of Militant Rhetoric: Black Protest during World War II." *Journal of American History* 55 (December 1973): 692–713.

Fishback, Price. "Segregation in Job Hierarchies: West Virginia Coal Mining, 1906–1932." *Journal of Economic History* 64 (September 1984): 755–74.

Fisher, Robert. "Organizing in the Modern Metropolis: Considering New Social Movement Theory." *Journal of Urban History* 18 (February 1992): 222–37.

Forbath, William E. "Caste, Class, and Equal Citizenship." *Michigan Law Review* 98 (October 1999): 1–91.

Fox-Genovese, Elizabeth, and Eugene D. Genovese. "The Political Crisis of Social History: A Marxian Perspective." *Journal of Social History* 10 (Winter 1976): 205–19.

Frank, Dana. "Symposium on Tera Hunter: To 'Joy My Freedom—The Labor Historian's New Clothes." *Labor History* 39 (May 1998): 169–71.

Frederickson, Mary. "Four Decades of Change: Black Workers in Southern Textiles, 1941–1981." In *Workers' Struggles, Past and Present: A "Radical America" Reader*, edited by James Green, 62–82. Philadelphia: Temple University Press, 1983.

———. "The Southern Summer School for Women Workers." *Southern Exposure* 4 (Winter 1977): 70–75.

Freeman, Joshua B. "Catholics, Communists, and Republicans: Irish Workers and the Organization of the Transport Workers Union." In *Working-Class America: Essays on Labor, Community, and American Society*, edited by Michael H. Frisch and Daniel J. Walkowitz, 256–83. Urbana: University of Illinois Press, 1983.

———. "Delivering the Goods: Industrial Unionism during World War II." *Labor History* 19 (Fall 1978): 570–93.

Gable, Richard W. "NAM: Influential Lobby or Kiss of Death?" *Journal of Politics* 15 (May 1953): 254–73.

Gavins, Raymond. "The NAACP in North Carolina during the Age of Segregation." In *New Directions in Civil Rights Studies*, edited by Armstead L. Robinson and Patricia Sullivan, 105–25. Charlottesville: University Press of Virginia, 1991.

Gay, Dorothy A. "Crisis of Identity: The Negro Community in Raleigh, 1890–1900." *North Carolina Historical Review* 50 (April 1973): 121–40.

Gerstle, Gary. "Race and the Myth of the Liberal Consensus." *Journal of American History* 82 (September 1995): 579–86.

———. "The Working Class Goes to War." In *The War in American Culture*, edited by

Lewis A. Erenberg and Susan E. Hirsch, 105–27. Chicago: University of Chicago Press, 1996.

———. "Working Class Racism: Broaden the Focus." *International Labor and Working Class History* 44 (Fall 1993): 33–40.

Gilkes, Cheryl Townsend. "Together and in Harness." In *Black Religious Leadership from the Slave Community to the Million Man March: Flames of Fire*, edited by Felton O. Best, 170–85. Lewiston, N.Y.: Edwin Mellon Press, 1998.

Glenn, Evelyn Nakano. "Symposium on Tera Hunter: To 'Joy My Freedom—Protest, Resistance, and Survival in the Jim Crow South." *Labor History* 39 (May 1998): 172–75.

Gluck, Sherna Berger. "Socialist Feminism between the Two World Wars: Insights from Oral History." In *Decades of Discontent: The Women's Movement, 1920–1940*, edited by Lois Scharf and Joan M. Jensen, 279–97. Boston: Northeastern University Press, 1978.

Goldfield, Michael. "Race and the CIO: The Possibilities for Racial Egalitarianism during the 1930s and 1940s." *International Labor and Working Class History* 44 (Fall 1993): 1–44.

Goldin, Claudia. "The Role of World War II in the Rise of Women's Work." *American Economic Review* 81 (September 1991): 741–56.

Goluboff, Risa L. "'Won't You Please Help Me Get My Son Home?': Peonage, Patronage, and Protest in the World War II Urban South." *Law and Social Inquiry* 24 (Fall 1999): 777–806.

Goodwyn, Lawrence. "The Cooperative Commonwealth and Other Abstractions: In Search of a Democratic Premise." *Marxist Perspectives* 3 (Summer 1980): 8–42.

———. "Hierarchy and Democracy: The Paradox of the Southern Experience." In *From the Old South to the New: Essays on the Transitional South*, edited by Walter J. Fraser Jr. and Winfred B. Moore Jr., 227–39. Westport, Conn.: Greenwood Press, 1981.

Gordon, Linda. "Race and Family: Studying the Arizona Orphans." *Chronicle of Higher Education* 66 (June 9, 2000): B4–B6.

Granger, Lester. "Industrial Unionism and the Negro." *Opportunity* 14 (January 1936): 29–30.

———. "Negroes and War Production." *Survey Graphic, Magazine of Social Interpretation* 31 (November 1942): 469–544.

Green, James. "The Struggle for Control." In *Workers' Struggles, Past and Present: A "Radical America" Reader*, edited by James Green, 21–23. Philadelphia: Temple University Press, 1983.

Gregory, James N. "Response." *Labor History* 39 (May 1998): 166–68.

———. "Southernizing the American Working Class: Post-War Episodes of Regional and Class Transformation." *Labor History* 39 (May 1998): 135–54.

Griffin, Larry J. "Why Was the South a Problem to America?" In *The South as an American Problem*, edited by Larry J. Griffin and Don H. Doyle, 10–31. Athens: University of Georgia Press, 1995.

Griffin, Larry J., and Robert R. Korstad. "Class as Race and Gender: Making and Breaking a Labor Union in the Jim Crow South." *Social Science History* 19 (Winter 1995): 425–54.

———. "Historical Inference and Event-Structure Analysis." *International Review of Social History* 43, no. 6 (1998), supplement, 145–65.

Grimes, William T. "The History of Kate Bitting Reynolds Memorial Hospital." *Journal of the National Medical Association* 64 (July 1972): 376–81.

Grundy, Pamela. "'We Always Tried to Be Good People': Respectability, Crazy Water Crystals, and Hillbilly Music on the Air, 1933–1935." *Journal of American History* 81 (March 1995): 1591–620.

Guthrie, Woody. "A Minstrel in Tobacco-Land." *The Worker Magazine*, January 18, 1948, 2.

Gutman, Herbert G. "The Negro and the United Mine Workers of America: The Career and Letters of Richard L. Davis and Something of Their Meaning, 1890–1900." In *The Negro and the American Labor Movement*, edited by Julius Jacobson, 49–127. Garden City, N.Y.: Anchor Books, 1968.

Hall, Jacquelyn Dowd. "'The Mind That Burns in Each Body': Women, Rape, and Racial Violence." In *Powers of Desire: The Politics of Sexuality*, edited by Ann Snitow, Christine Stansell, and Sharon Thompson, 350–70. New York: Monthly Review Press, 1983.

Hall, Jacquelyn Dowd, Robert Korstad, and James Leloudis. "Cotton Mill People: Work, Community, and Protest in the Textile South, 1880–1940." *American Historical Review* 91 (April 1986): 245–86.

Halpern, Rick. "The CIO and the Limits of Labor-Based Civil Rights Activism: The Case of Louisiana's Sugar Workers, 1947–1966." In *Southern Labor in Transition, 1940–1995*, edited by Robert H. Zieger, 86–112. Knoxville: University of Tennessee Press, 1997.

———. "Organized Labor, Black Workers, and the Twentieth Century South: The Emerging Revision." In *Race and Class in the American South since 1890*, edited by Melvyn Stokes and Rick Halpern, 43–76. Oxford and Providence: Berg Publishers, 1994.

———. "Symposium on Halpern and Horowitz: Packinghouse Unionism—Getting to Grips with the CIO: The Significance of the Packinghouse Experience." *Labor History* 40 (May 1999): 226–30.

Hamilton, Dona Cooper, and Charles V. Hamilton. "The Dual Agenda of African American Organizations since the New Deal: Social Welfare Policies and Civil Rights." *Political Science Quarterly* 107 (Fall 1992): 435–52.

Hammond, Martha. "Gideon Jackson Walks Again." *New Masses* 58 (January 1, 1946): 3–4.

Harley, Sharon. "Symposium on Tera Hunter: To 'Joy My Freedom—Leisure and Labor: Subversive at All Levels." *Labor History* 39 (May 1998): 175–79.

Harris, Abram L. "Race, Radicalism, and Reform." In *Race, Radicalism, and Reform: Selected Papers*, edited by William Darity Jr. New Brunswick: Transaction Publishers, 1989.

Harris, Howell John. "Give Us Some Less of That Old-Time Corporate History." *Labor History* 28 (Winter 1987): 75–83.

———. "Symposium on Halpern and Horowitz: Packinghouse Unionism—Meat and Men." *Labor History* 40 (May 1999): 216–19.

Hartmann, Heidi. "The Historical Roots of Occupational Segregation: Capitalism, Patriarchy, and Job Segregation by Sex." *Signs* 1 (Spring 1976): 137–69.

Henderson, Donald. "Agricultural Workers." *American Federationist* 43 (May 1936): 488–93.

———. "The Rural Masses and the Work of Our Party." *Communist* 14 (September 1935): 866–80.

Herod, Andrew. "Reinterpreting Organized Labor's Experiences in the Southeast: 1947 to the Present." *Southeastern Geographer* 37 (November 1997): 214–37.

Higginbotham, Evelyn Brooks. "African-American Women's History and the Metalanguage of Race." *Signs* 17 (Winter 1992): 251–74.

Hill, Herbert. "Herbert Hill Replies." *New Politics* 1 (Spring 1988): 61–71.

———. "Myth-Making as Labor History: Herbert Gutman and the United Mineworkers of America." *International Journal of Politics, Culture, and Society* 2 (Winter 1988): 132–200.

———. "Race, Ethnicity, and Organized Labor: The Opposition to Affirmative Action." *New Politics* 1 (Winter 1987): 31–82.

Hoffman, Erwin D. "The Genesis of the Modern Movement for Equal Rights in South Carolina, 1930–1939." In *The Negro in Depression and War: Prelude to Revolution, 1930–1945*, edited by Bernard Sternsher, 193–214. Chicago: Quadrangle Books, 1969.

Hogan, Michael J. "American Marshall Planners and the Search for a European Neocapitalism." *American Historical Review* 90 (February 1985): 44–72.

Honey, Michael. "Class, Race, and Power in the New South: Racial Violence and the Delusions of White Supremacy." In *Democracy Betrayed: The Wilmington Race Riot of 1898 and Its Legacy*, edited by David S. Cecelski and Timothy B. Tyson, 163–84. Chapel Hill: University of North Carolina Press, 1998.

———. "The Labor Movement and Racism in the South: A Historical Overview." In *Racism and the Denial of Human Rights*, edited by Marvin J. Berlowitz and Ronald S. Edari, 77–94. Minneapolis: Marxist Educational Press Publications, 1984.

———. "Operation Dixie: Labor and Civil Rights in the Postwar South." *Mississippi Quarterly* 45 (Fall 1992): 439–52.

Horowitz, Daniel. "Rethinking Betty Friedan and the Feminine Mystique: Labor Union Radicalism and Feminism in Cold War America." *American Quarterly* 48 (March 1996): 1–42.

Horowitz, Roger. "Symposium on Halpern and Horowitz: Packinghouse Unionism—The National Versus the Local: A Response to Commentators." *Labor History* 40 (May 1999): 231–35.

Horowitz, Roger, and Rick Halpern. "Work, Race, and Identity: Self-Representation in the Narratives of Black Packinghouse Workers." *Oral History Review* 26 (Winter/Spring 1999): 23–43.

Hunter, Tera. "Symposium on Tera Hunter: To 'Joy My Freedom—Response." *Labor History* 39 (May 1998): 185–87.

Huntley, Horace. "The Red Scare and Black Workers in Alabama: The International Union of Mine, Mill, and Smelter Workers, 1945–1953." In *Labor Divided: Race and Ethnicity in United States Labor Struggles, 1835–1960*, edited by Robert Asher and Charles Stephenson, 129–45. Albany: State University of New York Press, 1990.

———. "The Rise and Fall of Mine Mill in Alabama: The Status Quo against Interracial Unionism, 1933–1949." *Journal of the Birmingham Historical Society* 6 (January 1979): 5–13.

Isenberg, Cynthia. "Camel Caravan." *New Masses* 63 (June 3, 1947): 7–9.

Jackson, Augusta V. "A New Deal for Tobacco Workers." *The Crisis* 45 (October 1938): 322–24, 330.

Janiewski, Dolores. "Southern Honor, Southern Dishonor: Managerial Ideology and the Construction of Gender, Race, and Class Relations in Southern Industry." In *Work Engendered: Toward a New History of American Labor*, edited by Ava Baron, 70–91. Ithaca: Cornell University Press, 1991.

Jenkins, J. Craig, and Craig M. Eckert. "Channeling Black Insurgency: Elite Patronage and Professional Social Movement Organizations in the Development of the Black Movement." *American Sociological Review* 51 (December 1986): 812–29.

Jenkins, J. Craig, and Charles Perrow. "Insurgency of the Powerless: Farm Worker Movements (1946–1972)." *American Sociological Review* 42 (April 1977): 249–68.

Johnson, Charles S. "The Conflict of Caste and Class in an American Industry." *American Journal of Sociology* 42 (July 1936): 55–65.

———. "The Present Status of Race Relations in the South." *Social Forces* 23 (October 1944): 27–32.

———. "Social Relations and Their Effects on Race Relations in the South." *Social Forces* 23 (March 1945): 343–48.

Johnson, Charles S., and Davis McEntire. "Minority Labor Groups." In *Yearbook of American Labor*, vol. 1, *War Labor Policies*, edited by Colston E. Warne et al., 363–400. New York: Philosophical Library, 1945.

Johnson, Guion Griffis. "The Ideology of White Supremacy, 1876–1910." In *Essays in Southern History*, edited by Fletcher Melvin Green, 124–56. James Sprunt Studies in History and Political Science, no. 31. Chapel Hill: University of North Carolina Press, 1949.

Johnson, Howard. "The Negro Veteran Fights for Freedom." *Political Affairs* 26 (May 1947): 429–40.

Jolley, Harley E. "The Labor Movement in North Carolina, 1880–1922." *North Carolina Historical Review* 30 (July 1953): 354–75.

Jones, Beverly. "Race, Sex, and Class: Black Female Tobacco Workers in Durham, North Carolina, 1920–1940, and the Development of a Female Consciousness." *Feminist Studies* 10 (Fall 1984): 441–51.

Jones, Claudia. "An End to the Neglect of the Problems of the Negro Woman!" *Political Affairs* 28 (June 1949): 51–67.

Katznelson, Ira. "Symposium on Halpern and Horowitz: Packinghouse Unionism—Cases and Theory." *Labor History* 40 (May 1999): 219–22.

Katznelson, Ira, Kim Geiger, and Daniel Kryder. "Limiting Liberalism: The Southern Veto in Congress, 1933–1950." *Political Science Quarterly* 108 (Summer 1993): 283–306.

Kazin, Michael. "The Agony and Romance of the American Left." *American Historical Review* 100 (December 1995): 1488–512.

Keech, William R., and Michael P. Sistrom. "North Carolina." In *Quiet Revolution in the South: The Impact of the Voting Rights Act, 1965–1990*, edited by Chandler Davidson and Bernard Grofman, 155–90. Princeton: Princeton University Press, 1994.

Kelley, Robin D. G. "'We Are Not What We Seem': Rethinking Black Working-Class Opposition in the Jim Crow South." *Journal of American History* 80 (June 1993): 75–112.

Kellogg, Peter J. "Civil Rights Consciousness in the 1940s." *The Historian: A Journal of History* 42 (November 1979): 18–41.

Kendrick, Alex H., and Jerome Golden. "Lessons of the Struggle against Opportunism in District 65." *Political Affairs* 32 (June 1953): 26–37.

Kerns, Harvey. "The Southern Field." *Opportunity* 23 (Fall 1945): 175–77.

Kinkela, David. "Singing Once Again on Mermaid Avenue." *Radical History Review* 81 (Fall 2001): 153–61.

Klare, Karl E. "Judicial Deradicalization of the Wagner Act and the Origins of Modern Legal Consciousness, 1937–1941." *Minnesota Law Review* 62 (1978): 265–339.

———. "Labor Law as Ideology: Toward a New Historiography of Collective Bargaining Law." *Industrial Relations Law Journal* 4 (Summer 1981): 450–502.

Klehr, Harvey, and John Earl Haynes. "Moscow Gold, Confirmed at Last?" *Labor History* 33 (Spring 1992): 279–93.

Korstad, Karl. "Black and White Together: Organizing in the South with the Food, Tobacco, Agricultural and Allied Workers Union (FTA-CIO), 1946–1952." In *The CIO's Left-Led Unions*, edited by Steve Rosswurm, 69–94. New Brunswick: Rutgers University Press, 1992.

———. "Tobacco Road, Union Style." *New Masses* 59 (May 7, 1946): 13–15.

Korstad, Robert. "The Possibilities for Racial Egalitarianism: Context Matters." *International Labor and Working Class History* 44 (Fall 1993): 41–44.

Korstad, Robert, and Nelson Lichtenstein. "Opportunities Found and Lost: Labor, Radicals, and the Early Civil Rights Movement." *Journal of American History* 75 (December 1988): 786–811.

"Labor Drives South." *Fortune* 34 (November 1946): 134–40, 230, 232, 234, 237.

Lasseter, Dillard B. "The Impact of the War on the South and Implications for Postwar Developments." *Social Forces* 23 (October 1944): 20–26.

Leab, Daniel J. "'United We Eat': The Creation and Organization of the Unemployed Councils in 1930." *Labor History* 8 (Summer 1967): 300–315.

Lee, Wallace. "Negro Digest Poll: Which Union Is Fairer to the Negro: AFL or CIO?" *Negro Digest* 3 (June 1945): 50.

Lens, Sid. "Meaning of the Grievance Procedure." *Harvard Business Review* 26 (November 1948): 713–22.

Levine, Lawrence W. "Symposium on Tera Hunter: To 'Joy My Freedom—Imagining Freedom." *Labor History* 39 (May 1998): 179–82.

Lewis, Diane K. "A Response to Inequality: Black Women, Racism, and Sexism." *Signs* 3 (Winter 1977): 339–61.

Lewis, Earl. "Invoking Concepts, Problematizing Identities: The Life of Charles N. Hunter and the Implications for the Study of Gender and Labor." *Labor History* 34 (Spring 1993): 292–308.

Lichtenstein, Alex. "Antiliberalism and the Working-Class Politics of Nostalgia." *Labor History* 39 (May 1998): 158–61.

———. "The Cold War and the 'Negro Question.'" *Radical History Review* 72 (Fall 1998): 185–93.

———. "Exploring the Local World of Interracialism." *Labor History* 41 (Winter 2000): 61–90.

———. "Putting Labor's House in Order: The Transport Workers Union and Labor Anti-Communism in Miami during the 1940s." *Labor History* 39 (Winter 1998): 7–23.

———. "'Scientific Unionism' and the 'Negro Question': Communists and the Transport Workers Union in Miami, 1944–1949." In *Southern Labor in Transition, 1940–1995*, edited by Robert H. Zieger, 58–85. Knoxville: University of Tennessee Press, 1997.

Lichtenstein, Nelson. "Ambiguous Legacy: The Union Security Problem during World War II." *Labor History* 18 (Spring 1977): 214–38.

———. "The Communist Experience in American Trade Unions." *Industrial Relations* 19 (Spring 1980): 119–39.

———. "From Corporatism to Collective Bargaining: Organized Labor and the Eclipse of Social Democracy in the Postwar Era." In *The Rise and Fall of the New Deal Order*,

1930–1980, edited by Steve Fraser and Gary Gerstle, 122–52. Princeton: Princeton University Press, 1989.

———. "Great Expectations: The Promise of Industrial Jurisprudence and Its Demise, 1930–1960." In *Industrial Democracy in America: The Ambiguous Promise*, edited by Nelson Lichtenstein and Howell John Harris, 113–41. New York: Cambridge University Press, 1993.

———. "Industrial Democracy, Contract Unionism, and the National War Labor Board." *Labor Law Review* 33 (August 1982): 524–31.

Lichtenstein, Nelson, and Howell John Harris. "Introduction: A Century of Industrial Democracy in America." In *Industrial Democracy in America: The Ambiguous Promise*, edited by Nelson Lichtenstein and Howell John Harris, 1–19. New York: Cambridge University Press, 1993.

Lieberman, Robbie. "The Culture of Politics: Communism, Americanism, and the People's Songs Hootenanny." *South Atlantic Quarterly* 85 (Winter 1986): 78–88.

Locke, Alain. "The Unfinished Business of Democracy." *Survey Graphic* 31 (November 1942): 455–59.

Lott, Eric. "'The Seeming Counterfeit': Racial Politics and Early Blackface Minstrelsy." *American Quarterly* 43 (June 1991): 223–54.

Love, Richard. "In Defiance of Custom and Tradition: Black Tobacco Workers and Labor Unions in Richmond, Virginia, 1937–1941." *Labor History* 35 (Winter 1994): 25–47.

MacNeill, Ben Dixon. "The Town of a Hundred Millionaires." *North American Review* 232 (August 1931): 101–10.

Marcello, Ronald. "The Politics of Relief: The North Carolina WPA and the Tarheel Elections of 1936." *North Carolina Historical Review* 68 (January 1991): 17–37.

Martin, Charles H. "The Civil Rights Congress and Southern Black Defendants." *Georgia Historical Quarterly* 71 (Spring 1987): 25–52.

Marx, Gary T. "Religion: Opiate or Inspiration of Civil Rights Militancy among Negroes." *American Sociological Review* 32 (February 1967): 64–72.

Mason, Lucy Randolph. "The CIO and the Negro in the South." *Journal of Negro Education* 14 (Fall 1945): 552–61.

McAdam, Doug. "Recruitment to High-Risk Activism: The Case of Freedom Summer." *American Journal of Sociology* 92 (July 1986): 64–90.

McAdam, Doug, John D. McCarthy, and Mayer N. Zald. "Social Movements." In *Handbook of Sociology*, edited by Neil J. Smelser, 695–737. Newbury Park, Calif.: Sage Publications, 1988.

McCallum, Brenda. "The Gospel of Black Unionism." In *Songs about Work: Essays in Occupational Culture for Richard A. Reuss*, edited by Archie Green, 108–33. Bloomington: Folklore Institute, Indiana University, 1993.

———. "Songs of Work and Songs of Worship: Sanctifying Black Unionism in the Southern City of Steel." *New York Folklore* 14 (Summer 1988): 9–33.

McColloch, Mark. "The Shop-Floor Dimension of Union Rivalry: The Case of Westinghouse in the 1950s." In *The CIO's Left-Led Unions*, edited by Steve Rosswurm, 183–99. New Brunswick: Rutgers University Press, 1992.

McCusker, Kristine M. "Interracial Communities and Civil Rights Activism in Lawrence, Kansas, 1945–1948." *The Historian: A Journal of History* 61 (Summer 1999): 783–99.

McDonnell, Lawrence T. "'You Are Too Sentimental': Problems and Suggestions for a New Labor History." *Journal of Social History* 17 (Summer 1984): 629–54.

Meier, August, and Elliot Rudwick. "Attitudes of Negro Leaders toward the American Labor Movement." In *The Negro and the American Labor Movement*, edited by Julius Jacobson, 27–48. Garden City, N.Y.: Anchor Books, 1968.

———. "Communist Unions and the Black Community: The Case of the Transport Workers Union, 1934–1944." *Labor History* 23 (Spring 1982): 165–97.

Mezerik, A. G. "The C.I.O. Southern Drive." *The Nation* 164 (January 11, 1947): 38–40.

———. "Dixie in Black and White." *The Nation* 164 (April 19, 1947): 448–51.

Montgomery, David. "Labor and the Political Leadership of New Deal America." *International Review of Social History* 39 (December 1994): 335–60.

Moore, Barrington, Jr. "The Communist Party of the USA: An Analysis of a Social Movement." *American Political Science Review* 34 (February 1945): 31–41.

Murray, Philip. "Round Table: Which Union Is Fairer to the Negro: AFL or CIO?" *Negro Digest* 3 (June 1945): 39–49.

Naison, Mark. "Claude and Joyce Williams: Pilgrims of Justice." *Southern Exposure* 1 (Fall/Winter 1974): 38–50.

———. "Marxism and Black Radicalism in America: Notes on a Long (and Continuing) Journey." *Radical America* 5 (May–June 1971): 3–25.

———. "Paul Robeson and the American Labor Movement." In *Paul Robeson: Artist and Citizen*, edited by Jeffrey C. Stewart, 179–94. New Brunswick: Rutgers University Press, 1998.

———. "The Southern Tenant Farmers' Union and the CIO." *Radical America* 2 (September–October 1968): 36–56.

Nasstrom, Kathryn L. "Down to Now: Memory, Narrative, and Women's Leadership in the Civil Rights Movement in Atlanta, Georgia." *Gender and History* 11 (April 1999): 113–44.

"The Negro's War." *Fortune* 25 (June 1942): 76–80, 157, 158, 160, 162, 164.

Nelson, Bruce. "Class and Race in the Crescent City: The ILWU, from San Francisco to New Orleans." In *The CIO's Left-Led Unions*, edited by Steve Rosswurm, 19–45. New Brunswick: Rutgers University Press, 1992.

———. "Class, Race, and Democracy in the CIO: The 'New' Labor History Meets the 'Wages of Whiteness.'" *International Review of Social History* 41 (December 1996): 351–74.

———. "Organized Labor and the Struggle for Black Equality in Mobile during World War II." *Journal of American History* 80 (December 1993): 952–88.

———. "Working-Class Agency and Racial Inequality." *International Review of Social History* 41 (December 1996): 407–20.

Nelson-Cisneros, Victor B. "UCAPAWA and Chicanos in California: The Farm Worker Period, 1937–1940." *Aztlan* 7, no. 3 (1978): 453–76.

Newman, Kathy M. "The Forgotten Fifteen Million: Black Radio, the 'Negro Market,' and the Civil Rights Movement." *Radical History Review* 76 (Winter 2000): 115–35.

Norrell, Robert J. "Caste in Steel: Jim Crow Careers in Birmingham, Alabama." *Journal of American History* 73 (December 1986): 669–94.

———. "Labor at the Ballot Box: Alabama Politics from the New Deal to the Dixiecrat Movement." *Journal of Southern History* 57 (May 1991): 201–34.

Northrup, Herbert R. "The Negro in the Tobacco Industry." In *Negro Employment in Southern Industry: A Study of the Racial Policies of Five Industries*, edited by Herbert R. Northrup and Richard Rowan, 1–18. Philadelphia: Industrial Research Unit, Department of Industry, Wharton School of Finance and Commerce, University of Pennsylvania, 1970.

———. "The Tobacco Workers International Union." *Quarterly Journal of Economics* 56 (August 1942): 606–26.

Oestreicher, Richard. "Urban Working-Class Political Behavior and Theories of American Electoral Politics, 1870–1940." *Journal of American History* 74 (March 1988): 1257–86.

Olson, James S. "Race, Class, and Progress: Black Leadership and Industrial Unionism, 1936–1945." In *Black Labor in America*, edited by Milton Canton, 153–64. Westport, Conn.: Negro Universities Press, 1969.

Painter, Nell Irvin. "The New Labor History and the Historical Moment." *International Journal of Politics, Culture, and Society* 2 (Spring 1989): 367–70.

Palmer, Edward Nelson. "Negro Secret Societies." *Social Forces* 23 (December 1944): 207–12.

Palmer, Phyllis Marynick. "White Women/Black Women: The Dualism of Female Identity and Experience in the United States." *Feminist Studies* 9 (Spring 1983): 151–70.

Patterson, William L., et al. "Round Table: Have Communists Quit Fighting for Negro Rights?" *Negro Digest* 3 (December 1944): 57–70.

Patton, Randall. "The CIO and the Search for a 'Silent South.'" *Maryland Historian* 19 (Fall/Winter 1988): 1–14.

Peace, Clifford H. "Pastoral Care in an Industrial Setting." *New Christian Advocate* 1 (September 1957): 15–18.

Perry, Pettis. "Next Stage in the Struggle for Negro Rights." *Political Affairs* 28 (October 1949): 33–46.

———. "Press Forward the Struggle against White Chauvinism." *Political Affairs* 29 (May 1950): 138–49.

Phillips, Kimberley L. "Symposium on Halpern and Horowitz: Packinghouse Unionism—Dismembering Heroic Unions." *Labor History* 40 (May 1999): 222–26.

Pitzele, Merlyn S. "Can American Labor Defeat the Communists?" *Atlantic Monthly* 179 (March 1947): 27–32.

Pollitt, Daniel H. "The Fifth Amendment Plea before Congressional Committees Investigating Subversion: Motives and Justifiable Presumptions—A Survey of 120 Witnesses." *University of Pennsylvania Law Review* 106 (June 1958): 1117–37.

Poston, Ted. "The Making of Mamma Harris." *New Republic* 36 (November 4, 1940): 624–26.

Preece, Harold. "The South Stirs: I. Brothers in the Union." *The Crisis* 48 (October 1941): 317–18, 322.

———. "The South Stirs: II. The Fight for Civil Rights." *The Crisis* 48 (November 1941): 350–51.

———. "The South Stirs: III. The Pulpit and the New South." *The Crisis* 48 (December 1941): 388–89.

Prichard, Robert W. "Winston-Salem's Black Hospitals Prior to 1930." *Journal of the National Medical Association* 68 (May 1976): 246–49.

Quam-Wickham, Nancy. "Who Controls the Hiring Hall?: The Struggle for Job Control in the ILWU during World War II." In *The CIO's Left-Led Unions*, edited by Steve Ross-wurm, 47–67. New Brunswick: Rutgers University Press, 1992.

"R. J. Reynolds' King-Sized Profits." *Fortune* 56 (December 1957): 235, 240, 242.

Rabinowitz, Howard N. "More Than the Woodward Thesis: Assessing the Strange Career of Jim Crow." *Journal of American History* 75 (December 1988): 842–56.

Ransom, Leon A. "Combating Discrimination in the Employment of Negroes in War Industries and Government Agencies." *Journal of Negro Education* 12 (Summer 1943): 405–16.

Reagon, Bernice Johnson. "My Black Mothers and Sisters, or On Beginning a Cultural Autobiography." *Feminist Studies* 8 (Spring 1982): 81–96.

Reuss, Richard A. "The Roots of the American Left-Wing Interest in Folksong." *Labor History* 12 (Spring 1971): 259–79.

Reynolds, Lloyd G., and Charles C. Killingsworth. "The Union Security Issue." *Annals of the American Academy of Political and Social Science* 224 (November 1942): 32–39.

Robinson, Armstead L. "Plans Dat Comed from God: Institution Building and the Emergence of Black Leadership in Reconstruction Memphis." In *Toward a New South?: Studies in Post–Civil War Southern Communities*, edited by Orville Vernon Burton and Robert C. McMath Jr., 71–102. Westport, Conn.: Greenwood Press, 1982.

Roediger, David. "Symposium on Tera Hunter: To 'Joy My Freedom—An Enthusiasm." *Labor History* 39 (May 1998): 182–85.

Rosen, Sumner M. "The CIO Era, 1935–1955." In *Black Workers and Organized Labor*, edited by John H. Bracey Jr., August Meier, and Elliot Rudwick, 170–84. Belmont, Calif.: Wadsworth Publishing Company, 1971.

Rosenzweig, Roy. "Organizing the Unemployed: The Early Years of the Great Depression, 1929–1933." *Radical America* 10 (July–August 1976): 37–60.

Ross, M. H. "Labor and the South." *The Nation* 183 (July 7, 1956): 14–16.

Ross, Nat. "Two Years of the Reconstituted Communist Party in the South." *Political Affairs* 26 (October 1947): 923–35.

———. "What's Happening in the South." *Political Affairs* 26 (July 1947): 612–23.

Rosswurm, Steve. "The Catholic Church and the Left-Led Unions: Labor Priests, Labor Schools, and the ACTU." In *The CIO's Left-Led Unions*, edited by Steve Rosswurm, 119–37. New Brunswick: Rutgers University Press, 1992.

———. "Introduction: An Overview and Preliminary Assessment of the CIO's Expelled Unions." In *The CIO's Left-Led Unions*, edited by Steve Rosswurm, 1–17. New Brunswick: Rutgers University Press, 1992.

Rosswurm, Steve, and Toni Gilpin. "The FBI and the Farm Equipment Workers: FBI Surveillance Records as a Source for CIO Union History." *Labor History* 27 (Fall 1986): 485–505.

Ruth, Kent. "Negro Labor in the Southern Crystal Ball." *Phylon* 10 (Summer 1949): 233–39.

Ryon, Roderick N. "An Ambiguous Legacy: Baltimore Blacks and the CIO, 1936–1941." *Journal of Negro History* 65 (Winter 1980): 18–33.

Sayles, Leonard R. "Wildcat Strikes." *Harvard Business Review* 32 (November–December 1954): 42–52.

Schrecker, Ellen W. "McCarthyism and the Labor Movement: The Role of the State." In *The CIO's Left-Led Unions*, edited by Steve Rosswurm, 139–57. New Brunswick: Rutgers University Press, 1992.

Schuyler, George S. "Reflections on Negro Leadership." *The Crisis* 44 (November 1937): 327–28, 340.

Shaffer, Robert. "Women and the Communist Party, USA, 1930–1940." *Socialist Review* 9 (May–June 1979): 73–118.

Shields, Art. "Meet Ed Crouch." *Labor Age* 18 (January 1929): 13–14.

Shields, Emma L. "A Half-Century in the Tobacco Industry." *Southern Workman* 51 (September 1922): 419–25.

Shields, James M. "Woes of a Southern Liberal." *American Mercury* 34 (January 1935): 73–79.

Simon, Bryant. "Rethinking Why There Are So Few Unions in the South." *Georgia Historical Quarterly* 81 (Summer 1997): 65–84.

Sitkoff, Harvard. "Racial Militancy and Interracial Violence in the Second World War." *Journal of American History* 58 (December 1971): 661–81.

Slichter, Sumner H. "How Much Trade-Unionism as Usual?" *Atlantic Monthly* 171 (January 1943): 74–82.

Smith, Margaret Supplee. "Reynolda: A Rural Vision in an Industrializing South." *North Carolina Historical Review* 65 (July 1988): 287–313.

Snow, David, et al. "Frame Alignment Processes, Micromobilizations, and Movement Participation." *American Sociological Review* 51 (August 1986): 464–81.

"The South Gets Rough with Wallace." *Life* 25 (September 13, 1948): 33–35.

Stark, David. "Class Struggle and the Transformation of the Labor Process." *Theory and Society* 9 (January 1980): 89–130.

Stebenne, David L. "The Postwar 'New Deal.'" *International Labor and Working Class History* 50 (Fall 1996): 140–47.

Stepan-Norris, Judith, and Maurice Zeitlin. "'Who Gets the Bird?' or, How the Communists Won Power and Trust in America's Unions: The Relative Autonomy of Intraclass Political Struggles." *American Sociological Review* 54 (August 1989): 503–23.

Stevenson, Marshall F. "Beyond Theoretical Models: The Limited Possibilities of Racial Egalitarianism." *International Labor and Working Class History* 44 (Fall 1993): 45–52.

Stone, Katherine Van Wezel. "The Post-War Paradigm in American Labor Law." *Yale Law Journal* 90 (June 1981): 1509–80.

Street, Paul. "The 'Best Union Members': Class, Race, Culture, and Black Worker Militancy in Chicago's Stockyards during the 1930s." *Journal of American Ethnic History* 20 (Fall 2000): 18–49.

Strom, Susan Hartman. "Challenging 'Woman's Place': Feminism, the Left and Industrial Unionism in the 1930s." *Feminist Studies* 9 (Summer 1983): 359–86.

Sugrue, Thomas J. "Crabgrass-Roots Politics: Race, Rights, and Reaction against Liberalism in the Urban North, 1940–1964." *Journal of American History* 82 (September 1995): 551–78.

———. "'Forget About Your Inalienable Right to Work': Deindustrialization and Its Discontents at Ford, 1950–1953." *International Labor and Working Class History* 48 (Fall 1995): 112–30.

———. "The Incredible Disappearing Southerner?" *Labor History* 39 (May 1998): 161–66.

———. "Segmented Work, Race-Conscious Workers: Structure, Agency, and Division in the CIO Era." *International Review of Social History* 41 (December 1996): 389–406.

Sweetland, Monroe. "The CIO and the Negro American." *Opportunity* 20 (September 1942): 292–94.

"'T' Stands for Tobacco." *People's Songs*, July/August 1947, 11.

Thomas, Glyn. "Hear the Music Ring." *New South* 23 (Summer 1968): 37–46.

Thompson, Bob. "Strengthen the Struggle against White Chauvinism." *Political Affairs* 28 (June 1949): 14–27.

Thornton, J. Mills, III. "Challenge and Response in the Montgomery Bus Boycott of 1955–1956." *Alabama Review* 33 (July 1980): 163–235.

Thrasher, Sue, and Leah Wise. "The Southern Tenant Farmers' Union." *Southern Exposure* 1 (Fall/Winter 1974): 6–32.

Townsend, Willard S. "One American Problem and a Possible Solution." In *What the Negro Wants*, edited by Rayford W. Logan, 163–92. Chapel Hill: University of North Carolina Press, 1944. Reprint, with a new introduction and bibliography by Kenneth Robert Janken, Notre Dame: University of Notre Dame Press, 2001 (page citations are to the reprint edition).

Trotter, Joe William, Jr. "African Americans in the City: The Industrial Era, 1900–1950." *Journal of Urban History* 21 (May 1995): 438–57.

———. "African-American Workers: New Directions in U.S. Labor Historiography." *Labor History* 35 (Fall 1994): 495–523.

Uesugi, Sayoko. "Gender, Race, and the Cold War: Mary Price and the Progressive Party in North Carolina, 1945–48." *North Carolina Historical Review* 77 (July 2000): 269–311.

Valien, Preston. "Expansion of Negro Suffrage in Tennessee." *Journal of Negro Education* 26 (Summer 1957): 362–68.

Valocchi, Steve. "The Racial Basis of Capitalism and the State, and the Impact of the New Deal on African Americans." *Social Problems* 41 (August 1994): 347–62.

Walker, Anders. "Legislating Virtue: How Segregationists Disguised Racial Discrimination as Moral Reform Following Brown v. Board of Education." *Duke Law Journal* 47 (November 1997): 399–424.

Weaver, Robert C. "The Employment of Negroes in United States War Industries." *International Labour Review* 50 (August 1944): 141–59.

———. "The Negro Comes of Age in Industry." *Atlantic Monthly* 172 (September 1943): 54–59.

———. "Recent Events in Negro Union Relationships." *Journal of Political Economy* 52 (September 1944): 234–49.

Wilkens, Mark. "Gender, Race, Work Culture, and the Building of the Fire Fighters Union in Tampa, Florida, 1943–1985." In *Southern Labor in Transition, 1940–1995*, edited by Robert H. Zieger, 176–204. Knoxville: University of Tennessee Press, 1997.

Williamson, John. "For a Mass Marxist Party of the Working Class." *Political Affairs* 25 (March 1946): 225–39.

———. "Improve and Build Our Communist Press—The Next Step in Building." *Political Affairs* 25 (September 1946): 811–17.

———. "New Organizational Problems of the Communist Party." *Political Affairs* 25 (December 1946): 1109–27.

———. "Trade Unions and the Negro Workers." *Political Affairs* 26 (November 1947): 1107–17.

Woodbury, Clarence. "They Put a Parson on the Payroll." *The American Magazine* 153 (January 1952): 18–19, 81–85.

Woodward, C. Vann. "Strange Career Critics: Long May They Persevere." *Journal of American History* 75 (December 1988): 857–68.

Wright, Gavin. "The Origins of American Industrial Success, 1879–1940." *American Economic Review* 80 (September 1990): 651–68.

"Yankee-Type Rebels." *Forbes* 70 (November 1952): 14–21.

Zahavi, Gerald. "Fighting Left-Wing Unionism: Voices from the Opposition to the IFLWU in Fulton County, New York." In *The CIO's Left-Led Unions*, edited by Steve Rosswurm, 159–81. New Brunswick: Rutgers University Press, 1992.

———. "Passionate Commitments: Race, Sex, and Communism at Schenectady General Electric." *Journal of American History* 83 (September 1996): 514–48.

———. "'Who's Going to Dance with Somebody Who Calls You a Mainstreeter?': Communism, Culture, and Community in Sheridan County, Montana, 1918–1934." *Great Plains Quarterly* 16 (Fall 1996): 251–86.

Zieger, Robert H. "The CIO: A Bibliographical Update and Archival Guide." *Labor History* 31 (Fall 1990): 413–40.

———. "Introduction: Is Southern Labor History Exceptional?" In *Southern Labor in Transition, 1940–1995*, edited by Robert H. Zieger, 1–13. Knoxville: University of Tennessee Press, 1997.

———. "Toward a History of the CIO: A Bibliographical Report." *Labor History* 26 (Fall 1985): 485–516.

———. "A Venture into Unplowed Fields: Daniel Powell and CIO Political Action in the Postwar South." In *Labor in the Modern South*, edited by Glenn T. Eskew, 158–81. Athens: University of Georgia Press, 2001.

Books

Abrams, Douglas Carl. *Conservative Constraints: North Carolina and the New Deal*. Oxford: University Press of Mississippi, 1992.

Adams, Frank. *James Dombrowski: An American Heretic, 1897–1983*. Knoxville: University of Tennessee Press, 1992.

Adams, Frank, and Myles Horton. *Unearthing Seeds of Fire: The Idea of Highlander*. Winston-Salem: John F. Blair, 1975.

Allen, Theodore W. *The Invention of the White Race*. Vol. 1, *Racial Oppression and Social Control*. London: Verso, 1994.

Amberg, Stephen. *The Union Inspiration in American Politics: The Autoworkers and the Making of a Liberal Industrial Order*. Philadelphia: Temple University Press, 1994.

Anderson, James D. *The Education of Blacks in the South, 1860–1935*. Chapel Hill: University of North Carolina Press, 1988.

Arnesen, Eric. *Brotherhoods of Color: Black Railroad Workers and the Struggle for Equality*. Cambridge: Harvard University Press, 2001.

———. *Waterfront Workers of New Orleans: Race, Class, and Politics, 1863–1923*. New York: Oxford University Press, 1991; reprint, Urbana: University of Illinois Press, 1994.

Atleson, James B. *Labor and the Wartime State: Labor Relations and Law during World War II*. Urbana: University of Illinois Press, 1998.

Ayers, Edward L. *Vengeance and Justice: Crime and Punishment in the 19th Century American South*. New York: Oxford University Press, 1984.

Banks, William H. *Black Intellectuals: Race and Responsibility in American Life.* New York: W. W. Norton, 1996.

Barbash, Jack. *Labor's Grass Roots: A Study of the Local Union.* New York: Harper, 1961.

Barrett, James R. *William Z. Foster and the Tragedy of American Radicalism.* Urbana: University of Illinois Press, 1999.

———. *Work and Community in the Jungle: Chicago's Packinghouse Workers, 1894–1922.* Urbana: University of Illinois Press, 1987.

Barthwell, Akosua. *Trade Unionism in North Carolina: The Strike against Reynolds Tobacco, 1947.* New York: American Institute for Marxist Studies, 1977.

Bartley, Numan. *The Rise of Massive Resistance: Race and Politics in the South during the 1950s.* Baton Rouge: Louisiana State University Press, 1969.

Bastin, Bruce. *Red River Blues: The Blues Tradition in the Southeast.* Urbana: University of Illinois Press, 1995.

Bates, Beth Tompkins. *Pullman Porters and the Rise of Protest Politics in Black America, 1925–1945.* Chapel Hill: University of North Carolina Press, 2001.

Beardsley, Edward H. *A History of Neglect: Health Care for Blacks and Mill Workers in the Twentieth-Century South.* Knoxville: University of Tennessee Press, 1987.

Beatty, Bess. *Alamance: The Holt Family and Industrialization in a North Carolina County, 1837–1900.* Baton Rouge: Louisiana State University Press, 1999.

Beck, Carl. *Contempt of Congress: A Study of the Prosecutions Initiated by the Committee on Un-American Activities, 1945–1957.* New Orleans: Phauser Press, 1959.

Belfrage, Cedric. *A Faith to Free the People.* New York: Dryden Press, 1944.

———. *South of God.* New York: Modern Age, 1941.

Bentley, Elizabeth. *Out of Bondage.* New York: Devin-Adair, 1951.

Berman, William C. *The Politics of Civil Rights in the Truman Administration.* Columbus: Ohio State University Press, 1970.

Bernstein, Carl. *Loyalties: A Son's Memoir.* New York: Simon and Schuster, 1989.

Bernstein, Irving A. *A Caring Society: The New Deal, the Worker, and the Great Depression.* Boston: Houghton Mifflin, 1985.

———. *The Lean Years: A History of the American Worker, 1920–1933.* Boston: Houghton Mifflin, 1972.

———. *Turbulent Years: A History of the American Worker, 1933–1941.* Boston: Houghton Mifflin, 1971.

Billings, Dwight B., Jr. *Planters and the Making of a "New South": Class, Politics, and Development in North Carolina, 1865–1900.* Chapel Hill: University of North Carolina Press, 1978.

Bledsoe, Thomas. *Or We'll All Hang Separately: The Highlander Idea.* Boston: Beacon Press, 1969.

Bloom, Jack M. *Class, Race, and the Civil Rights Movement.* Bloomington: Indiana University Press, 1987.

Blum, John Morton. *V Was for Victory: Politics and American Culture during World War II.* New York: Harcourt, Brace, Jovanovich, 1976.

Borchert, James. *Alley Life in Washington: Religions and Folklife in the City, 1850–1970.* Urbana: University of Illinois Press, 1980.

Bosmajian, Haig. *The Freedom Not to Speak.* New York: New York University Press, 1999.

Boyer, Richard O., and Herbert M. Morais. *Labor's Untold Story*. New York: United Electrical, Radio and Machine Workers of America, 1955.

Braden, Anne. *The Wall Between*. Knoxville: University of Tennessee Press, 1999.

Branch, Taylor. *Parting the Waters: America in the King Years, 1954–1963*. New York: Simon and Schuster, 1988.

Brattain, Michelle. *The Politics of Whiteness: Race, Workers, and Culture in the Modern South*. Princeton: Princeton University Press, 2001.

Braverman, Harry. *Labor and Monopoly Capital: The Degradation of Work in the Twentieth Century*. New York: Monthly Review Press, 1974.

Brinkley, Alan. *The End of Reform: New Deal Liberalism in Recession and War*. New York: Alfred A. Knopf, 1995.

Brody, David. *In Labor's Cause: Main Themes on the History of the American Worker*. New York: Oxford University Press, 1993.

———. *Workers in Industrial America: Essays on the Twentieth Century Struggle*. New York: Oxford University Press, 1980.

Brooks, Aubrey Lee. *A Southern Lawyer: Fifty Years at the Bar*. Chapel Hill: University of North Carolina Press, 1950.

Brooks, Thomas R. *Clint: A Biography of a Labor Intellectual, Clinton S. Golden*. New York: Atheneum, 1978.

Brown, Michael K. *Race, Money, and the American Welfare State*. Ithaca: Cornell University Press, 1999.

Brownlee, Fambrough L. *Winston-Salem: A Pictorial History*. Norfolk, Va.: Donning Company, 1977.

Buffa, Dudley W. *Union Power and American Democracy: The UAW and the Democratic Party, 1935–72*. Ann Arbor: University of Michigan Press, 1984.

Bunche, Ralph J. *The Political Status of the Negro in the Age of FDR*. Chicago: University of Chicago Press, 1973.

Burgess, Margaret Elaine. *Negro Leadership in a Southern City*. Chapel Hill: University of North Carolina Press, 1962.

Burrough, Bryan, and John Helyar. *Barbarians at the Gate: The Fall of RJR Nabisco*. New York: Harper and Row, 1990.

Caldwell, A. B., ed. *History of the American Negro, North Carolina Edition*. Vol. 4 of *History of the American Negro*. Atlanta: A. B. Caldwell Publishing Company, 1921.

Cantwell, Robert. *When We Were Good: The Folk Revival*. Cambridge: Harvard University Press, 1996.

Carawan, Guy, and Candy Carawan. *We Shall Overcome: Songs of the Southern Freedom Movement*. New York: Oak Publications, 1963.

Carlton, David L., and Peter A. Coclanis, eds. *Confronting Southern Poverty in the Great Depression: The Report on Economic Conditions of the South with Related Documents*. Boston: Bedford Books of St. Martin's Press, 1996.

Carson, Clayborne. *In Struggle: SNCC and the Black Awakening of the 1960s*. Cambridge: Harvard University Press, 1981.

Carter, Dan T. *Scottsboro: The Tragedy of the American South*. Baton Rouge: Louisiana State University Press, 1969.

Caute, David. *The Great Fear: The Anti-Communist Purge under Truman and Eisenhower*. New York: Simon and Schuster, 1978.

Cayton, Horace R., and George S. Mitchell. *Black Workers and the New Unions*. Chapel Hill: University of North Carolina Press, 1939.

Cecelski, David S., and Timothy B. Tyson, eds. *Democracy Betrayed: The Wilmington Race Riot of 1898 and Its Legacy*. Chapel Hill: University of North Carolina Press, 1998.

Cell, John W. *The Highest Stage of White Supremacy: The Origins of Segregation in South Africa and the American South*. New York: Cambridge University Press, 1982.

Chafe, William H. *Civilities and Civil Rights: Greensboro, North Carolina, and the Black Struggle for Freedom*. New York: Oxford University Press, 1980.

―――. *Unfinished Journey: American since World War II*. New York: Oxford University Press, 1986.

Chandler, Alfred D., Jr. *The Visible Hand: The Managerial Revolution in American Business*. Cambridge: Harvard University Press, 1977.

Chong, Dennis. *Collective Action and the Civil Rights Movement*. Chicago: University of Chicago Press, 1991.

Clark, Daniel J. *Like Night and Day: Unionization in a Southern Mill Town*. Chapel Hill: University of North Carolina Press, 1997.

Clark-Lewis, Elizabeth. *Living In, Living Out: African American Domestics in Washington, D.C., 1910–1940*. Washington, D.C.: Smithsonian Institution Press, 1994.

Cleaver, Harry. *Reading Capital Politically*. Austin: University of Texas Press, 1979.

Cobb, James C. *The Most Southern Place on Earth: The Mississippi Delta and the Roots of Regional Identity*. New York: Oxford University Press, 1992.

―――. *Redefining Southern Culture: Mind and Identity in the Modern South*. Athens: University of Georgia Press, 1999.

―――. *The Selling of the South: The Southern Crusade for Industrial Development, 1936–1980*. Baton Rouge: Louisiana State University Press, 1982.

Cochran, Bert. *Labor and Communism: The Conflict That Shaped American Unions*. Princeton: Princeton University Press, 1977.

Cohen, Lizabeth. *Making a New Deal: Industrial Workers in Chicago, 1919–1939*. New York: Cambridge University Press, 1990.

Cohen, Robert. *When the Old Left Was Young: Student Radicals and America's First Mass Student Movement, 1929–1941*. New York: Oxford University Press, 1993.

Cohen, William. *At Freedom's Edge: Black Mobility and the Southern White Quest for Racial Control, 1861–1915*. Baton Rouge: Louisiana State University Press, 1991.

Colburn, David R. *Racial Change and Community Crisis: St. Augustine, Florida, 1877–1980*. New York: Columbia University Press, 1985.

Collins, Charles Wallace. *Whither Solid South?: A Study in Politics and Race Relations*. New Orleans: Pelican Publishing Company, 1947.

Connor, R. D. W., and Clarence Poe. *The Life and Speeches of Charles Brantley Aycock*. Garden City, N.Y.: Doubleday, Page, 1912.

Cooper, Patricia A. *Once a Cigar Maker: Men, Women, and Work Culture in American Cigar Factories, 1900–1919*. Urbana: University of Illinois Press, 1987.

Cowie, Jefferson. *Capital Moves: RCA's Seventy-Year Quest for Cheap Labor*. Ithaca: Cornell University Press, 1999.

Cox, Oliver Cromwell. *Caste, Class, and Race: A Study in Social Dynamics*. Garden City, N.Y.: Doubleday, 1948; reprint, New York: Monthly Review Press, 1970.

Cripps, Thomas. *Making Movies Black: The Hollywood Message Movie from World War II to the Civil Rights Era.* New York: Oxford University Press, 1993.

Crow, Jeffery, and Robert F. Durden. *Maverick Republican in the Old North State.* Baton Rouge: Louisiana State University Press, 1979.

Crow, Jeffery, Paul Escott, and Flora J. Hatley. *A History of African Americans in North Carolina.* Raleigh: Division of Archives and History, 1992.

Culver, John C., and John Hyde. *American Dreamer: The Life and Times of Henry A. Wallace.* New York: W. W. Norton, 2000.

Daniel, Pete. *Breaking the Land: The Transformation of Cotton, Tobacco, and Rice Cultures since 1880.* Urbana: University of Illinois Press, 1985.

———. *Standing at the Crossroads: Southern Life in the Twentieth Century.* New York: Hill and Wang, 1986.

Daniels, Jonathan. *Tar Heels: A Portrait of North Carolina.* New York: Dodd, Mead, 1941.

Davis, Chester. *The Character of the Community.* Vol. 13 of *Winston-Salem in History*, edited by Manly Wade Wellman. Winston-Salem: Historic Winston-Salem, 1976.

Davis, Chester S., and Malcolm F. Mallette. *The Golden Years: 1915–1965.* Winston-Salem: Winston-Salem Rotary Club, 1965.

Davis, Lenwood G., William J. Rice, and James H. McLaughlin. *African Americans in Winston-Salem/Forsyth County: A Pictorial History.* Virginia Beach, Va.: Donning Company, 1999.

Davis, Paxton. *Being a Boy.* Winston-Salem: John F. Blair, 1988.

Denning, Michael. *The Cultural Front: The Laboring of American Culture in the Twentieth Century.* London: Verso, 1996.

Dickerman, Marion, and Ruth Taylor, eds. *Who's Who in Labor.* New York: Dryden Press, 1946.

Dickerson, Dennis C. *Out of the Crucible: Black Steelworkers in Western Pennsylvania.* Albany: State University of New York Press, 1986.

Directory of Social and Health Agencies. Winston-Salem: Community Council, 1946.

Dittmer, John. *Local People: The Struggle for Civil Rights in Mississippi.* Urbana: University of Illinois Press, 1994.

Dollard, John. *Caste and Class in a Southern Town.* 3d ed. New York: Doubleday Anchor Books, 1957.

Drake, St. Clair, and Horace R. Cayton. *Black Metropolis: A Study of Negro Life in a Northern City.* Rev. ed. New York: Harper and Row, 1962.

Draper, Alan. *Conflict of Interests: Organized Labor and the Civil Rights Movement in the South, 1954–1968.* Ithaca: ILR Press, 1994.

Draper, Theodore. *American Communism and Soviet Russia: The Formative Period.* New York: Octagon Books, 1977.

Duberman, Martin Bauml. *Paul Robeson.* New York: Alfred A. Knopf, 1989.

Dubofsky, Melvyn. *The State and Labor in Modern America.* Chapel Hill: University of North Carolina Press, 1994.

———, ed. *Technological Change and Workers' Movements.* Beverly Hills, Calif.: Sage Publications, 1985.

Du Bois, W. E. B. *Black Reconstruction in America: An Essay toward a History of the Part Which Black Folk Played in the Attempt to Reconstruct Democracy in America, 1860–1880.* New York: Atheneum, 1975.

————. *The Souls of Black Folk: Essays and Sketches.* Chicago: A. C. McClurg, 1903.

Dudziak, Mary L. *Cold War Civil Rights: Race and the Image of American Democracy.* Princeton: Princeton University Press, 2000.

Dunbar, Anthony. *Against the Grain: Southern Radicals and Prophets, 1929–1959.* Charlottesville: University Press of Virginia, 1981.

Durr, Virginia Foster. *Outside the Magic Circle: The Autobiography of Virginia Foster Durr.* University: University of Alabama Press, 1985.

Dyson, Lowell K. *Red Harvest: The Communist Party and American Farmers.* Lincoln: University of Nebraska Press, 1982.

Edmonds, Helen G. *The Negro and Fusion Politics in North Carolina, 1894–1901.* Chapel Hill: University of North Carolina Press, 1951.

Edsforth, Ronald. *Class Conflict and Cultural Consensus: The Making of a Mass Consumer Society in Flint, Michigan.* New Brunswick: Rutgers University Press, 1987.

Edwards, Laura F. *Gendered Strife and Confusion: The Political Culture of Reconstruction.* Urbana: University of Illinois Press, 1997.

Edwards, Richard. *Contested Terrain: The Transformation of the Workplace in the Twentieth Century.* New York: Basis Books, 1979.

Edwards, Richard C., Michael Reich, and David M. Gordon, eds. *Labor Market Segmentation.* Lexington, Mass.: D. C. Heath, 1975.

Egerton, John. *Speak Now against the Day: The Generation before the Civil Rights Movement.* New York: Alfred A. Knopf, 1994.

Escott, Paul D. *Many Excellent People: Power and Privilege in North Carolina, 1850–1900.* Chapel Hill: University of North Carolina Press, 1985.

Fairclough, Adam. *Teaching Equality: Black Schools in the Age of Jim Crow.* Athens: University of Georgia Press, 2001.

Fantasia, Rick. *Cultures of Solidarity: Consciousness, Action, and Contemporary American Workers.* Berkeley: University of California Press, 1988.

Fariello, Griffin. *Red Scare: Memories of the American Inquisition, An Oral History.* New York: W. W. Norton, 1995.

Faue, Elizabeth. *Community of Suffering and Struggle: Women, Men, and the Labor Movement in Minneapolis, 1915–1945.* Chapel Hill: University of North Carolina Press, 1991.

Federal Writers' Project, WPA of North Carolina. *North Carolina: A Guide to the Old North State.* Chapel Hill: University of North Carolina Press, 1939.

Filippelli, Ronald L. *Labor in the USA: A History.* New York: Alfred A. Knopf, 1984.

Filippelli, Ronald L., and Mark McColloch. *Cold War in the Working Class: The Rise and Decline of the United Electrical Workers.* Albany: State University of New York Press, 1995.

Fink, Gary M., and Merl E. Reed, eds. *Essays in Southern Labor History: Selected Papers/Southern Labor History Conference, 1976.* Westport, Conn.: Greenwood Press, 1977.

Fink, Leon. *Workingmen's Democracy: The Knights of Labor and American Politics.* Urbana: University of Illinois Press, 1983.

Fink, Leon, and Brian Greenberg. *Upheaval in the Quiet Zone: A History of Hospital Workers' Union, Local 1199.* Urbana: University of Illinois Press, 1989.

Fish, Gertrude Sipperly, ed. *The Story of Housing.* New York: Macmillan, 1979.

Flamming, Douglas. *Creating the Modern South: Millhands and Managers in Dalton, Georgia, 1884–1984.* Chapel Hill: University of North Carolina Press, 1992.

Flowers, Linda. *Throwed Away: Failures of Progress in Eastern North Carolina.* Knoxville: University of Tennessee Press, 1990.

Foley, Neil. *The White Scourge: Mexicans, Blacks, and Poor Whites in Texas Cotton Culture.* Berkeley: University of California Press, 1997.

Foner, Eric. *Reconstruction: America's Unfinished Revolution, 1863–1877.* New York: Harper and Row, Perennial Library, 1989.

Foner, Philip S. *Organized Labor and the Black Worker, 1619–1973.* New York: International Publishers, 1974.

Fones-Wolf, Elizabeth A. *Selling Free Enterprise: The Business Assault on Labor and Liberalism, 1945–60.* Urbana: University of Illinois Press, 1994.

Fosdick, Raymond B. *Adventure in Giving: The Story of the General Education Board, a Foundation Established by John D. Rockefeller.* New York: Harper and Row, 1962.

Foster, James Caldwell. *The Union Politic: The CIO Political Action Committee.* Columbia: University of Missouri Press, 1975.

Foster, William Z. *American Trade Unionism: Principles and Organization, Strategy and Tactics.* New York: International Publishers, 1947.

Frank, Dana. *Purchasing Power: Consumer Organizing, Gender, and the Seattle Labor Movement, 1919–1929.* New York: Cambridge University Press, 1994.

Fraser, Nancy. *Justice Interruptus: Critical Reflections on the "Postsocialist" Condition.* New York: Routledge, 1997.

Fraser, Steven. *Labor Will Rule: Sidney Hillman and the Rise of American Labor.* New York: Free Press, 1991.

Fraser, Steven, and Gary Gerstle, eds. *The Rise and Fall of the New Deal Order, 1930–1980.* Princeton: Princeton University Press, 1989.

Frazier, E. Franklin. *Black Bourgeoisie: The Rise of a New Black Middle Class.* New York: Free Press, 1957.

Frazier, E. Franklin, and C. Eric Lincoln. *"The Negro Church in America" and "The Black Church since Frazier."* New York: Schocken, 1974.

Frederickson, Kari. *The Dixiecrat Revolt and the End of the Solid South, 1932–1968.* Chapel Hill: University of North Carolina Press, 2001.

Freeland, Richard M. *The Truman Doctrine and the Origins of McCarthyism.* New York: Alfred A. Knopf, 1972.

Freeman, Joshua B. *In Transit: The Transport Workers Union in New York City, 1933–1966.* New York: Oxford University Press, 1989.

———. *Working Class New York: Life and Labor since World War II.* New York: New Press, 2000.

Friedlander, Peter. *The Emergence of a UAW Local, 1936–1936: A Study in Class and Culture.* Pittsburgh: University of Pittsburgh Press, 1975.

Fries, Adelaide, Stuart Thurman Wright, and J. Edwin Hendricks. *Forsyth: The History of a County on the March.* Chapel Hill: University of North Carolina Press, 1976.

Gabin, Nancy F. *Feminism in the Labor Movement: Women and the United Auto Workers, 1935–1975.* Ithaca: Cornell University Press, 1990.

Gaer, Joseph. *The First Round: The Story of the CIO Political Action Committee.* New York: Duell, Sloan and Pearce, 1944.

Gaines, Kevin G. *Uplifting the Race: Black Leadership, Politics, and Culture in the Twentieth Century.* Chapel Hill: University of North Carolina Press, 1996.

Garfinkel, Herbert R. *When Negroes March: The March on Washington Movement in the Organizational Politics of FEPC.* Glencoe, Ill.: Free Press, 1959.

Gaston, Paul. *The New South Creed: A Study in Southern Mythmaking.* New York: Alfred A. Knopf, 1970.

Gavins, Raymond. *The Perils and Prospects of Southern Black Leadership: Gordon Blaine Hancock, 1884–1970.* Durham: Duke University Press, 1977.

Genovese, Eugene D. *Roll, Jordan, Roll: The World the Slaves Made.* New York: Vintage Books, 1976.

George, Carol V. R. *God's Salesman: Norman Vincent Peale and the Power of Positive Thinking.* New York: Oxford University Press, 1993.

Gerstle, Gary. *Working-Class Americanism: The Politics of Labor in a Textile City, 1914–1960.* New York: Cambridge University Press, 1989.

Gholson, Edward. *The Negro Looks into the South.* Boston: Chapman and Grimes, 1947.

Gilmore, Glenda Elizabeth. *Gender and Jim Crow: Women and the Politics of White Supremacy in North Carolina, 1896–1920.* Chapel Hill: University of North Carolina Press, 1996.

Glazer, Nathan. *The Social Basis of American Communism.* New York: Harcourt, Brace, 1961.

Glen, John M. *Highlander: No Ordinary School.* Knoxville: University of Tennessee Press, 1996.

Glickman, Lawrence B. *A Living Wage: American Workers and the Making of Consumer Society.* Ithaca: Cornell University Press, 1997.

Goldfield, David R. *Black, White, and Southern: Race Relations and the Southern Culture, 1940 to the Present.* Baton Rouge: Louisiana State University Press, 1990.

Goldfield, Michael. *The Color of Politics: Race and the Mainsprings of American Politics.* New York: New Press, 1997.

Goodman, James. *Stories of Scottsboro: The Rape Case That Shocked 1930s America and Revived the Struggle for Equality.* New York: Pantheon Books, 1994.

Goodman, Walter. *The Committee: The Extraordinary Career of the House Committee on Un-American Activities.* New York: Farrar, Straus, and Giroux, 1968.

Goodwyn, Lawrence. *Breaking the Barrier: The Rise of Solidarity in Poland.* New York: Oxford University Press, 1991.

———. *Democratic Promise: The Populist Moment in America.* New York: Oxford University Press, 1976.

Gordon, David M., Richard Edwards, and Michael Reich. *Segmented Work, Divided Workers: The Historical Transformation of Labor in the United States.* New York: Cambridge University Press, 1982.

Gornick, Vivian. *The Romance of American Communism.* New York: Basic Books, 1977.

Gottlieb, Peter. *Making Their Own Way: Southern Blacks' Migration to Pittsburgh, 1916–30.* Urbana: University of Illinois Press, 1987.

Gould, Stephen Jay. *Wonderful Life: The Burgess Shale and the Nature of History.* New York: W. W. Norton, 1984.

Graham, Shirley. *Paul Robeson: Citizen of the World.* New York: J. Messner, 1946; reprint, Westport, Conn.: Negro Universities Press, 1971.

Green, Archie. *Only a Miner: Studies in Recorded Coal-Mining Songs.* Urbana: University of Illinois Press, 1972.

Greene, Lorenzo J., and Carter G. Woodson. *The Negro Wage Earner*. Washington, D.C.: Association for the Study of Negro Life and History, 1930.

Greenstone, J. David. *Labor in American Politics*. New York: Alfred A. Knopf, 1969.

Greenwood, Janette Thomas. *Bittersweet Legacy: The Black and White "Better Classes" in Charlotte, 1850–1910*. Chapel Hill: University of North Carolina Press, 1994.

Gregory, Charles O., and Harold A. Katz. *Labor and the Law*. New York: W. W. Norton, 1979.

Griffith, Barbara S. *The Crisis of American Labor: Operation Dixie and the Defeat of the CIO*. Philadelphia: Temple University Press, 1988.

Griswold, Erwin N. *The 5th Amendment Today: Three Speeches*. Cambridge: Harvard University Press, 1955.

Gross, James A. *Broken Promise: The Subversion of U.S. Labor Relations Policy, 1947–1994*. Philadelphia: Temple University Press, 1995.

———. *The Making of the National Labor Relations Board: A Study in Economics, Politics, and the Law*. Albany: State University of New York Press, 1974.

———. *The Reshaping of the National Labor Relations Board: National Labor Policy in Transition*. Albany: State University of New York Press, 1981.

Grossman, James R. *Land of Hope: Chicago, Black Southerners, and the Great Migration*. Chicago: University of Chicago Press, 1989.

Grubbs, Donald. *The Cry from Cotton: The Southern Tenant Farmers Union and the New Deal*. Chapel Hill: University of North Carolina Press, 1971.

Guichard, Parris, and Lester Brooks. *Blacks in the City: A History of the National Urban League*. Boston: Little, Brown, 1971.

Gullan, Harold I. *The Upset That Wasn't: Harry S. Truman and the Crucial Election of 1948*. Chicago: Ivan R. Dee, 1998.

Gutman, Herbert G. *The Black Family in Slavery and Freedom, 1750–1925*. New York: Pantheon Books, 1976.

———. *Work, Culture, and Society in Industrializing America*. New York: Alfred A. Knopf, 1976.

Hahamovitch, Cindy. *The Fruits of Their Labor: Atlantic Coast Farmworkers and the Making of Migrant Poverty, 1870–1945*. Chapel Hill: University of North Carolina Press, 1997.

Hale, Grace Elizabeth. *Making Whiteness: The Culture of Segregation in the South, 1890–1940*. New York: Pantheon Books, 1998.

Hall, Jacquelyn Dowd. *Revolt against Chivalry: Jessie Daniel Ames and the Women's Campaign against Lynching*. New York: Columbia University Press, 1979.

Hall, Jacquelyn Dowd, et al. *Like a Family: The Making of a Southern Cotton Mill World*. Chapel Hill: University of North Carolina Press, 1987.

Hall, William James, and Helen Johnson McMurray. *Tanglewood: Historic Gem of Forsyth County, North Carolina*. Winston-Salem: Hunter Publishing Company, 1979.

Halpern, Rick. *Down on the Killing Floor: Black and White Workers in Chicago's Packinghouses, 1904–54*. Urbana: University of Illinois Press, 1997.

Halpern, Rick, and Roger Horowitz. *Meatpackers: An Oral History of Black Packinghouse Workers and Their Struggle for Racial and Economic Equality*. New York: Twayne Publishers, 1996.

Hanchett, Thomas W. *Sorting Out the New South City: Race, Class, and Urban Development in Charlotte, 1875–1975*. Chapel Hill: University of North Carolina Press, 1998.

Harris, Howell John. *The Right to Manage: Industrial Relations Policies of American Business in the 1940s.* Madison: University of Wisconsin Press, 1982.

Harris, William H. *The Harder We Run: Black Workers since the Civil War.* New York: Oxford University Press, 1982.

———. *Keeping the Faith: A. Philip Randolph, Milton P. Webster, and the Brotherhood of Sleeping Car Porters, 1925–37.* Urbana: University of Illinois Press, 1977.

Harrison, Alferdteen, ed. *Black Exodus: The Great Migration from the American South.* Jackson: University Press of Mississippi, 1991.

Haynes, John E. *Red Scare or Red Menace?: American Communism and Anticommunism in the Cold War Era.* Chicago: Ivan R. Dee, 1996.

Haynes, John Earl, and Harvey Klehr. *Venona: Decoding Soviet Espionage in America.* New Haven: Yale University Press, 1999.

Hewitt, Nancy. *Southern Discomfort: Women's Activism in Tampa, Florida, 1880s–1920s.* Chicago: University of Illinois Press, 2001.

Higginbotham, Evelyn Brooks. *Righteous Discontent: The Women's Movement in the Black Baptist Church, 1880–1920.* Cambridge: Harvard University Press, 1993.

Hill, Herbert. *Black Labor and the American Legal System.* Madison: University of Wisconsin Press, 1985.

Hill, Robert A., ed. *The Marcus Garvey and Universal Negro Improvement Association Papers.* Berkeley: University of California Press, 1983–84.

Hill's Winston-Salem City Directory. Richmond, Va.: Hill Directory Company, 1938.

Hill's Winston-Salem City Directory. Richmond, Va.: Hill Directory Company, 1947–48.

Hinson, Glen. *Virginia Work Songs.* Ferrum, Va.: BRI Records, 1983.

Hinton, James. *The First Shop Stewards' Movement.* London: G. Allen and Unwin, 1973.

Hirschhorn, Bernard. *Democracy Reformed: Richard Spencer Childs and His Fight for Better Government.* Westport, Conn.: Greenwood Press, 1997.

Holt, Rackham. *Mary McLeod Bethune: A Biography.* Garden City, N.Y.: Doubleday, 1964.

Honey, Michael. *Black Workers Remember: An Oral History of Segregation, Unionism, and the Freedom Struggle.* Berkeley: University of California Press, 1999.

———. *Southern Labor and Black Civil Rights: Organizing Memphis Workers.* Urbana: University of Illinois Press, 1993.

Hook, Sidney. *Common Sense and the Fifth Amendment.* New York: Criterion Books, 1957.

Horne, Gerald. *Black Liberation/Red Scare: Ben Davis and the Communist Party.* Newark: University of Delaware Press, 1994.

———. *Communist Front?: The Civil Rights Congress, 1946–1956.* Rutherford, N.J.: Fairleigh Dickinson University Press, 1988.

Horowitz, Daniel. *Betty Friedan and the Making of the Feminine Mystique: The American Left, the Cold War, and Modern Feminism.* Amherst: University of Massachusetts Press, 1998.

Horowitz, Roger. *"Negro and White, Unite and Fight!": A Social History of Industrial Unionism in Meatpacking, 1930–90.* Urbana: University of Illinois Press, 1997.

Horton, Aimee Isgrig. *The Highlander Folk School: A History of Its Major Programs, 1932–1961.* Brooklyn: Carlson Publications, 1989.

Horton, Myles, with Judith Kohl and Herbert Kohl. *The Long Haul: An Autobiography.* New York: Doubleday, 1990.

Howe, Irving, and Lewis Coser. *The American Communist Party: A Critical History*. New York: Praeger, 1962.

Hunnicutt, Benjamin Kline. *Work without End: Abandoning Shorter Hours for the Right to Work*. Philadelphia: Temple University Press, 1988.

Hunter, Tera W. *To 'Joy My Freedom: Southern Black Women's Lives and Labor after the Civil War*. Cambridge: Harvard University Press, 1997.

Hurston, Zora Neale. *Their Eyes Were Watching God*. Urbana: University of Illinois Press, 1991.

Hutchinson, Earl Ofari. *Blacks and Reds: Race and Class in Conflict, 1919–1990*. East Lansing: Michigan State University Press, 1995.

Irons, Janet. *Testing the New Deal: The General Textile Strike of 1934 in the American South*. Urbana: University of Illinois Press, 2000.

Isserman, Maurice. *Which Side Were You On?: The American Communist Party during the Second World War*. Middletown, Conn.: Wesleyan University Press, 1982.

Jackson, Walter A. *Gunnar Myrdal and America's Conscience: Social Engineering and Racial Liberalism, 1938–1987*. Chapel Hill: University of North Carolina Press, 1990.

Jacoby, Sanford M. *Modern Manors: Welfare Capitalism since the New Deal*. Princeton: Princeton University Press, 1997.

Jacoway, Elizabeth, and David R. Colburn, eds. *Southern Businessmen and Desegregation*. Baton Rouge: Louisiana State University Press, 1982.

Jameson, Fredric. *Postmodernism, or, The Cultural Logic of Late Capitalism*. Durham: Duke University Press, 1991.

Jamieson, Stuart. *Labor Unionism in American Agriculture*. New York: Arno Press, 1976.

Janiewski, Dolores E. *Sisterhood Denied: Race, Gender, and Class in a New South Community*. Philadelphia: Temple University Press, 1985.

Jefferys, Steve. *Management and Managed: Fifty Years of Crisis at Chrysler*. New York: Cambridge University Press, 1986.

Jenkins, Philip. *The Cold War at Home: The Red Scare in Pennsylvania, 1945–1960*. Chapel Hill: University of North Carolina Press, 1999.

Johanningsmeier, Edward P. *Forging American Communism: The Life of William Z. Foster*. Princeton: Princeton University Press, 1994.

Johnson, Charles S. *Patterns of Negro Segregation*. New York: Harper and Brothers, 1943.

Jones, Jacqueline. *Labor of Love, Labor of Sorrow: Black Women, Work, and the Family from Slavery to the Present*. New York: Basic Books, 1985.

Jones, Raymond M. *Strategic Management in a Hostile Environment: Lessons from the Tobacco Industry*. Westport, Conn.: Quorum Books, 1997.

Kantrowitz, Stephen. *Ben Tillman and the Construction of White Supremacy*. Chapel Hill: University of North Carolina Press, 2000.

Kaplan, Judy, and Linn Shapiro, eds. *Red Diapers: Growing Up in the Communist Left*. Urbana: University of Illinois Press, 1998.

Kaufman, Stuart B. *Challenge and Change: The History of the Tobacco Workers International Union*. Urbana: University of Illinois Press, 1986.

Kazin, Michael. *The Populist Persuasion: An American History*. New York: Basic Books, 1995.

Keech, William R. *The Impact of Negro Voting: The Role of the Vote in the Quest for Equality*. Chicago: Rand McNally, 1968.

Keeran, Roger. *The Communist Party and the Auto Workers Unions.* Bloomington: Indiana University Press, 1980.

Kelley, Robin D. G. *Hammer and Hoe: Alabama Communists during the Great Depression.* Chapel Hill: University of North Carolina Press, 1990.

———. *Race Rebels: Culture, Politics, and the Black Working Class.* New York: Free Press, 1994.

Kelly, Brian. *Race, Class, and Power in the Alabama Coalfields, 1908–1921.* Urbana: University of Illinois Press, 2001.

Kennedy, Stetson. *Southern Exposure.* Garden City, N.Y.: Doubleday, 1946.

Key, V. O. *Southern Politics in State and Nation.* New York: Alfred A. Knopf, 1949.

Kimeldorf, Howard. *Reds or Rackets?: The Making of Radical and Conservative Unions on the Waterfront.* Berkeley: University of California Press, 1988.

King, Richard H. *Civil Rights and the Idea of Freedom.* Athens: University of Georgia Press, 1996.

Kirby, Jack Temple. *Rural Worlds Lost: The American South, 1920–1960.* Baton Rouge: Louisiana State University Press, 1987.

Kirby, John B. *Black Americans in the Roosevelt Era: Liberalism and Race.* Knoxville: University of Tennessee Press, 1980.

Klehr, Harvey. *Communist Cadre: The Social Background of the American Communist Party Elite.* Stanford: Hoover Institution Press, 1978.

———. *The Heyday of American Communism: The Depression Decade.* New York: Basic Books, 1984.

Klehr, Harvey, and John Earl Haynes. *The American Communist Movement: Storming Heaven Itself.* New York: Twayne, 1992.

Klein, Joe. *Woody Guthrie: A Life.* New York: Alfred A. Knopf, 1980.

Kousser, J. Morgan. *Colorblind Injustice: Minority Voting Rights and the Undoing of the Second Reconstruction.* Chapel Hill: University of North Carolina Press, 1999.

———. *The Shaping of Southern Politics: Suffrage Restriction and the Establishment of the One-Party South, 1880–1910.* New Haven: Yale University Press, 1974.

Kraditor, Aileen S. *"Jimmy Higgins": The Mental World of the American Rank-and-File Communist, 1930–1958.* New York: Greenwood Press, 1988.

Kraus, Henry. *The Many and the Few: A Chronicle of the Dynamic Auto Workers.* 2d ed. Urbana: University of Illinois Press, 1985.

Krueger, Thomas A. *And Promises to Keep: The Southern Conference for Human Welfare, 1938–1948.* Nashville: Vanderbilt University Press, 1967.

Kryder, Daniel. *Divided Arsenal: Race and the American State during World War II.* New York: Cambridge University Press, 2000.

Kusmer, Kenneth L. *A Ghetto Takes Shape: Black Cleveland, 1870–1930.* Urbana: University of Illinois Press, 1976.

Ladd, Everett Carll, Jr. *Negro Political Leadership in the South.* New York: Atheneum, 1969.

Larkins, John R. *The Negro Population of North Carolina: Social and Economic.* Raleigh: North Carolina State Board of Charities and Public Welfare, 1944.

Lasch-Quinn, Elisabeth. *Black Neighbors: Race and the Limits of Reform in the American Settlement House Movement, 1890–1945.* Chapel Hill: University of North Carolina Press, 1993.

Lawson, Steven. *Black Ballots: Voting Rights in the South, 1944–1969*. New York: Columbia University Press, 1976.

———. *Running for Freedom: Civil Rights and Black Politics in America since 1941*. Philadelphia: Temple University Press, 1991.

Lears, T. J. Jackson. *Fables of Abundance: A Cultural History of Advertising in America*. New York: Basic Books, 1994.

Lee, Chana Kai. *For Freedom's Sake: The Life of Fannie Lou Hamer*. Urbana: University of Illinois Press, 1999.

Leloudis, James L. *Schooling the New South: Pedagogy, Self, and Society in North Carolina, 1880–1920*. Chapel Hill: University of North Carolina Press, 1996.

Lemert, Ben F. *The Tobacco Manufacturing Industry in North Carolina*. Raleigh: National Youth Administration of North Carolina, 1939.

Lerner, Gerda. *Black Women in White America: A Documentary History*. New York: Vintage Books, 1973.

———. *Fireweed: A Political Autobiography*. Philadelphia: Temple University Press, 2002.

Letwin, Daniel. *The Challenge of Interracial Unionism: Alabama Coal Miners, 1878–1921*. Chapel Hill: University of North Carolina Press, 1998.

Levenstein, Harvey A. *Communism, Anti-Communism, and the CIO*. Westport, Conn.: Greenwood Press, 1981.

Levine, Lawrence W. *Black Culture and Black Consciousness: Afro-American Folk Thought from Slavery to Freedom*. New York: Oxford University Press, 1977.

Lewinson, Paul. *Race, Class, and Party: A History of Negro Suffrage and White Politics in the South*. New York: Grosset and Dunlap, 1965.

Lewis, Earl. *In Their Own Interests: Race, Class, and Power in Twentieth-Century Norfolk, Virginia*. Berkeley: University of California Press, 1991.

Lewis, Hylan. *Blackways of Kent*. Chapel Hill: University of North Carolina Press, 1955.

Lewis, Ronald L. *Black Coal Miners in America: Race, Class, and Community Conflict, 1780–1980*. Lexington: University Press of Kentucky, 1987.

Lichtenstein, Alex. *Twice the Work of Free Labor: The Political Economy of Convict Labor in the New South*. London: Verso, 1996.

Lichtenstein, Nelson. *Labor's War at Home: The CIO in World War II*. New York: Cambridge University Press, 1982.

———. *The Most Dangerous Man in Detroit: Walter Reuther and the Fate of American Labor*. New York: Basic Books, 1995.

———. *State of the Union: A Century of American Labor*. Princeton: Princeton University Press, 2002.

Lichtenstein, Nelson, and Howell John Harris, eds. *Industrial Democracy in America: The Ambiguous Promise*. New York: Cambridge University Press, 1996.

Lieberman, Robbie. *"My Song Is My Weapon": People's Songs, American Communism, and the Politics of Culture, 1930–1950*. Urbana: University of Illinois Press, 1989.

Lincoln, C. Eric, and Lawrence H. Mamiya. *The Black Church in the African American Experience*. Durham: Duke University Press, 1990.

Link, William A. *The Paradox of Southern Progressivism, 1880–1930*. Chapel Hill: University of North Carolina Press, 1992.

Linn, Jo White. *The Gray Family and Allied Lines*. Salisbury, N.C.: Privately published, 1976.

———. *People Named Hanes*. Salisbury, N.C.: Privately published, 1980.

Lipsitz, George. *Class and Culture in Cold War America: "A Rainbow at Midnight."* South Hadley, Mass.: J. F. Bergin Publishers, 1982.

———. *A Life in the Struggle: Ivory Perry and the Culture of Opposition*. Philadelphia: Temple University Press, 1988.

Litwack, Leon F. *Trouble in Mind: Black Southerners in the Age of Jim Crow*. New York: Alfred A. Knopf, 1998.

Logan, Rayford W., ed. *What the Negro Wants*. Chapel Hill: University of North Carolina Press, 1944. Reprint, with a new introduction and bibliography by Kenneth Robert Janken, Notre Dame: University of Notre Dame Press, 2001.

Luebke, Paul. *Tar Heel Politics: Myths and Realities*. Chapel Hill: University of North Carolina Press, 1990.

Lynd, Staughton, ed. *"We Are All Leaders": The Alternative Unionism of the Early 1930s*. Urbana: University of Illinois Press, 1996.

Lyons, Paul. *Philadelphia Communists, 1936–1956*. Philadelphia: Temple University Press, 1982.

Mabry, William Alexander. *The Negro in North Carolina Politics since Reconstruction*. Durham: Duke University Press, 1940.

MacDougall, Curtis D. *Gideon's Army*. New York: Marzani and Munsell, 1965.

Marable, Manning. *Race, Reform, and Rebellion: The Second Reconstruction in Black America, 1945–1982*. Jackson: University Press of Mississippi, 1984.

Markowitz, Gerald, and David Rosner, eds. *"Slaves of the Depression": Workers' Letters about Life on the Job*. Ithaca: Cornell University Press, 1987.

Markowitz, Norman D. *The Rise and Fall of the People's Century: Henry A. Wallace and American Liberalism, 1941–1948*. New York: Free Press, 1973.

Marshall, F. Ray. *Labor in the South*. Cambridge: Harvard University Press, 1967.

———. *The Negro and Organized Labor*. New York: John Wiley and Sons, 1965.

———. *The Negro Worker*. New York: Random House, 1965.

Martin, Charles H. *The Angelo Herndon Case and Southern Justice*. Baton Rouge: Louisiana State University Press, 1976.

Mason, Lucy Randolph. *To Win These Rights: A Personal Story of the CIO in the South*. New York: Harper and Row, 1952.

Matles, James M., and James Higgins. *Them and Us: Struggles of a Rank-and-File Union*. Englewood Cliffs, N.J.: Prentice-Hall, 1974.

Matthews, Donald R., and James W. Prothro. *Negroes and the New Southern Politics*. New York: Harcourt, Brace and World, 1966.

Mayer, Barbara. *Reynolda: A History of an American Country House*. Winston-Salem: John F. Blair, 1997.

McAdam, Doug. *Political Process and the Development of Black Insurgency, 1930–1970*. Chicago: University of Chicago Press, 1982.

McAdam, Doug, Sidney Tarrow, and Charles Tilley. *Dynamics of Contention*. London: Cambridge University Press, 2001.

McKiven, Henry M., Jr. *Iron and Steel: Class, Race, and Community in Birmingham, Alabama, 1875–1920*. Chapel Hill: University of North Carolina Press, 1995.

McLaurin, Melton Alonza. *The Knights of Labor in the South*. Westport, Conn.: Greenwood Press, 1978.

McMillen, Neil R. *Dark Journey: Black Mississippians in the Age of Jim Crow.* Urbana: University of Illinois Press, 1989.

McWilliams, Carey. *Brothers under the Skin.* Rev. ed. Boston: Little, Brown, 1964.

Meier, August, and Elliot Rudwick. *Black Detroit and the Rise of the UAW.* New York: Oxford University Press, 1979.

Meyerson, Michael. *Nothing Could Be Finer.* New York: International Publishers, 1978.

Milkman, Ruth. *Gender at Work: The Dynamics of Job Segregation by Sex during World War II.* Urbana: University of Illinois Press, 1987.

Minchin, Timothy J. *The Color of Work: The Struggle for Civil Rights in the Southern Paper Industry, 1945–1980.* Chapel Hill: University of North Carolina Press, 2001.

―――. *What Do We Need a Union For? The TWUA in the South, 1945–1955.* Chapel Hill: University of North Carolina Press, 1997.

Mitchell, Harry L. *Mean Things Happening in This Land: The Life and Times of H. L. Mitchell, Co-Founder of the Southern Tenant Farmers Union.* Montclair, N.J.: Allanheld, Osmun, 1979.

Mitford, Jessica. *A Fine Old Conflict.* New York: Alfred A. Knopf, 1977.

Montgomery, David. *The Fall of the House of Labor: The Workplace, the State, and American Labor Activism, 1865–1925.* New York: Cambridge University Press, 1987.

―――. *Workers' Control in America: Studies in the History of Work, Technology, and Labor Struggles.* New York: Cambridge University Press, 1979.

Moon, Henry Lee. *Balance of Power: The Negro Vote.* Garden City, N.Y.: Doubleday, 1949.

Morgan, Edmund S. *American Slavery, American Freedom: The Ordeal of Colonial Virginia.* New York: Norton, 1995.

Morris, Aldon. *The Origins of the Civil Rights Movement: Black Communities Organizing for Change.* New York: Free Press, 1984.

Morrison, Joseph L. *Governor O. Max Gardner: A Power in North Carolina and New Deal Washington.* Chapel Hill: University of North Carolina Press, 1971.

Myrdal, Gunnar. *An American Dilemma: The Negro Problem and Modern Democracy.* New York: Harper and Row, 1944.

Naison, Mark. *Communists in Harlem during the Depression.* Urbana: University of Illinois Press, 1983.

National Education Department, Communist Party. *Theory and Practice of the Communist Party: First Course.* Marxist Study Series, vol. 1. New York: New Century Publishers, 1947.

Navasky, Victor S. *Naming Names.* New York: Viking Press, 1991.

Nelson, Bruce. *Divided We Stand: American Workers and the Struggle for Black Equality.* Princeton: Princeton University Press, 2001.

―――. *Workers on the Waterfront: Seamen, Longshoremen, and Unionism in the 1930s.* Urbana: University of Illinois Press, 1988.

Nelson, Daniel. *Management and Workers: Origins of the New Factory System in the United States, 1880–1920.* Madison: University of Wisconsin Press, 1975.

Nelson, Steve, James R. Barrett, and Rob Ruck. *Steve Nelson, American Radical.* Pittsburgh: University of Pittsburgh Press, 1981.

Newbold, N. C. *Five North Carolina Negro Educators.* Chapel Hill: University of North Carolina Press, 1939.

Noble, David F. *Forces of Production: A Social History of Industrial Automation.* New York: Alfred A. Knopf, 1984.

Noel, Mrs. Henry M., Jackson D. Wilson, and Mrs. Jackson D. Wilson. *Roaring Gap.* Winston-Salem: Excalibur Enterprises, 1976.

Norrell, Robert J. *Reaping the Whirlwind: The Civil Rights Movement in Tuskeegee.* New York: Alfred A. Knopf, 1985.

Northrup, Herbert. *Organized Labor and the Negro.* New York: Harper and Brothers, 1944.

Obadele-Starks, Ernest. *Black Unionism in the Industrial South.* College Station: Texas A&M University Press, 2000.

O'Brien, Gail Williams. *The Color of the Law: Race, Violence, and Justice in the Post–World War II South.* Chapel Hill: University of North Carolina Press, 1999.

Odum, Howard W. *Race and the Rumors of Race.* Baltimore: Johns Hopkins University Press, 1997.

Packer, Herbert L. *Ex-Communist Witness: Four Studies in Fact Finding.* Stanford: Stanford University Press, 1962.

Painter, Nell Irvin. *The Narrative of Hosea Hudson: His Life as a Negro Communist in the South.* Cambridge: Harvard University Press, 1979.

Payne, Charles. *I've Got the Light of Freedom: The Organizing Tradition and the Mississippi Freedom Struggle.* Berkeley: University of California Press, 1995.

Peale, Norman Vincent. *The Power of Positive Thinking.* Englewood Cliffs, N.J.: Prentice-Hall, 1952.

Peck, Sidney M. *The Rank-and-File Leader.* New Haven: College and University Press, 1963.

Petrone, Gerard S. *Tobacco Advertising: The Great Seduction.* Atglen, Pa.: Schiffer, 1996.

Pintzuk, Edward C. *Reds, Racial Justice, and Civil Liberties: Michigan Communists during the Cold War.* Minneapolis: Marxist Educational Press Publications, 1997.

Piven, Frances Fox, and Richard A. Cloward. *Poor People's Movements: Why They Succeed, How They Fail.* New York: Random House, 1977.

Pleasants, Julian M., and Augustus M. Burns III. *Frank Porter Graham and the 1950 Senate Race in North Carolina.* Chapel Hill: University of North Carolina Press, 1990.

Plotke, David. *Building a Democratic Political Order: Reshaping American Liberalism in the 1930s and 1940s.* New York: Cambridge University Press, 1996.

Polenberg, Richard. *America at War: The Home Front, 1941–1945.* Englewood Cliffs, N.J.: Prentice-Hall, 1968.

———. *War and Society: The United States, 1941–1945.* Philadelphia: J. B. Lippincott, 1972.

Powell, William, ed. *Dictionary of North Carolina Biography.* Chapel Hill: University of North Carolina Press, 1979–96.

Prather, H. Leon. *We Have Taken a City: Wilmington Racial Massacre and Coup of 1898.* Cranbury, N.J.: Associated University Presses, 1984.

Preece, Harold, and Celia Kraft. *Dew of Jordan.* New York: E. P. Dutton, 1946.

Prichard, Robert W. *Medicine.* Vol. 11 of *Winston-Salem in History,* edited by Manly Wade Wellman. Winston-Salem: Historic Winston-Salem, 1976.

Puryear, Elmer L. *Democratic Party Dissension in North Carolina, 1928–1936.* Chapel Hill: University of North Carolina Press, 1962.

Rabinowitz, Howard N. *Race Relations in the Urban South, 1865–1890.* New York: Oxford University Press, 1978.

Raboteau, Albert J. *Slave Religion: The "Invisible Institution" in the Antebellum South.* New York: Oxford University Press, 1978.

Rachleff, Peter. *Black Labor in the South: Richmond, Virginia, 1865–1890.* Philadelphia: Temple University Press, 1984.

Record, Wilson. *The Negro and the Communist Party.* Chapel Hill: University of North Carolina Press, 1951.

———. *Race and Radicalism: The NAACP and the Communist Party in Conflict.* Ithaca: Cornell University Press, 1964.

Redding, J. Saunders. *No Day of Triumph.* New York: Harper and Brothers, 1942.

Reed, Linda. *Simple Decency and Common Sense: The Southern Conference Movement, 1938–1963.* Bloomington: Indiana University Press, 1991.

Reich, Michael. *Racial Inequality: A Political-Economic Analysis.* Princeton: Princeton University Press, 1981.

Reynolds, Patrick, and Tom Shachtman. *The Gilded Leaf: Triumph, Tragedy, and Tobacco— Three Generations of the R. J. Reynolds Family and Fortune.* Boston: Little, Brown, 1989.

Richter, Irving. *Labor's Struggles, 1945–1950.* New York: Cambridge University Press, 1994.

Rifkin, Jeremy. *The End of Work: The Decline of the Global Labor Force and the Dawn of the Post-Market Era.* New York: G. P. Putnam's Sons, 1995.

Robert, Joseph C. *The Story of Tobacco in America.* Chapel Hill: University of North Carolina Press, 1967.

Robinson, Cedric J. *Black Marxism: The Making of the Black Radical Tradition.* London: Zed Press, 1983.

Robnett, Belinda. *How Long? How Long?: African-American Women in the Struggle for Civil Rights.* New York: Oxford University Press, 1997.

Roediger, David R. *Toward the Abolition of Whiteness.* London: Verso, 1994.

———. *The Wages of Whiteness: Race and the Making of the American Working Class.* London: Verso, 1991.

Rosengarten, Theodore. *All God's Dangers: The Life of Nate Shaw.* New York: Alfred A. Knopf, 1974.

Rosswurm, Steve, ed. *The CIO's Left-Led Unions.* New Brunswick: Rutgers University Press, 1992.

Ruck, Rob. *Sandlot Seasons: Sport in Black Pittsburgh.* Urbana: University of Illinois Press, 1987.

Ruiz, Vicki L. *Cannery Women, Cannery Lives: Mexican Women, Unionization, and the California Food Processing Industry, 1930–1950.* Albuquerque: University of New Mexico Press, 1987.

Rymer, Russ. *American Beach: A Saga of Race, Wealth, and Memory.* New York: Harper-Collins, 1998.

Salmond, John A. *Gastonia, 1929: The Story of the Loray Mill Strike.* Chapel Hill: University of North Carolina Press, 1995.

———. *Miss Lucy of the CIO: The Life and Times of Lucy Randolph Mason, 1882–1959.* Athens: University of Georgia Press, 1988.

———. *A Southern Rebel: The Life and Times of Aubrey Willis Williams, 1890–1965.* Chapel Hill: University of North Carolina Press, 1983.

Santino, Jack. *Miles of Smiles, Years of Struggle: Stories of Black Pullman Porters.* Urbana: University of Illinois Press, 1989.

Savage, Barbara Dianne. *Broadcasting Freedom: Radio, War, and the Politics of Race, 1938–1948*. Chapel Hill: University of North Carolina Press, 1999.

Scales, Junius Irving, and Richard Nickson. *Cause at Heart: A Former Communist Remembers*. Athens: University of Georgia Press, 1987.

Schatz, Ronald W. *The Electrical Workers: A History of Labor at General Electric and Westinghouse, 1923–60*. Urbana: University of Illinois Press, 1983.

Schrecker, Ellen. *The Age of McCarthyism: A Brief History with Documents*. Boston: Bedford Books of St. Martin's Press, 1994.

———. *Many Are the Crimes: McCarthyism in America*. Boston: Little, Brown, 1998.

———. *No Ivory Tower: McCarthyism and the Universities*. New York: Oxford University Press, 1986.

Scott, James C. *Weapons of the Weak: Everyday Forms of Peasant Resistance*. New Haven: Yale University Press, 1985.

Sensbach, Jon F. *A Separate Canaan: The Making of an Afro-Moravian World in North Carolina, 1763–1840*. Chapel Hill: University of North Carolina Press, 1998.

Shapiro, Herbert. *White Violence and Black Response: From Reconstruction to Montgomery*. Amherst: University of Massachusetts Press, 1988.

Shaw, Stephanie. *"What a Women Ought to Be and to Do": Black Professional Women during the Jim Crow Era*. Chicago: University of Chicago Press, 1996.

Shields, James M. *Just Plain Larnin'*. New York: Coward-McCann, 1934.

Shirley, Michael. *From Congregation Town to Industrial Community: Culture and Social Change in a Southern Community*. New York: New York University Press, 1994.

Siewers, Charles N. *Forsyth County: Economic and Social*. A Laboratory Study at the University of North Carolina, Department of Rural Social Economics. New Bern, N.C.: O. G. Dunn, 1924.

Simmons, Furnifold. *F. M. Simmons, Statesman of the New South: Memoirs and Addresses*. Edited by J. Fred Rippy. Durham: Duke University Press, 1936.

Simmons-Henry, Linda. *Heritage of Blacks*. Edited by Philip N. Henry and Carol M. Speas. Charlotte: North Carolina African American Heritage Foundation with the Cooperation of the Delmar Company, 1990.

Simon, Bryant. *A Fabric of Defeat: The Politics of South Carolina Millhands, 1910–1948*. Chapel Hill: University of North Carolina Press, 1998.

Sitkoff, Harvard. *A New Deal for Blacks: The Emergence of Civil Rights as a National Issue*. New York: Oxford University Press, 1978.

Smith, James Howell. *Industry and Commerce: 1896–1975*. Vol. 8 of *Winston-Salem in History*, edited by Manly Wade Wellman. Winston-Salem: Historic Winston-Salem, 1976.

Smith, Jane Webb. *Smoke Signals: Cigarette Advertising and the American Way of Life*. Chapel Hill: University of North Carolina Press, 1990.

Smith, Margaret Supplee, and Emily Herring Wilson. *North Carolina Women: Making History*. Chapel Hill: University of North Carolina at Chapel Hill, 1999.

Sobel, Richard. *They Satisfy: The Cigarette in American Life*. Garden City, N.Y.: Anchor Press/Doubleday, 1978.

Solomon, Mark I. *The Cry Was Unity: Communists and African Americans, 1917–1936*. Jackson: University Press of Mississippi, 1998.

Sosna, Morton. *In Search of the Silent South: Southern Liberals and the Race Issue*. New York: Columbia University Press, 1977.

Southern, David W. *Gunnar Myrdal and Black-White Relations.* Baton Rouge: Louisiana State University Press, 1987.

Spero, Sterling D., and Abram L. Harris. *The Black Worker: The Negro and the Labor Movement.* New York: Columbia University Press, 1931.

Starobin, Joseph R. *American Communism in Crisis, 1943–1957.* Cambridge: Harvard University Press, 1972.

Starobin, Robert S. *Industrial Slavery in the Old South.* New York: Oxford University Press, 1970.

Stein, Judith. *Running Steel, Running America: Race, Economic Policy, and the Decline of Liberalism.* Chapel Hill: University of North Carolina Press, 1998.

———. *The World of Marcus Garvey: Race and Class in Modern Society.* Baton Rouge: Louisiana State University Press, 1986.

Stepan-Norris, Judith, and Maurice Zeitlin. *Talking Union.* Urbana: University of Illinois Press, 1996.

Storrs, Landon R. *Civilizing Capitalism: The National Consumers' League, Women's Activism, and Labor Standards in the New Deal Era.* Chapel Hill: University of North Carolina Press, 2000.

Sugrue, Thomas J. *The Origins of the Urban Crisis: Race and Inequality in Postwar Detroit.* Princeton: Princeton University Press, 1996.

Sullivan, Patricia. *Days of Hope: Race and Democracy in the New Deal Era.* Chapel Hill: University of North Carolina Press, 1996.

Taft, Philip. *Organizing Dixie: Alabama Workers in the Industrial Era.* Revised and edited by Gary M. Fink. Westport, Conn.: Greenwood Press, 1981.

Tarrow, Sidney. *Power in Movement: Social Movements, Collective Action, and Politics.* New York: Cambridge University Press, 1994.

Taylor, Gwynne Stephens. *From Frontier to Factory: An Architectural History of Forsyth County.* Raleigh: North Carolina Division of Archives and History, 1981.

Tennant, Richard. *The American Cigarette Industry: A Study in Economic Analysis and Public Policy.* New Haven: Yale University Press, 1950.

Thomas, Audrey, and Elaine M. Smith, eds. *Mary McLeod Bethune: Building a Better World—Essays and Selected Documents.* Bloomington: University of Indiana Press, 1999.

Tilley, Nannie Mae. *The Bright-Tobacco Industry, 1860–1929.* Chapel Hill: University of North Carolina Press, 1948.

———. *The R. J. Reynolds Tobacco Company.* Chapel Hill: University of North Carolina Press, 1985.

———. *Reynolds Homestead, 1814–1970.* Richmond, Va.: R. Kline, 1970.

Tindall, George Brown. *The Emergence of the New South, 1913–1945.* Baton Rouge: Louisiana State University Press, 1967.

Tise, Larry Edward. *Building and Architecture.* Vol. 9 of *Winston-Salem in History*, edited by Manly Wade Wellman. Winston-Salem: Historic Winston-Salem, 1976.

———. *The Churches.* Vol. 10 of *Winston-Salem in History*, edited by Manly Wade Wellman. Winston-Salem: Historic Winston-Salem, 1976.

———. *Government.* Vol. 6 of *Winston-Salem in History*, edited by Manly Wade Wellman. Winston-Salem: Historic Winston-Salem, 1976.

———. *Publications.* Vol. 12 of *Winston-Salem in History*, edited by Manly Wade Wellman. Winston-Salem: Historic Winston-Salem, 1976.

Tomlins, Christopher L. *The State and the Unions: Labor Relations, Law, and the Organized Labor Movement in America, 1880–1960.* New York: Cambridge University Press, 1985.

Trotter, Joe William, Jr. *Black Milwaukee: The Making of an Industrial Proletariat.* Urbana: University of Illinois Press, 1985.

———. *Coal, Class, and Color: Blacks in Southern West Virginia, 1915–32.* Urbana: University of Illinois Press, 1990.

Tursi, Frank. *Winston-Salem: A History.* Winston-Salem: John F. Blair, 1994.

Tyson, Timothy B. *Radio Free Dixie: Robert F. Williams and the Roots of Black Power.* Chapel Hill: University of North Carolina Press, 1999.

Vittoz, Stanley. *New Deal Labor Policy and the American Industrial Economy.* Chapel Hill: University of North Carolina Press, 1987.

Von Eschen, Penny M. *Race against Empire: Black Americans and Anticolonialism, 1937–1957.* Ithaca: Cornell University Press, 1997.

Washington, Booker T. *The Booker T. Washington Papers.* Edited by Louis R. Harlan et al. Urbana: University of Illinois Press, 1981.

Waynick, Capus M., John C. Brooks, and Elsie W. Pitts, eds. *North Carolina and the Negro.* Raleigh: North Carolina Mayors' Co-operating Committee, 1964.

Weare, Walter B. *Black Business in the New South: A Social History of the North Carolina Mutual Life Insurance Company.* Urbana: University of Illinois Press, 1973.

Weaver, Robert C. *Negro Labor, a National Problem.* New York: Harcourt, Brace, 1946.

Weems, Robert E. *Desegregating the Dollar: African American Consumerism in the Twentieth Century.* New York: New York University Press, 1998.

Weinstein, Allen, and Alexander Vassiliev. *The Haunted Wood: Soviet Espionage in America—the Stalin Era.* New York: Random House, 1999.

Weiss, Nancy J. *The National Urban League, 1910–1940.* New York: Oxford University Press, 1974.

Wellman, Manly Wade. *The Founders: 1766–1775.* Vol. 1 of *Winston-Salem in History*, edited by Manly Wade Wellman. Winston-Salem: Historic Winston-Salem, 1966.

———. *Transportation and Commerce.* Vol. 4 of *Winston-Salem in History*, edited by Manly Wade Wellman. Winston-Salem: Historic Winston-Salem, 1976.

———. *The War Record.* Vol. 2 of *Winston-Salem in History*, edited by Manly Wade Wellman. Winston-Salem: Historic Winston-Salem, 1966.

Wellman, Manly Wade, and Larry Edward Tise. *A City's Culture: Painting, Music, Literature.* Vol. 5 of *Winston-Salem in History*, edited by Manly Wade Wellman. Winston-Salem: Historic Winston-Salem, 1976.

———. *Education.* Vol. 3 of *Winston-Salem in History*, edited by Manly Wade Wellman. Winston-Salem: Historic Winston-Salem, 1976.

———. *Industry and Commerce, 1766–1896.* Vol. 7 of *Winston-Salem in History*, edited by Manly Wade Wellman. Winston-Salem: Historic Winston-Salem, 1976.

Western North Carolina Conference of the Methodist Church. *Journal of the 1967 Session.* Western North Carolina Annual Conference of the Methodist Church, 1967.

White, Deborah G. *Too Heavy a Load: Black Women in Defense of Themselves, 1894–1994.* New York: W. W. Norton, 1999.

Who's Who. New York: St. Martin's Press, 1948–49.

Who's Who in Colored America. New York: Who's Who in Colored America Corporation, 1950.

Widick, B. J. *Detroit: City of Race and Class Violence.* Detroit: Wayne State University Press, 1989.

Wilkes, Alfred W. *Little Boy Black.* New York: Charles Scribner's Sons, 1971.

Williamson, Joel. *The Crucible of Race: Black-White Relations in the American South since Emancipation.* New York: Oxford University Press, 1984.

Willmann, John B. *The Department of Housing and Urban Development.* New York: Praeger, 1967.

Wilson, Charles, and William Ferris, eds. *Encyclopedia of Southern Culture.* Chapel Hill: University of North Carolina Press, 1989.

Winkler, John K. *Tobacco Tycoon: The Story of James Buchanan Duke.* New York: Random House, 1942.

Wood, Phillip J. *Southern Capitalism: The Political Economy of North Carolina.* Durham: Duke University Press, 1986.

Woodward, C. Vann. *Origins of the New South, 1877–1913.* Baton Rouge: Louisiana State University Press, 1951.

———. *The Strange Career of Jim Crow.* 3d ed. New York: Oxford University Press, 1974.

Wright, Gavin. *Old South, New South: Revolutions in the Southern Economy since the Civil War.* New York: Basic Books, 1986.

Wright, Richard. *Black Boy.* New York: Harper and Brothers, 1945; reprint, New York: Harper and Row, 1966.

Yaeger, Patricia. *Dirt and Desire: Reconstructing Southern Women's Writing, 1930–1990.* Chicago: University of Chicago Press, 2000.

Young, Douglas M. *Morobullia: Seventy-Five Years of Winston-Salem Rotary.* Winston-Salem: Winston-Salem Rotary Club, 1992.

Zahavi, Gerald. *Workers, Managers, and Welfare Capitalism: The Shoeworkers and Tanners of Endicott Johnson, 1890–1950.* Urbana: University of Illinois Press, 1988.

Zieger, Robert H. *The CIO, 1935–1955.* Chapel Hill: University of North Carolina Press, 1995.

———, ed. *Organized Labor in the Twentieth-Century South.* Knoxville: University of Tennessee Press, 1981.

Zogry, Kenneth Joel. *The University's Living Room: A History of the Carolina Inn.* Chapel Hill: University of North Carolina, 1999.

Conference Papers, Dissertations, and Theses

Anderson, David M. "The Battle for Main Street U.S.A.: Welfare Capitalism, Boosterism, and Labor Violence in the Industrial Heartland, 1896–1963." Ph.D. diss., University of North Carolina at Chapel Hill, 2002.

Badger, Tony. "The Transformation of North Carolina: From Kerr Scott to Jesse Helms." Harrelson Lecture, North Carolina State University, Raleigh, N.C., November 3, 1997.

Boyette, Lawrence J. "Mine Mill in the South, 1933–1950: A New Analysis." Senior thesis, University of North Carolina at Chapel Hill, 1983.

Brown, Elsa Barkley. "Uncle Ned's Children: Richmond, Virginia's Black Community, 1890–1930." Ph.D. diss., Kent State University, 1994.

Brown, Leslie. "Common Spaces, Separate Lives: Gender and Racial Conflict in the 'Capital of the Black Middle Class.'" Ph.D. diss., Duke University, 1997.

Burns, Augustus M., III. "North Carolina and the Negro Dilemma." Ph.D. diss., University of North Carolina at Chapel Hill, 1969.

Carlson, Craig. "Frank Porter Graham and the National War Labor Board." Unpublished paper, University of North Carolina at Chapel Hill, 1993. In possession of author.

Clark, Wayne Addison. "An Analysis of the Relationship between Anti-Communism and Segregationist Thought in the Deep South, 1948–1964." Ph.D. diss., University of North Carolina at Chapel Hill, 1976.

Dunston, Aingred Ghislayne. "The Black Struggle for Equality in Winston-Salem, 1947–1977." Ph.D. diss., Duke University, 1981.

Emspak, Frank. "The Break-Up of the Congress of Industrial Organizations (CIO), 1945–1950." Ph.D. diss., University of Wisconsin, 1972.

Fehn, Bruce. "Striking Women: Gender, Race, and Class in the United Packinghouse Workers of America, 1938–1968." Ph.D. diss., University of Wisconsin at Madison, 1991.

Fields, Barbara J., and Fields, Karen. "Remarks at Closing Plenary Session." Presented at the Fourth Southern Conference on Women's History, Southern Association for Women Historians, Charleston, S.C., June 14, 1997.

Frederickson, Mary Evans. "A Place to Speak Our Minds: The Southern School for Women Workers." Ph.D. diss., University of North Carolina at Chapel Hill, 1981.

Glenn, Joanne. "The Winston-Salem Riot of 1918." Master's thesis, University of North Carolina at Chapel Hill, 1979.

Goldfield, Michael. "The Failure of Operation Dixie: A Critical Turning Point in American Political Development." Presented at the Seventh Southern Labor Studies Conference, Atlanta, Ga., October 10–13, 1991.

Haessly, Jo Lynne. "Mill Mother's Lament: Ella May, Working Women's Militancy, and the 1929 Gaston County Strikes." Master's thesis, University of North Carolina at Chapel Hill, 1987.

Huntley, Horace. "Iron Ore Miners and the Mine Mill in Alabama: 1933–1952." Ph.D. diss., University of Pittsburgh, 1977.

Jones, Craig T. "Communism, Rheumatism, and Cigarettes: The Roots of Revolution in the New South." Honor thesis, Brown University, 1983.

Jones, William Powell. "Cutting through Jim Crow: African American Lumber Workers in the Jim Crow South, 1919–1960." Ph.D. diss., University of North Carolina at Chapel Hill, 2000.

Korstad, Karl. "An Account of the 'Left-Led' CIO Unions' Efforts to Build Unity among the Workers in Southern Factories during the 1940s." Presented at the Civil Rights Seminar conducted by Professors William Chafe and Lawrence Goodwyn, Duke University, Durham, N.C., April 9, 1979.

Korstad, Robert Rodgers. "Daybreak of Freedom: Tobacco Workers and the CIO, Winston-Salem, North Carolina, 1943–1950." Ph.D. diss., University of North Carolina at Chapel Hill, 1987.

Miller, Bertha Hampton. "Blacks in Winston-Salem, North Carolina, 1895–1920: Community Development in an Era of Benevolent Paternalism." Ph.D. diss., Duke University, 1981.

Modell, John. "Why War Engenders Social Change: Black Americans and Military Service in WWII." Presented at the Institute for Research in Social Science, University of North Carolina at Chapel Hill, April 7, 1987.

Obadele-Starks, Ernest. "The Black Working and Middle Classes and the Politics of Racial Separatism along the Upper Texas Gulf Coast, 1883–1945." Presented at the Southern Historical Association Conference, Birmingham, Ala., November 13, 1998.

Ramsey, Sonya Yvette. "More Than the Three R's: The Educational, Economic, and Cultural Experiences of African American Female Public School Teachers in Nashville, Tennessee, 1869 to 1983." Ph.D. diss., University of North Carolina at Chapel Hill, 2000.

Reagon, Bernice Johnson. "Songs of the Civil Rights Movement, 1955–1965: A Study in Cultural History." Ph.D. diss., Howard University, 1975.

Ritterhouse, Jennifer Lynn. "Learning Race: Racial Etiquette and the Socialization of Children in the Jim Crow South." Ph.D. diss., University of North Carolina at Chapel Hill, 1999.

Rosswurm, Steve. "Communism and the CIO: An Assessment." Presented at the "Perspectives on Labor History: The Wisconsin School and Beyond" conference of the State Historical Society of Wisconsin, Madison, March 9–10, 1990.

Sparks, Holloway. "Dissident Citizenship: Lessons on Democracy and Courage from Activist Women." Ph.D. diss., University of North Carolina at Chapel Hill, 1999.

Steelman, Joseph Flake. "The Progressive Era in North Carolina, 1884–1917." Ph.D. diss., University of North Carolina at Chapel Hill, 1955.

Thomas, Karen Kruse. "The Wound of My People: Segregation and the Modernization of Health Care in North Carolina, 1935–1975." Ph.D. diss., University of North Carolina at Chapel Hill, 1999.

Troxell, John P. "Labor in the Tobacco Industry." Ph.D. diss., University of Wisconsin, 1931.

Uesugi, Sayoko. "'Jim Crow Must Go!': Women's Activism, the Cold War, and the Making of the Progressive Party in North Carolina, 1945–1948." Master's thesis, University of North Carolina at Chapel Hill, 1997.

Urmann, Michael Francis. "Rank and File Communists and the CIO (Committee for Industrial Organization) Unions." Ph.D. diss., University of Utah, 1981.

Walker, Harry J. "Changes in Race Accommodation in a Southern Community." Ph.D. diss., University of Chicago, 1945.

Warlick, Robert P. "Organization of the Leaf-House Workers in the Bright-Leaf Tobacco Belt by the CIO." Unpublished paper, Rutgers University, 1948. In possession of author.

Windham, Lane. "Greenhands: A History of Local 10 of the Food, Tobacco, and Agricultural Allied Workers of America in Greenville, N.C., 1946." Senior thesis, Duke University, 1991.

Workman, Andrew. "Creating the Center: Liberal Intellectuals, the National War Labor Board, and the Stabilization of American Industrial Relations, 1941–1945." Ph.D. diss., University of North Carolina at Chapel Hill, 1993.

ACKNOWLEDGMENTS

Learning the craft of history takes much time and many teachers. I have been blessed to have had both in abundance. The time came from the generous support of institutions. Wise tutors always seemed to be there when I needed them. Writing *Civil Rights Unionism* has been a long journey, and the route has been circuitous, but it has been rewarding each step of the way.

My greatest teachers have been my parents, Karl and Frances Korstad, who participated in the final battle to retain Local 22 as the bargaining agent for workers at Reynolds. They met in Charleston, South Carolina, during the war. Karl, whose parents were Norwegian and Scotch-Irish, grew up in the small towns of northern Minnesota. The war cut short his graduate studies in English literature (which introduced him to the Marxist literary critics that he so respected), and he landed in Charleston, writing press reports for the army. Frances had grown up across the harbor on James Island, where the Rodgers family ran a nursery business. She had graduated from the College of Charleston and worked on a graduate degree in social work at Tulane before returning to a job with the Charleston County welfare office.

When FTA Local 15 struck the American Tobacco Company plant in Charleston, Karl and some of his army buddies started raising money and handing out leaflets for the strikers. When the war ended, FTA president Donald Henderson offered him a job as the business agent for Local 10 in Memphis, Tennessee. In 1947 Karl became Southeast regional director for FTA, and he and Frances moved to Raleigh and then to Carrboro, North Carolina. Frances worked as a volunteer in the Progressive Party campaign while she was pregnant with me, and Karl put thousands of miles on the car negotiating contracts and meeting union members from Virginia to Florida. In 1949 they moved to Winston-Salem. Karl joined the organizing staff there as the union desperately tried to recruit white workers. His assistant, Moranda Smith, was the first black woman to become a regional director for an international union.

By the time I became conscious of the world, the fight for Local 22 had been lost and the left-wing labor movement was in retreat. Although a union job awaited Karl in New York, my parents decided they wanted to stay in the South and make whatever contribution they could. They moved to nearby Greensboro and borrowed money and plants from my grandfather in Charleston. In a rented storefront with an apartment in the rear, they opened Sedgefield Garden Center and started selling bedding plants, seeds, and shrubs. A few years later they bought four acres down the highway and built a shop and a home for my recently arrived brother David and me. My father took up the shovel and hoe by day while maintaining his voracious intellectual curiosity at night. My mother minded the store and the house and read alongside him when the chores were done.

Having lost the mass movement that made his Marxism come alive, Karl returned to the books and writing that had been his original entrée to the culture and politics of the left. From then on, he was always reading three or four books at a time: fiction, history, politics, and literary criticism. He also continued to write, although the short stories he sent to the *New Yorker* got returned and the opinion pieces seemed never to get published. Frances, herself an ardent reader and political observer to this day, put her formidable social skills to work developing a new network of friends and keeping us connected to her large extended family.

Our record collection included Chopin's nocturnes and preludes, but there were also albums by Pete Seeger, Woody Guthrie, Paul Robeson, and even the Red Army Band. The hardback copies of Marx, Lenin, and Stalin in my father's study must have startled some of my parent's new middle-class friends who came to parties and dinners. But I don't remember anyone ever saying anything about them, and they were still there when the house burned down in 1973. Actually, the neighbors probably found his large collection of English literature just as odd.

The FBI's periodic visits must have been chilling, but Karl and Frances did not allow them to intrude on our lives. Then, in 1958, eight years after the demise of Local 22, the House Committee on Un-American Activities called Karl to testify at one of its final hearings in Atlanta. All I remember about the trip was the swimming pool at the motel. But the *Greensboro Daily News* made sure that everyone in town knew about it with a picture and front-page story. A few customers called to say that they would no longer be requiring our services, but the company had developed a loyal following and most people turned a blind eye.

Robert "Chick" Black, the cochairman and one of the key leaders of Local 22, worked alongside my parents. I first became aware of the daily humiliations of Jim Crow because of him. One summer, when I was twelve or so and helping Chick with a landscaping job, I wanted to eat at the newly opened McDonald's. Chick pulled into the parking lot and handed me some money for his lunch, explaining that I would have to go to the window since McDonald's didn't serve blacks. Although I remember being disturbed by this, segregation was such a routine aspect of my world that I wasn't especially surprised. I came back to the truck with our fifteen-cent hamburgers and we ate them there. I hope I felt embarrassed by my insistence on eating at a place where he couldn't be served. I hadn't been out on the truck much before, and I'm sure we usually took our lunch with us; at least Chick and other black workmen did.

I don't remember many such incidents, for Chick was a masterful navigator of the etiquette of Jim Crow. He also exuded a dignity and presence that rebuffed most insults before they could occur. The charm and strength that had made Chick a great mass leader and a formidable foe of Winston-Salem's industrialists served him well in his dealings with Greensboro's white elite, in whose yards we worked.

In subtle and not so subtle ways I was being brought up to continue Karl, Frances, and

Chick's struggle. They didn't hide their history or beliefs, but neither did they dwell on the past. They were neither bitter nor boastful. They were keen observers, always interested in the present, to which they brought a critical yet always generous eye. They resolutely thrust themselves into a new social world, practicing their politics in quiet ways, primarily in the education of their children and their support of the civil rights, antiwar, and cultural politics of my generation. Karl, in particular, took it upon himself to bring unfamiliar ideas, ways of seeing, and interpretations into his conversations, whether he was talking to members of our extended family, his colleagues in the landscaping business, or the hoards of young people who passed through their business for over forty years.

Chick was also a patient teacher, about how to trim boxwoods or spread pine needles, how to cope with injustice, and, most important, how to live with dignity and decency in an imperfect world. My parents taught me by example and instruction. But I am sure that Chick's affirmation and personification of those same democratic lessons helped to burn them in my soul.

I went off to the University of North Carolina at Chapel Hill in the fall of 1967 and soon became involved in the antiwar movement. Although I didn't make much connection between what I was doing and my parents' past (we were the "New Left," after all), I soon found myself reading many of the same writers that my father always read, and I even developed an interest in the Marxist literary critiques he studied in graduate school. As I looked to combine my activism with my scholarly interests, however, I never envisioned that I would become the chronicler of his union days.

After a few years spent living in Boston in the early 1970s and trying to figure out what to do with my life, I decided I needed a more structured environment for my political studies. I enrolled in a master's program at the Graduate Faculty at the New School for Social Research in New York, where my professors included Robert Heilbroner, David Gordon, Heidi Hartman, and Harry Cleaver. My classmates were mostly a fascinating group of twenty-somethings, veterans of the recent student mobilization with more questions than answers at that point. The courses in economic history, political economy, and labor economics were just what I needed to help me understand what was going on in the world. The effort to unite theory and practice came together in a weekly study group whose goal was to read Marx's *Capital* "politically," that is, to understand how Marx's theory grew out of his revolutionary practice and to see how *Capital* could be applied to the struggles in the 1970s. The group included Peter Bell, Rich Bethel, Harry Cleaver, Bill Cleaver, Amy Hirsh, Rick McGahey, Phil Mattera, and Rayna Rapp, and I have often drawn on those discussions in writing *Civil Rights Unionism*.

Casting around for a topic for my master's paper, I "discovered" FTA. I wrote the thesis as part of a labor economics class with David Gordon, one of the founders of the Union for Radical Political Economics and a leading leftist critic of American domestic policy until his death in 1996. David helped me to refocus my paper from a rambling institutional history of FTA to a case study of the tobacco workplace. He was very patient as I struggled to put some of the pieces together, and his comments on the final draft greatly influenced the direction of the later work. He lived a few blocks down from me on East Tenth Street and went out of his way to make me feel welcome in the city.

After I finished my master's paper, I begin to think that the story of Local 22 might be expanded into a book. I wrote to a few historians and publishers and sent a description to Bob

Conrad, a friend from my Chapel Hill days who had just taken a job in economics and public policy at Duke University. He passed it on to Carol Stack, who in turn showed it to William Chafe and Lawrence Goodwyn, history professors and directors of Duke's Oral History Project. In the summer of 1978, they offered me a six-month fellowship so that I could come to Durham and work on the project.

The Oral History Project's office, overseen by Thelma Kithcart, was home base for a number of African American graduate students and a meeting place for Bill and Larry's many friends and colleagues. Bill Chafe, whose book on the civil rights movement in Greensboro was about to come out, was extremely supportive and encouraging. He has remained a good friend, a mentor, and a colleague, and our collaboration, along with Ray Gavins, on "Behind the Veil: Documenting African American Life in the Jim Crow South," a project for the Center for Documentary Studies at Duke, has deepened my insight into the era of segregation. Although I had reservations about returning to graduate school, Bill convinced me that additional training would improve my work. Little did I imagine that one day I would end up back at Duke as a tenured professor. I can't imagine how I could ever thank him for his encouragement and inspiration. I hope this book is at least partial payment.

I gave Larry Goodwyn an early draft of Chapter 1. We met mid-afternoon at a deli off campus and proceeded to drink a few beers and smoke a pack of cigarettes. Although I had given Larry the manuscript a few days earlier, I don't think that he had read it. He took it from a stack of papers, found a black felt-tipped pen in his pocket, and over the next few hours brought me down to earth. I try not to remember how bloodless the prose was; I threw those early drafts away. But without making me feel incapable, Larry prodded me toward a drastic rewriting of the chapter. I learned a lot about being a historian and a writer in those few hours, and any trace of verisimilitude that exists in this book is there in part because of that encounter. Larry's books on Populism and Solidarity have been guideposts in my own work.

Coming back to Chapel Hill for graduate study in history changed my life. Having majored in political science as an undergraduate and studied economics in graduate school, I was overwhelmed by the study of *all* of American history and wondered what the colonial period could possible say to me about the twentieth-century world. But I became enchanted with the study of history, in large part because of the faculty and my graduate student peers. In courses taught by Bill Barney, Leon Fink, Don Mathews, John Nelson, Nell Painter, and Joan Scott, and by Peter Wood at Duke, I began to understand the political importance of the past. Among my student colleagues, Wayne Durrill and Jim Leloudis, in particular, taught me how to think historically. Wayne and I took our comprehensive exams together, but Jim, who had taken his the previous year, worked with us every step of the way as we tried to craft our own synthetic overview. Jim, who is now on the UNC faculty, has remained a close friend and constant collaborator. We have team taught joint classes with Duke and UNC students and are coauthoring a history of antipoverty activism in North Carolina in the 1960s.

In the fall of 1982 I started working on a dissertation about Local 22. But before I had gotten very far, I embarked on a different, and tremendously rewarding, project. A group that had gathered around the Southern Oral History Program at UNC decided to write a book based on interviews the program had recently completed with industrial workers in the Piedmont. It was a risky venture, but I welcomed the opportunity to work collaboratively and to try to write a book that workers, as well as scholars, might read. Chris Daly, Jacquelyn Hall, Lu Ann Jones, Jim Leloudis, and Mary Murphy, my coauthors on *Like a Family: The Making of a Southern Cotton Mill World*, taught me so much about being a writer and a historian. *Civil Rights Unionism* is a child of *Like a Family*, and they all share in its parentage.

A predoctoral fellowship at the Smithsonian Institution's National Museum of American History provided an opportunity to really launch my dissertation, but, more important, it gave me a new community of scholars who challenged me in new ways. My Smithsonian mentor, Pete Daniel, was at the center of a large social network that included Rob Snyder, Hartmut Keil, Chris Clark, Peter Kuznick, Sally Stein, and others. Pete had also worked at Reynolds one summer while he was a student at Wake Forest, and his comments on my work were informed by his personal experiences and deep knowledge of southern history. He has continued to be a close friend and colleague. It was also during this year in Washington that Jacquelyn Hall and I began our lifelong partnership. But more on her later.

My dissertation committee consisted of Larry Goodwyn, Nell Painter, Peter Coclanis, Don Reid, and Leon Fink. Leon served as my advisor, but he was so much more than that. As a student and a teaching assistant, I had the opportunity to learn from his deep knowledge and understanding of American workers and their past. His work on the Knights of Labor and Local 1199 deeply influenced the questions I asked about events in Winston-Salem. We also became close friends, sharing our mutual interests in gardening, squash, and Tar Heel basketball, as well as history. Leon and his wife, Susan Levine, welcomed me into their family and nurtured me with many years of food, talk, and laughter. The thoughtful criticisms of each person on my committee provided the road map I have followed in turning the dissertation into a book.

While in Washington, I had gotten to know Nelson Lichtenstein, who was teaching at Catholic University. He had started work on his biography of Walter Reuther, and we talked about the similarities between Local 22 and Local 600 of the United Auto Workers and the important role that black workers and their unions had played in the civil rights activism of the 1940s. We presented a paper together at the 1986 meeting of the Southern Historical Association. Buoyed by the comments of Sara Evans and Harvard Sitkoff, we then published a revised version in the *Journal of American History*. Much of the framework we hammered out in comparing Winston-Salem and Detroit remains at the heart of *Civil Rights Unionism*.

In 1990–91 a fellowship from the National Endowment for the Humanities allowed me to join Jacquelyn in Palo Alto, California, where she was a fellow at the Center for Advanced Study in the Behavioral Sciences. The staff and the other fellows, particularly Associate Director Bob Scott, welcomed us warmly. For me, a critical aspect of that experience was another fruitful collaboration with Larry Griffin, a professor of sociology at Vanderbilt University and an expert on labor and labor relations. We prepared a conference paper on how the events in Winston-Salem helped delineate the complex relationship between race, class, and gender identity and subsequently published two articles together. *Civil Rights Unionism* greatly benefits from Larry's sociologist's gaze.

When we returned to North Carolina, I began teaching part-time in Public Policy Studies at Duke and, along with Bill Chafe and Ray Gavins, directing the Behind the Veil project at the Center for Documentary Studies. The graduate students who served as research coordinators on that project, Leslie Brown, Annie Valk, and Paul Ortiz, shaped the project fundamentally. I am deeply grateful to my coeditors on *Remembering Jim Crow: African Amer-*

icans Talk about Life in the Segregated South—Bill Chafe, Ray Gavins, Paul Ortiz, Robert Parrish, Jennifer Ritterhouse, Keisha Roberts, and Nicole Waligora-Davis. Ray, like Bill, has been a valuable mentor, colleague, and friend. I also want to thank Iris Tillman Hill for her leadership at the center and her commitment to the Behind the Veil project.

In the fall of 1994, I began teaching full-time as an assistant professor in Public Policy Studies and became director of the Hart Leadership Program. My colleagues in Public Policy have always been supportive and encouraging, particularly Bruce Kuniholm, who, as chair of the department and as the only other historian, has helped me understand the role of historical thinking in public policy making. Phil Cook and Bruce Jentleson, who have succeeded Bruce as departmental chairs during the past six years, have supported me at every turn. My colleagues in the Hart Leadership Program were amazingly tolerant when I needed time to work on "the book." Thanks to Alma Blount, Bridget Booher, Tony Brown, Teddie Brown, Kirk Felsman, Alex Harris, Susan King, Joy Mischley, and Bruce Payne.

I have had the privilege of working with a number of excellent graduate assistants over the years. Lisa Hazirjian has served as an insightful reader, interviewer, and researcher. Derek Chang helped greatly with the research on life in Winston-Salem's African American community. Kathy Walbert, Bruce Baker, Melyn Glusman, Katie Otis, Andy Arnold, Tim Timmons, Rod Clare, and Dave Anderson all provided important assistance at key times.

A number of history colleagues have read and commented on this project. Jim Barrett, Mark Naison, and Garry Gerstle provided insightful comments on the dissertation. Nancy Hewitt, Steven Lawson, Syd Nathans, Howell Harris, Bruce Nelson, Bryant Simon, and Mike Honey read various drafts of the book. Glenda Gilmore has shared in many lively discussions about race and politics in North Carolina. Her work has been a model of engaged scholarship, and her comments on this manuscript have made it better in ways big and small.

Fellowships from the Duke/UNC Center for Research on Women and the National Endowment for the Humanities allowed me uninterrupted time for writing. The staffs of the many archives and libraries I have used over the years have been indispensable. Many thanks to Robert Anthony, Alice Cotton, and Harry McKown at the North Carolina Collection and John White at the Southern Historical Collection, both at the University of North Carolina at Chapel Hill.

As this project moved toward closure, I had the great good fortune to connect with Grey Osterud, whose historical insights and editorial talents immensely improved the book. It is hard to imagine how I could have finished the journey without David Perry, who somehow combined the qualities of an astute editor with those of a great friend. I feel privileged to have worked with the University of North Carolina Press on two book projects. Each experience has deepened my respect for that premier institution. The Press's Mary Lauer, Mark Simpson-Vos, Mary Reid, and Ron Maner have helped make this book a reality.

Another stroke of good luck occurred when Gerda Lerner took up part-time residence in Chapel Hill. She read the final manuscript with a fine, writerly eye, and her suggestions helped me wrestle the manuscript into its final shape.

Kathleen Kearns and Mike Sistrom also stepped in to make this project, like everything I have done, a collaborative work. Kathleen helped to prepare the photographs. To say that Mike painstakingly checked the footnotes is an understatement: he worked with me, sometimes day and night, to prepare a book that has evolved over many years, and through many moves and technological changes, for press. I am grateful to them both.

I owe a great debt to the men and women who "brought that big giant down to earth" and who made the history I write about. They helped me tell their story. I can only hope that that telling helps keep their struggle alive.

Finally, to Jacquelyn, my wife and fellow chronicler of the insurgent South. These few words cannot begin to convey my deep appreciation for her love and support over the years. She has endured countless conversations, endless drafts, and the vicissitudes of historical research and writing with patience and humor. But more than that, she engaged the project with the passion and wisdom that infuse her own work. This book and my life are so much richer thanks to her.

INDEX

Italic page numbers refer to illustrations.

strike of 1947, 316–17; and National Urban League, 377; and Committee of 100, 380

Black churches: as support base, 3; and civil rights movement, 11; and Tobacco Workers Organizing Committee, 22, 27, 30–31, 32, 39; and black community, 30–31, 85–86; and Jim Crow laws, 60; and segregation, 75; and class inequalities, 79, 86–87; and black working class, 87, 92, 164; and political activism, 87, 139–40, 161; and DeBerry, 152, 153; and women's leadership, 155; and union organizing, 158, 241, 353, 391; and Wellman, 161; and Emancipation Day, 234; millennialism of, 274; and commercial laundries workers, 304; and strike of 1947, 315, 316, 331; and race relations, 414

Black community: and black churches, 30–31, 85–86; and rural migration, 78; and racial solidarity, 91, 164–65, 405; and relief, 335; and union's standing, 337, 376; and segregation, 345; and class solidarity, 357; and Wallace, 358, 360; and Community Relations Project, 379; leadership of, 379–80, 469 (n. 34)

Black elites: and education, 76–78; and leadership, 78–79; and morality, 87; and public debate about union, 181–86; and Emergency Citizens Committee, 198

Black history, 233, 234

Black men: and racial division of labor, 95; and white women, 95, 134, 160, 241–47, 281, 319; and gender division of labor, 96; education of, 105; and marriage, 105; and workers' ages, 105; and sexual exploitation of women, 110; and foremen, 111; stereotypes of, 117, 339

Black middle class: and unionization, 1, 132, 165, 259, 306, 337; and Winston-Salem politics, 9; in Winston-Salem, 61; neighborhoods of, 78, 80–81, 183; and rural migration, 78–79; and black business, 79–80; and social welfare programs, 82–83; and black churches, 86, 87; and Jim Crow, 91; and racial division of

labor, 97; and black tobacco workers, 141; and black working class, 164–65, 184, 415; and public debate about union, 183, 184, 190, 196, 198; and Emergency Citizens Committee, 196, 198; and race relations, 259; and Local 22, 329, 368, 407, 408; and Progressive Party, 367; and white supremacy, 376, 380; and Community Relations Project, 379; leadership of, 379–80; and white elites, 406; and gradualism, 415; and civil rights movement, 418

Black nationalism, 123, 355

Black neighborhoods: and black working class, 71, 74–75, 81–82, 82, 84, 369, 373, 435 (n. 49); and pocket neighborhoods, 71; map of, 72; conditions of, 74, 75, 81–82, 84, 373; and segregation, 74–75, 373; and black middle class, 78, 80–81, 183; and white press, 373–74

Black Panther Party, 415

Black press, 142, 234

Blacks: and labor movement, 4; and voter registration, 51, 264, 383, 386, 414; and class inequalities, 79, 183–84; and Comintern, 123; and United Cannery, Agricultural, Packing, and Affiliated Workers of America–Congress of Industrial Organizations, 149; stereotypes of, 208; and sports, 235–36; and Communist Party, 268, 326; and Wallace, 359

Black sharecroppers, 144

Blackshear, Benny, 114

Black tobacco workers: and civil rights, 1, 4; and R. J. Reynolds Tobacco, 2; and union organizing, 37, 99–100, 121, 131, 276, 443 (n. 29); white textile workers compared with, 43–44; and drive system, 47; and racial subordination, 48–49; and rural migration, 61; and education, 69–70; and racial division of labor, 95, 96–98, 103, 438 (n. 12); education of, 105; and music, 118–19; and union contracts, 130; and black middle class, 141; and public debate about union, 183, 186; and political activism, 188, 255, 258–59, 297; and sports, 236, 236; and Communist Party,

268, 269, 340–41; and strike of 1947, 312, 313–14, 318; and kinship networks, 347; and unemployment, 369; and Peace, 391–92; and Kenneth R. Williams, 405. *See also* Foremen-worker relations

Black voters: disfranchisement of, 49, 51–54, 60, 90, 138, 162, 383; and Democratic Party, 137, 139, 252, 361, 385, 443 (n. 43), 444 (n. 47); and voter registration, 138, 139, 162; mobilization of, 143; and diluting black vote, 383; and gerrymandering tactics, 383–84, 469 (n. 53)

Black women: and Republican Party, 49; and domestic service, 70–71, 73, 91, 106, 371, 434 (n. 22); and rural migration, 70–71, 87–88; and education, 79, 165, 232, 435 (n. 43); and black churches, 86, 90, 232; leadership of, 86, 90–91, 155, 380, 404; stereotypes of, 87, 173; and gender division of labor, 95; and racial division of labor, 95; and commercial laundry workers, 304; and Progressive Party, 360

Black women tobacco workers: percentage of, 2, 71, 434 (n. 22); and stemming, 14–18, 277, 442 (n. 27); and stemmers' sitdown strike, 17–29; and Tobacco Workers Organizing Committee, 17; and foremen, 38, 109–10, 173; textile workers compared to, 44; and leaf houses, 71, 106, 189–90; and leadership, 90–91, 155, 165, 232, 252; and domestic service, 91; and gender division of labor, 95, 96, 173; ages of, 105; education of, 105, 165; and marriage, 105–6; and working conditions, 107, 108; and sexual favors, 117; and stemmers' sit-down strike negotiations, 171; and racial division of labor, 172; and shop floor democracy, 218; and Mathews, 323; and layoffs, 369, 370; and unemployment problem, 372. *See also* Foremen-worker relations

Black working class: and union organizing, 37, 142, 143; and rural migration, 68–70, 105; in Winston-Salem, 68–92, 433 (n. 19); and black neighborhoods, 71, 74–75, 81–82, *82*, 84, 369, 373, 435 (n. 49); and Jim

Crow laws, 71, 75, 92; and proletarianization, 71, 73, 434 (n. 27); and health care, 84–85; and black churches, 87, 92, 164; and entertainment, 88–89; and sports, 89–90; and black nationalism, 123; and wages, 127; and political activism, 162, 163, 164–65, 224, 382; and black middle class, 164–65, 184, 415; stereotypes of, 209, 224; and leadership, 380; and alderman candidate, 405–6; and poverty, 418

Blaine, J. S., 139, 140, 185, 384

Blakely, Evan, 226, 244

Blevins, Eva, 208, 220–21

Blue Monday, 114

Blum, Jewel, 409

Bonaparte, Carnell, 171, 175

Bonneau, Anna Lee, 239

Bonner, Herbert, 337, 339

Boulware, Wardell, 105

Bourbon Democrats, 5, 291

Branon, Neil, 208

British-American Tobacco Company, 190

Brotherhood of Sleeping Car Porters–AFL, 142

Broughton, J. M., 161

Browder, Earl, 267, 268, 274

Brown, Charlotte Hawkins, 404–5

Brown, Clark, 181, 186, 259, 378

Brown, James, 99

Brown, Shurley, 186

Brown, Viola, 2, 107, 217, 235, 259, 271, 325, 416

Brown & Williamson Tobacco Company, 34, 101, 112, 124, 129–30, 131, 135, 180, 397

Brown v. Board of Education (1954), 414

Bruce, Vivian, *199*, 200, 203, 242, 259, 273, 325

Bruce, W. H., 139, 141

Bumgardner, Edgar: and stemmers' sit-down strike, 19, 24, 27; and industrial democracy scheme, 100; and racial division of labor, 108; and O'Neal, 196; and union contracts, 203; and grievance procedures, 216, 218, 219; and Communist Party, 341; management style of, 388

Burke, Alice, 268

and unions, 10, 337; and political repression, 11; and Truman, 265, 342, 357; and racial discrimination, 288, 343; and Local 22, 301; and Communist Party, 340; and civil rights, 344, 416

Colored Improvement League, 139

Colored Men's Ticket, 50

Commandoes, 415

Committee of 100, 380–82, 383, 469 (n. 38)

Committee on Civil Rights, 343, 357

Committee on Negro Affairs, 138

Commonwealth College, 151

Communist International (Comintern), 123

Communist Party: and unionism, 1, 6, 7; and race/class linkage, 5; and union organizing, 122; in Winston-Salem, 122, 124–25, 253, 265–66, 456 (n. 39); and interracialism, 123, 124, 275, 299; in South, 123–24; and Scottsboro Boys, 126; and egalitarianism, 141; and Henderson, 143–44; and Congress of Industrial Organizations, 146, 263, 267, 291, 299, 322, 329, 398, 400; and fascism, 146–47; and New Deal, 146; and public debate about union, 180; and music, 237; and Local 22, 265–75, 321–33, 336–45, 398, 399, 401–3, 407–8, 409, 456 (n. 43); and Taft-Hartley Act, 303, 352, 466 (n. 47); and 1947 alderman election, 307, 405; and racial discrimination, 328, 355; and campaign against white chauvinism, 355; and Progressive Party, 357; and Soviet Union, 400. *See also* Popular Front

Community Relations Project (CRP), 9, 376–78, 382–83

Congress: and workers' movement, 10; and antilabor legislation, 311; and low-income housing, 373, 374. *See also* House Un-American Activities Committee

Congress of Industrial Organizations (CIO): and Operation Dixie, 3, 290–300, 307, 314, 400; and civil rights unionism, 4; and South, 4; and "structure of political opportunities," 7; and Cold War, 12; and public debate about union, 18, 179, 180–81, 184, 186, 194, 200, 207; and "no strike pledge," 22; and stemmers' sit-down strike, 32, 40; and tobacco industry, 130; and interracialism, 131, 132, 134, 142, 241, 299; and union organizing, 131; and black working class, 135; and voting campaigns, 137; establishment of, 141, 143; and Communist Party, 146, 263, 267, 291, 299, 322, 329, 398, 400; and union songs, 158; and white working class, 165; and bargaining units, 177; and certification election, 189, 192–93; and collective bargaining, 202; and wages, 209–10; and shop steward system, 212–13; and workers' education, 229; and music, 238; Political Action Committee, 252, 254, 255, 261, 262, 297, 307, 405; and Folger, 263; ideological rifts within, 299, 301, 357–58, 393, 394–95, 398, 404; and alderman election, 307; and right-to-work legislation, 308; and strike of 1947, 314, 320, 329; and white tobacco workers, 350; and anti-Communist affidavits, 352; defensive position of, 357; and Progressive Party, 359, 367, 394; and United Transport Service Employees, 393, 394–99, 401; weakening of, 416

Congress of Racial Equality, 415

Consumerist tactics: and union organizing, 100, 122; and public debate about union, 186; and strike of 1947, 320–21, 463 (n. 48); and Food, Tobacco, Agricultural, and Allied Workers, 335

Cook, Minnie Myers, 288

Cooper, Anna Julia Haywood, 77

Corporate maternalism, 68

Corporate welfare, 121

Cottage meetings, 157–58, 238, 292

Craftsmen, 42, 44

Crane, Frank, 171

Crowder, Orvelle, 217

Cuthrell, Albert, 168–69

Dalton, William, 262, 263

Daniel, Franz, 330

Daniels, Jonathan, 64, 66, 194, 304

Daniels, Josephus, 53, 64

Emergency Citizens Committee, 193–96, 198, 207, 246, 247, 376, 450 (n. 75)

Employment Act, 257

Equal educational opportunities, 3

Espe, Conrad, 32, 34

Ethiopia, 234

Evans, E. Lewis, 121, 122, 131

Export Leaf Tobacco Company, 190, 249, 282, 283, 292, 294, 296

Fain, James, 139

Fair Employment Practices Committee (FEPC), 143, 256, 257, 291, 370, 416

Fair Labor Standards Act (1938), 16, 132, 190, 289

Farley, John, 75, 76

Farmers' Alliance, 49, 50

Farm workers, 144

Fascism, 142, 143, 146, 147, 163, 180, 256, 338

Favoritism: and foremen-worker relations, 102; and stemmers' sit-down strike negotiations, 170; and O'Neal, 196; and union contracts, 209; and kinship networks, 347

Federal Bureau of Investigation (FBI): and Local 22, 267, 270–71, 321, 324, 456 (n. 39); and Communist Party, 324, 326, 327; and anti-Communist movement, 337; and un-Americanism, 416

Federal government: and unionism, 7, 10, 40, 202; and minimum subsistence of living, 16; and wage controls, 20, 129; and racial capitalism, 58–59; and labor-management relations, 136, 212, 223–24, 333, 353; and integration of armed forces, 142; and Communist Party, 336, 407–8; and low-income housing, 373; and integration of R. J. Reynolds Tobacco, 414

Federal Housing Authority, 373

Fellowship of Southern Churchmen, 330

Fields, Maso, 25

Fifth Amendment, 339, 402, 465 (n. 16)

Filipino cannery workers, 144

First Amendment, 339

Fishel, Blanche, 97–98, 113, 116, 187, 188, 391

Folger, Alonzo Dillard, 253

Folger, John, 253–54, 255, 260, 261–62, 264, 281, 309, 361

Food, Tobacco, Agricultural, and Allied Workers–Congress of Industrial Organizations: and labor-management relations, 2, 214; and social learning, 2, 6; and tobacco workers, 211; staff support of, 225; and leadership, 229–30, 302, 402; and interracialism, 240–41, 242, 246, 346, 394; and leftists, 267, 394; and leaf house strike, 283; and Operation Dixie, 290–300; and strike of 1947, 314, 316, 320, 330, 332, 333, 463 (n. 48); and Communist Party, 322, 325, 330–31, 396, 398–99, 400, 401, 403–4; and anti-Communist movement, 338; and House Un-American Activities Committee, 338; and white tobacco workers, 345, 346, 349, 350; and anti-Communist affidavits, 352, 393, 396, 397, 405, 466 (n. 47); and Wallace, 358, 400; and Progressive Party, 367; and Smith, 394; and Truman, 400; and certification election, 407–12, 413. See also Local 22

Foreman, Clark, 331, 338, 361, 362, 365

Foremen-worker relations: and black women tobacco workers, 38, 109–10, 173; and power of foremen, 101, 102, 103, 109, 217; and Reynolds, 102; slavery compared to, 108; and drive system, 109, 388, 439 (n. 45); and racial division of labor, 109–13, 414; and sexual exploitation, 110–11; and women's restrooms, 110–11, 174; and resistance, 114–19; and wages, 116, 172, 210, 282, 440–41 (n. 63); and industrial espionage, 117, 170; and union organizing, 121; and antiunion strategies, 134; and voter registration, 138; and stemmers' sit-down strike, 168; and stemmers' sit-down strike negotiations, 175–76; and public debate about union, 179; and certification election, 189; and shop stewards, 191–92, 204, 214–15; and union contracts, 208, 334; and grievance procedures, 216, 217, 219, 221, 347; and seniority, 281; and

India, 234

Industrial democracy scheme, 100

Industrial espionage, 117, 170, 209, 347

Industrial jurisprudence. *See* Labor-management relations; National Labor Relations Board; National War Labor Board

Ingle, John J., 192, 193, 203, 253

Insurance, 80, 99, 329

Integration: and Communist Party, 123; of armed forces, 142, 416; and Local 22, 228; and strike of 1947, 319; in Winston-Salem, 414–15. *See also* Segregation

International Fur and Leather Workers Union, 304

International Labor Defense, 126

Interracialism: and Tobacco Workers Organizing Committee, 32, 162–63, 176; and Communist Party, 123, 124, 275, 299; and unemployed councils, 125; and Congress of Industrial Organizations, 131, 132, 134, 142, 241, 299; and Tobacco Workers International Union–American Federation of Labor, 133–35; and Emergency Citizens Committee, 198; and union contracts, 205; and Food, Tobacco, Agricultural, and Allied Workers–Congress of Industrial Organizations, 240–41, 242, 246, 346, 394; and Local 22, 258, 346, 355, 401, 403, 411–12; and Community Relations Project, 376–79

Isley, E. T. "Jazz," 313

Jackson, Aunt Molley, 237

Jackson, Elijah, 299, 396

Jackson, James E., Jr., 89

Jackson, Marie, 294

Jackson, Thomas, 259

Jackson, Wilhelmina, 139, 140, 444 (n. 47)

Japanese cannery workers, 144

Jazz Age, 46

Jefferson, Thomas, 309

Jessup, Mabel, 183–84, 188

Jim Crow laws: and white elites, 9; and white supremacy, 55–56, 60; and black workers, 61; and black working class, 71,

75, 92; and black elites, 77; and union organizing, 99, 100, 164; and armed forces, 142, 252; and Tobacco Workers Organizing Committee, 160; and stemmers' sit-down strike negotiations, 169, 172; and public debate about union, 182; and grievance procedures, 219; and Local 22, 228; and voting rights, 254; and Communist Party, 271, 340; and leaf houses, 297; and Progressive Party, 359; and Wallace, 360; and black churches, 391

Johnson, B. C., 19, 27

Johnson, Charles S., 97, 104–6, 108–12, 117, 129, 131–32, 133

Johnson, Guy B., 161

Johnson, Hobart, 187, 188

Johnson, James Weldon, 237

Johnson, Louise, 242–44, 246, 247

Johnson, T. E., 81

Joint Committee on Labor-Management Relations, 353

Jonas, Glenn, 320

Jones, Brownie Lee, 228, 229, 231

Jones, Cal, 286, 288

Jones, David, 331

Jones, Madison, 260

Jones, Ruby: leadership of, 2, 7; and working conditions, 107, 108, 201–2; and foremen, 109, 173, 201, 214; and restroom breaks, 111, 174; aspirations of, 201; as shop steward, 214, 215; and Communist Party, 341; and Moranda Smith, 411

Juries, 140–41, 247, 345

Kate Bitting Reynolds Memorial Hospital, 84–85

Kellum, C. C., 270, 305, 306, 358

Key, V. O., 64

Keynes, John Maynard, 147

Kilgore, Thomas, 140, 153

King, Martin Luther, Jr., 11–12, 416

Knights of Labor, 49–50

Koger, Harry, 150, 152, 155, 156, 157, *157*, 160, 161, 162

Koger, Mary Lou, 346, 348

Korean War, 407

National Labor Relations Act. *See* Wagner Act

National Labor Relations Board: and Local 22, 8–9, 10, 393, 394, 396, 397; establishment of, 130; and R. J. Reynolds' labor-management relations, 134, 156, 204, 223; and certification elections, 162, 177–81, 186–93, 200, 202, 292, 296, 397, 407–12, 413; and grievance procedures, 205; and Taft-Hartley Act, 303; and anti-Communist affidavits, 352, 393; and decertification petitions, 352

National Negro Congress, 142, 304

National Negro Labor Congress, 274

National Recovery Administration (NRA), 104, 127, 129

National Textile Workers Union (NTWU), 123–24

National Urban League, 376–77, 378

National War Labor Board, 7, 29, 34, 100, 202, 205–10, 213–15, 223, 295, 337

Negro Chamber of Commerce, 304

Negro Chartered Democratic Club, 140

Negro History Week, 234

Negro Liberation Movement, 355

Negro Ministerial Association, 100

Negrophobe extremists, 52

Negro Voters' League, 138

Nesmith, Lonnie, 107, 112, 232

New Deal: and Democratic Party, 4, 252; momentum of, 4; and "structure of political opportunity," 7; and white workers, 11; and union organizing, 37, 120, 136, 155, 163; reforms of, 127–30; leftward drift of, 141; social democratic impulses of, 143, 147, 160; and Communist Party, 146, 267, 268, 336; and Southern Front, 148; and civic participation, 160; and collective bargaining, 202; and Chatham, 261; and Folger, 261, 264; and Truman, 268; and Wallace, 357; and Progressive Party, 359, 360; and public works employment, 370; and Congress of Industrial Organizations, 394

Newton brothers, 81

Nineteenth Amendment, 360

Nixon, E. D., 417–18

Nixon, Richard M., 1, 337–38

North Carolina: post–Civil War political system of, 49–54; and voter turnout, 51; and economic oligarchy, 64–65; and Communist Party, 124; and third-party election laws, 360–61, 386; and unemployment compensation law, 371

North Carolina Farm Bureau, 289

"No union" campaign, 186–87, 188, 189, 192–93

Odum, Howard, 161

Office of Price Administration, 163, 256–57

Old Town Country Club, 66

Oligopolistic pricing, 9

O'Neal, Frank, *197*, *259*; and union organizing, 22; and stemmers' sit-down strike, 28, 39, 169, 170–71, 174; and DeBerry, 152; and public debate about union, 184, 196, 199; militancy of, 266; and Communist Party, 269–70, 274; and leaf house strike, 283; and union contracts, 354; and Local 22, 391

Open shop, 207, 281

Page, Myra, 126

Paige, Satchel, 90

Pan African Congress, 123

Pan African movements, 234

Parker, Robert, 173

Paternalism: and welfare capitalism, 9; and Reynolds, 43, 47; and white poor, 58; and labor-management relations, 101–2, 103, 175, 214, 387; and antiunion efforts, 136; and economics, 141; and black middle class, 196; and union contract, 204; and gradualism, 415

Patterson, Frank, 174

Peace, Clifford H., 390–92

Peale, Norman Vincent, 1, 389–90, 391

Pearson, C. O., 363

Pease, John, 294

ism, 9; and Pitts, 30; and unions, 31, 415; and white supremacy, 55; and wages, 58, 104, 127–28; and racial division of labor, 98; and employment benefits, 103, 113; and welfare capitalism, 104; and National Industrial Recovery Act, 129; and juries, 140–41; and armed forces, 142, 160; in defense industries, 142–43, 160; and People's Institute of Applied Religion, 151; and class inequalities, 266; and leaf houses, 283; and Cold War, 288, 343; and Communist Party, 328, 355; and Progressive Party, 359; and Wallace, 360; and anti-Communist movement, 404

Racial division of labor: and R. J. Reynolds Tobacco production, 94, 103, 106–7; and white tobacco workers, 94, 96–98, 172, 280, 438 (n. 12); and white supremacy, 97, 372; and working conditions, 106–8, 112–13; and foremen-worker relations, 109–13, 414; and advancement opportunities, 114, 173, 205; and stemmers' sit-down strike negotiations, 172–73; and public debate about union, 179; and stemming workers, 278, 279; and leaf houses, 280; and seniority, 281, 369; and strike of 1947, 313–14, 319–20, 334

Racial inequalities: and stemmers' sit-down strike, 37–38, 40, 171, 172–73; and white supremacy, 55, 376; and shop floor democracy, 218; and wages, 281; and Communist Party, 328; and democracy, 343, 344, 357, 465 (n. 26); and Committee of 100, 381

Racial justice, 337

Racial solidarity: and class consciousness, 3, 5; and black community, 91, 164–65, 405; and Local 22, 307, 308, 310; and white tobacco workers, 351

Racial subordination: and white supremacy, 5, 41, 55, 57, 58, 59–60, 76, 92, 431 (n. 44); and white elites, 9, 59; and R. J. Reynolds Tobacco, 49; and post–Civil War politics, 52; and racial division of labor, 97, 172; and public debate about union, 194–95

Radicalism, 146, 163, 212, 240, 265, 267, 415, 416, 417

Radio: and black choral groups, 89; and Local 22, 232, 254, 401, 403; and Communist Party, 269, 327–28, 340; and certification elections, 292; and Kenneth R. Williams, 309; and strike of 1947, 314; and Woody Guthrie, 350; and United Transport Service Employees, 398; and anti-Communist movement, 408; and certification election, 410; black access to, 436 (n. 73)

Railroad brotherhoods, 308

Ramsay, John, 350

Rand, Remington, 192

Randolph, A. Philip, 142, 234

Ranson, Luther, 319–20, 351

Ratledge, Latta B., 366

Ray, A. H., 181

Reagan, Ronald, 341

Real estate industry, 74, 81, 316, 373, 375

Red-baiting: and R. J. Reynolds Tobacco, 8, 274; and Local 22, 301, 306, 326–27, 337; and Davis, 342

Redd, Jasper, 193

Red scare: and political repression, 9, 120; and post–World War I period, 101; and labor movement, 120; and Communist Party, 122; in Winston-Salem, 337; and white civic groups, 341–42; and McCarthy, 408; and white supremacy, 417

Reemployment Agreement, 128

Regionalism, 147

Rein, David, 338–39

Relief: and unemployed councils, 125–26; and leaf house strike, 283; and strike of 1947, 315, 316, 320, 329–30, 335; and Communist Party, 328; and white tobacco workers, 345; and unemployment, 370

Religion/business alliance, 389–92

Rent control board, 316, 375

Republican Party: Democrats allied with, 5, 148, 419; and Congressional control, 10, 302, 357; post–Civil War biracial coalition of, 49; and blacks, 50–51, 53; and white supremacy, 53; and tax codes, 57; and white primary, 58, 432 (n. 51); and black voters, 137; and mayoral election of 1939, 139; and anti-Communism, 264–65, 336; and Progressive Party, 357, 360

Reynolds, Kate Bitting, 66, 68

Reynolds, Katharine Smith, 66, 67–68, 78, 83

Reynolds, Richard Joshua: and tobacco industry, 43–47; and politics, 50; death of, 64; and Reynolda House, 66; and Cameron Park, 75; and black elites, 77–78; and labor-management relations, 102; and Peale, 389; and sexual exploitation of women, 440 (n. 49)

Reynolds, Richard Joshua, Jr., 65, 66, 364, 373

Reynolds, Will, 66, 84, 198–200

Reynolds Building, 46

Reynolds family, 64, 65, 66, 84

Right-to-work legislation, 303–4, 308, 312, 462 (n. 27)

Risher, Evelyn, 239

R. J. Reynolds Employees Association: and Ingles, 192–93, 253; and certification election, 200; and union contracts, 203; company support for, 207; and white unionists, 220; and grievance procedures, 221; and union organizing, 240, 246, 247; and DeBerry/Johnson incident, 242, 243–44; and anti-union strategies, 249, 351, 409; and strike of 1947, 312, 321

R. J. Reynolds Tobacco: and labor movement, 1, 3, 9; and tobacco industry, 2; history of, 6; strategies of, 8, 11, 98; and labor shortages, 14, 81, 98; and working conditions, 16–17; rise of, 41–49; and National Recovery Administration, 128; and antitrust violations, 264; profits of, 311

R. J. Reynolds Tobacco Employment Office, 101–3

R. J. Reynolds Tobacco Factory Council, 102

R. J. Reynolds Tobacco management: and mechanization, 8, 277–78, 458 (n. 4); and stemmers' sit-down strike, 24–26, 29, 32, 36, 39–40, 41, 167–78; and white workers, 32; and union contracts, 101, 203, 310–12,

333, 351–54, 398–99; antiunion strategies of, 133–36, 155–56, 165–66, 192, 194, 203, 204, 208, 247, 278, 319, 326, 328, 345, 350, 351, 353, 356, 376; and public debate about union, 178–90; and voting rights, 255; and decertification petition, 352; and seasonal workers, 369, 371–72; and post-contract labor relations strategies, 386–92; and blacklisting, 414

R. J. Reynolds Tobacco production: and mechanization, 8, 277–81, 334, 351, 369; and stemmers' sit-down strike, 33; centralization of facilities, 46–47; and division of labor, 93–98, 103; and union organizing, 98–101; and labor-management relations, 101, 114–19; and welfare capitalism, 101–4; and authority structures, 104–14; and layoffs, 278, 279, 369; and strike of 1947, 312–14, 319–20, 332, 333, 353, 463 (n. 47)

Robert E. Lee Hotel, 34

Robeson, Paul, 1, 10, 234, 237, 238, 335–36, 355, 361, 404, 411, 412

Robinson, Earl, 237

Rockefeller, John D., 44

Rogers, Evander, 39, 155, 208

Roosevelt, Eleanor, 404

Roosevelt, Franklin D.: and South's economic problems, 5; and Reynolds, 66; and New Deal, 127; and tobacco industry, 128; and white tobacco workers, 129; and racial issues, 137; and civil rights, 142; and conservative congressmen, 143; and Soviet Union, 180, 265, 394; and labor-management relations, 202; and black voters, 252; re-election of, 255; death of, 256; and Chatham, 261; and Win the War program, 271; and Bethune, 404

Roosevelt, Theodore, 45

Ross, Mike, 359

Royal, Sidney, 88

Rural migration: and social learning, 2; and women workers, 3, 70–71, 87; and black working class, 68–70, 105; and white working class, 72–73, 105; and black elites, 78